The Stories of English

The Stories of English

The Stories of English

David Crystal

ALLEN LANE
an imprint of
PENGUIN BOOKS

ALLEN LANE

Published by the Penguin Group
Penguin Books Ltd, 80 Strand, London WC2R 0RL, England
Penguin Group (USA) Inc., 375 Hudson Street, New York, New York 10014, USA
Penguin Books Australia Ltd, 250 Camberwell Road, Camberwell, Victoria 3124, Australia
Penguin Books Canada Ltd, 10 Alcorn Avenue, Toronto, Ontario, Canada M4V 3B2
Penguin Books India (P) Ltd, 11, Community Centre, Panchsheel Park, New Delhi – 110 017, India
Penguin Books (NZ) Ltd, Cnr Rosedale and Airborne Roads, Albany, Auckland, New Zealand
Penguin Books (South Africa) (Pty) Ltd, 24 Sturdee Avenue, Rosebank 2196, South Africa

Penguin Books Ltd, Registered Offices: 80 Strand, London WC2R 0RL, England

www.penguin.com

First published 2004
1

Designed by Richard Marston
Typeset by Rowland Phototypesetting Ltd, Bury St Edmunds, Suffolk
Printed in England by Clays Ltd, St Ives plc

ISBN 0–713–99752–4

Contents

Illustrations

Maps

Introduction

In fact, the book has two introductions, because there are two stories to be told.

On p. 3 there is an outline of the history of English, as often recounted. The past century has seen dozens of books which have presented the language in such terms, describing stages in the emergence of what has come to be called 'Standard English'. A standard is a variety of a language which has acquired special prestige within a community. It is an important focus of study, and one which will be routinely encountered as the chronology of the present book unfolds. But an account of the standard language is only a small part of the whole story of English. The real story is much, much bigger.

Accordingly, beginning on p. 5, there is an introduction to this real story, which is what this book is largely about. 'Real stories' would be more accurate, for in the history of something as multifaceted as a language, there are always several trends taking place simultaneously. A richness of diversity exists everywhere, and always has, over the language's 1,500-year history; but the story of Standard English has hitherto attracted all the attention. The other stories have never been given their rightful place in English linguistic history, and it is time they were.

Telling several stories simultaneously is not something which suits the linear expository method of a book, so to convey this message I have had to adopt a somewhat unorthodox structure. The main sequence of chapters provides a chronological narrative from Old English to Modern English, focusing on the interaction between standard and nonstandard; but they are separated by 'Interludes' illustrating topics to do with nonstandard English which fall outside the time framework. Also, within chapters, I have used panels to illustrate the nature of the nonstandard dimension, thereby emphasizing the dynamic tension which always exists between nonstandard and standard varieties.

It is a patchwork quilt of a book, as a result; but that is inevitable, given the constraints faced by any historian of nonstandard language. It is not easy to obtain data on the various kinds of nonstandard English, or even on what informal spoken Standard English was really like, in the years before broad-casting, tape-recorders, camcorders, and the Internet gave voices to daily personal interaction in all its regional and cultural diversity. Standard English presents us with no such problem because, as the community's prestige written form, it has been the medium of authorial expression over several centuries. The other varieties do not fare so well.

If the recorded linguistic echoes of the past are predominantly White and Anglo-Saxon, as they seem to be, how much will we ever learn about the language of the ethnic minorities which form an important part of British history? If past echoes are predominantly male, will we ever discover what role women played in the history of English? And if these echoes are all so closely tied to the standard dialect, with writers dismissing regional dialects as 'sadly battered and mutilated' or 'quaint and eccentric', will we ever discover our real sociolinguistic heritage?[1]

The Stories of English is an exploration of this heritage.

The standard story

The standard history of the English language usually goes something like this.

- In the year 449 Germanic tribes arrived in Britain from the European mainland, and displaced the native British (Celtic) population, eventually establishing a single language which was Anglo-Saxon in character.
- Most writings of the period are shown to be preserved in the West Saxon dialect, the language of King Alfred, spoken in the politically and culturally dominant region of southern England around Winchester. Descriptions of the language, known as Anglo-Saxon or Old English, therefore reflect this dominance.
- Fundamental changes began to affect Old English grammar during the later Anglo-Saxon period, and these, along with changes in pronunciation, innovative spelling conventions, and a huge influx of new words after the Norman Conquest, led to the language evolving a fresh character, known as Middle English.
- During the Middle English period, the literary language began to evolve, culminating in the compositions of Chaucer, and we see the first signs of a Standard English emerging in the work of the Chancery scribes in London.
- The introduction of printing by Caxton in 1476 brought an enormous expansion in the written resources of the language, and was the major influence on the development of a standardized writing system. Spelling began to stabilize, and thus became less of a guide to pronunciation, which continued to change.
- Further changes in pronunciation and grammar, and another enormous increase in vocabulary stimulated by the Renaissance, led to the emergence of an Early Modern English. Its character was much influenced by Elizabethan literature, notably by Shakespeare, and by the texts of many Bibles, especially those of Tyndale (1525) and King James (1611).
- The unprecedented increase in the language's range and creativity brought a reaction, in the form of a climate of concern about the unwelcome pace and character of language change. This led to the writing of the first English dictionaries, grammars, and manuals of pronunciation, in an attempt to bring the language under some measure of control.
- As a result, there emerged a sharpened sense of correctness in relation to a standard form of English, and this came to be encountered worldwide, as speakers of educated British English gained global influence throughout the British Empire. At the same time, the question of standards became

more complex, with the arrival of American English as an alternative global presence.

- By the end of the eighteenth century, the standard language had become so close to that of the present-day, at least in grammar, pronunciation, and spelling, that it is safely described as Modern English. But there continued to be massive increases in vocabulary, chiefly as a consequence of the industrial and scientific revolutions, and of the ongoing globalization of the language – a process which would continue throughout the twentieth century and into the twenty-first.

Just one story is being told here.[2] It is predominantly the story of what happened to English in England, and moreover to just one kind of English in England – the kind of English which we associate with the written language, with literary expression, and with speaking and writing in a formal, educated way. It is a story, in short, of the rise of Standard English – and, as we shall see, not even all of that. Yet it takes only a moment's reflection to deduce that this cannot be the whole story. The book needs a better introduction.

The real story

It is not what the orthodox histories include which is the problem; it is what they omit, or marginalize. 'The' story of English, as it has been presented in the mainstream tradition, is the story of a single variety of the language, Standard English, its special status usually symbolized through capitalization. But this variety is only a small part of the kaleidoscopic diversity of dialects and styles which make up 'the English language'. Indeed, for every one person who speaks Standard English, there must be a hundred who do not, and another hundred who speak other varieties as well as the standard. Where is their story told?

The marginalization has not been accidental. Several authors have taken the view that only Standard English is worth studying. One of the most influential, Henry Cecil Wyld, wrote *A Short History of English* in 1914, which I remember having to read as an English undergraduate nearly fifty years later. His opening sections could not have made the bias clearer. After referring to the great diversity of English dialects, he says:

> Fortunately, at the present time, the great majority of the English Dialects are of very little importance as representatives of English speech, and for our present purpose we can afford to let them go, except in so far as they throw light upon the growth of those forms of our language which are the main objects of our solicitude, namely the language of Literature and Received Standard Spoken English . . .

Only the dialects which gave rise to the standard are worth studying, therefore (though he does allow Scots, thinking doubtless of Burns):

> After the end of the fourteenth century, the other dialects, excepting always those of Lowland Scotch, gradually cease to be the vehicle of literary expression, and are no longer of importance to us as independent forms of English.

He concludes:

> In this book, therefore, the developments of the Modern provincial English dialects are not considered unless they can throw light on the history of Standard English.[3]

In this single-mindedness of vision, he was by no means alone, and such views coloured much of the thinking about the language, both in Britain and abroad, during the twentieth century.

The standard tradition

The focus on Standard English is understandable. We have only to look around us. Every country in the world is in the process of coming to terms with English, in its new role as a global lingua franca, and when we encounter the language in advertising, travel, and other international domains, it is invariably Standard English that we see. Within a country where English is the primary language, the impression is even stronger: it is unusual to see anything but the standard language in the press, on television, in public signage, on commercial products, in bookshops, or in schools.

That is what we would expect. The role of a standard language, whether it is used nationally or internationally, is to enable the members of a community to understand each other. Everyone needs to learn it, in the interests of efficient and effective communication. That is why in school we are taught to read and write Standard English, and are given opportunities to read it aloud and to hear others read it. The leading national institutions, such as the British Parliament, the US Congress, the BBC, and CNN, adopt it as their primary means of expression, in the interests of universal comprehensibility, so we hear it widely spoken in public as the language of power and prestige. Its expressive potential is exploited throughout English literature. It has an especially high profile among foreign learners of English. A small minority of families, from a certain class and educational background, speak it naturally at home as a mother dialect.

Nowhere in this book will there be any denigration of Standard English, therefore. Its role is crucial in fostering intelligibility within national and global society, and its adoption as the primary medium of literary expression has produced six centuries of authorial achievement. I am using it (with just a few exceptions) to write this book now. At the same time, we only have to listen to the English-speaking world around us to realize the absurdity of any account which identifies Standard English with the language as a whole, whether today or in previous centuries. Three facts are critical. Most English speakers do not speak Standard English. A significant number of English authors do not write in Standard English. And a large number of those using English in computer-mediated interaction do not use it either.

There are no reliable figures, but anyone who travels around the English-speaking world – or who simply stands and listens in a city centre or village shop – will be left in no doubt that nonstandard Englishes, in the form of regional and ethnic dialects, are the normal linguistic way of life for most people. And even if others do not use nonstandard English in their speaking and writing, they have an evident ability to process a great deal of it in their listening and reading. The exploitation of nonstandard varieties is the basis of many television sitcoms. And Standard English users often deviate from the rules of the standard, in speech or in writing, in order to convey a particular effect. As the title of one book on the electronic revolution playfully reads: 'We ain't seen nothin' yet'. It may be nonstandard in grammar, but everyone understands it.

A large number of terms have evolved to characterize nonstandard varieties of English, some of them scientific and objective, some popular and impressionistic, some positively insulting. Towards one end of the terminological spectrum we find 'regional dialects', 'modified standards', 'nonstandard speech', 'creoles', 'pidgins', 'vernaculars', and 'code-mixing'; towards the other end we find 'substandard speech', 'country talk', 'patois', 'brogue', 'argot', 'cant', 'lingo', 'broken English', and 'gutter speech'. They all have one thing in common: none of them are 'standard'.

Histories of English do not of course totally ignore all these varieties; but they do tend to marginalize them. Certainly they are not given the central position which they would receive if the balance of content in a survey were to reflect the corpus of national and international regional English usage. Accounts of Old or Middle English, for example, traditionally spend several chapters describing the language and literature of the period, but treat dialects as an isolated topic – usually somewhere towards the back of the book. Even in the modern period, when there is no shortage of literary dialect representation, language histories tend to treat regional usage in a disproportionately minimalist manner. *The Stories of English* is, accordingly, an attempt to redress the balance.[4] It deals with Standard English, as it must, for there are many stories to be told there, too; but it also reflects – insofar as the historical record (largely and inevitably expressed through the standard language) enables me to do so – the presence of nonstandard, and specifically regional varieties in earlier English linguistic history. The closer we come to modern times, the easier it becomes to represent the nonstandard perspective. But it has always been there.

Variation within Standard English

There are many stories to be told within Standard English, too . . . ? This is because the standard language is not a homogeneous phenomenon, internally consistent throughout in the way it uses pronunciation, spelling, grammar, vocabulary, and patterns of discourse. The common impression that such consistency exists, within an English-speaking community, derives from the fact that most of the written English we see around us is *formal* in character. It is

English on its best behaviour. When people compose books, articles, brochures, signs, posters, and all the other forms of printed English, they try to 'get it right', often employing personnel (such as copy-editors) or manuals (such as guides to house style) to ensure that the language does conform to the standard. The same applies to people who speak the standard professionally, such as radio announcers, political spokespersons, university professors, and court-room lawyers. The closer they can make their spoken style conform to the written standard, the less they will attract the criticism of being 'careless', 'lazy', or 'sloppy'. The public language that we hear and read is therefore characteristically at the formal end of the stylistic spectrum.

And a spectrum there is, within Standard English. Variation is everywhere. Even within the formal domain, there is variety. Lawyers, clerics, politicians, doctors, dons, radio announcers, scientists, and others, even when communicat-ing as carefully as they can, do not all talk and write in the same way. There are major linguistic variations between 'legal English', 'religious English', and all the other styles which we associate with leading social institutions. Most of these have received recognition. Books have been written on 'the language of the law' or 'religious language'. The properties of formal English, both spoken and written, have been quite thoroughly explored.

However, at the other end of the spectrum, informal Standard English has been much neglected. What happens to the speech of radio announcers in the BBC canteen? How do politicians talk when they meet up for a drink? How do lawyers express themselves when they go home in the evening? Do university professors on a foreign tour use the same language in their postcards or emails home as they do in their lectures and articles? Do off-duty copy-editors never split their infinitives? As soon as we begin to ask such questions, it is plain that there is another world here, waiting to be explored. It is common experi-ence that people 'slip into something comfortable', when they go off-duty. What is the linguistic equivalent of being 'comfortable', when people are no longer in the public eye? And do all these professionals slip into the same linguistic clothes, when they cease being professional? Very little information is available about such matters. This story has not been told either.

There is no question that a broad band of informal speech and writing exists. Anyone who has ever begun a postcard with the words 'Having a lovely time' is being informal, for omitting part of a sentence (*ellipsis* – here, the subject and auxiliary verb, *I'm* or *We're*) is one of the things we routinely do to make our writing or speech sound casual and familiar. Anyone who has allowed an expletive into their speech, whether a mild euphemism such as *blooming* or *darn* or one of the serious four-letter options, is being informal, for these forms by their nature have evolved to meet the demands of earthy, grass-roots interaction. Anyone who has used a piece of slang, whether popular or professional, is being informal, for slang primarily exists to foster rapport among individuals who wish to express their sense of belonging to a social group. Anyone = Everyone, in such contexts.

The wardrobe analogy is apt, for it suggests that we have several options for being informal. In clothing, we may choose something slightly casual or go for something totally outrageous, depending on our personalities and bank balances. In speech and writing, too, we have several options – levels of informality which also range from the slightly casual to the totally outrageous. Personality is relevant here, in the same way – though not bank balance, for language is the cheapest way of expressing identity – and our choice of language will also be conditioned by such factors as the subject-matter of the conversation, the number, age, and gender of the participants, and the type of situation in which the conversation is taking place. Unifying, universal features of informal English do exist, but there is a great deal of variation here as well.

The more options we have, within the formal–informal spectrum, the more we feel ready to meet the needs of a complex, multifaceted society. With clothing, a diverse wardrobe enables us to dress to suit the occasion; and so it is with language. The more linguistic choice we command, the more we find ourselves able to act appropriately as we move from one social occasion to another. It is obvious that anyone who lacks the ability to express English formally, with control and precision, is at a serious disadvantage in modern society. But the opposite also applies: anyone who lacks the ability to handle the informal range of English usage is seriously disadvantaged, too.

The latter point is not so relevant for native speakers of English, who will have grown up with an informal command of the language; but it is crucial for non-native learners, who comprise the vast majority of English language users today (see Chapter 17). For example, a multinational organization with headquarters in Britain or the USA may hold all its meetings in formal business English, but a great deal of the 'real' business often takes place in the corridors and cafes outside the meeting-room, carried on in a colloquial, idiomatic style which non-native managers may struggle to comprehend. Even within the meeting-room, a piece of casual repartee or a passing jokey usage can be enough to undermine the confidence of anyone who lacks a sense of the varieties of informal English. It is a familiar scenario. The British and American members of the management team all laugh, but not the managers from, say, Italy or Hong Kong.

Again, there are no reliable figures, but intuitively we sense that informal English is far more 'normal' than formal English. If we had some way of adding up all the occasions on which informal and formal English speech are used by Standard English speakers all over the world, I suspect the former would exceed the latter by a ratio of at least ten to one. If you are a Standard English speaker, think back over your past week, and recall the occasions when you spoke formal English. They will be islands of identifiable usage – such as at work, in public meetings, or during certain kinds of visit or phone call. It will not be possible to bring to mind so readily the occasions when you made informal use of English, because there will have been so many of them – conversations with family, friends, workplace contacts, neighbours, and passers-by; conversations at home or work, in shops, bars, restaurants, buses, trains, and sporting arenas. Informal English chat is the matrix within which formal English locates itself and with which it contrasts. It is the norm.

The story of informal conversation is beginning to be told, in dictionaries and grammars and manuals of style, but the account is patchy and the attitude typically suspicious. The impression is still widespread that there is something a little odd about informal English – that a casual style, with its half-formed thoughts, loosely constructed sentences, unfinished utterances, interruptions, changes of subject, vagueness, repetitiveness, and a general 'play it by ear' attitude to interaction, is somehow intrinsically inferior to a style where every-thing is carefully thought out, sentences are tightly organized and complete, the progression of meaning is logical and coherent, and conscious effort is made to be relevant, clear, and precise. This is a message which prescriptive grammarians and purist commentators have been drumming into us for the past 250 years. It may take another 250 to forget it, though the signs are that it will take much less (Chapter 20).

We need *both* stylistic domains to live a full linguistic life. 'Thanks a million' has its place alongside 'I am most grateful'. 'We've got all sorts of lovely grub and booze in the fridge' complements 'A wide variety of foodstuffs and beverages has been left in the refrigerator'. There are times at work when 'Hey, Dick, take a look-see here' will be appropriate, and those when we need something more like 'Excuse me, Mr Smith, would you please examine this'. Likewise, at the dinner table, there are occasions when it would be exactly right to say 'Be a dear and send the salt down . . . Ta', and occasions when we know it has to be 'Would you kindly pass the salt? . . . Thank you so much'. The exact character of the informal language will of course depend on such factors as the age of the participants and their cultural background: in 2003, I heard such expressions of thanks as 'Cheers', 'Wicked', 'Good one', 'Cool', 'Fierce', and there are many more. But the basic point remains, regardless of which particular words are used. To have only one style at our disposal, or to lack a sense of appropriateness in stylistic use, is disempowering and socially disturbing. Not only are we no longer in control of the situation in which we find ourselves, we soon discover that stylistic ineptitude is the first step on the road towards social exclusion.

The point applies to all cultures and to all languages, but it is especially an issue in the case of a language like English, which has developed so many nuances of formality and informality in the course of its long, socially diverse, technologically influenced, and increasingly global history. The more we understand these nuances the better, so that we can use them appropriately upon occasion, and also respond appropriately when others use them. Being in control also means that we can switch from one style to another, in order to convey a particular effect. Television weather-forecasters, for example, have developed this style-switching into a fine art, from formal, through various degrees of informal, to totally informal.

> A deep depression is approaching the British Isles, which will bring heavy rainfall by early morning.
> Another low coming in, so you'll need your umbrellas tomorrow.
> More rain on the way, I'm afraid, so get your brollies out for the morrow.

We also have to be in control to avoid incongruous or bizarre usage, or to appreciate a joke when it is made. We need to know that 'How's tricks, your grace?' is improbable outside the world of television satire. And we need to be very sure of our ground (or very drunk) before we say 'Yo, Officer'.

No account of the history of English should ignore the whole of the language's formality range, but the informal levels have been seriously underrepresented in the traditional accounts, partly because they have been so much associated with regional dialect speech. For centuries of language pedagogy, formal English has been lionized and informal English marginalized – often penalized, using such labels as 'sloppy' or 'incorrect'. But the more we look for informality in English linguistic history, the more we find it, and moreover in contexts which have an unequivocal literary pedigree. It is yet another story which is waiting to be told.

Standards and formality: further stories

The standard story; the nonstandard stories, the informality story . . . It should now be clear why I am dissatisfied with the kind of singular-noun approach to English, such as we find in the title of many a book or television programme: 'the story' of English, 'the heritage' of English. But there is more. The previous section has focused entirely on the formality range within Standard English. Yet contrasts of formality are an intrinsic part of all varieties, not just the standard. Although we tend to associate regional dialects with informal speech, this is purely an artefact of the standard perspective. Anyone who has lived within a linguistically nonstandard community knows that there are gradations of formality there, too.

I lived my entire secondary-school life in Liverpool, and can recall many a playground situation where everyone, teachers and pupils, was speaking Liverpudlian English, but in very different styles. There were forms of address, nicknames, wordplay, expletives, and all sorts of everyday words which we would happily use together, though never to the teacher, and vice versa. A new record might be described as *gear* ('fine') to a mate, but if the teacher asked about it, we would say something like *great*. I recall one of the most popular teachers once saying that something was *gear*, and causing a bit of a snigger by so doing. But that was why he was popular. He spoke our language.

Out of the playground and into the classroom, and Standard English ruled (albeit with a Liverpool accent). British Standard English, of course. And in that slight modification lies yet another story. My secondary-school anecdote has its myriad equivalents in the high schools of the United States, but there the move from playground to classroom would be a move from local dialect into American Standard English. In the US classrooms, the teachers would be allowing such expressions as *I've gotten* and *quarter of four*, whereas in the UK the corresponding standard usages would be *I've got* and *quarter to four*. Write something on the board, and the US teacher would allow *color* and *traveling*, whereas the British teacher would insist on *colour* and *travelling*. There are several thousand differences of pronunciation, spelling, grammar, vocabulary, idiom, and discourse between British and American English. There seem to be two standards in the world, and presumably each has its individual story.

The British/American distinction is of course well recognized and studied. But are these the only two global standards? The more we observe the way the English language is evolving in such parts of the world as Australia, South Africa, and India, the more we sense that new standards are emerging there, too – varieties which are not identical to British or American English, but which are fulfilling the same role in providing educated people within the community with an agreed set of conventions to facilitate efficient and effective intelligibility. Once upon a time, such international regional variations would have been treated with the same condescension and contempt as were the features of national regional dialects – as inferior, incorrect, and uneducated. Today, when we note that these features are in widespread educated use within those communities, when we see them used throughout the print media, and hear them in the speech of government ministers and chief executives, then we can no longer use such labels. If you want to sell your goods to other English-speaking countries, or wish to maintain good diplomatic links with them, it would be as well not to refer to their speech as 'inferior'.

One of the most important trends within the evolution of English during the second half of the twentieth century has indeed been the emergence of new standard usages within the world's English-speaking communities, as well as of new varieties of nonstandard English within those communities, many of them spoken by ethnic minorities. At the same time, older regional varieties which had previously received little attention outside their own country of origin, such as the English of the Caribbean, South Africa, or India, have come into international public prominence, especially through the medium of creative literature. Their stories are important, too, for they are stories of emerging identity – far too important nowadays to be briefly summarized in a single chapter on 'New Englishes'. They should be a significant presence in any book on the history of English.

There is something about such phrases as 'new varieties' and 'ethnic minorities' which does not well capture the scale of this dimension of the inquiry. They suggest a few thousand people, or perhaps tens of thousands. But when we consider the international locations where English is now established, we need to talk in terms of much larger figures – millions, and tens of millions. If only 5 per cent or so of the population of India, for example, speak English, then we are talking about as many people speaking English in that country as speak English in the whole of Britain. (The real figure is certainly much greater.) This can come as something of a shock to people who have not thought beyond the 'Standard British English' perspective. With over 1.5 billion speakers of English around the globe, the English of England is today a tiny minority dialect of 'World English', and getting tinier by the decade. Here, too, we ain't seen nothin' yet.

Identity, of course, is a much bigger notion than geography. The answer to the question 'Who are you?' cannot be reduced to 'Where are you from?', though that dimension is undeniably critical. There are many other possible answers, such as 'I am a doctor', 'I am a Sikh', 'I am a teenager', or 'I am a woman', and each of these identities exercises an influence on the way the speaker uses language – or has used language in the past. Sociolinguistics is the subject which investigates the nature of the linguistic variation that relates to identity. And during the past fifty years, sociolinguists have been highly successful in demonstrating the enormous range of variation in speech and writing which exists in modern society. The speech of ethnic minorities, such as African-American English in the USA or Caribbean English in the UK, has been given serious attention for the first time. And the linguistic features which differentiate male and female patterns of discourse have also come to be thoroughly explored.

We know these differences exist now – and we can guess that similar differences must have existed in the past. In this respect, sociolinguists are linguistic uniformitarians – appropriating here the term describing the view of James Hutton, the eighteenth-century Scots geologist, that the processes controlling the evolution of the earth's crust were of the same kind throughout geological time as they are today. Human nature hasn't changed that much during the past 2,000 years. Linguistic variation of the same kind as we encounter today must have existed throughout the history of English. English will always have been spoken by ethnic minorities in distinctive ways. Women will always have played their part in shaping the language, both as users and as commentators. But you would never guess this from the standard story of English.

New standards, non-standards, informalities, and identities. This is a book about the *real* stories of English, which have never, in their entirety, been told.

Chapter 1 The origins of Old English

There was variety from the very beginning. There must have been. No one has ever found a speech community which does not contain regional and social variation, and it is inconceivable that the human race has changed in this respect in the course of a mere 1,500 years. Indeed, the society which the Anglo-Saxons joined in Britain in the fifth century was notably heterogeneous. Old English, as we have come to call the earliest stage of the language, evolved in a land which was full of migrants, raiders, mercenaries, temporary settlers, long-established families, people of mixed ethnic origins, and rapidly changing power bases. The society was not very numerous – the total population of Britain in the fifth century cannot have been much more than half a million – but it was highly scattered, with people living in small communities, and groups continually on the move. These are ideal conditions for a proliferation of dialects.

Our main source of information about the period, Bede's *Ecclesiastical History of the English Nation*, written *c.* 730 (see panel 1.1), opens with a statement recognizing the existence of a multi-ethnic and multilingual Britain. In his first book, Chapter 1, we read:

> This island at present . . . contains five nations, the English, Britons, Scots, Picts, and Latins, each in its own peculiar dialect cultivating the sublime study of Divine truth. The Latin tongue is, by the study of the Scriptures, become common to all the rest.[1]

Subsequent chapters describe in detail how this situation evolved. The first arrivals, Bede says, were Britons (we would now call them Celts), and they gave their name to the land. The Picts then arrived in the north of Britain, from Scythia via northern Ireland, where the resident Scots would not let them stay. The Scots themselves arrived in Britain some time later, and secured their own settlements in the Pictish regions. Then, 'in the year of Rome 798' (= AD 43), Emperor Claudius sent an expedition which rapidly established a Roman presence in most of the island. The Romans ruled there until the early fifth century, when Rome was taken by the Goths, and military garrisons were withdrawn. Attacks on the Britons by the Picts and Scots followed. The Britons appealed to

Rome for help, but the Romans, preoccupied with their own wars, could do little. The attacks continued, so the Britons came to a decision. As Bede recounts in Chapters 14 and 15:

> They consulted what was to be done, and where they should seek assistance to prevent or repel the cruel and frequent incursions of the northern nations; and they all agreed with their King Vortigern to call over to their aid, from the parts beyond the sea, the Saxon nation . . .
>
> Then the nation of the Angles, or Saxons, being invited by the aforesaid king, arrived in Britain with three long ships.

The *Anglo-Saxon Chronicle* reports their landing in Ebbsfleet (Pegwell Bay, near Ramsgate, Kent) in AD 449. The fifth nation, led by the brother-commanders Hengist and Horsa, had arrived.

The account is clear and succinct, but the terms used to describe the peoples hide a deeper complexity which would have had linguistic consequences. The translators use such words as 'nation', 'race', and 'tribe', which suggest social groupings of a much more determinate and coherent nature than would have been the case. We need to be especially suspicious when we see Bede explaining (in Book I, Chapter 15), with apparent conviction, how the Germanic arrivals were the ancestors of the English peoples that surrounded him in the eighth century:

> Those who came over were of the three most powerful nations of Germany – Saxons, Angles, and Jutes. From the Jutes are descended the people of Kent, and of the Isle of Wight, and those also in the province of the West-Saxons who are to this day called Jutes, seated opposite to the Isle of Wight. From the Saxons, that is, the country which is now called Old Saxony, came the East-Saxons, the South-Saxons, and the West-Saxons. From the Angles, that is, the country which is called Anglia [Angulus, modern Angeln], and which is said, from that time, to remain desert to this day, between the provinces of the Jutes and the Saxons, are descended the East-Angles, the Midland-Angles, Mercians, all the race of the Northumbrians, that is, of those nations that dwell on the north side of the river Humber, and the other nations of the English.

The account was influential, and was incorporated into the *Anglo-Saxon Chronicle* for the year 449.

The 'nations' were 'Saxons, Angles, and Jutes'? We dare not trust the names and the descriptions. Nowadays we are used to interpreting community names as if they reflected a social reality that is essentially coherent, territorial, and culturally homogeneous: the Poles live in Poland and do things that are typically Polish, the Danes live in Denmark and do things typically Danish. Of course we know that such characterizations hide a host of variations, not least

1.1 Who was Bede?

Bede – in Old English, Bæda – was born *c.* 672 in Monkton, a Northumbrian settlement just south of the River Tyne (present-day Tyne and Wear). At the age of seven he was taken to the monastery of Wearmouth, near modern Sunderland, and soon after joined the monastery at Jarrow. He became a deacon at nineteen and a priest at thirty, working as a writer and teacher. He died in 735 and was buried at Jarrow, his remains later being moved to Durham Cathedral. A doctor of the Church, he was canonized in 1899. His feast-day is 25 May.

Almost everything we know about Bede comes from an autobiographical chapter at the very end of the *Ecclesiastical History of the English Nation*, which was begun in his late fifties, and finished only four years before he died. He lists in detail all his works until that point: biblical commentaries, treatises on language, biographies, letters, compilations, and histories. The *Ecclesiastical History*, written in Latin (*Historia ecclesiastica gentis Anglorum*), was his masterpiece. His aim was to tell the story of how Christianity arrived in Britain, but in so doing he became the first to give an account of the island's history, and he is the earliest literary source we have for the events which shaped the nation. He scrupulously acknowledged his sources and helpers in a Preface. One of his contacts, a London priest called Nothhelm, even travelled to Rome to search the papal archives for relevant letters from the popes. Bede's wide learning, reinforced by a historian's skills of synthesis and detachment, led to the book quickly becoming an authority throughout Europe, and it was frequently copied. A translation into Old English was instigated (some have thought, made) by King Alfred the Great, and this is the source of the extract on p. 16.

those arising from immigration, emigration, ethnic mixing, and different levels of language proficiency. But in the days described by Bede, the names bore an even greater unpredictability in relation to social conditions. As historian Peter Hunter Blair puts it, referring to Bede, 'there are many grounds for thinking that his threefold division reflects the orderliness of his own mind rather than the realities of the settlements'.[2] Bede himself in fact did not maintain his distinctions consistently, as the quotations suggest, referring to the same people sometimes as *Angli* and sometimes as *Saxones*.

Modern historians now know, thanks especially to twentieth-century archaeological discoveries, that the social setting for these events was much more complex than Bede's outline account suggested. This is hardly surprising. Bede was after all writing some 300 years after the arrival of the Germanic tribes, and even though some of his information came from an earlier source – a treatise written by a sixth-century British monk, St Gildas – that source was still a century away from the time of Vortigern. Both Bede and Gildas, moreover, had a particular focus – the history of Christianity – and the main forces and factors involved in this history did not need to take into account sociolinguistic realities. Any statement about these realities must always be tentative, given the limited evidence, but all conclusions point in the same direction, that fifth-century north-west Europe must have been a salad-bowl of languages and dialects.

The community names of the time were of several kinds. Some were 'tribal', in the sense that all the members of the group would be originally related through kinship: the Angles may well have been a tribe, in this sense, though doubtless mixed with other stock. Other names reflected a much looser sense of 'tribal', being little more than a collection of bands gathered together under a leader. The -*ing* names of English towns suggest this interpretation: *Reading*, for example, was where the 'people of Read' (the 'red one') lived – though Read, of course, might have founded a dynastic succession, and the group would have become more tribal (in the first sense) as time went by. Yet another interpretation of a name is as a label for a confederation of groups who came together for defence or attack: this description seems to suit the Saxons, whose identity was based on their fighting ability with the type of short sword known as the *seax*. As long as a man carried a seax, he would be called Saxon, regardless of his ethnic or geographical origins. (In a similar way, later, all Vikings would be called 'Danes', regardless of whether they came from Denmark or not.)

The names, accordingly, are not as clear-cut as they might appear. In particular, it was perfectly possible for an Angle to 'become' a Saxon by joining one of the seax-wielding groups. And as the Saxons moved westwards towards Normandy from their homeland in south-west Denmark, doubtless many Frisians, Franks, and others would have been incorporated into their ranks. We know least of all about the Jutes. The name Jutland, in northern Denmark (see panel 1.2), suggests an original homeland, but there is evidence that by the time the Jutes arrived in England they had lived elsewhere and adopted other ways. Their burial practice, for example, was inhumation – like that used by the Franks and other tribes on the middle Rhine – and not like that which was usual among the tribes of north-west Germany, who practised cremation. Many of the trappings found in graves in Kent, Sussex, and along the Thames are similar to those discovered in Frankish and Frisian territories. All this mixing suggests that the Jutes had no clear ethnic identity when they crossed the Channel: they may have given their name to Jutland, but they left no name in Britain. Indeed, as Bede never mentions the Jutes again, and as the name never appears in Kentish personal or place-names, a direct ethnic line of connection between Kent and the Continent has often been questioned.

The linguistic situation, always a reflex of social structure, must accord-

1.2 The general direction of the fifth-century Germanic invasions

Geography accounts for the location of the arrivals. Angles migrating from Denmark would arrive along the length of the east coast. Saxons migrating from the northern coast of Continental Europe would arrive in the area of the Thames and along the south coast.

ingly have been much messier than any simple classification could ever reflect. When the invaders arrived in England, they did not bring with them three 'pure' Germanic dialects – Anglian, Saxon, and Jutish – but a wide range of spoken varieties, displaying different kinds of mutual influence. Attempts to find neat origins of the English dialects on the Continent are misguided, notwithstanding the points of similarity which have been noted between, say, Kentish and Frisian. The notion of 'purity' was as mythical then as it is now. A modern analogy is hard to find, but television these days sometimes allows us to observe a battalion of British troops abroad. They are brought together by their military purpose, not by speech: when we listen to them talk, we hear all kinds of accents. Their Anglo-Saxon counterparts would have been no different. Or, if they were different, it would be because the situation was much more volatile, compared with today, and the variation would have been more marked. Their age, after all, was an 'age of migrations' – a period of upheaval following a rise in the Germanic population during the first centuries of the millennium, when small groups were often on the move, living in territories which had no defined political boundaries. Accents and dialects proliferate, in such circumstances.

Traditional accounts of the history of languages tend to minimize or ignore the inherent messiness found in real-life linguistic situations. Philologists have always tried to impose some order on the field by using the notion of a 'family' of languages – the Germanic family, in the present case, with its three main branches: North Germanic (Icelandic, Faeroese, Norwegian, Swedish, Danish), East Germanic (Gothic), and West Germanic (English, Frisian, Dutch, German, and derived languages). The metaphor of a 'family' is helpful, but it is also misleading in its suggestion that languages evolve through nice clear lines of descent, as in a human family. It does not allow for the kind of 'sideways' influence which individual languages have on each other. Varieties of a language which have begun to separate from each other can still influence one another in all kinds of ways, sometimes converging, sometimes diverging. The process never stops, being a reflex of the kind of mutual contact societies have. In these early centuries, communities which lived on the coast used sea-routes enabling them to maintain connections, and some shared linguistic features would have been one of the consequences. A group which moved inland would be less likely to maintain regular contact with its coastal associates, and be more likely to develop new features. Dialect convergence and divergence would be taking place at the same time, in different locations.

We can note both of these processes happening for the Germanic group of languages during the period. In the late second century, the Goths moved into Europe from southern Scandinavia, eventually arriving in the Mediterranean region. During the fourth century, Bishop Wulfilas translated the Bible into Gothic. The language had changed so much during this short time that scholars now consider it to be a distinct, eastern branch of the Germanic family. On the other hand, the westward movement of peoples along the north European coast and into England resulted in a group of languages which had much greater similarities. English and Frisian, indeed, were so close that they would probably have been mutually intelligible for many centuries, especially in Kent. Even today, though mutual intelligibility has long since gone, English people listening to modern Frisian sense a familiarity with its expression which is not present in the case of Dutch or German. Genetic anthropologists have discovered a significant Y-chromosome identity, too (p. 31).[3]

It is not possible to say how intelligible the Angles, Saxons, and Jutes found each other. There was a great deal that unified them culturally, of course. They had a common oral literary heritage and a common set of religious beliefs. Probably their dialects would have been mutually comprehensible, for the most part, though with islands of difficulty due to distinctive local pronunciations and vocabulary. The variation may have been no more than that which differentiates, say, present-day Glasgow, Newcastle, or London. The speech of these cities can be extremely difficult for outsiders to understand, when spoken rapidly and colloquially; but it becomes accessible when people speak slowly, and regular contact with the speakers quickly increases recognizability. Doubtless such variations in style existed in early Germanic, too. But there were significant differences separating the eastern and western branches of Germanic. If a Goth met a Saxon, in the fifth century, they would probably have had great difficulty understanding each other.

Not only was there a great deal of sociolinguistic variety among the Continental peoples before they crossed the Channel and the North Sea, there was substantial variation in Britain already. Bede gives the impression that there were no Germanic people in Britain before the Anglo-Saxon invasions; but we now know that Hengist and Horsa were by no means the first Germanics to arrive in Britain from the European Continent. There is archaeological evidence of a Germanic presence in the Roman towns and forts of the south and east before the end of the Roman occupation in *c.* 400. For example, Germans in Roman military service in Gaul wore belt buckles of a distinctive type, and these have been found in early fifth-century graves at locations along the River Thames. Early runic inscriptions have been found, of Continental origin (see panel 1.3). There is argument over whether the numbers of Germanic incomers were large or small, and what their role was (mercenaries? settlers? traders? invaders?), but there is no doubt that they were there. And their speech – whether a different language, dialect, or accent – would have been distinctive.

Kent must have been an especially mixed sociolinguistic region. The name long precedes the Anglo-Saxon invasions. It is Celtic in origin, from a hypothetical root form *canto-* probably meaning 'rim' or 'border' – hence, 'the land on the border' – and the British tribe that lived there were known as the *Cantii*. As the region on the 'rim' of England, and the part closest to the European mainland, it is likely that there had long been contact with the Germanic peoples. Indeed, Julius Caesar noticed the similarities as early as the 50s BC: he comments in his Gallic Wars (*Commentarii de bello Gallico*, Book V, 14), 'By far the most civilized inhabitants are those living in Kent [Cantium] . . . whose way of life differs little from that of the Gauls.' Soon after, Kent became a trade route to and from the Continent, and as a result was exposed to a wide range

1.3 The Caistor rune

The earliest runic inscription known in England was found in a cremation cemetery at the former Roman town of Caistor-by-Norwich, Norfolk (the name comes from Latin *castra*, 'fort'). It is written on a roe-deer's ankle-bone (*astragalus*), which was probably used as a plaything (perhaps a die in a game), and reads *raihan*, 'roe-deer'. The runic scholar R. I. Page draws attention to the shape of the H rune, which has a single cross-bar: this was typical of northern runic writing, rather than the system used further south in Frisia (where the H was written with two cross-bars).[4] It suggests that the person who used this script came from Scandinavia, possibly southern Denmark. The significance of the find is that it dates from *c.* 400. This person was living in East Anglia well before the Anglo-Saxon invasions began.

of Continental influences, especially from Frisians and Franks. During the late sixth century, in the reign of Æthelbert (who married the Christian daughter of a Frankish king), it would become a major cultural and political centre, doubtless highly cosmopolitan in outlook.

If there had long been Germanic people in Kent, then they may have been responsible – as some scholars have thought – for the naming of the Saxon peoples, as they heard of their arrival. Those to the south came to be called the South Saxons (Sussex) and to the west the West Saxons (Wessex), with those in between the Middle Saxons (Middlesex). Those to the north, curiously, were not called North Saxons (there is no Norsex) but East Saxons (Essex), which suggests that the naming took place at a time when the arrivals on the east coast had moved along the Thames until they could be seen to be 'east' of the other groups. The *-sex* name does not imply that the same people lived in all three areas; indeed, archaeologists have pointed out evidence of close links between Essex and Kent and relatively little in common with Wessex. The other interesting point is that these names are the names of the people, not the place they lived in: if it had been the latter, the names would have appeared as *Sussexland*, or the like – just as *Englaland* ('land of the Angles') would appear later.

A cross-section of British society in 449 would thus show people of many different backgrounds – Celts, Romano-Celts, Germanic immigrants of various origins, probably some Germano-Celts (for how many of the invaders would have brought their wives with them?) – living in tiny communities of perhaps just a few hundred people. But this synchronic picture is not the only dimension we have to consider, in understanding the sociolinguistic forces which influenced Old English. The diachronic dimension – the way language changes over time – must also be taken into account. We must not forget that the various waves of immigration and invasion did not take place all at once. If Germanic people were arriving in Britain in, say, 400, their speech would be very different from those who arrived a century later – even if the two groups of people originated in exactly the same part of the Continent. And at least a century was involved. It was some fifty years before the first waves of Angles and Jutes arrived (449, according to the *Anglo-Saxon Chronicle*), another twenty-five before the South Saxons came (477), and nearly twenty years later before the West Saxons did (495). A lot can happen to pronunciation in a hundred years. We listen today to recordings made by the BBC in the 1920s and are struck by the very different 'far back' sound of Received Pronunciation then (p. 472). How much more different would a century of pronunciation change have been, at a time when there was so little contact between people?

Once in the country, mobility did not cease. Population growth within the Anglo-Saxon groups, plus the continual pressure from new arrivals in the east, forced people to move inland. Although frequently halted through conflict with the British, the Anglo-Saxons rapidly spread throughout central, southern, and north-eastern England (see panel 1.4). By 600 they had reached the area of present-day Dorset, and occupied land north to the River Severn, across central England into Yorkshire, and north along the coast towards the River Tyne. The paths taken by the Anglians followed the major rivers. Some entered the country via the Wash, at the River Ouse, eventually moving north-west to form the kingdom of Lindsey. A major grouping moved south to form the kingdom of East Anglia. A group who settled in an area west of modern Cambridge in the early sixth century came to be known as Middle Angles. Some entered via the River Humber, taking the Trent tributary southwards towards central England: these came to be called Mercians (a name which meant 'marchmen' or 'borderers'). Some moved north from the Humber, along the Yorkshire River Ouse, forming the kingdom of Deira. Further north still, the kingdom of Bernicia came to be established through a series of incursions, initially from the sea and then from the south. There was no movement at that time into Cornwall, Wales, Cumbria, or southern Scotland, where the British were still dominant. Indeed, numerically the Anglo-Saxons were probably a minority until well into the eighth century.

In all this, we are talking about small groups meeting small groups: no national armies existed in the sixth century, or for some time after. Accordingly, it is not possible to generalize about the social consequences of the expansion.

1.4 Early domains of Anglo-Saxon power (seventh century)

In some places, an Anglo-Saxon victory would mean the total displacement of the British; in others, the British would have stayed near by (often preferring to live on the higher ground, while the Anglo-Saxons preferred the lower); in still others, cultural assimilation would have taken place. The traditional view that the Anglo-Saxons arrived and pushed all the British back into Wales and

Cornwall, destroying everything en route, is now known to be simplistic. Although there are several reports in the *Anglo-Saxon Chronicle* of towns being sacked (such as Pevensey, Sussex, in 491), the archaeological evidence suggests that most towns were not. And although some Britons fled to the Welsh mountains, the far north, the Cornish moors, or further afield to Brittany, many – probably the majority – stayed in subjection, and by degrees adopted the new culture.

There would have been a great deal of *accommodation* between people – that is, accents and dialects coming closer together when communities were at peace with each other, and diverging when they were at odds. A great deal of bilingualism must have been heard at the outset, and there must have been some language mixing. There are tantalizing hints of bilingual awareness in some of the place-names. The British name for *Dover*, for example, was *Dubris*, which was a plural form meaning 'waters'. When the name was adopted by the Anglo-Saxons it became *Dofras*, which was likewise a plural form. This suggests that those who named the place had some awareness of Celtic grammar. *Wendover* ('white waters' – a stream) in Berkshire and *Andover* ('ash-tree stream') in Hampshire had a similar history.

Place-names provide intriguing evidence about the developing relationships between the British and the Anglo-Saxons. There are large numbers of Celtic place-names in England. A small selection would include *Arden, Avon, Exe, Leeds,* and *Severn,* as well as the hundreds of compound names which contain a Celtic component. Most of the forms found in these names (insofar as they can be interpreted at all) have meanings to do with features of the landscape, such as *cumb/comb* 'deep valley', *dun* 'hill fort', *lin* 'lake', and several words for 'hill' – *torr, pen, crug, bre*. The Celtic element is italicized in the following selection: *Berk*shire, *Bray, Bre*don, *Cam*bridge, *Car*lisle, *Ciren*cester, *Don*caster, *Glou*cester, Ilfra*combe, Lan*caster, *Leic*ester, *Lin*coln, *Mal*vern, *Man*chester, *Pen*kridge, *Penrith, Pen*zance, *Wilt*shire, *Win*chester, *Wor*cester.

Lists of this kind hide an important point – that the names are not evenly distributed across England. If there are few such names in an area, presumably this was a location where few British people remained, or where the assimilation into Anglo-Saxon society was complete. Conversely, where there are clusters of Celtic names, we must assume a culture where the British survived with their own identity for some time, coexisting with their Anglo-Saxon neighbours, who were presumably fewer in number compared with their compeers in the east. On this basis, we can see a steady increase in Celtic place-names as we look from east to west across England, until we reach Wales and Cornwall, where there are hardly any Germanic names at all. Celtic names in the east are by no means entirely absent, but they do tend to be names of major centres and features, such as *Thames, London, Dover,* and *Kent.* In such cases, we are probably seeing the workings of convenience: the Anglo-Saxons took over the Celtic name simply because it was widely known. A similar pragmatism would be seen many times in the later development of place-names.

In an age of great mobility, contacts would have been very transient and of variable status. At one point, two groups might be trading partners; at another, they might be enemies. There was a continual shifting of local alliances between bands. There must have been dozens of fiefdoms throughout the period. By 600, ten independent domains had evolved south of the River Humber: Lindsey, East Anglia, and Essex in the east; Kent and Sussex in the south-east; Mercia and Middle Anglia in the midlands; Wessex in the south; and Magonsætan and Hwicce in the west, along the Welsh border. By 700, seven 'kingdoms' had been established throughout the country, the so-called Anglo-Saxon Heptarchy of Kent, Sussex, Wessex, Essex, East Anglia, Mercia, and Bernicia (Northumberland), though it would be misleading to think of these domains as being particularly large (some were more like a modern county in size) or as having clear-cut political boundaries. Nor is the balance of power between these kingdoms stable during the next 200 years. East Anglia and Kent were important areas in the seventh century, the latter especially following the arrival of St Augustine and other Roman Catholic missionaries in 597. By the end of that century Northumbria had become a major religious and cultural centre (as Bede would later demonstrate). Mercia's power grew in the eighth century, especially under King Offa. In the ninth century, political power moved south again, with Wessex dominant under King Alfred (reigned 871–99), and it remained there for some time.

1.5 Why England, not Saxonland?

If the Angles established themselves in one half of the country and the Saxons in the other, why did the name of the modern country derive from the former rather than the latter? The historical evidence, though meagre, does not suggest that the Angles were any more numerous than the Saxons, or had greater military successes. Why, then, is the country called *England*, and not *Saxonland, Saxland,* or some other such form? It is a puzzle, but we can make some guesses.

The original use of the name *Angli* (for the people) and *Anglia* (for the country) is found in Latin writers during the seventh century, but only with reference to the Angles (as opposed to the Saxons and Jutes). A king of Kent, Æthelbert, is called *rex Anglorum* – 'king of the Angles'. *Angl-* is later found in Old English as both *Angel-* and *Engl-*. In the Alfredian translation of Bede (Book IV, Chapter 26), for example, we find the phrase *on Engla lande*, translating Latin *in regione Anglorum*, which meant 'in the country of the Angles'. Bede never used

Anglia for the country as a whole: his name for it was *Brittania* or *Britannia* ('Britain').

There was one context, however, where the early Latin writers did give the *Angl-* element prominence. This was in the phrase *Angli Saxones*, used at least from the eighth century to mean the 'English Saxons' (of Britain) as opposed to the 'Old Saxons' (of the Continent). A long time afterwards, as the historical facts began to blur in the popular mind, *Anglo-Saxons* came to be interpreted as 'Angles and Saxons', the combined Germanic people of Britain, which is how the term is used today. But in the eighth century *Angl-* did not have this sense. Rather, it was the crucial, contrastive element in the phrase – the *English* Saxons, as opposed to other kinds. Issues of identity being so important, perhaps it was this prominence which fixed *Angl-* in the intuitions of the people, as a label for the people as a whole?

Whatever the reason, we can see the name broadening its meaning in the ninth century. The Old English translation of Bede uses the term *Angelcynn* (literally, 'race of the Angles', Bede's *gens Anglorum*) to refer to all the Germanic peoples. The adjective *English* makes its first appearance at that time, too – long predating the name *England*. In a treaty made between Alfred and the Dane Guthrum (*c*. 880) we see *English* opposed to *Danish*, and it plainly refers to all of the non-Danish population, not just the Angles. Also, at around the same time, *English* is used for the language: the translation of Bede at one point (Book III, Chapter 19) talks about a monastery *nemned on Englisc* ('called in English') *Cneoferisburh*, and Alfred quite often uses the name in this way.

It took over a century before we find the phrase *Engla lande* referring to the whole country, by the writers of the eleventh-century *Chronicle*. There was then a long period of varied usage, and we find such forms as *Engle land*, *Englene londe*, *Engle lond*, *Engelond*, and *Ingland*. The spelling *England* emerged in the fourteenth century, and soon after became established as the norm.

Then, as now (p. 434), power politics controlled language trends (see panel 1.5). Power residing in Kent meant that the Kentish dialect would gain prestige. Power in the north would lead to a corresponding boost for Northumbrian. And for the first time in the history of English we can see the effect of such power on language, through the medium of writing. The missionaries introduced the Roman alphabet to the country, and large numbers of manuscripts, initially all in Latin, were soon being produced by monastic scribes. By the middle of the seventh century, these scribes were beginning to incorporate Old English forms into their work, devising a new alphabet in the process. It was an uncertain, experimental period, for this was the first time anyone had tried to write down what English people said, and conventions of handwriting, layout, spelling, and style had to be established. The texts soon began to display distinctive features, some of which reflected the regional background of the scribe or the location where he was working. The written language immediately added a new dimension to the language, a fresh set of opportunities for expression, and a millennium later it would provide the data and motivation for a whole new field of study, Old English dialectology.[5]

Interlude 1
The Celtic language puzzle

In fact there are two puzzles. First, why did the Anglo-Saxons not end up speaking the Celtic languages of Britain? Arriving in such small numbers, we might have expected them to adopt the language of the country, as can easily happen after a period of settlement and intermarriage. This is what took place at the time in Normandy, for example, where the Scandinavian invaders ended up speaking French. It is also what took place in England after 1066, with the Norman invaders eventually speaking English. But the Germanic invaders of Britain retained their original language.

The second puzzle. When invaders arrive in a country and impose their own language, they take in words from the indigenous language, often in large numbers. To take a relatively recent example, there are thousands of words in the *Dictionary of South African English* which have come from Afrikaans, Xhosa, Zulu, and other African languages.[6] Although English arrived in South Africa as a language of power, it quickly began to reflect local concerns by assimilating new vocabulary. And we may generalize: even if an invading group ends up adopting the conquered people's language, that language leaves a sign of its presence. When the Vikings arrived in England in the late eighth century, they introduced many Scandinavian loanwords and even managed to exercise an influence on English grammar (p. 76). When the Normans took over England, they introduced thousands of French loanwords into the English they eventually adopted, as well as French conventions of spelling (p. 210). Why, then, are there so few Celtic loanwords in Old English? How can the Anglo-Saxons have failed to be influenced by the majority Celtic language around them?

Apart from the place-names referred to on p. 25, the influence is indeed small, and many of the words which are cited as of Celtic origin are of doubtful etymology. It is sometimes difficult to tell whether a word entered Old English from Welsh, after the Anglo-Saxons arrived, or whether it had been acquired on the Continent from Latin, and was thus already in their language. For example, *bin* 'receptacle' might have derived from an early British word *benna* (compare Welsh *ben* 'wagon') or from an even earlier Latin *benna*; *assen* 'ass' probably came from an Old British word *assen*, but it might have been earlier, from Latin *asinus*. There are also cases of words which probably came from Celtic, but because there are equivalent forms in some Germanic languages, the point is not certain. These include *puck* 'malicious spirit' (Welsh *pwca*), which had a similar form in Old Norse (*puki*), and *crock* 'pot' (Welsh *crochan*), also found in several Scandinavian languages (such as Icelandic *krukka*).

Old English words which do seem to have a clear Celtic connection include *bannoc* 'piece of a loaf or cake', *broc* 'badger', *cammoc* 'cammock, a type of plant', *crag* (compare Welsh *craig* or *carreg*), *dunn* 'grey-brown' (compare Welsh *dwn*), and *wan* 'dark' (compare Welsh *gwan*). *Wan*, for instance, a word not otherwise known in Germanic, turns up in *Beowulf* (l. 702): *Com on wanre niht scriðan sceadugenga* 'The creature of the shadows came stalking in the dusky night' (John Clark Hall's translation). Three other Celtic words turn up in Northumbrian texts, suggesting an ongoing British presence in the far north: *bratt* 'cloak', *carr* 'rock', and *luh* 'lake' (cf. modern *loch*). We must also add to the list a few words introduced by Irish missionaries, such as *ancor* 'anchorite', *clucge* 'bell', and *dry* 'sorcerer' (compare *druid*). There are several words of uncertain etymology with possible Celtic connections cited in the *Oxford English Dictionary*, but even if we included them all, we would only be talking of another twenty or so candidates. A number of other Celtic borrowings (such as *brogue*, *coracle*, and *plaid*) did come into English, but not until well after the Old English period.

There are various explanations, but all are speculation. Perhaps there was so little in common between the Celtic way of life as it had developed in Roman Britain, and the Anglo-Saxon way of life as it had developed on the Continent, that there was no motivation to borrow Celtic words. There might even have been a conscious avoidance of them. This could have happened if the Anglo-Saxons perceived themselves to be so socially superior to the 'barbarians' that Celtic words would have been seen as 'gutter-speak'. Or there could have been avoidance for the opposite reason: because many Celts would have become highly Romanized (for the Romans were in the country for the best part of 400 years), perhaps the Anglo-Saxons perceived them as 'nouveau riche' and wished to distance themselves from such 'posh' speech. Either factor could have been relevant, in different times and places.

Then again, a completely different line of reasoning might have been involved. Perhaps the two ways of life were so similar that the Anglo-Saxons already had all the words they needed. Celtic words which the Anglo-Saxons might most usefully have adopted might already have come into their language from Latin because of the Roman presence in Europe. At the very least they would have been familiar with many Latin words, from encounters with Romans on the Continent. From this point of view, Latin – as the language of political power – would have been a more attractive source of words than

Welsh; and this would have been consolidated when the Irish missionaries arrived in Britain, bringing Latin as the language of a different kind of power. The Celts, too, would have been familiar with Latin: there must have been many Latin-speaking Celts during the Romano-Celtic years. Latin certainly had an influence on early Celtic, as can be seen from such forms as Welsh *eglwys* 'church' from *ecclesia*, or *ysgol* 'school' from *schola*. Several early place-names show this influence, such as the many places whose names have a British form of *ecclesia* as their source: *Eccles*, *Eccleshall*, *Exhall*, *Eccleston* (see also panel 1.6).

1.6 The *cross* question

Was *cross* a Celtic loanword? It was not the normal word for 'cross' in Old English: that was a word with Germanic origins, *rod* 'rood', as in the triumphant line 56 of the Old English poem *The Dream of the Rood*: *Crist wæs on rode* 'Christ was on the cross' (p. 40). So how did *cross* arrive in English?

The word is known in Germanic, deriving from Latin *crux*: Old Norse has *kross*. And as it does not appear in Old English until the tenth century, it is very possible that the Vikings brought the word with them. The earliest usage is in the place-name *Normannes cros* (modern Norman Cross, near Peterborough, Cambridgeshire), which has a Scandinavian ring to it because of the way the specific term precedes the general one (contrast the opposite pattern in Celtic, as in Welsh *Llanfair* 'Church [of] Mary'). Then from the eleventh century it appears in other names, all in the north, such as *Crosby* and *Crosthwaite*.

But some have argued that a word with such Christian significance would be unlikely to have come from a Scandinavian source. Religious words did not on the whole enter English from Germanic, whereas the Irish missionaries brought many religious terms with them. The Latin word had entered Old Irish as *cros*; Welsh has it as *croes*. Certainly stone crosses were common in Ireland, and Irish art influenced the stone crosses of England; so perhaps there was linguistic influence there, too. The matter is unresolved, and probably unresolvable.

Genetic evidence is helping to throw some light on the situation. A study reported in 2002[7] showed a major difference in Y-chromosome markers between men from a selection of seven towns along an east–west transect from East Anglia to north Wales, suggesting a mass migration of Celts from England, with at least half the male indigenous Celtic population of England being displaced. The researchers, having also identified striking genetic similarities between English and Frisian men, concluded that the Welsh border was more of a genetic barrier than the North Sea. Such a significant population movement is suggestive of what we would today call 'ethnic cleansing' – and if this were so, one of the consequences would be a distaste for all things Celtic, especially the language. You do not borrow words from people you have just evicted.

But the linguistic evidence from personal names does not entirely support this scenario. There are not many Celtic names used by Anglo-Saxon personalities, but when they do occur they are of special interest. *Cædwalla, Ceadda, Cedd, Ceawlin, Cerdic*, and *Cumbra* are all Welsh names. *Cumbra*, for example, is very close to the Welsh word for 'Welshman', *Cymro*. But what is interesting is that these are all names of members of the Anglo-Saxon nobility. *Cædwalla*, for instance, was king of Wessex in 685, according to the *Anglo-Saxon Chronicle*, and his conversion to Christianity is described by Bede (Book V, Chapter 7). But *Cædwalla* is a distinctly Welsh name. Indeed, he has a namesake in the Welsh prince *Cadwallon* of Gwynedd – referred to as 'king of the Britons' by Bede (Book II, Chapter 20) – who killed the Northumbrian King Edwin in 633. What sort of society must it have been for Anglo-Saxon royalty to adopt Welsh names?

People are remarkably sensitive about choosing first names, as every parent knows. Great thought is devoted to the matter. No one would give their child the name of an enemy or of a person felt to be disreputable. When people are at war, they may even change their name to avoid being wrongly identified – as famously happened with the British royal family in 1917, when George V replaced Saxe-Coburg-Gotha by Windsor. On the other hand, choosing the name of a person whom one respects, or whom one wants to impress or thank, is a common practice – whether this be an older relative, a family friend, a business contact, or a political ally. People are also much influenced by social trends: some names become highly popular, and in modern times newspapers publish annual lists of the most fashionable choices. Religion exercises a strong influence, too, as with names of saints or biblical personalities. In older times – as still in many societies today – even greater significance was attached to the meanings of names, with children being deliberately called names which mean 'blessed', 'Christ-like', and so on.

So, if some Anglo-Saxon noblemen were giving their children British names, it must mean that, at the very least, there was respect for some members of Celtic society in some parts of the country. A likely scenario is that Anglo-Saxon chieftains would be living in accord with members of the Romano-Celtic nobility, and intermarrying with them. A child would be named for a senior member of one or other family, and this would just as easily be Celtic as Germanic. Some of these children would one day become nobility themselves, and use of the name would spread. And if senior members of the household did such things, then junior members would also find it a fashionable thing to do. We do not know who were the parents of Cædmon – the seventh-century monastery stable-lad who, according to Bede (Book IV, Chapter 24), became

England's first Christian poet – but they gave him a Welsh name. Why such intimate contact with Celtic tradition did not result in a greater influx of Celtic loanwords into Old English remains one of the great puzzles in the history of the language.

Chapter 2 The Old English dialects

The names of four of the Anglo-Saxon kingdoms have given us the names of the four Old English dialects recognized in philological tradition: West Saxon, Kentish, Mercian, and Northumbrian, with the last two sometimes grouped together as a northern variety, Anglian. The question which immediately arises is: why only four? If dialects are such important markers of identity (as modern studies have repeatedly shown), and if Anglo-Saxon society was so complex (as the account in Chapter 1 suggests), we would expect there to be many more. Was Britain at the time not so linguistically heterogeneous after all?

This initial impression derives from the nature of the evidence available to us from the Anglo-Saxon period, and is highly misleading. The four dialects are judgements based on the investigation of the surviving literary texts, and these are few and fragmentary. Toronto University's *Dictionary of Old English Corpus*[1] shows that the entire body of Old English material from 600 to 1150 in fact consists of only 3,037 texts (excluding manuscripts with minor variants), amounting to a mere 3 million words. A single prolific modern author easily exceeds this total: Charles Dickens' fiction, for example, amounts to over 4 million. Three million words is not a great deal of data for a period in linguistic history extending over five centuries, and it is a tiny amount when it comes to looking for signs of dialect variation, which by their nature are going to be occasional. That scholars have been able to find evidence of even four major dialect areas is quite an achievement, under these circumstances. In reality, there must have been many more. East Anglia is an example of a major gap. There would have been many dialects in this area, from what we know of early patterns of settlement, but there are no Old English texts which represent them. Doubtless thousands of manuscripts were destroyed in the Viking invasions.

The texts which do exist are thinly scattered throughout the period and around the country (see panel 2.1). They fall into three broad types. The first category comprises glossaries of Latin texts, where scribes added Old English equivalents to the Latin words between the lines or in the margins. Such glossaries vary greatly in size from just a few words to several thousand; for example, the Corpus manuscript (from Corpus Christi College, Cambridge) comprises over 2,000 glossed words; the Book of Psalms (the Vespasian Psalter) over 30,000. The second category comprises a varied range of prose works, several of which are associated with the names of King Alfred, Abbot Ælfric, and Bishop Wulfstan. These include charters, laws, local records, recipes, medical texts, inscriptions, cryptograms, lists of names (of kings, bishops, saints, abbots, martyrs), the *Anglo-Saxon Chronicle*, translations, homilies, devotional and liturgical texts, letters, dialogues, and imaginative writings. The third category comprises the poetry of the period, mainly found in four collections dating from around 1000 – the Vercelli, Exeter, Beowulf, and Junius texts – and including the major poems: *Beowulf, The Wanderer, The Seafarer, The Battle of Maldon*, and *The Dream of the Rood*. Also in the poetic corpus are some smaller works, such as 'Cædmon's Hymn' and 'Bede's Death Song', several riddles, verses on biblical themes, and various songs, charms, inscriptions, and fragments.

2.1 The textual sources for early Old English

Prob. date	Northumbrian	Mercian	West Saxon	Kentish
675	Franks Casket inscription			
700	Ruthwell Cross inscription	Epinal glosses Charters		
725	Person and place-names in Bede Cædmon's Hymn Bede's Death Song	Person and place-names in Bede Charters		
750	Leiden Riddle	Charters		Charters
775		Blickling glosses Erfurt glosses Charters		Charters
800		Corpus glosses		
825		Vespasian Psalter glosses Lorica Prayer Lorica glosses		Charters

Prob. date	Northumbrian	Mercian	West Saxon	Kentish
850			Charters	Charters Medicinal recipes
875			Charters Royal genealogies Martyrologies	
900			Cura pastoralis Anglo-Saxon Chronicle	
925			Orosius Anglo-Saxon Chronicle	
950		Royal glosses	Anglo-Saxon Chronicle Medicinal recipes	Charters Kentish Hymn Kentish Psalm Kentish proverb glosses
975	Rushworth Gospel glosses Lindisfarne Gospel glosses Durham Ritual glosses	Rushworth Gospel glosses		

This table summarizes the main sources which survive in the first 300 years of the Old English period, arranged chronologically and assigned to the four main dialect areas. The dates are for the language, not the manuscripts, which are often extant only in a later version. Several of the early texts are extremely small: the Franks Casket inscription is some fifty words; 'Bede's Death Song' is five lines; 'Cædmon's Hymn' is nine lines; the Leiden Riddle is fourteen lines. By contrast, the Vespasian Psalter gloss contains text from the 150 psalms, and the *Anglo-Saxon Chronicle* gives entries for several centuries.

The panel gives an indication of how the texts distribute themselves over time and place in the first three centuries of the period.[2] The evidence for a Kentish dialect is thin, with just a few documents, glosses, and poetic texts, chiefly ninth/tenth century, displaying features that seem to be south-eastern in character. Although not numerous, these features are none the less among the most interesting in the early history of English. Several, indeed, exercise a permanent influence on the language, being taken up by some Middle English writers (notably, Chaucer) and eventually entering Standard English. The case of *merry* (see panel 2.2) provides an illustration. By contrast, the bulk of the Old English corpus is West Saxon in character, reflecting the steady growth in West Saxon power during the tenth century – a hegemony which lasted until the arrival of the Normans. Not only is this dialect found in the texts of the

2.2 Why not Mirry England?

The earliest record of the word *merry* is in a translation of the sixth-century *De Consolatione philosophiae* (*Consolation of Philosophy*) by the Roman statesman Boethius, made by or for King Alfred in the last decade of his reign. It is spelled *myrige*, the *y* spelling representing a short vowel sound high up in the front of the mouth, pronounced with rounded lips, similar to the vowel in French *tu* or Scots *you*. Several other words had this vowel, such as *syn* 'sin', *fyllan* 'fill', and *mynster* 'minster'. As the modern spellings show, the pronunciation changed over time into the modern [i] sound. What seems to have happened is that people stopped pronouncing the vowel with their lips rounded. Judging by the way *i* spellings start to appear, this change was under way by the early Middle Ages.

So why didn't this change affect *myrige*? If the word had followed the trend, it would have appeared in Modern English as *mirry*. The answer lies in the dialects.

The vowel in *merry* had two other spellings in Old English. There was a spelling with *u*, which seems to relate to the south-west, and a spelling with *e*, which is found in the south-east. Judging by the sounds we associate with an *e* spelling, it would appear that Kentish people pronounced these words without the lip-rounding and in a much more open way. In Modern English, we can hear a similar lowering of the [i] vowel in some accents, such as when people from Glasgow pronounce *Jimmy* in a way which makes it sound more like *Jemmy*. *Sin* must have sounded like *sen*, in Anglo-Saxon Kent, and that is how we sometimes find it spelled.

Out of the tangle of spellings in Middle English (p. 211), in which many variants coexisted – Chaucer, for example, has spellings of *merry* with *e*, *u*, and *y* – it is the Kentish *e* form which has survived. A few other words went the same way, such as *hemlock*, *knell*, and *left* – a permanent memorial to an Old English dialect.

Alfredian era, shown in the chronology panel above, it is the dialect which unifies the major poetic works dating from year 1000 and beyond. For reasons of both quantity and literary quality, therefore, it is the West Saxon dialect of this period which is used as the standard introduction to Old English in textbooks and courses (p. 54).

The early appearance of Northumbrian texts is not surprising when we recall that by 700 several major centres of learning had emerged in the north, notably at Jarrow, Durham, and Lindisfarne, with Bede and later Alcuin producing influential works. The amount of language in these texts is not large, but there are enough variant forms used in a consistent way to indicate that a distinctive Northumbrian dialect existed by the beginning of the eighth century. An example is given on p. 45. Interlinear glosses from the late tenth century confirm the character of this dialect, notably those added to the Lindisfarne and Rushworth Gospels. The absence of Northumbrian texts between the eighth and tenth centuries is a further result of the Viking burnings.

The growth of Mercia as a political power and a centre of culture and learning, during the eighth century, is reflected in the survival of several texts from that period. The most important are glossaries in which many of the forms display a distinctive West Midlands character, notably the Corpus and Vespasian Psalter texts. A surprising number of charters, land records, and other official documents have also survived, reflecting the growth of political and legal frameworks during the period, especially under Offa, and they show many Mercian features. By no means all of these texts were actually written in Mercia, but they do contain features which could only have been produced by people who were either from Mercia or whose speech had been influenced by Mercians. Canterbury, in particular, attracted scholars from all over the country, given its status as an authoritative religious centre within England. Several eighth-century archbishops, indeed, were from the Midlands, and we can well imagine that their speech would have provided a prestigious model. Mercian dialect features would easily find their way into Kentish texts, as a consequence. The same influence was later apparent in Wessex, at the end of the eighth century, when Alfred began to realize his vision of a cultural renaissance. To achieve his aims, in the absence of local expertise, he needed help from outside, which he found by employing such scholars as Wærferþ and Plegemund, who came from Mercia. Although many texts which appeared during his reign, such as the *Cura pastoralis* (*Pastoral Care*) and the first parts of the *Anglo-Saxon Chronicle*, are predominantly West Saxon in dialect character, they display a noticeable admixture of Mercian forms.

There are several examples of this happening in the early years of the *Parker Chronicle*, a manuscript very much associated with Winchester and King Alfred.[3] *Æþelm ealdorman*, 'Aldorman Æthelm', is one of three chief shire officers identified in the year 893. The scribe reporting the events of that year spells the first vowel of this word with *ea*, which is a typically West Saxon spelling for an *a*-type vowel when it is followed by *l* and another consonant. But earlier in the *Chronicle*, in the handwriting of a different scribe, we read for the year 837: *Her Wulfheard aldormon gefeaht at Hamtune* – 'In this year Aldorman Wulfheard fought at Southampton'. Here, *alderman* is spelled with an *a*, which is a typically Mercian spelling for the vowel in the same context. If this were an isolated case, we might dismiss it as an error. But we see the same difference repeated in other words of the same kind, such as the forms for 'all', which in year 892 is *ealle* and in year 853 is *alle*, and those for 'gave', which in year 893 is *sealde* and in year 836 is *salde* (the form derives from *sellan*, which eventually gave Modern English *sell*). The likelihood is that the early part of the *Chronicle* was written by a Mercian, who left some dialect fingerprints on the West Saxon text.

2.3 The Dream of the Rood

This is an extract from an Old English manuscript: the last four lines of p. 105r of the Vercelli Book (MS *Vercelli Biblioteca Capitolare CXVII*) preserved in the Cathedral Library at Vercelli, northern Italy), dating from the end of the tenth century. It contains a poem known as *The Dream of the Rood*, in which the author recounts a dream about Christ's cross, which speaks to him about the burden it carried. The extract is part of the cross's reminiscence, beginning at line 55, *Crist wæs on rode* 'Christ was on the cross'. The words are spaced (unlike in the runic inscription), but the text is written in run-on lines, and editors have to 'find' the poetic units, using such clues as rhythm and patterns of alliteration. All five of the distinctive Old English letters are used:

æ ('ash'), close to Modern English *a* in *cat*
þ ('thorn'), the equivalent of Modern English voiceless *th* as in *thin*
ð ('eth'), the equivalent of Modern English voiced *th* as in *this*
ƿ ('wynn'), usually replaced by a *w* in modern editions
ȝ ('yogh'), usually replaced by a *g* in modern editions

Note also the use of 'long' letters for *r* and *s* in the word *Crist* and elsewhere. A transliteration of the extract reads as follows, with modern punctuation added,[4] along with a word-for-word translation and a modern equivalent.

Crist   þæs on rode.
Christ   was on cross
Hpæðere þær fuse   feorran   cpoman
Yet   there hasteners from afar came
to þam æðelinʒe. Ic þæt eall be heold.
to the   prince   I that all   beheld
Sare   ic pæs mid sorʒum ʒedrefed, hnaʒ ic h pæðre þam secʒum to handa,
grievously I was with sorrows troubled, bowed I yet   the men   to hands
eaðmod, elne   mycle. ʒenamon   hie þær ælmihtiʒne ʒod,
humble   strength great   took hold of they there almighty   god
ahofon hine of   ðam [hefian pite]
lift   him from the   [heavy torment]

Christ was on the cross.
Yet, hastening ones came there from afar
to the prince. I beheld all that.
I was grievously troubled with sorrows, yet I bowed to the hands of men
in humbleness with great zeal. There they took hold of Almighty God,
lifted him from the heavy torment.

A distinctive variant

Short extracts from the poem (less than fifteen lines in all) are spelled out in runes
along the edges of the huge (5.3 metres / 17 ft 4 in.) Ruthwell Cross, sited in a
church at Ruthwell, south of Dumfries, south-west Scotland, often said to be the
finest surviving piece of sculpture from the Anglo-Saxon period. Its date is uncertain, but thought to be the first half of the eighth century, perhaps *c.* 750. Some of
the lines in the manuscript page displayed on p. 40 are on the west face, including
line 56, *Krist was on rodi.* The runic lettering (there are no spaces between the
words) reads as follows:

ᛣ ᚱᛁᛋᛏ ᚹᚠᛋ ᚩᚾ ᚱᚩᛈᛁ

k r i s t w a s o n r o d i

Even in this fragment, we can see the presence of Old English variation. In the
manuscript text of the poem, the word for 'cross', *rode*, is what we would expect
to find in West Saxon. But the Ruthwell Cross inscription has the Northumbrian
form, *rodi*. Similarly, in the second line of the extract above, the word for 'came'
does not appear on the Cross in its West Saxon form, *cpoman*, but with the
final -*n* missing, *kwomu*. The omission of final -*n* is a characteristic of several
Northumbrian texts.

Examples like these suggest that we must regard dialect mixing as a normal part of the Old English linguistic situation (see panel 2.3). Mixing takes place when people from different dialect backgrounds come into contact and let themselves be influenced by each other. The amount and direction of the mixing (whether A influences B more than B influences A) is largely a matter of relative prestige, about which we know little, for we have only hints about the social background of individual Anglo-Saxon scribes. But we do know there was considerable mobility. Travel records of the time suggest that the monks moved around the country a great deal, often bringing copies of books with them and staying for long periods in their host monasteries. There they would continue their scribal activities, working in association with others who might display different dialect backgrounds, and influencing – and being influenced by – different scribal practices and conventions. A Mercian in a Wessex household would inevitably be much affected by the norms in use there, but he would not be able to eliminate his dialect origins completely. In the absence of a standardized spelling system, he would continue to operate with a phonetic spelling system: an Old English word would be spelled on the basis of how it sounded to the writer, who would instinctively follow his own pronunciation and assign the closest letters he could find.

The *alderman* example illustrates the process in action. The scribe who wrote the first vowel sound with a single symbol, *a*, was presumably used to hearing it as a sound with a steady-state quality (a single-element, or 'pure', vowel). The scribe who wrote it with two letters, *ea*, would only have done this if he had been used to hearing it differently. The likelihood is that he knew it as a sound with two successive qualities in it (a diphthong), the first *e*-like, the second *a*-like, and he scrupulously identified both. (An alternative is that he heard it as a sound which was neither *a* nor *e*, but somewhere in between, so he used the two letters as a way of trying to represent its middle-of-the-road character.) The scribes' different auditory preferences would stem from their different dialect backgrounds.

As long as a scribe lived his whole life in one place, we would expect this principle to produce a reasonably consistent writing system. But, as we have seen, the monks did not always stay in one place. A Mercian scribe newly arrived in a southern scriptorium, such as Canterbury, who found his workplace and colleagues congenial, would inevitably find his accent accommodating to those around him, and his new pronunciations would be likely to affect his spelling preferences, probably without him even noticing it. Such variations can be found today, even when we have a standardized spelling system. I often get letters from British scholars living in the USA whose spelling mixes British and American conventions – *theater* alongside *theatre*, *medieval* alongside *mediaeval*, and so on. Today people worry about such things, because we treat the consistent use of a standardized spelling system as a sign of an educated person. In Anglo-Saxon times, no such worry existed. Spelling variation was normal – and indeed remained so until the eighteenth century (p. 393).

There are many cases where, within a single text written by one person – sometimes even within a single line – we find two different spellings. A Kentish man called Abba made his will in the mid 830s,[5] and talks about what he (*man, mon* = 'one') will leave his brother: one clause begins *ond him man selle* 'and to him one gives . . .'; the next begins *ond mon selle him* 'and one gives to him . . .'. Why the variation? We first need to know that the word for 'man' was typically spelled *man* or *mann* in the south but *mon* or *monn* in the north. (The spelling variation can still be encountered today in written representations of Scots speech, p. 489, which regularly use *mon*.) Mercian and Northumbrian texts tend to use *mon(n)*. *hwet is **mon** ðæt gemyndig ðu sie his oððe sunu **monnes** forðon ðu neosas hine* ('What is man that you should be mindful of him or the son of man that you should care for him'), says the psalmist (Vespasian Psalter, Psalm 8). West Saxon and Kentish texts tend to use *man(n)*. *Ic heortan **mannes** gestrangie* ('I strengthen the heart of man'), says the baker in the late West Saxon *Colloquy* of Ælfric (l. 190). Most of the 'man' spellings in Abba's will are *mon* or *monn*, but both *man* and *mann* also appear. It rather looks as if Abba dictated his will to a Mercian scribe working in Kent, whose scribal preference for *mon* was being influenced by the *man* forms used around him.

Inconsistency would be especially likely to emerge if a sound in a word was not heard clearly – as is typically the case when a vowel occurs in an unstressed syllable. *Man* turns up again in the last syllable of *alderman*, but there it does not have the *a* vowel as we hear it when the word is spoken in isolation. It is a more relaxed pronunciation, articulated towards the centre of the mouth, sounding more like 'mun' (the precise phonetic symbol is [ə]). The same sort of reduction in vowel quality would have been found in Old English, and we can well imagine a scribe puzzling over which symbol to use for a sound which was not like the 'usual' *a*. For our Mercian scribe working in Canterbury, the 'pull' would be in two directions, towards *o* and *a*, and it is not surprising, accordingly, to find both spellings used: so, in the *Parker Chronicle*, we find *aldormon* used twice in the year 837 and *aldorman* a few lines later used twice in the year 843. The uncertainty would apply whatever dialect was used – as at the point later in the *Chronicle* where the second scribe talks about *Æþelm ealdorman*: one of Æþelm's colleagues is identified as *Æþered ealdormon* earlier in the same line.

The motivation to write phonetically was undoubtedly strong; but other factors could interfere with it. Local orthographic norms, in particular, could pull a spelling in a fresh direction. A Canterbury-based Mercian scribe would see other spellings of a word than the ones he himself used, and perhaps be influenced by them. Doubtless there was discussion within the scriptorium about how some words, especially the names of important people, should be spelled. Younger scribes would copy the habits of older ones. Traditional Latin spellings would exercise an influence, too. In a situation where copying is routine, factors such as tiredness and poor light would affect performance accuracy, especially when letter shapes and word sequences resembled each other. This would be reinforced by differences in personality: some scribes would have been meticulous copyists; others would have been cavalier. We know there were many errors from the corrections which some manuscripts show. For example, at the very end of the entry for the year 845 in the *Parker Chronicle*, we find the words 7 *siȝe namon* 'and won the victory', referring to a defeat of the Danes by aldorman Eanwulf and others. The very next sentence – the first sentence of the year 851 (there are no entries for the intervening years) – also ends with 7 *siȝe namon*, this time referring to a defeat by aldorman Ceorl. It is the kind of copying danger which has affected copyists and typesetters down the centuries: the eye jumps from the end of the first sentence to the end of the second, and you carry on copying (typesetting) the next sentence, leaving out the second one altogether. This is exactly what the scribe did. In this case, he fortunately noticed his error, erased the mistaken sentence (though leaving several words visible, which is how we know the error happened), and carried on correctly.

Most of the dialect conclusions about Old English are based on the spelling variations found in the texts, which are assumed to reflect differences in the way words were pronounced. But some of the evidence goes beyond pronunciation (phonology). In particular, a great deal can be deduced from the way words were constructed and the kinds of inflectional ending they had (morphology). Old English still retained a great deal of the grammatical structure of the Germanic family of languages. Certain types of meaning (such as the different nuances of time, manner, and mood in verbs) and the relationship between words in a sentence (such as between subject, verb, and object, 'who's doing an action, who's affected by an action') were very largely expressed by varying the actual shape of the words, especially by using different word endings (inflections). Modern English, by contrast, has very few such inflections, expressing meaning relationships either by using extra words or by varying the order of words in a sentence. Thus, we express most semantic relationships in the verb by adding an 'auxiliary verb' – *I walk* becomes *I have walked*, *I was walking*, *I will walk*, *I may walk*, and so on. The meaning of 'who does what to whom' is signalled by changing the order of the words: in *John kisses Janet*, we know that it is *John* who is doing the kissing; in *Janet kisses John*, we know that it is the other way round. Modern English does still have a few inflections, notably to express plural (*cat, cats*), possession (*cat, cat's*), comparison (*big, bigger, biggest*), the third-person singular (*walk, walks*), durational aspect (*walk, walking*), and the simple past tense (*walk, walked*). But in Old English far more meanings were capable of being expressed in this way, and variations in the inflectional endings are therefore an important potential source of dialect distinctiveness – just as they are today (p. 480).

Pronouns and the verb 'to be' provide good examples. How would you say 'they are' in Old English? In West Saxon, you had two choices, derived from different roots and slightly different in nuance. From the root verb *wesan*, you could say *hi sindon* or *hi sind* – forms which were sometimes also spelled with a *y*, and with *sind* sometimes ending with a *t* (as in the pronunciation of modern German *Sie sind*). From the root verb *beon*, you could say *hi beoð* – a form which might be compared with the present-day regional usage, *they be*. But in Northumbrian and Mercian texts, we would find *hi arun* or *earun* – and it is actually this form which eventually becomes the standard usage: 'are'. Or again, how would you say 'I love you' in Old English? In West Saxon, you would say, talking to a single beloved, *ic lufie þe* (*ic* was pronounced like 'itch'; the *f* of *lufie* was sounded like a *v*; and *þe* was roughly like Modern English 'they'). If talking to several beloveds, it would be *ic lufie eow*. You love me? *þu lufast me*. They love us? *hi lufiað us*. But early northern texts used a different form of the pronoun as an object of the verb: *þec, eowic, mec,* and *usic*. Up north, they said *ic lufie þec* (see further, panel 2.4).

Variations in phonology and morphology are especially useful as guides to dialect identity, because they are likely to turn up fairly frequently in a text. Phonological variations are the commonest, because several words containing a particular sound are likely to appear on a page. The present paragraph contains many instances of words containing the sound /e/, for example. In an inflected language, morphological variations are next in frequency: even in Modern English we can find several examples of an inflectional ending in a short text – a dozen instances of the plural -*s*, for example, just in the present paragraph. Vocabulary variations, however, are much less common: the chances of finding a particular dialect word in a text are fairly small. An everyday word such as *frozen*, for example, does not turn up at all on this page (apart from in this instance), or indeed anywhere else in the book. And when the entire corpus is so small, it is difficult to be sure whether a word is genuinely dialectal in any case. If a word is found only in a Northumbrian text, for example, it does not mean that it is a Northumbrian dialect word; it may well be just a word which happens not to be recorded in the texts of any of the other dialects.

Considerable progress has been made in the lexical domain in recent

2.4 Three Our Fathers

A good way of developing a sense of the nature and extent of textual variation is to find a passage which occurs in several manuscripts – such as one of the biblical texts. The Lord's Prayer is a convenient example (Matthew 6: 9–13), as it appears in West Saxon (WS), Northumbrian (N), and Mercian (M) versions. The texts chosen show just one set of regional possibilities: for example, an alternative Northumbrian version exists in which the first line has *ðu bist* instead of *ðu art*. In several places, the reason for the variant form is unclear.

The WS text is late eleventh century (taken from a Corpus Christi College, Cambridge, manuscript, 140); the N text is late tenth century (from the Lindisfarne Gospel); the M text is early tenth century (British Library Royal w.A.xx). The word order from the interlinear glosses has been rearranged for ease of comparison, following the procedure of Thomas Toon.[6] The fairly literal translation follows the WS text.

The terms 'further forward' and 'further back' refer to the position of the tongue when producing vowels. pron. = pronunciation

Area	Text	Selected points for comment
WS1	fæder ure þu þe eart on heofonum	*fæder*: pron. of *a* is further forward compared to N
N1	fader urer ðu art in heofnum	*art*: pron. of *a* is further back before *r* and a consonant
M1	feder ure þu eart in heofenum	*feder*: pron. of *a* is further forward compared to WS and N
	'our father thou who art in heaven'	
WS2	si þin nama gehalgod	
N2	sie ðin noma gehalgad	*noma*: northern pron. of *a* before a nasal consonant (p. 42)
M2	se þin noma is gehalgad	*noma*: northern pron. of *a* before a nasal consonant (p. 42)
	'be thy name hallowed'	
WS3	to becume þin rice, gewurþe ðin willa	*becume*: *u* is further back compared to N and M
N3	to cymeð ðin ric, sie ðin willo	
M3	to cyme þin rice, sie þin willa	
	'to come thy kingdom, be done thy will'	
WS4	on eorðan swa swa on heofonum	

Area	Text	Selected points for comment
N4	in eorðo suæ is in heofne	*suæ*: pron. of *a* is further forward compared to WS
M4	on eorþan swe in heofenum	*swe*: pron. of *a* is further forward compared to WS and N
	'on earth as in heaven'	
WS5	urne gedæghwamlican hlaf syle us to dæg	
N5	userne ofer wistlic hlaf sel us todæg	*userne*: northern form of pronoun
M5	ur deghweamlice hlaf sele us to deg	*deg*: pron. of *a* is further forward compared to WS and N
	'our daily bread give us today'	
WS6	7 forgyf us ure gyltas	
N6	7 forgef us usra scylda	*usra*: northern form of pronoun
M6	7 forgef us ussa scylda	
	'and forgive us our guilts'	
WS7	swa swa we forgyfað urum gyltendum	
N7	suæ uoe forgefon usum scyldgum	*uoe*: lip-rounding of *e* after *w*
M7	swe 7 us for gef ure scylde	*swe*: pron. of *a* is further forward compared to WS and N
	'as we forgive our guilty ones'	
WS8	7 ne gelæd þu us on costnunge	
N8	7 ne inlæd usih in costunge	*usih*: northern form of pronoun
M8	7 nu in læde is in costunge	
	'and not lead thou us into temptation'	
WS9	ac alys us of yfele	
N9	ah gefrig usich from yfle	*usich*: northern form of pronoun (p. 44)
		from: northern pron. of *a* before a nasal consonant
M9	a les us from yfele	*from*: northern pron. of *a* before a nasal consonant
	'but free us from evil'	

decades, thanks to several large-scale studies and the compilation of computer concordances. In particular, hundreds of words have been noted, from a good range of sources, which seem to be specifically Anglian – as opposed to being common Old English or specifically West Saxon in character. A few of these are listed in panel 2.5. It is even possible to go further, and to identify items that are specifically Mercian or Northumbrian: among the latter, for example, are *hæsere* 'master', *portcwen* 'prostitute', *hoga* 'prudent', and *utacund*

2.5 Some dialect word differences in Old English

Modern gloss	Found in Anglian only	Found in West Saxon or used more widely
bell	clucge	bell
blind	bisene	blind
border	fæs	fnæd
chalice	cælc	calic
disappear	acwincan	acwinan
false	lygge	leas
feed	alan	fedan
loss	los	lor
pride	oferhygd	ofermod
sell	bebycgan	sellan

'foreign', as well as some specifically Celtic words, such as *carr* 'rock' and *luh* 'loch' (p. 30). A detailed study of the words for 'pride, haughtiness' (Latin *superbia*) in a religious context demonstrated that a cluster of words based on *oferhygd* were exclusively northern, whereas other clusters based on *ofermod*, *prut*, and *modig* were found only in the south – *ofermod* in early texts, the others in later ones.[7]

Some elements of word formation also seem to have been dialectally restricted. One of the most thoroughly analysed elements is the use of the female agent noun ending (modern *-ess*, as in *actress, waitress*): this is *-estre* in West Saxon and *-icge* in Anglian. Thus we find the word for 'huntress' appearing as *hunticge* in the north and as *huntigestre* in the south; '(female) sinner' is *synnicge* in the north, whereas '(female) harpist' is *hearpestre* in the south. The form expressing the idea of '-bearing' is another example about which scholars are fairly confident: this was *-berende* in the north, as in *æppelberende* 'apple-bearing', but *-bære* in the south, as in *blostmbære* 'blossom-bearing'. Several other possible dialectally different forms have been proposed. But conclusions often have to be tentative, especially in the case of infrequent words. Even if the dialect provenance of a text is known, there is ultimately no guarantee that an isolated word belongs to that dialect. It might be a word from another dialect that the copyist has introduced, deliberately or in error – especially likely in the later period when a West Saxon scribe was copying manuscripts of Anglian origin. It might be a word preferred by a particular scribal centre (p. 52). It might be an archaic word, from an earlier period of Old English, not otherwise known. The uncertainties mean that definite conclusions about dialect lexical usage are often lacking, and our knowledge of Old English word-geography remains very limited.

Dialect variations affecting the arrangement of words in sentences (syntax) are also not commonly encountered. The basic patterns of word order (such as subject – verb – object) identify the language as a whole, and are not likely to show much dialect variation. And such syntactic variations as do exist turn up infrequently: as with vocabulary, we might read a whole text without encountering a single instance. For example, imperative constructions (commands) are conspicuous by their absence in this (or any) expository book. Also, in many Old English texts we cannot trust the syntactic information at all, because of the way the text was compiled: in particular, writing glosses above the words of a Latin text tells us very little about natural Old English word order. In Ælfric's *Colloquy*, for example, the glossator takes a sentence (l. 73) and handles it word by word:

Heortas ic ʒefelnʒc in nettum 7 bar   ic ofsloh
Ceruos   cepi   in retibus et aprum iugulawi
Harts I caught in nets and boar I slew[8]

How far such sequences illustrate a natural Old English word order it is difficult to say. Just occasionally, you see what must be a genuine Old English word order coming through – such as in line 13, where the Latin reads *Professus sum monachus*, literally 'professed I am monk', and the English gloss reads *Ic eom ʒeanpyrde monuc* – 'I am a professed monk'.

One thing is clear: because the entire corpus is the product of a scribal elite, it gives no information about the dialect variations which ordinary people would have used. So much of the material belongs to specialized stylistic varieties, such as religious and legal language, or is consciously innovative and poetic. A record of everyday conversational speech is hardly ever found, if we exclude the formulaic poetic haranguing of opposing army leaders (as in *The Battle of Maldon*). The earliest fragment of a plausible conversation between 'ordinary folk' is in Bede's *Ecclesiastical History* (Book IV, Chapter 24) – that between the cowherd Cædmon and a man who appears to him in a dream. As Bede reports the event, Cædmon leaves a banquet ashamed that he cannot take his turn at singing anything for the assembly, goes home, and falls asleep. The following exchange then takes place (omitting the linking phrases, such as 'he spoke'):

Cædmon, sing me hwæthwugu.
Cædmon, sing me something.
Ne con ic noht singan; and ic for þon of þeossum gebeorscipe ut eode ond hider gewat, for þon ic naht singan ne cuðe.

I can sing nothing; and for that reason I went out from this banquet and came
   hither, because I did not know how to sing anything.
Hwæðre þu meaht me singan.
However you can sing for me.
Hwæt sceal ic singan?
What shall I sing?
Sing me frumsceaft.
Sing me creation.[9]

Fascinating as this is, it gives us only the barest of hints about everyday speech.
'Sing me creation' might sound a little stilted – but it is a construction which
has lasted down the centuries. 'Sing me a story' is the name of an album of
children's songs compiled by *Sesame Street*'s Bob McGrath in 1998.

There is one recorded example of a fairly extensive Old English conversation – the pupil–teacher dialogue which forms the *Colloquy* of Ælfric. But
we can hardly take this as representative, for – apart from the odd syntax,
referred to above – it was designed as an instructional technique for use in
monastic schools, especially for teaching Latin. It has a question-and-answer
style, designed to elicit vocabulary, as this extract shows (ll. 50–58):

Canst þu æniȝ þinȝ?	'Do you know how to do anything?'
Scis tu aliquid?	
Ænne cræft ic cann.	'I know one occupation.'
Unam artem scio.	
Hƿylcne?	'Which?'
Qualem?	
Hunta ic eom.	'I am a hunter.'
Uenator sum.	
Hƿæs?	'Whose?'
Cuius.	
Cincȝes.	'The king's.'
Regis.	
Hu beȝæst þu cræft þinne?	'How do you carry out your work?'
Quomodo exerces artem tuam?	
Ic brede me max	'I knot myself a net'
Plecto mihi retia	
7 settle hiȝ on stoƿe ȝehæppre . . .	'and set it up in a convenient place . . .'
et pono ea in loco apto . . .	

A sequence like this shows some natural-sounding ellipsis (p. 8), and is probably
the closest we will ever get to Old English conversational style.

Even though the Old English corpus is small, it contains a remarkable amount of variation. The problem for the scholar is to decide which bits of the variation are random error and which reflect some aspect of the sociolinguistic situation of the time. Sometimes, external evidence can help. If we know, for example, that a particular charter was authorized by a Mercian king granting Mercian land to a Mercian nobleman, and the manuscript has stayed in a Mercian archive, then it is very likely that it was drawn up by a Mercian scribe, and so the words it contains would reflect Mercian speech. But such clear situations are far from typical. In a case where a Mercian king granted land in Kent to a Kentish monastery, it is unclear whether the deed would be drawn up by someone from the king's scriptorium or the monastery's: we might expect it to be the king's, but the information about Kentish land boundaries and contents would be more readily available to the local scribes, so perhaps they would have been involved. Perhaps both parties were involved in writing different sections of the charter. Perhaps a single Mercian scribe compiled the whole thing, but wrote a section down from the dictation of a Kentish man. And we must not discount what is probably the commonest scenario of all: the original document was entirely drawn up in Mercia, but the copy of the deed which has survived is one which was later made in Kent. It is plain, from such ramifications, that it will often be impossible to work out the provenance of a document from the linguistic features it contains. To say that a document is 'Kentish', therefore, is a judgement made on the basis of the balance of evidence, and will only occasionally be uncontentious.

Most texts display variations which provide possible evidence of more than one dialect. In some cases, because of the time-scale involved, features from several dialect areas are present, immensely complicating questions of origin. A text, as we have had it handed down to us today, might reflect many generations of scribal influence. This is especially so in the case of the more famous literary texts, which we can imagine to have been repeatedly copied over long periods of time by different scribes from different parts of the country, each of which might leave some dialect fingerprints. One of the best examples is the most famous text of all, *Beowulf*, which displays evidence of all four Old English dialects, and moreover of these dialects as they existed at different times, producing a text which one editor (Klaeber) has described as an 'unnatural medley of spellings'.[10] The word for 'guest, visitor, stranger' for example, turns up as *gist, gyst, gæst, giest*, and *gest*. The extant *Beowulf* manuscript was written probably some 250 years after it was first composed, allowing many opportunities for different dialects to manifest themselves, and for the text to display the stylistic preferences of different monastic schools or the linguistic eccentricities of individual scribes. An additional complication is that the extant manuscript was penned by two scribes (the second hand beginning at l. 1939),

2.6 Factors influencing Old English dialects in the eighth and ninth centuries in England

Main area of Scandinavian settlement

----- Diocesan areas

——— Navigable stretches of river

Major routes
I Ermine Street (Chichester – York)
II Icknield Way (Salisbury Plain – Norfolk)
III Watling Street (Dover – London – Wroxeter)
IV Fosse Way (Exeter – Lincoln)
V London Way (London – Dorset)
VI Dere Street (York – Firth of Forth)

Monastic centres
1 Winchester
2 Canterbury
3 Lichfield
4 York
5 Lindisfarne
6 Jarrow
7 Lincoln
8 Peterborough
9 Ely
10 Glastonbury

WHITHORN

LINDISFARNE

VI

NORTHUMBRIAN

HEXHAM

YORK

Ouse

LINDSEY

LICHFIELD

ELMHAM

MERCIAN

LEICESTER

HEREFORD

Severn

WORCESTER

DORCHESTER
Thames

DOMMOC

Wye

LONDON

WINCHESTER

WEST

SAXON

London

ROCHESTER

CANTERBURY

KENTISH

SELSEY

SHERBORNE

0   miles   50

0   km   80

whose different copying abilities and habits have been the source of much debate.

The four major dialect areas are the ones which have received all the attention; but undoubtedly there were further divisions within them (see panel 2.6). Over and above the question of their social diversity, as already discussed with especial reference to Kent (p. 21), three of the areas they covered were huge, as we can see from the map on p. 51. Mercian and Northumbrian, in particular, covered a territory which in later centuries would each be home to several distinct dialects. These later dialects did not suddenly appear; they slowly evolved; and it is likely that some of their linguistic features were present in Anglo-Saxon times. Certainly there are enough variations within both Mercian and Northumbrian for scholars to postulate northern forms of the former and southern forms of the latter. For example, a Northumbrian scribe, Owun, compiled the glosses to one part of the Rushworth Gospel; but his conventions are not identical with the type of Northumbrian found in the Lindisfarne Gospels. Some have called his dialect Southumbrian. And likewise, analysis of the considerable variation which can be found in Mercian texts suggests the existence of at least northern vs southern sub-dialects there. Later evidence suggests a West and East Midlands division.

What is particularly unclear – but highly intriguing – is whether we should be thinking exclusively in geographical terms in attempting to explain such variation. Some scholars think that, in the final analysis, what we have is a picture not of regions of the country but of diocesan preferences, given that most scribes came from just a few monasteries, such as Jarrow, Winchester, Lichfield, and Canterbury; and that is the motivation behind the map on p. 51, where we see an outline of the main diocesan areas in the eighth century, along with the main communication routes that will have facilitated dialect contact. The study of different handwriting preferences, illustration styles, and page-layout conventions – part of the subject of palaeography – is especially important in this connection. Some words are now known to have been preferred in West Saxon texts, especially texts originating in Winchester in the late tenth and early eleventh centuries. There are big differences between the early West Saxon of King Alfred and the literary standard which emerged in the 'Winchester' school associated with Ælfric and Æthelwold (late West Saxon), more than can be explained by linguistic change over the period of a century. Some of the variation may indeed be dialectal in origin; for there must have been a great deal of regional variation in West Saxon, given the enormous area it covered. But the variations could more plausibly be ascribed to the institutional norm used by the Winchester school. Alfred uses very few 'Winchester words', whereas Ælfric uses many. The word for 'foreign, strange' is *fremde* in Alfred, but almost always *ælfremed* in Ælfric; 'church' (in its sense of community) is *cirice* or *gesamung* in Alfred, and almost always *gelaðung* in Ælfric. Several dozen such differences have now been noted.[11]

The role of 'schools of practice' must not be underestimated, at any stage in the history of English. To take a modern analogy: a Martian studying modern orthographic variations in English printed books might think that such differences as *judgment/judgement* or *washing machine/washing-machine* reflect dialect differences, such as British vs American; in fact, they reflect only the preferences of individual publishing houses. Convenient as the Old English dialect names are, and illuminating as a first-generation (in the computational sense) attempt to impose some order on the variation observed in texts, they cannot be trusted as a guide to regional dialectology, any more than the racial labels discussed earlier reflected an ethnic reality. A second-generation stage of sociolinguistically informed inquiry is needed, and has hardly begun.

'Philologists' is the traditional way of describing scholars who work on older states of a language, but, as far as Old English dialects are concerned, a more accurate term would be 'linguistic detectives', given that so much of the time they are engaged in a painstaking search for clues. Sometimes, indeed, this search has taken them well outside the Anglo-Saxon time-frame – either earlier, in an attempt to argue for antecedents of Old English dialects in Continental locations, or later, in an attempt to justify postulated dialect distinctions for which there is little evidence. An impression that a particular feature is Kentish, for example, might be confirmed by looking at the way the Kentish dialect evolved in the Middle Ages, where (as we shall see in Chapter 9) the much larger number of surviving texts allows us to draw more accurate conclusions about regional origins. Regional linguistic norms hardly exist in Anglo-Saxon times, but they do eventually emerge, and they can be retrospectively informative. However, before we see what happened to dialects in Middle English, there is another sociolinguistic factor to be explored: the contact which Anglo-Saxons had with speakers of other languages, notably Latin and the Scandinavian languages, Danish and Norwegian. The lexical diversity which we associate with Modern English, and which accounts for so much of its stylistic versatility, had its origins here.

Interlude 2
The rise and fall of West Saxon

The second half of the Old English period is dominated by the rise of West Saxon as a standard literary dialect. The prestige of a language always reflects the power of its speakers (p. 27), and in Anglo-Saxon times the emergence of Wessex as the dominant and eventually unifying force in English politics inevitably resulted in an increase in the status of its dialect. But standards do not develop overnight; and in the case of Old English, the process can be seen operating over a century.

Early West Saxon is the name given to the dialect which characterizes the literature of the first part of this period. It is a literature almost entirely due to the motivation and influence of King Alfred, who introduced a revival of religion and learning – a programme designed to win God's support for victory over the pagan Danes and to consolidate loyalty to himself as a Christian king (see panel 2.7). That he was totally aware of the educational need is clear from his Preface to the translation of Gregory's *Cura pastoralis* (*Pastoral Care*), made in the early 890s, in which he writes to Bishop Wærferþ contrasting the early days of Christianity in England with his own time, following the destruction caused by the Vikings.

> It has very often come into my mind what learnèd men there once were throughout England, from both sacred and secular offices, and what happy times there were throughout England . . . and how people abroad looked to this country for learning and instruction, and how we should now have to get it from abroad, if we were to have it. So completely had it declined in England that there were very few people on this side of the Humber who could understand their service-books in English or translate even one written message from Latin into English, and I think there were not many beyond the Humber either. So few they were that I cannot think of even a single one south of the Thames when I came to the throne. Thanks be to almighty God that we now have any supply of teachers . . . Therefore I think it better, if you think so too, that we also translate certain books, which it is most needful for all men to know, into the language that we can all understand, and make it happen – as we very easily can with God's help, if we have peace – that all

young people who are now freemen in England, those that have the means, should devote themselves to study while they have nothing else to do, until the time that they know how to read written English well.

As far as we can tell from the surviving manuscripts, the results of Alfred's assiduous language planning were remarkable. Almost all prose texts during the late ninth century and throughout the tenth display a dialect which is very largely West Saxon – albeit, as we have seen in Chapter 2, with an admixture of forms from other dialects – and it is this which has been used as the primary input for introductory grammars and manuals of Old English today. The major texts from the early period include the translation of Bede's *Ecclesiastical History* (p. 15), the *Anglo-Saxon Chronicle*, and works by Alfred himself, such as the translation of the *Pastoral Care* and Boethius' *Consolation of Philosophy*.

2.7 Alfred the Great (849–99)

Alfred was born in Wantage in Oxfordshire, the fifth son of King Ethelwulf, and became king of Wessex in 871. When he came to the throne, the Danes had already conquered much of Northumbria, parts of Mercia, and East Anglia, and threatened to subdue Wessex itself. He inflicted on them their first major reverse at the Battle of Edington (878), and began to win back Danish-occupied territory by capturing the former Mercian town of London (886). He stole the military initiative from the Danes by reorganizing his forces into a standing army, building a navy, and establishing a network of *burhs* (fortified centres). He forged close ties with other English peoples not under Danish rule, and provided his successors with the means to reconquer the Danelaw and secure the unity of England. A famous story of his being scolded by a peasant woman for letting her cakes burn has no contemporary authority, and is first recorded in the eleventh century.

Late West Saxon is the name given to the development of this dialect towards the end of the tenth century, when we find the writings of Ælfric, Wulfstan, Æthelwold, Byrhtferth, and others, as well as the continuation of the *Chronicle*, all of which were widely and officially distributed through the political and Church networks. But there is an important difference between the Early and Late periods. In the Early period, the texts contain a great deal of variation, displaying dialect mixture (especially from Mercian, p. 34), personal variation, and scribal inconsistency. There is no sign of any real attempt to produce a consistent, universally standardized form of expression.

During the second half of the tenth century, just such an effort began to

2.8 Ælfric (c. 955–c. 1020)

Ælfric (pronounced alfritch) became a monk and then abbot at the new monastery of Cerne Abbas in Dorset, and was later appointed to be the first abbot of Eynsham in Oxfordshire. He composed two books of eighty *Homilies* in Old English, a paraphrase of the first seven books of the Bible, and a book of *Lives of the Saints*. He also wrote a Latin grammar and Latin–English glossary, accompanied by a Latin *Colloquium* (the *Colloquy*, p. 48) which gives a vivid picture of contemporary social conditions in England. The greatest vernacular prose writer of his time, he is often called *Ælfric Grammaticus* ('The Grammarian').

be made. A noticeable consistency appears in the work of scribes from monasteries all over the country. Writers as far apart as modern Wiltshire (Æthelwold), Dorset and Oxfordshire (Ælfric), and Worcestershire (Wulfstan) show remarkable similarity in spellings, words, and constructions. Many scholars think that the influence of the Winchester school was especially strong. We can even see signs of revision taking place, with authorial corrections suggesting a concern to use 'correct' language. Ælfric (see panel 2.8) was one who revised aspects of his earlier work, even to the extent of consistentizing his use of noun endings and verb forms (which were in a state of flux at the time, p. 42); for example, he went through his homilies changing his forms of the verb 'to be', replacing *sindon* by *beon* and *is* by *bið*. Several Early West Saxon manuscripts were also corrected by scribes to satisfy their sense of what was becoming standard.

The authors knew very well what they were doing, as they often discussed problems of translation and style in their work. And Ælfric spoke apocalyptically about the need to avoid copying errors:

> Now I desire and beseech, in God's name, if anyone will transcribe this book, that he carefully correct it by the copy, lest we be blamed through careless writers. He does great evil who writes carelessly, unless he correct it. It is as though he turn true doctrine into false error. Therefore everyone should make straight that which he before bent crooked, if he will be guiltless at God's doom.

But after all the effort, it is ironic to see that the West Saxon standard did not become the foundation of present-day Standard English. Although this dialect continued to have influence throughout the eleventh century, it gradually fell out of use. A different standard language would eventually arise, evolving in an area well north of Wessex (Chapter 10).

Chapter 3 Early lexical diversity

There is a curious myth widespread in the world: many people believe that their language can somehow be 'pure' – comprising a set of sounds, words, and structures that can all be traced back continuously to a single point of origin – and that anything which interferes with this imagined purity (especially words borrowed from other languages) is a corrupting influence, altering the language's 'true character'. In the case of English, it is the Germanic origins of the language, in their Anglo-Saxon form, which are supposed to manifest this character. In the sixteenth century, John Cheke wanted to have English 'pure, unmixed and unmangled with borrowing of other tongues', and suggested that words with Latin and Greek origins be replaced by words with Old English roots – *centurion* by *hundreder*, *prophet* by *foresayer*, *resurrection* by *gainrising*, and so on. The nineteenth-century English Romantics enthused even more strongly, with some authors (such as Dickens and Hardy) lauding the qualities of Anglo-Saxon vocabulary. The Dorsetshire poet William Barnes tried to remove all non-Germanic borrowings in his work, not only constructing Old English coinages, as Cheke did, but also resuscitating long-dead Anglo-Saxonisms, such as *inwit* for *conscience*. In the twentieth century, George Orwell was perhaps the best-known writer to continue flying this flag: 'Bad writers', he says in his essay 'Politics and the English Language' (1946), 'are nearly always haunted by the notion that Latin and Greek words are grander than Saxon ones.'

There are certainly important stylistic differences between Germanic and Romance words, as we shall see (p. 174); but support for any notion of a 'return to purity' is misplaced. No language has ever been found which displays lexical purity: there is always a mixture, arising from the contact of its speakers with other communities at different periods in its history. In the case of English, there is a special irony, for its vocabulary has never been purely Anglo-Saxon – not even in the Anglo-Saxon period. By the time the Anglo-Saxons arrived in Britain, there had already been four centuries of linguistic interchange between Germanic and Roman people on the European mainland. The Roman soldiers and traders borrowed Germanic words and the Germanic people borrowed Latin ones. The integration was at times quite marked: many Roman cohorts consisted of men from Germanic tribes. Language mixing was there from the very beginning (see panel 3.1).

3.1 Blank check

The intricate path words can trace between languages is well illustrated by the history of *blank*. Look in a dictionary, and you will find that the word arrived in English in the fourteenth century, a borrowing of French *blanc*, meaning 'white'. A quotation in the *Oxford English Dictionary* for *c.* 1325 talks of a robe furred 'with blaun and nere' (with white and black). In Modern English phrases, such as *blanc de blanc*, for a type of wine, there is no doubting the Gallic resonances of *blanc/blank*. This is one of the words which Orwell and the others would have condemned as resolutely non-native. But they would have been wrong.

We must first note that a word corresponding to *blanc* exists in other Romance languages, too – for example, in Spanish it is *blanco*, in Italian *bianco*, in Portuguese *branco*. So it must have existed in Vulgar Latin, the parent of all the Romance languages. Vulgar Latin evolved throughout western Europe over several centuries as the Roman Empire declined. But where did these speakers get the word from? There is no such form in Classical Latin, where the word for 'white' was *albus*.

The clue comes from the other Germanic languages. In Old High German, there is a form *blanc*, which meant 'white, shining'. In Old English, *blanca* turns up meaning a horse, presumably white or grey in colour. In *Beowulf* (l. 856) we read of *beornas on blancum* – 'warriors on steeds'. It is easy to deduce what must have happened. Roman soldiers or merchants in Europe encountered the word used by the Germanic peoples and borrowed it. We shall never know why, though some have speculated. Perhaps the Romans were especially impressed by the Germanic habit of painting their shields with 'choice colours' or by their buildings 'stained with a clay so clear and bright that it resembles painting' (both customs reported by Tacitus in his *Germania*). Something about colour must have impressed them, for *blanc* is not the only colour word to have entered Romance from Germanic during that period (*brun* 'brown', *gris* 'grey', and *bleu* 'blue' did also).

Whatever the reasons for the borrowing, *blank* turns out to be a Germanic word after all.

The Latin story

We know that this process happened very early on because Latin words entered several of the other old Germanic languages of Europe as well, such as Old High German, Gothic, and Old Saxon. The Anglo-Saxons, wherever they came from, would not have been immune to this influence. Thus we find, for example, Latin *scrinium*, meaning 'a chest for books or papers', appearing in Old Frisian *skrin*, Old High German *skrini*, and Old Norse *skrin* (pronounced 'screen', with a /sk-/) as well as in Old English *scrin* (where it was pronounced 'shreen', with a /ʃ-/). The distinctive pronunciation of the Old English form tells us that this word must have entered English very early, reflecting a time (perhaps as early as the third century) when the Anglo-Saxons were changing the pronunciation of words containing *sk* from /sk/ to /ʃ/. The process is called *palatalization*, and it can be seen in such other words as *fish* and *dish* (from Latin *piscis* and *discus*). It is a very natural pronunciation change – as can be heard in the speech of anyone who tries to pronounce /sk-/ words after having had too much to drink – and was one of the features which must have made Anglo-Saxons sound very different from their Old Scandinavian peers (p. 20). If *shrine* had entered the language later, after this pronunciation trend was over, it would have kept its /sk-/ sound, and we would have ended up pronouncing it as 'skrine' /skraɪn/ in Modern English. This is what happened to *school*, for example, which *did* enter English at a later period: it kept the /sk-/, which is why we now say 'skool' and not 'shool'.

It is not entirely clear just how many words entered English from Classical or Vulgar Latin during this Continental time of contact. In one influential work, Mary Serjeantson lists 183 words from the Continental period, another 114 words from the period between 450 and 650, and a further 244 from 650 to the Conquest.[1] But she, and everyone else who has studied this period, acknowledges that it is often impossible to be definite about the time-frame to which a loanword properly belongs. A Latin word might have arrived in English through any of several possible routes. To begin with, Latin words must have entered the Celtic speech of the Britons during the Roman occupation, and some might have remained in daily use after the Romans finally left in the early fifth century, so that they were picked up by the Anglo-Saxons in due course. Or perhaps Latin continued to exercise its influence following the Roman departure: it is possible that aristocratic Britons would have continued to use the language as a medium of upper-class communication. If so, then we might expect a significant number of Latin words to be in daily use, some of which would eventually be assimilated by the Anglo-Saxons. On the other hand, if these scenarios did *not* apply, the Latin words arriving in Britain would have been those brought in by the Anglo-Saxons themselves. A further possibility is that new Latin words would continue to arrive in Britain long after the Anglo-Saxons first arrived because of the ongoing trading activities between Britain and the Continent. And lastly, following the coming of St Augustine in 597, the influence of Latin-speaking monks must have grown, with Latinisms being dropped into speech much as they still are today, as a modus operandi which adds gravitas passim to one's magnum opus, inter alia (pace Orwell). Deciding how a particular Latin word entered English, accordingly, is quite problematic.

When we look at the lists which have been compiled for the Continental period, we find that the Latin words express a considerable semantic range. They include words for plants and animals (including birds and fish), food and drink, household objects, vessels, coins, metals, items of clothing, settlements, houses, and building materials, as well as several notions to do with military, legal, medical, and commercial matters. Most are nouns, with a sprinkling of verbs and adjectives. A selection is given in panel 3.2. As we move into the period of early Anglo-Saxon settlement in England, we find these semantic areas continuing to expand, with the growing influence of missionary activity reflected in an increase in words to do with religion and learning. A number of these are listed in panel 3.3.

These lists illustrate words which for the most part have survived in the language to the present-day; only a few are included which eventually fell out of use. But obsolescence was to be the fate of nearly half of all Latin borrowings during this early period. They died out for a variety of reasons. In some cases, they were replaced during the Old English period: *fossere*, for example, was in early competition with *spade*, which is given as the gloss for Latin *vangas* in the early eighth-century Epinal–Erfurt and Corpus glossaries (ll. 1087/2079), and *spade* won. More often, the word which formed the replacement arrived in medieval times, as with *pocket*, which entered English from Norman French in the thirteenth century, taking over the function earlier performed by Old English *bisæcc* 'pocket' (from *bisaccium*) – see also panel 3.4. Also quite common was the replacement of early Latin words by other Latinisms in much later periods of borrowing (p. 155): Old English *diht*, for example, meaning 'saying, direction', was from Latin *dictum*, but it is not the direct ancestor of Modern English *dictum* – a word which was borrowed (again) from Latin in the seventeenth century. Whatever the reason, many Latin words of this period failed to survive into Modern English. We no longer recognize such words as *fifele* 'buckle' (from *fibula*) and *fæcele* 'torch' (from *facula*), or *gellet* 'basin' (from *galletum*) and *gabote* 'small dish' (from *gabata*), or *sinop* 'mustard' (from *sinapis*) and *strægl* 'mattress' (from *stragula*). But they were live words in early Anglo-Saxon speech.

3.2 Some of the words borrowed from Latin during the Continental period

Old English word	Modern English gloss	Latin origin
belt	belt	balteus
butere	butter	butyrum
camp	field, battle	campus
candel	candle	candela
catt	cat	cattus
ceaster	city	castra
cetel	kettle	catillus
cupp	cup	cuppa
cycene	kitchen	coquina
cyse	cheese	caseus
draca	dragon	draco
mæsse	mass	missa
mil	mile	mille
minte	mint	menta
munuc	monk	monachus
mynster	minster	monasterium
panne	pan	panna
piper	pepper	piper
pise	pea	pisum
plante	plant	planta
port	door, gate	porta
port	harbour, town	portus
pund	pound	pondo
sacc	sack, bag	saccus
sinoð	council, synod	synodus
stræt	road	strata
tigle	tile	tegula
weall	wall	vallum
win	wine	vinum
ynce	inch	uncia

Borrowing from Latin continued throughout the Old English period, but it changed its character as Church influence grew. Whereas most of the earlier words had entered the language through the medium of speech, there was now an influx of learnèd and religious words through the medium of writing. Some domestic vocabulary did continue to come in, such as *rose* 'rose' from *rosa*, *bete* 'beetroot' from *beta*, and *cama* 'bridle' from *camus*, but over 60 per cent

3.3 Some of the words borrowed from Latin *c.* 450–*c.* 650

Old English word	Modern English gloss	Latin origin
cocc	cock	coccus
cugle	cowl	cuculla
cyrtan	to shorten, curtail	curtus
forca	fork	furca
fossere	spade	fossorium
græf	stylus	graphium
læden	Latin	ladinus (Vulgar Latin)
leahtric	lettuce	lactuca
mægester	master	magister
nunne	nun	nonna
pere	pear	pirum
pinsian	to reflect, consider	pensare
punt	punt, flat boat	ponto
relic	relic	reliquia
renge	spider	aranea
seglian	to seal	sigillare
segn	mark, sign	signum
stropp	strap	stroppus
torr	tower	turris
turl	ladle, trowel	trulla

of the later loans were more abstract, scholarly, or technical. This trend became especially strong after the Benedictine revival of the monasteries at the end of the tenth century (once the Viking attacks had stopped, p. 65), where most of the Latin loans had a distinctive educated character. The emphasis is not surprising: the teaching of the Church had to be communicated to the Anglo-Saxon people, and new vocabulary was needed to express the new concepts, personnel, and organizational procedures. Borrowing Latin words was not the only way in which the missionaries engaged with this task. Rather more important, in fact, were other linguistic techniques. One method was to take a Germanic word and adapt its meaning so that it expressed the sense of a Latin word: examples include *rod*, originally meaning 'rod, pole', which came to mean 'cross' (p. 31); and *gast*, originally 'demon, evil spirit', which came to mean 'soul' or 'Holy Ghost'. Another technique, relying on a type of word creation which permeates Old English poetry, was to create new compound words – in this case, by translating the elements of a Latin word into Germanic equivalents: so, *liber evangelii* became *godspellboc* 'gospel book' and *trinitas*

3.4 A gem example

It is sometimes difficult to tell, at first glance, whether a modern word has Old English or Middle English origins, in cases where both of the possible sources ultimately come from Latin. The French words which arrived in Middle English had their origins in Latin too. It is therefore possible to find a Latin word entering English in the Anglo-Saxon period in one form, and turning up in English again much later via French in another form – but with both forms very similar in appearance.

Modern English *gem* is an example. This appears in Old English as *ʒimm*, 'precious stone', from Latin *gemma*; it is often printed as *gimm*. Although this form closely resembles *gem*, the modern word actually came into the language in the fourteenth century, from Old French, *gemme*. *This gemme of chastite* is how Chaucer describes the widow's son in *The Prioress's Tale* (l. 609). How do we know that it was this word, and not the Anglo-Saxon one, which is the origin of the Modern English word?

The pronunciation is the clue. The first sound of *gem* /dʒ/ is an English adaptation of the French sound /ʒ/ (as heard, for example, at the beginning of the French name *Jacques*). The *ʒ* symbol in the Old English word represented the sound /j/, as in *year*. If *gimm* had stayed in the language, we would be pronouncing it today as 'yim'.

became *þriness* 'threeness' = 'trinity'. But Latin loans played their part, too, as the selection in panel 3.5 illustrates.

An interesting point about some of the loanwords from Latin is that they were borrowed twice, as can be seen in the selection in panel 3.6. For example, the translator of the early eighth-century Corpus glossary translated *coriandrum* 'coriander' as *cellendre* (l. 569), but in Ælfric (writing some 300 years later) we find it appearing as *coriandre*. It is not surprising to find doublets of this kind. In an age of poor communications and limited literary transmission between generations, a word could easily be borrowed more than once, without the translator being aware of previous usage. Alternatively, there might have been a conscious attempt to be different from earlier usage, especially in a scholarly age, when writers might wish to show their Latin learning. A third possibility is that the pronunciation might have changed in the interim, so that any sense of identity with the earlier word would be lost.

Of all the Latin words that came into Old English, only a hundred or so remain in modern Standard English. A few others can still be heard in regional dialects: for example, *sicker* 'secure, safe' is found as *sicor* in King Alfred's time, a borrowing of *securus*, and may still be heard in many parts of Scotland and Ireland, and in northern counties of England. Various reasons account for the

3.5 Some of the words borrowed from Latin c. 650–c. 1100

Old English word	Modern English gloss	Latin origin
alter	altar	altar
biblioþece	library	bibliotheca
cancer	crab	cancer
creda	creed, belief	credo
cucumer	cucumber	cucumer
culpe	guilt, fault	culpa
diacon	deacon	diaconus
fenester	window	fenestra
fers	verse	versus
grammatic	grammar	grammatica
mamma	breast	mamma
notere	notary	notarius
offrian	sacrifice, offer	offere
orgel	organ	organum
papa	pope	papa
philosoph	philosopher	philosophus
predician	preach	praedicare
regol	religious rule	regula
sabbat	sabbath	sabbatum
scol	school	scola

3.6 Some words borrowed twice from Latin during the Old English period

Early loan	Later loan	Modern English gloss	Latin origin
celc	calic	cup	calicem
cliroc	cleric	cleric, clergyman	clericus
læden	latin	Latin	latinus
leahtric	lactuca	lettuce	lactuca
minte	menta	mint	menta
spynge	sponge	sponge	spongea

lack of Latin survivors. In some cases, the objects and notions simply went out of use – such as *pilece* 'robe made from skin' (from *pellicea*), *buteric* 'leather bottle' (from *buta*), *dinor* 'coin' (from *denarius*), and *mydd* 'bushel measure of corn' (from *modius*). Also, some of the learnèd words never caught on, being

apparently restricted to the written language and used only occasionally there
– such as *cursumbor* 'incense' in the Lindisfarne Gospels. But the chief reason
is the overwhelming influence of French words in the Middle Ages (p. 144),
which entered the language in thousands. Older Latin words would have had
to be really well established to avoid being replaced by the more modern and
fashionable forms. The remarkable thing is that several of them were very well
integrated into Old English – so much so that today we cannot differentiate
them from Germanic words without the help of an etymological dictionary.
Twelve of the following twenty-four words are Latin, and twelve Germanic –
but which is which?

> belt, bin, cook, craft, cup, day, earth, god, good, gold, home, light, pan, pit, post,
> pot, red, sack, sock, stop, sun, wall, wife, work

(The answer is on p. 540.[2]) Cases such as these – as well as such 'basic' lexical
pairs as *dog* and *cat* (the first Germanic, the second Latin) – present a major
challenge to those who believe that Germanic words are always more authentic-
ally English than Latin ones (see panel 3.7).

The Scandinavian story

The second main source of lexical variation in Old English was Scandinavia;
but even though the Vikings made their presence felt in Britain in the 780s, it
was a further century before Old Norse words began to make their appearance.
The opening encounter was recorded in the *Parker Chronicle* in an entry for
the year 787 (actually 789, the scribe having made another of those copying
errors which complicate the study of Old English texts, p. 43, so that all the
years between 754 and 845 are two out):

> In this year King Beorhtric took to wife Eadburh, daughter of Offa. And in his
> days came for the first time three ships: and then the reeve [the King's local official]
> rode thither and tried to compel them to go to the royal manor, for he did not
> know what they were, and they slew him. These were the first ships of the Danes
> to come to England.[3]

This attack – probably by Norwegians, in fact, rather than by Danes – was in
the south, on the coast of Dorset, and it was followed by several raids in the
north. The monastery at Lindisfarne was plundered in 793, Jarrow in 794, and
Iona in 795. Then there is a lull, before the *Chronicle* records further incursions
from the mid 830s, all along the south coast, from Cornwall to London. Winter
camps in the Thames estuary became routine from 851. There was no permanent

3.7 Anglo-Saxon routes

Although the Latin element in Old English vocabulary is very limited, it is at times quite prominent in its presence. The names of Anglo-Saxon roads provide an example.

The map on p. 51 shows that, when the Anglo-Saxons arrived in Britain, a network of major roads had been built to supplement the many paths which dated from prehistoric times. Their linguistic significance has already been suggested. Dialects can influence each other only when people are in contact; and for that to happen, good communications need to be in place (a point we shall return to in the twentieth century, p. 472).

The Anglo-Saxons were well aware of the two types of route, because they gave them different names. A road which had been made artificially – usually by the Romans – was called a *stræt* 'street', from Latin *strata*. A track which had emerged over time through repeated usage was known by the Germanic word *weg* 'way' – as in *hrycgweg* 'ridgeway'.

The names of the four major routes reflect this difference. *Watling Street* and *Ermine Street* were Roman roads; *Icknield Way* was prehistoric. What we now call the *Fosse Way* – a Roman road – seems to go against this distinction, until we recognize that in early sources it was referred to simply as *Fosse* or *Fosse Street*; the name *Fosse Way* (formerly also spelled *Foss Way*) dates only from the fifteenth century.

The identifying names of these routes also display different language etymologies: in Old English, Watling Street was *Wæclinga stræt* or *Wætlinga stræt* – the Germanic name of a community living in the area of St Albans ('Wacol's people'). *Ermine* was another Germanic name: *Earninga stræt* – 'the Roman road of the Earningas – Earn's people'. However, *Fosse* is Latin: *fossa* was a ditch or dyke, and presumably the name was given because of ditches built on one or both sides of the route. The etymology of *Icknield* is not known, but the word has a resonance that is neither Germanic nor Latin, and it may well be a legacy of a pre-Roman era.

settlement during that time, and little movement inland, but in 865 a Danish army arrived in East Anglia, and within a year had reached York. The conquest of Northumbria followed, and from the mid 870s Danish settlements rapidly proliferated throughout the north-east. The *Parker Chronicle* for 876 reports of a Danish leader: 'in this year Halfdan shared out the lands of Northumbria, and they were engaged in ploughing and in making a living for themselves'.

Incursions into Mercia and Wessex brought allied resistance, especially in Berkshire from King Æthelred and his brother Alfred, who defeated the Danes at Ashdown (870). King Alfred's later defeat of the Danes at Ethandun (modern Edington) in 878 marked a turning-point. The Danish leader Guthrum agreed to leave Wessex, and retreated to East Anglia, where a further period of Danish settlement followed. And in 886 Alfred made a treaty with Guthrum which left Alfred in control of London and Guthrum in control over an area of eastern England which, because it was subject to Danish laws, came to be known as the Danelaw. This area ran from the northern shore of the Thames as far west as the River Lea (the boundary of Essex), then north along the Lea into Bedfordshire and from there along the Ouse to the line of Watling Street (p. 51); the boundaries further north are unclear, but it is evident from the place-names which eventually appeared that Danes were present in the whole of the northern and north-eastern third of the country, roughly between Cheshire and Essex (see the map on p. 51). Over 2,000 Scandinavian place-names are found throughout the area, chiefly in Yorkshire, Lincolnshire, and the East Midlands. The distribution of Scandinavian family names – such as those that end in -son (*Johnson, Henderson, Jackson . . .*) – also shows a concentration throughout the Danelaw, the bias visible early on, in the records of Domesday Book (1086–7). In Yorkshire and north Lincolnshire, 60 per cent of the names recorded in early Middle English sources are of Scandinavian origin.

The Scandinavian place-names are one of the most important linguistic developments of the period. Many are easily recognized. Over 600 end in -*by*, the Old Norse word for 'farmstead' or 'town', as in *Rugby* and *Grimsby*, the other element often referring to a person's name (Hroca's and Grim's farm, in these two cases), but sometimes to general features, as in *Burnby* 'farm by a stream' and *Westerby* 'western farm'. Many end in -*thorpe* 'village, outlying farm', -*thwaite* 'clearing', or -*toft* 'homestead': a mixed bag is *Althorp*, *Millthorpe, Braithwaite, Applethwaite, Lowestoft*, and *Sandtoft*. Sometimes the whole name is a single Norse word, or a combination of two such words: for example, there are half a dozen villages simply called *Toft*, and a dozen villages called *Thorpe*; combined forms appear in *Crosby*, 'farm near a cross' (from *kros* + *by*) and *Skokholm* island in Pembrokeshire (*stokkr* 'channel' + *holmr* 'small island'). In some cases, we have to be careful before confidently assigning a name to a Scandinavian source, because an Old English word of similar form and meaning also existed. *Thorpe* is a case in point: there was also an Old English word, *þrop* or *þorp*, meaning 'village'. There is a *Thorp* in Surrey, for example, and a *Throop* in Dorset, both well outside the Danish area of settlement. We also have to be careful about assuming that a Scandinavian name always reflects an original Danish or Norwegian settlement. It is likely that a local Danish aristocracy sometimes imposed a Scandinavian name on an Anglo-Saxon community, as the mark of a local 'empire'. Some of the relational names, such as *Netherby* 'lower farmstead' and *Westby* 'west farmstead', could easily have arisen in that way. It is also possible that some native Anglo-Saxon communities voluntarily adopted a Norse name, perhaps because of a social relationship which had evolved with the incomers. But whatever the social situation, the Danelaw displays a significant level of place-name influence throughout.

There is a further dimension to the mixing of languages in English place-name history. Words from Old Norse and Old English can exist side by side within the same name – so-called *hybrid* names. To see this, we need first of all to be aware of the common Anglo-Saxon elements in English place-names, such as those listed in panel 3.8. Most place-names of Anglo-Saxon Britain consist of these elements, either alone or in combination. Many of the combined forms use the ending *-ingas*, meaning 'people of', as in Hastings (*Hæstingas*, 'people of Hæsta') and Barking (*Berecingas*, 'people of Berica'). More complex compounds using all-English elements are Birmingham (*Beormingaham*, 'homestead of the people of Beorma') and Uppingham (*Yppingeham*, 'homestead of the people on the higher land'). And one can have some fun creating possible English places by combining Old English elements, then seeing whether such

---

3.8 Some Old English elements in English place-names

Old English word	Meaning	Some modern equivalents
bæce, bece	stream, valley	-bach, -badge, -bage, batch-, -beach, -bech
bearu	grove, wood	-barrow, -ber, -bear, -beare, -borough
beorg	hill, mound	-bar, berg-, -ber, -berry, -borough, -burgh
broc	brook, stream	brock-, -broke, -brook, brough-
burh, burg	fortified place	-borough, -burgh, -bury
cot	cottage, shelter	coat-, -cot, -cote, cott-
denu	valley	-dean, deane-, -den, den-
dun	down, hill	-den, -don, dun-, -ton
geat	gate, hole	-gate, yate-, -yate, -yatt, -yet
hyll	hill	-el, hel-, hil-, -hill, hul-, -le
lacu	stream	lack-, -lake, -lock
læcc	stream, bog	lach-, lash-, -leach, lech-, -ledge, letch-
leah	wood, glade	lee-, -leigh, -le, -ley, -low
mæd	meadow	made-, -mead, -meadow, med-, -mede,
mor	moor, fen	-moor, mor-, more-, -more, mur-
pol	pool, stream	pol-, -pole, -pool, poul-
stan	stone	stan-, -ston-, -ston, -stone
tun	enclosure, village	-ton, ton-, -tone
welle, wælle	well, spring	wal-, -wall, wel-, -well, wil-, -will
wic	dwelling, farm	-wich, -wick, -week, wig-, wych-

names actually exist: *Churchdean, Heathridge, Bridgecombe, Combebridge*...
But the game would fail when it encountered such hybrid names as *Stackpole*,
south-west Wales, 'pool by the steep rock' (from Old Norse *stakkr* + Old
English *pol*) or *Finedon*, Northumberland, 'valley of the folk assembly' (from
Old Norse *þing* + Old English *dene*). It would of course also fail with words
like *Bewcastle*, where an Old Norse element joins with an Old English word of
Latin origins: 'shelter at a Roman station' (*buð* + *ceaster*). Mixes of this kind
are remarkably common, especially a combination of a Scandinavian personal
name and an Old English locator, such as *tun* 'farmstead, village'. We know
that Ulfr, Skurfa, and Sigge settled in North Yorkshire, because their names are
recorded in *Oulston, Scruton*, and *Sigston* (see also panel 3.9).

3.9 Keswick and Chiswick, Skipton and Shipton

Scandinavian influence is to be found not only in the use of an Old Norse word.
Quite often, a place-name uses an Old English word, but its form is different
because of the way the invaders pronounced it. These must have been cases
where, rather than invent a new name, or find an equivalent in Old Norse, the
Scandinavians carried on using the Old English name they encountered, and
adapted the pronunciation to suit themselves. The meaning of *Chiswick* in Greater
London is 'cheese farm', from Old English *cese*, where the *c* was pronounced
'ch' /tʃ/. There was no such 'ch' sound in Old Norse, which had kept the old
Germanic /k/ in such words (compare modern German *käse*). *Keswick*, Cumbria,
also means 'cheese farm'. If the Norwegians hadn't settled there, the name would
probably be *Chiswick* today.

Similarly, the 'sh' sound found in *Shipton* ('sheep farm') was also lacking in
Old Norse, hence we find *Shipton* in Dorset but *Skipton* in Yorkshire. A further
development is illustrated by *Skipwith*, Yorkshire. Here, not only has the initial
sound been adapted, but the second element is entirely Norse – *viðr* 'wood' being
used instead of Old English *wic*. If there had never been any Scandinavian influence,
the village would probably today be called *Shipwich*.

Not only is there place-name variety between Old English and Old Norse,
there is some variation within the Norse names themselves. This is because the
Danes were not the only Scandinavian invaders at that time; the Norwegians
had come to Britain via a different route, attacking the Western Isles of Scotland,
Ireland (Dublin fell to them in 836), North Wales, and north-west England
(during the early tenth century). Their settlements, accordingly, are found in
the western areas of northern England, though there was no sharp dividing line
at the Pennines: Norwegians found their way into Yorkshire, for example, and
Danes into Cumbria. The two Old Norse dialects were by no means identical,

and it is sometimes possible to tell, from the spellings of a place-name, whether it is Norwegian or Danish in origin. The word for 'temporary shelter' is an example. This was *buð* in Norwegian, and in names using this element it appears today in such spellings as *bouthe* and *buthe*. The equivalent in Danish was *boð*, which resulted in such modern spellings as *bothe* and *booth*. There is a village called *Bouth* in Cumbria and one called *Booth* in Lancashire: the first is Norwegian, the second is Danish. The difference is even more interesting when we find place-names which suggest that the Norse originator had travelled to England via Ireland. There is a *Melmerby* in Cumbria and Yorkshire, for instance: 'Melmor's village' – but *Melmor* is an Irish name ('servant of Mary'). And names such as *Brigsteer*, Cumbria, have a Celtic resonance: the name means literally 'bridge Styr' – in other words, 'Styr's bridge'. Why wasn't the place called *Steerbridge*? Probably because Styr had been influenced by Irish, for in the Celtic languages names used adjectivally come after the noun.

We might expect Scandinavian place-names to be recorded relatively quickly after the period of Norse settlement began; but what about general words in speech and writing? The Treaty of Wedmore between Alfred and Guthrum (886) in fact contains the first Scandinavian loans known in Old English texts: *healfmarc* 'half a mark' comes from the Scandinavian currency unit, *mǫrk*, and *liesengum*, a variant of *liesing* 'freedmen' comes from *leysingiar*. A few more are found in the York and Peterborough versions of the *Anglo-Saxon Chronicle*, the northern Gospels (Lindisfarne and Rushworth), and a sprinkling of other sources. But they do not amount to very many. Only about thirty Norse words came into Old English during this period: a selection is listed in the first part of panel 3.10. Just a handful are general-purpose words. Most are terms reflecting the imposition of Danish law and administration throughout the region, social structure, or cultural objects or practices, such as seafaring and fighting. Very few had enough broad applicability to survive into later periods of English, once Scandinavian culture and power declined.

The decline in political power seems to have begun around the year 900, with the gradual retaking of the Danelaw by the West Saxons. By 920 English control had reached as far as Northumbria, and the change of fortunes seemed assured after the decisive battle of Brunanburh (937), which saw the defeat of a combined force of Scandinavians and Scots. In 954 the last of the Scandinavian kings of York, Eric Bloodaxe, was expelled. King Edgar (959–75) promulgated laws which recognized the right of Englishmen and Danes to keep their own customs. But the period of peace which followed was not to last long. During the 980s, Danish attacks began again, and were again successful. One such attack has achieved poetic immortality through *The Battle of Maldon*, which records the defeat of Byrhtnoth, earl of the East Saxons, at Maldon, Essex in 991. The subsequent period of conflict produced a string of Danish victories,

3.10 Some of the words borrowed from Old Norse in the Old English period

Old English word	Modern English gloss	Old Norse origin
Early borrowings (pre-1016)		
barða/barda	beaked ship	barð
ceallian	call	kalla
dreng	warrior	drengr
feolaga	fellow, mate	felagi
husting	tribunal	husþing
lagu	law	lǫg
ora	Danish coin	aurar
targe	small shield	targa
utlaga	outlaw	utlagi
wrang	wrong	vrang
Later borrowings (1016–1150)		
carl	man	carl
cnif	knife	knifr
diega	die	deyja
hæfene	haven	hǫfn
hamele	rowlock	hamla
hittan	come upon	hit
læst	fault, sin	lostr
sceppe	wheat measure	skeppa
scoru	score	skor
tacan	take, touch	taka

culminating in 1016, following the death of King Æthelred, with the ascent of the Danish king Cnut (Canute) to the English throne. A further wave of Danish settlement took place as a consequence, with many Danish soldiers choosing to stay in England, and this time they found land in parts of the country which extended well beyond the old area of the Danelaw.

This new period of Danish rule lasted from 1016 to 1042, first under Cnut (to 1035) and then for a few years under his son Hardecanute. The social status of Scandinavian words and usage must have increased greatly at the time, with the arrival of a whole new tier of Danish aristocracy, and Cnut's affirmation in 1018 that the laws of Edgar should continue to be respected. Whether the new usage was intelligible to English ears or whether it required translation is an issue we shall return to below. But the immediate impact must have been considerable, and very similar to that which accompanied the arrival of the Norman French a generation or so later, or the arrival of the Scottish court in London in the early seventeenth century. We can imagine words which previously might have been considered archaic or alien now acquiring fresh prestige. And a whole new tranche of Danish words would become fashionable. It was also likely that some of this prestige would have continued after Hardecanute's death. The election of the Anglo-Norman Edward the Confessor as king brought a new Norman influence into the English court, but both French and Scandinavian influences coexisted for a while, with several Danes continuing to hold senior court positions. Opinions vary about the balance of power, but the daily conflicts of position and power must have been reflected in a remarkable range of accents, styles of usage, and strong language attitudes at the time. Doubtless Danish and Norman voices provided the stock-in-trade of many a court jester.

Despite the extensive period of settlement and Danish becoming the language of power for a generation, the overall impact of Scandinavian words on Old English vocabulary continued to be slight during the eleventh century – just a few dozen more items being identifiable in English texts. Indeed, when we count up all the Scandinavian words which entered Old English between the ninth and the twelfth centuries, we arrive at a surprisingly small total – about 150. And only some twenty-five words from this period survived into Modern English. Much debate has been devoted to explaining this lack. One important factor would have been the rise of the West Saxon dialect as the literary language following King Alfred's extensive use of it; by the year 1000 it had achieved the status of a scribal standard, used throughout the country (p. 55). It would have been difficult for regionally restricted Danish forms to achieve public prominence, as a result. The political centres were in the south, at Winchester and later London, outside the Danelaw. A factor relevant to the later period would have been the rise of Norman influence, making Danish words less prestigious. But perhaps most important is the very short period of time overall that received Danish rule – little more than fifty years in the age of the Danelaw and only twenty-six years in the age of Cnut. No creative literature with a Danish theme has survived from this period which might have shown a typical Scandinavian vocabulary (a contrast, as we shall see, with the early Middle English period), and indeed very few manuscripts from this time have survived at all.

If that was the end of the linguistic dimension to the Scandinavian story, it would be no more than a ripple in English linguistic history. But something remarkable was taking place in the period between Old and Middle English. Although there are no written records to show it, a considerable Scandinavian vocabulary was gradually being established in the language. We know that this must have been so, because the earliest Middle English literature, from around 1200, shows thousands of Old Norse words being used, especially in texts coming from the northern and eastern parts of the country, such as the *Orrmulum* and *Havelok the Dane* (p. 196). They could not suddenly have arrived in the twelfth century, for historically there was no significant connection with Scandinavia at that time; England was under Norman French rule. And as it takes time for loanwords to become established, what we must be seeing is a written manifestation of an underlying current of Old Norse words that had been developing a widespread vernacular use over the course of two centuries or more. There is no doubt that many of these words *were* well established, because they began to replace some common Anglo-Saxon words. The word for 'take', for example, was *niman* in Old English; Old Norse *taka* is first recorded in an English form, *toc* (= *took*), during the late eleventh century in the *Anglo-Saxon Chronicle* (year 1072), but by the end of the Middle English period *take* had completely taken over the function of *niman* in general English. As was often the case, the Anglo-Saxon word remained for some time in regional dialects. *Nim*, from *niman*, developed the sense of 'steal', and was still being used regionally into the nineteenth century, and in slang (according to Eric Partridge) into the twentieth.[4] It would not be surprising to find it still in some dialects today, either as a verb or as a derived noun *nim* or *nym*, meaning 'thief' (cf. the name of Falstaff's crony, Nym).

To complete the Scandinavian story, we have to move forward an era. Old Norse words entered virtually all the word classes of the language in Middle English. From the noun *burðr* we have *birth*, from the verb *vanta* we have *want*, and from the adjective *illr* we have *ill*. The adverb *þrar* led to *throli* 'earnestly, furiously', though this word died out in the sixteenth century. Unusually, a number of words with a primarily grammatical function were also borrowed, and these will be discussed further below: the range included the pronoun *baðir*, which resulted in *baðe*, modern *both*, and the preposition *til*, which resulted in *till*. There was even a conjunction, *ok* 'and', which has a brief period of life in a few early Middle English texts, such as the *Orrmulum*, as *occ*.

The everyday flavour of the Scandinavian loans can be seen in these two dozen words, all of which survived into modern Standard English:

anger, awkward, bond, cake, crooked, dirt, dregs, egg, fog, freckle, get, kid, leg, lurk, meek, muggy, neck, seem, sister, skill, skirt, smile, Thursday, window

The total number of Scandinavian words from this period in Standard English today is unclear, partly because some etymologies are uncertain, and partly because some items are so restricted in their modern occurrence that they hardly count as productive forms – *gaggle* is a case in point, from Norse *gagl* 'young goose', but today used only with reference to a collection of geese. Most estimates suggest between 400 and 500. The total also very much depends on which words you choose to count: the word *sky*, for example, also appears in several dozen compound forms (*skyjack, skylight, skylark* . . .). If we included all of these, the total would be several thousand.

But there is no reason why we should restrict the count to the standard dialect (see further, panel 3.11). The regional dialects of England have in fact preserved a much greater number of medieval Scandinavian words – at least 600 are known from the dialect surveys which have so far been carried out, and the true total must be well over a thousand. Many of them are found in regions of the far north of England or in Scotland, such as *gleg* 'quick, sharp', *scaur* 'rock, crag', and *hooly* 'slowly, carefully'. Some are known in Ireland as well, such as *ettle* 'intend, propose' (*ætla*). Many are found further south in England, such as *skeer* 'clear out a fire, poke the ashes', known in Cheshire, Derbyshire, and Yorkshire. *Addle* 'earn' (from *øðla*) is another widespread Midlands word: *Can you credit the wages some chaps addle these days?* *Grum* 'angry' has a broad swathe of dialect usage between Yorkshire and as far south as Devon. *Frosk* 'frog' and *skep* 'basket' are also widely distributed. There are some excellent adverbs: my favourite is *owmly* 'lonely, dreary' (*aumligr*), used chiefly in Yorkshire as a descriptive term for old large houses.

3.11 Doublets

A language-contact situation such as existed between Danish and English readily yields many word pairs, where each language provides a word for the same object or situation. Usually, one usage ousts the other. The Danish word survived in such cases as *egg* vs *ey* and *sister* vs *sweostor*. The English word survived in such cases as *path* vs *reike* and *swell* vs *bolnen*.

But in a number of interesting cases, *both* words survived, because their meanings went in different directions. This is what happened to the following items:

Old Norse	Old English
dike	ditch
hale	whole
raise	rise
scrub	shrub
sick	ill
skill	craft
skin	hide
skirt	shirt

Also interesting are those cases where the Old English form has become part of Standard English while the Old Norse form has remained in a regional dialect.

Old Norse	Old English
almous	alms
ewer	udder
garth	yard
kirk	church
laup	leap
nay	no
scrive	write
trigg	true
will ['lost']	wild

Some of these words have become part of a regional standard, such as the Scots use of *kirk* 'church'. Several have become widely known through former literary use, such as *hap* 'luck, success': 'Be it art or hap, / He hath spoken true', says Antony of the Soothsayer (*Antony and Cleopatra*, II.iii.33). *Gate* 'way' is another example: in *King Lear* (IV.vi.237) disguised Edgar adopts a country accent and tells Oswald to *go your gate* (i.e., 'be on your way) (see p. 360). *Gate* in this sense is widely used throughout the north of England and in Scotland, and is often encountered in writing because of its frequency in street names such as *Micklegate* and *Gallowgate*. (This is not, incidentally, the same usage as the one which turns up in such London names as *Aldgate* and *Newgate*; there the sense of *gate* is 'portal' – an Anglo-Saxon, not a Scandinavian word.) Quite a few words are recorded both in general use and in place-names, such as *force* 'waterfall' (*Catterick Force, Stainforth Force*).

We must not overrate the impact of Scandinavian words on English: they are only a tiny number compared with the thousands of French words which entered the language during the Middle Ages. Moreover, the majority fell out of use. Modern readers would make no sense of most of the entries in a dictionary of Scandinavian words in Middle English: *crus, goulen, stor, scogh, hething, mensk, derfly, bleike* ... (The meanings, respectively, are 'fierce', 'scream', 'strong', 'wood', 'scorn', 'honour', 'boldly', 'pale'.) Yet some of the ones that did survive exercised a disproportionate influence, because (like *take* and *get*) they were very frequently used. And they were supplemented by another set of changes which were even more influential, because they made a permanent impact on the grammar of the language, both standard and nonstandard. The most important of these changes was the introduction of a new set of third-person plural pronouns, *they, them*, and *their*. These replaced the earlier Old

English inflected forms (p. 44): *hi* or *hie* (in the nominative and accusative cases, 'they / them'), *hira* or *heora* (in the genitive case, 'their, of them'), and *him* or *heom* (in the dative case, 'to them, for them') – several spelling variants were in use, with all forms. Pronouns do not change very often in the history of a language, and to see one set of forms replaced by another is truly noteworthy.

It did not, of course, happen overnight. In fact it took some 300 years for the substitutions to work their way through the whole pronoun system and throughout all parts of the country. The change started in the north and steadily moved south. The new forms must have been very welcome in the south, where a series of changes had been affecting the pronunciation of the Old English third-person pronouns *he* 'he', *heo* 'she', and *hi* 'they', so that they had begun to sound alike. Such a level of ambiguity would have been intolerable: people need to be able to tell, in such sentences as '/hiː/ said /hiː/ loved me', whether it is a male, female, or plural speaker referring to a male, female, or plural lover. The *they* form solved the problem for the plural pronoun; and around the same time *she* emerged (though its source is more obscure) to provide a solution for the female form.

By 1200, *they* (it appears in various spellings – *thei*, *þeȝȝ*, etc.) had replaced *hi* in the North Midlands. In the *Orrmulum* (p. 196), written in the East Midlands around 1200, we can see the two sets of forms in competition. The author, Orrm, always uses *þeȝȝ* 'they' instead of *hi*, when the word is subject of the clause, but when it comes to other functions, he uses *hemm*, *heore*, and *here* alongside *þeȝȝm* and *þeȝȝre*. The two systems can be seen together even in short phrases, such as *þeȝȝ hemm self* ('they themselves'). *They* was in general Midlands use by 1300, and had begun to move south, where it coexisted with *hi* until about 1400. At the same time, the other forms were changing, at different rates in different parts of the country. Chaucer uses *þei* alongside *her/ here* and *hem*. *Hi* disappeared completely from the language by around 1450, and the final sightings of the other *h*- forms can be seen soon after. There is still occasional variation between *h*- and *th*- forms in William Caxton's early prose: in the final Epilogue of his *History of Troy* (c. 1473), for example, we find both *hem* and *them*: 'I have promysid to dyverce gentilmen and to my frendes to adresse *to hem* as hastely as I myght this sayd book' is followed a few lines later by certain authors who 'wryten favorably for the Grekes and gyve *to them* more worship than to the Trojans'. But by the end of his publishing career, the *th*- forms are everywhere. The only later trace of the pronunciation of the old *h*- forms is when *them* is colloquially reduced to *'em*, a usage very common in Shakespeare, and still around today (*Give 'em to me*).

Several other influences of Old Norse on English grammar can be seen. A development closely associated with *they* was the use of *are* as the third-person plural of the verb *to be*. This form had already been used sporadically in northern texts during the late Old English period – for example, in the Lindisfarne Gospels – but in Middle English it steadily moves south, eventually replacing the competing plural forms *sindon* and *be*. *Sindon* disappeared completely by the mid 1200s, but *be* remained in use for several centuries, entering generations of intuitions through the style of the Book of Common Prayer and the King James Bible (e.g., *They be blind leaders of the blind*, Matthew 15:14). Modern Standard English has almost entirely lost sight of this form, though it is occasionally encountered in subjunctive contexts (e.g., *if they be there*), poetry, proverbial phrases (e.g., *Medicines be not meat to live by*), and idioms (e.g., *the powers that be*). However, it continues to be a major feature of the language in regional dialects, both in Britain and abroad (p. 481). What is standard for one era can be regional for another.

Among other Scandinavian grammatical features which survived are the pronouns *both* and *same*, and the prepositions *til* 'till, to' and *fro* 'from'. *Fro* (also found as *fra* and *frae*) is still widespread in regional dialect, though in Standard English it is used only in the fixed phrase *to and fro*. The negative response word, *nay*, is also Norse in origin (*nei*). From Old Norse *munu* we find an auxiliary verb *mun*, in various forms, as in this example from the northern chronicle poem *Cursor Mundi*, written in the early 1300s: *him mond forbede / To haf don suilk an ogli dede* 'he would refuse to do such a dreadful deed' (l. 1105). *Mun* is still heard today in regional dialects with the meaning 'must', a famous nineteenth-century example being the last line of Tennyson's 'Northern Farmer, Old Style': *an' if I mun doy I mun doy* (p. 494). Finally, the *-s* ending for the third-person singular present-tense form of the verb (as in *she runs*) was almost certainly a Scandinavian feature. In Old English, this ending was usually -ð, as in *hebbað* 'raises' and *gæð* 'goes'; but in late Northumbrian texts we find an *-s* ending, and this too spread south to become the standard form (see further, p. 218).

Several other Norse grammatical forms entered early Middle English, though they did not survive. For example, in the *Cursor Mundi* we find several instances of *at* appearing as a relative pronoun: *þis palais at was sua rike* – 'this palace that was so splendid', l. 415). And *sum* meaning 'as' is found replacing *so* in the word *hu sumeuer* 'howsoever' (l. 2,339). Also worth noting are those words, such as *few*, *though*, *against*, and *at*, which, although not new to the language (they were all in Old English), had their usage influenced by Old Norse patterns. There are several colloquial or idiomatic uses of *with* and *at*, for example, which were introduced or reinforced by awareness of an analogous Norse construction.[5] Examples include its 'contact' use (*he's always at his desk*) and a usage which did not exist in Old English, of the type *She lives at Mary's* (i.e., house). Both constructions were common in Old Norse, and it is notable that they begin to appear with some frequency in Middle English.

The early French and Saxon stories

Telling the Scandinavian story takes us well into the Middle Ages. But there are other foreign linguistic elements which need to be identified in the Old English mosaic before we leave the Anglo-Saxon period. Although Celtic, Latin, and Norse elements do account for almost all the lexical diversity in the early language, they do not account for its whole range. Old French, in particular, was already beginning to make its presence felt; and there were some Old Saxon words, too.

The major impact of French on English would not take place until after the Norman Conquest (p. 144), but French influence in Britain did not suddenly start in 1066. Trading relationships with the north European mainland had been growing throughout Anglo-Saxon times. During the eighth century, for example, King Offa and Emperor Charlemagne signed a trading treaty, and promptly fell out over it: Charlemagne complained about the length of the English woollen cloaks he received; Offa found the Frankish lava grindstones of poor quality. The result was a (short-lived) ban on English merchants entering Gaul and Frankish merchants entering England. The export of wool was a significant feature of the period – some historians say it was *the* significant feature, the basis of Anglo-Saxon wealth[6] – and the fame of English cloth reached as far afield as the Arab world. From records of the dues paid at customs posts throughout Europe, it is known that English traders regularly visited towns in Gaul and around the Mediterranean. It would have been surprising if merchants had not brought some French words back to England.

An even stronger influence came from religious and political contacts. The *Anglo-Saxon Chronicle* reports regular visits to Rome during Alfred's reign (from 887). Then, during the tenth century, the lull following the Danish defeat (p. 67) gave an opportunity for a renewal of monastic life and learning (the *Benedictine revival*) – a revival which began on the Continent. The Benedictine abbey at Cluny (in the French Bourgogne) was founded in 910, and became known for its monastic reforms, promoting a stricter observance of the Benedictine rule. Soon after, monastic centres were established at Fleury, Ghent, and elsewhere, and several English religious leaders visited them. St Dunstan, for example, spent an enforced year on the Continent after a quarrel with King Eadwig in 956. At the political level, contacts with France grew following the marriage in 1002 of Ethelred II (the *unræd*, or 'ill-advised' – misleadingly translated in Modern English as 'unready') to Emma, daughter of Duke Richard of Normandy. This was the first dynastic link between the two countries. Ethelred's son, Edward (the Confessor), was later exiled to Normandy, during the period of Danish rule, and lived there for twenty-five years, returning to England in 1042 with many French courtiers (p. 72).

Given the nature of the contact, it is perhaps surprising that so few French loans of the period have been recorded, though this can probably be attributed to the time-lag effect noted earlier (p. 73). A foundation of familiarity with French was being laid down during the eleventh century, which doubtless facilitated the onset of the later period of massive borrowing. A number of the words first known from the twelfth century were likely to have been around in the eleventh. As it is, we have just a sprinkling of French loans recorded in such eleventh-century sources as Ælfric and the *Anglo-Saxon Chronicle*: *bacun* 'bacon', *gingifer* 'ginger', and *capun* 'capon' come from this period, as do a number of words illustrating a more general kind of cultural contact: *tumbere* 'dancer', *servian* 'serve', *arblast* 'weapon', *prisun* 'prison', *serfise* 'service', and *market* (appearing in a 963 charter, though the word was probably added at a later date). *Battle* is discussed in panel 3.12. The most influential loan was certainly *prut* or *prud* 'proud', along with *pryd* 'pride', which were important terms in religious exposition. These began to appear regularly in the eleventh century, and prompted a series of derived forms, such as *prytscipe* (literally 'prideship'), *prutness* ('prideness'), and *prutlic* ('pridelike'). The forms also entered into several compounds, such as *oferprut* 'haughty', *woruldpryde* 'worldly pride', and *prutswongor* 'overburdened with pride'.

In all such cases, we need to look carefully at the meaning of the words,

---

3.12 Battle Abbey

'Then the king went to Hastings at Candlemas, and while he was there waiting for a breeze he had the abbey at Battle consecrated . . .' [*he let halgian þæt mynster æt þære Bataille*]

This reference in the *Laud Chronicle* to 2 February 1094 reports the building of the abbey at Battle, East Sussex, on the site of the Battle of Hastings. What is linguistically interesting is that the name of the abbey is the first recorded instance of the word *battle*, a French loanword which in general usage does not appear until the end of the thirteenth century. The *Chronicle* shows the French spelling.

A year later, another building is mentioned, in the north of England, and this time the French origin is explicitly recognized. 'The king . . . ordered a castle to be built in front of Bamburgh, and called it in his language "Malvoisin", which in English means "Evil Neighbour"'. [. . . *& hine on his spæce Malueisin het þæt is on Englisc Yfel nehhebur* – literally: 'and it in his language Malueisin called that is in English Evil neighbour'] not just at their form, before we assign a French origin. *Castel* is a case in point. This word, from Latin *castellum*, is found in the late West Saxon Gospels in the sense of 'village'; but in the *Chronicle* we see it used very definitely in its Norman sense of 'fortress', with references being made to castles being 'built'. *þa hæfdon þa welisce menn gewroht ænne castel on Herefordscire*, writes the Laud chronicler for 1048: 'at that time the foreigners had built a castle in Hereford-shire'. Another cautionary point is that it is not always clear whether a word came into English at the time from Old French or directly from Latin – an etymological problem which we will encounter again in the Middle English period. *Sot* 'foolish', for example, could have come from either source, as could *tur* 'tower'.

There is one other source of foreign words in Old English: the other Germanic languages which had been developing in parallel with Old English in other parts of Europe, such as Frisian and Old Saxon. Contacts had been maintained between England and the Baltic territories. English missionaries had worked there. King Alfred had employed scholars from the European mainland during his cultural revival, and a few words in West Saxon have been attributed to that influence, notably *macian* 'make'. The Old English word for 'island', spelled variously *iȝland*, *iland*, or *eȝland*, is probably Frisian in origin. A text known as *Genesis B* – so-called because it is embedded within the old English poem *Genesis* – is a late ninth-century translation of an Old Saxon original, copies of which were still being made during the tenth century. Several of its words are found in a ninth-century Old Saxon poem on the Gospels called the *Heliand*. They include: *sima* 'chain', *hearra* 'master', *strið* 'struggle', *landscipe* 'region', *heodæg* 'today', *hearmscearu* 'affliction', *suht* 'illness', *wær* 'true', and a few more. The closeness in form to Old English words means that there may be other lexical relationships still not identified. For the most part, though, Old Saxon words made no permanent mark on English. Their presence in the late Anglo-Saxon period is more symbolic: an indication of the readiness of the language (by which one means the people) to tolerate foreign expressions and incorporate them where there is felt to be a need. Already in Old English we find the foundation being laid of the lexical eclecticism which would become a future hallmark of the language (see further, panel 3.13).

Loanwords have been a focus of this chapter because they are the main way of demonstrating the scale and multiplicity of the social forces affecting the language during the Anglo-Saxon period – forces which produced a range of dialects and styles whose variety has often been obscured by the concentration on West Saxon as the literary standard (p. 54). This first period in the history of English is truly remarkable in the number and type of language-contact situations which the Anglo-Saxons experienced within their own borders. In the six centuries between 500 and 1100, the people had to deal routinely with

3.13 A Slavic arrival

The *Parker Chronicle* for 1031 (actually reporting 1027) reports a visit of King Cnut to Rome. It goes on: 'As soon as he arrived back in England, he gave to Christ Church [in Canterbury] the port at Sandwich, together with all the dues that there accrue from both sides of the harbour, so that whenever the tide is at its highest and to the full, and a ship is afloat in closest proximity to the shore, and a man is standing on that ship and has a small tapering-axe in his hand . . .' [*and þar beo an mann stande on þan scipe and habbe ane taper-æxe on his hande* . . .]

Tantalizingly, the rest of the charter is erased in the manuscript. But G. N. Garmondsway adds the likely continuation from a fuller version in the Red Book of Canterbury, now at Canterbury Cathedral (No. 16): 'the monastery shall receive the dues from as far inland as can be reached by a small axe thrown from the ship'.

Doubtless the monks had a real interest in following the prowess of this Anglo-Saxon ancestor of the javelin or shot-put. But for linguists, the interest is in the word *taper-æxe*. Although there was a word *taper* earlier in Old English, that was in the sense of 'candle', ultimately an alteration of the Latin word *papyrus*. (That plant did much more than form the basis for early paper; part of it could be used to make candle-wicks.)

Taper-æxe seems to be a quite separate development, entering the language from Old Norse. But where did the Danes get it from? The most likely candidate is an Old Slavic word, *toporu*. Modern Russian has it still, in *topor* 'axe'. If so, it is the first example of an originally Slavic word in English.

---

speakers of no fewer than four language families – Celtic (chiefly Old Welsh), Italic (Vulgar Latin, Classical Latin), Romance (Old French, Norman French), and other branches of Germanic (Old Norse, Old Saxon, Frisian). No subsequent period in British history introduced such a diverse set of linguistic influences within the British Isles. Indeed, to find anything comparable, we must turn to the present-day, when the forces set loose by globalization have once again subjected the language to a remarkable process of expansion (Chapter 17).[7]

Interlude 3
Understanding Danes

To understand the great influence of Old Norse on English, we have had to leave our original focus of inquiry into Old English, and move forward into Middle English. There was a time when philologists and literary historians felt that there was a major break between the Old and Middle English periods, with the language having to 'begin again' in the Middle Ages. The Scandinavian effect is a clear argument against this, as we shall note again in Chapter 5 – a demonstration of linguistic continuity in the early history of the language. It is a continuity which can be seen even in the south of England, where Scandinavian influence was weakest. Several Norse words appear in the earliest Middle English texts, and steadily increase in frequency, especially in the fourteenth century. (Chaucer, writing in the London area towards the end of that century, uses over sixty Scandinavian words.) Indeed, by following the Scandinavian theme to its conclusion – the spread of Norse usage from the north of England throughout the rest of the country – the thrust of the argument takes us right through the Middle English period, as far forward as the beginning of the fifteenth century. It is a time-scale of some 250 years.

None the less, when we note the starting-point of the written evidence, around 1175, we cannot ignore the fact that there was a notable gap between the final occasion Anglo-Saxons and Scandinavians were in routine contact (roughly 1050) and the time when the linguistic repercussions of that contact started to appear in significant numbers in the language. That is 125 years. Why did it take so long? Some delay is natural, when languages come into sudden contact with each other (as we shall see again with the arrival of French loanwords in Middle English, p. 120); but in the present connection the delay was probably greater because West Saxon, not Mercian or Northumbrian, was becoming the standard literary language. The 200 years following the reign of King Alfred saw the political dominance of Wessex, centred on Winchester, and the vast majority of the literary canon of Old English is written in the West Saxon dialect (p. 55). It is unlikely that the few texts written in the Danelaw would have had literary influence outside the region; nor would Norse words, resonating with associations of invasion, have been likely to appeal to southern authors and scribes. A considerable body of vernacular usage would have had to be in place before authors would have begun to use such words unselfconsciously, and for scribes to have introduced them without a second thought. A delay of a century or more is not unlikely, for this to happen.

But this still leaves unanswered three other questions. Why was there such extensive borrowing from Old Norse? Why was this borrowing so intimate, eventually affecting the expression of all areas of everyday life? And why did Norse linguistic features become so pervasive in the country as a whole, given that the area of Danish settlement was originally so restricted? The answers largely lie in the nature of the cultural assimilation which took place – an issue which has attracted a great deal of debate and speculation.

Much of this debate has addressed the question of intelligibility. When the Danes first arrived, would the Anglo-Saxons have been able to understand what they were saying? Or would they have needed interpreters? Some scholars have argued that there was a great deal of mutual intelligibility, because the time when the Danelaw was being settled, around 900, was only some 500 years since the time when the Anglo-Saxons and Danes would have been neighbours in Continental Europe, speaking similar north Germanic dialects (p. 21) – and 500 years is no time at all, in terms of linguistic history. If this was the case, then there would have been a great deal of linguistic interaction as the people began to live side by side, and this would have eventually involved a huge amount of accommodation (p. 25) in everyday speech. But the primary direction of influence for some time would have been from Scandinavian into English. After all, the Danes were the conquerors, and conquerors do not usually have the sort of benevolent mindset which makes them look kindly on the vocabulary of the conquered. The Anglo-Saxons living in the Danelaw, on the other hand, would have been under considerable linguistic pressure to acquire the vocabulary which accompanied the invaders. Large numbers of everyday words would have quickly come into use, few of which would ever be likely to appear in official documents. Things would have been different if there had been a Danelaw Chaucer to use them in literary narration.

Did this scenario apply? It all depends on how much linguistic change would have taken place in that 500 years. What can happen, linguistically, in half a millennium? We can compare the period between 1500 and 2000, which roughly coincides with the growth of American English as distinct from British English. How different are these two varieties today? If we examine the written standards of Britain and the USA, the answer has to be 'not very much'; educated Britons and Americans do, on the whole, understand each other. But these standards are not the relevant points of comparison for an age when such varieties were absent or (in the case of tenth-century English) at the earliest stage of evolution. We need to compare *nonstandard* varieties – the everyday forms of regional speech, such as those heard in working-class rural areas or city suburbs in Britain and the USA – and here we find many examples of dialects that would be to a large extent mutually unintelligible today (p. 21), notwithstanding the cultural and media contact which has linked the two nations for so long. Some movies and documentary films have even had to resort to subtitles for regional dialects, to ensure that the dialogue is intelligible when it crosses the Atlantic. How much less would mutual intelligibility have been, one imagines, in an age when communications were so much more sporadic, and the North Sea a greater barrier than the present-day Atlantic. At best, people might have been able to grasp the gist of each other's speech, but only if the subject-matter was domestic and utterances not too long or complicated.

If Danish and Old English were mutually unintelligible in the Danelaw, then an alternative scenario has to be envisaged – one of emergent bilingualism. Here, we can imagine the Anglo-Saxons being at first unable to understand the speech of the new settlers other than through an interpreter, and vice versa. But, as with the first scenario, the pressure would have been on them to learn Danish. In such cases, we know from sociolinguistic studies that it takes three generations for such pressure to have its full effect. In the first generation, adults gradually pick up bits of the incoming language – younger members learning it quite well, at least for everyday purposes, with older members perhaps knowing only a few words and phrases relating to common objects and activities, such as greeting. The children of this generation are in a different situation, growing up in a bilingual environment, and, as with such children the world over, taking to the two languages quite naturally. But the two languages are not usually of equal status – especially not, in a situation of invasion. Here, the incoming language becomes prestigious at the expense of the other – as has happened in the case of colonial languages all over the world (p. 121) – because it offers greater economic and political opportunities. When the second-generation children grow up, therefore, they opt to use the new language and allow their parental language to go to seed. And when that generation has its own children, the ancestral language is dropped completely: the third-generation children hear only the incoming language from their parents. In this way we see arising the situation – all too familiar these days, with so many of the world's languages endangered – of grandchildren and grandparents being unable to understand each other.

If Danish power had lasted longer, all this might have happened in the Danelaw, and again in Cnut's time. But in neither period did Danish political power last long enough. Even allowing for shorter life-spans than today, the fifty years of Danelaw rule was hardly enough for two generations of language shift; the twenty-six years of Cnut's was hardly enough for one. And even before the first generation of Danelaw rule was over, as we have seen, the West Saxon retaking of the area had begun (p. 70). Accordingly, as the political balance of power shifted, so the reasons for learning Danish would diminish. In such circumstances, the eventual linguistic outcome reflects the numbers of people involved. With Anglo-Saxons far outnumbering Danes, and English political power in the ascendant, second-generation Danish children would find it much more useful to maintain their English language skills. Their sense of ethnic identity would probably result in a kind of English liberally sprinkled with Norsisms, and many of these would eventually assimilate into the speech of the community. Being everyday words and having no particular prestige, they would be unlikely to be written down, at least not until an age emerged where the conflict which had given rise to them was so far in the past that the words had lost all their cultural associations. The arrival of the Cnut regime would have reversed this process to some extent, but it did not last long enough to alter the underlying trend.

We are left with the question of how long it would take, in these circumstances, for Norse usage to move out of the Danelaw region into the country as a whole. After 1066, the impediment caused by the standard language being the dialect of Wessex was becoming less serious. Its literary heyday was over, and by the end of the Middle Ages a quite different part of the country was to produce the dialect which would become the standard language (p. 243). The centre of political power was moving from Winchester to London, and communications between London and the north were improving and increasing. There would of course be a certain linguistic inertia for Scandinavian words to overcome. The south was probably much more conservative, linguistically, than the north, being less used to the kind of innovation that turns up routinely in bilingual communities, so doubtless there would be a certain antipathy to 'foreign' words, just as there is today.

Our question is therefore a speculative one. After the Norman Conquest, how long would it take for Scandinavian culture to be so lost sight of in England that its loanwords and grammatical constructions would shed all their foreign associations, and become part of the common stock of English literary usage? Linguistic intuitions acquired through direct cultural transmission would soon diminish once the grandchildren of the children of Cnut's era had died. It is difficult to believe that a strong sense of cultural connection would last much beyond a century. If this is the case, we would expect Nordic resonances to have disappeared by the late twelfth century, and for Norse words to begin appearing regularly from then on in texts which have a provenance and subject-matter completely unrelated to anything Scandinavian. The conclusion is tempting, for this is indeed the period, as we have seen, when such words do begin to be common in a wide range of English texts from all over the country.

Chapter 4 Stylistic variation in Old English

Twentieth-century studies have begun to demonstrate the considerable amount of systematic variation which exists within Old English. When I first studied this subject, in the 1960s, the overriding impression I received was of a language which existed in a homogeneous literary standard, with regional and social variation limited and marginal, the stuff of footnotes only. Today, we have begun to appreciate the range of sociolinguistic factors which must have governed the dynamics of the language, and the influence of these factors is slowly being revealed through the sophisticated investigative techniques available to modern scholarship. The true diversity of Old English is steadily emerging. Regional dialect variation provides one dimension, as we have seen in the first two chapters. Social variation arising out of language contact is another, most noticeable in the use of loanwords, which contribute in strong measure to the impression of linguistic heterogeneity (Chapter 3). Institutional variation is a third dimension, arising out of the distinctive procedures and practices of the major scriptoria – an early encounter with language planning. A fourth dimension is chronological variation, with texts representing a period of over 400 years, and thus displaying many signs of language change. And we must not forget stylistic variation.

Stylistic variation here refers to the range of linguistic effects that speakers or writers use when they express themselves as individuals or relate to other people within their own milieu. A group of people from the same regional and social dialect background do not all speak or write in the same way. Their language can vary in level of formality, for example, ranging from a style whose effects are governed by ritual and propriety to one which is casual and colloquial. Style can also reflect the nature of the subject-matter or reflect the user's occupation, as in the case of religious and legal language. It can vary in terms of the method of exposition, which includes such major genre variations as poetry and prose, as well as more specific types such as speeches, homilies, letters, songs, and riddles. Many of these distinctions can be found in Old English, though there are some limitations arising out of the nature of the material. The colloquial level of expression, in particular, is not well represented

– though there are fragments of relatively informal expression in a few texts, as we shall see (p. 97). Most Old English texts show a style of language appropriate for formal occasions.

None the less, even within this formal level, there are important variations to be found. Most obviously, there is the contrast between poetry and prose. But then within poetry we find important differences between the heroic narrative style displayed in such works as *Beowulf*, *Finnesburh*, and *Widsith*, the Christian texts and commentaries illustrated by *Genesis*, *Exodus*, and *The Dream of the Rood*, and the elegiac reflections found in many short pieces, such as *The Wanderer*, *The Seafarer*, and *The Ruin*. There are also several minor genres, such as the riddles, or the sententious sayings often referred to as 'gnomic poetry' ('A hall shall stand, grow old itself. A tree which lies low grows least. Trees shall spread out and faith increase . . .'). Within the domain of prose, we also find a wide range of variation, extending from the isolated items encountered in glossaries, inscriptions, and cryptograms to the extended discourses typical of liturgies, homilies, charters, laws, and wills. Some texts are translations from Latin; some are of Anglo-Saxon origin. Variation in subject-matter includes the legal (e.g., charters, wills, laws), religious (e.g., prayers, creeds, penitential texts, monastic rules, biblical translations), scientific (e.g., medical, folkloric, botanical, grammatical), and historical (e.g., town records, lists of kings, chronicles, martyrologies). Style is also affected by audience, so that we might expect differences to appear in texts directed at professionals (e.g., fellow-monks), congregations, students, families (e.g., wills), or the general public. And some authors, such as Ælfric and Wulfstan, developed distinctive personal modes of expression. We know from Modern English that these variables promote significant stylistic differences in written texts. There is no reason to expect Old English to be any different – though with such small amounts of written data extant, the task of detecting stylistic distinctiveness ranges from the difficult to the impossible.

A distinctive use of language has, however, been identified with reference to the major genre distinction of poetry vs prose, especially in relation to vocabulary. While many Old English words are genre-neutral, several appear only in poetry, while others predominate in prose. For example, in the study of the words for 'pride, haughtiness' referred to on p. 79, *prut* forms were found only in prose, whereas the *ofer-* forms appeared in poetry. The heroic poems use a wide range of 'warrior' words, such as *rinc*, *secg*, *hæleð*, *beorn* (related to the word for 'bear'), and *freca* (related to the word for 'wolf') – all with roughly the same meaning of 'hero, man' – and these rarely occur in prose. When they do, it is usually because the prose writer is attempting an elevated style. A poetic word like *hæleð* appears many times in *Beowulf*, where its poetic resonance grows as we repeatedly encounter its use in expressive rhythmical and alliterative contexts – *hæleð under heofonum* (l. 52, 'heroes beneath the heavens'), *hæleð in hoðman* (l. 2,458, 'heroes in the grave'), *hæleð hiofende* (l. 3,142, 'heroes lamenting'). When we find an instance of this word in a piece of Alfredian prose, therefore, it comes as something of a surprise – until we see that it appears in a passage which is a translation of Latin verse. Plainly, there is nothing to stop prose authors introducing poetic forms into their texts if they want to achieve a more elevated style. The distinction between poetry and prose is not absolute: there has been poetic prose and prosaic poetry in all periods of English literature. Modern poetry, too, uses words (usually archaisms) that are rarely or never found in prose – such as *morn* 'morning', *ere* 'before', and *oft* 'often'. But in Old English the possibilities were very much greater.

It is the poetic words and expressions which have attracted most attention because the lexical processes they display are, for many people, the most important features of Old English linguistic creativity. Most notable is the use of a wide range of synonymous words and phrases to express a particular notion, such as 'sea', 'ship', or 'warrior'. A ship, for example, might be described straightforwardly as a *scip* or *ceol* 'keel', but in addition will be found described using a variety of short phrases or compound words – some fairly literal, such as *wægflota* 'wave floater', *sægenga* 'sea goer', and *brimwudu* 'water wood', some more imaginative, such as *merehus* 'sea-house', *sæhengest* 'sea steed', and *yþmearh* 'wave horse'. There are at least fifty expressions to describe the sea itself, such as 'seal bath' (*seolbæþ*), 'fish home' (*fisceseþel*), 'swan road' (*swanrad*), and 'whale way' (*hwælweg*). In many cases it is difficult to establish whether the forms are indeed genuine synonyms, or whether there is some subtle element of meaning difference. Is a *beorn* just a 'warrior' or is it a particular kind of warrior? Is a *bil* the same as a *sweord*, or is it a particular kind of 'sword'? In Modern English, we know that *horse* and *mare* do not have the same meaning, and that *horse* and *steed* do – the only difference being that *steed* is more poetic. In Old English, we often cannot be sure.

Lexical variation is of course commonplace in narrative to avoid having to use the same word repeatedly. In modern football journalism, for example, players are rarely described as merely *kicking* the ball; rather, they *lift* it, *hoof* it, *slip* it, *slam* it, *power* it, and much more . . . But we have little today that quite compares to the imaginative range and allusive expressiveness of the Old English poetic synonyms. We do make some efforts in that direction: footballers, for example, might be called, rather pedestrianly, *goal-scorers* or *team-members*; but we do not typically describe them as *ball-kickers* or *net-aimers*, and even journalists do not engage in such flights of descriptive fancy as *field-lords* or *hoof-dandies*. But it is just such leaps of imagination which we repeatedly find in Old English poetry: the human body is described as a *banhus* or *bancofa* 'bone-house, bone-coffer'; a sword as a *beadoleoma* 'battle-light'; thunder as *wolcna sweg* 'sound of the clouds'; the eye as a *heafodgim* 'head-gem'. The descriptive phrases are so distinctive that a term from Old Norse poetic treatises, *kenning*, has been used to describe them.

Why are there so many synonymous expressions? What lies behind the creation of a kenning? One reason is the way such devices help to create a more expressive and varied poetry. They enable the poet to maintain the rhythmical structure of lines of poetry and the repeated pattern of sounds they contained. To see this, we must first take a look at the nature of the Old English poetic line, which is probably the most structurally distinctive verse form to have emerged in the history of English. Its basic principles of construction are straightforward, and can be found with little variation throughout the whole of the Old English poetry corpus (in all, some 30,000 lines). In the original manuscripts, the texts are written out in continuous lines, just as prose would be, though with occasional marks to show metrical divisions. In modern editions, editors space out the lines and add modern punctuation (see panel 4.1).

- Each line is made up of two half-lines (in Old English studies usually called *verses*) of contrasting rhythms separated by a brief pause.

  Hroðgar maþelode,   helm Scyldinga (*Beowulf*, l. 371)
  Hroðgar replied,   protector of the Scyldings

- Each half-line consists of two rhythm units (*feet*).

  Hroðgar maþelode,   helm Scyldinga
     A   B   A   B

- Each foot contains a stressed (or *accented*) syllable, shown here underlined, preceded or followed by one or more unaccented syllables. (The rhythmical sequences produced are not further described here.)

  Hroðgar ma<u>þe</u>lode,   helm Scyldinga

- The two halves are joined by the repetition of the initial sound of certain accented syllables (*alliteration*), shown below in bold. One such syllable in each half-line must alliterate. In the second half-line, the first accented syllable is the dominant one, and this may alliterate with either or both the accented syllables in the first half-line.

  Hroðgar maþelode,   helm Scyldinga

- The rules governing alliteration are simple: a pair of accented syllables alliterate when they both begin with the same consonant, or when they both begin with a vowel. Any vowel can alliterate with any other vowel. (This last point is different in Modern English, where we require words to begin with the *same* vowel before they are felt to alliterate: we feel that *Albert the ant* alliterates, but *Albert the octopus* does not. In Old English, both forms were felt to alliterate.)

Panel 4.2 shows these rules operating over a few lines from *Beowulf*. If one of the rules of poetic composition is that the initial sounds of certain words must duplicate each other in every line, then the more words which are available to express a particular notion, the more the poet has creative opportunities. If the only word for 'man' were *man*, for example, then this would limit the number of things which could be said in a given line; whereas if there were several synonyms for *man*, the options would be much increased. We can consider a hypothetical case where a writer wanted to say, in Old English:

ADJECTIVE and ADJECTIVE   was the man of steel.

The Old English word for man was, indeed, *man* or *mon*, often spelled with two *n*'s. In this position in the line, the rules require one or both adjectives to

---

4.1 *The Wanderer*

The task facing the editor is apparent from this reproduction of a text from the poetic anthology found in the Exeter Book.[1] It shows the first thirty-three lines of *The Wanderer*, an elegy on the theme of transience and loneliness, uttered by a man remembering happy times in his lord's hall. It is not obvious, at first sight, that it is a poem. Nor does the text have a title: titles were added much later, in the nineteenth century, when published editions of the texts came to be made. The poem's opening lines are here laid out in modern poetic style. The original Old English letters ʒ and þ (p. 39) are here shown in modern equivalents, *g* and *w* respectively (a practice continued throughout this chapter).

> Oft him an-haga   are gebideð
> Meotodes mildse,   þeahþe he mod cearig
> geond lagu lade   lange scolde
> hreran mid handum   hrimcealde sæ,
> wadan wræclastas.   wyrd bið full anræd!
> Swa cwæþ eardstapa,   earfoþa gemyndig,
> wraþra wælsliehta,   winemaga hryre.
> Oft ic scolde ana   uhtna gehwelce
> mine ceare cwiþan;   nis nu cwicra nan
> þe ic him modsefan   minne durre
> sweotule asecgan.

> Often the solitary man prays for favour
> the mercy of the Lord, though he with sad heart
> through the watery way must long
> stir with hands the frost-cold sea,
> travel the paths of exile. Fate is totally uncompromising.
> So spoke the wanderer, mindful of hardships,

of cruel slaughters, of the death of dear kinsmen:
'Often I alone every dawning have had to
bewail my sorrows; there is now no one among the living
to whom I dare speak my heart openly . . .'

4.2 Old English poetry

The structure of Old English poetic lines is illustrated here by an extract from *Beowulf* (ll. 102–6): the description of the monster Grendel. Accented syllables are underlined; alliterating sounds are in bold.

wæs se **g**rimma **g**æst **G**rendel haten,	That grim spirit was called Grendel,
mære **m**earcstapa, se þe **m**oras heold	Famous waste-wanderer that held the moors
fen ond **f**æsten; **f**ifelcynnes eard	Fen and fastness; the land of the race of monsters
wonsæli **w**er **w**eardode hwile	The unhappy creature occupied for a while
siþðan him **Sc**yppend for**scr**ifen hæfde.	After the Creator had condemned them.

alliterate with *man*, so the only choices for the poet would be to find words beginning with *m* – such as *mære* 'famous', *micel* 'great', *modig* 'courageous', or words based on *mægen* 'might'. As we can imagine, there will not be many of these. But if the author had *rinc, secg, beorn, freca*, and others at his disposal, as alternatives to *man*, then several more possible combinations would be available in the first half-line – such as *rice* 'powerful' and *rof* 'renowned' to go with *rinc, sarig* 'sad' and *searo-grim* 'fierce in battle' to go with *secg*, or *from* 'bold' and *frod* 'wise' to go with *freca*. When kennings are involved as well, offering further word combinations, there is an extremely wide range of expressive possibilities.

But why did such a heavily structured style of poetry emerge in the first place? Why did the poets burden themselves with all these rules of balance and alliterative linkage? The answer is that they were *not* a burden; on the contrary, they were a major means of making the task of poetic creativity easier. This is because the Anglo-Saxons, as other Germanic peoples of the time, worked at first through the oral medium; poems were composed, performed, and passed on without any use being made of writing. Later during the Anglo-Saxon period, poems began to be composed in writing – such as the four attributed to Cynewulf, who must have written these pieces because he incorporated his name into the lines as a runic acrostic – but the bulk of the surviving poetic literature represents a much earlier process. We know very little about the date of most Anglo-Saxon poems – debate continues, for example, over the composition of *Beowulf*, whether eighth century or much later – but there is no doubt, from parallels with other early Germanic poems, such as the Old Saxon *Heliand*, that we are dealing with an ancient and widespread oral tradition.

The tradition is referred to several times in Old English heroic poetry, where we hear of the *scop* (pronounced 'shop'), the professional minstrel, singing the old stories while playing a small harp-like instrument. Early on in *Beowulf* we hear of the revelry in the hall of Heorot: 'the sound of the harp, the clear song of the minstrel' (l. 89). And Bede tells the story of Cædmon, the first English poet of known name, who learned his gift miraculously, after a long life of embarrassment: 'being sometimes at entertainments, when it was agreed for the sake of mirth that all present should sing in their turn, when he saw the instrument come towards him, he rose up from table and returned home' (Book IV, Chapter 24; see p. 48). That an oral transmission was widespread over time and space in Britain is suggested by the fragment from *The Dream of the Rood* which appears on the Ruthwell Cross (p. 39). The full text is in a copy made in Canterbury in the tenth century; but the Cross inscription shows that it was known in southern Scotland during the eighth.

Alliterative structuring is one of the ways in which an orally transmitted text can be remembered for accurate retelling. The point has been given some analysis in modern times, in relation to the feats of recall occasionally seen on stage and television, where people do such things as memorize telephone directories or long lists of numbers.[2] One of the ways this can be done is by imposing structure onto the text, associating particular sequences with sounds, rhythms, words, word sets, and so on. Alliteration and rhythm both prove to be valuable 'phonological mnemonics' (memorizing devices which make use of a language's sound system), as can be seen elsewhere in language when the need to grab the listener's or reader's attention is paramount, such as in news headlines and advertising slogans. Although the extent of the longest text, *Beowulf* (3,182 lines), is not exceptionally great – about twice the number of lines which would have to be learned by an actor playing Hamlet – the task of remembering it all is much facilitated by the phonological structuring. It is something which is at the heart of language learning, as we know from the way a nursery rhyme appeals to very young children, who rapidly pick up and repeat its rhyming and rhythmical patterns.[3]

Literature which is transmitted orally also relies greatly on formulaic expressions, partly as an aide-memoire, but also as a means of identifying characters, recurring scenes, and common events. Formulae add familiarity, and satisfy expectation – as in such present-day instances as children's story-telling: 'Once upon a time . . .', '. . . lived happily ever after'. In most renditions of *The Three Little Pigs*, the wolf is only ever described as a *big, bad wolf*, though several alternative accounts of his wickedness and size might be imag-ined. Listeners home in on such devices very quickly, and part of the pleasure of the response is to hear them repeated – or, on occasion to be deliberately varied. A big bad wolf might, in a sequel, become a big *good* wolf – an issue actually addressed in Jon Scieszka's *True Story of the Three Little Pigs*, where the wolf insists that he was framed! In Modern English, such narrative formulae, whether norms or playful deviations, are infrequent. In Old English, they are ubiquitous.

In *Beowulf*, we hear such set phrases as *wið ord ond wið ecg* (l. 1,549, 'against point and edge') and *wigum ond wæpnum* (l. 2,395, 'with warriors and weapons'); the hero himself is repeatedly described as *heard under helme* (ll. 342, 404, 2,539, 'brave under helmet'). An imaginative phrase associated with a particular object or action is used whenever the situation warrants it: *ealdsword eotenisc* ('ancient sword made by giants') describes no fewer than three swords – Beowulf's (l. 1,558), Wiglaf's (l. 2,616), and Eofor's (l. 2,979). It is even possible to sense a certain playfulness, when the poet takes a formula usually used routinely for one type of being, and applies it to another. Warriors are often described using the phrase 'X weard' ('guardian of X'): Hroðgar is described as *beahhorda weard* (l. 921, 'guardian of ring-hoards') and *rices weard* (l. 1,390, 'guardian of the realm'), and Beowulf describes himself as *folces weard* (l. 2,513, 'guardian of the people'). The associations are positive and heroic. So when the poet describes the monster as *beorges weard* (ll. 2,524, 2,580, 3,066, 'guardian of the barrow'), we can imagine the description to be somewhat tongue-in-cheek. We do not know how the poems were performed – whether chanted, sung, or recited – but their oral character is evident, and presumably poets would gain in reputation through their ability to embellish their tellings with fresh coinages and to introduce variations into familiar phrases (see panel 4.3).

All poets want to be fresh and original, both in what they say and in the way they say it. No writer wishes to attract the charge of banality today, and Anglo-Saxon poets would have been no different. Prose writers, however, often had other priorities and constraints. What they might write, and the way they

---

4.3 Poetic riddles

That the Anglo-Saxons had a quirky sense of humour we can tell from the riddles, ninety-five of which are found along with other major texts in the Exeter Book, a tenth-century compilation. Some were probably written down during the eighth century, but their authorship – presumably several writers – is unknown. Three of the shorter riddles are reproduced in this panel. The numbers are those assigned by George P. Krapp and Eliott Dobbie in their edition of 1936; the numbers in brackets are those assigned by Craig Williamson in a later edition (1977). He combined Krapp–Dobbie Riddles 1–3 as Riddle 1, 75–6 as Riddle 73, and 79–80 as Riddle 76, thereby producing ninety-one texts. The interpretation of the riddles is given on p. 541.[4] Special care should be taken with Riddle 42, which suggests, perhaps more than any other, that human nature has not changed much over the past thousand years.

32 [34]

Ic wiht geseah in wera burgum	I saw a creature in the towns of men
seo þæt feoh fedeð. Hafað fela toþa;	which feeds the cattle. It has many teeth;
nebb biþ hyre æt nytte, niþerweard gongeð,	its beak is useful, it points downward,
hiþeð holdlice ond to ham tyhð,	it plunders gently and returns home,
wæþeð geond weallas, wyrte seceð	it searches along the slopes, seeks roots,
Aa heo þa findeð, þa þe fæst ne biþ;	always it finds those that are not firm;
læteð hio þa wlitigan, wyrtum fæste,	it leaves the fair ones fixed by their roots,
stille stondan on staþolwonge,	quietly standing in their proper place,
beohrte blican, blowan ond growan.	brightly gleaming, blowing and growing

42 [44]

Wrætlic hongað bi weres þeo,	A wondrous thing hangs by a man's thigh,
frean under sceate. Foran is þyrel.	full under the clothes. In front is a hole.
Bið stiþ ond heard, stede hafað godne;	It is stiff and hard, it knows its proper place;
þonne se esne his agen hrægl	when a young man lifts his tunic
ofer cneo hefeð, wile þæt cuþe hol	above his knee, he wants to be able
mid his hangellan heafde gretan	to enter with the head of his hanging thing
þæt he efenlang ær oft gefylde.	the hole that it has often filled before.

43 [45]

Moððe word fræt; me þæt þuhte	A moth ate words; it seemed to me
wrætlice wyrd þa ic þæt wundor gefrægn,	a strange event when I heard of that wonder,
þæt se wyrm forswealg wera gied sumes,	that a worm, a thief in darkness, should devour
þeof in þystro, þrymfæstne cwide,	the songs of men, glorious utterance,
ond þæs strangan staþol. Stælgiest ne wæs	and a place of strong being. The thievish visitor
wihte þy gleawra, þe he þam wordum swealg.	was no whit the wiser for swallowing the words.

might write it, would often be bound by legal or religious considerations – such as the need to be faithful to a Latin original; and even if there was no formal requirement, most prose works of the period had Latin texts as a source, which would inevitably be an influence on their content and style. Where vernacular materials might have been available as sources, as would probably have been the case with parts of the *Anglo-Saxon Chronicle*, creativity would have been constrained by the standard pattern of exposition to be followed. And we must not forget that most writings were produced for public consumption, often with official status – for example, Alfred sent a copy of the *Pastoral Care* to every diocese in his kingdom. That alone would impose serious restrictions on any tendency to idiosyncrasy that a writer might have. The kind of personal prose style which we shall encounter in the Middle English period (p. 178) is hardly to be seen in Old English.

On the other hand, Old English prose style is by no means uniform. When Alfred began his revival, this was the first time (apart from in a few legal documents) that English had been used for prose exposition, and certainly there are no surviving precedents for prose writings of any length. There was no standard language, no set of agreed expectations as to how a prose text should be written. There was thus an opportunity for experimentation, with writers searching for stylistic levels which they felt would be appropriate for different kinds of text. Several parameters were available to be varied. Writers could choose their sentence length, introduce antithetical structures, make use of parallel phrases, link sentence parts with alliteration, or change word order for emphasis. In vocabulary they also had considerable choice – in some ways, a greater choice than the poets, who tended to exploit the traditional stock of poetic forms. The use of Germanic or Norse words would result in vernacular styles; Latin words would make the language more elevated, especially if the words were particularly learnèd.

Another stylistic initiative was to borrow from the poets, using their words, phrases, rhythms, or alliterative patterns. Anglo-Saxon poets sometimes used very ordinary language to make a point – as with the 'everyday' vocabulary frequently used by the writer of *The Dream of the Rood* (p. 39) – and prose writers found they could work in reverse, as it were, achieving a 'high' style by incorporating balanced constructions and poetic diction. Later writers could add an extra resonance to their work by using archaic words or spellings. And for the Christian writer, there was the option of either staying with trad-itional Latin expressions or adapting the language of Anglo-Saxon heroic poetry to do the job. Christ might then become a warrior, with all the attributes of a Beowulf. One parameter that was not used was dialect variation: writers did not yet have a sense of dialect as a contrastive expressive option; such a possibility would become available only after the emergence of one dialect as a recognized standard, which took place towards the end of the Middle English period (p. 163). However, there are clear indications of moves in the direction of a more informal style, as in this extract from Ælfric's Preface to *Genesis* (ll. 110–15), as well as in the extract given in panel 4.4.

> God gesceop us twa eagan and twa earan, twa nosðyrlu, twegen weleras, twa handa and twegen fet, and he wolde eac habban twa gecyðnyssa on ðisre worulde gesett, ða ealdan and ða niwan; for ðan ðe he deð swa swa hine sylfne gewyrð, and he nænne rædboran næfð, ne nan man ne ðearf him cweðan to, Hwi dest ðu swa?

4.4 Everyday speech

It is impossible to know how close Old English prose could get to the constructions and rhythms of everyday speech. But occasionally it is possible to sense a colloquial tone and a naturalness of pace, as in this extract.

Apollonius of Tyre

The story of Apollonius of Tyre is found in an eleventh-century manuscript.[5] It is a translation from Latin, but it displays little sign of a Latinate style, and contains some very natural-sounding pieces of dialogue. At this point in the tale, Apollonius has been shipwrecked, but finds his way to the castle of the king, whom he impresses by his skill in a ball-game taking place in the public baths. Afterwards, the king sends a servant to find out who the stranger is:

> þa wænde he ongean to ðam cynge and cwæð: 'Se iunga man þe þu æfter axsodest is forliden man.' Ða cwæð se cyng: 'Þurh hwæt wast ðu þæt?' Se man him andswerode and cwæð: Þeah he hit silf forswige, his gegirla hine geswutelað.' Ða cwæð se cyngc: 'Ga rædlice and sege him þæt se cyngc bit ðe þæt ðu cume to his gereorde.' Ða Apollonius þæt gehyrde, he þam gehyrsumode and eode forð mid þam men oð þæt he becom to ðæs cynges healle. Ða eode se man in beforan to ðam cynge and cwæð: 'Se forlidena man is cumen þe ðu æfter sendest ac he ne mæg for scame in gan buton scrude.' Ða het se cyngc hine sona gescriden mid wurðfullan scrude and het hine in gan to ðam gereorde.

> Then he went back to the king and said: 'The young man that you were asking after is a shipwrecked man.' Then the king said: 'How do you know that?' The servant answered and said: 'Though he didn't say anything himself, his garments revealed it.' Then the king said: 'Go quickly and tell him that the king asks that you come to his feast.' When Apollonius heard this, he obeyed and went along with the men until he came to the king's hall. Then the servant went in before the king and said: 'The shipwrecked man that you sent for has arrived, but he is too ashamed to come in without proper clothing.' Then the king commanded that he be clothed at once with worthy garments and called him in to the feast.

One feature of this extract has particular stylistic significance as a marker of informal speech: when the king gives his servant the instruction to fetch Apollonius, he says, 'Go quickly and tell *him* that the king asks that *you* come to his feast.' In spontaneous speech this rapid switching of perspective, even within a single sentence, is perfectly normal. In his excitement, the king is jumping ahead and anticipating what the servant will actually say to Apollonius. In any formal narrative, care would have been taken to ensure that the pronouns agreed: 'Go quickly and tell him that the king asks that *he* come to his feast.'

> God made us with two eyes and two ears, two nostrils, two lips, two hands and two feet, and he would also have two testaments established in this world, the old and the new; for he does whatever becomes himself, and he has no counsellors, nor needs anyone to say to him, Why do you so?

What is notable, in fact, is how many prose writers of the period seemed to avoid the use of Latin words, as part of an apparently conscious effort to develop an indigenous style. The point is explicitly addressed by Ælfric in the Preface to his translation of *Genesis*, where he remarks that:

> Latin and English do not have the same *wise* in the arrangement of the language; anyone who teaches or translates from Latin into English must always arrange it so that the English has its own *wise*, otherwise it is very difficult to read for someone who does not know the Latin *wise*.

(*Wise* meant 'manner, way, wise, fashion', and might here be translated as 'style'.)

At the same time, some writers went in the other direction, aiming for a heightening of style which would live up to the canons of Classical Latin rhetoric. For example, Byrhtferth, master of Ramsey school in the early eleventh century, employed a style which made copious use of learnèd words in both Old English and Latin, as in this observation on writing from his *Manual* of ecclesiastical computation, composed in 1011:

> Eac me com stiðlice to mode hu þa getyddustan boceras gewyrceað sinelimpha on heora uersum. Hwæt, hig ærost apinsiað wærlicum mode þa naman and þa binaman and heora declinunga . . .[6]

> It also came strongly into my mind how the most learnèd authors make synaloepha in their verses. Lo, they first reflect with a careful mind the nouns and the pronouns and their declensions . . .

Synaloepha? A Latin term for the coalescence of two syllables into one (as when *you are* becomes *y'are*). Bishop Wulfstan, in particular, developed a highly crafted rhetorical style, praised by his contemporaries, which in its balanced constructions, formulaic expressions, and pairs of words linked by alliteration and often rhyme is very close to verse. His 'Sermon of Wolf to the English' (*Sermo Lupi ad Anglos*), composed in 1014, contains such passages as the following:

> Nis eac nan wundor þeah us mislimpe forþam we witan ful georne þæt nu fela geara men na ne rohtan foroft hwæt hy worhtan wordes oððe dæde. Ac wearð þes þeodscipe swa hit þincan mæg swyþe forsyngod þurh mænigfealde synna 7 þurh fela misdæda: þurh morðdæda 7 þurh mandæda, þurh gitsunga 7 þurh

gifernessa, þurh stala 7 þurh strudunga, þurh mannsylena 7 þurh hæþene unsida, þurh swicdomas 7 þurh searacræftas . . .

It is also no wonder that things are going badly for us since we now know very well that many men of long ago did not care very often what they did in word or deed. And the people, as it can seem, became very corrupted through numerous sins and through many evil deeds: through deadly sins and through crimes, through greed and through gluttony; through theft and through robbery; through slave-trafficking and through pagan vices, through deceits and frauds . . .

Detailed stylistic studies of individual writers, much aided by compu-tational techniques, are now beginning to demonstrate that it is possible to show principled stylistic variation in Old English prose. There are inconsistencies and awkwardnesses of composition, as the medium evolved, especially in the early period. But by the eleventh century, it is possible to see the emergence of an expressive maturity, through which authors made conscious choices about the way in which they wrote. These choices involved much more than contrasts of genre, such as the distinction between chronicle and homily. 'Styles within styles' can be seen, and several authors, such as Alfred, Ælfric, and Wulfstan, display marked personal stylistic traits. When we combine this observation with that already made about the importance of poetic variation, it is plain that the Old English period, despite its limited textual sources, is able to provide us with an invaluable insight into the origins of English linguistic diversity.

It is a scholarly commonplace to point to the literary brilliance of the Old English period, and to draw attention to the importance of its contribution to philological, historical, religious, legal, and social studies.[7] But its linguistic importance goes well beyond its role as the first stage in the formal evolution of the English language. All the issues to do with regional and social variation which will exercise us in later chapters – issues which attract widespread interest today, both in their own right and as factors in understanding social trends – have their antecedents in the Anglo-Saxon period. It is therefore a matter of some concern to observe the marked trend in the last quarter of the twentieth century for Old English to be sidelined in university courses. Popular awareness of this crucial period of the language is virtually non-existent. It is time for a revival. Indeed, I could do no better at this point than adapt King Alfred's message (p. 54) to the present educational situation.

It has very often come into my mind what learnèd men there once were throughout England, from both sacred and secular offices, and what happy times there were throughout England . . . and how people abroad looked to this country for learning and instruction in Old English, and how we should now have to get it from abroad, if we were to have it. So completely has it declined in England that there are very few people on this side of the Humber who can understand Old English or translate even one written message from Old English into Modern English, and I think there are not many beyond the Humber either.

Is it going too far to suggest, as does Alfred, that anyone with the means who has nothing better to do should take up Old English studies? Perhaps. But I strongly believe that the subject should again become obligatory for those seriously interested in the history of their language. For too many people, the English language does not begin until we reach what is Chapter 6 of this book, Middle English. Yet so much has already happened by that period. It is surely time for the rehabilitation of Old English studies.

Interlude 4
Grammatical transition

The transition from Old English to Middle English is primarily defined by the linguistic changes that were taking place in grammar. Old English, as we have seen (p. 43), was a language which contained a great deal of inflectional variation; Modern English has hardly any. And it is during Middle English that we see the eventual disappearance of most of the earlier inflections and the increasing reliance on alternative means of expression, using word order and prepositional constructions rather than word endings to express meaning relationships. But we must be careful not to overstate the nature of the change. The phrase 'increasing reliance' is meant to suggest that there is a great deal of continuity between the grammatical systems of Old and Middle English. Word order was by no means random in Old English, nor was it totally fixed in Middle English.

To develop a feel for this change, it is important to look briefly at all the word-order possibilities in the basic construction of a sentence. In Modern English, word order controls virtually everything. In the sentence *the man saw the woman*, it is the order of the three main elements which is the key to understanding what the sentence is saying. These three elements are traditionally called subject (S), verb (V), and object (O), and it is the order SVO which tells us this sentence means that it is the man who was doing the seeing and not the other way round. That meaning cannot be unambiguously expressed by any of the five other possible patterns:

S + O + V	the man the woman saw
O + S + V	the woman the man saw
O + V + S	the woman saw the man
V + O + S	saw the woman the man
V + S + O	saw the man the woman

With inflectional endings, we avoid ambiguity when the word order changes. If 'the man' always has a subject ending and 'the woman' always has an object ending, then there will be no problem, whichever order is used:

the man-SUBJECT saw the woman-OBJECT
the woman-OBJECT saw the man-SUBJECT

In Old English, because such endings existed, we might expect to find all six patterns in use, and so we do; but some are much more frequent than others. What is interesting is that the 'favourite' patterns then are also important in later periods. SVO is by no means a modern innovation. And what is even more interesting is to find that texts in later periods also show all six patterns. There is significant continuity as well as difference between Old, Middle, and Modern English.

Here are the number of instances of S, V, and O found in samples of 300 clauses from four texts spread throughout the Old and early Middle English periods.[8]

	Parker Chronicle (734–892)	Alfred's Pastoral Care (c. 900)	Peterborough Chronicle (1122–54)	Orrmulum (1200)
SV	64	82	67	84
VS	36	18	33	16
SVO	30	26	51	62
SOV	35	44	17	14
OSV	11	21	15	8
OVS	3	2	3	4
VSO	18	6	13	11
VOS	3	1	1	1
VO	18	51	91	75
OV	82	49	9	25

All the patterns can be found in texts of both periods, though with very different frequencies. At the same time, we can see in these figures a definite trend towards the modern system. Putting the object before the verb is a striking feature of the pre-900 *Parker Chronicle*, for example: two thirds of the patterns are like this (see the lines SOV, OSV, OVS, OV); but in the *Orrmulum*, dated around 1200, we find that no less than three quarters of the patterns are the other way round.

Several instances of a classic Old English word order can be seen in this word-for-word translation of a sentence from an early text of the *Anglo-Saxon Chronicle* (755):

> *Ond þa ongeat se cyning þæt,   ond he on þa duru eode,*
> And when <u>realized the king</u> this,   and he <u>to the door went</u>,
> *ond þa unheanlice hine werede,   oþ he on þone æþeling locude,*
> and then bravely <u>himself defended</u>, until he <u>at the   nobleman looked</u>,
> *ond þa ut ræsde on hine, ond hine miclum gewundode.*
> and then <u>out rushed</u> on him, and <u>him</u> severely <u>wounded</u>.

And when the king realized this, he went to the door, and bravely defended himself until he noticed the nobleman; and then he rushed out at him and severely wounded him.

We see the strong tendency to put the verb element at the end of the clause, so that the object comes forward. The extract also shows how it was normal practice to invert the subject–verb order if a clause began with an adverb – here, the linking word *þa* 'then'. This is especially noticeable in *Chronicle* texts, where the phrase *Ond þa* 'and then . . .' is a major feature of the style, but it is widespread in the language, with several other adverbs involved. The inversion continued to be used throughout Middle English, and did not really start going out of use until the sixteenth century. It can even be heard today, for we still obligatorily invert subject and verb after a few initial adverbs with negative meaning, such as *hardly*, *barely*, and *scarcely*. We say *Scarcely had she left when . . .* and not *Scarcely she had left when . . .* In this phrasing we are listening to an echo of what was distinctive about Old English word order.

The grammatical picture is complex, and still not entirely understood.[9] Whether a clause pattern appeared as SVO or SOV, or something else seems to have depended on what sort of clause it was (e.g., whether main or subordinate – as in modern German), and what else was happening in the clause. To take just one example: the object would be very likely to come forward if it were a pronoun (*ealle þa biscopas _him_ underfengen*, 'all the bishops received him'), and less likely if it were a noun phrase, especially one which had some 'weight' in it (by containing adjectives or other elements, which would add extra meaning to the phrase). A very long noun phrase would tend to stay at the end of the clause, as in this coordinate sequence, where the verb is underlined and the object is everything which follows:

> and _namen_ þone eorl Waleram and Hugo Geruieses sunu and Hugo of Munford
> and fif and twenti oðre cnihtes
> and they took Count Waleran and Hugo Gervase's son and Hugo of Mundford
> and twenty-five other knights

The relative weight of the elements in a sentence continues to affect word-order patterns today. Genre could be a factor also: a word-order change might appear in poetry in order to preserve the rhythm of a poetic line, as also still happens today. And stylistic variation is always possible, as again can be encountered today. When we meet Yoda, in the Star Wars series of films, we find him regularly inverting his word order, placing the object initially: *If a Jedi knight you will become . . .* (OSV). This is another echo of Old English. We do not have any difficulty understanding this exceptional pattern today, and when it was beginning to fall out of use in Middle English doubtless it would have been just as comprehensible then.

A major grammatical frequency change of the kind described above is none the less of real significance in the history of a language. Grammar is, after all, the basis of the way in which we organize our utterances so that they make sense, through the processes of sentence construction, and it is not an aspect of language that changes very easily – unlike vocabulary and pronunciation. New words come into English on a daily basis, but new habits of grammatical construction do not. Indeed, only a handful of minor grammatical changes have taken place during the past four centuries, as we shall see in Chapter 18, though that period saw huge numbers of new words and many changes in accent. So when we see English altering its balance of grammatical constructions so radically, as happened chiefly during the eleventh and twelfth centuries, the kind of language which emerges as a consequence, Middle English, is rightly dignified by a different name.

Chapter 5 The transition to Middle English

Because of the shortage of texts, it is difficult to draw firm conclusions about the facts of regional linguistic variation in Old English. By comparison, the Middle English period is a textual goldmine. Not only are there vastly more documents, as we shall see, but it has proved possible to locate many of them geographically with a level of accuracy that is hardly ever practicable for texts of the Anglo-Saxon era, so that genuine dialect features can be brought more sharply into focus. To call Middle English a 'dialect age', as some do, is not meant to suggest that dialects were any more or any less frequent or important than in Anglo-Saxon times or in later periods of the language. It is just that we can, for the first time, see them more clearly. And it is the only time, in the whole history of the language, that we can see them without having our vision clouded or distorted by the existence of a standard variety of English. For, during much of the Middle English period, there was no such thing.

When was Middle English? The question is as difficult to answer as 'When were the Middle Ages?' Some people define it with reference to historical events, usually selecting the Norman invasion of 1066 as its starting-point and the beginning of the Tudor dynasty, the accession of Henry VII in 1485, as its close. Some use a mixture of literary, linguistic, and cultural criteria, starting with the earliest texts that show significant differences from Old English towards the end of the twelfth century, and finishing with Caxton's introduction of printing towards the end of the fifteenth (1476). Some take 1100 as the starting-point; some leave it as late as 1200. But no one feels really comfortable with an identification in terms of boundary-points. As the name 'Middle' suggests, we are dealing with a period of transition between two eras that each has stronger definition: Old English and Modern English. Before this period we encounter a language which is chiefly Old Germanic in its character – in its sounds, spellings, grammar, and vocabulary. After this period we have a language which displays a very different kind of structure (p. 117), with major changes having taken place in each of these areas, many deriving from the influence of French. From a modern perspective, we can sum up the effects of the Middle English period in a single word: it made the English language 'familiar'.

This feeling of familiarity is quite striking. Although the earliest surviving writings in Middle English are only about a century after the latest writings in Old English, Middle English texts do feel very much closer to Modern English. By the time we get to Chaucer, in the fourteenth century, we can find many phrases and sentences which – disregarding the spelling differences – look just like an archaic version of Modern English, as in these extracts from *The Reeve's Tale* (p. 163):

> How fares thy fair daughter and thy wife?
> And John also, how now, what do ye here?

By contrast, most of the extracts from Old English in earlier chapters give the impression of a totally different language, even if the old letters are replaced (pp. 96–7):

> Tha wande he ongean to tham cynge
> God gesceop us twa eagan and twa earan.

But familiarity is not just a linguistic matter. There is also a continuity of literary content between Middle and Modern English which had not existed previously. English readers today are aware of the subject-matter of the Middle English period in a way that they are not in relation to Old English. The status of Chaucer as the 'father of English poetry' has put at least some of *The Canterbury Tales* in front of every generation of schoolchildren since the fifteenth century. Several modern Christmas carols are medieval in origin. There are published collections and recordings of Middle English folk-songs, lullabies, and love lyrics (see panel 5.1).[1] Children still learn the verse mnemonic for the number of days in a month, first found in a fifteenth-century collection, albeit in a somewhat different form:

> Thirty dayes hath November,
> April, June, and September;
> Of xxviii is but oon [one],
> And all the remenaunt xxx and i.

The story of King Arthur and the knights of the Round Table has been continuously retold since Caxton printed Thomas Malory's *Le Morte Darthur* (*The Death of Arthur*) in 1485. Again, by contrast, hardly anyone would be able to retell the story of Beowulf.

This later, literary continuity – between Middle and Modern English – has tended to put the earlier continuity – between Old and Middle English – rather in the shade. Indeed, people often talk about a 'break' between Old and Middle English. But there was never any break. From a linguistic point of view, there could not have been. A spoken language does not evolve in sudden jumps:

it consists of many thousands of working parts – in the case of English, over three dozen vowels and consonants, some three or four thousand features of sentence structure, and tens of thousands of domestic words – and they do not all shift at once. If they did, different generations would not be able to understand each other. So, although the pace of linguistic change between Anglo-Saxon and early medieval times does seem to have been quite rapid, it was still gradual, and we will encounter texts which are amalgams of Old and Middle English and texts which fall 'midway' between Old and Middle English. The eleventh and twelfth centuries have a transitional character of their own: they might well be described as a transition within a transition.

The continuity is mainly to be seen in texts of a religious, political, or administrative character, thousands of which have survived. Most of the surviving material in English is religious in character – about a third are collections of homilies, especially by Ælfric and Wulfstan. There are also three collections of laws, two copies of the *Anglo-Saxon Chronicle*, two copies of the Old English Gospels, two Psalter glosses, some works of Alfred, and various saints' lives, monastic guidelines, proverbs, dialogues, and medicinal texts. The writings of Ælfric, in particular, continued to be copied throughout the eleventh and twelfth centuries, and these overlap with sermons from the twelfth century that are very clearly in an early form of Middle English. The overlap is not difficult to identify. A copy of the Old English Gospels (Bodleian MS Hatton 38), made in Christ Church, Canterbury, probably in the 1190s, has been called 'the last Old English text'. That is very much later than a manuscript which has been called 'the earliest Middle English text': the *Sermo in festis Sancti Marie uirginis* ('Homily for Feasts of the Blessed Virgin Mary'), a translation of a Latin sermon by Ralph d'Escures, who was archbishop of Canterbury between 1114 and 1122. It forms one of the *Kentish Homilies*, compiled *c.* 1150 or somewhat earlier, most of which are copied straight from Ælfric's *Catholic Homilies*. About fifty years later we find the *Lambeth Homilies*, several of which (the group known as MX1) incorporate much earlier material, the Old English texts being turned into a more contemporary orthography. Homily 2 actually includes most of Wulfstan's *Be godcundre warnunge* ('About divine admonition'), discussed further below; Homilies 9 and 10 are transcriptions of two of Ælfric's sermons; and Homily 11 also contains a passage from Ælfric. They must have been popular works. Five of the sermons also appear in another early thirteenth-century collection, the *Trinity Homilies*.[2]

The fact that these texts are copies does not diminish their importance in the least. In a manuscript age, a copy can be as significant as its source, in that it displays the influence of a constellation of fresh factors reflecting the circumstances in which the copyist worked. The study of copies can yield valuable linguistic insights – in this case, both into the nature of the transition

5.1 A well-known lyric

The familiar feel of Middle English, even in its earliest manifestations, can be illustrated by the best known of the several hundred lyrics of the period which have survived. It is the only English song in a collection of French and Latin texts compiled by monks at Reading Abbey, Berkshire. Nothing is certain about its composer or context of composition, but it is the oldest known *rota* ('round') in English, and the oldest to use six voices. There has been much debate about the meaning and tone of the text – whether it is an innocent 'spring poem' or whether the cuckoo has a ribald significance, as was the case with several other poems of the period. The scribe has added a Latin text on Christ's Passion, written in red ink below the black English lettering (though the words do not fit the tune very well). There are also some Latin instructions about how it should be sung.

Reading Abbey did not have a scriptorium, so the manuscript was probably copied at Oxford. The text is usually dated 1225–50, though it could be later, and the music may be as late as *c.* 1310. The only punctuation in the manuscript is the raised dot. The Old English letter *þ* ('th') is still in use; *u* is found for *v*; and the single letter *w* is used for the first two letters of *wude*. It is difficult to be certain about the dialect, but the *-þ* verb ending at this time tells us that it is definitely not Northern (p. 209), and most of the spellings (such as the voiced *v* in *uerteþ*) suggest a Southern or possibly Midlands origin.

Two linguistic cautions are in order. First, notwithstanding the apparent meaning of the word with which the lyric begins, this is indeed a text for springtime – as we would expect from the theme, the cuckoo arriving in England during April. There is no contradiction, because in Middle English *sumer* was the only word available to describe the period between the vernal and autumnal equinoxes. The word *spring* to refer to the season is not recorded in English until the mid sixteenth century.

Second, since the Middle Ages, the word *fart* has become risqué or taboo, replaced in polite expression by such euphemisms as 'break wind' and 'flatulence'. The Victorian era, in particular, searched desperately for alternative readings. However, it is unlikely that the word had any offensive associations in the thirteenth century. (This lyric, incidentally, provides us with the first recorded use of that verb.)

Sumer is icumen in·	Spring has come in·
Lhude sing cuccu·	Loudly sing, cuckoo!
Groweþ sed and bloweþ med	Seed grows and meadow blooms
And springþ þe wde nu·	And the forest springs up now.
Sing cuccu	Sing, cuckoo!
Awe bleteþ after lomb·	Ewe bleats after lamb,
Lhouþ after calue cu·	Cow lows after calf,
Bulluc sterteþ bucke uerteþ	Bullock leaps, buck farts.
Murie sing cuccu·	Merrily sing, cuckoo!
Cuccu cuccu·	Cuckoo, cuckoo,

Wel singes þu cuccu·	You sing well, cuckoo.
Ne swik þu nauer nu·	Nor cease you never now!
Sing cuccu nu sing cuccu·	Sing cuckoo now, sing cuckoo!
Sing cuccu sing cuccu nu·	Sing cuckoo, sing cuckoo now!

between Old and Middle English, and into the demands of the sociolinguistic situation to which scriptoria writers were responding. The situation raises the same kind of issue that we have seen to be of importance in relation to Old English (p. 41), but with the difference that in the twelfth century we have an increasing amount of material surviving to provide us with evidence about scribal practice, and much more reliable data on where copies were made. Most twelfth-century manuscripts were produced by a small number of scriptoria, especially those at Peterborough, Rochester, Christ Church in Canterbury, and Worcester. Catalogues of library holdings have often survived – not having suffered the firestorm fate of their Anglo-Saxon antecedents (p. 34) – and it is thus often possible to be reasonably precise about the origins of a copied text, and to be more confident about drawing conclusions relating to such matters as handwriting fashion, scriptorium conventions, and dialect background.

The primary task of the scriptoria was the copying of Latin texts. Only a small proportion of time and energy was evidently devoted to English manuscripts, judging by the few scribes which seem to have been assigned to such work. But the fact that there were *any* vernacular manuscripts being copied is intriguing; for, if Latin was so dominant, why did monasteries bother to deal with anything in English at all? One reason could have been an antiquarian interest – a concern to preserve the past. We can easily imagine that this would have been an important motivation following the Conquest, at least among those Anglo-Saxon monks who had developed a sense of indigenous heritage in the face of an encroaching Norman language and culture. But this cannot have been the sole, or even the main motivation. The preservationist temperament is one which is much concerned with accuracy of transmission, and any scribe who saw himself[3] contributing to this goal would have been likely to produce copies which attempted to preserve as exactly as possible the linguistic features of the sources. But such meticulousness of copying practice is unusual, in the twelfth century. Repeatedly we find copied texts where the scribes were plainly acting more as editors than as transcribers.

The evidence comes from the many manuscripts which are fresh compilations of older material, in which Old English texts, or parts of these texts, have been selected to be part of a new publication whose aim was to address a particular theme or fulfil a contemporary need. Ælfric's *Catholic Homilies* were repeatedly used in this way. His homilies sometimes appeared whole in a collection along with work by other authors; sometimes they were excerpted; and sometimes they were represented by fragments of text introduced into a single composite work of various sources.[4] The amount of creative editing was at times substantial, especially in the homiletic manuscripts, with source texts not only updated in their use of language, but also abridged or simplified, and at times given a new emphasis through the addition of fresh content.

A good example of scribal adaptation is found in the way one of the *Lambeth Homilies* handles material from Ælfric's *Catholic Homilies*.[5] A sentence in the source text reads (ignoring punctuation marks):

> Ðæt geoffrode lamb getacnode cristes slege se þe unscæðði wæs his fæder
> geoffrod for ure alysednysse
> that offered-up lamb signifies Christ's slaying he who innocent was to his father
> offered for our redemption

In the copy, it appears like this (again, ignoring punctuation):

> þet i-offrede lomb þet þe engel het offrian bitacneð cristes deðþe þet wes milde
> and wiðutan gulte his feder i-offrad for ure alesendnesse
> that offered-up lamb that the angel ordered to be offered signifies Christ's death
> who was mild and without guilt to his father offered for our redemption

The changes are of two kinds. Some are motivated by a sense of linguistic change, such as the replacement of *se þe* by *þet*, or the substitution of the Old English *ge-* past-time prefix by *i-* (later often spelled *y-*, before it eventually disappears from the language). But others are more to do with an altered sense of what the content should be, shown above by underlining. In the first instance, an extra element – a whole new point about an angel – is added to the account. In the second, the meaning of an unusual word is being glossed. Although *unscæðði*, 'innocent, harmless', was quite common in Old English, and even appears in an early Middle English text (*Orrmulum*, l. 2,889), it disappears from the language around this time, and its replacement here by a fuller and simpler phrase suggests that it was already unfamiliar. The impression we receive, here and elsewhere, is that the scribe is 'spelling things out', perhaps for a readership which was not as well versed in religious thought as the earlier monastic audience.

Or perhaps for a readership for whom times had changed. An example is Wulfstan's *Be godcundre warnunge* ('About divine admonition'), written in the early eleventh century. Part of its content relates to the military situation at the time. Danish rule had come about as a result of the Viking invasions (p. 65), and Wulfstan interprets the hardships inflicted on the Anglo-Saxon people as a punishment for their sinful ways. There is much reference to being beset by enemies.[6]

> and ic eow awerige wið hearma gehwylcne þæt eow bite ne slite, here ne hunger,
> ne feonda mægen ahwar ne geswenceþ
> and I will protect you against every harm so that neither sting nor bite, ravage
> nor hunger, nor the strength of enemies may anywhere afflict you

Whoever 'copied' this in the twelfth century, long after the Norman Conquest, must have felt that the force of this passage was either irrelevant or unclear, for what we find is a much shortened version:

> *and ic eou wulle werien wið elene herm. Ne þet eou ne scal derien nouðer here ne hunger*
>
> and I will protect you against every harm so that neither ravage nor hunger shall afflict you

The reference to enemies has gone. By the late twelfth century, those who had beset everyone in Wulfstan's time, or even in the time of William the Conqueror, would have been a distant memory. The new version focuses on notions that are more timeless in character. It also drops some of Wulfstan's distinctive and (presumably by then) old-fashioned rhetoric.

Why change prestigious texts in this way? The explanation must lie in a pastoral concern to provide material to aid those finding themselves increasingly responsible for preaching to the lay public. However, it is unlikely that texts of this kind were intended for direct public use, such as by pupils in classrooms. The appearance of the extant manuscripts rather argues against it: they are relatively unworn, lacking the tell-tale signs of a well-thumbed text.[7] Much more likely is that they were intended for library use, among the monks themselves or by members of the secular clergy making use of nearby monastery facilities. Compilations of classical spiritual material would make excellent source material for sermons. They would also provide a useful source for devotional reading, performing much the same function as a modern anthology of essays or a book of quotations. There is little sign of such texts being used as 'scripts' to be read aloud in a church. Few of the manuscripts contain the kind of 'marking up' which is typical when a text is used in that way – orthographic signs, such as underlining and intonational diacritics, which remind the reader how a text is to be pronounced.

From a comparison of source and copy, it is plain that some scribes did pay close attention to literal accuracy, reproducing a purely visual image of a text. But this would have become increasingly difficult to carry out, as Old English grew increasingly unfamiliar, and the nature of the errors can offer information about the way the scribe was coping with linguistic change. At any time an old letter-shape, orthographic abbreviation, spelling, grammatical ending, or word might fail to be recognized. It might then be copied wrongly, or the scribe might consciously modernize – in effect, interpreting rather than transcribing. A lot would have depended on the type of text being copied: the constraint to 'get things right' in a legal text would probably have been greater compared with a literary text, in which individual variations are not only acceptable but often expected. It would also have depended on the amount of training the scribes had received, and in which language (Latin, French, English), for – as we know from Modern English – it is no small task to accurately spell a language where the letters no longer reflect contemporary pronunciation.

This unphonetic situation already existed in the twelfth century: the spelling of Old English, which had become largely standardized in the late Old English period (p. 56), was by then a century or so behind the contemporary pronunciation. In some respects – such as the spelling of vowels in unstressed syllables – there would have been very little correlation. Under these circumstances, it is not surprising to find a great deal of inconsistency, not only between scribes, but even within the work of an individual scribe, and an error analysis of the inconsistent patterns can be illuminating, as we see in panel 5.2. For example, with English grammar changing so radically (p. 101), there would be a general tendency to ignore older word endings, or to respell them (usually with an *e*), and to alter patterns of word order. *On þyssum geare* 'In this year' begins the *Peterborough Chronicle* for 1123 (p. 117); *On þys gear* begins the corresponding text for 1140. It is easy to see how copyists working in this period, concerned to make their texts more intelligible to their contemporaries, might simply omit the earlier inflections and make compensatory changes in syntax to produce a result which would be more a new edition of a source than a facsimile. People do the same sort of thing today: when we read a modern edition of a Shakespeare play, we do not notice the many changes which the editor has silently introduced – altering the Elizabethan typeface, spelling, and punctuation to make the text more accessible to a modern reader.

The copying practices of twelfth-century scribes also provide evidence of an ongoing oral tradition between Old and Middle English. In several texts it is possible to identify examples of formulaic phrases, aphoristic expressions, and other rhetorical features, dealing with a particular theme, which cannot be related to any known written source. When such locutions are found in several texts of different times and places, the conclusion is unavoidable that we are seeing here examples of oral transmission. The only way such material could have been incorporated into a piece of 'copying' is for the scribe to have been remembering such expressions and judging them to be appropriate for the text he was working on. An example is the homily *Be heofonwarum and beo helwarum* ('Heaven-dwellers and hell-dwellers'), where we find the theme of Judgement Day addressed: the congregation is exhorted to lead a holy life and give alms in order to deserve heaven and avoid hell. To add some colour, the homilist gives a vivid description of hell's torments, using several formulaic constructions.[9] The attributes of the Monster of Hell, for example, are described in 'hundreds':

> *He hæfað hundteontig heafda, 7 he hafað on alcum heafde hund eagena*
> He has a hundred heads, and he has on each head a hundred eyes

Torments are often listed in formulaic pairs:

on helle . . . þær bið hunger 7 þurst. þær bið ungemet cyles 7 hætan.
in hell . . . there is hunger and thirst. there is excessive chill and heat.

The same kinds of locution turn up in other places and in other texts. There is nothing in any surviving Old English source to warrant such additions. They must have been part of collective memory.

The religious material is of great sociolinguistic significance. If Ælfric's work was still being copied or quoted as late as *c.* 1200, this gives us the strongest of hints that the language had not moved so far from Old English as to be totally unintelligible. It is inconceivable that the huge labour involved in copying would have been undertaken if nobody had been able to understand them. On the other hand, we can sometimes sense a growing linguistic difficulty from some of the contemporary decision-making, as when the monks of Worcester requested William of Malmesbury to have the Old English life of Wulfstan translated into Latin – presumably because they found it easier.[10] And sometimes there is a frank admission of failure. Around 1300, we find someone adding the following note in the margin of an Old English text: *non apreciatum propter ydioma incognita* – 'not appreciated because unknown language'.[11] Perhaps

5.2 Looking over a scribe's shoulder

Great insight can be gained into the scribal copying process in cases where the sources of a copied text are known. By taking parallel passages from the source text and the copy, we can identify the changes and draw conclusions about the reliability of a transcription and the way the scribe was approaching his task. In a case studied by Roy Liuzza (who provided the image used in the heading of this panel), it is even possible to see changes operating twice over – across *three* versions of the Old English Gospels.[8] The latest version (referred to as H below) is kept in the Bodleian Library in Oxford (Hatton 38); it was made in Christ Church, Canterbury, around the very end of the twelfth century. This is a copy of a mid twelfth-century manuscript (R) now held in the British Library in London (Royal I A.xiv) and probably also made at Christ Church. This in turn is a copy of an earlier manuscript (B), held in the Bodleian (Bodley 441), whose origin is unknown. That the three are related in this way can be deduced from various common errors: for example, a particular page missing in B is also missing in R and H.

The following selection of lines from Matthew 7: 17, 22 illustrates three patterns. (I have added the Latin Vulgate text for comparison, along with a Modern English translation.) In the first – a continuation of the sentence 'A sound tree cannot bear bad fruit' – we find a very accurate rendition, with just one spelling change between B and R:

Latin	autem arbor fructus malos [facit]
English	nor a rotten tree [bears] good fruit
B	ne þæt yfele treow gode wæstmas
R	ne þæt yfele treo gode wæstmas
H	ne þæt yfele treo gode wæstmas

On the other hand, in this next line R makes a silly mistake, adding an extra *drihten* ('Lord') to the two in the source. H, evidently more scrupulous, restores the original.

Latin	multi dicent mihi in illa die Domine Domine
English	Many will say on that day to me Lord Lord
B	Manege cweþað on þam dæge to me dryhten dryhten
R	Manege cweðeð on þam daige to me drihten drihten drihten
H	Maneʒe cweðeð on þam daiʒe to me drihten drihten

This passage also illustrates some changes in spelling, and one of these hints at a change in pronunciation: the *æ* vowel in *dæge* becomes *ai*, suggesting that the pronunciation was becoming more like a diphthong (as is still heard in modern *day*). Also to be seen is a sign of the grammar changing: the verb ending -*að*, with its *a* symbol marking an open vowel, becomes the nondescript -*eð*. The letter *e* is often used as a 'default' letter when a vowel is losing its original distinctive sound.

In the third, we find the R scribe deciding to expand the meaning of his source – making good sense, but doing something that is not in the Latin text. However, in this case, H seems to approve of the addition.

Latin	et in tuo nomine virtutes multas fecimus
English	and in your name we worked many miracles
B	and on þinū naman we worhton mycle myhta [the ˜ marks an abbreviated -m]
R	and on þinum name we worhte mycele wundra and myhte ['wonders and miracles']
H	and on þinen name we worhte mychele wundre and mihte

Plainly the R and H scribes did not have a strong sense of the values of the Old English inflectional endings. We see them dying away, to be replaced by forms with an *e*:

-um > -en   -an > -e   -on > -e   -a > -e

The later spelling of *mycle* 'many' as *mychele* anticipates the form which would eventually become standard in English as *much*.

Analyses of this kind show that, far from being an uninteresting mechanical exercise, scribal copying can bring to light all kinds of evidence about ongoing language change and the purpose for which a new text was being made.

the overall situation was something like a modern preacher reading and including in a sermon extracts from the Authorized Version of the Bible of 1611 – generally comprehensible but with an archaic resonance and occasionally difficult or incomprehensible words and passages. But there is a more general sociolinguistic point which must not be overlooked: the fact that, during the twelfth century, English was available as a medium for vernacular copying at all.

Interlude 5
Two *Peterborough Chronicles*

The *Anglo-Saxon Chronicle* did not stop in 1066: in one manuscript we find entries continuing for nearly a century after the Norman Conquest. This is the *Peterborough Chronicle*, so called because it was first copied in the Benedictine monastery at Peterborough, Cambridgeshire, probably to replace a manuscript destroyed in a devastating fire five years earlier.[12] It was copied in 1121, and updated to that year, and various scribes kept it going until 1131. No further additions were then made for twenty-three years – a period largely coinciding with the reign of King Stephen, whose anarchic times would have allowed little opportunity for historical reflection and recording. But following the death of Stephen in 1154, the *Chronicle* was immediately updated to that year – probably the work of a single continuator making an individual effort – by the addition of six annals dealing with several events of the period, one of which (for the year 1137) is a famous description of the torments and misery which had affected everyone.[13]

That gap of twenty-three years proved to be of immense linguistic significance for later historians of English. The *Peterborough Chronicle* entries up to and including 1131 were written in Old English, in the West Saxon literary standard (p. 54); but the later entries are sufficiently different in spelling, grammar, and vocabulary that they have to be considered an early example of Middle English. The *Chronicle* is not quite the earliest example of Middle English: that accolade probably has to go to one of the *Kentish Homilies* (p. 107); but it is the earliest text we have written in the East Midland dialect, from which Modern Standard English was to develop (p. 243). Also, the final continuation of the *Peterborough Chronicle* is of special interest because of the way its style can be directly compared with an analogous sample of Late West Saxon of only twenty-five years before. Nowhere else is the transition between Old and Middle English so visible.

The two extracts below illustrate this transition. They are very similar in some respects, yet distinctively different in others. The first is the beginning of the entry for 1123; the second is the beginning of the entry for 1137 (but written *c.* 1154). In the first, at this late stage in Old English, we can already see some changes from earlier usage (e.g., *cyning* is now *king*), but many defining features are still there, such as the dative endings in *On þyssum geare* and *to þam kyng*, the Old English definite article *se*, the accusative form of *he* (*hine*), the inverted word order of subject and verb (p. 101), and several Old English locutions, such as *on an half him*.

> *On þyssum geare wæs king Henri on Cristes   tyde at Dunestaple,*
> In this   year   was   king Henry at   Christmas time at Dunstable,
>
> *7   þær   comen þes   eorles sandermen of Angeow to him.*
> and there came   of the earl   messengers of Anjou   to him.
> [= there came to him messengers of the Count of Anjou]
>
> *7   þeonen   he ferde   to Wudestoke, 7   his biscopes 7   his hird*
> *eal mid him.*
> and from there he travelled to Woodstock, and his bishops and his retinue
> all with him.
>
> *Þa   tidde   hit on an Wodnesdei,   þet   wæs on iiii   Idus Ianuareii,*
> then happened it   on a   Wednesday, that was on fourth Ides of January,
> [= the fourth day before the Ides of January, i.e., 10 January]
>
> *þet se   king rad in his derfald;   and se   biscop Roger of Seresbyrig on*
> *an   half   him*
> that the king rode in his deer-park; and the bishop Roger of Salisbury   on
> one side of him
>
> *and se   biscop Rotbert Bloet of Lincolne on oðer   half   him, 7   riden*
> *þær   sprecende.*
> and the bishop Robert Bloet of Lincoln   on other side of him, and were riding
> there talking.
>
> *Þa   aseh dune se   biscop of Lincolne 7   seide to þam kyng, Laferd kyng, ic*
> *swelte.*
> then sank down the bishop of Lincoln and said to the   king, Lord   king, I
> perish.
>
> *7   se   king alihte   dune of   his hors 7   alehte   hine betwux his*
> *earmes*
> and the king jumped down from his horse and lifted down him between his
> arms
>
> *7   let   hine beran   ham to his inne,   7   wearð þa sone   dead.*
> and had him carried home to his lodging, and became then straight away dead.

The later text continues to show some Old English features (in word order, for example, we see the inversion after *þa*, and the adjective following the noun in *Henri king*), but there are a number of contrasts: the definite article is now *þe* (also spelled *te* and *the*), the accusative of *he* is now *him*, and in several places a gloss is hardly needed because the word order is more familiar and the syntax moves along in a more modern way – as in the sequence about arresting Bishop Roger. Also, when we examine the *Chronicle* as a whole we find many signs of ongoing change – inconsistency in the use of word endings and word order, and quite frequently a rather awkward manner of expression (as in the glossed clause below), giving the impression of a writer trying to create an appropriate style using a new set of linguistic resources.

Ðis gære for þe king Stephne ofer sæ to Normandi and ther wes underfangen,

This year went the king Stephen over sea to Normandy and there was received,

forþi ðat hi uuenden ðat he sculde ben alsuic alse the eom wes,

because they expected that he would be just such as the uncle was,

and for he hadde get his tresor; ac he to-deld it and scatered sotlice.

and because he had still his treasure; but he squandered it and dissipated foolishly.

Micel hadde Henri king gadered gold and syluer, and na god ne dide me for his saule thar-of.

Much had Henry king amassed gold and silver, but no good not did one for his soul with it.

[= but no good did it do him for the salvation of his soul]

Þa þe king Stephne to Englalande com, þa macod he his gadering æt Oxeneford,

When king Stephen to England came, then held he his council at Oxford,

and þar he nam þe biscop Roger of Sereberi, and Alexander biscop of Lincoln

and there he arrested the bishop Roger of Salisbury, and Alexander bishop of Lincoln

and te canceler Roger, hise neues, and dide ælle in prisun.

and the chancellor Roger, his nephews, and put all in prison.

til hi iafen up here castle. Þa the suikes undergæton ðat he milde man was

until they gave up their castles. When the traitors perceived that he mild man was

and softe and god, and na iustise ne dide, þa diden hi alle wunder.

and easy-going and kindly, and no punishment not inflicted, then did they all atrocities.

> *Hi   hadden him manred maked and athes suoren, ac hi   nan treuthe ne heolden.*
>
> They had   him homage done   and oaths sworn, but they no loyalty not kept.

One of the most notable features of these extracts is what hardly appears in either of them: French vocabulary. The Normans had been in England for over 50 years – nearly 100, by the time of the second extract – and yet the *Peterborough Chronicle* as a whole has very few new French loanwords (about 30). *Castle* in the second extract is indeed Old French, but that is a pre-Conquest loan (p. 80). The only modernisms are *canceler*, *tresor*, and *iustise*, and there are few other examples in the rest of the *Chronicle* continuation. Nor, as we shall see in Chapter 6, is there very much French vocabulary in other early Middle English literary texts. But it is not long before the French loanwords turn from a trickle into a flood.

Chapter 6 A trilingual nation

Logically, we might have expected the English language to die out, after 1066. That is what usually happens, when one nation subjugates another. The Portuguese arrived in Brazil in 1500, and what language is the norm in present-day Brazil? None of the indigenous Indian languages, but Portuguese. With few exceptions, the pattern repeats itself throughout history: the Spanish in Central and South America, the British in North America and Australia, the Anglo-Saxons in England (p. 29), and a host of lesser-known but locally just as dramatic scenarios involving Russian, Chinese, Arabic, and many other languages whose cultures are associated with periods of political expansion and dominance. Norman French in England is one of those exceptions. It failed to establish itself, and by the time of Chaucer it was learned only as a foreign language. It took less than 300 years for English to be officially reasserted – notably, being used for the first time as the language at the opening of Parliament in 1362. How could this have happened?

At the outset, there seemed no likelihood of it happening. Within ten years of the arrival of William I, 'the Conqueror', local English rebellion had been crushed with great severity; within twenty years, the manifestation of an increasingly centralized government resulted in the first national survey of land resources, Domesday Book (1086–7); and during the next seventy years Norman rule was consolidated through the reigns of William II and Henry I. There was in effect a single Anglo-Norman kingdom, with the Channel perceived as a bridge rather than as a barrier. Even when this period was over, the French connection did not cease: the 'second invasion' in 1153–4 of Henry II of Aquitaine, resolving the chaotic situation left by Stephen, the last Norman king, established the Angevin, or Plantagenet, dynasty on the English throne – a dynasty which lasted until 1399. The French language, in various northern varieties – Norman French, to begin with – thus became established in the corridors of power. French-speaking barons were given senior posts and huge tracts of land, and they arrived with their French-speaking retinues – a process which continued into the reign of Henry I. The senior Church positions were given to French-speaking abbots and bishops: Abbot Lanfranc of Caen was made archbishop of Canterbury in 1070, replacing the Anglo-Saxon Stigand, and thereafter all English bishoprics and the headships of religious houses were given to French-speaking clerics. French merchants and craftsmen arrived in England to take advantage of the commercial opportunities provided by the new regime. French – Anglo-Norman French, to be precise – seemed secure.

Its position seemed even stronger, at the outset, because of the continuities which were maintained between England and Normandy. Aristocratic links with the Continent continued to be important, because many nobles maintained estates there. The monarchs themselves were regularly in France. William I actually spent about half his reign in Normandy, in at least five of those years not visiting England at all. William II and Henry I also spent half their reigns there, as did several later kings – Henry II for as many as twenty years. The crusading Richard I spent only six months or so in England. We do not know just how much English these monarchs knew, but it was probably very little. The chronicler Ordericus Vitalis, writing in the 1130s, reports that William I did at one point try to learn English, when he was forty-three (c. 1071), but, being somewhat preoccupied by the pressures involved in imposing his rule throughout the kingdom, in the face of ongoing local rebellions, he made little progress. He probably would not have been able to understand the English-language charters which he promulgated at the outset of his reign (see panel 6.1). His youngest son, as Henry I, married an English wife, Eadgyth, the daughter

6.1 William's writ

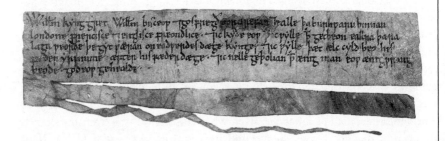

If we needed a symbol of continuity for the English language immediately *after* the Norman Conquest, we could do no better than look at the writs issued in 1067 to the citizens of London by William I, such as the one illustrated here.[1] The language is English – an uncommon usage in an era when official documents had long been, and for over a century would continue to be, in Latin. (The illustration shows all four distinctive Old English letters (p. 39), but in the transcript, for ease of reading, yogh has been transliterated as *g*, and wynn as *w*. The scribal abbreviations have also been expanded – 7 as *and* and þ as *þæt*.)

Willm kyng gret Willm bisceop and gosfregð portirefan and ealle þa burhwaru binnan londone frencisce and englisce freondlice· and ic kyðe eow þæt ic wylle þæt get beon eallre þæra laga weorðe þe gyt wæran on eadwerdes dæge kynges· and ic wylle þæt ælc cyld beo his fæder yrfnume æfter his fæder dæge· and ic nelle geþolian þæt ænig man eow ænig wrang beode· god eow gehealde·

King William greets Bishop William and Port-reeve Geoffrey and all the burgesses within London, French and English, in a friendly way. And I make known to you that I wish you to enjoy all the rights that you formerly had in the time of King Edward. And I want every child to be the heir of his father after his father's lifetime. And I will not permit any man to do you any wrong. God preserve you.

It would be some 200 years before English monarchs and other officials would routinely use English, as opposed to Latin or French, on public occasions (p. 138).

---

of the Scots king Malcolm, which perhaps gave him a more intimate awareness of the language than would otherwise have been gained from official encounters. But we know nothing about his command of English really, nor that of his successor, Stephen, who spent his whole reign in England because of the civil strife of the time, nor that of King John, who lived mainly in England after 1204. We must assume that French continued to be the norm in court until at least the early thirteenth century, and that most of the nobles were largely or wholly monolingual.

The fact that William promulgated anything in English at all is interesting – a recognition of the established nature of the language in England. Unlike Celtic, 500 years before, English had a considerable written literature and a strong oral tradition. There was a public awareness of historical continuity, not least because of the events recorded in the *Anglo-Saxon Chronicle*. A vibrant strand of vernacular religious expression could be traced back for well over a century (Chapter 5). Contributions were still being made to Anglo-Saxon imaginative literature – whether original or copied is often a matter of dispute – but the fact that so many of the well-known Anglo-Saxon texts survive in eleventh-century manuscripts (not least, *Beowulf*) suggests that the heroic tradition was alive and well. It could hardly have been otherwise when several of the events it commemorated – such as the Battle of Maldon (991) – were at the boundaries of living memory when William came to the throne.

It would have taken a sociolinguistic shift of immense proportions to knock English off course, and the factors which would have created the conditions for such a shift were just not present in the decades following 1066. To begin with, there was political uncertainty. William's decision in 1087 to bequeath Normandy to one of his sons (Robert Curthose) and England to another (William Rufus) was a major source of conflict, and split the Norman aristocracy's loyalties. Henry I resolved the matter, defeating Robert at Tinchebrai in 1106, but then complicated things by dying without a legitimate male heir. Further feuds followed, which peaked during the reign of Stephen, as recounted in the *Peterborough Chronicle* (p. 117). Meanwhile, Normandy itself was vulnerable to invasion by its neighbours in Anjou and France. Good relations between England and Normandy in fact lasted only for some 150 years. Following the accession of John in 1199, there was outright war; England lost control of Normandy, and the English nobility lost their estates in France. Within England, there was a growing spirit of nationalism. Antagonism grew between the two countries, leading ultimately to the Hundred Years War (1337–1453) between England and France. Whatever opportunity there may have been for the French language to recover was crushed for ever once Edward III declared himself 'King of England and France' in 1340. 'At Crécy field our clouds of warlike smoke / Choked up those French mouths and dissevered them', says Edward the Black Prince in Shakespeare's *King Edward III* (IV.iv.4). French was now the language of the enemy. The point was never forgotten. Much later in historical drama, it is acknowledged by the rebel Jack Cade, in his attack on Lord Say, who 'can speak French, and therefore he is a traitor' (*Henry VI Part 2*, IV.ii.157). Cade goes on:

> Nay, answer if you can; the Frenchmen are our enemies; go to, then, I ask but this: can he that speaks with the tongue of an enemy be a good counsellor, or no?

And the rabble respond, 'No, no; and therefore we'll have his head'. Which, in due course, they do.

But apart from a deteriorating political situation, it is plain that the number of Normans in England was never sufficient for their language to have made much of an impact on the general population. It has been estimated that they may have been no more than 10,000 or 15,000 soldiers – perhaps as few as 5,000 – plus an uncertain number of camp followers and opportunistic settlers: but this is a tiny number compared to the general English population, which by the time of Domesday Book totalled 1.5 million.[2] By 1300 that population had reached at least 3 million. The vast majority of the population would have had little or no contact with French at all, and would continue to speak Old English. A bilingual class would indeed have emerged – it probably already existed, given the dynastic connections with Normandy long predating the Conquest, and the evidence of early French loanwords (p. 78) – but this would have stayed small, consisting of the aristocracy, senior clergy, and merchant traders and settlers. A few English would have learned French: we can easily imagine a number of astute individuals, not wanting to miss an opportunity, who would have picked up the language in order to gain advantages from the new local aristocracy after 1066. But the pressure on the French to learn English was much greater. Baronial staff would have had to learn English in order to mediate between their lords and local communities. French-speaking clergy would have found acquiring the language essential in order to carry out their mission to the people. Of critical importance is the fact that few French women made the voyage to England, so there was an enormous amount of intermarriage between Normans and English, and – whatever the difficulties in communication between spouses – their children would have grown up bilingually. It would only have taken one generation to establish the first peer group of young, ambitious, bilingual landed gentry. It would have been a maintained bilingualism: the need to keep up a local position would have fostered the role of English; and the need to keep in with the court would have preserved the role of French. But this would have lasted only for as long as French remained the language of prestige there.

We know that the effects of intermarriage were immediate and significant because contemporary commentators referred to them. Richard Fitz Neal (or Fitz Nigel, d. 1198) was one: he was treasurer both to Henry II and Richard I, and bishop of London, and now best known as the author of *De necessariis observantiis Scaccarii dialogus*, commonly called the *Dialogus de Scaccario (A Dialogue on the Exchequer)* – a two-volume account, begun in 1176–7, of the procedures followed by the Exchequer in the author's time. In Book I, Chapter 10, he writes (as part of an exposition of the notion of 'murder': see panel 6.2):

> during the time that the English and Normans have now dwelt together, and mutually married, and given in marriage, the nations have become so intermingled that one can hardly tell to-day – I speak of freemen – who is of English and who of Norman race; excepting, however, the bondsmen who are called 'villani' [villeins], to whom it is not free, if their lords object, to depart from the condition of their station.[3]

6.2 The meaning of murder

What has Richard Fitz Neal's reference to English and Norman intermarriage got to do with murder? The modern word comes from Latin (*murdrum*), and is found in Old English, but not with exactly the same meaning it has today. In Anglo-Saxon times a murder was any killing that society condemned as particularly wicked or hateful. In *Beowulf*, where the word is first recorded, Cain in the Old Testament is described as committing *morðor* (l. 1,264) and a blood-feud is described as *morþor-hete* 'murderous hate' (l. 1,105).

But there is a further nuance. A *morðor* was a killing carried out in secret. In Germanic society, a killing which took place in public view was not considered a crime, but a wrong done to an individual that could be righted through a revenge killing or some sort of compensation. Only a killing which took place in secret justified the term, for then there could be no natural justice.

This is the sense which Fitz Neal recognizes when his protégé asks him 'what is murder and why is it so called?' (Section X of Book I). His answer also gives us an insight into the relationships between Normans and Anglo-Saxons in the years after the Conquest (see further below):

> Murder (*murdrum*), indeed, is properly called the secret death of somebody whose slayer is not known. For 'murdrum' means the same as 'hidden' or 'occult'. Now, in the primitive state of the kingdom after the Conquest, those who were left of the Anglo-Saxon subjects secretly laid ambushes for the suspected and hated race of the Normans, and, here and there, when opportunity offered, killed them secretly in the woods and in remote places. As vengeance for whom – when the kings and their ministers had for some years, with exquisite kinds of tortures, raged against the Anglo-Saxons; and they, nevertheless, had not, in consequence of these measures, altogether desisted – the following plan was hit upon: that the so-called 'hundred' in which a Norman was found killed in this way – when he who had caused his death was to be found, and it did not appear from his flight who he was – should be condemned to a large sum of tested silver for the fisc [exchequer]; some, indeed, to £36, some to £44, according to the different localities and the frequency of the slaying. And they say that this is done with the following end in view: namely, that a general penalty of this kind might make it safe for the passers-by, and that each person might hasten to punish so great a crime and to give up to justice him through whom so enormous a loss fell on the whole neighbourhood.

The student, quite rightly, follows this answer up with another question: 'Ought not the occult death of an Anglo-Saxon, like of a Norman, to be reputed murders?' Fitz Neal replies: 'By the original institution it ought not to, as thou hast heard', but – he continues with the quotation on p. 125 – because we cannot tell Normans and English apart these days, 'almost always when any one is found thus slain to-day, it is punished as murder'.

Fitz Neal's account also provides confirmation of the mutual suspicion and antagonism which must have existed in the years following the Conquest. It is an atmosphere which is reported at the very beginning of the period by the monk–chronicler Ordericus Vitalis (of Norman stock, though born in Shropshire *c.* 1175), who writes in Chapter 14 of his *Ecclesiastical History* of the events on King William's Coronation Day – Christmas Day 1066:

> Meanwhile, at the instigation of the devil, the enemy of all good, an unforeseen occurrence, pregnant with mischief to both nations, and an omen of future calamities, suddenly happened. For when Aldred the archbishop was demanding of the English, and Geoffrey, bishop of Coutances, of the Normans, whether they consented to have William for their king, and the whole assembly loudly gave

their willing assent, with one voice though not in one language, the men-at-arms, who formed the guard outside the abbey, upon hearing the shouts of joyful acclamation raised by the people in the church in a language they did not understand, suspected some treachery and imprudently set fire to the neighbouring houses. The flames quickly spreading, the people in the church were seized with panic in the midst of their rejoicings, and crowds of men and women, of all ranks and conditions, eagerly struggled to make their escape from the church, as if they were threatened with immediate danger. The bishops only, with some few of the clergy and monks, maintained their post before the altar, and trembling with fear completed the coronation office with some difficulty, the king himself being much alarmed. Almost all the rest hastened to the scene of conflagration, some to make vigorous efforts to extinguish the flames, and more in the prospect of committing robberies in the confusion that prevailed. The English were greatly enraged when they understood the origin of this unfortunate affair, which leading them to suspect the Normans and consider them faithless, they waited for some future opportunity of revenge.[4]

There were several opportunities, though none, in the long run, successful. A series of rebellions during the next five years was put down with great ruthlessness. The campaign known as the 'harrying of the north' (1069–70) was so severe, as the twelfth-century Benedictine monk–chronicler Simeon of Durham put it, 'that there was no village inhabited between York and Durham'. Over 100,000 people died of hunger, following the destruction of the land, according to Ordericus Vitalis. Throughout the country, the Anglo-Saxon nobility was systematically eliminated: by the time of Domesday Book (1086–7), some 4,000 thegns – the landholding warriors of Anglo-Saxon times – had been replaced by some 200 barons. Many English noblemen became refugees and fled into Scotland, where they were welcomed by King Malcolm Canmore and significantly increased the number of English speakers in the region (p. 203). The resentment which any nation must feel against such an army of occupation would have found a natural outlet in antagonism towards the language. Anyone speaking French would have been immediately identified with 'the suspected and hated race of the Normans' (as Fitz Neal, reporting contemporary attitudes, described them). Under these circumstances, it is inconceivable that ordinary people would have taken up the learning of French in large numbers. Only those for whom it was a matter of profit or survival would have done so.

Accordingly, with spoken French restricted to the court, the regional aristocracy, the well-educated clergy, and a handful of others, and written French an elite language of government, the new language made very few inroads into English society. Even at the official level, there were constraints on its use, because Latin had for centuries been accepted as the language of law, administration, literature, and the Church. Domesday Book was written in Latin, not French, and most of the ensuing administrative record-keeping continued to be in Latin. Latin also continued to be the primary language of religious expression – as indeed it would remain, in the Roman Catholic tradition, up to the present-day. And there seems to have been an expectation that intelligent people would know Latin as a matter of course – this, at least, seems to be the implication from the comment of the lady in Piers Plowman's dream vision (Passus 1), who is sharply critical of his slow thinking:

> 'Thou doting duffer,' quoth she, 'dull are thy wits;
> Too little Latin thou learnest, man, in thy youth.'[5]

So although French came to be used more and more in formal domains, such as law, literature, and the arts, it never became the sole voice of officialdom. English, on the other hand, found its social role very sharply defined: in speech, it was the second-class language, the language of the defeated. It would never have been heard at court, or on formal occasions when Norman lords were present. And it would rarely have been used in writing – apart from in the domain of religion where, as we have seen, it was making respectable progress.

The linguistic situation of Anglo-Norman England is, from a socio-linguistic point of view, very familiar. It is a situation of *triglossia* – in which three languages have carved out for themselves different social functions, with one being a 'low-level' language, and the others being used for different 'high-level' purposes. A modern example is Tunisia, where French, Classical Arabic, and Colloquial Arabic evolved different social roles – French as the language of (former) colonial administration, Classical Arabic primarily for religious expression, and Colloquial Arabic for everyday purposes. Eventually England would become a *diglossic* community, as French died out, leaving a 'two-language' situation, with Latin maintained as the medium of education and the Church (p. 155) and English as the everyday language. And later still, the country would become *monoglossic* – or monolingual, as it is usually expressed. But monolingualism is an unusual state, and in the twenty-first century there are clear signs of the reappearance of diglossia in English as it spreads around the world (p. 522).

That the situation in the early Middle Ages was diglossic is supported by this extract from a verse chronicle attributed to the monk Robert of Gloucester (though in fact a compilation of at least three writers), written around the end of the thirteenth century, or soon after. He reports the arrival of the Normans, first mentioning that they were monolingual:

> And þe Normans ne couþe speke þo bote hor owe speche,
> And speke French as hii dude atom, and hor children dude also teche . . .

And the Normans could speak nothing but their own language,
And spoke French as they did in their own country, and also taught it to their
children . . .

But then, referring to the nobility (*heiemen*) descended from the Normans, he draws specific attention to the contrast in language use between the upper and lower classes. Indeed, the modern contrast between 'high' and 'low' language is anticipated: the *heiemen* ('high men') are opposed to humble folk, *lowe men*.

Vor bote a man conne Frenss me telþ of him lute.
Ac lowe men holdeþ to Engliss, and to hor owe speche ʒute . . .

Unless a man knows French he is thought little of
And low-born men keep to English, and to their own speech still . . .

But he is a modern in his thinking, for this section of the chronicle concludes:

Ac wel me wot uor to conne boþe wel it is,
Vor þe more þat a mon can, þe more wurþe he is.

And I know very well that it is good to know both
For the more a man knows the worthier he is.

An early proponent of the value of bilingualism.

By the end of the twelfth century, references are being made to children of the nobility who have English as a mother tongue, and who have to learn French in school. The number of French-teaching handbooks increased greatly during the thirteenth century, as did bilingual dictionaries and word lists and the frequency of translations into and out of French – further signs of the changing balance of linguistic power. Two writers, at different points in the thirteenth century, provide an insight. Ranulph Higden, a monk at St Werburgh's at Chester, wrote in Latin a book he called *Polychronicon* – a chronicle of many ages (in fact, from the Creation to 1352). After his death (1364), it was translated into English by John of Trevisa (Trevessa, near St Ives, Cornwall), who became vicar of Berkeley, Gloucestershire. Completed in 1387, it became well known following its publication by Caxton in 1482. It is written in a South-Western dialect, with some Midland influence – and thus a rather different South-Western from that used by Robert of Gloucester – Robert spells *for* with a *v*, for example, reflecting that region's tendency to voice its fricatives (as it still does today in such pronunciations as 'Zummerzet' for *Somerset*), whereas John does not.

At one point (Chapter 59), we find Higden reviewing the language-teaching situation in England, and giving two reasons for the decline of English as a mother tongue:

On ys for chyldern in scole, aȝenes þe vsage and manere of al oþer nacions, buþ compelled for to leue here oune longage and for to construe here lessons and here þinges a Freynsch, and habbeþ suþthe þe Normans come furst into Engelond. Also gentil men children buþ ytauȝt for to speke Freynsch fram tyme þat a buþ yrokked in here cradel, and conneþ speke and playe wiþ a child hys brouch; and oplondysch men wol lykne hamsylf to gentil men, and fondeþ wiþ gret bysynes for to speke Freynsch, for to be more ytold of.

One is for children in school, contrary to the usage and custom of all other nations, [who] are compelled to abandon their own language and to carry on their lessons and their affairs in French, and have done so since the Normans first came to England. Also the children of gentlemen are taught to speak French from the time that they are rocked in their cradle, and learn to speak and play with a child's trinket; and rustic men will make themselves like gentlemen, and seek with great industry to speak French, to be more highly thought of.

This seems clear enough; but Trevisa is anxious to point out that times have changed, so he adds a long paragraph of his own.

Þys manere was moche y-vsed tofore þe furste moreyn, and ys seþthe somdel ychaunged. For Iohan Cornwal, a mayster of gramere, chayngede þe lore in gramerscole and construccion of Freynsch into Englysch; and Richard Pencrych lurnede that manere techyng of hym, and oþer men of Pencrych, so þat now, þe ȝer of oure Lord a þousond þre hondred foure score and fyue, of þe secunde kyng Richard after þe Conquest nyne, in al þe gramerscoles of Engelond children leueþ Frensch, and construeþ and lurneþ an Englysch, and habbeþ þerby avauntage in on syde, and desavauntage yn anoþer: Here avauntage ys, þat a lurneþ here gramer yn lasse tyme þan childern wer ywoned to do. Disavauntage ys þat now childern of gramerscole conneþ no more Frensch þan can here lift heele, and þat ys harm for ham and a scholle passe þe se and trauayle in strange londes, and in meny caas also. Also gentil men habbeþ now moche yleft for to teche here childern Frensch.

This practice was much used before the first plague [the Black Death of 1349], and has since been somewhat changed. For John Cornwall, a teacher of grammar, changed the teaching in grammar school and the construing of French into English; and Richard Penkridge learned that method of teaching from him, and other men from Penkridge, so that now, 1385 AD, the ninth year of the reign of the second King Richard after the Conquest, in all the grammar schools of England, children abandon French, and compose and learn in English, and have thereby an advantage on the one hand, and a disadvantage on the other. The advantage is that they learn their grammar in less time than children used to do. The disadvantage is that nowadays children at grammar school know no more French than their left heel, and that it is a misfortune for them if they should cross the sea and travel in foreign countries, and in other such circumstances. Also, gentlemen have now largely abandoned teaching their children French.

Know no more French than their left heel? That sentence has a peculiarly modern ring about it.

Higden, writing in the 1350s, was already somewhat behind the times, if we are to believe the very clear statement about the changed situation made by William of Nassington (a village in Northamptonshire), written in 1325. An administrative official at York, he is known for his Latin translations into English, in northern dialect, including an English version of his own *Speculum vitae* (*Mirror of Life*). In 1384 there is a record of the English text being read before senior staff at Cambridge University for four days, before being pronounced free from heresy. At the beginning of this work (lines 61–78), he explains why he is using English:

In English tonge I schal ȝow telle,	In the English tongue I shall you tell,
ȝif ȝe wyth me so longe wil dwelle.	If you with me so long will dwell.
No Latyn wil I speke no waste,	No Latin will I speak nor waste,
But English, þat men vse mast,	But English, that men use most,
Þat can eche man vnderstande,	That is able each man to understand,
Þat is born in Ingelande;	That is born in England;
For þat langage is most chewyd,	For that language is most displayed,
Os wel among lered os lewyd.	As much among learnèd as unread.
Latyn, as I trowe, can nane	Latin, as I believe, know none
But þo that haueth it in scole tane.	Except those who have it in school done.
And somme can Frensche and no Latyn,	And some know French and no Latin,
Þat vsed han cowrt and dwellen þerein.	Who have used it at court and there remain.
And somme can of Latyn a party	And some know of Latin partly
Þat can of Frensche but febly.	Who know of French but feebly.
And somme vnderstonde wel Englysch	And some understand well English
Þat can noþer Latyn nor Frankys.	Who know neither Latin nor French.
Boþe lered and lewed, olde and ȝonge,	Both learnèd and unread, old and young,
Alle vnderstonden english tonge.	All understand the English tongue.

There can be no clearer statement about the linguistic character of the new era. Yet the amount being written in English was still very limited, even fifty years later, if we accept the poet John Gower's statement in the Prologue to his long poem about courtly love, *Confessio amantis* (*Confession of Love*), written in the 1380s and revised in 1393 (l. 21):

> Som man mai lyke of that I wryte:
> And for that fewe men endite [compose]
> In oure englissh, I thenke [plan to] make
> A bok [book] for Engelondes sake,
> The yer [year] sextenthe of kyng Richard.

And his contemporary, Thomas Usk, in the Prologue to his prose essay *The Testament of Love* (1384–5), also finds it necessary to make a case for using his 'dame's tongue' (the earliest reference I have found to a 'mother tongue'):

> In Latyn and French hath many soverayne wyttes had gret delyte to endyte [compose] and have many noble thynges fulfylde; but, certes [certainly], there ben [be] some that speken their poysye [poetic] mater in Frenche of whiche speche the Frenche men have as good a fantasye as we have in heryng [hearing] of Frenche mennes Englysshe.

An English poet composing in French, he suggests, does as badly as a Frenchman trying to speak English. And Usk concludes:

> Let than clerkes endyten [compose] in Latyn, for they have the propertie of science and the knowynge in that facultie; and lette Frenchmen in their Frenche also endyten their queynt [strange] termes, for it is kyndely to their mouthes; and let us shewe our fantasyes [imaginations] in suche wordes as we lerneden [learned] of our dames tonge.

All understand this 'dames tongue', William of Nassington had suggested. But what sort of tongue was it, after 200 years of French influence?

The impact of French

Language reflects society; language change reflects social change. It is hardly surprising, therefore, to find French having such a dramatic effect on English when we consider the social implications of a 'Conquest' and the many areas where Britain found itself assimilating the culture of France. By the end of the twelfth century, people were trying to use their vernacular language to express a wide range of new functions. It must have been an uncomfortable situation, coping with the unfamiliar domains of expression introduced by the Normans.

The pressure was growing to use English, but there was no suitable English to use. Writers could not rely on the vernacular varieties available from earlier times, such as had evolved to meet the needs of chronicle history and religion, because the ancient language was no longer in use: Old English had become Middle English. And in the case of the domains most affected by the Norman invaders, such as law, architecture, estate management, music, and literature, there was a new, francophone vision to be expressed. Here, an Anglo-Saxon perspective, with all its associated vocabulary and conceptualization, was irrelevant. People had no alternative but to develop new varieties of expression, adopting Continental models, and adapting traditional genres to cope with the French way of doing things.

The development of new domains of expression involves all aspects of language. A distinctive vocabulary is the most noticeable feature – not individual words arriving one at a time, but large clusters of words introduced to express sets of related concepts. In ecclesiastical architecture, for example, French architects in England adapted Continental sources for their cathedral designs, so that in due course the buildings are better described as Romanesque or Gothic rather than as Early English. The associated specialist terminology needed to express this fundamental shift of vision was very large, covering everything from building tools to aesthetic abstractions. But the 'language of buildings' involves far more than vocabulary. New words from abroad bring new patterns of sound, so pronunciation changes. These pronunciations need to be written down, so new spellings appear. The character of phrases and sentences also changes, with the adoption of foreign compounds, idioms, formulaic expressions, and other multi-word constructions. And individual authors, schools, and genres influence general patterns of style. Several of the new domains of expression would prove to be influenced by French habits of discourse – legal English, for instance, reflecting a barrage of unfamiliar procedures and practices.

The realm of ecclesiastical architecture also illustrates how the language of a newly emerging variety could soon become widely encountered. The new cathedrals being built in the decades after the Conquest were all over the country, in such widely separated locations as Lincoln, St Albans, Hereford, Ely, Worcester, Exeter, Carlisle, and Durham. Other locations saw a great deal of rebuilding, perhaps because a church had become too small for the growing population or because it had been devastated by fire, such as happened to the foundations at Peterborough (1116) and Canterbury (1174). New monasteries and nunneries had to be built, to meet the needs of the religious orders being introduced throughout England. Early arrivals from the Continent included the Carthusians (in the eleventh century) and Cistercians (twelfth century), to be followed by the orders of friars, the Franciscans and the Dominicans. In addition to the leading houses, smaller abbeys sprang up everywhere, often founded by local lords who placed members of their family in charge. In these circumstances, a new English – but French-inspired – architectural nomenclature would quickly spread.

The religious developments had significant linguistic effects. New religious houses meant new scriptoria, more scribes, and thus more manuscripts. The scribes were needed, because there was so much more to be written about. Within the monastic setting, there were new rules and guidelines to be circulated, not least to meet the needs of the burgeoning number of nunneries, as women came to play a more prominent role in religious life.[6] And all aspects of the Catholic Church were being affected by the canons of a flurry of General Councils. After a long period during which there were no Councils at all (Constantinople had been the last, in 869–70), there were six in less than 200 years: the four Lateran Councils (1123, 1139, 1179, 1215), two at Lyons (1245, 1274), and one at Vienne (1311–12). Each event generated new literature, and, though this was all in Latin, the need to interpret and apply the recommendations demanded English. The Middle Ages was the period when the importance of the vernacular as a religious medium was beginning to be emphasized. The work of the friars as preachers and teachers to all classes of the population, especially the poor, had been sanctioned by the Fourth Lateran Council in its Tenth Canon: 'we decree that bishops provide suitable men, powerful in work and word, to exercise with fruitful result the office of preaching; who in place of the bishops, since these cannot do it, diligently visiting the people committed to them, may instruct them by word and example'. As a result, with more preachers meeting the public, the spoken vernacular language developed fresh oratorical modes of expression which soon exceeded the range and quantity of their Old English counterparts; and much of this new output came to be written down.

A similar story can be told for other major domains, such as political administration. Domesday Book (1086–7) was the first national survey carried out by a government whose character was becoming increasingly centralized, and it proved to be the stimulus for an unprecedented amount of legal formulation and record-keeping. About 2,000 writs and charters survive from the Anglo-Saxon period; in the twelfth and thirteenth centuries the surviving legal manuscripts number hundreds of thousands. Everyone was affected by documentation, from landowner to serf. The amount of work passing through the new civil service offices – the Chancery and the Exchequer – grew immensely. From 1199 Chancery clerks began to keep parchment copies of letters sent out under the great seal. Even though many manuscripts have been lost, it is still possible to get a sense of the growth in administrative load from such details as the amount of sealing wax used by Chancery clerks. In the late 1220s the office was using 3.63 lb a week; by the late 1260s the weekly outlay had risen to 31.9 lb.[7]

A remarkable amount of administrative ephemera built up during the late eleventh century and throughout the twelfth: records of apprenticeship, guild membership, and military conscription (muster rolls), records of assize courts and quarter sessions, enclosure awards, and parish registers. Manorial records, for example, listed such matters as land transfers within a manor, and the names and deaths of tenants. Occasional taxes, or subsidies, were collected by local assessors, who kept detailed accounts on behalf of the Exchequer. The Pipe Rolls of the Exchequer are the earliest surviving series of public records, running almost without a break from 1155 until 1834, with one roll from 1129–30 also surviving. They contained accounts of the royal income, arranged by county, for each financial year. (The name comes from the pipe-like appearance of the parchments which resulted when the individual pages were sewn together and rolled up.) It might be thought that the vast increase in documentation in early Middle English is of little importance for the history of the language, because they were almost entirely written in Latin – often (as in the case of the Pipe Rolls) in a highly abbreviated style. But this is to forget the importance of names – both of people and of places – as the next Interlude illustrates (p. 140). A great deal of information can be deduced about social and regional background from the choice and spelling of proper names. And it would in any case not be long before this documentation began to be written in English.

Record-keeping affects everybody. Today, we are so used to maintaining records and having them available for information retrieval that it is difficult to imagine a world without them – a world where everything depended on verbal memory.[8] That was very largely the case in the Anglo-Saxon world, and it remained so until the twelfth century, when it proved no longer possible to ignore the daily demands imposed by a society which depended on literacy in order to function. Writing became increasingly visible to all, its significance not lost on the illiterate majority, whose lives were governed by it. Some time later, Shakespeare would put into the mouth of Jack Cade a comment about the almost magical power of the written language. Agreeing to his rebel associate's call to 'kill all the lawyers', Cade reflects on the way writing can condemn a man to death: 'Is this not a lamentable thing, that of the skin of an innocent lamb should be made parchment? That parchment, being scribbled o'er, should undo a man?' (*Henry VI Part 2*, IV.ii.73). Literacy became a priority during the twelfth century. The number of schools rapidly increased. And, at a higher level, advanced literacy began to manifest itself in the establishment of the first universities (Oxford in 1249, Cambridge in 1284), as well as through that series of intellectual and cultural developments in Continental Europe known as the 'twelfth-century Renaissance'.

This Renaissance affected all areas of knowledge, and new language emerged to express fresh thinking in such domains as theology, philosophy, logic, law, cosmology, medicine, and mathematics. A renewal of interest in the Classics and the nature of ancient learning increased the prestige of Latin, but other languages – notably, Arabic and Greek – also received fresh attention. Vernacular literature also benefited. Not only did the rebirth of learning lead to a great increase in the number of translations into English from other languages, foreign influence also manifested itself in the world of English secular music and literature. The two domains had been inseparable in the performances of the virtuoso poet–musicians who emerged in the eleventh century, travelling around the courts and taverns of Europe, romanticizing the high ideals of courtly love, recounting long-past epics, and capturing events of the moment in satirical and bawdy ballads. These professional entertainers performed a variety of roles, used a range of dialects and styles, and were known by various names (depending on the time and place), such as *trouvères*, *troubadours*, *minnesinger*, *jongleurs*, *goliards*, and *gleemen*. We find a reference to their role in an early Middle English text, the thirteenth-century *Lay of Havelok the Dane* (ll. 2,327–40), in which the celebrations taking place at Havelok's coronation include both the reading and singing of romances (*gestes* is derived from the name of the French epic poems, the *chansons de geste*):

Leyk of mine, of hasard ok,	Sports of dice, of gambling, too,
Romanz-reding on þe bok;	Reading romances from the book;
þer mouthe men here þe gestes singe,	There might you hear the epics sung
þe glevmen on þe tabour dinge.	The gleemen beating on the drum.

The development of a more sophisticated musical genre was also to be found in France, in the works of such composers as Pérotin Magister (*c.* 1160–1240), Philippe de Vitry (1291–1361), and Guillaume de Machaut (*c.* 1300–1377), the last decisively influencing the emergence of polyphonic singing. And in due course, all these developments crossed the English Channel, bringing their language with them (see panel 6.3).

It was accordingly during this period – chiefly in the thirteenth century – that we find French coming to be viewed as the first international language of culture and fashion. But it was a new kind of French, learned in a new kind of way. The Anglo-Norman variety, which had been the mother tongue of the power-wielding class after the Conquest, had by this time virtually died out, to be replaced by a more prestigious variety, the language of the French court, taught as a foreign tongue in homes and schools. This was the key to social advancement: one could not be thought civilized if one did not speak the 'French of Paris', with its fashionable pronunciation, vocabulary, and style. The point

6.3 Eleanor of Aquitaine

The changing character of a language is usually the result of anonymous social trends; but every now and then we can identify an individual whose influence has been exceptional. In the twelfth century, such a person was Eleanor of Aquitaine. Thanks to her lifelong patronage, no one had more influence on the spread through-out France of troubadour music and song. And we must note that 'lifelong', in this instance, is no cliché: her eighty-two years (1122–1204) was remarkable, almost twice the average life expectancy in the early Middle Ages.

Eleanor was heiress of the duchy of Aquitaine in south-west France – a huge patrimony covering almost a third of the country, and much influenced by the musical and artistic traditions of nearby Spain and Moorish Africa. A first marriage to Louis VII of France was annulled, and in 1152 she married Henry of Anjou, who became Henry II of England. Two of her eight children became English kings – Richard I and John. In 1173 she supported a rebellion against Henry, which resulted in her being imprisoned for fifteen years; but after his death she was effectively ruler of England for four years (1190–94), when Richard I was away on the Third Crusade.

Eleanor was already famous for her patronage in her home region, and her arrival in the English court heralded a new musical era, during which she received many Continental musicians. The troubadour movement took time to establish itself, partly because its dialect (the *langue d'oc* of the southern region of France) was different from the Anglo-Norman dialect which had grown up in England (derived from the *langue d'oil* of the French north). But in its various genres, French music eventually became fashionable and influential. Richard I was himself a composer and singer – an accomplishment which has achieved legendary status. (Richard was imprisoned in Austria on the way home from the Crusades. His friend Blondel de Nesle (1155–*c*. 1200) went in search of him, singing a song they had jointly composed, in the hope that Richard would recognize it and sing a response. The strategy worked, when the song was answered from a cell in the castle of Dürrenstein, and Blondel was able to inform the English where Richard was being held.)

Legend aside, there is no doubt that French musical expression was a signifi-cant influence on the subject-matter, vocabulary, and style of the language of English secular music during the thirteenth century.

was still relevant a century later, when Chaucer pokes some fun at the presum-ably nonstandard linguistic ability of the Prioress, who had learned her French at the Benedictine nunnery in Stratford (now part of Greater London):

| And Frenssh she spak ful faire and fetisly | And French she spoke very well and gracefully |

After the scole of Stratford atte Bowe,	After the school of Stratford at Bow,
For Frenssh of Parys was to hire	For French of Paris was to her
unknow.	unknown.

But French was not only in vogue for the sake of fashion. Even more than previously it was an important career language, for by the middle of the thirteenth century it was regularly being used as an alternative to Latin in administrative settings. Although the Church continued to use Latin for ecclesiastical purposes, in court circles it was steadily being replaced by French. Officials would still use Latin for letters abroad or to senior clergy, but otherwise French was the norm for royal letters. French also gradually supplanted Latin in parliamentary debate, retaining its position until itself later supplanted by English. And in the business world, scribes carried on their recording and accounting in French until well into the fifteenth century.

The relationships between the three languages were immensely complex during the later part of the period. We must not forget that not only was English changing during this time, but so was French, especially in the law courts, where it remained for some time, becoming more specialized and different from that of Paris, with large numbers of arcane legal expressions and a syntax increasingly influenced by English word order. The notion of 'English supplanting French' does not refer to a swift change. A statute of 1362 indeed recognized the role of English for the first time in Parliament, but that did not suddenly stop the use of French. On the contrary, French had a routine presence in parliamentary records until well into the fifteenth century, and is actually still encountered there as late as the seventeenth century.[9] The context of the 1362 statute was a concern over the way plaintiffs were unable to understand spoken proceedings in the courts: ordinary people could not follow the French of their lawyers and judges. The 1362 statute applied basically to the spoken language, not to the written records of the courts and Parliament, which continued to operate with a mixture of French, Latin, and English for a very long time. As late as 1549, in the reign of Henry VIII, Archbishop Cranmer is recorded as saying that plaintiffs complained because their lawyers pleaded their causes 'in the French tongue which they understood not'.[10] And when, in Shakespeare's *Henry VIII*, Cardinal Wolsey visits Queen Katherine to persuade her to cooperate with Henry's plans, he begins in Latin – only to be abruptly checked by the Queen (III.i.41):

O, good my lord, no Latin!
I am not such a truant since my coming
As not to know the language I have lived in.
A strange tongue makes my cause more strange, suspicious;
Pray speak in English.

By the sixteenth century, trilingualism would have been restricted to a specialized, chiefly legal elite. But during the Middle Ages in Britain, educated English people would have been trilingual as a matter of course. English would have been their mother tongue, as we have seen (p. 131).[11] They would have learned Latin as the required language of the Church, the Roman Classics, most scholarship, and some politico-legal matters. And they would have found French essential both for routine administrative communication within Britain and in order to be considered fashionable throughout Western European society. The situation would not last. As the Middle Ages progressed, we find English gradually making inroads into domains of discourse which had previously been the prerogative of Latin or French. Legal English, medical English, philosophical English, literary English, parliamentary English, and other varieties started to appear, and quite quickly evolved the distinctive and sophisticated styles of expression still used today. But in every domain, the new vernacular displays the influence of its linguistic antecedents. And by the end of the Middle English period, the Germanic element in the English vocabulary had been firmly put in the shade by a Romance and Italic lexical invasion of unprecedented proportions.

Interlude 6
Lay Subsidy dialects

When the king was in special need of revenue, such as to pay an army or to build ships, he would levy a tax on the entire population of towns and villages, based on the value of lands and possessions, with only the poorest exempted. An Act would grant one or more subsidies, with payment to be made over a period of time. The returns of those liable to pay were inscribed on parchment rolls which came to be called Lay (as opposed to Clerical, whose property was exempt) Subsidy Rolls. Over 20,000 such documents are held by the Public Record Office in London. Although in Latin, they contain a surprising amount of linguistic information about Middle English.[12]

Introduced by Parliament in 1332 to provide funds for Edward III's 'great and arduous affairs in Ireland and elsewhere', they contain lists of names of the people assessed, arranged by location for each hundred in the country, identifying the various demesnes, boroughs, villages, hamlets, and tithings. For example, in the returns for Frampton in Lincolnshire in 1332 we find the following (in the pre-decimal British monetary system, one pound consisted of 20 shillings [s.], and each shilling consisted of 12 pence [d.]):

Nicholas filius Ricardi	5s.
Thomas Hardepeny	2s.
Walter filius Willelmi	8d.
Robert de Bekyngham	1s. 4d.
Richard de Cobeldyck	5s. 8d.
William Echard	1s.

The lists, it is plain, are phrased in Latin ('Nicholas son of Richard', 'Walter son of William'), but not everything is Latinized to the same extent. Given names were more likely to be in Latin than surnames, and bynames (names which distinguish people by occupation, nickname, or provenance, such as William Miller, William Black, William of Buckingham) were generally left in English. So, by examining the way that personal names or place-names were spelled, various conclusions about the state of the language at the time can be drawn.

In particular, spelling variations can tell us a great deal about the way the dialects of Middle English were evolving. An illustration of the way they can be used is provided by the Swedish scholar Gillis Kristensson, who has been painstakingly working through the various counties of England studying the variant forms in these Rolls.[13] If we take the first sound in the name *White*, for example, and look at the Rolls representing the East Midland counties between 1296 and 1334 (see the map on p. 142 for county locations), we find three types of spelling: *wh-*, *w-*, and various combinations beginning with *q-*. This sound was spelled *hw-* in Old English (*hwit*), a 'voiceless *w*' /ʍ/. It is still heard today in many accents which distinguish between, say, *whales* and *Wales* (p. 466), but from Old English times the trend was to replace it by the 'voiced *w*' (/w/, as in *Wales*), and this probably motivated the changed order of the letters, with the more dominant *w* being written in front of the *h*. Why the sound was changing in this way is not entirely clear: it was probably the continuation of a development from within Old English, when the /h/ sound in a consonant cluster was beginning to be dropped in many words – *hnutu* became later *nut*, *hlaf* became *loaf* – but the process was also very likely influenced by Norman pronunciation, where /w/ was the only form. Whatever the reason, we find clear evidence in the Rolls of the existence of variation and change.

Throughout the southern part of the region, we see *wh-* spellings everywhere, reflecting the Old English norm – *White, Whyte, Whitman, Whitbread, Whitlock, Hwyte* . . . – alternating with a sprinkling of *w-*. In Suffolk we see *Whyting* as well as *Wyting*, in Essex *Whiteman* as well as *Wyteman*. In seven counties, as can be seen in panel 6.4, there is a massive preponderance of *wh-* names – out of 262 instances, only 39 (15 per cent) have a *w-* spelling. In Cambridgeshire, however, the usage is the other direction – 15 *w-* forms and only 1 *wh-* form – and in Rutland there are no *wh-* forms at all. Evidently *w-* is infiltrating the Old English pronunciation, and in some areas more than others, though why it is making such rapid progress in the north is unclear. Even more distinctive, we find a cluster of spellings with a *q-* – *Qwarles, Qwytewell* (modern *Whitwell*), *Quite, Qwytside, Qwhitbred*, 79 in all – just in one county, Norfolk. The letter *q*, though common in Latin, was rarely used in Old English, but it became common after the Conquest, and the French scribes used it as a means of representing a velar fricative – the /x/ sound heard in such modern words as Scots *loch* or Welsh *bach*. We will encounter this sound again as we move north towards Scotland (p. 204); but its presence in such quantity in Norfolk suggests that it was more than just a traditional spelling. Mr White of Norwich was probably for some time pronounced 'chwite', before the /x/ weakened, and eventually disappeared.

If this were just an isolated case, we might not be able to draw many conclusions from it. But again and again we see pattern in the variant spellings

6.4 The distribution of *q-*, *wh-*, and *w-* spellings in personal names and place-names in East Midlands Lay Subsidy Rolls (adapted from Kristensson, 1995)

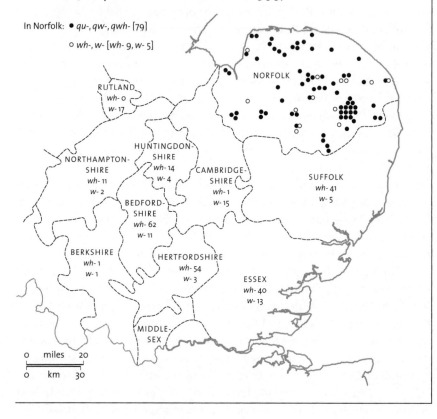

of people and places, and when the patterns start to coincide we can begin to sense dialects emerging out of the mist. For instance, in this same part of England there are clear differences in the words for 'mill' (Old English *mylen*) further inland. In the south-east – Suffolk and Essex, and also Cambridgeshire – the forms are almost without exception spelled with an *e*: *Melne, Melle, Melner, Meller*. Villages that have kept the *e* into modern times include *Meldreth* and *Melford*. In the west, in Bedfordshire, the names are entirely spelled with *u*: *Mulne, Mulle, Mulner, Muller*. A modern example is *Mulbarton*, south of Norwich. And in the north – Norfolk, Huntingdonshire, and Rutland – the names are almost entirely spelled with *i*: *Milne, Mille, Milner, Miller*, which is the standard modern form. Hertfordshire is an interesting mix of *e* and *u* forms: modern *Millhouse* appears in the Rolls as *Melne*; modern *Westmill* appears as

Westmulle. Forms with an *e* spelling are otherwise very rare in Hertfordshire, so why do the 'meller' words appear there at all? Perhaps it was as Kristensson suggests: 'mellers' from the south-east may have been especially good craftsmen, and travelled further inland to find fresh trade.

Name lists have several other linguistic uses apart from being valuable as dialect evidence, and apart, of course, from their intrinsic interest to genealogists and social historians. The history and use of names is a discipline of study in its own right (*onomastics*), and of considerable popular interest – as we see annually today, when newspapers publish their lists of the 'top ten' first names. What were the most popular names in, say, Worcestershire in 1346? The Lay Subsidy Rolls can tell you.[14] For the record, *John* was by far the most popular male name, followed by *William, Robert, Thomas, Richard*, and *Henry*. Less common names included *Milo, Odo*, and *Gelfridus*. Women were not strongly represented in the Rolls, so few names appear more than once or twice; some are still familiar today, such as *Beatrix, Cristina, Elizabetha*, and *Katerina*, but several are no longer used, such as *Amicia, Agnete, Athelyna*, and *Hawisia*. However, the dialect evidence is particularly special, because it is so precise in the information it provides about provenance. One of the problems in using literary texts for dialect study – as we saw repeatedly for Old English (p. 50) – is that, although a text may be full of distinctive dialect forms, it is often impossible to be sure where it was composed or written down. A poem might be composed anywhere. But with data of the kind provided by the Lay Subsidy Rolls, Pipe Rolls, and other such documents, we have definite information. It is hardly possible for a regional point of origin to be more specific than in the case of a place-name.

Chapter 7 Lexical invasions

The trilingual situation which evolved in England during the early Middle Ages was to leave an indelible impression on English. The combined influence of French and Latin – with French at the outset by far the more important – radically altered the character of the language. The impact was most noticeable in vocabulary, though all aspects of language were affected to some degree. As we have seen in Chapter 3, around the year 1000, non-Germanic words in English could be numbered in the hundreds; by 1500 the language had incorporated tens of thousands. English was moving in a direction from which there would be no turning back. Eventually it would become the most etymologically multilingual language on earth.

The scale of the invasion can easily be seen if the lexicons of two texts are compared, one from the early years of Middle English, before the period of French borrowing, the other from the later years, once the peak momentum of borrowing was over. The first text is an extract from a long early thirteenth-century verse chronicle called *Laȝamon's Brut*. We know little of Layamon – as the name is usually spelled these days – other than what he says at the beginning of his poem: that he was a parish priest of *Ernleȝe*, modern Areley Kings, in Worcestershire. He tells the story of the history of Britain, beginning with the landing of Brutus (the *Brut* of the title, and the reputed founder of the British race); he includes some tales of King Arthur, and ends with the last Saxon victory over the British in 689. The poem has many features of interest, not least that it is written in an alliterative line, intriguingly suggestive of Old English models (p. 89). However, the approach also shows the influence of French chivalric romances, and uses as a source a French verse chronicle, *Roman de Brut*, made by a twelfth-century Anglo-Norman poet, Robert Wace.

Under these circumstances, it is perhaps surprising that the *Brut* contains very few French loanwords. The following extract (l. 21,739) about a haunted lake in fact contains none at all:

> *Þat is a seolcuð mere, iset a middelærde,*
> That is a marvellous lake, placed in the world:
> *Mid fenne and mid ræode, mid watere swiðe bræde,*

With marsh and with reeds, with water very extended,
Mid fiscen and mid feoȝelen, mid uniuele þingen.
With fish and with birds, with very many creatures.
Þat water is unimete brade, nikeres þer baðieð inne,
The lake is extremely wide, water monsters there swim within,
Þer is æluene ploȝe in atteliche pole.
There is sport of supernatural creatures in that terrible pool.
Sixti æit-londes beoð i þan watere longe,
Sixty islands are in that extensive lake,
In ælc of þan æit-londe is a clude hæh and strong
In each island is a rock high and strong
Þer næstieð arnes and oðere græte uoȝeles.
Where nest eagles and other great birds.

It may well have been the poem's content – stories of ancient battles in atmospheric settings – which motivated the poet to use an older indigenous vocabulary; or perhaps it was the association with the rhythms and resonances of the Old English metrical tradition. But the fact remains that, although the text exists in two manuscripts, written with about twenty-five to fifty years between them, only some 250 French words appear in the combined total of over 30,000 lines.[1] Interestingly, two thirds of these are in the later manuscript, where the scribe seems to have made an effort to modernize the text, replacing some of the older words with French equivalents, presumably reflecting what he felt to be contemporary taste (see panel 7.1). Most of the replaced words would have

---

7.1 Some of the Old English words replaced by French loans in the later version of *Laȝamon's Brut*

Earlier version (c. 1200)	Later version (c. 1250)	Modern English
æhte	tresur	treasure
boc-runen	lettre	letter
bolle	coupe	cup
gauel	truage	tribute
heren	serve	serve
marmon-stane	marbre	marble
milce	grace	grace
munuccliff	abbey	abbey
munstre	nonnerie	nunnery
wisen	atyr	attire

been unfamiliar if not unintelligible in the thirteenth century, but not all were altered because they had gone out of use. The scribe replaces *chireche* 'church' by *chapel*, for example, though both were current in Middle English (as they are today). He also replaced *axe* by *gisarme*, and here it was the replacement word which would later fall out of use.

The contrast with a much later heroic poem, *Sir Gawain and the Green Knight*, is striking. It is preserved in a manuscript dated about 1400, and tells the story of a green knight arriving at the court of King Arthur, and issuing a challenge which is taken up by Sir Gawain.[2] The following extract, towards the beginning of the poem (l. 161), is part of the description of the green knight and his horse. The French loanwords are underlined (but *richly* is discussed separately in panel 7.2).

> *And alle his vesture uerayly watȝ clene verdure,*
> And all his clothing truly was completely green,
> *Boþe þe barres of his belt and oþer blyþe stones,*
> Both the bars of his belt and other bright gems,
> *Þat were richely rayled in his aray clene*
> That were richly arranged in his elegant dress
> *Aboutte hymself and his sadel, vpon silk werkeȝ*
> About himself and his saddle, upon silk embroidery
> *Þat were to tor for to telle of tryfles þe halue*
> That were too hard for to tell of details the half
> *Þat were enbrauded abof, wyth bryddes and flyȝes,*
> That were embroidered upon it, with birds and flies,
> *With gay gaudi of grene, þe golde ay inmyddes.*
> With bright verdant hue of green, the gold always in the middle.

7.2 *Rich* choice

Rich is one of those intriguing words where it is difficult to be sure just how much influence French had in its origins. In the beginning, in Roman times, there was Latin *rex* 'king' – a term whose importance seems to have been universally valued, for it was adopted throughout Europe, appearing in early Celtic (as in modern Irish *rioghachd* 'kingdom'), the Germanic languages (as in modern German *reich*), and the Romance languages (as in modern Italian *ricco*).

A parallel English/French development took place. In Old English, the form emerged as *rice*, pronounced /ˈriːtʃə/, used both as an adjective meaning 'powerful, of high rank' or 'wealthy' and as a noun meaning 'kingdom'. In Old French, the form emerged as *riche* /ˈriːʃə/. There was also an Old English form *riclice* 'richly', which appears in a Middle English form in the *Gawain* extract above.

In early Middle English, we find two groups of spellings, representing different dialect developments. One group represented the /tʃə/ sound, as in *rycche*, *ricce*, and *riche*, and these are found mainly in southern texts. The other group represented a /k/ sound, as in *rike* and *ryke*, and these are found in northern texts, such as the *Cursor Mundi* (*c.* 1300). Other words showed a similar distinction. *Wic* 'dwelling place' appears in place-names both as *-wick* (*Chiswick*) and as *-wich* (*Norwich*), as we saw on p. 69.

The interesting question is: why did *rich* become the standard form, and not *rike*? It could have been the other way round, especially as so many northern forms became standard. The suffix *-like* appears in Middle English both as *-lich* /liːtʃ/ in the south and as *lik* /liːk/ in the north. In this case, though, it is the *k* form which survives, as in Modern English *lifelike*, *alike* (earlier *y-like*, Old English *ʒelic*), and so on.

It was probably the arrival of the French form which tipped the balance in favour of *rich*. The pronunciation with /ʃ/ would have reinforced the Old English form in /tʃə/, and we can easily imagine the indigenous pronunciation being pulled in the direction of the more prestigious foreign form. With Normans and Anglo-Saxons both using words which were pronounced so similarly, and with *riche* being part of the language of power, *rike* didn't stand a chance.

All the content words in the next two lines are French (*proud* was borrowed during the Old English period); however, these are somewhat exceptional in their loanword density, for the remaining lines of horse-description are largely Old English in character (*stayned* and *glent* are Old Norse).

> Þe *pendauntes* of his *payttrure*, þe *proude cropure*,
> The pendants of his horse's breast-trappings, the splendid crupper,
> His *molaynes*, and alle þe *metail anamayld* was þenne,
> His bit-studs, and all the enamelled metal was then,
> Þe *steropes* þat he stod on *stayned* of þe same,
> The stirrups that he stood on coloured of the same,
> And his *arsounʒ* al after and his *apel sturtes*,
> And his saddle-bows all behind and his noble tail,
> Þat euer glemered and *glent* al of *grene* stones.
> That continually gleamed and glinted all of green stones.

Romance words are supplementing Germanic words, providing a richer vocabulary; and once Latin words enter the equation (p. 155), the lexicon becomes richer still.

The mention of Old Norse reminds us that there had already been a steady tradition of lexical borrowing dating back to Old English, in which some French words had played their part (Chapter 3). But the impact of French in the Middle

Ages was much greater, both in quantity and stylistic range, and there are more ramifications to analyse. To begin with, the words were entering English through both the written and the spoken mediums, and at various stylistic levels within each medium. Many loans were general in character, but some were informal, and others were technical. Large numbers of terms related to restricted domains, such as horse-riding (as in the *Gawain* extract), law, religion, politics, society, and culture. Some domains attracted more loans than others: literature on courtly themes contained a relatively large number, as did writing which was a translation from French. The loans took their time to move north: in early Middle English there were far more French loans in southern texts, and an even spread does not emerge until the later period. The people who introduced the borrowing changed, too (p. 136): in the early centuries they were generally native-speakers of (Anglo-Norman) French; in the later, they were almost entirely speakers of (Parisian) French as a foreign language. And the fact that two varieties of French were involved must also be taken into account. The Parisian variety ultimately became the prestigious norm, and this led to some words actually being borrowed twice – once relatively early on from Anglo-Norman, and again some time later from Parisian French. The spellings typical of each variety provide the clue: we find Norman *calenge* and Parisian *challenge*, Norman *prisun* and Parisian *prison*. In a few cases, both forms stayed in English, some of them evolving different meanings (see panel 7.3). We explore these issues further in the next chapter.

French words began as a trickle and soon became a stream and then a flood. In the mid twelfth-century *Peterborough Chronicle* (p. 117) we find only twenty-nine new words, and they belong to just a few domains of discourse. There are religious words, such as *abbat* 'abbot', *cardinal*, and *miracle*; words to do with social position, such as *duc* 'duke', *cuntesse* 'countess', and *curt* 'court'; administrative words, such as *canceler* 'chancellor', *concilie* 'council',

7.3 Some loanword doublets from Norman and Parisian French

Norman loan	Parisian loan
conveie [convey]	convoye [convoy]
gaol	jail
reward	regard
warden	guardian
warrant	guarantee
wile	guile

and *rent*; and general terms of law and politics, such as *iustise* 'justice', *werre* 'war', and *pais* 'peace'. The numbers quickly increase. In a text probably written less than fifty years later, but with no manuscripts extant before the early thirteenth century, we find nearly 250. This is *Ancrene Riwle* (*Anchorites' Rule*), also known as *Ancrene Wisse* (*Anchorites' Guide*), a lengthy work providing spiritual direction for a group of three female recluses. Of particular note is that the religious subject-matter has motivated many specialized terms, such as *grace*, *letanie* 'litany', *sauter* 'Psalter', and *scrowe* 'scroll'. There is a large increase in abstract words, especially to do with morality and behaviour, such as *chastete* 'chastity', *daunger* 'arrogance', *defaut* 'fault', *delice* 'pleasure', *deuout* 'devout', *kurteisie* 'courtesy', and *largesse* 'generosity'. But there are also many everyday words, such as *avancen* 'advance', *broche* 'brooch', *cite* 'city', *flur* 'flower', *jurneie* 'journey', *manere* 'manner', *messager* 'messenger', *propre* 'suitable', *reisun* 'reason', and *tendre* 'tender'. In a sentence such as the following there is a real sense of lexical mixing (the French words are underlined):

> A leafdi wes mid hire fan biset al abuten, hire lond al <u>destruet</u>, & heo al <u>poure</u>, inwið an eorðene <u>castel</u>.

> A lady was by her foes besieged on every side, her land entirely laid waste, and she completely poor, within an earthen castle.[3]

The mixing can even be seen within individual words, as in *bisaumpleð* 'moralizes', which is a combination of an Old English prefix *be* and an Old French root *saumple*.

We need to consider this last type of example at greater length, because words formed by juxtaposing elements from two languages became increasingly common in Middle English. The *be-* prefix was attached to several other Old French words, such as *befool*, *besiege*, and *beguile*, and a number of Old English affixes were used to produce hybrid forms. The suffix *-ful*, for example, had been used earlier to form adjectives from abstract nouns – essentially, 'full of X', as when *sorhful* is used to describe Grendel's mother, 'sorrowful' after the death of her offspring (*Beowulf*, l. 2,119). In Middle English, it generated many adjectives from Old French nouns, such as *beautiful*, *graceful*, *merciful*, *faithful*, and *pitiful*. The opposite process also took place: French affixes used with Germanic words. *Soothship* appears in the fourteenth century, for instance, a combination of an Old English root and an Old French suffix. The French *-able* suffix combined with English roots to produce *knowable*, *findable*, *speakable*, *doable*, *makeable*, and hundreds more. Often the two languages both added an affix to a single word: in *unknowable* we have an English prefix and a French suffix sandwiching an English word; in *discovering* (used first as a noun) we have a French prefix and an English suffix sandwiching a French word.

Nation ... nationalize ... nationalization ... denationalization ... antidenationalization ... Our facility to build words by using prefixes and suffixes is so ingrained that we tend to forget just how important the process of affixation is in accounting for the character of English vocabulary. Excluding inflectional endings, there are just over a hundred prefixes and suffixes available for use in everyday English, and at least one of these will be found in 40–50 per cent of all the words in the language.[4] It is during Middle English that we find the first great flood of these affixed words, with French introducing such (Latin-derived) prefixes as *con-, de-, dis-, en-, ex-, pre-, pro-,* and *trans-,* and such suffixes as *-able, -ance/-ence, -ant/-ent, -ity, -ment,* and *-tion* (at the time, usually spelled *-cion*). The suffixes were especially productive, a trend typified in *tournament, defendant, solemnity,* and *avoidance.* The *-tion* ending alone produced hundreds of creations, such as *damnation, temptation, mortification, contemplation,* and *suggestion.* Prefixes, as seen in *conjoin, despoil, disobedient,* and *enchant,* were important, too, but not so widespread; we have to wait until the end of the Middle English period before we find a comparable explosion in their use (p. 303).

Each of the major literary works of the Middle English period provides evidence of the way new French loans were continuing to arrive and older loans being consolidated. Some texts contain relatively few such words, and some contain many, but all texts have some. By the time we reach the opening lines of *The Canterbury Tales,* the French lexical content is a major linguistic feature:

> When that Aprill with his shoures soote
> The droghte of March hath perced to the roote,
> And bathed every veyne in swich licour
> Of which vertu engendred is the flour . . .

> When April with its sweet showers has pierced the drought of March to the root, and bathed every vein in such liquid from which strength the flower is engendered . . .

The proportion of French vocabulary in Chaucer varies a great deal, depending especially on the subject-matter: the more courtly narratives attract more French words, as do his scholarly expositions. The opening of his scientific *Treatise on the Astrolabe,* where he addresses *Lyte Lowys my sone* ('little Lewis my son'), is full of French words:

> I apercyve wel by certeyne evydences thyn abilite to lerne sciences touching nombres and proporciouns; and as wel considre I thy besy praier in special to lerne the tretys of the Astrelabie.

> I can well see from several signs your ability to learn about the sciences to do with

numbers and proportions; and I also take note of your earnest request especially to acquire knowledge about the treatise on the astrolabe.

The style continues in this vein throughout the work, becoming highly technical in places. One wonders how much little ten-year-old Lewis would have understood!

There are of course several ways of putting neologisms, or new words, across to a readership so that they can begin to understand what is being said. One is the familiar technique of glossing – a procedure which the previous sentence has just exemplified. For example, in this description of the cock Chauntecleer, in *The Nun's Priest's Tale* (l. 2,854), if you do not know what an *orlogge* is, you can guess it from the more familiar word used in the earlier part of the line.

> *Wel sikerer was his crowyng in his logge*
> More reliable was his crowing in his resting-place
> *Than is a clokke or an abbey orlogge*
> Than is a clock or an abbey timepiece

There are many such pairings of old and new words in Middle English, and they often link a Germanic word to a French one: *harm and routhe* has the French word second, as does *grenehede or folye* 'wantonness', whereas the opposite order is found in *pleasance or lykyng* and a *bokeler or a targe* 'shield'.[5] Three words might be linked together in this way, such as the expressions for 'knife' in *The Reeve's Tale* (l. 3,960): nobody messes around with Symkyn's wife, the narrator says, *But if he wolde be slayn of Symkyn / With panade, or with knyf, or boidekyn* 'Unless he wanted to be killed by Symkyn with [one type of] knife or [another type of] knife or [another type of] knife'. The first term is derived from a French root, the second is Old English, and the third is of unknown origin, though it may well be Celtic. (Chaucer's is the first recorded use of *bodkin*.) The words in groups of this kind may not have identical senses – it is often difficult to be sure exactly how they differ – but because they belong to the same field of meaning, it is possible to use the content of the more familiar item(s) to help grasp the less-known ones. The glossing could of course go in any direction: in many cases an English word is used to clarify a new French or Latin word; but there are also instances (explaining Anglo-Saxon legal terminology, for example) where it is the English word which is not so familiar, and the author finds it necessary to use a French or Latin gloss. Indeed, law was the domain where lexical doublets would in due course become a major stylistic feature (see panel 7.4).

Certain domains of everyday vocabulary also displayed considerable French influence. It has become a textbook commonplace to report the new

7.4 Take heed and care

As the profession of the law became regularized during the thirteenth century, French replaced Latin as the primary language of legal expression. The court reports known as the Year Books run from around 1260 to 1535 and are entirely in French. French also begins to compete with Latin in the statutes, and by the fourteenth century was the dominant voice (p. 138). Then, during the fifteenth century, law French was gradually replaced by law English. It is not difficult to imagine the state of mind of the medieval lawyer, working in such a transitional period. Caxton's later complaint, 'Loo, what sholde a man in thyse dayes now wryte?' (p. 207) – must have been anticipated thousands of times.

The problem was: how can tradition be respected yet precision maintained when there are three languages competing for attention? It is plain that lawyers spend a great deal of their time worrying about the precise significations of words: David Mellinkoff even begins his classic account with the statement: 'The law is a profession of words'.[6] So what words should be chosen when Latin, French, and English each provide a copious supply of relevant items? How does one choose between synonyms, or – even more difficult – between two words which seem to be synonymous, but which might just have enough differential meaning to allow a lawyer one day to make an argument based on the difference?

The solution, in many cases, was: don't choose; use both. In Middle English we see the rise of the legal lexical doublets which would become one of the stylistic hallmarks of that profession. Old English *goods* and Old French *chattels* resulted in Middle English legalese *goods and chattels*. The words were often paired to cover distinct nuances, thereby avoiding ambiguity; but sometimes the pairing seems to be no more than a more emphatic expression of a single meaning; and sometimes it seems to be just a stylistic habit, perhaps fostered by its undoubted rhythmical appeal in oral performance. But whatever the reason, it became a major feature of legal style which continues to the present day.

The table gives a small selection of mixed-language doublets which have entered English since the Middle Ages. There were also triplets, such as *give, devise, and bequeath* (English / French / English) or *right, title, and interest* (English / English / French); and even quadruplets, such as *in lieu, in place, instead, and in substitution of* (French / French / English / French or Latin). And it was not long before the habit of doubling became extended to pairs of words regardless of their language of origin. In such pairings as *null and void, cease and desist, heirs and assigns*, and *aid and abet* we see French words together. In *have and hold, let or hindrance*, and *each and every*, English words are together. But *have and hold* requires a further comment: it reminds us that lexical coupling is an ancient English stylistic tradition (p. 98). *Heold mec ond hæfde Hreðel cyning*, reminisces Beowulf (l. 2,430) – 'King Hrethel had and held me' (i.e., looked after me). The rhythmical appeal of lexical doubling has well-established historical roots.

Doublet	Sources
acknowledge and confess	English / French
breaking and entering	English / French
final and conclusive	French / Latin
fit and proper	English / French
give and grant	English / French
had and received	English / French
keep and maintain	English / French
lands and tenements	English / French
made and provided	English / Latin
new and novel	English / French
pardon and forgive	French / English
peace and quiet	French / Latin
shun and avoid	English / French
will and testament	English / Latin
wrack and ruin	English / French

terms for food which supplemented the Old English ones, such as *veal* alongside *calf*, *pork* alongside *pig*, and *mutton* alongside *sheep*. But it was the whole culinary lexicon which was affected, as can be seen from any of the hundreds of recipes collected in English cookery books of the fourteenth and fifteenth centuries.[7] Two examples are *Mortreus de Chare* 'mortress of flesh', a dish of ground meat thickened with eggs and breadcrumbs, and *Chike Endored* 'glazed chicken', a dish of chicken glazed with a golden batter. In each case the words of French origin are underlined. (*Morter* 'mortar' is a problem case, as there was such a word in Old English; but the medieval usage seems to be a fresh borrowing.)

Mortreus de Chare

Take porke, and seth [boil] it ynow [enough]; and take it vppe, and bawde hit [slice it thinly], and hewe it and grinde it, and in a morter; And cast therto grated brede [bread], and then drawe the same broth thorgh [through] a streynour [strainer], And temper hit with ale, and do al into a potte, and lete [let] boile, and aley [mix] hit with yolkes of egges, And then lete it boile no more, And caste thereto powder of ginger, Salt, And put hit in disshes in maner of Mortrewes, And cast thereto powder of ginger, & serue [serve] it forth.

Chike Endored

Take a chike, and drawe him [take out its entrails], and roste him, And lete the fete [feet] be on, and take awey the hede; then make batur of yolkes of eyron and floure, and caste there-to pouder of ginger, and peper, saffron and salt, and pouder hit faire til hit be rosted ynogh [enough].

The coexistence of the two words for 'eggs' – *egges* and *eyron* – should be noted, as we shall find these alternatives turning up again as an issue in the later history of English (p. 208).

It is difficult to be precise about the number of French words entering English during Middle English, because no dictionary has yet found it possible to take into account the lexical content of the thousands of manuscripts which exist, and many words and senses await identification. An example is *mortreus*, in the first recipe, which is not to be found even in the primary source for English lexical history, the *Oxford English Dictionary* (*OED*). We also have to remember that some words which did arrive had a very short life-span, often being used just once, or having a recorded history of only a few decades or centuries. But in order to assess the general impact of French on English we can none the less gain a great deal of relevant information by examining the earliest-recorded instances of words contained in the *OED*. Between 1250 and 1450 just over 27,000 words are identified as having a first recorded usage in at least one sense in a particular year, and (excluding the derived forms, such as *advisedly* from *advise*) around 22 per cent of these are words of French origin. Over three quarters of them are nouns. The peak of borrowing was the last quarter of the fourteenth century, when over 2,500 French words are identified.[8]

If we look more closely at the period, we find that there are first usages recorded for every year during that century, and in only four years is there an absence of anything French: 1301, 1317, 1318, and 1335. By contrast, there are a dozen years each represented by over a hundred French loans: 1300, 1325, 1330, 1340, 1374, 1375, 1380, 1382, 1386, 1387, 1398, and 1400. In 1383 just nine new words are recorded as having come into English, and they are all French: *assieged*, *authorize*, *baboonery*, *benefice*, *benet* (one of the lesser orders of the Catholic Church), *decrease* (as a noun), *spigot* (probably from Provençale), *superfluli* ('superfluously'), and *sustaining*. The actual year-dates, of course, do not mean very much. If a word is recorded in a manuscript of 1383, it does not necessarily follow that the word actually arrived in English in that year. In most instances – certainly, in the case of everyday words – it will have been present in the language for some time. And the fact that there is no French word recorded for, say, 1335, is purely an artefact of the selection of texts made by the lexicographers – some periods having been sampled more thoroughly than others – along with a general uncertainty about manuscript dating. It is the total impression which is important, and by the end of the Middle English period we find that – regardless of exactly when the words came into the language, and including the derived forms – around 30 per cent of English vocabulary is French in origin.

The flow of French loanwords into English reduced during the fifteenth century, but the overall rate of foreign borrowing did not, because of the growing influence of Latin. Indeed, thanks chiefly to its role as the language of scholarship and science, Latin words would eventually have a much greater impact on English than French ones: today, just over 30,000 words (excluding derived forms) have French identified as part of their history in the *OED*; for Latin, the corresponding figure is over 50,000. But even within the Middle English period, it had been an important source of vocabulary, directly or indirectly (via French). The two languages were intimately related, not only historically (French evolving from Vulgar Latin some 500 years previously) but also synchronically. For most of the Middle Ages, Latin was taught in England through the medium of French, and was presumably pronounced, and certainly sometimes spelled, in a French way. In many cases, the French and Latin words are so similar in form that it is impossible to say whether a word has come into English directly from French or directly from Latin, or is the result of some mutual influence. The adjective *expectant* arrives in English around 1400, but did it come directly from medieval French *expectant* or medieval Latin *exspectant-em* (a form of *exspectare*)? It is impossible to say. *Contrite, dissimulation, theatre, meridian, signification,* and *impression* represent dozens of examples which present similar problems. If an English author encounters a Latin word and decides to use it with a French suffix, then what should we call it? When Chaucer (in *Boece*, Book V, Prosa iv, l. 202) says that *a man is a thyng ymaginable and sensible* – the first recorded use of *imaginable* – are we to assume that he took the adjective directly from Latin *imaginabilis*, or did he take the verb *imagine*, which had arrived in English around the time he was born, and add a French -*able* ending to it? Probably quite a few of the words included in the above total for French are Latin words in disguise. Many more show an admixture of Latin and French influences. It can be an intricate yet frustrating matter, tracing the history of a loanword during the Middle English period (see panel 7.5).

7.5 An adventurous etymology

The history of the word *adventure* shows an interesting interaction between French and Latin influences. The word is first recorded as *auenture* in the thirteenth-century *Ancrene Riwle* (p. 149). The spelling shows that its source is definitely Old French, for the Latin original form was *adventura*.

Auenture stayed in literary writing, becoming a popular word to describe the comings and goings of romantic heroes. Chaucer uses it in *The Knight's Tale* (l. 1,160), for instance: at one point, Arcite says to Philemon, *I tolde thee myn aventure*. But in popular speech, and especially in Northern dialects, people pronounced the word in shortened form, as can be seen from such spellings as *awnter*, *aunter*, and *anter*. In one of the Wakefield Mystery Plays (*The Conspiracy*, l. 735), Malchus describes the plot to kill Jesus as an *awnter*. It was a usage which remained in the north, especially in Scotland, for several hundred years. Indeed, derived forms, such as *antrin* 'strange', may still be found today.

But *auenture* became the standard usage – with one modification. In the sixteenth century it was one of the words to be refashioned by those who felt that English words should have their connection to Latin made explicit. If the Latin source had a *d*, the reasoning went, then so should the English version. We can see an uncertainty already in William Caxton's works, where in *The Golden Legend* we find *auenture* and in *The Knight of the Tower* we find *aduenture* (both were published within a few months of each other, *c.* 1484). A century later, *adventure* was the norm.

Many other words were remodelled under Latin influence. During the later part of the Middle English period, *conferm* changed to *confirm*, *aorn* to *adorn*, and *det* or *dette* to *debt*. *Forȝiue us oure dettes*, says a version of the Lord's Prayer in 1400; *forgeue vs our debtes*, says the corresponding version in the Geneva Bible of 1557. The changes anticipate the etymological purism which would become one of the most influential fashions of the sixteenth century (p. 292).

Fortunately, there are large numbers of clear cases too, where a direct Latin origin is indisputable. Because Latin was the language of the Church, medieval scholarship, and early political administration, many are technical terms or part of a domain's standard nomenclature. Here is a representative sample from some of the chief domains. (In several cases, such as the names of many minerals, Latin is being used as a 'relay' language, re-expressing a term which was originally found in Greek.)

> Alchemy: dissolve, distillation, elixir, essence, ether, mercury
> Astronomy: ascension, comet, eccentric, equator, equinoxial, intercept
> Biology: asp, cicade, juniper, locust, lupin, pine
> Education: abacus, desk, et cetera, formal, major, minor
> Language and literacy: allegory, clause, index, neuter, scribe, simile
> Law: client, debenture, executor, gratis, legitimate, proviso
> Medicine: diaphragm, digit, dislocate, ligament, orbit, saliva
> Mineralogy: antimony, arsenic, chrysolite, garnet, lapis lazuli, mineral
> Religion: collect, diocese, lector, limbo, psalm, redemptor

The vast majority entered English through the written language, and were probably uncommon in speech. Some of the 'routine' elements of the liturgy – such as *pater noster* 'Our Father', *credo* 'I believe', or *confiteor* 'I confess' – would have had both a spoken and a written presence. Just a few may have come directly from spoken Latin: *benedicite* ('bless you'), perhaps, or the praise-word *alleluia*.

Not everything was domain-restricted. The period also saw the arrival of a large number of non-specific words. Nouns, as always, were in the majority: their generally abstract character is illustrated by *adoption, collision, colony, conflict, depression, exclamation,* and *impediment*. But there were significant numbers of adjectives and verbs: *communicative, compact, complete, effeminate, imaginary,* and *infirm; admit, combine, commit, conclude, import,* and *infect*. Many of the technical terms also developed more general senses: this is what happened to *equivalent, extravagant, implement, mediator, pauper,* and *persecutor,* for example. The broadening of meaning sometimes took place very quickly: *mediator* is found in the *Cursor Mundi* as a religious term *c.* 1300 (referring to Christ as the one who mediates between God and humanity), but as early as 1375 it is being recorded in a general sense ('go-between'). On the other hand, *extravagant* is first recorded in 1387, as a technical term from canon law, referring to a type of uncodified papal decree; its next recorded usage, in the general sense of 'straying, roaming', is not until Shakespeare – the 'extravagant spirit' of *Hamlet,* I.i.155. Other extensions of usage could take even longer: *implement* as a noun arrives in 1454; as a verb it does not appear until the early 1800s.

As in the case of French, the frequency with which Latin loanwords are used is very dependent on subject-matter. They are dispersed throughout Chaucer's *Treatise on the Astrolabe,* for example – *latitude, longitude, ascension, equinoxiall* 'equinoctial', *firmament, equaciouns* 'equations', *umbra* – doubtless adding to little Lewis' comprehension problem (p. 150). But there are very few in most fourteenth-century texts. They are sporadic in John of Trevisa's translation of *Polychronicon,* from which I have already quoted (p. 130, and see again p. 168): in the same paragraph of some 250 words we find just four Latinisms: *confederat, commyxstion* 'intermingling', *construe,* and *construccion* 'construction'. And they are hardly to be found in the lively colloquial exchanges between Satan, Jesus, the devils, and the biblical characters in *The Harrowing of Hell,* one of the early fifteenth-century York Mystery Plays. Despite using several Latin quotations, there are only two English Latinisms in over 400 lines: *obitte* ('dead', l. 269) and *sacrament* (l. 316). The patterns of future use are beginning to be laid down: the more formal or 'elevated' the language level, the more likely that it will contain words of Latin origin.

In due course, the term *aureate* would be used by the fifteenth-century poet John Lydgate to describe a style which attempted to emulate the great Classical writers, with intricate sentence patterns and erudite, euphonious vocabulary. He introduces it at the end of the opening sentence of the Prologue to his *Troy Book* – a huge work of over 30,000 lines commissioned by King Henry IV in 1412. Addressing Mars, he asks:

So be myn helpe in this grete nede
To do socour [help] my stile to directe
And of my penne the tracys [writing] to correcte
Whyche bareyn [empty] is of aureat lycour [golden fluid]
But [unless] in thi grace I fynde som favour
For to conveye it wyth thyn influence,
That stumbleth ay [always] for faute [lack] of eloquence
For to reherse or writen any word;
Now help, O Mars, that art of knyghthod lord
And hast of manhod the magnificence.

Those ten lines complete an elaborate 37-line sentence (see panel 7.6). Words borrowed directly from Latin are certainly in evidence: there are three just in

---

7.6 A Lydgate sentence

The reference to sentence construction above reminds us that language character, variation, and change are only partly to be identified with vocabulary. Grammar plays an important part, as also does pronunciation and spelling. The extract from John Lydgate is an illustration of the level of elaborate syntax which some writers were trying to achieve in the late Middle English period, and which was to become highly fashionable in the sixteenth century. But the true complexity can be seen only by examining an entire sentence. The opening sentence of the Prologue to the *Troy Book* is therefore laid out below in a way which demonstrates its internal structure. The line endings in the poem are marked by /.

The basic structure is simple: 'O Mars . . . Now . . . Help me . . .' (said three times). Within this outline, however, there is much complication, as one thought leads to a sub-thought, and then to another. It is impossible to read this sentence aloud and retain any sense of its overall structure; it far exceeds the normal processing ability of memory for language, and is at the opposite extreme from the kind of conversational discourse illustrated by the extract from Chaucer on p. 176. Parallel and subordinate constructions interweave in intricate ways – not always successfully, it has to be said, in that it is not always clear which parts relate to which other parts – and variations in word order, usually responding to the needs of the poetic metre, add a further complication. But the discipline imposed by the rhyming couplets and the metre generates a dynamic of its own which carries the reader along, regardless of the number and length of constructions. The technique is not far removed from the kind of 'ongoing sentence' typical of modern conversational storytelling, where people process the language 'a bit at a time'.[9]

O Myghty Mars, /
    that wyth thy sterne lyght / In armys hast the power and the myght /
    And named art from est [east] til occident / The myghty lorde, the god
        armypotent [omnipotent], /

That wyth schynyng of thy stremes rede [streams of red light] / By influence dost
the brydel lede / Of chevalry as sovereyn and patrown, /
  Ful hoot [hot] and drye of complexioun, /
  Irows and wood [angry and mad] and malencolyk /
  And of nature brent [hot] and coleryk, /
  Of colour schewyng lyche the fyré glede [like the burning coal], /
Whos feerce lokes [looks] ben [are] as ful of drede/ As the levene [lightning]
  that alyghteth [strikes] lowe / Down by the skye from Jubiteris bowe /
  (Thy stremes ben so passyng despitous [spiteful], / To loke upon, inly
    furious, /
  And causer art wyth thy fery bemys [fiery beams] / Of werre [war] and stryf
    in many sondry rewmys [realms]),
  Whos lordschype is most in Caprycorn /
    But in the Bole [Taurus] is thy power lorn [lost]
  And causer art of contek [anger] and of strif; /
Now for the love of Vulcanus wyf [wife] /
  Wyth whom whylom [once] thou wer at meschef take,
So helpe me now, only for hyr sake, /
  And for the love of thy Bellona /
    That wyth the [thee] dwellyth byyownd [beyond] Cirrea / In Lebyelonde
    [Libya] upon the sondes rede [red sands]; /
So be myn helpe in this grete nede /
  To do socour my stile to directe /
  And of my penne the tracys [writing] to correcte /
    Whyche bareyn is of aureat lycour /
    But [unless] in thi grace I fynde som favour /
      For to conveye it wyth thyn influence, /
That stumbleth ay for faute [lack] of eloquence /
    For to reherse or writen any word;
Now help, O Mars,
  that art of knyghthod lord /
  And hast of manhod the magnificence.

this short passage (*direct, correct, aureate*). In a few cases, Lydgate is also the
first recorded user of a Latinism: examples include *abortive, donative,* and
unrecured 'unalleviated'. However, most of the words that might be described as
'aureate' – such as *amypotent* 'omnipotent', *cristallyn* 'crystalline', *rethoricyens*
'rhetoricians', *enlumine* 'illuminate', and *magnificence* – although ultimately
derived from Latin, also had a history in Old French, and it is a matter of
speculation which etymological element would have been foremost in Lydgate's
linguistic intuition. The point is perhaps academic. The important issue is the
general effect, and here Lydgate's Latinate style proved to be distinctive and

influential, being emulated by Renaissance poets of the following century both in England and Scotland.

Although French and Latin were the major influences on English vocabulary in the Middle Ages, we must not forget that other foreign language sources were contributing to its growing lexical diversity. Chapter 3 has already described the way Scandinavian words had begun to surface in Middle English, and panel 7.7 provides a further illustration of the linguistic distance which by then existed between English speakers and their Danish predecessors. In addition we find a sprinkling of words from other European languages. Contact with the Netherlands, both abroad and as a result of Flemish settlement by weavers and farmers in England and Wales, brought in some Dutch words from as early as the end of the thirteenth century – *poll* 'head' was one of the first, and later borrowings included *boor, booze, bounce, dote, firkin, hobble, huckster, kit, sled, splint,* and *wainscot.* Maritime contacts brought in *buoy, deck, hoist, hoy, marline,* and *skipper. Boy,* a word of uncertain origin, is very likely to have come from the Low Countries, too, given that it is known from Old Frisian as *boi* in the sense of 'young gentleman'. Within the British Isles, Celtic words continued to provide a small but steady trickle: Welsh *crag* is recorded first in the *Cursor Mundi* (*c.* 1300); Irish *kern* (a type of foot-soldier) some fifty years later. Both Irish and Scottish forms of *lough/loch* appear in the fourteenth century. Scottish Gaelic words also include *mull* 'headland', *inch* 'small island', and *clan*. And Celtic words arrive from the Continent, too: *gravel, lawn, league, marl, quay/cay, truant, valet, varlet,* and *vassal* are some of the Gaulish words which first entered French and thereby came into English.

7.7 Much atdo

When people borrow words from a language they do not know, they sometimes analyse the borrowing wrongly. This is what happened with the word *ado*. In Old Norse, *at* was a preposition used with the infinitive form of a verb, equivalent to English *to*. It is recorded in English from the thirteenth century, turning up especially in the north. For example, it appears in *The Conspiracy*, one of the fifteenth-century Towneley cycle of mystery plays from Wakefield, Yorkshire (Towneley was the name of the family that long had possession of the manuscript). Jesus says to Peter at one point: *Take vp this clothe and let vs go, ffor we haue othere thyngys at do –* 'for we have other things to do' (l. 383). *At* was still being used in this way, in parts of the north-west, during the twentieth century, and may still be heard there.

In southern English the form developed differently. People heard *at do*, but did not recognize the two parts of the Old Norse construction. Because /t/ and /d/ are pronounced in the same part of the mouth, it was a natural process to run the sounds together, producing *ado*. It then passed into Standard English as a noun, in such phrases as *without more ado* and, most famously, in the name of Shakespeare's play.

Ado was not alone. The origins of the verb *thwart* lie in an Old Norse adjective *þverr*, meaning 'transverse, cross'. But the final *-r* in that word was the inflectional ending used along with masculine nouns; this ending was replaced by a *-t*, when the adjective was used with neuter nouns, producing *þvert*, and this is the form which came into English as *þwert*, later changing to *thwart*. Why the English adopted this form rather than the other is not clear – perhaps because the *-rr* form sounded more foreign – but what is plain is that they cannot have realized that it was an ending, for otherwise the word would have entered the language as *þver*, and we would be saying today *I thwarred his evil designs*.

We do quite often hear a similar sort of process in action when someone is learning a foreign language and fails to recognize the structure of a new word. Anyone learning English who failed to recognize the plural ending in *children*, for example, might end up saying *I gave it to a children*. But misanalysis of this kind is fairly unusual, as a source of loanwords.

French found itself in the position of being a relay language very often during the Middle Ages. In fact it is rare to find words coming into English from other languages without some evidence of French influence en route – as in the case of *cork*, from Spanish, and a few dozen Greek words which entered English via Latin (such as *agony, asylum, echo, history*, and *mechanic*). It is not until the sixteenth century, following the growth in Continental travel and trade, an increased awareness of European literature and the Italian Renaissance, and a renewed interest in Classical authors, that we find words from a range of other languages coming into English directly (p. 300). In the Middle English period, virtually all loanwords from languages other than French and Latin were French-mediated. These included words from the other Romance languages: *marmalade* from Portuguese; *cordwain* from Spanish; *alarm, bark, brigand, florin, million*, and *alarm* (*all' arme* 'to arms!') from Italian. *Sable* arrived from Russian. *Bible, character, climate, fantasy, horizon, rheumatic, rhubarb, treacle*, and *tragedy* arrived from Greek. A large number came from the Middle East. From Arabic we find a virtual alphabet of forms, from *admiral* to *zenith* – *amber, azimuth, caliph, cotton, elixir, hazard, lute, mattress, mosque, saffron, syrup*. The distinctive *al-* forms begin to appear: *alchemy, alembic, almanac*. And from Persian we find *azure, mummy, scarlet*, and *taffeta*, as well as several terms to do with the game of chess: *check, rook, checkmate* – and *chess* itself. Some words had travelled a very long way before eventually reaching France and then Britain. *Arsenic* had at least three relay languages: first known in Persian, it reaches English via Greek, Latin, and Old French.

When we combine all these sources of vocabulary, we begin to get a sense of the scale of the lexical change that had taken place during the Middle Ages. At the end of the Old English period the size of the lexicon stood at something over 50,000 different words. Many words then fell out of use, but the rate of replacement was such that by the end of the Middle English period we see this total doubled; and, as we shall see (p. 317), the Early Modern English period would more than double it again. By 1450, something like half of the available word stock was non-Germanic, and half of the Germanic words were not Old English but Old Norse. Thanks to the nature of English grammar, which continued to give a high profile to such words as *the*, *of*, *and*, and *have*, the fundamental Anglo-Saxon character of the language was maintained. And in vocabulary, too, if we were to order Middle English words in terms of their frequency of use, we would find that around half of the most commonly used words were from Old English. Things have not changed. In one modern frequency list of the top 100 words in American written English, virtually all the grammatical words (*the*, *of*, *and*, *to*, etc. – the exceptions are listed on pp. 75–7) and all of the content words (*say*, *only*, *other*, *new*, *first*, *now*, *time*, *like*, *man*, *even*, *make*, *also*, *year*, *way*, *well*) are from Old English. The first French word occurs only at number 105 (*just*).[10]

Such statistics are interesting, but they tell us nothing about the significance of what was going on. The real importance of the Middle English period was the way in which this additional vocabulary became the primary means of introducing new concepts and new domains of discourse into the language, as well as a means of giving novel ways of expression to familiar concepts within old domains of discourse. In a word, the period was offering people a much greater linguistic *choice*. In 1200, people could only *ask*; by 1500 they could *question* (from French) and *interrogate* (from Latin) as well. What could be done with such newfound linguistic opportunities? During Middle English we see the evolution of a language which is increasingly exploiting the potentialities of regional, social, and stylistic variation.

Interlude 7
The first dialect story

There are several regional dialect features in Old English, as we have seen in Chapter 1, but when they appear they are incidental to the subject-matter. They do no more than reflect the regional background of the writer. If we see some features of the Northumbrian dialect, for example, we assume they are there because the scribe was Northumbrian. Today, when we see dialect features in a text, we usually find them being used for a different reason. We expect a novelist, for example, writing about a love affair between an American and a Scot, and where the contrast between their backgrounds is part of the plot, to represent their regional identities by choosing appropriate language. This contrastive use of dialect, to express character, becomes a major element in the history of English literature, and is thus an important part of the argument of this book (Chapter 19). So when did it first appear?

It seems to be in one of Chaucer's *Canterbury Tales*. The various characters in the tales come from all walks of life and regional backgrounds, from within England and abroad, but in only one story do they talk as if they do – in *The Reeve's Tale* (in the Middle Ages, a reeve was an official involved in the administration of an estate). Osewold the Reeve tells the story of how two Cambridge undergraduates, John and Aleyn, get revenge on Symkyn (a diminutive form of Simond), a miller who has been stealing corn belonging to their college. They arrive at the mill with their corn, intending to keep a careful watch on it as it is being ground; but Symkyn unties their horse's bridle, and it runs off. The students chase it, but by the time they catch it the miller has managed to steal some corn. Because it is now late at night, they stay at the mill, and find themselves sleeping in the same room as Symkyn, his wife, their six-month-old baby (who is in a cot at the foot of the miller's bed), and their twenty-year-old daughter. During the night, Aleyn seduces the daughter, who tells him where the stolen corn is stored. John, envious of Aleyn's success, then decides to seduce the wife. He moves the cot to the foot of his own bed; the wife pays a visit to the lavatory; and when she returns feels her way to the cot in the dark, thereby getting into John's bed. In the best manner of bedroom farces, Aleyn then tries to find his way back to his own bed, thinks the bed without the cot is his own, and gets into bed with Symkyn. Thinking Symkyn is John, he tells him of his success with the daughter. Symkyn gets up in a fury and starts to beat Aleyn, but trips and falls on top of his wife. She wakes in a panic, looks for a staff in the melee, but by mistake hits her husband on the head. The students then beat Symkyn, find their stolen corn, and leave in triumph.

We are not told very much about the students' background other than they are from a town 'fer [far] in the north' called Strother. No one has been able to identify a real-world Strother, though the name is known – there was a Castle Strother in Northumberland, and there still is a Strothers Dale, south of the River Tyne – but Chaucer certainly makes them talk in a Northern way, and some scholars have concluded on the basis of the dialect features represented that the town must have been somewhere in the north-east. The students are given only just under a hundred lines of speech, but several features are used repeatedly. In pronunciation, the most noticeable feature is that several words which in the south would have been written with an *o* or *oo* appear with an *a* or *aa*. In the text of the tale the contrast is often striking, as we find the Northern form in the speech of the students and the Southern form in the speech of Symkyn and his family, as well as in the voice of the narrator, the Reeve (see panel 7.8). (Line numbers follow the edition of the *Tales* by F. N. Robinson.)

7.8 A piece of north–south dialogue

Text	Literal translation
Aleyn spak first, 'Al hayl, Symond, y-fayth!	Aleyn spoke first, 'All hail, Symond, in faith!
Hou fares thy faire doghter and thy wyf?'	How fares thy fair daughter and thy wife?'
'Aleyn, welcome,' quod Symkyn, 'by my lyf!	'Aleyn, welcome,' said Symkyn, 'by my life!
And John also, how now, what do ye heer?'	And John also, how now, what do you here?'
'Symond,' quod John, 'by God, nede has na peer.	'Symond,' said John, 'by God, need has no equal.
Hym boes serve hymself that has na swayn,	It behoves him serve himself that has no servant,
Or elles he is a fool, as clerkes sayn.	Or else he is a fool, as scholars say.
Oure manciple, I hope he wil be deed,	Our catering officer, I think he will be dead,
Swa werkes ay the wanges in his heed;	So ache ever the molar teeth in his head;

And forthy is I come, and eek Alayn,	And therefore am I come, and also Aleyn,
To grynde oure corn and carie it ham agayn;	To grind our corn and carry it home again;
I pray yow spede us heythen that ye may.'	I pray you help us hence as soon as you can.'
'It shal be doon,' quod Symkyn, 'by my fay!	'It shall be done,' said Symkyn, 'by my faith!
What wol ye doon whil that it is in hande?'	What will you do while it is in hand?'
'By God, right by the hopur wil I stande,'	'By God, right by the hopper will I stand,'
Quod John, 'and se howgates the corn gas in.	Said John, 'and see how the corn goes in.
Yet saugh I nevere, by my fader kyn,	Yet saw I never, by my father's kin,
How that the hopur wagges til and fra.'	How the hopper wags to and fro.'

(ll. 4,022–39)

Word	Aleyn / John	Reeve	Symkyn, wife, daughter
both	bathe l. 4,087	bothe l. 4,076	
fro	fra l. 4,039	fro l. 3,921	
go	ga l. 4,102	gon l. 4,064	go l. 4,081
goes	gas l. 4,037	goth l. 4,018	goth l. 4,080
		gooth l. 3,922	gooth l. 4,098
no	na l. 4,026	no l. 4,020	no l. 4,048
so	swa l. 4,030		so l. 4,082
two	twa l. 4,129	two l. 3,969	
who	wha l. 4,073	who l. 4,300	who l. 4,271

We also find in this edition 'bones' as *banes* (l. 4,073), 'atones' as *atanes* (l. 4,074, 'at once'), 'home' as *ham* (l. 4,032), 'long' as *lange* (l. 4,175), 'own' as *awen* (l. 4,239), 'roe' as *raa* (l. 4,086), 'soul' as both *sale* (l. 4,187) and *saule* (l. 4,263), 'song' as *sang* (l. 4,170), 'take' as *taa* (l. 4,129), 'told' as *tald* (l. 4,207), and 'wrongly' as *wrang* (l. 4,252). Some manuscripts have other words in Northern dialect. The representation of the dialect is not entirely consistent: the word for 'know', *wot*, appears in the students' speech both as *waat* (Northern) in l. 4,086 and as *woot* (Southern) in l. 4,255; the word for 'also' appears both as *alswa* (Northern) in l. 4,086 and as *also* (Southern) in l. 4,256 – the latter probably because the word had to rhyme with *mysgo* in the previous line.

As several of these pronunciations appear a number of times, the effect is quite marked. But they are reinforced by an even more noticeable effect: the use of distinctively Northern grammatical features. The Reeve consistently uses a *-th* ending for the third-person singular form of the present tense, whereas the students almost always use the *-s* ending (p. 218; there is just one exception, in this edition: l. 4,256, where Aleyn says *lith* 'lies'). The tale begins (l. 3,921): *At Trumpyngtoun, nat fer fro Cantebrigge, / Ther gooth a brook, and over that a brigge* ('At Trumpington, not far from Cambridge, / There goes a brook, and over that a bridge'); but John tells the miller that he wants to see how *the corn gas* [goes] *in* (l. 4,037). The contrast is seen in other places: John uses *has* (l. 4,026), whereas the Reeve uses *hath* (l. 4,059); Aleyn uses *says* (l. 4,180), whereas the Reeve uses *speketh* (l. 4,151). And several other verbs are shown with the Northern ending, such as *brynges* (l. 4,130), *falles* (l. 4,042), *fyndes* (l. 4,130), *makes* (l. 4,254), and *wagges* (l. 4,039). The Reeve, by contrast, uses such forms as *gynneth* (l. 4,064, 'begins') and *looketh* (l. 4,059). The *-s* ending also turns up in some third-person plural forms. Aleyn says *fares* (l. 4,023), and John says *werkes* (l. 4,030); but the other characters and the Reeve use the Southern ending, which was *-e*, *-en*, or *-n* at the time, as in *make* (l. 4,051), *rennen* (l. 4,100, 'run'), and *han* (l. 4,090, 'have').

The forms of the verb *to be* are always dialect markers of some significance, because of their frequency (p. 44). Aleyn tells John: *I is as ille a millere as ar ye* (l. 4,045, 'I am as bad a miller as you are'), where we see two such forms, *I is* and *ye ar*, both Northern; probable Southern forms would have been *I am* and *ye ben* (or *been*), respectively. A little later, John uses *are* in *Now are we dryve til hethyng* (l. 4,110, 'Now are we brought into contempt'). By contrast, the Southern plural form is seen in the Reeve's *For jalous folk ben perilous everemo* (l. 3,961, 'For jealous people are always dangerous'). There are dialectal forms of verb past participles, too (as in Modern English *I have **walked**, They were **seen***). In Southern speech these usually appeared with a *y-* prefix, as in *ymaked* (l. 4,245), and often without an *-n* ending, as in *yronne* (l. 4,090, 'run'). However, Aleyn and John use such forms as *born* (l. 4,109), *lorn* (l. 4,073, 'lost'), *stoln* (l. 4,183), and *payen* (l. 4,133), without the *y-* and with a final *-n*. Again, there is not total consistency, as Aleyn uses *yshapen* at one point (l. 4,179). Some irregular verbs have dialect variants also, as in *geen* 'gone' (l. 4,078) instead of Southern *gon*, and *pit* instead of *put* (l. 4,088).

Some of the grammatical words are shown with Northern variants. For example, the Reeve says *hir corn* (l. 4,008, 'their corn') and Symkyn *hir art* (l. 4,056, 'their art'), both still using the Southern form derived from Old English (p. 76); but Aleyn talks about *thair bodyes* (l. 4,172, 'their bodies'), using the Norse form (which eventually became standard). Similarly, the Reeve says *to mille* (l. 4,008) and Symkyn *to the wolf* (l. 4,055), but John says *til scorn* (l. 4,110) – and also *til and fra* 'to and fro' (l. 4,039). The Reeve also says *no wyf* (l. 3,947, 'no wife') and Symkyn *no man* (l. 4,048), but Aleyn says *neen amendement* (l. 4,185, 'no amends'). *Ymel* (l. 4,171) is a Northern preposition, equivalent to Southern *among*. And there are a few other grammatical differences:

Word	Aleyn / John	Reeve	Symkyn, wife, daughter
if	gif l. 4,181	if l. 3,959	if l. 4,120
shall	sal l. 4,043	shal l. 4,321	shal l. 4,034
such	swilk l. 4,171	swich l. 4,318	swich l. 4,121
	slyk l. 4,130		
which	whilk l. 4,078	whiche l. 3,923	which l. 4,246

Again, there is a certain amount of inconsistency in the manuscripts: in this edition, *sal* turns up as *shal* in the students' speech at one point (l. 4,102).

The students also use some Northern vocabulary, though it is often impossible to be sure how far such words were in fact restricted to the north. Examples include *hayl* 'luck' (l. 4,022), *heythen* 'hence' (l. 4,033), *ilhayl* 'bad luck' (l. 4,089), *fonne* 'fool' (l. 4,089), *hethyng* 'scorn' (l. 4,110), *il* 'bad' (l. 4,184), and *wrang* (l. 4,252). These all come from Old Norse, originating in the settlement of Northumbria by the Danes (p. 51), but because the Danelaw covered such an extensive area, it is probable that at least some of these words were known further south – as in the case of *swayn* 'servant' (l. 4,027), *wight* 'active' (l. 4,086), and *lathe* 'barn' (l. 4,088), which turn up in other Middle English texts without any obvious Northern associations.

When we list all the dialect features – phonological, grammatical, and lexical – we find about 125 of them, averaging over one per line of student speech. Northern English is very evident in the way they talk. But a word of caution has to be inserted at this point. Scholars who have examined the eighty or so manuscript texts of Chaucer have noted that the number of Northern features varies from text to text. Some scribes doubtless did not notice that the features were Northern, thought them errors, and replaced them by 'correct' Southern forms. But in several manuscripts the movement is in the other direction. Here the scribes must have noticed that Chaucer was attempting to represent dialect speech, and decided to 'help him out', adding Northernisms that they were aware of. This is the most likely explanation, for example, of the use of *boes* 'behoves, is fitting', which is found in Robinson's edition, though it is not in the oldest manuscript of the *Tales*, the Hengwrt manuscript, where the word appears as *bihoues*. Similarly, John uses a distinctively Northern form of 'how' when he says *wil I . . . se howgates the corn gas in* (l. 4,037, 'I will . . . see how the corn goes in'), whereas Aleyn says *wil I . . . se how that the mele falles doun* (l. 4,042, 'I will . . . see how the meal falls down'). In the Hengwrt manuscript, both students use *how*.[11]

The significance of Chaucer's use of these dialect features, however, extends well beyond the range and frequency of their use. What is really interesting is what they suggest about his attitude towards the dialect. In Modern English, we are used to seeing regional dialects criticized and condemned (p. 524), and the first signs of these attitudes were already present in Middle English. In the 1387 translation of Ranulph Higden's *Polychronicon* (p. 129), we read: 'All the language of the Northumbrians, and especially at York, is so harsh, piercing, and grating, and formless, that we Southern men may hardly understand it.' And he adds, perceptively: 'I believe that this is because they are near to strange men and foreigners, who speak in a foreign tongue, and also because the kings of England always dwell far away from that part of the country.' But there is none of this sense of disapproval or inferiority in the Chaucer story. Here, regional dialect speech is given to two educated young men, students at Cambridge. They are not rustics. Indeed, if anyone appears to be rustic and provincial, at least in attitude, it is Symkyn himself – but he speaks in a Southern way. At no point do the miller, his wife and daughter, or the tale-teller poke fun at the students' manner of speech. Symkyn may be prejudiced about students – he plainly doesn't like their intellectual ideas very much ('the greatest clerks are not the wisest men', he says at one point, l. 4,054) – but he doesn't display any prejudice about their speech. Moreover, the Northern speakers come out on top, in this tale. Dialect wins.

We must conclude that the regional dialect features in this story are not carrying any loaded message. They are not part of any satire at the expense of the characters. Nor are they carrying any kind of hidden agenda, as they would in an Early Modern English tale, where – as later examples will show (p. 345) – regional dialect speakers in a story are often uneducated, immoral, or criminal. The dialect features are simply characterizing the speakers. There is no more to say.

The Reeve's Tale is a fine example of dialect democracy. If only things had stayed that way.

Chapter 8 Evolving variation

An emerging theme of the Middle English period is the way writers notice that the English language is evolving and begin to talk about it. Linguistic discussion in Old English, insofar as it existed at all, was Latin-orientated, focusing on Latin grammar, the nature of translation, the use of Latinate rhetorical figures, and the differences between Latin and English style. It is possible to see, from the range of stylistic variation in Old English texts (Chapter 4), that some authors were beginning to explore the expressive potential of their language; their writing plainly manifests a growing linguistic awareness. But there is very little evidence of a corresponding *metalinguistic* awareness. Only in the occasional reflection, notably by Ælfric (p. 98), do we see writers taking a step back and reflecting on what it is they and their contemporaries are doing with – or to – the language. Nor was there much change after the Conquest, despite increasing comment being made about the relative merits of English and French (Chapter 6). Remarks about the way English was developing do not appear until the end of the fourteenth century; and when they do, the focus is almost entirely to do with the problems of coping with a new sense of regional and social variation as manifested in the proliferating domains of English discourse.

A domain of discourse is a distinctive manner of expression reflecting the subject-matter and social context which bring a group of people together. Several such domains have already been encountered in earlier chapters. Some have their origins in regional or ethnic groupings, or in distinctions of social class, and these are expressed through the varieties known as *dialects*. Others have their origins in occupational activities – such as law, religion, political administration, medicine, farming, sailing, and cooking. In each case we find the evolution of a variety of language which partly reflects the domain's subject-matter (the 'jargon'), partly the social context in which the people find them-selves (e.g., formal or informal, professional or amateur, regulated or unregulated), and partly the nature of the users (e.g., male or female, old or young, educated or uneducated). Any aspect of language structure can function as a distinguishing feature of a domain – a particular set of sounds, spellings, grammatical patterns, or words. In practice, the most noticeable features, and the ones which elicit the most frequent reactions, are the words, because there are so many of them. Linguistic change is always easiest to observe in the lexicon – that is why so much attention has been paid in previous chapters to vocabulary. Although pronunciation and grammar contribute greatly to the underlying identity of a domain, and are important dimensions of change during the Middle English period (p. 117), it is the vocabulary which proves to be the most distinctive marker, and the area which therefore attracts most comment by the writers of the period.

Chaucer was one of the first to comment – or, at least, his characters were – and in each case the observation is to do with the nature of a domain's vocabulary. Scholarly nomenclature, in particular, tends to get short shrift. In *The Franklin's Tale* (l. 1,266) the narrator – attempting to explain the way a magician was going to perform an illusion – is quite open about his ignorance: *I ne kan no termes of astrologye* – 'I'm not familiar with any astrological terms'. In *The Merchant's Tale* (l. 1,567), sixty-year-old January, looking for a wife, asks advice of his two brothers. One of them makes a point by quoting the Roman philosopher Seneca [*Senek*] – which greatly upsets the old man:

> Straw for thy Senek, and for thy proverbes!
> I counte nat a panyer ful of herbes
> Of scole-termes.

School-words can't be valued as much as a basketful of herbs, he says; or, as nineteenth-century Americans would later say, 'They 'ain't wuth a hill of beans!'[1]

The Shipman, in the Epilogue to *The Man of Law's Tale* (l. 1,188), is another who has little time for scholarly jargon. He promises to tell his tale,

> But it schal not ben [be] of philosophie,
> Ne phisylas, ne termes queinte of lawe.
> Ther is but litel Latyn in my mawe! [stomach]

He is well aware of the way Latin words characterize the discourse of philosophy, and knows his stylistic limitations. Indeed, he may already have overreached himself in his use of *phisylas*: although the meaning of this word is unclear – some think it is a scribal corruption of a legal or medical term – it is more likely, given Chaucer's acute sense of character, that the Shipman was trying to say *physick* and getting it wrong. He would not have been the first to muddle his terminology; Harry Bailey the Host does so, too. At one point (Introduction to *The Pardoner's Tale*, l. 304), he wishes the Physician well, attempts the names of several medical implements, then realizes he may have made a mess of it:

Seyde I nat wel? I kan nat speke in terme;
But wel I woot [know] thou doost myn herte to erme [grieve],
That I almoost have caught a cardynacle.

I cannot speak with formal accuracy, he says, but your sad tale has got to me so much that I have almost had a heart attack. He is telling the truth, for *cardynacle* seems to be a mixture of the unfamiliar *cardiacle* (from Latin *cardiaca*, a short form of *cardiaca passio*, 'cardiac passion' , referring to heartburn or palpitations) and the well-known *cardinal*. It is one of the first recorded English malapropisms.

The Shipman's use of the word *quaint* is an interesting indication of stylistic awareness. A recent arrival from French, in the late fourteenth century, the word did not have the often patronizing modern sense of something being cutely attractive in an old-fashioned way. 'Quaint law terms' would have referred to words which were elegant and refined, ingeniously or carefully constructed, perhaps also unfamiliar or strange in appearance. The Canon's Yeoman uses the word, too (*The Canon's Yeoman's Tale*, l. 751). His employer was evidently an alchemist as well as a cleric, but though the subject is a closed book to him – 'With this Channon I dwelt have seven yeer, / And of his science am I never the neer' – he is aware of the obfuscating power of technical terminology, and how this can make people seem 'wonderfully wise':

we semen wonder wise,
Oure termes been so clergial and so queynte.

Chaucer's is the first recorded usage of *clergial*, meaning 'clerkly, scholarly'. The Yeoman has none the less picked up a great deal of terminology from his employer; he can certainly make himself *sound* like an alchemist, as can be seen during his tale, when he is describing what is in their laboratory (l. 790):

As boole armonyak, verdegrees, boras,
And sondry vessels maad of erthe and glas,
Oure urynales and oure descensories,
Violes, crosletz, and sublymatories,
Cucurbites and alambikes eek,
And othere swiche . . .

There is no point in glossing all the terms, for they are as technical today as they would have been then: *bole armeniac*, a type of medicinal clay, *verdegris* and *borax*. *Urinal* is deceptive: a glass used for making solutions. *Descensories*, *sublymatories*, *cucurbites*, and *alembics* are all vessels used in distillation or sublimation. A *croslet* is a crucible.

Quaint these words are indeed, and hardly the sort of thing to be used outside of their proper domain. Certainly it would be most inappropriate to use such words in a love letter. It might be thought unlikely that anyone would ever want to, but perhaps in an age when stylistic norms were evolving, the possibility was real enough (and in a later metaphysical age would become a reality). At any rate, Pandarus thinks it worth while drawing Troilus' attention to the point when advising him how to write a letter to Criseyde (*Troilus and Criseyde*, Book II, l. 1,037):

> Ne jompre [jumble] ek [also] no discordant thyng yfeere [together]
> As thus, to usen termes of phisik
> In loves termes; hold of thi matere
> The forme alwey, and do that it be lik [like].

His advice: don't use hard words, and make the form always suit the content.

Pandarus gives the impression that he and Troilus are sufficiently aware of the nature of medical terms that they could have used them if they had wanted to. And this is certainly the impression given by the eagle in Chaucer's dream, reported in *The House of Fame* (l. 854), who has just made, as he thinks, a convincing point to the author, and done so in straightforward language:

> Have y [I] not preved [proved] thus symply,
> Without any subtilite
> Of speche, or gret prolixite
> Of termes of philosophie,
> Of figures of poetrie,
> Or colours of rethorike?
> Pardee [by God], hit oughte the [thee] to lyke!
> For hard langage and hard matere [subject-matter]
> Ys encombrous [cumbersome] for to here
> Attones [at the same time]

His advice: keep the words simple if there is a difficult thought to be expressed. The eagle should be the mascot of the Plain English Campaign.

These quotations demonstrate that a sense of the linguistic norms associated with different specialist domains was growing, as well as an associated readiness to disparage professional jargon. At the same time, we can find evidence of an awareness of other, more general stylistic norms, unrelated to individual professions. The distinction between poetry and prose is one such norm. At one point the Host interrupts Chaucer himself, in the middle of a rhyming story about Sir Thopas, and criticizes his *drasty* [worthless] *speche*: *Thy drasty rymyng is nat woorth a toord!*, he says (l. 930), and suggests he start again *in prose somwhat*. The Parson concurs in his Prologue (l. 46) – *I wol yow telle a myrie tale in prose* – as does the Man of Law, in the preamble to his own tale (l. 96): *I speke in prose*. A little earlier, in apologizing for his difficulty in finding a subject to talk about, the Man of Law draws attention to the presence of another general stylistic dimension: contemporary vs archaic language (l. 46). What's the point in trying to find a good story, he says, when Chaucer – notwithstanding his many faults as a writer – has already told them all in an old-fashioned way?

> I kan right now no thrifty [serviceable] tale seyn [tell]
> That Chaucer, thogh he kan but lewedly [badly]
> On metres and on rymyng craftily,
> Hath seyd hem [them] in swich [such] Englissh as he kan
> Of olde tyme, as knoweth many a man;

He adds, with tongue in cheek:

> And if he have noght seyd hem, leve [dear] brother,
> In o [one] book, he hath seyd hem in another.

With so much literature around, readers must have had a sophisticated intuition about the character of 'old-time' language.

The new varieties appearing in Middle English are not totally different from each other in the words they use. Then as now, a scholarly variety made use of a large number of words of a generally intellectual kind that had no particular relation to the specialist content of the domain – words like *accord*, *assent*, *character*, *convey*, *maintain*, *notable*, and *portray* – and in due course, many of these words (at least, in some of their senses) became part of the everyday language of educated people. Indeed, it was the use of vocabulary which, at the time, distinguished an educated from an uneducated person. In modern times, we can tell that someone has an educated background if they use Standard English (p. 6); but in the fourteenth century there was no Standard English, and regional accents and dialects were heard in all walks of life. How, then, could you show you were 'a cut above the rest'? By using high-sounding words. This is the linguistic message we can extract from an account such as the one we read a century later in Thomas Malory's *Morte Darthur* (Book VIII, Chapter 3), describing the way Sir Tristram grows to adulthood:

> And after, as he grew in might and strength, he laboured ever in hunting and in hawking, so that never gentleman more, that ever we heard read of. And as the book saith, he began good measures of blowing of beasts of venery [hunting], and beasts of chase, and all manner of vermin [wild beasts], and all these terms we have yet of hawking and hunting. And therefore the book of venery, of hawking, and hunting, is called the book of Sir Tristram. Wherefore, as meseemeth, all gentlemen that bear old arms ought of right to honour Sir Tristram for the goodly

terms that gentlemen have and use, and shall to the day of doom, that thereby in a manner all men of worship may dissever [distinguish] a gentleman from a yeoman, and from a yeoman a villain [villein].

The point is clear: it is by the use of 'goodly terms' that you can recognize someone as a gentleman.

Middle English, accordingly, saw the emergence of a language which was able to operate at two stylistic levels (see panel 8.1). At one extreme there was a learnèd, literary style, typically formal and elaborate, characterized by a lexicon of French and Latin origin, and employed by the aristocratic and well

---

8.1 Words seemly or boistous

Thomas Usk, writing at the same time as Chaucer, addresses the two-level issue directly in the opening lines of his Prologue to *The Testament of Love*. Although written in 1384–5, the first text we have of it dates from 1532, when it was included by mistake in a collected edition of Chaucer by a member of Henry VIII's household, William Thynne. Usk knows about learnèd styles of writing: he will have none of them. There will be no embellished rhetoric (*semelych colours*) in his writing – just straightforward, down-to-earth speech (*rude wordes and boystous*). He wants ordinary people to understand him. Only plain English, he says, will 'pierce the heart to the innermost point':

> Many men there ben [be] that with eeres openly sprad [spread] so moche swalowen the delyciousnesse of jestes and of ryme by queynt knyttyng coloures [strange complicated rhetorical figures] that of the goodnesse or of the badnesse of the sentence take they lytel hede [heed] or els none. Sothely [in truth], dul wytte and a thoughtful soule so sore have myned [undermined] and graffed in [dug a grave in] my spyrites that suche craft of endytyng [composition] wol not ben of myn acqueyntaunce. And, for [because] rude wordes and boystous, percen [pierce] the herte of the herer to the inrest [innermost] poynte and planten there the sentence [meaning] of thynges, so that with lytel helpe it is able to spring [grow], this boke, that nothyng hath of the great floode of wyt ne of semelych colours, is dolven [cultivated] with rude wordes and boystous, and so drawe togyder to maken the catchers [audience] therof ben the more redy to hent sentence [grasp the meaning].

He draws a striking analogy between language and different styles of visual art:

> Some men there ben [be] that peynten with colours ryche and some with vers [verse] as with red ynke and some with coles [charcoal] and chalke; and yet is there good matere [content] to the leude [lay] people of thilke [the same] chalky purtreyture [portraiture], as hem [they] thynketh for the tyme; and afterwarde the syght of the better colours yeven [given] to hem more joye for the first leudenesse [former lack of skill].

It is a rather backhanded compliment: ordinary speech is good for you, but only because it will help you to appreciate a more richly coloured style if you manage to improve yourself. *Leude leudenesse commendeth*, he adds: 'The uneducated approve of uncultured matters.'

In actual fact, Usk's English was nowhere near what we might conceive of as 'lewed' speech. Here are the opening lines of *The Testament of Love*:

> Alas, Fortune, alas; I that somtyme in delycyous houres was wont to enjoy blysful stoundes [times] am nowe dryve [driven] by unhappy hevynesse [sadness] to bewayle my sondrye yvels [sundry evils] in tene [sorrow]. Trewly, I leve [believe] in myn herte is writte of perdurable [everlasting] letters al the entencyons [notions] of lamentacion that nowe ben ynempned [named], for any maner disease outwarde in sobbyng maner sheweth sorowful yexynge [distress] from within.

Perdurable letters is a boistous style? *Entencyons of lamentacion* lewed? I think not.

---

educated; at the other, there was an everyday, popular style, typically informal and casual, full of words with Germanic roots, and used by ordinary folk.[2] It is essentially the opposition noted in Chapter 6 between 'high' and 'low', *lered* and *lewed* ['learnèd and unlearnèd'], though now realized through bidialectism rather than through bilingualism. The phrase *lered and lewed* (or *lewed and clerks*) turns up from the very beginning of the period, in Orrm and Layamon, and continues well into the sixteenth century. It was a distinction which had been hinted at in Old English (p. 98), but the shortage of texts there made it difficult to draw firm stylistic conclusions. In Middle English, by contrast, in addition to the metalinguistic observations of the writers (and their characters), there is a wealth of material to demonstrate the widespread presence of these two general levels of style. Both were idealizations, to some degree. The 'lered' level would have been full of terms that even the supposedly learnèd would not have fully understood. This is very much the impression given by Thomas Usk, in his Prologue to *The Testament of Love*:

> many termes there ben in Englysshe whiche unneth [hardly] we Englysshmen connen declare the knowlegynge [comprehension]; ... the understandyng of Englysshmen wol not stretche to the privy [peculiar] termes in Frenche whatsoever we bosten [boast] of straunge langage.

And the 'lewed' level would have been some distance removed from the realities of medieval colloquial English. This is the greater problem, in fact. Because our only evidence comes via the medium of writing, we shall never know what the most colloquial varieties of English were. There are, however, some hints to be obtained from the writing of a number of authors.

Here, Chaucer ranks supreme. His contemporaries found his ability to handle the 'lered' varieties of English particularly impressive. John Lydgate sums it up in a parenthetic piece of praise in the middle of Book III of his *Troy Book* (l. 4,237):

For he owre Englishe gilte [gilded] with his sawes,
Rude [unpolished] and boistous [rough] firste be olde dawes [days],
That was ful fer [far] from al perfeccioun
And but of litel reputacioun,
Til that he cam and thorugh his poetrie
Gan [began] oure tonge firste to magnifie
And adourne it with his elloquence . . .

The language was being magnified and adorned with eloquence. Caxton would reiterate the point, when he published Chaucer a century later. It was an eloquence which gives us an insight into both formal and informal upper-class speech – the formal represented by elegantly elaborated descriptions, the informal by conversational exchanges between learnèd individuals – in this case, an author and a bird. Here is a piece of dialogue between Chaucer and an upper-class (a companion of Jupiter, after all) eagle who has visited him in a dream (*The House of Fame*, l. 991):

With that this egle gan to crye,
'Lat [let] be,' quod he, 'thy fantasye!
Wilt thou lere [learn] of sterres [stars] aught?'
'Nay, certeynly,' quod y, 'ryght naught.'
'And why?' 'For y am now to [too] old.'
'Elles I wolde the [thee] have told,'
Quod he, 'the sterres names, lo,
And al the hevenes sygnes therto,
And which they ben [be].' 'No fors [no matter],' quod y.
'Yis, pardee [by God]!' quod he; 'wostow [do you know] why?'

And he goes on to tell him. There is no denying the informal tone – *lat be, ryght naught, no fors, pardee* – the last reminiscent of other French-derived fashionable expressions of the period, such as *ma foy* and *grant mercy*. And it is a striking contrast with other aspects of the eagle's style – a bird that is capable of rhyming *dissymulacions* with *reparacions*, and *renovelaunces* with *aqueyntaunces*. The eagle is a powerful language-user, because he is in command of both styles: he is conversant with the language of the divine court, for he obeys Jupiter's commands; but he can 'speak down-market' when he has to: 'I can / Lewedly to a lewed man / Speke' (l. 865). The eagle has done what all present-day English language-learners need to do: achieve and be proud of a bidialectal ability. It is an important principle to which I shall return in the final chapter. The eagle could be a mascot for sociolinguists, too.

Chaucer was equally impressive in his representation of informal speech at the lower end of the social scale. Throughout *The Canterbury Tales*, in particular, we find a regular sprinkling of colloquialisms in the speech of some of the characters, especially the 'rude speche and boold' of the Host.[3] We hear a great deal of swearing, especially of a religious kind – *by my fay*, *a Goddes name*, *by Seynt Ronyon*. Several dismissive idioms reflect an everyday working-class world: *I counte hym nat a flye*, *I rekke* [reckon] *nat a bene*, *straw for your gentilnesse!* Narratives are interrupted by colloquial phrases, some of which have a very modern ring about them – *ye woot wel what I mene* ('know what I mean?'), *but wyte ye what* ('you know what?'). Interjections occur, such as *allas* and *weylaway*. There is even a feminine giggle: *tehee*.[4] At the same time, it has to be acknowledged that we do not know just how class-related any of these usages were. Several of the colloquial interpolations – such as *ywys* ('indeed'), *God woot* ('God knows!') and *bishrewe me* – could have been used by people from any social background. An informal discourse marker such as *well* (as in '*Well*,' *said she* . . .) is used by such diverse characters as old January in *The Merchant's Tale*, the Manciple, Pandarus, Criseyde, and the Host (see Interlude 8, p. 190). The same point applies to the many 'literary colloquialisms', such as *for the nonce*, *shortly for to say*, and *as I guess*. These formulaic units provide a convenient rhyme or complete the rhythm of a line, and can turn up in the speech of virtually anybody.

Chaucer is aware of what he is doing. At the very beginning of the *Tales*, after introducing the pilgrims, he promises to tell their stories, and – bearing in mind that there is probably going to be some strong or risqué language – says he will *speke hir* [their] *wordes proprely* (*General Prologue*, l. 729). He is going to 'tell it as it is', and hopes that the company will not think badly of him for doing so. He justifies his position in an aphorism: *The wordes moote be cosyn to the dede* (l. 742): 'the words must be cousin to the deed'. Everyone seems happy with this. Even in the rudest story, *The Miller's Tale* (ll. 3,734, 3,810), where characters fart noisily, where an insistent suitor is fooled by his uninterested lady into kissing *hir naked ers* [arse], and where another suitor has a hot iron thrust *amydde the ers*, the earthy words do not seem to upset the assembled listeners – which include a prioress, a nun, a parson, and several other presumably sensitive souls. After hearing the tale, *for the moore part they loughe and pleyde* [laughed and rejoiced]. Even Chaucer seems to have been a bit surprised by that: *Ne at this tale I saugh no man hym greve*, he says – 'I saw nobody upset by this tale' – apart from Oswald the Reeve, who was a carpenter by trade, and who evidently didn't like the way the butt of the tale was a member of his profession. It was as if Chaucer were expecting a comment from a good Kentish citizen – the medieval equivalent of 'appalled of Tunbridge Wells'. But the 'rude words' seem not to bother anybody – doubtless because they were not 'rude', in the modern sense, at all. *Piss*, for example, is used by the Parson and the Wife of Bath, as well as by the Miller and the Canon's Yeoman. It was ordinary, down-to-earth, informal language, but not 'rude'. The presumably really rude words of the period, such as *cunt*, are not found in the *Tales* (though sometimes hinted at in such words as *queynte*).

The stylistic opposition we see emerging in Middle English, accordingly, is between a level of language which brings together the domains of the noble, the gentleman, and the scholar – *faire speche*, 'courteous', 'gentle', 'learnèd' – and a level of language characterized by 'churl's terms' and 'foul words' – *knayvssh speche*. It is a contrast between 'lered and lewed', the former typically formal, the latter typically informal, and it extends well beyond creative literature. It can be seen very clearly in the letters being written during the period, such as those between members of the nobility and those between members of

8.2 Two fifteenth-century letters

On 28 February 1418, King Henry V had this letter written from Caen during his French campaign:

> By þe Kyng Worshipful fader in god Ryht trusty and wel beloued. For as moche [much] as we haue granted of oure grace speciale to oure welbeloued Esquier Piers Gerueys þe londes and tenementes þat weren hugh ffastolfs knyght as ye may se [see] moore cleerly by þe supplicacion whiche þe saide Piers putte vnto vs closed wiþinne þis lettre: We wole þat ye do make vpon þe same supplicacion by vs graunted. lettres patentes vnto þe said Piers Garueys vnder oure greet seel beynge in youre kepynge in due forme. Yeven vnder oure signet in oure Castel of Caen þe xxviij. day of ffeuerer.

On 2 April 1449 Margaret Paston wrote a long letter to her husband John with these opening and closing words:

> To my ryt3 [right] wurschipful mayster Jon Paston be þis delyverid in hast, dwelling in þe Innere Tempill.
>
>   Ryt3 wurschipful hosbond, I recommawnd me to 3ou, praying 3ou to wete [know] þat my kosyn [cousin] Clere dynyd wyth me þis day, and sche told me þat Heydon was wyth here 3isterevyn [yesterday evening] late. And he told here þat he had a letter from þe Lord Moleynys, and schewyd [showed] here þe same letter, praying hym þat he wold seyn [would say] to his frendys and wele-willerrys [wellwishers] in þis contré [country] þat he thankyth hem of here [their] godewill and for þat þei haue don for hym, and also praying Heydon þat he wold sey to Rychard Ernold of Crowmer þat he was sory and evyl payd þat his men maden þe

afray up-on hym, for he seyd it was not be [by] his will þat his men xuld [should] make afray on noman [no one] in þis contré wyth-owth ryt3 [right] grett cawse; and as for þat was don to 3ou, jf it myt3 ben prevyd [proved] þat he had don oþerwise to 3ou þan ryt3 wold as for 3owr mevabyl godis [moveable goods], 3e xuld ben content so þat 3e xuld haue cawse to kon hym þank [offer him thanks] . . .

þe blisseful Trinyté haue 3ou in his keping. Wretyn [written] at Norwyche in hast [haste] on þe Wedenysday nexst be-fore Palm Sonday. 3owrys, M. P.

With no national standard to use as a guide, both letters are idiosyncratic in spelling and punctuation, but in other respects they well illustrate the contrast between a 'lered' and a 'lewed' style (p. 178). The royal letter is ceremoniously formulaic and professional in its phrasing, uses elaborate greetings and farewells, and has a learnèd vocabulary, lexical doublets (*londes and tenementes*), and a well-planned cohesive sentence structure. It is a courtly style that has been labelled 'curial' or 'clergial' (p. 171). Chaucer knew of it: speak in 'heigh style', he has his Host advise the Clerk, 'as whan that men to kynges write' (*The Clerk's Prologue*, l. 18).

The domestic letter illustrates an informal level of writing between people who are forming a new 'middle' class of literate landed gentry, and who no longer need to rely on scribes. The sentences are long and loosely structured, plainly representing an outpouring of thoughts such as would occur had the content been spoken aloud. In this respect, there is little difference between the informal epistolary style then and now.

The Paston letters are a remarkable collection, over 400 letters (*c.* 200,000 words) written over three generations by a Norfolk family who rose from peasantry to junior aristocracy during that time. At the time of this letter, John Paston was often away from home, and he kept in regular touch with his wife Margaret, and she with him. Many letters in the sequence are by women, a significant development in an age when correspondence was the prerogative of upper-class men or male scribes.[5]

The letters are between people who know each other well, and – as with any modern letter between intimates – they assume a great deal of prior knowledge, so that the content is not entirely intelligible to outsiders. Those from the middle decades of the century coincide with the Wars of the Roses, but you would hardly guess that there was a war on. They deal with private matters – children, business dealings, local lawlessness, and conflicts over land with the local nobility, especially over the Caister estate after the death of its owner, the Pastons' kinsman Sir John Fastolffe. That surname, known also to Henry V, would surface again in English literature, over a century later, but in a different context, as Falstaff.

the newly literate middle class (see panel 8.2). At the upper end, we have such locutions as the ones used by King Henry V in 1418: *we haue granted of oure grace speciale to oure welbeloued Esquier Piers Gerueys*. At the lower end, we have John Paston writing to his brother in 1473 and using the first recorded instance of the 'watchamacallit' type of nonsense word: *as whatcalle-ye-hym seyde to Aslake*. Just occasionally, we find individual texts or words identified as belonging to one level or the other. In Passus 5 of the allegorical dream vision of life, *Piers Plowman*, attributed to William Langland, the character of Sloth, it seems, knows only the 'low-life' stories:

> I know not *Paternoster* · as the priest it singeth,
> But I know rhymes of Robin Hood · and Earl Randolph of Chester,
> But of our Lord or our Lady · not the least ever made.[6]

And in *The Manciple's Tale*, when Phebus' wife sends for her *lemman* 'lover', the use of the word immediately makes the narrator apologize (l. 205):

> Hir lemman? Certes [certainly], this is a knavyssh speche!
> Foryeveth [forgive] it me, and that I yow biseche.

And he then goes on to justify it. *The word moot nede be cosyn to the werkyng*, he reaffirms (l. 219). The only difference between an unfaithful upper-class married woman and an unfaithful lower-class married woman, he says, is in the language used to describe them:

> . . . the gentile, in estaat above,
> She shal be cleped [called] his lady, as in love;
> And for that oother is a povre womman,
> She shal be cleped his wenche or his lemman.

Lady-love vs whore. It is an early example of the way society manipulates language to cope with the unpalatable. Such nuances are inexpressible without a developed vocabulary of synonymous expressions, and it is just such a multi-dimensional lexicon which, chiefly as a result of French and Latin borrowing, evolves during Middle English, and becomes the major part of the language in the next two centuries. Part of this legacy is an enormous range of euphemistic words and phrases in Modern English. In polite society, people *perspire, defecate*, and *copulate*; elsewhere (excuse my French: see panel 8.3), they *sweat, shit, and fuck*.

Literacy and its outcome

This chapter has taken its illustrations chiefly from poetry, because it was the poets of the period who provided the clearest evidence of the growth in stylistic awareness taking place in Middle English. Chaucer is the primary source because his undisputed pre-eminence in portraying the range of his social milieu has a

8.3 Excuse my French

Why the name of the French language should have emerged in the late nineteenth century as a coy apology for someone unable to control the emission of an Anglo-Saxon swear-word is something of a mystery. The connotations for French during the eighteenth century had been largely positive, as befitted the language of international diplomacy and fashionable society, and had led to the language's name entering English in a number of genteel eighteenth- and nineteenth-century locutions, such as *French clock*, *French hem*, and *French window*. But the name had its darker side.

From the sixteenth century, venereal disease was known as the *French disease*, and the connection generated several associated expressions, such as *French marbles*, *measles*, *crowns*, *goods*, and *gout*. 'Some of your French crowns have no hair at all,' says Quince to Bottom, alluding to the way the disease can cause baldness (*A Midsummer Night's Dream*, I.ii.90). The long English military campaigns in France probably provided the original motivation. Samuel Butler, in *Hudibras* (II.ii.456), refers to the 'amorous French aches'.

During the eighteenth century, a certain spiciness crept into the associations – French novels and prints were thought to be very daring. The *Oxford English Dictionary*'s earliest recorded instances of the term *French letter* are from the 1850s. Perhaps it was the rise of the music hall, with its bawdy repartee, that finally extended the appellation to risqué language. *OED* references date from 1895. One language commentator of the time, J. R. Ware, defines *loosing French* as 'violent language in English'.[7] And by the 1930s we are begging people's pardon for it.

linguistic reflex in his ability to provide so many language varieties of the time with a literary voice. Although overlaid with stylistic features of a specifically poetic kind – notably, a remarkable creativity in the use of different metres, verse forms, and rhetorical figures of speech – his characters, belonging to different classes, occupations, and regional backgrounds, come alive in a way that had not previously been seen in English. No one else would reflect more of a country's linguistic life until Shakespeare. But Chaucer was not alone. The poetic style of his contemporary John Lydgate has already been referred to (p. 158), and along with the poetry of John Gower (p. 132) we have a named group of writers who have been called the 'literary triumvirate' of Middle English.[8] Some critics would make the group a quadrumvirate, to include William Langland, whose portrayal of the miserable conditions of peasant society adds a level of representation not seen in the prosperous middle-class world portrayed in *The Canterbury Tales*. A little later the poets would be joined by Thomas Malory, whose Arthurian saga raised the level of achievement for narrative prose. And also in the fifteenth century, there would be the proliferation of mini-dramas in the play cycles of York, Wakefield, and elsewhere. It was an age, in short, when literary genres were maturing, becoming recognizable and imitatable.

The reference to the 'naming' of authors is significant This is the first period in English when it is possible to identify a poetic elite. Anonymity surrounds the poems of the Old English period, and little changed when poetry resurfaced in early Middle English. For centuries, outside the largely Latinate tradition of religious writing (Chapter 5), there had been no major figure to copy. Indeed, for quite some time, in the years following the Conquest, there had been nothing to copy at all: the linguistic continuities which can be identified between Old and Middle English can be seen only in prose. The reasons for this lack of poetry are not well understood, though they must relate to the sociolinguistic climate in Britain during the early Middle Ages. With French and Latin the prestige languages, and providing all the literary norms, it would have taken a great visionary nationalistic poet indeed to make English the language of poetic choice. And an unworldly one. Poets write in order to be read – and in the twelfth century, the preferences of the only people who could read were decidedly Continental. An associated factor must have been the radical linguistic changes taking place between Old and Middle English. The grammatical restructuring of the language, along with the absence of a standard spoken language and a standardized writing system, must have provided a very uncertain linguistic climate for the creative writer. Poets make their impact by operating within a language system that is essentially stable. As Robert Graves once put it: 'A poet . . . must master the rules of grammar before he attempts to bend or break them.'[9] In an age when rules were undergoing such change, it would not be obvious how best to bend and break. To depart from norms, one first needs norms.

Matters began to settle down during the second half of the fourteenth century. This was partly a consequence of numbers. More English was being spoken by more people across the whole social scale, so there was more scope for consensuses of usage to emerge. By 1300 the population had doubled from its level at the time of the Conquest (p. 124), and although the mid fourteenth-century Black Death reduced the English population by between a third and a half, by 1450 the population was still around 2 million, and would approach 2.5 million by 1500. With few people maintaining an instinctive rapport with French, the demand grew for reading material in the vernacular, and with that, an interest in seeing indigenous (as opposed to translated) themes addressed. A large part of the popularity of The Canterbury Tales lay in the recognition of home-grown characters in familiar settings. And some authors began to be household names.

A text such as the Tales not only reflected contemporary varieties of speech and writing, it also helped to shape them. Literary elites, and the successes they have penned, by their nature have great influence; other writers copy them, and shared preferences of literary expression emerge. The outcome is of importance not only for the student of literature but also for the historical linguist, as it provides the chief evidence for the evolution of language variety. In an age when writing is the only source of information about language structure and use, a great deal can be deduced from the way authors opt for particular conventions of expression, sometimes producing such a distinctive literary milieu that in due course it attracts labelling as a 'school' (such as the 'Scottish Chaucerians'). An associated dimension, even more illuminating in its linguistic detail, is the shaping of literary genres – no longer just 'poetry' vs 'prose', but 'romance', 'dialogue', 'satire', 'fable', 'allegory', and much more – which introduce new dimensions of expressive variation into the language, and greatly contribute to its evolving mosaic of styles. It is always in the oeuvre of the highest-ranking authors that we see a language's stylistic range most fully represented. And the more popular the text, the more likely it is that its characteristics of language or style will influence others, and become part of the language as a whole.

It is during the late Middle English period that we see developments of this kind taking place. As texts became popular, they became available in more manuscripts, and these manuscripts achieved a much wider distribution across the country, thanks to improved communications. *Piers Plowman*, for example, exists in three distinct versions, of which as many as fifty-four manuscripts have survived. Other works were even more popular, if the number of surviving manuscripts is taken as evidence – around a hundred, in the case of the long didactic poem *The Prick of Conscience*. The extent to which a text could become nationally known is illustrated by a letter written by John Ball to the Essex members of the Great Society of Peasants in 1381, on the eve of the Peasants' Revolt. 'Stand together in God's name,' he writes, *and biddeþ* [bid] *Peres Plouȝman go to his werk* of chastising those in power.[10] In another example, John Wycliffe argues the case for translating the Bible into English, casually referring to a (now lost) play from the York cycle of mystery plays: *freris han tauȝt in Englond þe Paternoster in Engliȝsch tunge, as men seyen in þe pley of ȝork, and in many opere cuntreys* – 'friars have taught in England the Paternoster in the English language, as they tell in the Play of York, and in many other countries'.[11] Today, we do not think twice about dropping a literary name into the conversation, referring to a 'Big Brother mentality' (in the Orwellian, not television sense) or a 'Micawber-like philosophy'. But this kind of received literary wisdom, in which literary names enter the language as a whole, is possible only when the literature itself is widely transmitted and widely read and listened to. That was a fourteenth-century development. The only comparable event previously had been the nationwide circulation of religious events and personalities through Bible readings and sermons – for the vast majority, a purely oral–aural experience.

The development of a literary national language consciousness presupposes a significant increase in the ability to read; and by the beginning of the fifteenth century, literacy was no longer the province of an aristocratic and scholarly elite, but was becoming widespread among the new middle classes.[12] Some 10 per cent of the male population could sign their names in 1500; this had doubled by 1550 (the corresponding figures for women were 1 and 5 per cent). Although verse was much more popular than prose, and courtly tales in particular, it was not only creative literature which was being read. Homes were acquiring manuscripts of many kinds, as well as producing their own in the form of letters, journals, and business papers. Religious literature was the primary genre, with biblical readings, spiritual and moral tracts, saints' lives, Psalters, sermons, and other devotional material now receiving a wide secular circulation. There were manuscripts dealing with medicine, domestic affairs (such as cookery, p. 153), and pastimes (such as hunting). Ballads, folk-tales, and secular lyrics were popular. So, too, were histories (of the world, of Britain, of King Arthur, of Troy, of the Crusades . . .), reports of current affairs, and accounts of exotic travel abroad. Biographies and autobiographies began to be written. Educational resources proliferated, such as dictionaries, grammars (of Latin and French), reading primers, and alphabet books. Ranulph Higden (p. 129) is one of the first to refer in Latin to an *abecedary* – which his translator John of Trevisa helpfully glosses in English as 'a þing wiþ letters for to spel'. Although Latin remained the language of serious intellectual expression (with the occasional exception, such as the religious writing of Reginald Pecock), a huge number of translations ensured the vernacular transmission of texts from all over Europe. And once printing arrived, in 1476 (p. 255), the availability of home reading material, from Bibles to epic romances, greatly increased.

Printing eliminated the huge amount of distortion due to scribal variation and the vagaries of memory in oral performance which had bedevilled the transmission of texts in the Middle Ages. The authors themselves were well aware of the problem. Chaucer actually went so far as to wish disease onto his own scrivener (*scriveyn*), Adam, unless he improved his copying skills:

> Adam scriveyn, if ever it thee befalle
> Boece or Troylus for to wryten newe,
> Under thy long lokkes thou most [must] have the scalle [scabs],
> But [unless] after my makyng [composition] thou wryte more trewe;
> So ofte a-daye I mot [must] thy werk renewe,
> It to correcte and eek [also] to rubbe and scrape;
> And al is thorugh thy negligence and rape [haste].

Printing was not at first the perfect solution, because it introduced a fresh set of problems: negligent scribes were followed by negligent typesetters (p. 257). But it did add an element of stability to literature, as well as an apparatus which made the recapitulation and retrieval of information so much easier. Today, we are so used to the presence of title pages, contents pages, page numbers, footnotes, running heads, indexes, and all the other facilities provided by the printed book that we can easily fail to appreciate the problems facing people who lived in an era when such facilities did not exist. How can one refer a person to a favourite line or passage in a text, when there are no page or line numbers? Today, we simply say: Book II, line 364. How can authors quote from each other? There are severe limits to what can be done through a purely manuscript-mediated medium. The printed book did much more than just increase the number, range, and availability of texts; it permitted the development of a sophisticated intertextuality, on the part of both author and reader. And from a specifically linguistic point of view, it exposed people, far more than had been possible previously, to writing whose source lay outside their locality. The climate needed for the emergence of a standard variety of the language was slowly being formed.

Indeed, by the end of the Middle English period there had been a fundamental change in the literary and linguistic climate in England. There was also a greater consciousness about the nature of English. One of the benefits of multilingualism in society (and of bilingualism in an individual) is that the coexistence of languages makes people more alert to the languages' particular properties. As George Steiner has put it: 'is it not the duty of the critic to avail himself, in some imperfect measure at least, of another language – if only to experience the defining contours of his own?'[13] The point applies as much to authors, and in England during the Middle English period this experience was unavoidable (Chapter 6), especially when, as a natural command of French died away, it was made more conscious through the growth of language-teaching classes, language-learning materials (such as bilingual or trilingual word lists), and translations.[14] One consequence was a growing sense that English was not as 'good' as French and Latin, and needed to be improved – a mindset which became a dominant theme of the sixteenth century, but which was already present in the fifteenth century in the minds of writers such as Lydgate and Caxton who, as we have seen (p. 176), praised Chaucer for doing precisely that.

The first rumblings of discontent laid down the pattern of complaint that all subsequent generations would follow. One of the first was the splenetic monk, Ranulph Higden, whom we have already encountered being critical of language teaching and dialect variation in Britain (pp. 130, 168). In the same section of his *Polychronicon* (Chapter 59) we find him – as translated by John of Trevisa – complaining about the way English was being corrupted by foreign influences:

> by commyxstion and mellyng, furst wiþ Danes and afterward wiþ Normans, in menye þe contray longage ys apeyred, and som vseþ strange wlaffyng, chyteryng, harryng, and garryng grisbittyng.

> by intermingling and mixing, first with Danes and afterwards with Normans, in many people the language of the land is harmed, and some use strange inarticulate utterance, chattering, snarling, and harsh teeth-gnashing

He is thinking chiefly about regional variations in accent and dialect (Chapter 9), but it is quite plain where he lays the blame – on the invading foreigner. And in due course it was the massive borrowing of vocabulary from French which became the chief butt of criticism. The arrival of loanwords may have made the language elegant, in the eyes and ears of some, but – as we have seen in the mouths of some of Chaucer's characters – it also made it alien. The world of non-fiction provided its critics, too. An early comment is made by the mystical writer Richard Rolle of Hampole, who precedes his early fourteenth-century translation of the Psalter with the remark that he will 'seke no strange Inglis' – he means words from French, because he makes it clear that he has no objection to expressions which display the influence of Latin. Osbern Bokenham, who made a fifteenth-century translation of Higden's *Polychronicon* (in *Mappula Angliae*), comments on the way French has 'barbarized' English – an early use (not recorded in the OED) of a word which would later become a favourite in the purist lexical arsenal. In all of this, it is typically the vocabulary which is the focus of controversy. French had a limited but important influence on English grammar, too, but grammatical issues are rarely brought into the foreground of the debate. It was in Middle English, for example, that English took on board a number of constructions modelled on the French phrasal pattern *faire X, prendre X, tenir X*: this is where such locutions as *do homage, have mercy on, make complaint,* and *hold dear* come from. I know of no one who chose patterns of this kind to instantiate an argument either for or against French influence on English.

As we have already seen with Thomas Usk (p. 174), it is one thing to claim adherence to a principle of linguistic usage, and quite another to stick to it oneself. People who readily complain about language always have an unreal perception of what they do themselves: they routinely break the principle they most ardently commend. It is so today, as we shall see in Chapter 15, and it was so in Middle English, when we find principles of usage being adumbrated for the first time. If Richard Rolle had been scrupulous in his avoidance of French words, he would have been unable to write much of what he did. As an illustration, consider this sentence taken from a tract in which he draws an analogy between bees and human beings (the French words are underlined):

> They kepe thaire wynges clene [clean], that es, þe twa <u>commandementes</u> of <u>charyté</u> þay fulfill in gud <u>concyens</u> [conscience], and they hafe othyre <u>vertus</u>, vnblendyde with þe fylthe of syne and vnclene luste.

Nor are these the only foreign loans in this sentence: *wings* is Old Norse.

The battle-lines are being laid down for a controversy which would preoccupy the sixteenth century, in the form of the 'ink-horn' controversy (p. 291), and which we will see regularly in later chapters, as we encounter seventeenth-century debates about correctness, eighteenth-century concerns about the 'language of the age', nineteenth-century revivals of interest in Anglo-Saxon, and twentieth-century antipathies towards Classicism. On the one hand, there are writers such as Thomas Elyot, who writes (in *The Gouernour*, 1531) of the value of Latin terms for the 'necessary augmentation of our langage'. On the other hand, we have George Orwell, who has as one of his rules for cultivating a 'good prose style': 'to reduce the amount of Latin and Greek in the average sentence, to drive out foreign phrases'.[15] The core antagonism is between those who value linguistic ornateness and those who value linguistic simplicity, between those who welcome foreign influence and those whose taste is only for native words. The linguistic dimension of the debate is often related to a deeper social, religious, or aesthetic issue – a 'simpler' English to enable ordinary people to understand the Bible, perhaps, or a 'native' English to enable poets to come closer to the land. But it is just as often argued purely as a linguistic issue – such as whether it is desirable for the language to contain 'hybrid' words (words which combine elements from different language backgrounds, as illustrated on p. 149).

Although this two-sided controversy still has plenty of life in it, in the twenty-first century, the presence of a third position has been growing in prominence. 'Neither part of the language is good or bad absolutely, but in relation to its subject,' said the essayist Thomas De Quincey in 1839,[16] and this view has come to be reflected in the principle of appropriateness which emerged within twentieth-century sociolinguistics and which informs a great deal of contemporary work in stylistics. It is an eclectic vision, in which foreign elements, regardless of their source, are seen as contributing to the expressive resources of the language, giving writers more options than had previously been available. From this perspective, the main linguistic legacy of the Middle English period was the enhancing of the opportunities for lexical stylistic choice. Lexical doublets became available: Latin *ascend* supplemented Old English *climb*; French *desire* supplemented Old English *wish*. In many cases there were triplets, of the *ask / question / interrogate* type (p. 162), with both Latin and French supplementing Old English (see panel 8.4).

The lexical alternatives offered authors multiple possibilities. The rhythmical differences between the words allowed for different choices within a line of verse. The fact that the words began with different sounds would permit alternative possibilities for alliteration. Their different internal structures would allow new relationships of assonance. Their different endings gave fresh options for rhyme. Thus at one point Chaucer can write (in *The Miller's Tale*, l. 3,355):

> And forth he gooth, jolif and amorous,
> Til he cam to the carpenteres hous

And at another (in *The Knight's Tale*, l. 1,973):

> In thilke colde, frosty regioun
> Ther as Mars hath his sovereyn mansioun.

8.4 Lexical alternatives

The table illustrates the kind of lexical alternatives which were available by the end of the Middle English period, including some which arrived soon after. The dates are those of their first recorded usage in the *Oxford English Dictionary*.

Germanic	French	Latin
ask *c. 885*	question *c. 1470* (*c. 1300 as noun*)	interrogate *1483*
climb *c. 1000*		ascend *1382*
clothes *c. 800*	attire *1250*	
fast *c. 888*	firm *c. 1340*	secure *c. 1533*
fire *c. 825*	flame *c. 1340*	conflagration *1555*
guts *c. 1000*	entrails *c. 1300* courage *c. 1300*	
holy *c. 825*	sacred *c. 1380*	consecrated *1552*
house *c. 950*	mansion *1340*	
kingly *1382* (*king 836*)	royal *c. 1374*	regal *c. 1374* (*c. 1330 as noun*)
rest *c. 825*	remainder *1424*	residue *1362* (*via French*)
rise *c. 1000*	mount *1362*	ascend *1382*
sorrow *c. 888*	distress *c. 1290*	
wish (*verb*) *c. 897*	desire *c. 1230*	
weariness *c. 900*		lassitude *1533* (*via French*)

Hous was from Old English; *mansioun* arrived in the early fourteenth century from Old French. As the new loanwords found their place within the lexicon, they began to associate (*collocate*) with other words in selective ways and to take on different nuances. Germanic *kingly*, for example, was definitely a male word, but French *royal* and Latin *regal* applied to both sexes. *Kingly* was only used before a noun, whereas *royal* (and sometimes *regal*) were often used after (as in *blood royal, banners royal*). In due course, each word developed its own range of collocations: *royal* accreted a range of technical uses and became increasingly used with proper names (*rhyme royal, royal blue, Royal Highness, Royal Shakespeare Company*); *regal* developed a range of associations to do with behaviour and appearance (*regal look/performance/confidence/splendour*). Only in humour can we break these collocations: *The Kingly Shakespeare Company* might be a headline accompanying a review of a play in which the actor playing some monarch had done especially well; a headline referring to *The Regal Shakespeare Company* would probably be making a not entirely kind point about local theatre politics.

Middle English gave us stylistic choice. And by the end of the period, one of these choices was between standard and nonstandard English.

Interlude 8
Well well

Well, this interlude presents another feature of conversational style.

We would not expect to see such an opening in a formal written text. *Well* is out of place. When the word is used in this way, it does not express such meanings as the adjectival 'healthy' or 'satisfied', the adverbial 'successfully' or 'properly', or the nominal 'spring of water'. It is one of a group of words that has a range of subtle functions marking the way a discourse is structured or the relationship between the participants in a dialogue. And they are characteristic of the more informal kind of conversational English.

Well can mark a change of topic or action (*well what book did you read, then?*) or introduce a piece of reported speech (*he said well not everybody thinks like that*). It can mitigate the force of a confrontation: *well I don't think so* is more pacifying and less abrupt than the bare *I don't think so*. It can express rapport: *Well how are you!* And it can be used to emphasize uncertainty (*well I'm not sure about that*), express an attitude (*well!*), or just fill a silence (*well . . .*). In all cases we are dealing with one of the most distinctive and frequent features of colloquial style.[17]

The first examples of this range of use are in Middle English, and provide an important indication of the way styles were evolving during that period. *Well* was often used in Old English in its adjectival, adverbial, and nominal meanings, but not in a clear discourse-marking way. The nearest we get to this function is the way *wella* or *wel la* was used as an attention-getting device before important statements, equivalent perhaps to 'Listen!', and sometimes translated as 'Alas!'. Old English made more use of *Hwæt!*, used at the beginning of a discourse as a call to the listener to focus attention on a familiar point or story which is to follow. Its most famous literary manifestation was as the opening word of the *Beowulf* saga. Its closest modern conversational equivalent would be *you know?* or *do you know?*

Neither *wel la* nor *hwæt* survived in Middle English. But Chaucer, with his sharp ear, shows that *wel* was already established in a discourse function introducing a piece of direct speech. The Manciple has been a little reluctant to tell his story, having stepped in to replace the drunken and incapable Cook, and his opening remark shows the softening force of the word (Prologue, *The Manciple's Tale*, ll. 25, 104):

> 'Wel,' quod the Maunciple, 'if it may doon ese
> To thee, sire Cook, and to no wight displese . . .'

In other words: if people don't mind my stepping in . . . The Host is delighted:

> Telle on thy tale, Manciple, I thee preye.

And off the Manciple goes with the new topic:

> 'Wel, sire,' quod he, 'now herkneth what I seye.'

Wel (also in *now wel*) is used ten times by Chaucer's characters in its discourse function, always preceding a *quod – quod she, quod oure hoost, quod Pandare*. It is also used in prose. At about the same time as Chaucer was writing, we find it in Thomas Usk's *The Testament of Love* (1384–5; Book II, Chapter 7, l. 7). This particular instance is striking, as it contrasts with *well* in a different sense:

> 'Wel,' quod I, 'this inpossession [imposition] I wol [will] wel understande.'

A century later we see *well* preceding the verb *said* in *The Morte Darthur*. In Book I, Chapter 1, for example, we find two *well*-users interacting:

> Then for pure anger and for great love of fair Igraine the king Uther fell sick. So came to the king Uther Sir Ulfius, a noble knight, and asked the king why he was sick. I shall tell thee, said the king, I am sick for anger and for love of fair Igraine, that I may not be whole. Well, my lord, said Sir Ulfius, I shall seek Merlin, and he shall do you remedy, that your heart shall be pleased. So Ulfius departed, and by adventure he met Merlin in a beggar's array, and there Merlin asked Ulfius whom he sought. And he said he had little ado to tell him. Well, said Merlin, I know whom thou seekest, for thou seekest Merlin; therefore seek no farther, for I am he; and if King Uther will well reward me, and be sworn unto me to fulfil my desire, that shall be his honour and profit more than mine; for I shall cause him to have all his desire. All this will I undertake, said Ulfius, that there shall be nothing reasonable but thou shalt have thy desire. Well, said Merlin, he shall have his intent and desire. And therefore, said Merlin, ride on your way, for I will not be long behind.

Merlin is evidently being very accommodating.

But for the full range of discourse uses of *well*, we have to wait for Early Modern English. We find rapport uses, for example, in the second act of Nicholas Udall's *Ralph Roister Doister* (1566):

> TALKAPACE   Well, Truepenny, never but flinging! [*rushing around*]
> ALYFACE   And frisking!
> TRUEPENNY   Well, Tibet and Annot, still swinging and whisking! [*dashing about*]
> TALKAPACE   But ye roil abroad. [*gad about*]

And earlier in the play we find Talkapace softening a caution with an early use of *well* inside a sentence:

> If ye do so again, well, I would advise you nay.

It is Shakespeare who illustrates virtually every *well* usage in his plays, and puts them into the mouths of characters from all social ranks. The only usage which is missing is the one introducing direct speech – unsurprisingly, as these are plays not narratives – but even this function is touched upon when the rebel Holland reflects (*Henry VI Part 2*, IV.ii.7, with First Folio punctuation):

> Well, I say, it was never merry world in England, since Gentlemen came up.

Apart from this, we have *well* expressing group rapport, as when Horatio invites Barnardo to tell his story (*Hamlet*, I.i.33):

> Well, sit we down . . .

There is *well* expressing change of event, as when Hamlet gives the players leave to go (III.ii.55):

> Well, go make you ready.

We see *well* offering the chance of a new topic when Hamlet, after an aside to Horatio, turns to Osrick once again (V.ii.134):

> Well, sir?

The word seems to be just filling the silence in Hotspur's account of his boredom in listening to Glendower ranting on (*Henry IV Part 1*, III.i.152):

> I cried 'Hum', and 'Well, go to!'

And it becomes a substitute for articulate speech in *All's Well That Ends Well* when Parolles, returning from a battle, expostulates (II.v.87):

> Lose our drum? Well.

Shakespeare actually gives us a discoursal gloss when he has Hamlet warn his fellows (I.v.175) that he does not want the game given away when he puts 'an antic disposition on'

> by pronouncing of some doubtful phrase,
> As 'Well, well, we know' . . .

And in this dialogue (*Henry IV Part 1*, I.ii.45) *well* marks someone wanting to reduce the force of a confrontation. Falstaff has addressed Prince Hal in typical blustering style, but when he receives an equally forceful response, he yields:

> FALSTAFF What a plague have I to do with a buff jerkin?
> PRINCE HAL Why, what a pox have I to do with my Hostess of the tavern?
> FALSTAFF Well, thou hast called her to a reckoning many a time and oft.

This is a scene full of linguistic fencing: as many as seven of the sixty exchanges begin with a discourse *well*. And one of them shows an expansion of the usage:

> PRINCE HAL Well then, once in my days I'll be a madcap.

Well then is one of several ways of adding emphasis. *Well now* is another, used by the countess in *All's Well That Ends Well* (I.iii.94). It is an interesting usage, as they are the very opening words of a private conversation with her steward, an invitation to speak intimately:

> COUNTESS Well, now.
> STEWARD I know, madam, you love your gentlewoman entirely.

Doubling the *well* is another way of adding emotion to an interaction. Somerset's tension is apparent when he asks the others which rose they will choose, white or red, to show which side they are on (*Henry VI Part 1*, II.iv.55):

> Well, well, come on; who else?

In *Coriolanus* (II.i.26) the tribunes Brutus and Sicinius are so irritated by Menenius' long-windedness that they break out into a joint exclamatory prompt:

> Well, well sir, well.

And in *Macbeth* (V.i.51) the Doctor uses a triple *well*, at a loss to know how to react on hearing the profound sigh from the sleepwalking Lady Macbeth:

> GENTLEWOMAN I would not have such a heart in my bosom, for the dignity of
>   the whole body.
> DOCTOR Well, well, well.
> GENTLEWOMAN Pray God it be, sir.

What is interesting about the Gentlewoman's response, of course, is her taking the Doctor's words literally. This must be the first recorded instance in written English of someone failing to understand a discourse function of *well*.

Chapter 9 A dialect age

Middle English may have been a stylistic age; but it was above all a dialect age. It is the only period in the history of English when we can see regional variation reflected in the written language so widely and so unselfconsciously. Systematic variation was difficult to see in the Old English period, because most parts of the country had no manuscripts surviving, and even in those areas which *were* represented, the texts were few, their authorship often uncertain, and the dialectal status of their distinguishing features frequently unclear (p. 34). We need a lot of text before the properties of a dialect begin to show up clearly. Dialects are, after all, no more than varieties of an individual language, and they share in most of the properties of that language; they have far more sounds, words, and grammatical patterns in common than actually differentiate them. So, to get a complete picture of the way the dialects of a language work, we need a wide range of texts, on a wide variety of topics, written by a wide range of people, from all over the country. It is an ambitious set of goals, which even surveys of modern dialects find hard to achieve; and in the Old English period it was not possible. But in the Middle English period, especially from the fourteenth century, we have enough material to piece together a reasonably full picture of what the dialect situation must have been like.

The medieval age in Britain also allows us to come as close as it is possible to get in writing to the 'natural state' of a group of English dialects. It was an age before printing, and before one of these dialects had grown in prestige and become the language's 'standard dialect' – what we shall later identify as 'Standard English' (p. 222). Standard English changed everything. It turned the nonstandard dialects into second-class citizens, and those who would previously have written unselfconsciously in them found themselves no longer able to do so. Once we are taught to write a language in its standard form – as everyone is who goes to school – it becomes very difficult to write down a dialect in a way which realistically captures its linguistic character. Indeed, most people would see no point in doing so. There have been some literary successes, as we shall see in later chapters, but on the whole the norms of the standard language act as a glass through which we can see other dialects but darkly. So, to encounter a period when there was no standard language to obscure the view is a rare treat. Standard English, as we know it today, did not emerge in a recognizable form until the very end of the Middle English period. For a glorious 300 years, people could write as they wanted to, and nobody could say they were wrong.

No standard language? But what had happened to the Late West Saxon which had begun to emerge as a literary standard towards the end of the Old English period (p. 54)? The impetus to write in this dialect largely died out during the eleventh century, as the centre of gravity of the new kingdom moved away from Winchester and towards London, and a whole new set of factors began to influence the language. It did not disappear immediately. A great deal of twelfth-century religious writing displays uniformities of usage among scribes, which suggests the continuing influence of West Saxon norms (p. 56). And even in the early thirteenth century there is evidence of a continuing tradition, notably in the Herefordshire region of the West Midlands. This can be seen especially in two prose works – the rule for anchoresses, the *Ancrene Wisse* (p. 149), and the Bodley manuscript of a group of saints' lives and homilies known as the Katherine Group (named after one of the texts, the *Life of Saint Katherine*).[1] The manuscripts are written in different hands, but the linguistic similarities are so striking that scholars have concluded that they manifest a single direction of influence stemming from the Old English literary tradition, which was strong in this region. *Ure ledene . . . is ald Englis* ('Our language . . . is old English'), says one of the writers (in *Seinte Margarete*). Bishop Wulfstan had worked in nearby Worcestershire (p. 98), and it is here that Layamon was probably based (p. 144). The Katherine Group uses a strongly alliterative style, whose preservation seems to be particularly associated with the West Midlands, as it is still evident in the *Gawain* poet a century later (p. 146). There must have been a literary awareness and a continuity of tradition in local scriptoria which had managed to maintain its identity, despite the massive changes in linguistic practice taking place elsewhere. Doubtless this was due to the fact that Herefordshire, lying to the west of the Cotswold escarpment, was relatively isolated geographically, and – on the Welsh borders – subject to a very different set of political, social, and military influences. Many Anglo-Saxon lords had moved to the area to distance themselves as much as possible from the Norman invaders. Whatever the reasons, the so-called 'AB-dialect' (Ancrene/Bodley) is unique in its inter-scribal uniformity. Some scholars have suggested that it could be viewed as a kind of 'local standard', but if so, it was one which did not spread very far or last for very long. We need more than two manuscripts to justify calling a dialect a 'standard'. And the same sort of limitation applies to other localized varieties displaying mutual influence which can be detected at various points during the Middle English period.

The lack of a national standard opened up the orthography to all kinds of innovative practices. One of the earliest writers went so far as to devise a whole new system of spelling. This was Orrm, an English monk writing around 1200 in an East Midland dialect. Nothing is known of the author. His name – he calles himself both Orrm and Orrmin – suggests he was of Scandinavian descent (the name meant 'serpent' in Old Norse). The dedication to his book tells us that he had a brother, Walter, who was, like him, a canon of the Augustinian (or Austin) order. A possible location for them would have been at Elsham Priory, near Brigg, north Lincolnshire. He calls his book the *Orrmulum – forrþi þatt Orrm itt wrohhte* 'because it was Orrm who wrote it'. His idea was to provide a collection of homilies intended for church reading, based on the Gospel readings used in church throughout the year. He has a table of contents listing Latin texts for 243 homilies, but only about an eighth of these have survived – if indeed they were all completed. It was an immensely ambitious undertaking: the surviving English text is 10,220 full poetic lines.[2] If he did complete it in the manner of what remains, the whole work would have been three quarters of a million words.

Orrm was really the first English spelling reformer, with a methodical temperament, a disciplined style, and an almost obsessive concern for clarity of exposition which at times became repetitive to the point of tediousness. His text does not loom large in literary reviews of the period. But from a language point of view, he is unique (see panel 9.1). He was a linguistic individualist: he did not use the alliterative and rhyming style employed by virtually all other Middle English poets. Each of his lines has fifteen syllables, divided into two half-lines of eight and seven syllables respectively. But the primary linguistic interest is the idiosyncratic – yet highly consistent – spelling system, probably devised to give preachers some help in reading aloud, at a time when the language had been undergoing a relatively rapid period of change. In pronunciation alone, since Old English, there had been changes in both the length and quality of vowels, some diphthongs had altered, the articulation of several consonants had changed, and there was much less variety in the range of vowels in unstressed syllables (p. 114). Orrm sorts this out. He senses that there is a problem in distinguishing between 'long' vowels (as in modern *sea, seat, say, so, saw*, etc.) and 'short' vowels (as in *sit, set, sat*, etc.), so he devises a way of telling the difference. The most noticeable feature is that, when a syllable ends in a consonant and the vowel is short, he doubles the following consonant. This would be like writing *sitt, sett, satt* today – and indeed we do actually use this distinction in such contrasts as *sitting* (where the vowel is short) and *siting* (where it is long), *hopping* and *hoping, stagger* and *stager*, and so on. It's the extra consonant that counts. He is scrupulous in the application of his method: high-frequency grammatical words like *and, with*, and *under* all have their

9.1 The opening of the *Orrmulum*

The dominating graphic feature of the opening lines of the *Orrmulum* is the use of double consonants marking short vowels. These lines also contain examples of some of Orrm's other spelling conventions. He was particularly careful to distinguish the different kinds of sound represented by ʒ in Old English:

- ʒ shows that the sound is [j], as in *yet*, written *ʒĕt*;
- ʒʒ shows that it is an [i] sound at the end of a diphthong, as in *may*, written *maʒʒ*;
- ʒh shows that it is a type of consonant sound, a voiced velar fricative [ɣ], as in *hallʒhe* 'holy'.

The double acute accent on *ʒĕt* is interesting, as it gives a hint of Orrm's reasoning. In Latin, a vowel before a *t* would usually be short, so any preacher seeing the word *ʒet* would assume it was pronounced as in modern English *yet* [jet]. In fact its pronunciation at the time was more like *yate* [jeːt]. So Orrm provides his readers with a reminder, in the form of the diacritic.

> *Nu broþerr Wallterr, broþerr min, affterr þe flæshess kinde,*
> Now brother Walter, my brother, according to the way of flesh,
> *Annd broþerr min i Crisstenndom þurrh fulluhht annd þurrh trowwþe,*
> And my brother in Christendom through baptism and through faith,
> *Annd broþerr min i Ḡodess hus, ʒĕt o þe þride wise,*
> And my brother in God's house, moreover in the third way,
> *Þurrh þatt witt hafenn tăkenn ba an reʒhellboc to follʒhenn,*
> Because we have both chosen to follow a monastic rule,
> *Vnnderr kanunnkess had annd lif, swa summ Sannt Awwstin sette;*
> According to the order and life of canon, just as St Augustine laid down;
> *Icc hafe don swa summ þu badd, annd forþedd te þin wille,*
> I have done as you asked, and fulfilled your desire,
> *Icc hafe wennd inntill Ennglissh Ḡodspelless hallʒhe láre,*
> I have translated into English the Gospel's holy wisdom,
> *Affterr þatt little witt tatt me min Drihhtin hafeþþ lenedd.*
> With the little intelligence that my Lord has granted me.

There is also an interesting grammatical usage in the fourth line. *Witt* is one of the dual pronouns (meaning 'we two') which were already becoming obsolete in Old English (p. 44). Orrm uses them several times. To find them still being used in the thirteenth century is a little surprising, and presumably they had become something of an archaism by then. That this might be the case is suggested by another word later in the line, *ba* 'both'. If the 'dual' meaning of *witt* had been strong in the minds of readers, 'both' would have been unnecessary. That Orrm chose to use it is perhaps an indication of *witt*'s growing archaic status.

consonant doubled – *annd, wiþþ, vnnderr* – even though the prospect of misreading in such cases is remote.

Because the spelling is so systematic, and the text is so long, we can gain a particularly clear indication of the accent Orrm must have had. For example, there are a number of words which, depending on dialect, are spelled with either an *a* or an *o* vowel before an *n* (as in Old English, p. 42), and these are all spelled with *a* by Orrm: *mann* 'man', *maniȝ* 'many', *þannkenn* 'thank', and *stannt* 'stand' all occur in the first twenty lines. Another variant is in the use of a short *e*-type vowel in such words as *ȝerne* 'eagerly' instead of *ȝeorne*. There are a dozen or so features of this kind, of known diagnostic value in differentiating Middle English dialects, and when these are used as a yardstick for the spellings in the *Orrmulum*, they point fairly clearly at a location somewhere in the northern part of the East Midlands. They would probably have spoken like that in and around Elsham Priory.

Conclusions of this kind are always a little suspect, especially early on in the Middle English period when the texts are still quite sparse, and little is known about some parts of the country. But even in the twelfth and thirteenth centuries, we are dealing with more data than was available in Old English. We have already seen one reason for the increase: the spread of religious houses and scriptoria all over the country, producing more manuscripts in local dialects. Even the earliest texts are quite substantial: the twelfth-century Lambeth group of homilies, for example, were written in the West Midlands dialect (on the borders of north Herefordshire and Shropshire), and contain over 20,000 words; the *Trinity Homilies* were written in the East Midlands dialect, and contain over 40,000. As the period progresses, we find increasing numbers of manuscripts surviving from known locations in all parts of England and southern Scotland, and it is possible to draw conclusions about Middle English dialects with increasing confidence.

At the same time, there are complications. The Middle English period lasts for over 300 years, and during that time there were major changes in the language, which affected all dialects. Not only would an East Midlands text look different from a West Midlands text; but an East Midlands text of 1200 would look very different from an East Midlands text of 1400. When we see distinctive forms in a Middle English manuscript, therefore, the regional and the chronological dimensions have to be disentangled. For example, in Old English the word for *stone* was *stan*, with a long 'ah' vowel. The change to the modern form took place in Middle English. At the beginning of the period, we find the *stan* form in the twelfth-century *Peterborough Chronicle* and the early thirteenth-century *Ancrene Wisse*, from the East and West Midlands respectively. But *ston* forms are also making their appearance across the Midlands in the thirteenth century – we can find examples in the West, in a tale called *The Vox and the Wolf*, and in the East, in an early Bestiary.[3] *Ston*, also spelled *stoon* (as in Chaucer) then becomes the norm throughout the south and Midlands, and spreads up into Yorkshire and the Lancashire/Cheshire area: we find *ston* or *stone* in the Towneley Plays and *Sir Gawaine and the Green Knight*. Only in the far north and in Scotland do we continue to find *stan* – as in John Barbour's *Bruce*, in the late fourteenth century (see panel 9.2).

The general trend is clear: *stone* spreads from south to north in the thirteenth century. But each time we encounter one of its forms in a manuscript, we need to make a decision. The word *stan* by itself tells us nothing: it could be a twelfth-century Southern form, a thirteenth-century Midlands form; or a

---

9.2 *Stane* stayed

Although *stone* became the norm in Standard English, *stane* by no means disappeared. It continued to be used throughout the north of England and in Scotland, where it became the normal form in Scottish literary English. It was still being used in the great Scots revival in the eighteenth century: for example, we find it in Robert Burns' *Tam O'Shanter* (l. 89):

> By this time he was cross the ford,
> Whare in the snaw the chapman smoor'd [Where in the snow the merchant
>   suffocated];
> And past the birks and meikle stane, [birch wood and great stone]
> Whare drucken Charlie brak's neckbane [Where drunken Charlie broke his neck]

We see it today in such place-names as *Dwarfie Stane*, a rock-cut tomb in Orkney, northern Scotland, *The Loupin' Stanes* 'Leaping Stones' near Lockerbie, and *The Hill o' Many Stanes*, a fan-shaped alignment of large stones near Wick, Caithness. But it is not just a fossilized word in place-names; it is a living part of modern Scots (p. 489), used in several varieties. In the Bible, David kills Goliath with a stane. And Irish folk-singer Johnny McEvoy has it in the title of his Scottish epic, *Wee Magic Stane*:

> O the Dean o' Westminster wis [was] a powerful man,
> He held a' [all] the strings o' the State in his hand
> And a' this great power it flustered him nane [none]
> Til some rogues ran away wi' his wee magic stane.
> Wi a tooreli ooreli ooreli ay, etc.

The usage is not restricted to Scotland. It can also be heard in local dialect speech and folk-song in many parts of north-east England and in Northern Ireland (in Ulster Scots). As the Scots proverb says: *A rowin stane gaithers nae fug* ('A rolling stone gathers no moss').

fourteenth-century Northern form. If we definitely know the text is Southern, then we can guess the date. If we definitely know the text is fourteenth-century, then we can guess the region. But if we do not know either of these things for certain, then we have a problem. And if it is a thirteenth-century text, we have an especial problem, for *stan* and *ston* forms were both still being used at that time, at least in the Midlands and possibly elsewhere. That is when the dialectology detective-work begins. What are we to make of the situation we find in the early thirteenth-century *Brut* (p. 144), written by Layamon in Worcestershire, in the south-west Midlands? This exists in two manuscripts, one (Otho) copied some twenty-five years later than the other (Caligula). The earlier manuscript has *a* forms (*þat weorc is of stane*); the later manuscript has *o* forms (*walles of stone*). Is this because the pronunciation of 'stone' had changed in Worcestershire during that period, or is the spelling the result of a copy made in some other part of the country, or by a Southern (or Southern-trained) scribe who ended up in Worcestershire doing the work?

The situation becomes more complicated still when we find such forms appearing in the mouths of characters. The fifteenth-century York Mystery Plays use *stone* throughout – apart from in a single instance, in the dialogue between Joseph and Mary, when Joseph says *stille als stane*. This might be a character note for a provincial Joseph, as with the students' dialect in *The Reeve's Tale* (p. 163) – King Herod, for example, says *still as stone* later in the play. More likely – given that it is an isolated instance – *stane* is there simply to help the rhyme at the end of the line; *mane* and *nane* end two of the preceding lines. In one of the Towneley Plays, *The Pilgrim*, there is a similar situation, with *stane* turning up just once, in the speech of Lucas. Here, the character-note explanation is definitely ruled out, for Lucas additionally uses the word spelled as *stone*. The usage has to be motivated by the need to meet the rhyme:

> [Christ] was of the crosse tayn [taken]
> he was layde full sone [immediately] agane
> In a graue, vnder a stane . . .

Examples such as these suggest that the *stane* form was still part of the linguistic intuitions of Yorkshire playgoers in the fifteenth century, even though their everyday pronunciation had moved on.

Stone is just one word showing regional dialect variation, taken at random from a lexicon of tens of thousands. Not all the words show such variation, of course. In particular, there is little regional differentiation to be seen in the many scholarly loanwords from French and Latin, characteristic of the 'high style' (p. 174). Doubtless, when it came to using 'termes of philosophie', such as *notable* and *dissimulation*, the pronunciation norms and spelling preferences of educated people greatly overlapped. It would be the everyday words, such

9.3 Major Middle English dialect areas

The continuous lines should be thought of as representing transitional areas between dialects, not clear-cut boundaries. The broken lines identify areas where – depending on the linguistic criteria used – a part of the country could be assigned to alternative dialects. The dotted lines identify the 'triangle' of special influence (p. 217).

as *stone, church, bridge, cheese,* and *fox,* which would most likely display regional variation, and it is these which have been meticulously studied to establish the broad pattern of Middle English dialects (see panel 9.3). These major dialect areas correspond very largely to those already present in Old English (p. 51), but there has been some renaming. What was *Northumbrian* is now called *Northern,* and distinguished from the very different developments taking place in Scotland (see below). What was *West Saxon* is now called *South-Western,* or *Southern,* though not extending quite as far north as in Anglo-Saxon times. *Kentish* is usually referred to as *South-Eastern,* and – depending on the linguistic criteria used – either had a northern boundary along the Thames or extended as far as Norfolk. The most important difference, however, is the development of the old *Mercian* dialect area into two distinct regions, now called *East Midlands* and *West Midlands,* the dividing line broadly following the path of the southern Pennines and the Cotswold Hills. An *East Anglian* area is sometimes separately distinguished. The East Midlands – taking this to include the London area – proves to be of special significance for the later history of English, as it is the region which had greatest influence on the evolution of the standard language (Chapter 10). But we must not anticipate. During the early Middle English period, all dialects were equal, though some were more fully represented by texts than others.

The Scottish dimension

The map on p. 201 gives a traditional picture of the dialects of Middle English in England. But all such maps ignore the fact that in Scotland, at this time, the English language was also developing its character, and in a highly distinctive way. Indeed, when we consider the literature which was being created there during the medieval period, we have to conclude that English was already showing signs of the multi-track development which would be the keynote of its later history. Perhaps similar developments in speech were taking place in Wales and Ireland, but there is no evidence. In Ireland, following the arrival of the Anglo-Normans in 1169, Latin and French were the norms. English, although used to some extent as a language of administration from the mid thirteenth century, made very little progress as a vernacular, losing ground to French and Irish, so much so that in 1366 the Statutes of Kilkenny actually had to insist 'that every Englishmen use the English language, and be named by an English name'. In Wales, there is no real evidence of a Welsh English until the sixteenth century (p. 341). Only in Scotland, during the Middle English period, do we find the emergence of a dialectally distinctive English literary tradition.[4]

There was no clear boundary to be seen between Scotland and England during the Old English period. The Anglo-Saxons had moved into Scotland during the second half of the sixth century, defeating the Celts in several battles, and establishing settlements in various parts of the south of the country. Following the union of the Scottish and Pictish kingdoms, *c.* 850, there was a long struggle between Celts, Saxons, and Vikings for control of the whole border area, and in the early eleventh century a political boundary eventually emerged along the River Tweed. During that time, there is little evidence of English in Scotland, other than a sprinkling of Anglian place-names (such as *Haddington* and *Whittinghame*) and the occasional inscription or legal document, and what there is shows the area to be a linguistic extension of Northumbrian. It is this dialect that can be seen in the inscriptions on the Ruthwell Cross (p. 40), discovered near the town of Dumfries.

The stimulus for the independent development of a Scottish dialect of English came after the Norman Conquest, when English loyalists fled to Scotland, to be welcomed by Malcolm III (reigned 1058–93). Malcolm spoke English – he had been an exile in England during the reign of Macbeth (the protagonist of Shakespeare's play) – and his marriage to Margaret (later, St Margaret), the sister of Edgar the Atheling, resulted in an anti-Norman alliance which must have given the language considerable prestige. English, rather than Gaelic, influences were widespread. Margaret established at Dunfermline a Benedictine priory of monks from Canterbury. Most new townships were given English names, as were Margaret's four eldest children – Edward, Edmund, Ethelred, and Edgar (nor was Gaelic used for any of the others – Alexander, David, Matilda, and Mary). Malcolm, and later his sons and grandsons, began the development of a feudal society of trading settlements (*burghs*) based on the Norman model, in which English emerged as the lingua franca. The burghs quickly grew in size, incorporating the steady number of refugees escaping the anti-Anglo-Saxonism of the Norman kings, and – following the growth of trading links with Europe – immigrants from Scandinavia and Holland. Flemish mercenaries had also sometimes been employed on English campaigns, and were encouraged to settle in the border territories (in south-west Wales as well as in Scotland) – a trend which would lead to *Fleming* becoming a common Scottish surname. The Flemings and Scandinavians both spoke Germanic languages, so they would have readily assimilated into the English-speaking (rather than the Gaelic-speaking) sector of Scottish society. In any case, with English rapidly rising in prestige (much earlier in Scotland than in England, p. 138), there would have been little motivation for incomers to learn Gaelic, even though that was the mother tongue of most of the Scottish population. The problems facing Gaelic in modern times had early origins.

By the thirteenth century, English was the dominant language in the Lowland south and east, being used widely in commerce and (along with Latin) in law. Although French had been taken up as the language of the court and of aristocratic culture, following the pattern found throughout Western Europe (p. 136), the personal background of the royal family must have promoted a considerable degree of bilingualism. And once that royal line died out, at the end of the thirteenth century, the position of English was strengthened by the new royal lines coming from English-speaking Lowland houses: the Balliols, Bruces, and Stewarts. By the end of the fourteenth century, English had replaced French in the court, and soon after (1411) it replaced Latin in parliamentary proceedings. As in England, the amount of administrative documentation steadily grew, with local charters, burgh records, letters, and other forms of prose now appearing in a distinctive local dialect. It was a dialect which had evolved largely independently of the linguistic changes taking place in England. We have already seen how the Hundred Years War affected the relationship between English and French (p. 124); in Scotland there was a Three Hundred Years War, following Edward I of England's invasion in 1296. There would be no motivation for Scottish English to accommodate to the speech patterns of England in such circumstances, and every motivation to make local speech as different as possible. No growing influence of the London dialect here. The situation continued throughout the whole of the Middle English period.

By 1400 the Scottish dialect had evolved a character quite different from anything to be found south of the Tweed, and already had an epic piece of literature to be proud of. This was John Barbour's verse chronicle of the wars of independence in the early fourteenth century, *The Bruce*. Written in 1375 (though the earliest extant copy dates from a century later),[5] the text displays forms typical of the Northern speech of England, as well as a wide range of distinctively Scottish variants. The use of *they*- forms of the pronoun is Northern (p. 75), as are the *-and* and *-s* endings in verbs (*byrnand* instead of *burning*, *has* instead of *hath*), which we will discuss further below. There is widespread use of the Northern long *a* vowel instead of the Southern *o* (already noted in the case of *stane* 'stone'): *sa* 'so', *ane* 'one', *gane* 'gone', *ga* 'go', *stanys* 'stones'. At the same time there are many words, spellings, and grammatical endings which indicate its evolving local character, several of which are still associated with Scots speech and writing today, such as *gang* 'go', *gude* 'good', *richt* 'right', *sare* 'sore', *syne* 'afterwards', *mekill* 'great', *sic* 'such', and *till* 'to'. The past forms of the verb are typically *-it*, as in *pressit* 'pressed' and *provit* 'proved'. Among Old English words which are rarely or never found outside Scotland are *anerly* 'alone', *scathful* 'harmful', *sturting* 'convention', and *umbeset* 'surround'; French loans into Scottish include *dour* 'stern', *moyen* 'means', *fasch* 'annoy', and *ladroun* 'rascal'. A particularly distinctive feature is the spelling of *wh-* as *quh-*, suggesting a strongly aspirated sound, as in *quhelis* 'wheels', *quhar* 'where', and *quhill* 'while'. In aggregate, these features combine to make a highly differentiated dialect, whose flavour can be captured even in a brief extract. Here are some lines from Barbour's account of the siege of Berwick in 1319 (Book XVII, l. 738):

Thai war within sa stratly stad	They were within so severely placed
That thar wardane with him had	That their commander, [who] with him had
Ane hundreth men in cumpany	A hundred men in company
Armyt, that wicht war and hardy	Armed, who valiant were and bold,
And raid about for till se quhar	And rode about for to see where
That his folk hardest pressit war.	That his people hardest pressed were.

The language was still being called *Inglis* 'English' at the time. The term *Scottis* 'Scots' or 'Scottish' does not appear with reference to English (its earlier application was to Gaelic) until the end of the fifteenth century, and the distinction really only becomes noteworthy after the writing of the poet–scholar Gavin Douglas, who makes a number of linguistic observations in the Prologues to his books of *Eneados*, translating Virgil's *Aeneid* (1513). He is self-deprecating about his own ability and about the qualities of Scottis – described as *bad harsk speche and lewit barbour tong* 'bad harsh speech and ignorant barbarous tongue' – compared with Latin (Prologue to Book I, l. 19). The description is understandable, given the standing in which Latin was held by everyone in the Middle Ages. But compared to the rest of English literature, even as early as 1377, it is a travesty of the truth (see panel 9.4).

9.4 A royal love lyric

The Kingis Quair (*The King's Book*), written *c.* 1430, illustrates the heights to which poetry written in the Scottish dialect would eventually rise.[6] Its 1,379 lines are divided into seven-line stanzas, whose length and rhyme scheme follow the pattern used by Chaucer in *Troilus and Criseyde*. Its subject-matter – a dream-allegory dealing with the vagaries of fortune and the joys of love – shows the influence of Chaucer's *Romaunt of the Rose*. The authorship of the poem has long been ascribed to King James I of Scotland (1394–1437), following a prefatory sentence in the manuscript: 'Maid be [by] King Iames of scotland the frist callit the kingis quair and Maid quhen [when] his Maiestie Wes In Ingland.'
    This is Stanza 63, in which the author addresses the goddess Venus:

O Venus clere, of goddis stellifyit,	O Venus clear, of gods made a star,
to quhom I yelde homage and sacrifis,	to whom I yield homage and sacrifice,
fro this day forth your grace be magnifyit,	from this day forth your grace be magnified,
thet me ressavit have in suich wise	that I have received in such a manner
to lyve under your law and do servis;	to live under your law and do service;
now help me furth, and for your merci lede	now help me forth, and your mercy lead
my hert to rest, that deis nere for drede.	my heart to rest, that near dies for dread.

The poem's scale, sophistication of subject-matter, and linguistic ingenuity have given it a particular significance in Scottish literary history. It is seen as a defining moment in the rise of the fifteenth-century poetic movement known as the Scottish Chaucerians, whose later members would include Robert Henryson, William Dunbar, and Gavin Douglas.

The emerging north–south divide

The most noticeable dialect differences in Middle English, as we would expect, are those between the parts of Britain furthest away from each other – the north and the south. From a London perspective, there would be nothing more different than the speech of Scotland. That is how the story is normally told. From an Edinburgh perspective, of course, there would be nothing more different than the speech of London. But the story is never told from a Scottish point of view, presumably because, when we encounter comments about dialect usage during this period, what we find is a mindset which is either wholly southern in character, or one which finds it natural to defer to it.

Ranulph Higden, as translated by John of Trevisa, had already noticed the changes in English caused by the arrival of the French (p. 130), and in the same chapter of his work he comments on the dialect situation, too. He is the first to recognize explicitly the existence of a dialect chain in English. 'The Saxon tongue,' he says, 'is divided into three' – it should really have been four, remembering Scotland – and he observes:

ys gret wondur, for men of þe est wiþ men of þe west, as hyt were vnder þe same party of heuene, acordeþ more in sounyng of speche þan men of þe norþ wiþ men of þe souþ. Þerfore hyt ys þat Mercii, þat buþ men of myddel Engelond, as hyt were parteners of þe endes, vnderstondeþ betre þe syde longages, Norþeron and Souþeron, þan Norþeron and Souþeron vnderstondeþ eyþer oþer.

It is remarkable that men from the east and men from the west, as it were under the same part of heaven, agree more in pronunciation than do men from the north with men from the south. Therefore it is that Mercians, who are from middle England, as it were sharers with the extremes, understand the marginal languages, Northern and Southern, better than Northern and Southern people understand each other.

It was not only southerners, such as John of Trevisa, who noticed the difference. Northerners did too. The author of the verse chronicle *Cursor Mundi*, written *c.* 1300 somewhere in the north-east, perhaps Yorkshire or Durham, is in no doubt about it. At one point in his long poem (l. 20,061) he mentions how he had found an account of the Assumption of the Virgin Mary, which he wanted to incorporate into his work, but there was a problem: *In sotherin englis was it draun* – 'it was written in southern English'. His solution?

And turnd it haue I till our aun
Langage o northrin lede
Þat can nan oiþer englis rede.

I have translated it into our own language for northern folk who can read no other English.

It is difficult to know just how seriously to take these comments about dialect difference. Would it really have been so difficult for northerners to read a Southern text? Then as now, there may have been a tendency to overemphasize or overinterpret the existence of a difference. A famous case in point comes just at the close of the Middle English period, in *c.* 1490, when William Caxton tells a story in his Prologue to the translation of Virgil's *Aeneid, The Booke of Eneydos*. It seems that a shipful of sailors were becalmed in the Thames estuary, and decided to make a shore visit 'for to refreshe them' while they waited for the wind to pick up. Caxton continues (the extract modernizes his punctuation):

And one of theym named sheffelde a mercer cam into an hows and axed [asked] for mete, and specyally he axyd after eggys. And the good wyf answerde that she coude speke no frenshe. And the marchaunt was angry, for he also coude speke no frenshe, but wold haue hadde egges, and she vnderstode hym not. And thenne at laste a nother sayd thet he wolde haue eyren. Then the good wyf sayd that she vnderstod hym wel.

Caxton is very impressed with this story, and sees in it a reflection of a general malaise:

Loo, what sholde a man in thyse dayes now wryte, egges or eyren? Certaynly it is harde to playse euery man by cause of dyuersite & chaunge of langage.

The reason for the good lady's difficulty is clear: *egges* was a Northern form, a development from Old Norse, whereas *eyren* was a Southern form, a development from Old English. Caxton would indeed have to choose, and as a publisher this is a real problem. But was he right to take the story at face value? The many recipe books of the period show that both words, *egges* and *eyren*, were still in use, as suggested by the cookbook examples on p. 153, though doubtless *eyren* was beginning to die out. It is difficult to believe that two common domestic terms would not have been well known to a cafe-owner on the banks of the Thames. More likely, the story arose from a piece of banter, much as one might find today in a London pub when someone with, say, an American accent orders some drinks, the barman fails to catch what was said, and another customer intervenes with a comment about the Americans 'not speaking English'. Caxton was of course making a point. Well aware of the huge amount of dialect variation in his century, and worried about how to print his books in a language that everyone would understand, the Sheffield story was a good way of deflecting possible reader criticism.

'That comyn [common] englysshe that is spoken in one shyre varyeth from a nother,' says Caxton, and repeatedly we find references being made to the differences between north and south. But why should these parts of the country be so different? The main reason was the pervasive influence that Old Norse continued to exercise throughout the northern area. As we have seen (p. 65), the Scandinavian contribution to English as a whole had been significant, and many Norse words – such as *call, knife*, and *give* – had become part of the language by the twelfth century, appearing in texts from all parts of the country. But in the north, in the areas where Scandinavian settlement had been strongest, there were a large number of Norse words still being used which had not travelled south, as well as Norse features of grammar and pronunciation. Where southerners would say *nimen*, northerners would say *taken* 'take'; Southern *cherle* would be Northern *carl* 'churl'; and other pairs were (South) *ich* vs (North) *ik* 'I', *ey* vs *egg* 'egg', *sterre* vs *sterne* 'star', *chirche* vs *kirke* 'church', *theigh* vs *though* 'though', and *hundred* vs *hundreth* 'hundred'. Several of the Northern words eventually become standard, but the majority do not, and are known today only from their sporadic occurrence in Northern texts in Middle English or from present-day regional dialect use. The *Cursor Mundi* provides an example: this contains such Norse words as *dill* 'hide', *brixel* 'shame', *nowcin* 'hardship', *serk* 'shirt, shift', *gleg* 'quick, sharp' [in perception], and *laire* 'clay, mud'. The first three did not survive the early Middle English period; the second three continued to have strong dialect use. *Gleg*, for example, is still widely heard in Scotland and in several parts of northern England, along with a number of derived forms, such as *glegly, gleg-witted, gleg-eyed*, and *gleg-tongued*.

We have already seen the long-term influence of Old Norse on Standard English grammar in the *they-* pronouns and the verb *to be* (p. 75). But when these forms first arrived in English they were dialectally distinctive, being used just in the north of England and in Scotland; only later in the Middle English period did they spread to other areas. The same trend can be observed in the third-person ending *-s* in the present tense – as in modern *he/she/it makes* vs *I/you/we/they make*. This ending appeared as *-es*, *-as*, or *-s* in the North and as *-eð*, *-að*, or *-ð* in the South: 'he loves' would thus be *he lufas* and *he lufað* respectively. Where the ending came from is discussed in Interlude 9 (p. 218), but once it arrived it spread steadily. By the end of the Middle English period, *-s* forms were being used throughout the Midlands, and were beginning to make their appearance in the South, replacing the form which by then was being routinely spelled as *-th*. The process of replacement took a long time: although the *-s* form eventually prevailed, the choice between such pairs as *he loves* and *he loveth* was still available in the age of Shakespeare, and would prove to be a useful literary option in metrical composition (p. 275).

This choice already had some literary value in the medieval period, in fact. Only some of the variation in third-person forms which we observe in Middle English texts can be explained with reference to regional factors. There is no doubt that the third-person *-s* ending was recognized in the South as a distinctively Northern form. Chaucer puts these forms into the mouths of his north-country students in *The Reeve's Tale* (p. 166): they use *has* and *says*, whereas the narrator (along with the south-country miller in the tale) uses *hath* and *speketh*. On the other hand, Chaucer and his contemporaries also use *-s* forms which have no dialectal significance. As with the case of *stane* above, the availability of *-s* endings allows a further option for an author to provide a satisfactory rhyme. In *The Clerk's Tale* (l. 1,079), for example, we find *fall* used with Chaucer's usual *-th* form:

> Whan she this herde, aswowne [in a swoon] doun she falleth
> For pitous [piteous] joye, and after hire [her] swownynge
> She bothe hire yonge children to hire calleth . . .

But in *The Book of the Duchess* (l. 257) we find *fall* used with an *-s* form, introduced purely to complete the rhyme:

> And I wol yive [give] hym al that falles [belongs]
> To a chambre; and al hys halles
> I wol do peynte with pure gold . . .

This is poetry, not dialect, talking.

A similar example had appeared more than half a century earlier, making use of the dialect variations which affected the present-participle ending on verbs (as in *I am running*). In early Middle English this was appearing as *-and* or *-ande* in Northern, as *-end* or *-ende* in the East Midlands, as *-ind* or *-inde* in the West Midlands, and in Southern and South-Eastern as *-ing* or *-inge*. In *Handlyng Synne*, a long morality poem begun in 1303 by Robert of Brunne (modern Bourne, in Lincolnshire), we find a group of people singing Christmas carols: at one point (l. 9,137) they are said to be *karolland* 'carolling', which is what we would expect from a work written so far north at this date; but a few lines earlier we find a group *karollyng* (l. 9,042):

Beune ordeyned here karollyng;	Bevo arranged their carolling;
Gerlew endyted what þey shuld	Gerlew dictated what they should
syng . . .	sing . . .
Þese men þat ȝede so karolland,	These men that went thus
	carolling,
Alle þat ȝere, hand yn hand . . .	All that year, hand in hand

In cases of this kind, the dialect resonance, if it is there at all, is very much in the background. Certainly there would be no rustic or humorous associations, such as we would find in a modern piece of verse which attempted a similar rhyme:

> I walked with her into the halls
> But on the staircase down I falls.

Some present-day humorists rely greatly on such effects – the oeuvre of Pam Ayres comes to mind. No one would have laughed at it in the fourteenth century.

Non-dialectal variation is widespread in Middle English texts. This is the down side of having a large number of manuscripts available for study. Many variations in usage appear which have nothing to do with the regional background of the writers. The early period, in particular, was an age when the orthography of English was subject to an unprecedented range of partly conflicting influences. One set of spelling conventions had come down from Old English, another arrived from French, and a third came in from medieval Latin. French scribal practice, for example, introduced such spellings as *qu-* (as in *quick*) to replace *cw-*, and this spelling became the norm by the end of the thirteenth century. However, French practice was not the same throughout the period; the usage of Parisian scribes differed in several respects from that of their Norman counterparts (p. 148). We find such Anglo-Norman spellings as *dulur*, *prisun*, and *finisshed*; the Parisian equivalents are *dolour*, *prison*, and *finissed*. Nor was the Old English legacy itself straightforward, as it had long displayed many differences in scribal practice (p. 52). In particular, the letters which the Irish monks had added to the Latin alphabet in order to write down Old English (*æ*, *þ*, *ð*, *ƿ*) all showed considerable variation in use, both chronologically and geographically. Letter *æ* sometimes appears as *ae*, *þ* as *u* or *uu*, and *þ* and *ð* as *th*. A ninth-century Kentish charter includes the names *ecgferð*, *sigefreð*, and *hunfreð*. The *Liber Vitae*, from the same century, lists hundreds of benefactors to the church in Durham: they include *ecgfrith*, *bugsuith*, and *heregyth*.[7] There are no names in the charter ending in *-th*, but several in the *Liber Vitae* do end in *-ð*. There was evidently a northern preference to use the *-th* spelling at the end of a name, but not to the total exclusion of the runic letters. And in other texts, we find yet further variation in the use of *þ* instead of *ð*. For the early Middle English French-trained scribe, the Anglo-Saxon orthographic heritage must have seemed not a little confusing, increasing the motivation to use French conventions, even though the long-term result of this process would be additional confusion.

Without a standard to act as a guide, it is not surprising to find a remarkable number of spelling variations in Middle English texts, as scribes attempted to cope with this welter of influences in individual ways. A selection of spellings for *day*, for example, includes *dai, day, daye, dæi, daiȝe, deai, dey, dei, dæȝ*, and *dawe*. For *knight* we find *knight, knighte, knyght, knyghte, knyht, knyhte, knith, kniȝt, knyȝt, knyȝte, knict, kincth, cniþte*, and *cniht*. Some words had hundreds of variants. There is variation even within the work of the same author, especially in the late fourteenth and early fifteenth centuries. Thus in Chaucer we find *passion* and *passioun*, *privee* and *privy* 'private', *offencioun* and *offensioun* 'offence', *norice* and *norys* 'nurse', and many more. The problem for Middle English dialectologists is plain. How can they discover, within all this variation, those spellings which represent genuine regional differences of accent? Which spellings, on the other hand, are simply 'free' variation – acceptable alternatives conveying no sociolinguistic implication, much as, today, we can spell *judgement* with or without the *e*, regardless of our regional, social, or professional background? And which are the result of scribal misjudgement or carelessness – a not unusual occurrence, to judge by Chaucer's cynical remark about his own scribe (p. 184)? Indeed, some studies of scribal practice have brought to light remarkable amounts of inconsistency, sometimes within a few lines of each other. There is even a case of a Chaucerian scribe who had a bad habit of duplicating passages from the text he was engaged in copying; we might imagine that here, at least, we would find identity, but we do not. When the duplicate passages are compared, they display many differences, not only in spelling, but in grammatical endings and the choice of words as well.[8]

The most sensible solution is the one adopted by Middle English dialectologists towards the end of the twentieth century: meticulous pattern-matching.[9]

The process begins by examining manuscripts which are definitely known, on non-linguistic grounds, to have been written in particular locations (*anchor texts*). Within each manuscript there will be distinctive linguistic features – spellings, words, and grammatical constructions – that can be assumed to be diagnostic of their locality. A manuscript from Kent, for example, might contain the word for 'church' as *cherche*; one from Devon might have it as *churche*; one from Oxfordshire might have it as *chirche*; one from Yorkshire might have it as *kirke*; and one from Cumbria might have it as *kyrk*. As each manuscript is studied, the distinctive forms for 'church' are placed on a map of the country. After a while, the numbers start to build up. Dozens of forms like *kirk*, *kirke*, *kyrk*, and *kyrke* are found, and it turns out that – with just a few exceptions – they belong to locations in the northern half of the country. Throughout the south, we find the forms using *ch*. Towards the east and south-east the *cherch* forms predominate; towards the west and south-west, the *church* forms; and down the centre of the country we find a large number of *chirch* or *chyrch* forms. Armed with this grid, it is now possible to take manuscripts of unknown provenance, and if they contain the word 'church' – which is quite often the case, as it is a very common word – we can see where its form could possibly fit. A manuscript containing *kirk* is bound to be Northern or the northern part of the East Midlands; a manuscript containing *cherche* is likely to be the southern or eastern part of the East Midlands or from the South-East (see panel 9.5). A single word, of course, is of limited value; but after carrying out this kind of exercise on hundreds of words, and taking into account a wide range of spelling variations, some very plausible conclusions about provenance can be achieved. The localization of a text can sometimes be narrowed down to just a few miles.

Dialectologists pray daily for neatly demarcated clusters of the kind illustrated in the panel – but rarely find them. The reality is much more complex. Preponderances of usage do exist, but so do all kinds of overlaps. In the West Midlands, there are places where *church* and *chirch* forms appear next to each other; in the East Midlands *chirch* and *cherch* forms coexist. In the north of Devon, where *churche* forms are the norm, there is a small, unexpected cluster of *cherche* forms. An isolated *chirche* form appears in the very north of Lancashire, surrounded by *kirk* forms. An isolated *kyrk* form appears as far south as Oxfordshire, surrounded by *church* and *chirch* forms. Panel 9.6 presents a more detailed picture of the distribution of 'church' forms from one region, the northern part of East Anglia. It is easy to see that *k*- forms die out as we move south, and *ch*- forms as we move north. But it is less easy to work out what is happening to the *ch*- forms, in this part of the world. *Cherch* and *chirch* seem to be in real competition during this period (roughly 1300–1500). The only

9.5 *Church* forms in England

kyrk

kirk

kirke

kirk

chirche   kirke

chirche

cherch

chirche

cherche

churche

churche

chirch   cherche

churche   cherche

0   miles   50

0   km   80

Plotting known locations of words for *church* during the Middle English period. If *kirk* appeared in a manuscript of unknown origin, the 'fit' would make it likely to have been written in the north.

consolation for the dialectologist, desperate for something simple and definite to say, is that there is no sign of any *church* forms.

Procedures of this kind will not find order in everything. Much variation is bound to remain inexplicable – other than by reference to idiosyncratic factors, such as copying error. The analysis has hardly begun of the descriptive material so far collated, but the pattern-matching approach has already demon-

9.6 *Church* forms in East Anglia

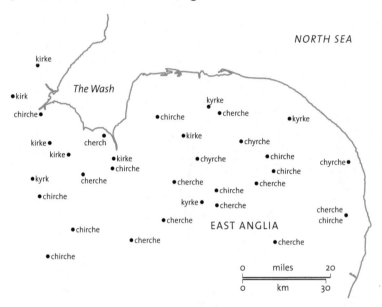

A selection of *church* forms in northern East Anglia during the Middle English period. The overlap between *k*- and *ch*- forms is evident, as is the overlap between *chi*- and *che*- forms. No *chu*- forms have travelled this far north and east, however.

strated its potential for discovering some degree of order within the remarkable range of forms displayed by Middle English manuscripts. It is so important to take their variability seriously – as at any period of linguistic history – and not to dismiss it as a random consequence of fortuitous or unknown circumstances. The fact that variation *can* be random does not mean that it always is. And when variation is studied systematically, it transpires that it usually isn't. Only in the twentieth century, with sophisticated recording and analysis of speech at last available, has it been possible to determine the range of factors involved. The age and sex of speakers and writers have proved to be critical, as has their social and economic background. Their perception of audience is relevant, language varying subtly in relation to those whom speakers and writers are addressing. Subject-matter is a further factor, motivating different kinds of spoken and written style. Several such variables have to be taken into account before an analyst would conclude, reluctantly, that a particular usage was 'random' or a 'slip of the brain'. These variables operate today, and they operated just as strongly in medieval times; but with only the written language available to access them, the goal of demonstrating system within variation becomes tantalizingly distant.

With no standard language to act as a control, Middle English illustrates an age when all dialects were equal, in the sense that the written language permitted the use of a wide range of variant forms, each of which was acceptable. There was no hint of a prescriptive attitude. People wrote differently – and in the case of literary characters, such as the Northern students in *The Reeve's Tale* – spoke differently; but they did not write or speak wrongly. One person may not have liked the way other people spoke or wrote – that is a character-note for the human race – but there was no suggestion that they were somehow 'incorrect' as a result of doing so. Chaucer's Parson evidently cannot stand stories which rhyme or which use the Northern alliterative style of composition. When the Host asks him for a story, he replies:

> But trusteth wel, I am a Southren man,
> I kan nat geeste 'rum, ram, ruf' by lettre,
> Ne, God woot, rym holde I but litel bettre

'I can't tell a tale in which words have to begin with the same letter', he says, 'Nor, God knows, do I rate rhyme any better'. So he opts for prose. But nowhere in *The Canterbury Tales* do we find him, or anyone else, condemning a regional way of talking. They may not like each other much, or like the subject-matter of a tale, or like someone's propensity for difficult words or for swearing,[10] but they don't pick on the accent or dialect in which they talk. Content seems to rule. If you don't like what you read, says Chaucer at one point, 'Turne over the leef and chese [choose] another tale ... Blameth nat me if that ye chese amys' (Prologue to *The Miller's Tale*, l. 3,177).

Variation, whether regional or personal, was routine. Nobody seemed to mind if a writer spelled a word differently from one part of a text to another. At one point in *The Wife of Bath's Tale*, we find *a draughte of sweete wyn* (l. 459); a short while after, we find *hym thoughte the tale swete* (l. 734). Nobody would have noticed the difference. That is one reason why we encounter so much scribal error at this time, of course: in the absence of a standard, copying mistakes can look like intentional choices. The instinct of modern editors, whose linguistic intuitions have been shaped by an era in which standardized usage is the norm, is to eliminate what would be perceived as unnecessary variability, seeing it as interfering with the reader's easy accessibility to the content of a text. It is a spellchecking age, and has been, since the eighteenth century (p. 394). The point is made by way of general acknowledgement, and is not intended as a criticism of editorial practice. A policy of standardization does often meet the expectations of the reader, who shares these intuitions, and a failure to standardize can at times introduce an unnecessary barrier to comprehension. That is why, for example, I standardized the punctuation in my extract from Caxton above (p. 207). But readers need to be told when this is happening, and must appreciate that the sanitized texts which result are some remove from the linguistic character of the original. The problem is at its greatest when we encounter language which has to be spoken aloud, in the case of drama, and where editorial intervention can radically alter the interpretation of a text.

Nobody seemed to mind . . . The contrast with modern attitudes is striking. The Middle English period illustrates a level of tolerance of language diversity which had disappeared by the eighteenth century. Nor, it must be admitted, did it last very long in Middle English either. Already, during the fourteenth century, we find the storm-clouds gathering. The contrast between 'lered' and 'lewed' was becoming a regular issue (p. 174), and we begin to see uncomplimentary remarks being made about regional speech. One of the earliest examples is Ranulph Higden, who follows his comment about north/south differences (p. 206) by these words (in Trevisa's translation):

> Al þe longage of þe Norþumbres, and specialych at ȝork, ys so scharp, slyttyng, and frotyng, and vnschape, þat we Souþeron men may þat longage vnneþe vnderstonde.

> All the speech of the Northumbrians, and especially at York, is so harsh, piercing, and grating, and formless, that we Southern men can hardly understand such speech.

Poor York, the earliest town to be publicly berated by a southerner for the accent of its inhabitants! In fact, the condemnation long predates the fourteenth century. Higden presumably held this attitude, though the passage is actually a borrowing from the Latin writer William of Malmesbury, written as early as 1125.[11] But the good people of York had their attitudes, too. In 1364, a skinner from Peebles who had been captured at the Battle of Neville's Cross (1346) between the Scots and the English was called as a witness in York, but his way of speaking – according to the record, a mixture of Scottish, Southern, and Northern – was judged by a York magistrate to be untrustworthy.[12] The fourteenth century evidently saw a growing tendency to stigmatize speakers 'from elsewhere', and this case shows that dialect labelling was current. The age, it seems, was not so linguistically innocent after all.

Although Higden has an unpalatable puristic streak, he also displays commendable sociolinguistic realism. He knows why the dialect difference with the North exists.

> Y trowe þat þat ys bycause þat a buþ nyȝ to strange men and aliens, þat spekeþ strangelych, and also bycause þat þe kynges of Engelond woneþ alwey fer fram

þat contray; for a buþ more yturnd to þe souþ contray, and ʒef a goþ to þe norþ contray, a goþ wiþ gret help and strengthe.

I believe that this is because it is near to outlandish men and foreigners, who speak in a foreign language, and also because the kings of England always live far from that region, being more inclined to the southern part of the country, and if they go to the northern part, they go with great force and might.

And he adds perceptively:

Þe cause why a buþ more in þe souþ contray þan in þe norþ may be betre cornlond, more people, more noble cytés, and more profytable hauenes.

The reason why they are more in the south than the north may be better cornland, more population, more noble cities, and more profitable harbours.

Quite so. Already by the early twelfth century the south was becoming a political, social, economic, and cultural magnet. By the fourteenth, it had consolidated its position, so that Higden's attitude would not have been unusual. Trevisa – a man always ready to add his own opinion when he thinks his source wrong – translates it without comment.

Things could not go on like this. There was a tension between the regionally and socially inspired linguistic diversity apparent in manuscripts and the growing sense of cultural division whereby one part of the country was felt to be socially superior to others. The south-east, and in particular the triangular area with focal points in London, Oxford, and Cambridge (p. 201), had become a region of special influence. And social change always has a linguistic sequel. It was inevitable that the speech of the south-east – or, at least, of those south-easterners in routine contact with the worlds of courtly culture, commerce, and learning – would increase in prestige, and begin to be evaluated as a more polished, elegant, and altogether more desirable medium of communication than the varieties available elsewhere. The stage was set for the emergence of a standard dialect.

Interlude 9
Where did the -s ending come from?

These were the most common endings for the present tense of Old English verbs, using *tellan* 'count' (later, 'tell') as an illustration:

first-person singular	-e	ic telle	I count
second-person singular	-est, -ast, -st	þu tellest	thou countest
third-person singular	-eð, -að, -ð	he/heo/hit telleð	he/she/it counts
first-person plural	-að, -ð	we tellað	we count
second-person plural	-að, -ð	ge tellað	you count
third-person plural	-að, -ð	hi tellað	they count

However, in the north, during the 800s, a new system was evolving alongside this one. Northumbrian texts of the late ninth century illustrate a simpler set of endings: an -*s* form is used for every person apart from the first person singular. For *tellan*, that system would probably have looked like this:

ic telle	we tellas
þu tellas	ge tellas
he/heo/hit tellas	hi tellas

The -*s* forms became increasingly widespread during early Middle English. They moved south into both the East and West Midlands, and north into Scotland, where even first-person singular forms are sometimes found ending in -*s*. During the fourteenth century, the plural -*s* endings began to die out in the Midlands, losing ground to a new form, -*en* – as in *we tellen* 'we count' – and this eventually became the dominant form in the south as well. But the third-person singular -*s* remained, and during the fifteenth century we see this moving south too, in due course becoming part of Standard English, and remaining with us today.

The intriguing question is: where did the -*s* ending come from?

There is no sign of it elsewhere in Old English, so it must have come from outside; and as the only influence in Northumbria during the ninth century was from Scandinavia, it must have been the result of contact between the Anglo-Saxons and the Danish incomers. We know that Old English was much influenced by Old Norse words and word forms (p. 71). The -s must be a further instance. But it could not have been a straightforward borrowing of the present-tense ending, because the equivalent present-tense forms of the verb in Old Norse had no -s.

ek tel	I tell	ver teljum	we tell
þu telr	thou tellest	er telið	you tell
hann/hon/þat telr	he/she/it tells	þeir/þær/þau telja	they tell

This was an even richer set of endings than had existed in Old English. A simplified system could hardly have come from here.

There are really only two possible explanations, and both are to do with the way people from one group in language-contact situations are known to misinterpret or mislearn what people from the other group are saying. Word endings are especially prone to error. Foreigners learning English often say things like 'he go', until they learn the correct system; likewise, the English, on their rare incursions into foreign-language learning, routinely say such things as *vous faisez* 'you make' (instead of *vous faites*). French people unable to pronounce English *th* consonant sounds will replace them by /s/ or /z/ – 'I sink zis is ze way'. English people unable to pronounce French nasal vowels will replace them by an oral vowel followed by a nasal consonant – 'tray bong resterong' (*très bon restaurant*).

There is no reason to think that the language-contact situation in the ninth century would have been any different. As Anglo-Saxons and Danes began to accommodate to each other's ways of talking, there would have been many occasions for errors to arise, as we have already seen in other connections (p. 160). And the errors could have come either from the Anglo-Saxon side or from the Danish side.

- In the first scenario, Anglo-Saxons heard other -s forms in Danish speech, assumed they were present-tense forms, and began to use them as part of their own system.
- In the second scenario, Danes tried to use the English present-tense -ð forms, but mispronounced them as -s. The Anglo-Saxons then found the -s forms congenial, eventually using them as part of their own system.

A case could be made for either of these explanations – or, of course, both may have exercised joint influence.

In relation to the first explanation, an -s ending (actually, -sk) was common in Old Norse verbs – in the second and third persons of verbs in the so-called 'middle voice'. This voice was used to express a wide range of meanings, such as reflexive and reciprocal – *hann telsk* 'he tells himself', *þeir teljask* 'they tell each other'. The *-s* forms appear with singulars and plurals, indicatives and subjunctives, and present and past tenses, so they would have been a frequent feature of Danish speech. They would also have been very noticeable: auditorily, [s] is a highly sonorous consonant; [k], by contrast, is a short and non-sonorant sound.

It would not have been surprising for the *-sk* to have been 'misheard' as *-s*. (Indeed, the dropping of the final *-k* did take place later in the development of most of the modern Scandinavian languages.) It would also be very natural for Anglo-Saxons to have assumed that such an ending was valid for English present-tense verb forms. Anglo-Saxons would have been able to make nothing of the 'middle' voice, as this category did not exist in Old English. To translate an Old Norse reflexive form would have required a circumlocution, such as those illustrated in the preceding paragraph. Generalizing *-s* into the present-tense system would have been the easiest of Anglo-Saxon errors.

In relation to the second explanation, we need only assume that the Danes had trouble distinguishing the *th* sound at the end of a word in English. This was likely, even though the *th* sound did exist in Old Norse. To understand why, we have to appreciate that there are two possible *th* sounds – one where the vocal cords are vibrating (the voiced sound [ð], as in *this*), and one where the vocal cords are not (the voiceless sound [θ], as in *thin*). In modern English, the two sounds are different phonemes (substituting one for the other can produce a change of meaning, as in *wreath* vs *wreathe* or *thigh* vs *thy*). But this was not the case either in Old English or in Old Norse, where the two sounds were variants of the same phoneme – much as, in Modern English, there are two variants of the /l/ phoneme, one of which occurs at the beginning of a word (the 'clear *l*' heard in *leap*), the other at the end of a word (the 'dark *l*' heard in *peel*).

Old English and Old Norse both had the two *th* variants, voiceless and voiced, but they used them in different ways. Old English, at the end of a word, used only the voiceless sound; Old Norse, in that position, used only the voiced sound. So, when the Danes heard an English final [θ], weakly articulated as inflectional endings always are, they would have had difficulty identifying it. It would not have sounded much like their own more strongly articulated [ð]. On the other hand, it *would* have sounded quite like their own [s] sound, which was always voiceless, or for that matter the English [s] sound. We know that [θ] and [s] are easy to mix up: this is the typical substitution that French learners of English make (and also, incidentally, is a common confusion in young English children when they are learning to talk). Generalizing *-s* into the present-tense system would have been the easiest of Danish errors.

Other factors may also have been relevant. The fact that the second-person singular ending contained an [s] element, as in *þu tellest*, could well have reinforced the illusion that this sound was an important person-marking feature of the English verb system. But the primary explanation for the emergence of -*s* in the English present tense requires reference to a much more powerful set of sociolinguistic and psycholinguistic considerations.

Chapter 10 The emerging standard

Standards exist to avoid the dangers of variability. We rely on a uniform system of weights and measures, because we know the scientific problems which would arise if we did not. We require our coins to be of a fixed shape, weight, and design, to safeguard ourselves against forgery. In relation to language, where the primary aim is to communicate meaning, the danger we face is breakdown in comprehension, which might range from a mild problem of mutual understanding to total unintelligibility. For the most part, there is no problem. Language is such a complex, flexible, and sensitive mode of human behaviour that most people use it instinctively to meet their local communicative needs without any need for special measures. This is especially so when a society consists of small and relatively isolated groups. But when societies become large and regionally diverse, or experience rapid periods of social change, the ability of its members to communicate successfully with each other can be put under great strain. An increasingly varied society will be reflected in an increasingly diversified language, with dialectal and stylistic variation growing to the extent that one sector may have difficulty in understanding another. In such circumstances, the emergence of a standard form of the language, to be learned by all, is a very natural development.

Standard languages arise in many ways. They can evolve over a long period of time associated with a particular body of religious or literary writing. Or an official body can be created (an Academy) which 'institutionalizes' a language by organizing the compilation of dictionaries, grammars, and manuals of style. In a further scenario, a standard can arrive, quite literally, overnight: a government selects a dialect of a language, prepares its people, and on a certain legally defined day it becomes the medium of national communication. Sometimes, more than one dialect is selected as the basis of the standard, and a planned amalgamation of forms takes place, as happened to Romansh in Switzerland in the 1980s when Rumantsch Grischun was devised, based on a collation of forms from the major dialects. It is even possible for a country to have two standard varieties of a language, as in the case of Norway, where Bokmål and Nynorsk have been in official coexistence since 1884.

In England, at the end of the Middle Ages, a standard language began to emerge, but it was in no way planned or institutionalized. There was no government intervention. No official bodies were established – the age predated the arrival of Academies in Europe (the first such body, in Italy, was not established until 1582). There were no pundits arguing for a policy of standardization. There was not even a long-standing body of comprehensible English classical literature to look back to: Old English was a foreign language to most people by then, as William Caxton observed in his Preface to *Eneydos* (*c.* 1490):

> And also my lorde Abbot of Westmynster ded [did] do shewe to me late certayn evydences wryton in olde Englysshe for to reduce it into our Engylysshe now usid. And certaynly it was wreton in suche wyse that it was more lyke to Dutche than Englysshe: I coude not reduce ne [nor] brynge it to be understonden.

In 1400 Chaucer's writing had yet to achieve classical status, and English translation of the Bible had hardly begun, notwithstanding Wycliffe's pioneering role in the 1380s. At the beginning of the fifteenth century, anyone who might have reflected on the need for a standard English language would have found it difficult to see where it could possibly come from. Yet, by the end of the century, its basis was definitely there.

It is difficult to resist the conclusion that Standard English, like Harriet Beecher Stowe's Topsy, 'just growed' – largely unselfconsciously during the fifteenth century, and increasingly self-aware thereafter. The growth took a long time – some 300 years, indeed, before the phenomenon, as we recognize it today, was firmly established. It is important to reiterate: only the *basis* of Standard English existed by 1500. Comparing the kind of language which was being written and spoken in those days to the kind of language we associate with Standard English now, we see a wide range of differences. The clear-cut distinction between 'correct' and 'incorrect' did not exist in late Middle English – that was an eighteenth-century development (p. 400). There was much greater flexibility over the range of forms which educated people were able to use. And a great deal of variation, a legacy of earlier Middle English (Chapter 9), was still in evidence. Apart from anything else, the language was still experiencing the consequences of the period of radical grammatical change which had begun at the end of the Old English period. In the fifteenth century it was undergoing a major shift in pronunciation norms (the Great Vowel Shift, p. 251). And its lexicon was continuing to grow rapidly through the introduction of large numbers of loanwords. A standard language presupposes a certain amount of stability: people have to be using the same set of rules, enabling them to distinguish between what is 'right' and what is 'wrong'. It would take a while before these judgements would be made with the kind of arrogant confidence which later became routine.

Language, however, is not like weights and measures, or coins. It is a human behaviour, and consequently susceptible to all the vagaries of the human condition. No standard language is ever completely immune to variability. No variety of language ever stands still, or is used by everyone in exactly the same way, not even the standard variety. Even after all the efforts of the eighteenth-century prescriptivists to fix English for ever, the present-day standard still has many points of variation, as a glance at any usage manual will show (see further, Chapter 18). There would have been no need for the Fowlers, Gowers, and Partridges of this world if it had been otherwise. The intention of books giving guidance about usage is to remove the uncertainty in the mind of the educated user who, having been brought up to believe that Standard English is an unvarying monolith, then discovers that it is not, because other educated users do not speak or write in the same way that he or she does – ?he/she does, ?(s)he does, ?they do. Everyone is affected. Each time an author writes a book, the text goes through the hands of a copy-editor employed by the publishing house, whose job is to make the text consistent according to the 'house style' of the publisher. Journalists have the same problem. House-style guidelines contain long lists of items whose standard usage is variable – such as the spelling choice between words ending in -*ise* vs -*ize*, hyphenation differences such as *washing-machine* vs *washing machine*, capitalization differences such as *the moon* vs *the Moon*, and grammatical differences such as *the car which was stolen* vs *the car that was stolen*. Indeed, my own style has been pulled in so many different directions over the years by different publishers that anyone doing a statistical analysis of usage in my oeuvre would encounter innumerable contradictions. If Standard English were truly invariable, none of this would ever happen, and usage manuals would not need to exist.

The notion of a 'standard language' is more complicated than a notion of 'standard weights and measures' for another reason: it operates differently in different mediums. It may apply only to the written language, or to the spoken language, or to both.[1] Present-day Standard English is primarily a written (and very largely a printed) phenomenon: the chief rules we follow are those governing the way we spell, and the vast majority of these are clear-cut (for the exceptions, see p. 477). *Accommodate* is 'right' and *accomodate* is 'wrong'. A much smaller number of rules govern the choices we make in grammar and vocabulary, and here it is more difficult to be definite about 'right' and 'wrong'. Only about 1 per cent of the grammatical rules of English (such as the proscription of *ain't*, or of double negatives, p. 403) are actually relevant to [for?] the distinction between standard and nonstandard, and debate can rage about the correctness or otherwise of some of the proscriptions (such as the concern over 'split infinitives', as in *to really agree*). Similarly, only a small number of dialect or slang words, by comparison with the lexicon as a whole, have a status as nonstandard, and several of these, as in the case of grammar, also generate a debate about their acceptability (such as *ungetatable* and *comeuppance*). The standardness of English is actually characterized with reference to a very small part – chiefly in spelling and grammar – of the language's structural resources.

When it comes to the spoken language, the rules governing the way we speak are even fewer and still less tightly constrained. Among the educated people who automatically use standard spelling in what they write, we hear a wide range of accents. Throughout the recent history of English it is possible to see, within a country, a trend towards giving normative status to a single accent – Received Pronunciation did in fact achieve such a status in England for some 200 years (p. 468) – but the rules governing the pronunciation of words in a prestige accent are never as all-inclusive or as determinate as those which govern spelling. All letters of the English alphabet are involved in the task of spelling, but only a few English sounds are involved in distinguishing types of accent – chiefly certain vowels, such as the contrast between long and short *a*, but also the occasional consonant, such as the use of [h] at the beginning of a word (p. 411). And there also exists a wide range of 'mixed accents', spoken by people who have lived in more than one locality; by contrast, the notion of a 'mixed spelling system' hardly exists.[2]

When people discuss the rise of Standard English, accordingly, they are usually talking about the way agreement emerged among writers in the fifteenth century about how to spell and punctuate the language. Their discussion would also include the way a consensus grew over which words or grammatical forms to use in writing, in cases where alternatives existed. But it would not normally include reference to the way people actually spoke. This is something which came later, in the sixteenth century. It seems that only after English was written down in a standardized form, and began to be taught in schools, did observers start to reflect about it, study it, and express their worries over how best to pronounce it, at which point the notion of a standard took on a spoken dimension. In this chapter, therefore, the focus is on the way a consensus gradually emerged, between 1400 and 1500, in the use of the written language. And the initial question has to be: why should a standard written system have begun to appear at this particular juncture in the history of English?

We have to look further back than the fifteenth century to answer this question. The emergence of a dialect as a written or spoken standard is the result of a long process of largely unconscious mental preparation. Influential people have to want it to happen. They have to feel a need – a sense of difficulty in communication. And then they have to make it happen. They have to spread it regionally and socially (*diffusion*) and maintain it (by teaching it and writing about it). A standard dialect arrives only when the intellectual and social climate warrants it, and that climate can take a considerable time to evolve, and depend upon a range of different factors. Histories of the English language have traditionally looked for a single factor – a major causative influence or a single point of origin – to explain the rise of Standard English. Indeed, several candidates have been proposed. The leading orthodoxy is that Standard English is a straightforward development of the Central or East Midland dialect of Middle English, as brought to London by large numbers of incomers from throughout the Midlands region. This is an important element in the history, undoubtedly, but it is by no means the only element. There are several stories behind the rise of Standard English.

The stories of Standard

The first storyline is psycholinguistic in character. From Chapter 9 we can deduce that by 1400 a sense of communicative difficulty must have been present among literate people. They were trying to operate in a written language where variation had become so uncontrolled that words could be spelled in dozens or hundreds of different ways. A scribe might write a form, and it would be impossible to say whether it was an intentional usage or a mistake. The literary authors were well aware of the dangers, knowing the extent to which their works could be contaminated by scribal error. Towards the end of *Troilus and Criseyde* (l. 1,793), in an address to his 'litel bok', Chaucer is one who expresses an earnest hope:

> And for there is so gret diversite
> In Englissh and in writyng of oure tonge,
> So prey I God that non myswrite the [thee] . . .

The problem, of course, is not the writer's (or miswriter's), but the reader's. If I am allowed to spell my words any way I want, this makes my task as a writer easier, but it makes the task of my reader more difficult. I might decide to write the word *flower* as *flower, flowr, flour, floor, flouer*, or in other ways, and I will know what I mean when I do so. But my reader has to work out what I meant. In the sentence *I smelled a flower*, the reader would hardly be confused if I used the other spellings, because the context of the sentence makes the meaning clear: *I smelled a flour*. But in many cases, the context would not help. *I saw the flour? The floor was green?* There must have been a point, in late Middle English, when the variable ways of spelling different words began to overlap so much that ambiguity started to become a real issue. With a growing number of homonyms (words which look the same but which have different meanings), texts would have become increasingly difficult to interpret, and learning to read and write would have become increasingly problematic. Moreover, the difficulty of making an accurate copy of a manuscript, with so many possible points of overlap, must have greatly increased. And anyone trying to produce an alphabetical list, such as a concordance, would have been greatly hampered. The compiler of a concordance to the Wycliffe Bible in the early fifteenth century – the first known concordance to an English book – was well aware of this. He goes so far as to warn his reader that the decisions he has made about alphabetical ordering may not meet everyone's expectations:

> Sumtyme þe same word & þe self þat is writen of sum man in oo [one] manere is writen of a-noþir man in a-noþir manere. þese diuerse maneris of writyng ben [are] to be considerid in þis concordaunce. ffor per chaunse [perchance], aftir my manere of writyng, sum word stondiþ in sum place, which same word, aftir þi maner of writying, shulde stonde in anoþir place.[3]

If this happens, he suggests, a reader has no choice but to write his own concordance:

> If it plese to ony man to write þis concordaunce, & him þenkiþ þat summe wordis ben not set in ordre aftir his conseit & his manere of writyng, it is not hard, if he take keep wiþ good avisement [attention] in his owne writyng, to sette suche wordis in such an ordre as his owne conseit acordiþ wel to.

But a language is a shared set of communicative conventions. It cannot be left to the 'conceit' [i.e., private opinion] of individuals.

A standard language will only arise if a community is cognitively ready for it, and this state of mind was very likely present by 1400. But people have to be socially ready for it, too, and this leads to a second storyline. The problems presented by a burgeoning range of nonstandard Englishes would not have become apparent until English became the language of the nation, to be used in a wide range of social settings, and this did not happen, as we have seen (Chapter 6), until the middle of the Middle English period. Before that, there was a trilingual situation which allowed educated people to talk and write to each other using either Latin or French. Latin, in its Classical incarnation, had a well-established standard form; and, before the period had much progressed, French had gained one also, in its Parisian form (p. 148). With two standard languages meeting communicative needs, there was hardly a need to provide a third.

The situation altered when French began to fall out of general educated use. People had to rely on English to perform the range of functions previously carried out by French, and, as we saw in Chapter 8, the range of varieties grew to meet the need. At the same time, a feeling was growing that perhaps the vernacular language could not live up to its new responsibilities. The view that the language had shortcomings, especially when compared to Latin, can be seen early on in medieval writing. The foreign influences on English were a particular source of disquiet. As early as 1193, in the Latin *Descriptio Kambriae* (*Description of Wales*, Chapter 6), Giraldus Cambrensis, noting the ancient character of the Cornish language, makes a passing observation about the similar situation in English:

> As in the southern parts of England, and particularly in Devonshire, the English language seems less agreeable, yet it bears more marks of antiquity (the northern parts being much corrupted by the irruptions of the Danes and Norwegians), and adheres more strictly to the original language and ancient mode of speaking.

The point was reiterated by Ranulph Higden, as we have seen (p. 186), who added the Normans to the list of corrupters. And Osbern Bokenham, in *Mappula Angliae* (*c.* 1440), regrets what he perceives to be a lack of purity in English: the 'dyuersites of toungis and languagis' found in Britain are 'not alle pure, but sum ben mixte and medlid on sundry ways'.

Notions of purity, corruption, elegance, decorum, correctness ... We should not underestimate the influence Latin had on the way English medieval writers thought about English. Classical Latin itself was perceived to be a model of the most desirable style, the result of agreed usage among cultured people and the best authors. Throughout Europe, in the Middle Ages, Horace's *Art of Poetry* and the rhetorical texts of Cicero were used as prescriptive guides to composition, and many treatises on the subject (*artes poetriae*, 'arts of poetry', *artes rhetoricae*, 'arts of rhetoric') were written by teachers during the thirteenth century. The notion of purity loomed large. A language should not use foreign or provincial words. Even Latin itself was often said to have been 'corrupted' as it spread through Europe; Italian was sometimes referred to as 'corrupt Latin', for example, and when Chaucer's Constance asks for help, at one point in *The Man of Law's Tale* (l. 519), her speech is described as *a maner Latyn corrupt* 'a kind of corrupt Latin'. English, because of its waves of foreign borrowing, was therefore held to be in a particularly bad state. The fact that those who inveighed against the supposed corruption themselves used many loanwords in order to do so was not noticed – or if it was, it was ignored. Because of the great 'commyxstion and mellyng' of Danish and Norman words, Trevisa translating Higden says, 'in menye þe contray longage is apeyred' (p. 186) – 'in many people the language of the country is harmed'; but to express this sentiment he has to use a Latin word, *commyxstion*, and four French words, *mellyng, contray, longage*, and *apeyred*, and in other places he does not shrink from using Norse words (such as *take*) either. I shall return to the self-contradictions inherent in the purist mentality in later chapters.

But just because an attitude is internally inconsistent does not make it any the less real or strongly held. And in the Middle English period there was universal agreement that the best writing would avoid foreign impurities, as well as provincialisms, everyday slang, obsolete terms, and arcane scholarly words. Rather it would aim for clear and elegant expression, employing euphonious polysyllabic words, balanced syntax, structures within structures (*hypotaxis*), skilful figurative language, and other features reflecting a dignified latinity (*Latinitas*). It bothered no one that these attributes were highly subjective – *euphonious*, after all, means no more than 'pleasing to the ear', and what might please one person might displease another. When there are stylistic models about whose excellence everyone agrees (such as those provided by Cicero), it matters little that the attributes are incapable of scientific definition. As a consequence, in medieval England, the virtues of such a style came to be widely recognized and emulated – such as by the thirteenth-century scholar Roger Bacon. By 1400, the desirability of 'agreed usage among cultured people', with reference to English, must have loomed large in many writers' minds.

Agreed usage was in any case evolving naturally: a third storyline. The huge amount of variation which we have noted must not blind us to the fact that there was also a great deal of consensus. As we have seen in the earliest scriptoria (p. 41), house styles readily develop. People accommodate to each other, when they work together, and consciously or unconsciously evolve a common style. During the Middle English period, all kinds of local linguistic consensuses must have emerged as lawyers, physicians, merchants, civil servants, court officials, families (such as the Pastons, p. 178), and other occupational and social groups began to produce increasing quantities of written material. One study finds 20 medical manuscripts in English in the thirteenth century, 140 in the fourteenth, and 872 in the fifteenth – a sixfold increase.[4] Much of this writing was not ephemeral (in the manner of private correspondence): it included national and local historical records, literary translations, travelogues, political and religious tracts, legal judgments, financial reports, and other accounts of long-term significance. People were writing about the past and the present with the future in mind. It is easy to be misled by the famous literature of an era – the Chaucers, Gowers, and Lydgates – into thinking that this is the only material of linguistic significance. On the contrary, in any century, literary creation forms but a tiny fraction of the published output of a society.

For the basis of a standard language to have emerged so quickly, during the fifteenth century, its roots must have been present in a broad cross-section of society. There must have been a growing sense of shared usage, as individual scriveners (a term recorded from the end of the fourteenth century) with different backgrounds came into contact and began to influence each other. Language change then will have been no different from language change now, and today sociolinguists have repeatedly drawn attention to the important role social networks play in fostering the diffusion of features throughout a community. Norms quickly grow when a social network is dense – that is, when many people interact regularly and frequently – and the network to which scriveners belonged in fifteenth-century London was, by all accounts, of great density.[5] Large numbers of people were involved in literary activities in the city area. Not only did they work there; they lived there – or, at least, in the residential wards in close proximity to the centre. Paternoster Row, near St Paul's, emerged as a centre of the book trade in the early 1400s, and by the end of the century the area around the cathedral was known for its books. Legal scriveners gathered in the vicinity, in the cathedral walks and taverns, to advertise for business. Many worked out of small offices, and would hang samples of their work outside to attract the attention of passing clients. Larger concentrations of scriveners were also located in the area. The important Chancery offices were only a few hundred yards away (see panel 10.1).

10.1 The city of London c. 1400

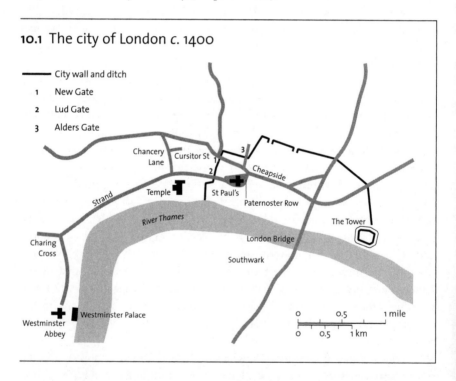

As society became more literacy-dependent (p. 180), more and more people took up scrivening as a profession. As early as 1373, legal scriveners organized themselves into a guild: the Writers of Court Letter. Parish clerks did the same: there were over a hundred churches in the central part of London, and they formed themselves into an organization in 1442. Over 260 stationers and book craftsmen have been identified as working in the area between 1370 and 1500; in due course their profession would come to be formalized as the Stationers' Company (1557). But none of these professions operated in social isolation. The busy streets and taverns of central London mixed everyone together. Then as now, professionals would have looked at each other's work to admire it, to rubbish it, to copy it. We must never forget that, although we talk abstractly about 'social networks', we are always referring to interaction between individual human beings.

Individuals belong to more than one network; and literary authors perhaps more than most. When it comes to discussing the sources of influence upon the development of the standard language, it makes no sense to draw sharp dividing lines around the concept of 'literature'. If we wish, we may talk about Chaucer having an influence on the development of the language; but if we do so we must remember that Chaucer was not only a poet, he was also a civil servant – first as a controller of customs in the port of London, later as a clerk of the king's works – as well as a soldier, diplomat, intelligence officer, and parliamentarian. And the same point applies to any of the clusters of scriveners who worked together in those days. If we identify one group as being potentially of great significance, as in the case of the scriveners of Chancery, we need to do so with a great deal of caution. Chancery records by their nature are better preserved than the records of many other influential groups of the time, and it is a moot point what role those other groups played in fostering a sense of linguistic standards. The teaching institutions, in particular, must have been important in shaping the intuitions of future scriveners – the big London grammar schools of St Paul's, St Martin-le-Grand, and St Mary-le-Bow, or the London convents of Greyfriars, Blackfriars, and Whitefriars. At the very least, Chancery writers would have mixed with teachers, clerics, merchants, and lawyers from the Inns of Court, along with the scriveners who worked for them, and been familiar with current linguistic trends. Today, language variation and change provides a subject of interest – in the broadest sense, to include delight, puzzlement, concern, and complaint. It will have been no different in medieval England.

We can imagine that linguistic discussion would have been particularly intense in areas outside London, as the influence of the capital made itself increasingly felt through the medium of English. This is another strand in the story of Standard. Centralization was of course nothing new, in the fifteenth century. Its post-Conquest origins can be seen in the Domesday Book, and the eventual establishment of a permanent civil service based in London. The legal and financial reforms instituted by Henry II in the mid twelfth century were a critical stage. Henry was duke of Aquitaine before succeeding to the English throne, and he continued to manage a wider Angevin Empire in Europe. This was an expensive matter, whose funding required new taxation measures, as well as efficient systems of debt collecting and enforcement, in which the role of a reconstituted Exchequer was crucial. Because he was often abroad, he had to implement an administrative framework which would run smoothly in his absence. A network of royal representatives – justiciars, chancellors, sheriffs, and others – became established throughout the country, all of whom were required to maintain full records of their activities and to be in regular contact with London. Taxes, rents, and fines were in the hands of a system of royal debt collectors. Common law evolved, and judicial procedures were reorganized and unified through a series of assizes. A permanent court sat regularly at Westminster, and royal justices went routinely on circuits. The issuing of writs became standardized, and there was an increased use of juries. It was a complex, integrated system. For example, if you had a grievance arising out of an assize visit, you (or your representative) would have to travel to Chancery and obtain the appropriate writ. You would pay for this writ, and take it back to the sheriff in your area. Your case would then be heard by a jury of twelve local people. In a writ of 'Mort d'Ancestor', for instance, the jury would be asked to decide whether someone was the legal heir to a piece of land, and whether his father had legal rights over it. The amount of written record-keeping and correspondence to support this kind of administrative framework was enormous, especially in the thirteenth century, when the making of copies of important documents became routine (p. 134)

Written material emanating from the civil service, law offices, ecclesiastical bodies, and business centres always operates with a rather special cachet. It is likely to be important and authoritative, and the language in which it is written will be formal – 'lered' rather than 'lewed' (p. 174). Its receipt is accompanied by a mixture of feelings, ranging from respect to trepidation. Its content may not always be fully understood, and may generate local debate among neighbours and a turning to local experts for advice. In the fifteenth century, most such missives would have originated in London, and whatever linguistic norms were developing there (see below) would have been slowly but persistently transmitted around the country. It is difficult to estimate the extent of the influence of this level of non-regional textual material, but we should certainly not underestimate it. All regions would have been exposed to it, and the language it contained would effectively have been the first contact most people had with a supra-local written English.

The role of Chancery, often cited as the primary influence on the rise of Standard English in medieval times, has to be seen within this context (see panel 10.2). The legal side of life is important, but it is not the only side. The documentation produced in London and being sent around the nation in the fifteenth century dealt with an enormous range of subject-matter and will have

10.2 Chancery

After the Conquest, the first great judicial court in England was the Aula Regis ('King's Court'), in which the monarch administered country-wide justice himself. It was held in various places, as the king moved round the country – a system which caused litigants great trouble and expense, and which came to an end following Provision 17 of the Magna Carta (1215) that 'common pleas shall not follow our court, but shall be held in some fixed place'. The growth of London-based permanent offices for the civil service was an immediate consequence.

The Aula Regis was eventually replaced by a system of three common-law courts: the Court of the King's Bench (the highest tribunal), the Court of Common Pleas (which dealt with ordinary civil actions), and the Court of Exchequer (which dealt with actions relating to the royal revenues). A system of ecclesiastical courts was also in operation – the Curiae Christianitatis ('Courts Christian') – with its own clerical civil service.

The term *Chancery* first appears in English in the late fourteenth century, referring to an additional court, presided over by the Lord Chancellor of England. It sat at Westminster and consisted of two tribunals. The *ordinary* tribunal was a court of common law, which formulated all original writs and issued writs for a new Parliament. The *extraordinary* tribunal heard cases and gave judgments based on rules of equity, invoked when the statutes of common law did not provide an adequate remedy. *Equity* was the Chancellor's sense of fair dealing – one of his titles was the Keeper of the King's Conscience – and the Chancery was often called the Court of Conscience. Its procedures differed in its methods of proof, trial, and relief, and did not involve the presence of a jury.

The administrative workload of Chancery was immense. In the fifteenth century it was staffed by around 120 clerks, and operated a strict hierarchy and system of apprenticeship. There were twelve senior clerks 'of the first form', and twelve 'of the second form', along with their assistants. In addition there were twenty-four cursitors, whose role was to make out all original writs *de cursu* (i.e., to do with routine official matters) in relation to the various English shires.

A Cursitor Street still exists, off Chancery Lane, in the EC4 part of London. The scrivener legacy of the area lasted for centuries, and eventually earned its place in literature. It is in Cursitor Street where 'Mr Snagsby, law-stationer, pursues his lawful calling' (Charles Dickens, *Bleak House*, Chapter 10).

---

had many sources other than Chancery. Having said that, we should not ignore the scale and status of the Chancery operation, which was such that its preferences in the use of language would very likely have been influential among those whose role routinely involved communication with the public – notably, the scriveners, teachers, and publishers. There is something about the legal situation which fosters linguistic sensibility. The need for clarity and precision in formulation, and for accuracy in transmission, is much greater in the case of the law than in any other profession. Lawyers love standardized words and expressions, because they know where they are with them: in this domain more than anywhere else, familiarity breeds content. Much of the training of a lawyer – or a legal scrivener – involves becoming familiar with the formulaic words and expressions which have been tried and tested in the courts. Indeed, when it comes to drafting, the scriveners are more important than the lawyers, in much the same way as today the formulation of acts of Parliament is not left to the elected power-makers – linguistic amateurs in this domain – but to highly trained parliamentary draftsmen. So if a concern for linguistic standards is going to arise anywhere, it is likely to be here.

Chancery was an organization well used to dealing with issues of standardization. Long before it had to deal with these problems in English, it had been dealing with them in French or Latin – languages where the question of stylistic standards had been a matter of early debate. The civil service had worked with disciplined, elegant, elevated styles for generations. Indeed, it might be argued that the standardizing tradition in legal writing can be traced as far back as Old English. In Anglo-Saxon times, those centres which came to be associated with the exercise of power also had writers who evolved shared forms of expression; and the study of Old English laws, written by different scribes in different places, has brought to light several characteristic features of style. To take just one example, a statement relating a crime to a punishment tended to use a fixed sequence of *if*- clause + main clause, as in this example from Æthelbert:

> *Gif man þone man ofslæhð, XX scillingum gebete*
> If a man kills another man, he must pay twenty shillings.[6]

Several such formulaic tendencies have been noted, and although the agreements are not sufficiently many and permanent to suggest that the law-writers were using a standard language, in the modern sense, there is undeniably a supra-local, standardizing temperament at work (see p. 56). Law-writers of the fifteenth – or of any – century would have recognized this temperament, too. They would know what an appropriately formal style was. And in managing the transition from French and Latin to English, they would have made full use of this experience.

We must not assume that all the features which eventually formed the standard language originated within the Chancery itself; Chancery scriveners could just as well have taken over and given an official seal of approval to features which were already in use elsewhere. There are two research tasks: we need to establish what the supposedly standard forms were, and then we have to establish the direction of the diffusion. If Chancery was indeed exercising a standardizing linguistic influence on scribal variation in the fifteenth century, we should be able to find it operating in the output of other writers of the time – in the other departments of government, the guilds and corporations, the Inns of Court, and the commercial record-keepers. Some studies have claimed to find such influence. One[7] examined the archives of the Bridge House Estates, the medieval trust responsible for the administration of old London Bridge – an important trust, as the bridge, constructed in 1176, was the only crossing-place in the city area until Westminster Bridge was built in 1750 – and noted the presence in the records, routinely kept in English from 1480, of several Chancery forms. By contrast, another study found no such influence present in a group of fifteenth-century medical manuscripts.[8]

We must be prepared for conflicting impressions when so little empirical research has been carried out. Given the huge amount of unanalysed material in this period, a partial picture is all that is currently available. A great deal of scientific writing, for example, took place in the fifteenth century, but little of this has been given a linguistic analysis. More important, however, is that so little statistical investigation of Chancery language has taken place either. The impression which is often given, that certain spellings were in 'standard' use, is certainly misleading if we take it to mean that there was no variability at all. On the contrary, even a cursory description of any collection of Chancery documents immediately displays large amounts of variation.[9] We can see this if we take a selection of the features thought to be indicative of a Chancery house style. An extract from a typical document is shown in panel 10.3, with some of its characteristic spellings noted. Additional typical Chancery spellings, it is claimed, are *these* for *thise*, *not* for *nat*, *but* for *bot*, *fro* for *from*, the use of *-gh* in *thorough* or *thurgh* for *thurch*, and *such(e)* or *soch(e)* for *swich(e)*, *sich*, and a range of other possibilities. Let us see what we find, if we search for competing patterns in a Chancery corpus of nearly 250 texts.

It turns out that several standardizing trends can indeed be demonstrated, but there is some degree of variability in *every* feature investigated. At one extreme, there are features which have hardly any spelling variation at all. The *-ly* category is a case in point, as this table shows:

Chancery form: number of instances		Alternative spellings: number of instances	
gretely 4		-	
goodly 9		-	
yerely ('yearly') 36		-	
mekely 30		mekelich 2	
lowely 5		loweli 1	lowelich 1
humbly 10	humblely 2	humblie 1	
graciously 7		graciousli 1	

10.3 Chancery house style

This is the beginning of a petition in the Commons concerning the *stews* (houses of ill repute) of Southwark in 1436. It contains several spellings which have been associated with the Chancery style of writing:

> Please hit to the Wisedomes and hye discrecions of the Worshipfull Comunes in this present parlement assembled to consider two grete meschiefs nowe in late dayes bygonnen by vntrywe lyvers and people with owte consciens and yet dwellyng in the Burgh of Suthwerk in the Shire of Surrey / Oon is that howe nowe late by Auctorite of parlement was ordeyned and stablet that no person that had dwelled at the comune Stywes shulde hald any comune hostryes ne comune Tavernes with yn the saide B(urg)h ne thay shulde not passe in no maner enquestes with yn the saide Shire safe only at the saide comune Stywes the whiche ordenaunce hath been to grete weel of alle the honest people of the saide Burgh and Shire and put awey mony and grete periuries robberyes and other inconueniences . . .

Among the features which have been suggested as typical of Chancery style are:

- past-tense verb endings typically *-ed* (*assembled, dwelled, ordeyned*)
- present-participle ending in *-yng* (*dwellyng*)
- third-person singular forms in *-th* rather than *-s* (*hath*)
- third-person plural pronoun in *th-* rather than *h-* (*thay*)
- 'said' as *saide* rather than *seide*
- 'should' as *shulde* rather than *schulde*
- 'which' as *whiche* rather than *wiche*
- 'any' as *any* rather than *ony*
- the double *o* spelling in 'one' (*oon*)
- *-ly* ending on adverbs (*only*) rather than *-li*, *-lich*, etc.
- prefix 'in-' as *en-* rather than *in-* (*enquestes*)
- 'tion' suffix is *-cion* (*discrecions*)

It should be noted that not all of these forms continued into modern Standard English.

A total of 103 *-ly* forms to 6 non-*ly* forms is good evidence of a standardizing trend. And we would have to allow a similar trend operating if we were to compare *hath* (169 instances) vs *has* (5 instances), *but* (115) vs *bot* (3), *not* (187) vs *nat* (30), *shal-/shul-* forms (293) vs *schal-/schul-* forms (22), *which(e)* (381) vs *wich(e)* (17), and *such(e)* (120) vs other spellings (23). On the other hand, several features show genuinely divided usage, in one case (*them*) the figures going against the expected trend:

Chancery form: number of instances	Alternative spellings: number of instances	
oon / oonly 55	one / onely 32	only 12
any 142	eny 112	ony 36
fro 79 froo 1	from 49	
these 31	thise 8	
said(e) 1,065	seid(e) 838	sayd(e) 66
them 21	hem 155	

Some items show a bewildering number of forms. Within the 'other spellings' for *such(e)* we find *soche, swiche, swich, sich, seche,* and *sych.* The predominant form for the third-person plural pronoun is *they* (111), but we also find *thei* (16), *thay* (11), and *thai* (1); alternatives to *them,* in addition to *hem,* are *theym* (33), *theyme* (2), *thaym* (32), and *thayme* (1). The point hardly needs further illustration. Although there are definite standardizing trends to be seen, there is still a remarkable amount of variation in Chancery texts – far too much to enable this source to be viewed as the only point of reference for the rise of Standard English. Chancery may well have speeded up the process of standardization, but other sources must have played their part, too.

What might these other sources have been? What other kinds of text carried sufficient weight in the early fifteenth century to be capable of exercising general influence on the way people wrote? For a standard to grow, two conditions need to be present: not only must there be internal consistency in usage, there needs to be widespread dissemination; and if a text is to be considered formative there must be clear evidence that it was being read outside of its place of origin – by large numbers of people in all kinds of places. This leads to two other storylines, for there are really only two candidates which satisfy this second criterion: the Bible translations initiated by John Wycliffe, and the work of Chaucer. Both have been called 'incipient standards',[10] though in neither case is the range of usage represented sufficiently uniform to warrant such a label. Rather, they should be seen as standardizing forces – additional influences promoting a climate in which people became increasingly familiar with supra-local texts. Their writing does indeed contain distinctive linguistic features, some of which reflect their geographical origins, and in principle any of these features – such as an idiosyncratic spelling or an innovative word or expression – could be picked up and used by others, as they encountered the texts, and eventually become part of Standard English. In fact, relatively little in their writing can be interpreted as uniquely influential in this way.

In the case of the Bible, an important factor which would have limited its standardizing effect was the amount of linguistic variation it contained. Wycliffe actually inspired the making of two translations: one before his death *c.* 1382, the other *c.* 1388 – it is not known just how much of the earlier translation he carried out himself – and when we compare the versions, we find many orthographic, lexical, and stylistic differences. A use of *unction* in the early version becomes *anointing* in the later, and similarly *captive* becomes *prisoner*, *veil* becomes *covering*, *concision* becomes *division*, and so on. Psalm 1 in the early version begins like this:

> (1) Blisful the man, that went not awei in the counseil of vnpitouse, and in the wei off sinful stod not; and in the chayer of pestilence sat not, (2) But in the lawe of the Lord his wil; and in the lawe of hym he shal sweteli thenke dai and ny3t [day and night].

In the later version, it is like this:

> (1) Blessid is the man, that 3ede not in the councel of wickid men; and stood not in the weie of synneris, and sat not in the chaier of pestilence. (2) But his wille is in the lawe of the Lord; and he schal bithenke in the lawe of hym dai and ny3t.

The spelling variations, in particular, should be noted: *chayer / chaier, counseil / councel, stod / stood, shal / schal*, etc. Even within the later version, which is the one usually read, we can certainly see some preferred forms, such as *fro* 'from', *silf* 'self', *seide* 'said', *schal* 'shall', and *ony* 'any', but several variants occur, and in some cases the variations appear side by side, as in the uses of *him* and *them*:

> Psalms 21:3   And my soule schal lyue to *hym*; and my seed schal serue *him*.
> Psalms 124:5   But the Lord schal lede *them* that bowen in to obligaciouns, with *hem* that worchen wickidnesse

We are a long way from a standard here, notwithstanding the fact that Wycliffian usage influenced scribes throughout the Midlands, as well as further south,[11] in both secular and religious texts, and was still to be seen in the writing of the anti-Lollard theologian Reginald Pecock half a century later.

Even if there had been no variation, it would have been difficult for the language of the Wycliffe Bible to have exercised a major influence on the emergence of the standard language, given the profound controversy caused by his religious views (see panel 10.4). His rejection of the doctrine of transubstantiation was denounced as heresy – it was the only heresy to flourish in medieval England – and it generated a fierce reaction. Several years before it was officially condemned at the Council of Constance (1415), the government brought in the Act *De Haeretico Comburendo* (1401, 'On the Burning of Heretics'). The Church limited the use of translations to those who had a bishop's licence. A

10.4 Wycliffe and the Lollards

John Wycliffe – the name appears in several variations, such as Wyclif, Wiclif, and Wickliffe – was born in Yorkshire, became an Oxford scholar, and held livings in the East Midlands, at Fillingham (Lincolnshire) and Lutterworth (Leicestershire), as well as further south at Ludgershall (Buckinghamshire). His political and religious views were highly controversial. He argued that the Church should be disendowed of its property, attacked episcopal privileges, rejected papal authority, and denied the doctrine of transubstantiation. Caught up in the reaction which followed the Peasants' Revolt of 1381, he was expelled as a preacher from Oxford, his writings were banned, and his manuscripts burned. He died in 1384.

He was especially concerned that lay people should be able to read the Bible in their own language. If the people of France can have the Bible in French, he argues (in *De Officio Pastorali*, Chapter 15), why not in England? If the Lord's Prayer can be heard in English in the York Mystery Plays, why not the whole Gospel?

> Crist and His apostlis tauȝten þe puple [taught the people] in þat tunge þat was moost knowun to þe puple. Why shulden not men do nou [now] so?

Several forms, such as *moost* (vs *most, mast*, etc.), *puple* (vs *peple, people*, etc.), *knowun* (vs *knowen, knawen*, etc.), and *shulden* (vs *sholden, schulden*, etc.), would have been dialectally distinctive at the time. Wycliffian manuscripts display forms indicative of the Midlands, with some Southern influences, and this is the character of the Bible translations, too.

convocation held at Oxford in 1408, under Archbishop Arundel, made the position perfectly clear (the text is in modern spelling):

> that no man hereafter by his own authority translate any text of the Scripture into English or any other tongue, by way of a book, booklet, or tract; and that no man read any such book, booklet, or tract, now lately composed in the time of John Wycliffe or since, or hereafter to be set forth in part or in whole, publicly or privately, upon pain of greater excommunication, until the said translation be approved by the ordinary of the place, or, if the case so require, by the council provincial. He that shall do contrary to this shall likewise be punished as a favourer of heresy and error.

This is hardly the climate required for a text to be able to influence the rise of a standard!

The ruling was aimed at the followers of Wycliffe, members of the order of Poor Preachers, or Lollards, who were taking the translation to all parts of the country. The term *Lollards* – a Dutch word meaning 'mumbler, mutterer'

– had been applied pejoratively during the fourteenth century to various kinds of semi-monastic orders, often with connotations of heresy and hypocrisy. It was also used to describe anyone whose views were considered to be anti-clerical or anti-social (e.g., a parish member who refused to pay tithes), and certainly a person who was fanatical, visionary, or just plain eccentric might find themselves referred to in this way. It was first used as a nickname for Wycliffe's followers in 1382, and this application quickly became the everyday sense, if we can judge from the allusion to them in the Epilogue to Chaucer's *Man of Law's Tale* (l. 1,173). The Parson has just criticized the Host for swearing, and the Host responds: *I smelle a Lollere in the wynd*. The Host asks the Parson to preach a sermon to the group, but the Shipman will have none of it: *He schal no gospel glosen here ne teche* – 'no interpreting or teaching of the Gospel here'. Everyone knew who Lollards were and what they did. All parts of England were eventually affected, with a Lollard presence especially strong in some areas (such as the eastern counties) during the first decades of the fifteenth century.

This reference to the way Wycliffe's followers 'interpreted' the Bible lies behind the Oxford convocation's opposition to Lollardry: it was not so much the translation *per se* which was the problem – for it was possible to use the text in an 'approved' way – but the interpretation placed upon it. And it would not be difficult to detect this emphasis, in someone's usage, given that the language of the translation was in so many respects distinctive. The two texts contain substantial lexical innovation. The *Oxford English Dictionary* has over 1,100 entries, many derived from Latin, whose first usage is recorded in one or other of the translations – either new words or new applications (senses) of older words. Under the former heading we find *actor, leviathan, lightful, merchandising, miseration, money-changer, neckerchief, observation*, and *reprehensible*. An example under the latter heading is *mystery*, here given a theo-logical as opposed to a secular sense. Not all of these would have been Wycliffian coinages, of course. For example, in the 1382 version we find the earliest recorded use of the word *interpretation*, but as this word also appears within the decade in writing by both Gower and Trevisa, it was doubtless in fairly general currency. Similarly, both Wycliffe and Chaucer, writing at about the same time, illustrate the first uses of such words as *jubilee, novelty*, and *persuasion*. However, many words would have been distinctively Wycliffian – *cognation* 'kinship, kindred' and *burnt-offering*, for example, with no recorded instances for another century, or words such as *again-rise* and *adjurement*, where there is no later usage recorded in the OED at all. And even the words which were not Wycliffian in origin would very likely have accreted some level of Wycliffian identity through association, because of the widespread circulation of the translation and the acknowledged enthusiasm of the preaching based upon it. No English text would have reached so many people before. A very large number of copies must have been made and circulated, judging by the remarkable number of manuscripts (some 200) which have survived.

The growth of anti-Lollard sentiment during the early fifteenth century will undoubtedly have exercised a strong counter-influence on the taking-up by the general public of the translation's preferred spellings (several reflecting their Midlands dialect origin) and innovative forms. The use of such language could easily have been seen as an affirmation of identity with Lollard beliefs, in much the same way that, today, certain words and phrases can identify someone as belonging to a particular background or holding a particular viewpoint. For example, until quite recently the phrase 'the power and the glory' would identify the speaker of the Lord's Prayer as coming from a Protestant and not a Catholic background. People in the fifteenth century would have been no less ready to notice linguistic markers of this kind, and – given the sanctions – to avoid using them. For whatever reason, a remarkably high percentage of the Wycliffian innovations did not survive in the language: only about half of the first usages recorded in Wycliffe's Bible actually remain in Modern English. Among those that did were *absent, adoption, adulteress,* and *allegory*; among those that didn't were *acception, aftercoming, againcoming,* and *aloneness*.

The Bible is often called 'literature', but it is a very different kind of literature from that illustrated by such authors as Chaucer. Wycliffe, as others after him, was concerned to develop a kind of English which ordinary people could understand – a style which would be close to everyday speech. Literary authors, by contrast, typically do the opposite, avoiding the linguistically banal, aiming for artistic excellence, and searching for originality of expression. Even when features of everyday speech can be found in a literary work – and some authors take great pains to represent it – they are inevitably highly crafted features. Whoever once described Harold Pinter as having 'a tape-recorder for an ear', in his ability to represent everyday conversation, was wrong: Pinter's conversations are carefully constructed exchanges, and do not convey the repetitive, loosely constructed, incomplete, and non-fluent character of our normal speech. It would have been the same with Chaucer, whose conversations – vivid and lively as they are – would have been at a considerable remove from daily spoken realities. Moreover, the simple fact that we are dealing with poetry makes his written expression quite unlike that which would be encountered in the other domains of written Middle English, let alone the fact that we are dealing with poetry acknowledged to display an especial brilliance. Poetic language is the domain where linguistic rules are maximally bent and broken (p. 182). It is this distance between literary language and everyday language which makes it unlikely that any literary writer, or group of writers, would ever exercise much of an influence on the emergence of a linguistic standard for general use. The best such writers might do is reinforce trends that are already there.

This is the context within which we should view Chaucer's role in relation to Standard English. As a London-based writer, working in and around the court, his idiolect (his personal dialect) would most naturally reflect whatever dialect was in use there. Because the written form of this dialect was highly varied, as we have seen, when using his literary persona he (or his scribes) would have had to make choices. Sometimes these choices turned out to be ones which in due course became features of Standard English. Quite often, they did not: typical Chaucerian spellings and forms such as *nat* 'not', *bot* 'but', *hir* 'their', *swich* 'such', *yaf* 'gave', and *sholde* 'should' did not become standard. This should not surprise us. In a manuscript age, it takes time for an author's work, no matter how popular or prestigious it is, to travel; and when it is eventually read, there is no compulsion on the reader to adopt the spellings or forms it contains. On the contrary. People know what literature is, and they can see that it is different from what is 'normal' language – that is one of the reasons they enjoy reading it. The only people who would want to be influenced by the language of an author are other authors; and they form only a tiny part of the population. It is unusual for the linguistic conventions adopted in a literary author's work to have a directly innovating effect on the standard language. What authors do is help to spread conventions that already have some presence within the community. Authors can highlight a usage, make readers familiar with it, give it prestige. This role would have been important in the case of an author as prestigious as Chaucer, who would be read by the most powerful people in the land.

Other important literary manuscripts of the period would have played a similar role. Chief among these is the Auchinleck manuscript, a large book (of 332 vellum leaves) produced by six scriveners working in the London area in the 1330s.[12] Probably compiled for some affluent member of the local populace, it contains a wide range of religious, historical, political, and literary texts, notably several metrical romances, such as *Guy of Warwick*, *Sir Orfeo*, *Arthour and Merlyn*, and *Sir Tristrem*. Some, such as the *Lay le Freine*, are known only from this book. Analyses of Chaucer's sources, such as the *Tale of Sir Thopas*, suggest that he knew this manuscript well (and he may even have owned it). It has been much studied for the light it sheds on literacy and book production in the fourteenth century, and some commentators have seen in the way it adapts its sources a socio-political trend indicative of a mood of national unity. Be this as it may, its preferences in word forms and spellings (just one of the scriveners is responsible for the majority of the work) are also seen in several other mid fourteenth-century manuscripts, and the text has consequently been taken as further evidence of a standardizing trend in Middle English.

The East Midlands story

Evidently, the first half of the fifteenth century is a period which sees the rise of a number of major factors capable of exercising some influence on the emergence of a standard language: the choices made by the City of London scriveners (especially those in Chancery), the choices made by the translators of the Wycliffe Bible and its promulgators, the choices made by the imaginative writers (notably, Chaucer) or their scriveners, and the choices made by other producers of literary manuscripts, such as those involved in the Auchinleck. The common element is the East Midlands dialect, and the dialect of the London area in particular. The influence of a capital city is always critical in the emergence of a standard. Just as the written forms of the Paris dialect had earlier been the major influence on the rise of Standard French (p. 136), so the written forms of the London dialect eventually shaped Standard English. The London dialect is particularly interesting, however, because it did not develop along the lines we might assume from its location, as shown on the dialect map of Middle English (p. 201). London was the place where three dialect areas met – Southern, South-Eastern, and East Midlands – and we might therefore expect the speech of the city, and thus its written representation, to have been a real hybrid, and Standard English to have emerged in due course as a mixture of three dialect sources. But this did not happen. Although there is some evidence of regional variation, the written 'London dialect' which emerged from around 1400 was far closer to the writing characteristic of the East Midlands area than of any other. The kind of writing we find among the legal scriveners, Wycliffian translators, Chaucer, and the Auchinleck scribes displays considerable overlap, suggesting the existence of diffused linguistic features, operating in different directions, among the various groups. Everyone seems to have been influenced, to a greater or lesser extent, by the Midlands dialects, with the East Midlands region particularly important. This includes Wycliffe: though not a Londoner, his life was spent largely in the Midlands, and the East Midlands was the area in which the Lollards had greatest influence.

Why should the East Midlands have exercised more influence than the dialects of the north, west, south, and south-west? The magnetic influence of the capital would have been the most critical factor – not because it was a political centre, but because of its economic importance. Economics is a much more important factor than politics in motivating language change among the general population, and in the fourteenth and early fifteenth centuries the economic prospects of the south-east began to emerge in earnest.[13] The East Midlands had always been the most populated and the most prosperous part of the country, having developed strong agricultural and textile centres during the early Middle Ages. As its towns grew in size, the area saw a corresponding increase in urban markets. Farming of all kinds was fundamental, and one consequence was the development of the wool trade with Flanders, causing the expansion of east-coast ports, such as Hull, Lynn, and Boston. This trade flourished until the fourteenth century, when wool was gradually replaced as the chief English export by cloth, with eastern towns, especially in East Anglia (e.g., Bury St Edmunds), again becoming the main manufacturers and suppliers to the Continent. Norfolk was an area of special significance, in view of its strategic commercial location. Norwich was the second-largest city in England in the late fourteenth century.

Panel 10.5 shows the distribution of lay and clerical wealth in the mid fourteenth century. The regional imbalance in favour of the south-east can be clearly seen, and this became more marked as the century progressed. Then as now, the capital opened up prospects for a better quality of life for people from other parts of the country, most of whom were living in extreme poverty. As farming declined in the Midlands, people moved south-east. There is evidence of a marked population shift during the fourteenth century, with immigration to the London area highest from the counties of Norfolk, Essex, and Hertford-shire, and later from counties further north and west. People travelled to London from all over the country, but the majority would have been from the Midlands area, their journey facilitated by the availability of the two major communi-cation routes, the Great North Road and Watling Street. The motivation to move grew after the series of plague outbreaks between 1348 and 1375. It is thought that the Black Death killed between a third and a half of the English population.[14] One of the consequences was an employment vacuum in London, much of which was soon filled by arrivals from the relatively heavily populated East Midlands counties.

The dialect character of London would have changed quite rapidly during this time, becoming increasingly Midlandish during the 1400s. Higden had already noticed that the Midlands dialect was easier for most people to under-stand (p. 206), as a communication conduit between Northern and Southern speech, and it is easy to imagine it becoming attractive as a 'dialecta franca' in London. It is important to appreciate that an East Midlands accent in 1400 would not have sounded as provincial as the corresponding rural accent would today. It would have conveyed several kinds of prestigious associations. Some of these would derive from the way it would have been spoken, perhaps in an upmarket accent, by the staff and students at the University of Cambridge; and certainly their writing would have displayed its influence. Depending on how far west we locate the boundary-line between East Midland and South-Western (p. 201), the University of Oxford would have added its academic associations, too. And in Norfolk, this dialect had emerged quite early on as a functional

10.5 The distribution of wealth in England and Wales in 1334 (after Bolton, 1985)

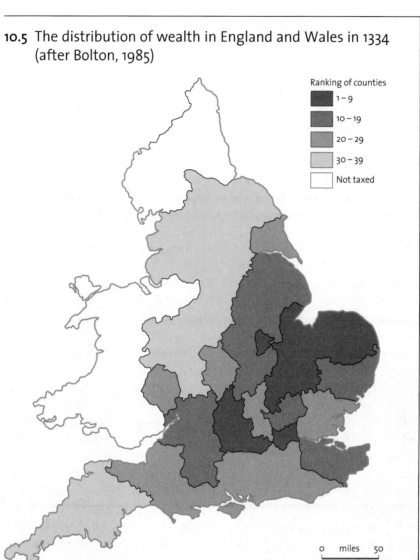

Ranking of counties

- 1 – 9
- 10 – 19
- 20 – 29
- 30 – 39
- Not taxed

tool for business communication. An area of relatively high population, the practical needs of commerce in the Norfolk area may well have fostered the replacement of Latin and French by English much earlier than in other parts of the country. In 1388–9, for example, Norfolk was the only place outside London to have its guild certificates written in English.[15] Standardizing tendencies would very likely have appeared here, among the more wealthy and literate growing merchant class, many of whom had begun to marry with the aristocracy (as later happened to the Pastons, p. 178). As contact with London grew, East Anglian usage would have made a further contribution to the dialect melting-pot out of which a written standard language would emerge.

Standard English evolved as a consequence of the coming together of a range of different but overlapping forces fostering a uniform written usage. No single factor could explain the outcome, because the genres involved were too diverse, representing legal, literary, religious, and other sources. The linguistic trend was much broader than could have been mediated by any one social group, whether they were lawyers, politicians, aristocrats, businessmen, scriveners, translators, or authors. The language of the court, in this respect, and the increased social prestige arising out of the presence of London as the political capital, was only one part of the story. Nor was the social direction of the language changes single and simple. Modern investigations of the factors which promote the diffusion of a linguistic feature have shown that change operates simultaneously in several directions.[16] It is not always 'top down', with higher-status people being copied by lower-status people; it is also 'bottom up', with higher-status people copying lower-status people, driven by such factors as the need for effective communication in administration or the impact of a work of popular literature. There is no reason to think that these processes would have operated any differently in the Middle Ages.

The early story of Standard English is essentially one in which we see the gradual spreading of usages which were at first socially, professionally, and regionally restricted – a process of slowly coinciding usage which is often referred to as *levelling*. The interaction was both multidimensional (any stylistic domain might be influenced by any other domain) and multifaceted (any or all aspects of language structure – sounds, spellings, grammar, vocabulary – might be affected). An individual writer would have had to resolve the competing pull of a multiplicity of linguistic forms from different genres, some of which would be by nature relatively conservative in their usage (as in legal English), some relatively innovative (as in literary English). During the fifteenth century there was no uniform rate of development of the standard form, and no single text could possibly have represented it in its entirety. Nor did a fixed written standard appear in the following century either. The process of levelling can take a very long time.

Levelling is something which happens through regular personal inter-action – daily conversation, shared reading, exchanges of correspondence, classroom teaching, visits away from home, and the like. People begin to accommodate to each other (p. 83), allowing their usage to converge or diverge depending on the nature of their ongoing social relationship. It is a twofold process: in some cases, people warm to a particular linguistic feature and begin to use it; in others, they veer away from a feature, and try to avoid it. Of the two processes, it is the latter which is probably more influential. People tend to be more conscious of features which are socially stigmatized, for whatever reason – a sense of upper class vs lower class, rural vs urban, one set of beliefs vs another (as we have seen in the case of Lollardry). It is easier to think 'I don't want to sound like X' than 'I do want to sound like Y'. Stigmatized features are also more widely encountered because they work in both directions: lower-class people can stigmatize upper-class features, and upper-class people can stigmatize lower-class features.

The sense of stigma can be spread in all kinds of ways. The entertainers – the writers, actors, and minstrels – are usually in the forefront, singling out and satirizing features of dialects or individuals. In the Wakefield *Second Shepherd's Play*, Mak the sheep-stealer claims to be a royal official, and adopts a special way of talking, but the other shepherds aren't fooled, perhaps because Mak wasn't making a very good job of his assumed accent:

MAK
   ich be a yoman [yeoman], I tell you, of the king;
   The self and the same, sond from a greatt lordyng, [messenger from a great lord]
   And sich [such].
   Fy on you! goyth [go] hence
   Out of my presence!
   I must haue reuerence;
   Why, who be ich?
PRIMUS PASTOR
   Why make ye it so qwaynt? [posh, see p. 171] Mak, ye do wrang.

Although there are some Southern features represented, such as 'quaint' French words, *ich be* (for *I am*), and the *-th* verb ending (instead of *-s*, p. 218), there is a great deal of inconsistency: *goyth* has a *-th* ending, but contains a Northern *oy* diphthong, and 'I' turns up as both *I* and *ich*. When Mak tries again, the first shepherd tells him to shut up in no uncertain terms:

   Ich shall make complaynt and make you all to thwang [be flogged]
   At a worde,
   And tell evyn how ye doth.
PRIMUS PASTOR
   Bot, Mak, is that sothe?
   Now take outt that sothren tothe, [southern tooth]
   And sett in a torde! [turd]

This is the mid fifteenth century. The allusion is interesting because it shows that by this time there was a consciousness (at least in Yorkshire) that 'official' language was something 'southern'. It might be thought, therefore, that by this point the story of Standard English was over. In fact, it was only just beginning.

Interlude 10
Complaining about change

There is a long-standing tradition in English-speaking countries of complaining about the way the language is developing (see further, Chapter 20). People are very ready to comment about usages they dislike – writing letters to the press, telephoning radio stations, forming protective societies, or (in the best-known cases) publishing manuals of personal hates. It is a complaint tradition: people do not usually write, phone, or band together to commend usages they like. Of the 5,000 or so letters about usage sent to me at the BBC during the broadcasting of my series *English Now* in the 1980s, only a handful did anything other than complain. When and why did this tradition start?

It is important first to appreciate that only a very small fraction of the language is ever the source of complaint – less than 1 per cent – but that each of the points does generate a great deal of fuss. The same complaints have been made for generations: not ending sentences with prepositions (*That's the book I was talking about* vs *That's the book about which I was talking*), not splitting infinitives (*I want to really understand* vs *I want really to understand*), not paying attention to a word's etymology (e.g., *decimate* must mean 'kill one in ten'), avoiding double negatives (*He didn't see no point* vs *He didn't see any point*), maintaining a word's traditional stress pattern (e.g. *controversy* rather than *controversy*), and so on. One of the most thorough compendiums (?compendia) of the nineteenth century was Henry Alford's *The Queen's English*; all the issues which worried him would turn up in any usage book today.

In the fourteenth and fifteenth centuries we have seen writers occasionally being critical about regional accents and stylistic usage (pp. 168, 216), but a build-up of complaints about the way the language was developing did not appear until the middle of the sixteenth. Why did it take so long? The answer lies in the multifarious linguistic changes which were taking place in the Middle Ages. People who complain do so because they have a clear belief in their mind as to what the 'correct' form of their language should be, and this is generally derived from the way the language is used in the written standard or in its expression as formal, careful speech. However, a standardized version of the written language began to appear only in the fifteenth century (Chapter 10), and became a serious talking point only in the sixteenth (Chapter 11). Without a standard, there is very little scope for notions of correctness to develop.

Correctness also needs a stable frame of reference in which to operate. If a language is in a process of rapid change, it is very difficult to develop a sense of norms. When a change – a new pronunciation, a new spelling, a new feature of grammar, a new word – begins to appear, it does not affect everyone and everywhere at once. Some parts of a country use it before others. Within any one part of the country, some speakers/writers use it before others. And within any one speaker/writer, some sentences and words manifest the change before others. A cross-section of society, at any given time, presents a complex picture of mixed usage. And when several aspects of a language are changing rapidly and radically, the picture is messy indeed.

This is how it was in Middle English. The fundamental shift in the grammar of the language, from an inflected pattern to one based on word order, took place by the beginning of the period (p. 101), but the consequences of this shift took several hundred years to work through. We can still see the old 'object before the verb' word-order patterns in fifteenth-century prose. (It is always an option in metrically disciplined poetry, even today.) It is still there in the informal interaction of the Paston letters, for example (p. 178), but only in a small number of sentence patterns and in some fixed phrases (e.g., *so God him help*).[17] We can see it dying away during that century: later Paston letters (after 1442) have fewer than half as many instances as early ones (*c.* 1400 or earlier). There are fewer still in another surviving set of correspondence, the letters of the Cely family of London wool merchants (1472–88). And the object–verb pattern finally disappears from English prose during the sixteenth century.

During Middle English we can see the language adapting in its grammar, finding new ways of expressing the meanings which in Old English were handled by word endings, and developing some new kinds of construction. The progressive form emerged (as in *I am going*), as did the range of auxiliary verbs in various functions (*I have seen*, *Does she know?*, *I didn't go*, *They can ask*, etc.). The infinitive form of a verb starts to be marked by the use of a particle (*to go*, *to jump*). A new form of expressing relationships such as possession appeared, using *of* (as in *the pages of a book*). In addition, as we have seen, several new grammatical forms appeared through the influence of Old Norse (p. 219). All areas of grammar were involved.

Other areas of language structure were also strongly affected. We have already seen the extensive impact foreign languages had on the evolving lexicon of Middle English (Chapter 7), and noted some of the new spelling conventions introduced by French scribes (p. 210). The pronunciation system, too, was undergoing significant change. We see several consonants and vowels altering their values, and new contrastive units of sound (*phonemes*) emerging. In particular, the distinction between the /f/ and /v/ consonants began to differentiate words (e.g., *grief* vs *grieve*), as did that between /s/ and /z/ (e.g., *seal* vs *zeal*). The *ng* sound at the end of a word also became contrastive (in Old English the *g* had always been sounded), so we now find such pairs as *sin* vs *sing*. But the biggest set of changes took place at the very end of the period, when all the long vowels underwent a series of changes.

The *long vowels* can be heard today in the Received Pronunciation (p. 468) of words like *seat* (as opposed to the *short vowel* of *sit*) and *lose* (vs *loose*). In Middle English, there were seven such vowels, and their values are shown in the table below, along with an approximate equivalent in modern Received Pronunciation.

Word	Vowel quality in c. 1400	Nearest Modern English (RP) vowel
time	/iː/	*teem* /iː/
see	/eː/	first part of *say* /ei/
sea	/ɛː/	first part of *Sarah* /ɛə/
fame	/aː/	*farm* /ɑː/
so	/ɔː/	*saw* /ɔː/
do	/oː/	first part of *doe* /ou/
now	/uː/	*new* /uː/

Around 1400, some of these vowels began to change their values, and by around 1600 all of them had done so. We can tell when a shift was taking place because of the way the spellings changed: if we see a word like *blod* 'blood', which was traditionally spelled with an *o*, beginning to be spelled with a *u*, as in *bloud* or *blud*, it suggests that some sort of pronunciation change in the direction of /uː/ is taking place. Taking into account these changes, and those that took place after 1600 also, we end up with the modern system, again illustrated here from Received Pronunciation.

Vowel quality in c. 1400		Vowel quality today	Modern English word (RP)
/iː/	>	/ai/	time
/eː/	>	/iː/	see
/ɛː/	>	/iː/	heath
/aː/	>	/ei/	fame

Vowel quality in c. 1400		Vowel quality today	Modern English word (RP)
/ɔː/	>	/əʊ/	so
/oː/	>	/uː/	do
/uː/	>	/aʊ/	now

The cumulative difference is striking. A sentence such as

We do say it's time to go now

would have roughly sounded, in Chaucerian pronunciation, as

Way doe sah it's teem to gaw noo.

It only took a few generations before the changes formed a real comprehension barrier. Today, if we hear Chaucer read in a Middle English pronunciation, it can be very difficult to understand him. It would have been difficult for Shakespeare, too.

The phenomenon is traditionally called the 'Great Vowel Shift', but the label is misleading in its suggestion that it was a single shift operating at a standard rate. The evidence of spellings, rhymes, and commentaries by contemporary language pundits suggests that it operated in more than one stage, affected vowels at different rates in different parts of the country, and took over 200 years to complete. Nor did it apply in the same way everywhere. The /uː/ value became a diphthong in most parts of England, as we hear in modern *now* and *house*, but this change did not happen in the north-east, or in Scotland, where the 1400 value may still be heard, as can be seen in such Scots spellings as *noo* and *hoose*.

Nobody has been able to establish why the change began – the causes of a sound-change are never easy to determine – and studies plotting its spread are still ongoing. Some parts of the country seem to have been more involved at the outset than others. One analysis has suggested that the low vowels, such as /aː/, began to change first in the North, specifically in the Yorkshire area, and the high vowels (such as /iː/) in the North Midlands and the South-West.[18] A varied dialect pattern is very likely: we know that the speakers of some dialects are more conservative than others, and take more time to assimilate a change.

The first of these changes was well under way when Caxton was born, and by the time he set up his press in London several words would have had competing pronunciations in the speech of those around him. Many people from the Midlands would have brought the change with them. Doubtless older people were more conservative, younger ones more innovative. Perhaps women were more ready to be innovative than men, as they are often known to be today (p. 418). Whatever the situation, it increased Caxton's problem. Not only were there variant non-regional spellings common in London for a word with a single pronunciation; several words were being spoken by Londoners with different non-regional pronunciations. These were not the best circumstances for fostering a standard written language. Nor was it a conducive climate for people to develop an intuition about norms of usage. It would take a further fifty years before people found that the language had settled down enough to be able to feel sufficiently comfortable to start complaining about it.

Chapter 11: Printing and its consequences

The story of Standard English, like Dylan Thomas' childhood, is one which has a beginning but no end.[1] No variety of language ever stands still, not even the standard variety. As we have seen in Chapter 10, standardizing trends emerged from the welter of variation which characterized the written language in the early fifteenth century, and these became more apparent as the century progressed. However, it took another 200 years before a standard language became established in its modern sense – that is, as a variety characterized by an agreed spelling system and a normative set of grammatical rules. The turning point was the eighteenth century, when an unprecedented concern for correctness in usage led to the composing of explicit prescriptions about usage which were universally taught in schools (Chapter 15). But even then, there was no total agreement about what counted as 'correct'. Dispute surrounded the prescriptions as soon as they were made, and there was never complete uniformity of usage. This scenario has continued. Despite the best efforts of prescriptive grammarians and usage pundits to get everyone writing in exactly the same way, a considerable amount of variability exists within the standard variety still – much more than people think (p. 474) – and the language continues to change. The point applies even more to those people – in Britain, between 12 and 15 per cent of the population[2] – who model their speech on the rules of the written standard, and who have to cope with variations in pronunciation. Standard English today, in either its written or spoken form, is not the same as it was a century ago, and will be different again a century hence.

As we have seen, the standard variety of English is the outcome of a long-term accumulation of formative influences, which affected different aspects of the language at different rates at different periods. Sometimes the changes (and the debate which accompanied them) chiefly related to vocabulary; sometimes to grammar; sometimes to general matters of discourse and style; and sometimes to spelling, or to the relationship of spelling to pronunciation. Throughout the history of standardization, the primary focus has been on the way the language is written – an emphasis which grew more noticeable over time as written English increasingly diverged from spoken English. The view that a writing system is a way of representing a speech system became steadily less relevant, as the standard evolved. Few of the developments which took place in writing bore any relationship to what was going on in speech. The written language, we might say, was taking on a life of its own – speech developing in one way; writing in another. We live with the consequences today: a language where there is a stark contrast between the dynamic world of spoken regional English and the static world of written Standard English. It is difficult to bring these two worlds together, though recent decades have seen highly successful efforts in adapting the standard written language to reflect the realities of speech once again (Chapter 19).

The development of a radically divergent written and spoken English is very much bound up with the eventual impact of the printing press; but the operative word is 'eventual'. Although printing was introduced into England by William Caxton as early as 1476, it was not until a century later that we find significant levels of standardization in printed books. Caxton, it must be noted, was not a language specialist or a professional writer; he was a businessman who wanted to make a living by selling books (see panel 11.1). As an intelligent observer, he would have been well aware of some aspects of language change and dialect variation. Anyone who returns to a country after living abroad for an appreciable period notices linguistic change, and Caxton was no exception. In the Prologue to *Eneydos* he comments: 'certaynly our langage now vsed

---

11.1 William Caxton

'I ... was born & lerned myn Englissh in Kente in the Weeld, where I doubte not is spoken as brode and rude Englissh as in ony place of Englond.' Thus writes William Caxton in the Prologue to the first English printed book, his translation of *The Recuyell* [compilation] *of the Historyes of Troy*. The reference to a *rude* ('unpolished') *English* is a conventional expression, used by many writers of the time (p. 287) as part of the 'humility formulae' requesting the reader's indulgence. Caxton would certainly have acquired some degree of linguistic polish in school, where he also learned Latin and probably French.

It is not known exactly when he was born – sometime around the year 1420, if we work back from the record of his apprenticeship in 1438 to a leading London mercer (a dealer in textiles). His later career as a merchant engaged in the cloth trade is obscure, though from the same Prologue we learn that he spent many years on the Continent, in the Low Countries. During the 1440s he went to one of the textile trading centres, Bruges, where in the early 1460s he became governor of the English Nation (the English merchant adventurers based in the town). There is some evidence that he was involved in importing and selling manuscripts, before he turned to printing, a technique which he learned in Cologne, Germany.

He established his first press in Bruges, where in 1473–4 he printed the 700-page *Recuyell*. Then, after returning to England in 1476, he set up another in a shop somewhere in the precincts of Westminster Abbey, to be near the court. On 29 September of that year (Michaelmas), his name is recorded in the account roll of the sacristan of Westminster Abbey as paying a year's rent in advance for his new premises.

Caxton published over a hundred separate items. They include several of his own translations, as well as popular prose works, such as Malory's *Morte Darthur*, and the work of the courtly poets – notably, Chaucer (two editions of *The Canterbury Tales*), Gower, and Lydgate. Among a range of miscellaneous pieces is a Latin grammar.

After his death (*c.* 1491) his business was taken over by his assistant, Jan Wynkyn de Worde (Worde was his home town of Worth), who around the end of 1500 moved the press to London's Fleet Street, nearer the City, occupying a house opposite Shoe Lane, at the sign of the Sun. The street's association with publishing would last nearly 500 years.

---

varyeth ferre [far] from that whiche was vsed and spoken whan I was borne'. But if pressed on the point, he would have been as vague about identifying these changes as most people would be today. It would seem he was aware of regional variation in vocabulary, as we have noted with the 'egg' story recounted in the same Prologue (p. 207), and this is to be expected, for new words are probably the most readily noticeable aspect of language change. But there is no reason to think he would have been especially conscious of the nature of the other changes which were taking place during his lifetime, all of which would play their part in shaping the standard language – the subtle changes in grammatical expression, the spelling trends emanating from London scriveners, or the major pronunciation changes which were moving through the population, in the form of the Great Vowel Shift (p. 252).

Caxton's work displays all the characteristics we would expect of any publisher trying to make a living while coping with new technology, manuscripts of diverse origin, and foreign staff (only the Continent could provide a supply of typesetters, in the early years), let alone satisfying the diverse expectations of a critical (and socially powerful) upper- and middle-class readership. Analyses of his writing and translations have brought to light many errors and inconsistencies, suggestive of someone publishing in haste and responding to the needs of the moment. In a modern publishing house, a hierarchy of decision-making (at least, in theory!) controls the quality of the final product, with an in-house editor ultimately responsible for a text whose accuracy has been repeatedly checked by professional copy-editors, proof-readers, and printer's readers. The printing process in medieval times involved similar people, responsible for estimating the number of lines per page (*casting off*), composing a complete page of metal type within a holding-frame (*forme*), and making textual corrections; but pressures of time and a limited availability of type made effective supervision difficult, even in cases where a master printer or editor was in charge of an operation.

Because type was in short supply, a book would be broken down into sections (*signatures*); a signature would be composed, checked, and printed, and the type would then be removed from the formes and used again to prepare other signatures. To maintain a high rate of production, several compositors would work simultaneously on a signature, and without a strict system of supervision it is easy to see how they might personalize their typesetting, fail to follow instructions, or introduce corrections at their own discretion. In the typical checking process, a proof sheet was pulled from a forme and compared with the original manuscript by two people: a *reader* would read aloud the original and the *corrector* would follow the text on the proof. The process would pick up several errors, and the appropriate corrections would be made to the type in the forme. However, a two-person process, where one person's dictating speed may not be the same as the other person's receptive speed, is obviously fallible; unfamiliar words, or words uttered in a foreign or regional accent, would not be easy to decode, and the large number of variant spellings in circulation would promote laxity – something would have to be really serious to count, or even be noticed, as an error. Correction was also a time-consuming business. Some errors would require whole lines of type to be reset, or words abbreviated, or extra letters (such as an optional final -*e*) added. Even if all the original errors had been noticed, further errors might be introduced at that point. As a result, pages would be checked again, even after the press run had begun. New errors would inevitably be spotted, and further changes made to the forme. That is why, in early books, we can compare two editions of the same print run and find that the pages are not identical. A century later, the teacher Richard Mulcaster was still worried about printing errors, so much so that in his *Elementarie* (see below) he focuses his spelling rules on handwritten texts rather than on printed ones, because 'the printers, setters, and correcters ouersights somtimes plaieth a part, and letteth manie errors abide in their work'.

The larger the number of compositors, readers, and correctors involved on the various signatures of a book, the more variability we would expect to find. In the case of compositors from abroad, we additionally have to allow for a lack of intuition about English spelling norms and what would count as an error. For example, at a time when -*e* was sometimes found at the end of a word and sometimes not, sometimes pronounced and sometimes not, a foreign compositor would be particularly likely to assume that its use was random, and to insert it or remove it (in cases like *Englissh*/*Englisshe*, *good*/*goode*) to meet a criterion of no linguistic relevance, such as when a line of type needed to be made to fit neatly into a forme. Foreign printing-staff, used to working with the spelling norms of their own language, would also find it difficult to avoid letting these norms influence the spelling of English words. Interference from Dutch presumably explains such spellings as *gh* (in place of *g*) in such words as *ghost* and *ghesse* ('guess') in several Caxton texts. To a certain extent it is the old story of scribal error all over again (p. 43) – except that this time the mistakes and inconsistencies would be replicated hundreds of times and come to be more widely distributed than any handwritten manuscript could ever have been.

It is plain, from the variety of spellings in Caxton's books, that he had no coherent spelling policy. Although many words are spelled consistently, there is a noticeable lack of standardization. In his own writing, as shown in the various Prologues and Epilogues, there is a great deal of variation, as can be seen from a glance at the extract from the 'egg' story (p. 207) in the *Eneydos* Prologue. There we find 'asked' spelled in two ways within a few words of each other: Sheffelde the mercer *axed for mete and specyally he axyd after eggys*. And throughout the text we find 'wife' as *wyf* and *wyfe*, 'little' as *lytyl* and *lityl*, 'good' as *good* and *goode*, 'them' as *them* and *theym*. The word 'book' is spelled as *booke* ten times in this Prologue, and as *boke* five, at one point both spellings turning up within three words of each other. In his Prologue to the *Recuyell*, Margaret is described as the *Duchesse/Duches* of *Bourgoyne/Bourgoine/Bourgone*. Caxton's translations vary in a different way, as they show the influence of a manuscript's language of origin. If he is translating a Dutch text, his spellings can reflect Dutch conventions, such as *oe* instead of *o* or *oo*: 'good', for example, appears as *goed* in the Dutch *Reynard the Fox*, but as *gode* and *good* in his Prologue to the Latin *Eneydos*. In translating a French text, such as the *Recuyell*, we find such French spellings as *musycque*, where elsewhere (such as in *The Canterbury Tales*) we find *musik*. The implication of all this variability should again be noted: with more copies being reproduced and widely circulated, proportionately more people would have been exposed to these inconsistencies than would have been possible before. It is quite possible that, in the late 1400s, the arrival of printing actually slowed down the process of standardization taking place elsewhere.

Although linguistic quotations from Caxton figure in every history of English, including this one, his observations about language were actually sporadic and incidental, and not a reflection of any language policy on his part, or perhaps even of any particular interest in the language as such. The way he carried out his translations – the adaptations he made, his choice of words – suggests that he was a man of the moment, devising ways of solving the immediate task presented by a text. Words used to solve a problem in one translation might never appear in any other: *enseygnement*, for example, is used often in the translation of the *Knight of the Tower*, and turns up three times in its Prologue and Colophon. It is probable that Caxton considered it a new word, for he uses it in association with a more familiar synonym – a translation doublet (p. 151) – to help the reader: *good enseygnementis and lernynges*, he writes at one point in the Prologue; *the booke of th'enseygnementes and techynge*, he writes at another. But that is where the usage ends. He does not use it elsewhere in his personal writing in relation to other books – as a translator interested in 'improving' the English language would have done – but stays with the words *learning* and *teaching*. It is as if he used the new word while it was 'on his mind', and then forgot about it.

Several examples of this kind are given in Norman Blake's extensive study of the nature of Caxton's personal vocabulary, and it is difficult to resist Blake's conclusion, that Caxton was 'an opportunist in linguistic matters'.[3] This can be sensed, also, in his choice of words: when he is writing his Prologues and Epilogues, his vocabulary is really quite small, and of a largely Germanic character; by contrast, when he is translating, he uses many words of Latin and French origin. His personal vocabulary, moreover, is minimally innovative: hardly any 'first usages' in English are attributed to Caxton in the *Oxford English Dictionary*. According to Blake, there are only about thirty anyway (most of which are not cited by the *OED*): they include *ample*, in two of its senses, and *maternal*, in the context of *maternal tongue* (= 'mother tongue'), and a number of *-ly* adverbs derived from adjectives which had entered the language in earlier decades, such as *prosperously*, *necessarily*, and *sempiternally* ('everlastingly'). These usages are generally of a mundane quality, suggesting that they were probably in common use. There is little sign of the linguistic energy and exploitation of the language's resources which we find in the creative writers of the time. The overall impression is that Caxton was someone who saw the written language as a functional tool, to be manipulated as required in order to get a job done.

None of this should be interpreted as belittling Caxton's considerable achievement. It could not have been easy for a Kentish man, brought up with a dialect at some remove from that of London, whose apprenticeship was spent in a trade which would have given him little contact with the more refined intuitions of Chancery scriveners, and who had spent so much time abroad, to have taken up a profession as demanding in its attention to linguistic detail as book production. He had to deal with material from a variety of sources, both native and foreign, in manuscripts which displayed considerable scribal and sometimes dialectal variation. Several manuscripts, such as those by Chaucer and Malory, were extremely long. He had to act as publisher, printer, and editor, writing his own supplementary material in the form of his Prologues and Epilogues. There was no one he could really turn to for help. There was no official body concerned with standards, and indeed no one at the time seemed to be particularly concerned about orthographic matters – this was a movement which developed half a century later. In addition, he had to cope with a rapidly changing language, a significant growth in literacy, and readers who were becoming increasingly conscious of regional and stylistic variation.

We get a sense of how critical his readers could be from the account of his tentative first steps in the translating business in the Prologue to the *Recuyell*. There he says that he had written about forty or fifty pages (*fyve or six quayers*, 'quires'), then got fed up:

> Y fyll [fell] in dispayr of thys werke and purposid no more to have contynued therin, and tho [those] quayers leyd apart; and in two yere aftyr laboured no more in thys werke.

However, during a meeting with Lady Margaret, the sister of the king, he happens to mention what he has done, and she asks to see it. The result was both bad news:

> And when she had seen hem, anone [anon] she fonde [found] a defaute in myn Englissh whiche sche comanded me to amende

and good news:

> and moreover comanded me straytli to contynue and make an ende of the resydue than [then] not translated.

Lady Margaret would certainly not have been the only person ready to find *defaute* ('fault'). The complaint tradition, as we have seen in the case of Higden (p. 186), was already under way.

Nor should the lack of a conscious standardizing policy in Caxton's printing house blind us to the fact that his books did introduce several features which would eventually help to shape Standard English. An important decision was his modernization of the orthography, using *g* and *th* instead of the manuscript symbols ʒ, þ, and ð; this immediately gave his texts a more modern appearance; it is a relatively easy matter to read Caxton's own writing (once punctuation has been added: see panel 11.2). The 'egg' story shows that he was aware of the need to make choices, and we can readily imagine that a discussion of individual cases would have been routine in the printing house, even though, as we have seen, the results would not always have lived up to expectations. Becoming part of the London business 'network' (p. 230) would have inevitably developed his sense of emerging written norms in the area. Certainly, his spellings on the whole do have a great deal in common with those preferred by the Chancery scriveners.

11.2 Punctuating

Early manuscripts had no punctuation or, even, spaces between words. The earliest conventions were introduced as a guide to phrasing when reading aloud became an important activity, such as on literary and liturgical occasions. There was a great deal of experiment: over thirty marks – various combinations of dots, curls, and dashes – can be found in medieval manuscripts, most of which disappeared after the arrival of printing. Some of them look like modern marks, but their function was not the same: a point, for example, represented a pause, rather than a sentence ending, and the height of the point could vary to express degrees of pause.

Printers had to make decisions about punctuation and capitalization as well as about spelling. The earliest European printers generally followed the marks they found in the manuscripts, the actual shapes depending on the typeface used.[4] Most recognized three kinds of pause, represented by a point, a virgule (/), and a mark of interrogation. Caxton chiefly used a virgule and point (.), occasionally a colon (:) and paragraph mark (¶). Word breaks at the end of a line were shown by a double virgule (//).The comma began to replace the virgule in the 1520s, though some printers used them interchangeably for a while.

Towards the end of the fifteenth century, semicircular parentheses, the question mark, and the semicolon, as well as the comma, were introduced in Europe, but it took some time for them all to appear in England. A single semicolon (until the mid seventeenth century called by various names, such as *comma-colon* and *hemi-colon*) turns up in the dedication to Coverdale's 1538 New Testament translation, which was printed in Paris. English printers did not begin using it until the 1570s.

Compositors found most of the new marks confusing, and there is a great deal of inconsistency of usage, especially when several people worked on the same book – most famously, in Shakespeare's First Folio (1623), where there is notable inconsistency in the use of the question mark vs exclamation mark, or the colon vs semicolon; and the apostrophe and hyphen turn up in some very unexpected places (as in *advan'st* 'advanced' and *the State . . . Cannot with safetie cast-him*, in *Othello*, l. 164). Some marks were virtually interchangeable – and indeed even in modern editions a comparison of two editions (e.g., of Shakespeare's *Sonnets*) will bring to light a remarkable range of decisions about which sets of lines should be separated by a colon, semicolon, comma, or point.

Uncertainty always surrounds a new punctuation mark. Long before the First Folio, there had been inconsistency among compositors over the use of the apostrophe, at first used only as a mark of omission, from 1559 (its use as a marker of possession was an eighteenth-century development). The hyphen, used to identify a compound word, and the exclamation mark (the *note of admiration*) arrived towards the end of the century. It took a long time for the use of these marks to stabilize.

Great uncertainty also surrounded the use of capital letters. First used for proper names as well as for sentence and verse-line openings, they were extended to any words thought to be important (such as titles, terms of address, and personification) as well as to words receiving special emphasis. During the seventeenth century, virtually any word might be capitalized, if it were felt to be significant, and compositors – to be on the safe side – tended to over-capitalize. A reaction set in against excessive capitalization in the eighteenth century, and we find the present-day system emerging.

Then as now there were heavy and light capitalizers, as well as heavy and light punctuators. Indeed, this is one of the areas where Standard English is still most unstable, as a glance at the 'sometimes capitalized' note in modern dictionary entries suggests – is it *prime minister* or *Prime Minister, moon* or *Moon, bible* or *Bible* (see further, p. 478)?

If Caxton did not show any great concern to standardize orthography, nor did his immediate successors. His assistant, Wynkyn de Worde, employed English compositors, which would have eliminated one source of uncertainty in textual transmission, but a comparison of texts (such as Caxton's and Wynkyn's editions of *Reynard*) still shows considerable variation in the later version.[5] The same applies to the work of the other London printers who arrived on the scene, such as John Lattou, who established the first press in the City of London in 1480; Julian Notary, who set up his press around 1496; and Robert Pynson, who began work in the parish of St Clement Dane's, just outside Temple Bar, some time before the century came to a close. It took another fifty years before the different printing houses began to produce work which, from a linguistic point of view, was difficult to distinguish because they were using broadly similar conventions, and it is only at this point that we can affirm the importance of the printing press as a means of consolidating a standard. When this happened, the results were dramatic. A standard can evolve without printing; but printing makes it spread more rapidly and widely. And once the standard is in the hands of the printers, they do not let it go.

Changing fashions

Attitudes to language are very much bound up with the conscious appreciation of the social trend which we refer to as *fashion*. Because language is quintessentially a social tool, we inevitably end up doing what other people do, even if we do not realize that we are doing it. Fashionable usage particularly affects the written language, where changes in practice are easy to see.[6] In recent times emailing and text-messaging are two illustrations of the speed with which a new orthographic style can emerge and become widespread. In business letters we have lived through a period in which indented paragraphs have become non-indented, and the lines in an address have lost their end-punctuation. In public places we have likewise seen the emergence of an 'uncluttered' style of graphic design, which has resulted in a diminution in the use of punctuation marks, such as the apostrophe (as when *St Paul's* appears as *St Pauls*). What we do in public affects what we do in private. Our formal correspondence eventually exercises an influence on our informal. If we routinely receive formal letters containing, for example, the word *judgment* without a medial *e*, or *advertize* with a *z* instead of an *s*, our replies will tend to adopt these spellings, even if we were brought up to do otherwise. And this in turn affects our private letters, emails, and computer writing (the latter no doubt reinforced by the insidious pressure from the pedants who program our spellchecking software). We accommodate to each other in writing, as well as in speech (p. 83).

The sixteenth century is the first time we can see fashion exercising a real influence on the developing standard. The term *standard language* was not yet in use – it is not recorded in English until the early nineteenth century – but the concept of a 'recognized exemplar of correctness in behaviour', or 'a practice recommended as universal', is known from the mid fifteenth century. The word *standard* had actually been in English since the twelfth century, when it arrived from Old French in the sense of 'a military or naval ensign'. Soon there was a derived sense ('an exemplar of measure or weight') which was probably a figurative extension, the king's standard being associated with authority and the issuing of commands. The more abstract notion emerged shortly after, and the application of the word to money ('a legal rate for the intrinsic value of coins') appeared at about the same time. It was plainly an age when people were beginning to think about norms, for the term turns up in a wide variety of contexts, such as alchemy and religion. Several other expressions referring to general use of language make their appearance from the late fourteenth century on: *usual* and *common* are applied to language by Caxton – *oure vsual and moder tongue* (Epilogue to *Boethius*), *comyn English* (Prologue to *Eneydos*); *corrector*, as we have seen, turns up in the context of printing; and *normal* is used with reference to language as early as 1530 (in Palsgrave, where a regular verb is described as *a normal*). In due course these words acquire a normative connotation, through their association with other words of a plainly evaluative character – George Puttenham, for example, referring to 'the vsuall speach of the Court'.

Although this quotation from Puttenham is quite late – it appears in *The Arte of Poetrie* in 1589 – it reflects the kind of locution which was current in the preceding decades. I choose it because the passage in which it appears is one of the most illuminating in the insight it provides us into the language fashions of the period, and it deserves to be studied at length. Puttenham is advising poets about the kind of language they should use, if they are to be successful (in Book III, 'Of Ornament', Chapter 4, 'Of Language'). It should, he says,

> be naturall, pure, and the most vsuall of all his countrey: and for the same purpose rather that which is spoken in the kings Court, or in the good townes and Cities within the land, then in the marches and frontiers, or in port townes, where straungers haunt for traffike sake, or yet in Vniuersities where Scholers vse much peeuish affectation of words out of the primatiue languages, or finally, in any vplandish village or corner of a Realme, where is no resort but of poore rusticall or vnciuill people:

The ideal norm is evidently aristocratic usage, for even university people are excluded. And even within the 'good towns and cities', the poet needs to be careful to find the right class of person:

> neither shall he follow the speach of a craftes man or carter, or other of the inferiour sort, though he be inhabitant or bred in the best town and Citie in this Realme, for such persons do abuse good speaches by strange accents or illshapen soundes, and false ortographie. But he shall follow generally the better brought vp sort, such as the Greekes call *charientes*, men ciuill and graciously behauoured and bred.

Following the usage of great writers of the past will not do:

> Our maker therfore at these dayes shall not follow *Piers plowman* nor *Gower* nor *Lydgate* nor yet *Chaucer*, for their language is now out of vse with vs:

And regional speech will not do either, even if you are upper class (a clear indication, incidentally, that regional speech was still current among the aristocracy):

> neither shall he take the termes of Northern-men, such as they vse in dayly talke, whether they be noble men or gentlemen, or of their best clarkes all is a matter: nor in effect any speach vsed beyond the riuer of Trent, though no man can deny but that theirs is the purer English Saxon at this day, yet it is not so Courtly nor so currant as our Southerne English is, no more is the far Westerne mans speach: ye shall therfore take the vsuall speach of the Court, and that of London and the shires lying about London within lx. myles, and not much aboue.

Sixty miles. It is a rhetorical point, for the sixty-mile circle would include not only Oxford and Cambridge, but also Ipswich and the whole of Kent, where regional dialect ruled (p. 343). Puttenham in any case immediately backtracks, realizing that 'good Southern' can be found anywhere. It is an explicit acknowledgement that, especially in writing, a standard now exists.

> I say not this but that in euery shyre of England there be gentlemen and others that speake but specially write as good Southerne as we of Middlesex or Surrey do, but not the common people of euery shire, to whom the gentlemen, and also their learnèd clarkes do for the most part condescend, but herein we are already ruled by th'English Dictionaries and other bookes written by learnèd men, and therefore it needeth none other direction in that behalfe.

'Condescend'? Presumably this meant that the gentry were able to 'talk down' to the locals, using the regional dialect – in other words, they were bidialectal. But just as interesting is the acknowledgement that 'we are already ruled' by the textbooks; 'it needeth none other direction'. We see here the beginning of the institutionalization of English in manuals perceived to be authoritative. But there is a sting in the tail even for the learnèd men:

> Albeit peraduenture some small admonition be not impertinent, for we finde in our English writers many wordes and speaches amendable, & ye shall see in some many inkhorne termes so ill affected brought in by men of learning as preachers and schoolemasters: and many straunge termes of other languages by Secretaries and Marchaunts and trauailours, and many darke wordes and not vsuall nor well sounding, though they be dayly spoken in Court.

Not even courtly language, it seems, is beyond the scope of criticism. So poets must take care:

> Wherefore great heed must be taken by our maker in this point that his choise be good. And peraduenture the writer hereof be in that behalfe no lesse faultie then any other, vsing many straunge and vnaccustomed wordes and borrowed from other languages: and in that respect him selfe no meete Magistrate to reforme the same errours in any other person, but since he is not vnwilling to acknowledge his owne fault, and can the better tell how to amend it, he may seeme a more excusable correctour of other mens: he intendeth therefore for an indifferent way and vniuersall benefite to taxe him selfe first and before any others.

That last piece of advice was not thereafter much heeded. Very few usage pundits would ever take the trouble to search out the linguistic mote in their own eye before discovering it in others.

In the mid sixteenth century, the 'English Dictionaries and other bookes written by learnèd men' could only have referred to works written in or about Latin. The first grammar written in English was by William Bullokar (1530?–1609): his full *Grammar at Larg[e]* is now lost, but an abbreviated version, which he called *Pamphlet for Grammar*, is known from 1586, prepared, as he puts it in an introductory statement to the reader, 'for the speedy parsing of English speech, and the easier coming to the knowledge of Grammar for other languages'.[7] This quotation is in modern spelling; the original is in Bullokar's reformed orthography, illustrated in panel 11.3. The grammar is heavily indebted to William Lily's *Short Introduction of Grammar* (i.e. Latin grammar), published in 1509. In an earlier work, *A short Introduction or guiding to print, write, and Reade Inglish speech: conferred with the olde printing and writing* (1580), Bullokar addresses the reader in rhyme, promising a family of books: there is to be a 'brother', in the form of a work on spelling reform ('the amendment of ortographie'), a 'sister' (his grammar), which 'lieth at home, abyding my good chaunce', and a 'Cousin Dictionarie', which 'I know doth lack me much'. Indeed it did. Nothing more is heard of that project. One of the early dictionaries of hard words (p. 280) is by his son, John – *An English Expositor* (1616), but this seems to be an independent work.

Not only were there no grammars on English in the sixteenth century, there were no English-language dictionaries either. Bilingual dictionaries existed, such as Thomas Thomas' *Dictionarium Linguae Latinae et Anglicanae* (*Dictionary of the Latin and English Languages*), compiled c. 1588, and they provided a model for the monolingual dictionaries when they eventually appeared. About half the words and definitions in the first such work, Robert Cawdrey's *A Table Alphabeticall* of 1604, are Anglicized versions taken from Thomas (see Interlude 11). But this is to jump ahead. In the sixteenth century, the linguistic energy of 'learnèd men' was almost entirely devoted to one thing: spelling reform. From c. 1540, a movement grew to impose order on what was perceived to be the chaotic state of English spelling. The earliest reformers were the Greek scholar Sir John Cheke (1514–57) and the scholar and statesman Sir Thomas Smith (1513–77), but they were soon followed by the leading enthusiasts, the Chester Herald John Hart (d. 1574) and William Bullokar, as well as by the teachers Alexander Gil (1565–1635) and Richard Mulcaster (1530?–1611), the last reputed to be the model for Holofernes in Shakespeare's *Love's Labour's Lost* (see below). It was not a purely programmatic movement: several of the reformers published whole works in the reformed spelling they advocated, such as Bullokar's *Aesops Fablź* (1585), over 64,000 words long.

John Hart is unequalled in the phonetic detail of his proposals, and a great deal can be learned about pronunciation in the sixteenth century from his descriptions. He wrote three books advocating spelling reform, notably *The opening of the unreasonable writing of our inglish toung* (1551, but not published until after his death) and *An Orthographie, conteyning the due order and reason, howe to write or paint thimmage of mannes voice, most like to the life of nature* (1569), which is as good a characterization as one might find of a definition of a phonetic alphabet. He is a strong advocate of radical reform,

11.3 A page from Bullokar's abridged grammar, the first to be written in English, illustrating his reformed orthography

Wil. Bullokarz abbreuiation of hiz Gram-　1
mar for english extracted out-of hiz Grammar at-larg, for the spedi parcing of
english spech, and the æzier coming
too the knowledg of Gram-
mar for other lan-
gagez.

Spech may be diuid-　{ Noun,
ed intoo on of thez　{ Pronoun, } declined
eiht partz: too wit,　{ Uerb,

Speech is diuided into eight parts.

Participl,　　　　{ So, that ther iz no-on
Aduerb,　　　un-declined　word too be uttered in
Conjunction,　　　　our spech, but it iz on
Prepozition,　　　　of the eiht partz befor
Interjection,　　　　mentioned.

The nam of any thing that may be sen,
feltt, heard, or understanded iz caled a nown,
az a hand, a hows, an pi, God, goodnes, hær-
ing, lærning: and may the æzilver be known,
from euery other part of spech, by som-on of
thez articlz, A, An, or The, sett befor such
word, which may comunly be uzed befor any
nown-substantiu named alon: but if a substantiu being in sentenc gouern a nown-ad-
iectiu, the adiectiu iz comunly sett betwen
such articl and substantiu, their prepozition
　　　　　　B 1　　　　　　being

The name of a thing that may be seen, felt, heard, or vnderstand-ed is a nown, & æsily perceiued by A, 2 : 17; An, or The, set before it.

2 : 11 : 21 : 57 :

believing that only a phonic basis in the spelling system – one sound, one letter – would rid the language of its 'divers vices and corruptions'. He perceptively sees that the problem is the reader's (p. 226): 'confusion and disorder' in spelling, he says at one point, 'bringeth confusion and uncertainte in the reading'.[8] And he itemizes the various difficulties, such as the use of one letter for several sounds (e.g., the 'double powers' of *g* in *gentle* and *together*) and of several letters for one sound. He particularly objects to a 'superfluite' of letters – 'more letters than the pronunciation neadeth of voices' – where he is thinking of the extra letters introduced into words by printers (p. 257) as well as the letters added by scholars wanting to show where words came from – such as the *b* added to *doubt* (because it was there in the Latin source, *dubitare*) or the *o* added to *people* (Latin *populum*). He would like to eliminate all silent letters, preferring a system in which, for example, an accent over a vowel would show that it is long. And he attacks cases where he thinks the letters are in the wrong order: *fable*, he says, should be written *fabel*.

None of the proposals from any of the reformers were taken up, despite Hart and others devoting a great deal of space to articulating the arguments in favour. The reason then is the same as the reason in later centuries, when many more proposals for spelling reform arose. The new symbols and conventions introduced by the different reformers were unfamiliar, complex, idiosyncratic, and not entirely self-consistent. No two systems agreed in what counted as the best set of 'improvements'. Spelling reform kingdoms have always been divided against themselves. Nor does English (i.e., the English people) seem to favour 'top down' proposals, made by authoritative individuals or institutions (though with one important exception, see p. 420). The English linguistic temperament seems to be more laissez-faire. When English spelling did standardize (between the sixteenth and eighteenth centuries), it did so 'bottom up', with a consensus of usage gradually favouring some traditional spellings at the expense of others. Only two real innovations were ever accepted, after Hart's time: the 24-letter alphabet of Middle English grew to 26, as vowel *i* came to be distinguished from consonant *j*, and vowel *u* from consonant *v*.

The case in favour of spelling using the long-established letters was first expounded by the headmaster of Merchant Taylors' School, Richard Mulcaster, in his *Elementarie*, a work on the principles of early education. Mulcaster agreed with Hart that it is 'a very necessary labor to set the writing certain, that the reading may be sure', but firmly rejected the view that radical spelling reform was the way to do it. According to Mulcaster, even though spelling had originated as a phonic system, it could no longer in the sixteenth century be regarded as the primary rationale for a writing system. Custom – 'a great and naturall governour' – had proved to be a much more powerful force, he says, reflecting the various influences which society had introduced over time, and allowing for differences in regional pronunciation in a way that a phonic system would be unable to do. In the phase of development reached by English spelling, he maintains that the chief governor is 'Art', the process whereby people start writing down collections of words, organizing them into types, and systematizing spelling rules ('gathering all those roaming rules, that custom had beaten out, into one body') – in a word, codification. He allows that there are some problems – inconsistencies and irregularities to be eliminated – but adding new letters or changing the shapes of existing letters is not the solution:

> though we grant some imperfection, as in a tongue not yet raked from her troubled lees, yet we do not confess, that it is too be perfected either by altering the form, or by increasing the number of our acquainted letters, but only by observing, where the tongue of her self, and her ordinary custom doth yield too the fining [refining], as the old and therefore the best method doth lead us.

Mulcaster starts the codification off himself, adding an alphabetical list of over 8,500 words with recommended spellings. He was wrong in one point – two new letters would be added to the alphabet in due course – but otherwise his views anticipated the outcome. Over the next two centuries, allowing custom to take its course produced a standardized system using the traditional alphabet. And if we compare the spellings of the words in his list with their spellings today, well over half are the same, and most of the differences are either of the *i/j* or *u/v* kind or minor variants at the ends of words (e.g., *elementarie, equall*).

The printing consensus which began to grow during the sixteenth century was itself prompted by social trends. Well aware of the debate raging (it is not too strong a word) about the nature of English spelling, printers had a professional interest in observing the way the climate was evolving; and they did respond to it, in all kinds of detailed ways. An example is the rationalization of the distinction between long and short vowels. By this period, a long vowel had come to be indicated by either a doubled vowel (as in *moon*) or a final silent *-e* (as in *ride*), and if it was necessary to distinguish a short vowel, this would be shown by a following doubled consonant (as in *running*, p. 196). However, the tendency had grown to double a consonant after a short vowel even when there was no possibility of confusion, and also to add a final *-e*, so that we commonly find such forms as *sette* and *hadde*. 'To sette foorth his most worthye prayse', occurs in the Exhortation to Morning Prayer (in the Book of Common Prayer, 1552). These 'superfluous' letters attracted a great deal of criticism from the reformers, and this was one of the points where they could claim to have had some influence, for the extra consonant and the final *-e* in words of this kind gradually fell out of use. In Shakespeare's First Folio (1623) we find 447 instances of *set* and only one each of *sett* and *sette*; similarly, we find 1,398 instances of *had* and only one of *hadde*.

The fashionable linguistic climate was not solely concerned with writing. The phonetic awareness evinced by Hart and the other reformers led to a natural focus on everyday pronunciation, and matters of regional accent came to the fore. Now it was not only the written language which was being evaluated, but speech, and here, too, the Court was seen as the place 'where the best englysshe is spoken'. This comment is from a French-teaching text written by the scholar John Palsgrave (d. 1554), *Lesclarcissement de la langue francois* (1532). It was reinforced by Hart, who in his *Orthographie* talks of London speech as being 'that speach which euery reasonable English man, will the nearest he can, frame his tongue therevnto'. And Sir Thomas Elyot, in *The Boke named the Governour* (1531, Chapter 5), is clear about what should be done to a nobleman's son before he is seven:

> hit shall be expedient that a noble mannes sonne, in his infancie, haue with hym continually onely suche as may accustome hym by litle and litle to speake pure and elegant latin. Semblably [similarly] the nourises [nurses] and other women aboute hym, if it be possible, to do the same: or, at the leste way, that they speke none englisshe but that which is cleane, polite, perfectly and articulately pronounced, omittinge no lettre or sillable, as folisshe women often times do of a wantonnesse, wherby diuers noble men and gentilmennes chyldren, (as I do at this daye knowe), haue attained corrupte and foule pronuntiation.

A notion of correct speech was now being recognized, and was being taught. Furthermore, it was being seen as a criterion of good breeding.

One of Elyot's phrases is worth noting: 'omitting no letter or syllable'. A viewpoint which gained sway in the sixteenth century was that all the letters in a word should be pronounced. If writing best represents the standard form of a language, this thinking went, then special care should be taken to pronounce every bit of it. The view is still respected today, and anyone who 'pronounces the t in *often*' has, consciously or unconsciously, been influenced by it. In the sixteenth century, it seems, there were pedants who insisted on pronouncing even the silent letters which had been added to a word to show their etymology. Shakespeare was one of the first to poke fun at this, when he displays Holofernes' shock at the way Don Armado pronounces his words (*Love's Labour's Lost*, V.i.17):

> I abhor such fanatical phantasims [extravagantly behaved persons], such insociable and point-device [affectedly precise] companions, such rackers of orthography as to speak 'dout', sine [without] 'b', when he should say 'doubt'; 'det' when he should pronounce 'debt' – 'd, e, b, t', not 'd, e, t'. He clepeth [calls] a calf 'cauf', half 'hauf', neighbour vocatur [is called] 'nebour' – 'neigh' abbreviated 'ne. This is abhominable – which he would call 'abominable'.

This is a modernized spelling. In the First Folio, as we shall see (p. 318), the orthography was by no means modern, and still quite variable.

This reference to Shakespeare draws attention to another characteristic of an age in which linguistic fashions were being formed: the emergence of prestigious texts, some aimed at adults and some at children in school. A standard language both facilitates and is facilitated by a national literature; and during the sixteenth century we see the publication of several important texts which were intended for use nationwide, and whose language would thus become privileged and influential. The dramas of the Elizabethan and Jacobean period in fact come at the end of this period of textual influence. It is a period which began with the printing of major literary authors by Caxton, but in the following 130 years the primary influence was less from literature than from religion, for the sixteenth century was the age of printed Bibles.

The biblical impact

The first English text to be printed was the New Testament of William Tyndale (c. 1494–1536), published in 1525–6, and revised in 1534. Its repercussions lasted for almost a century, stimulated by the religious intolerances and confrontations of the age (Luther's anti-Catholic protest at Wittenberg took place in 1517). By 1611, when the King James Bible appeared, over fifty different translations had been made, several of which appeared in many editions. During Edward VI's reign alone (January 1547 to July 1553) about forty editions of various texts were published, including Tyndale's, Coverdale's, Matthew's, and the Great Bible (see panel 11.4). They differed mainly in their scholarly notes, which attracted varying amounts of controversy because of their theological stances; and there were heated arguments over the linguistic choices the translators had made – such as *congregation* or *church*, *repentance* or *penance*, *seniors*

11.4 The age of Bibles

Between Tyndale (1525) and the King James Bible (1611), six translations had especial influence within Britain, and they display a single thread of influence.

Coverdale's Bible (1535)

This was the first complete Bible to be printed in English, including both Old and New Testaments. A translation from German, it was published in Cologne by the Protestant scholar Miles Coverdale. Much influenced by Tyndale, he made few changes to the earlier text, thereby introducing a linguistic conservatism which would later influence the authorized versions.

Matthew's Bible (1537)

This complete Bible was the first to be printed in England, under the royal licence of Henry VIII. The text is attributed to the chamberlain of Colchester, Thomas Matthew, but it was compiled by John Rogers, a friend of Tyndale. The translation is based largely on Tyndale, with some influence of Coverdale.

The Great Bible (1539)

This was the first of many official versions for use in Protestant England, so-called because of its physical size ($9'' \times 13\frac{1}{2}''$); it is a revision of Matthew's Bible by Coverdale, and was revised itself in 1540. It is often called *Cranmer's Bible*, because Archbishop Thomas Cranmer wrote a Preface to it. Its influence was unprecedented: a copy was placed by law in every parish church in the country, and the public (and often controversial) reading aloud of the Scriptures became widespread.

The Geneva Bible (1560)

This translation, showing the influence of Tyndale and the Great Bible, was made in 1557 by William Whittingham and other exiles in Geneva during the reign of Queen Mary. It was published on his return to England in 1559 after Queen Elizabeth's accession, the first English Bible in roman type, and an injunction went to all churches to obtain a copy. Its portable size made it popular, especially for use in the home, and 140 editions appeared in the following decades. It was published in Scotland in 1579, and became the standard version in churches there. Several Elizabethan authors quoted from it, including Shakespeare. It received a nickname, the *Breeches Bible*, because of the use of that word for the clothing worn by Adam and Eve in Genesis 3:7.

The Bishops' Bible (1568)

This was a revised version of the Great Bible, initiated by Archbishop Parker, which became an authorized version of the Church in 1571, replacing the Geneva version (which did, however, continue to be widely used in homes). It was a primary text for the scholars working on the King James Bible.

The Douay/Rheims Bible (1582, 1609–10)

This version was directed by William Allen and other Roman Catholic translators in Europe. The New Testament appeared first in Rheims, and a two-volume Old Testament at Douai in the year before the appearance of the King James Bible. Based on the Latin Vulgate, it was used by English Catholics for the next century.

or *priests*, and *charity* or *love* – as when Tyndale was condemned by Sir Thomas More for 'certain wordes euill & of euyll purpose changid'.[9] Linguistically, despite variations in vocabulary and style, the dependency on Tyndale is apparent throughout, and this influence continued via the widely used Geneva Bible until we reach the King James translation, commonly known as *the* Authorized Version.

Tyndale (often spelled Tindale) makes his position plain in his Preface. He wanted a translation which ordinary people would understand, even 'the boy who plows the field':

> I had perceaved by experyence, how that it was impossible to stablysh the laye people in any truth, excepte the scripture were playnly layde before their eyes in their mother tonge, that they might se the processe, ordre and meaning of the texte.

His was a fresh translation, using the Latin Vulgate, Luther's German translation, and the Greek text recently published by Erasmus (1516), but it was unauthorized, and the conditions of the 1408 ban on biblical translations applied (p. 238). Unable to print his text in England, he published it in Europe. Copies smuggled into England were seized or bought by the authorities and publicly burned, so much so that only two copies of this edition are known to survive today. A prohibition of 24 October 1526 gave all London citizens thirty days to hand over 'all and every one of the books containing the translation of the New Testament in the vulgar tongue'. Tyndale began again, working on a new translation of the Old Testament (which he never completed) and revising the New. But opposition continued to be great. Imprisoned by the authorities in Antwerp, he was executed in 1536, his last words being 'Lord, open the King of England's eyes' – a death-wish full of irony, as Coverdale's translation had been published the year before (an event which Tyndale was probably unaware of). The irony lies in the fact that Coverdale had been Tyndale's assistant, and his translation closely followed Tyndale's. The 1534 Convocation of Canterbury had petitioned Henry VIII 'that the holy scripture should be translated into the vulgar English tongue', and the Coverdale Bible contained a dedication to the king. As a result, ten years after Tyndale's translation was banned in England, Coverdale's version was welcomed. A decade was a long time in that period of English biblical history.

Tyndale's translation was highly influential in its choice of vocabulary and phrasing. Most of the language of the King James Bible (some studies have suggested over 80 per cent) can be traced back to him. It can be seen in the vocabulary and grammar of such passages as the following, from St Paul's Epistle to the Romans (13:8–9), with the texts placed in parallel (spelling is modernized):

Tyndale (1534 version)	King James (1611)
Owe nothing to any man: but to love one another. For he that loveth another, fulfilleth the law. For these commandments: Thou shalt not commit adultery: Thou shalt not kill: Thou shalt not steal: Thou shalt not bear false witness: Thou shalt not desire and so forth (if there be any other commandment) they are all comprehended in this saying: Love thine neighbour as thy self.	Owe no man any thing, but to love one another: for he that loveth another hath fulfilled the law. For this, Thou shalt not commit adultery, Thou shalt not kill, Thou shalt not steal, Thou shalt not bear false witness, Thou shalt not covet; and if there be any other commandment, it is briefly comprehended in this saying, namely, Thou shalt love thy neighbour as thyself.

Most memorable biblical allusions are Tyndale's – such as *let there be light, the truth shall make you free, am I my brother's keeper?, let my people go, the powers that be, blessed are the peacemakers, the signs of the times,* and *eat, drink, and be merry.* In vocabulary he was extremely conservative, and he hardly ever incorporated new coinages or learnèd terms (p. 237), or coined words himself. Only 120 entries in the *Oxford English Dictionary* have a first recorded use attributed to Tyndale, and the character of many of them – such as *fisherman, jesting,* and *weakling* – is so everyday that the attribution is undoubtedly fortuitous. The figure includes a number of compounds which also have an everyday flavour, such as *broken-hearted, fellow-soldier, house-top, long-suffering, rose-coloured, sea-shore, stumbling-block, two-edged* (of a sword), and *wine-press.* Several already existing words are found in new grammatical uses: *abrogate* as a verb, *beggarly* as an adjective, *brotherly* as an adverb, *nurse* as a verb ('bring up'). It is difficult to say how many genuine Tyndalisms there might be. He certainly introduced *viper* in such phrases as 'O generacion of vipers' (Matthew 3:7), and among other interesting possibilities in the list of first recorded uses are *betrayer, busybody, castaway, childishness, excommunicate, matrix* 'womb', *momentary, murmurer, prophesying, sanctifying* (noun), *sorcerer, unbeliever, ungodliness, ungodly, whoremonger,* and *zealous.* The totals are small. Tyndale, interested in reaching the ploughboy rather than the professor, was no lexical innovator.

It is this continuity of language – from King James back to Tyndale via various intermediary Bibles – which more than anything else consolidated the emerging standard in the sixteenth century. No other factor caused a variety of language to be so widely respected and circulated. The impact of biblical writing – as of any sacred text – on a nation's evolving standard language can hardly be overestimated. It can even save a language from extinction, as happened with Welsh following the translation of the Bible by Bishop William Morgan in

1588. But when people talk, as they do, about the King James Bible being an important influence on the English language, we need to realize that we are making a sociolinguistic point. The crucial issue is that the King James Bible was the one, as its title page stated, 'appointed to be read in Churches' (not 'authorized', incidentally, notwithstanding its popular name as 'The Authorized Version'). This gave its language of choice a national presence and level of prestige which would prove to be more widespread and longer lasting than any Bible of the previous century. And the language chosen by the translators was ultimately derived from the London dialect which had been showing signs of standardization in Caxton's time.

The conservative temperament of the King James translators is made clear in their Preface. Their aim, they say, is not to make a new translation, 'but to make a good one better, or out of many good ones, one principall good one'. One of their rules was:

> The old Ecclesiastical Words to be kept, viz., the Word *Church* not to be translated *Congregations*, &c.

They had little choice in the matter, as the guidelines for their work, which had been approved by the king, required them to use the Bishops' Bible as their first model, making as few alterations as possible; when this was found wanting, they could refer to earlier versions, including Tyndale. They often opt for older forms of the language, accordingly, even when modern alternatives were available – older word orders (e.g., *speak ye unto, things eternal*) and verb forms (e.g., *digged, wist* 'knew', *brethren*). Their conservatism is clearly seen if their choices are contrasted with Shakespeare's: in the First Folio, for example, we find eighty-three instances of *broke* (the past tense of *break*), which had

11.5 Contrasts in usage between the King James Bible and the First Folio of Shakespeare

King James old form	King James new form	First Folio old form	First Folio new form
bare 175	bore 1	bare 10	bore 25
clave 14	cleft 2	clave 0	cleft 8
gat 20 gotten 25	got 7	gat 0 gotten 5	got 115
goeth 135	goes 0	goeth 0	goes 166
seeth 54	sees 0	seeth 0	sees 40
spake 585	spoke 0	spake 48	spoke 142
yonder 7	yon 0 yond 0	yonder 66	yon 9 yond 45

begun to displace *brake* during the sixteenth century; but there are no instances of *broke* in the King James Bible, whereas there are seventy-three instances of *brake*. Several other examples of the contrast with the more modern language of Shakespeare are shown in panel 11.5. The avoidance of *yon* and *yond* in favour of *yonder* is interesting: although the three words are independent historical developments, there has been a tendency to view the first two as an abbreviation of the third (in the seventeenth century, *yon* would sometimes appear with an apostrophe, *yon'*). The King James translators, aiming for a dignified style, evidently found any suggestion of a colloquial contraction unpalatable.

The continuing presence of a word like *brake* as an archaism in Modern English is probably very much due to its use at a critical moment in the biblical narrative (*Jesus took bread, and blessed, and brake ...* Mark 14:22). Bible translations are like that. Because certain parts of the text are of special significance, and encountered frequently in Church services or home reading, the language they employ has a greater chance of becoming part of popular linguistic consciousness (often, of course, with an extended or figurative meaning) than in the case of other famous literature. Not every biblical allusion can be allowed to count as a lexical unit within Standard English, of course. A usage has to have achieved some degree of linguistic autonomy; it must be capable of being meaningful outside of its original biblical context, usable by English speakers who do not read (or even know) the Bible as well as those who do. (The same point applies to expressions derived from Shakespeare or any other author.) *Whited sepulchre* in Matthew's Gospel is a case in point: it is not important to know its etymology – who in the Gospel were originally described in this way – in order to appreciate its sense in Modern English, where it is used in all kinds of contexts. A usage that does not meet this criterion is really only a quotation. Thus, for example, the various expressions in the Christmas story in Matthew's Gospel (e.g., *a virgin shall be with child*; *gold, and frankincense, and myrrh*) are not used in contexts outside of this setting, and cannot really be seen as independent items within the Standard English lexicon, notwithstanding the fact that they are very familiar to many people.

The King James Bible – either directly, from its own translators, or indirectly, as a glass through which we can see its predecessors – has contributed far more to English in the way of idiomatic or quasi-proverbial expressions than any other literary source. Its lexicon is less than half that of Shakespeare, for example (p. 317), but its impact has been much greater. Matthew's Gospel alone, for example, yields over forty locutions which, directly or indirectly, are part of Modern English (see panel 11.6). The phrasing is sometimes exactly as it is in the Bible (e.g., *whited sepulchre, the signs of the times*), and sometimes it is a modernization (e.g., avoiding *thy* and *ye*). Quite often it is a shortening

11.6 Extracts from the King James version of St Matthew's Gospel, from which Standard English expressions have been derived:

man shall not live by bread alone (4:4)

the salt of the earth (5:13)

the light of the world (5:14)

let your light . . . shine (5:16)

an eye for an eye and a tooth for a tooth (5:38)

turn . . . the other [cheek] (5:39)

let not thy left hand know what thy right hand doeth (6:3)

our daily bread (6:11)

treasures in heaven (6:20)

no man can serve two masters (6:24)

ye cannot serve God and mammon (6:24)

O ye of little faith (6:30)

sufficient unto the day (6:34)

the mote . . . in thine own eye (7:3)

cast your pearls before swine (7:6)

seek and ye shall find (7:7)

straight . . . and narrow (7:14)

[wolves] in sheep's clothing (7:15)

by their fruits ye shall know them (7:20)

built his house upon the sand (7:27)

weeping and gnashing of teeth (8:12)

sick of the palsy (9:2)

new wine into old bottles (9:17)

lost sheep (10:6)

every kingdom divided against itself . . . shall not stand (12:25)

one pearl of great price (13:46)

a prophet is not without honour, save in his own country (13:57)

the blind lead the blind (15:14)

the signs of the times (16:3)

take up his cross (16:24)

two or three are gathered together in my name (18:20)

suffer little children (19:14)

the last shall be first, and the first last (20:16)

den of thieves (21:13)

out of the mouth of babes (21:16)

many are called, but few are chosen (22:14)

render . . . unto Caesar the things that are Caesar's (22:21)

whited sepulchre (23:27)

well done, thou good and faithful servant (25:21)

divideth his sheep from the goats (25:32)

thirty pieces of silver (26:15)

the spirit . . . is willing, but the flesh is weak (26:41)

all they that take the sword shall perish with the sword (26:52)

or an adaptation: for example, *straight and narrow* is from 'strait is the gate, and narrow is the way'; and the full form of this next expression is shown within brackets: *every kingdom divided against itself [is brought to desolation; and every city or house divided against itself] shall not stand* (12:25). We are never going to reach a precise total for the number of expressions of this kind which are genuinely part of the English lexicon, because there are no clear dividing lines between idioms and allusions and quotations. The Matthew total would be further increased if we were to add such locutions as *the voice of one crying in the wilderness, love your enemies, blessed are the poor in spirit*, and *take therefore no thought for the morrow*. What is really intriguing, of course, is why some expressions entered English in this way, and others did not. Why did such similes as *wise as serpents* or *harmless as doves* (10:16) not become everyday phrases? As always, when we consider lexical innovation, the bigger puzzle is to explain why so many apparently vivid or useful items did *not* appeal.

The biblical influence on the developing standard in the sixteenth century was supplemented by another source, the appearance of a Book of Common Prayer – or, to give it its full original title, *The Booke of the Common Prayer and administracion of the Sacramentes, and other Rites and Ceremonies after the Use of the Churche of England*. The version in general use today derives from the revision made in 1661–2, but this preserved much of what had appeared a century earlier, in the reign of Edward VI, in texts of 1549 and 1552. Its appearance was motivated both by a desire for liturgical reform and a concern for the use of the vernacular beyond that already being seen in the Bibles. The Commons addressed a supplication to Henry VIII in 1546:[10]

> Let them not perswade you that God is or can be better served in the Latine tong then in the Englysh.

They sensed a trend. English was by this time beginning to be used in Church services. English readings from the Scriptures are known from 1538, and an English Litany appeared in 1544. A comment of a contemporary chronicler, William Harrison, is interesting, because it draws attention to the impact these new texts would have been having on children's developing linguistic intuitions:[11]

> Vpon the 18 of October, the Letany in thenglish toung is, by the kinges commaund-ement, song openly in Pawles in London; & commaundement geuen [given] that it should be song in the same toung thorow out all England . . . & the children of Pawles schole, whereof I was one at that time, inforced to buy those bookes . . .

Following the accession of Edward VI, the amount of English used in church increased. In 1548 an English supplement to the Mass appeared, *The Order of the Communion*, and in the following year the first Book of Common Prayer, compiled by 'the Archbishop of Canterbury [Thomas Cranmer] and certain of the most learnèd and discreet bishops, and other learnèd men of this realm'. Along with various supplements and revisions, this text has remained in official use – apart from the two short periods under Queen Mary and Cromwell, during which it was banned – until the present-day.

It is impossible to distinguish the linguistic influence of the Prayer Book from that of the King James Bible, because of the extent to which the former incorporates extracts from the latter. Both sources have such familiar phrases as *go from strength to strength* and *they that go down to the sea in ships*. The Prayer Book makes use of a similar conservative style of usage as we have seen in the Bible, with such forms as *brake* (p. 276), the possessive construction *for Jesus Christ his sake*, the *-eth* verb ending, and the *thou/you* distinction (p. 307). However, the Prayer Book's various liturgical activities did generate a few phrases which entered the language as a whole, in the sense that they were later found in contexts outside of religion, such as *for better or worse* or *read, mark, learn and inwardly digest*, and gave currency to certain words which might otherwise have gone out of use, such as *banns* and *eschew*. Its language also provided the writers of novels, plays, television series, and newspaper headlines with a rich mine of possibilities (p. 515), such as *to have and to hold, ashes to ashes*, and *till death us do part* (the 1662 version, replacing the earlier *till death us depart*, where *depart* meant 'separate').

The Book of Common Prayer was the first real attempt to develop a formal liturgical style for English, one capable of meeting the needs of speech as well as of writing. Along with the Bible it added a fresh stylistic dimension – a new variety – to the language's resources in the sixteenth century. But the conservative inclination of these two texts did relatively little to develop the linguistic resources of English as a whole, especially its lexicon. The number of religiously motivated words was small compared with the number of French words which had arrived in Middle English (Chapter 7), and they formed only a small part of the huge numbers of Latin words which were beginning to make their appearance in the sixteenth century. Other domains prove to be more important in shaping the lexical character of the period usually referred to as Early Modern English.

Interlude 11
The first English dictionary

A dictionary is more than a list of words in alphabetical order: it is an alphabetical word list with definitions, compiled for no other purpose than to explain meaning and usage; and the first such book appeared at the very beginning of the seventeenth century.

The concept of the word list was not new: Richard Mulcaster, for example, included one at the end of his *Elementarie*, listing recommended spellings (p. 268). There had also been bilingual glossaries in Anglo-Saxon times (p. 35), and in the early Middle English period even a trilingual list: Alexander Neckham's *De nominibus utensilium* ('Of Useful Nouns'), giving Latin, French, and English equivalents. Printing brought several bilingual dictionaries, including a four-language work, John Baret's *Alvearie or Quadruple Dictionary* (1583), adding Greek. And explanations of hard words had been incorporated into Edmund Coote's *The English Schoole-Master* (1596), but that was a primer in several subjects, including religion and grammar. There had been no book with a purely lexical focus, entirely devoted to an alphabetical word list with definitions solely in English and on English, until *A Table Alphabeticall*, published in 1604 by the schoolteacher Robert Cawdrey, with the assistance of his schoolteacher son, Thomas.

The title page explains why he compiled it:

> A Table Alphabeticall, conteyning and teaching the true writing, and vnderstanding of hard vsuall English wordes, borrowed from the Hebrew, Greeke, Latine, or French, &c.
>
> With the interpretation thereof by plaine English words, gathered for the benefit & helpe of Ladies, Gentlewomen, or any other unskilfull persons.
>
> Whereby they may the more easilie and better vnderstand many hard English wordes, which they shall heare or read in Scriptures, Sermons, or elswhere, and also be made able to vse the same aptly themselues.

He had a point. A large number of learnèd words had entered the language during the previous half-century (p. 288), and it seemed like a sound educational proposition. The book proved to be popular, going through four editions, and several other 'dictionaries of hard words' would soon follow in its footsteps. In Cawdrey's address to the reader, we can tell just how unfamiliar such a book was, for he even feels it necessary to give detailed instructions about how to look words up – a necessary precaution, noted by others before him (p. 227):

> If thou be desirous (gentle Reader) rightly and readily to vnderstand, and to profit by this Table, and such like, then thou must learne the Alphabet, to wit, the order of the Letters as they stand, perfectly without booke, and where euery Letter standeth:

Not content with this, he adds an illustration:

> as (b) neere the beginning, (n) about the middest, and (t) toward the end.

And in case even this was not clear, he gives two examples of the method:

> Nowe if the word, which thou art desirous to finde, begin with (a) then looke in the beginning of this Table, but if with (v) looke towards the end. Againe, if thy word beginne with (ca) looke in the beginning of the letter (c) but if with (cu) then looke toward the end of that letter. And so of all the rest. &c.

And so of all the rest. This innocent-sounding remark actually sums up several centuries of thinking about alphabetization. In the earliest glossaries, alphabetization was by initial letter of the word only: so, in the Epinal glossary, for example (p. 35), we find the opening words in the list: *Amites, axungia, argillus, andeda, arula* . . . The Corpus glossary took a step forward, grouping words by the first two letters only: it begins, *Abelena, abies, absinthium, abortus, ablata* . . . The Wycliffe concordance (p. 227) was the first fully alphabetized English work to apply the alphabetic ordering principle to all the letters in the word, but practice had remained sporadic.

As dictionaries go, *A Table Alphabeticall* was not very large. It contained 2,521 headwords, but 65 of these were pairs or triplets of combined forms (joined by a brace, as shown in the illustration, p. 282) with a single definition, and there were also a few cross-references (e.g., *A E, see E; heathen, see Gentile*), so the total number of defined items was really 2,449. The bracketed words are a mixture of types: some bring synonyms together (*abbreviat / abbridge*), some link different word classes (*arive / ariuall*), and some link alternative spellings (*embark / imbark*).

Twenty letters of the alphabet were represented (A–I, L–T, U/V together, and Z). The printing left something to be desired: most letters were given an introductory heading, but there was none for G, L, and S. Notwithstanding the Preface, words were occasionally out of alphabetical order, as can be seen in panel 11.7.

11.7 A page of Cawdrey's dictionary

of hard Englifh words.
combuftible, eafily burnt
combuftion, burning o2 confuming with
fire.
comedie, (k) ftage play,
comicall, handled merily like a comedie
commemoration, rehearfing o2 remem=
b2ing
§ comencement, a beginning o2 entrance
comet, (g) a blafing ftarre
comentarie, expofition of any thing
commerce, fellowfhip, entercourfe of mer=
chandife.
commination, th2eatning, o2 menacing,
commiferation, pittie
commodious, p2ofitable, pleafant,fit,
commotion, rebellion, trouble, o2 difqui=
etneffe.
communicate, make partaker, o2 giue
part vnto
§ communaltie, common people, o2 com=
mon=wealth
communion, ⎫ fellow=
communitie, ⎭ fhip.
compact, ioyned together, o2 an agræmet.
compafsion, pitty,fellow=feeling
compell, to fo2ce, o2 conftraine
compendious, fho2t, p2ofitable
                                          com=

The notion of 'hard words' has to be taken with a pinch of salt. The book did include many Latinate words which by any definition would have to be considered arcane:

dilacerate, ebulliated, falcinate, ignominie, illiquinated, refulgent, salubritie, vnguent but the following examples show that some other principle must also have been at work:

alarum, all haile, ay 'ever', boate, bonnet, centre, dittie, fame, halaluiah, helmet, hush/husht, idiot

And whether the ladies, gentlewomen, and other unskilful persons would have found *baud, buggery, concubine, eunuch, genitalles,* and *incest* 'hard' or not, it is impossible to say.

The same inconsistency can be seen in the definitions. The whole point of a dictionary of hard words is to have the difficult words glossed by easier ones, and this for the most part Cawdrey does (headwords are shown in italic):

agglutinate, to ioyne together
assistance, helpe
ebulliated, boyled
illiquinated, unmelted

But what the intended reader would have made of the following explanations is difficult to know:

affirme, auouch, acertaine
allegation, alledging
diocesse, (g) iurisdiction
fantacie, imagination

The (g) is one of two etymological abbreviations in the book, used – along with (gr) – to identify words of Greek origin (there are 213 of them); the other is §, marking words of French origin (343); the remainder are Latin. In one case, the dictionary slips over into bilingualism: *peccaui* is glossed as 'I have offended'.

About a fifth of the definitions are single-word, sometimes preceded by the abbreviation (k), for 'kind of'. These are the weakest treatments, because of their lack of distinguishing detail:

barbell, (k) fish
chibball, (k) fruit
chough, (k) bird
citron, (k) fruit

But most headwords have two or three glosses, some of which are perceptively phrased:

allegorie, similitude, a misticall speech, more than the bare letter

We can sense here a lexicographical temperament, making good the limitations of a first gloss through a steadily amplifying and simplifying sequence.

Some definitions would be difficult to better for succinctness in a modern dictionary:

> *allude*, to speake one thing that hath resemblance and respect to another.
> *circumlocution*, a speaking of that in many words, which may be said in few.
> *competitor*, hee that sueth for the same thing, or office, that another doth.

Others, less succinct, are none the less informative:

> *cypher*, (g) a circle in numbering, of no value of it selfe, but serueth to make up the number, and to make other figures of more value.
> *hipocrite*, (g) such a one as in his outward apparrell, countenaunce, & behauiour, pretendeth to be another man, then [than] he is indeede, or a deceiuer.

And some are of particular interest to linguists:

> *dialect*, the manner of speech in any language, diuers from others.
> *etymologie*, (g) true expounding.

A Table Alphabeticall is a remarkable compilation, containing many surprises. Cawdrey's originality is not so much in his coverage as in his treatment. Over half the words he deals with were actually taken directly from the books by Coote (see above) or Thomas' Latin–English dictionary (p. 266) – a tradition of 'borrowing' in lexicography which is not unknown today. But he gives far more glosses – and far more thought to his glosses – than his predecessors. And the general style of his approach influenced the more ambitious dictionary-makers, over a century later (p. 380).

Chapter 12 Early Modern English preoccupations

The linguistic jump from Middle English to Modern English is too great to make in one step, and for this reason scholars have identified a transitional period which usually goes under the name of Early Modern English. It is fairly easy to assign a conventional date to the beginning of this period; less easy to say when it ends. The introduction of the printing press into England is a turning-point of acknowledged significance, even though its consequences for the language took some time to manifest themselves (Chapter 11), and several accounts recognize 1476 as a starting-point. Others opt for an earlier onset, such as the death of Chaucer (1400) or the century mid-point (1450); and some a later one, attracted by the nicely rounded appeal of 1500. Candidates for the end-point have been even more various, offering the date of the first declaration of American independence (1776), the date of publication of Dr Johnson's *Dictionary* (1755) or some other significant literary work of the time, or the century mid-point (1750). 1700 has appealed to some, as has 1800. A few writers avoid precise dates altogether, preferring a less specific time reference, such as 'fifteenth to eighteenth century', a historical notion such as 'Renaissance English', or a descriptive statement such as 'English from Caxton to Johnson'.

The common focus for the end of the period is evidently the eighteenth century, and looking at developments in linguistic structure it is indeed possible to sense a qualitative difference between 1700 (which plainly is within the Early Modern English period) and 1800 (which plainly isn't). The spelling, punctuation, grammar, and vocabulary of Jane Austen or William Hazlitt are appreciably closer to Modern English than is the language of John Dryden or Jonathan Swift. But more important than the structural changes which were taking place in English at the time are the changes in attitude towards the language, in particular the emergence of an explicit prescriptivism midway through what has been called the 'century of manners', and the clear recognition, as a consequence, of what a 'correct English' should be. Publications such as Bishop Robert Lowth's *Short Introduction to English Grammar* (1762) and John Walker's *Pronouncing Dictionary of English* (1774), along with Johnson's

Dictionary, identify a two-decade period which, sociolinguistically speaking, was a defining moment, after which things were never the same again.

The Early Modern English period is essentially an age of linguistic awareness and anxiety, in which Caxton's writing represents a dawning appreciation that the language is in a mess and needs sorting out, and the rise of the prescriptive movement represents the feeling that the matter is about to be satisfactorily resolved. And it was during the sixteenth century that anxiety levels about the nature of the English language rose noticeably. People began to 'notice' the language, and many did not like what they saw. We have already observed in Chapter 11 how printers, spelling reformers, and biblical translators were at various times and in various ways uncertain and confused, both about the state of the language and the direction in which it seemed to be moving. But the malaise was general, attracting comment from writers of diverse backgrounds. Everyone, whether expert in linguistic matters or not, felt entitled to have an opinion – as indeed they still do today.

'Notice' is an understatement. The period is notable for the intense interest writers displayed in linguistic matters. Much of the early interest was stimulated by the Bible translators and their critics, who displayed an enormous amount of creative linguistic energy. The mood is well captured by the authors of the King James Bible, who make their position plain in their Preface. Referring to the choice of such alternatives as *think* vs *suppose*, or *pain* vs *ache*, they say:

> wee have not tyed our selues to an vniformitie of phrasing, or to an identitie of words, as some peraduenture would wish that we had done . . .

On the contrary:

> For is the kingdome of God become words or syllables? why should wee be in bondage to them if we may be free, vse one precisely when wee may vse another no lesse fit, as commodiously?

We might expect plenty of controversy over the choice of particular words and expressions to express theologically contentious concepts (p. 271), but even the tiny details of a translation were scrutinized and commented upon. For example, right at the very beginning of the 'age of Bibles', we find Sir Thomas More attacking William Tyndale not only for his use of such loaded words as *senior* instead of *priest*, but even for mixing up 'two so plain englishe wordes, and so commen as is *naye* and *no*'.[1] The scrutiny led Tyndale to complain that his critics

> haue yet now so narowlye loked on my translatyon, that there is not so much as one I therin if it lack a tytle over his hed, but they haue noted it, and nombre it vnto the ignorant people for an heresy.[2]

They think it a heresy even if an *i* is left undotted, he avers.

We even find evidence in the period of amateur linguistic experiments. William Camden reports one, illustrating the way that the orthographic standard, even at the beginning of the seventeenth century, was still a long way from uniformity. He has been reflecting on the nature of English pronunciation:

> This variety of pronuntiation hath brought in some diversitie of Orthographie, and heere-vpon Sir John Price, to the derogation of our tongue, and glorie of his Welsh, reporteth that a sentence spoken by him in English, & penned out of his mouth by foure good Secretaries, severally, for trial of our Orthography, was so set downe by them, that they all differed one from the other in many letters: whereas so many Welsh writing the same likewise in their tongue varied not in any one letter at all.

Not wishing to let English seem subordinate to Welsh, Camden reports on another investigation:

> Well, I will not derogate from the good Knights credite; yet it hath beene seene where tenne English writing the same sentence, have all so concurred, that among them all there hath beene no other difference, than the adding, or omitting once or twice of our silent E, in the end of some wordes.

John Price's report reflected the times more accurately, it would seem, judging by the amount of variation seen in Shakespeare's First Folio twenty years later, where we find *briefly* spelled *breefely*, *briefelie*, *briefely*, and *briefly*, and *aid* spelled *aide*, *aid*, *ayde*, and *ayd*.

The most general worry in the early part of the period was whether English could really carry out the range of communicative functions that French and Latin had previously performed. As early as Caxton's time, we find it routine to comment about English being 'symple and rude', whereas French would be described as 'fayr' (in Caxton's *Recuyell,* for example), and although these comments were usually conventional, self-effacing expressions, they helped to inculcate a mindset that the language was inferior. Other European languages were often commended in similar terms. The traveller and physician Andrew Boorde, for example, draws the contrast pointedly in *The Fyrste Boke of the Introduction of Knowledge* (*c.* 1550):

> The speche of Englande is a base speche to other noble speches, as Italion Castylion [Spanish] and Frenche, howbeit the speche of Englande of late dayes is amended.

The emendations Boorde was thinking of were the many word-borrowings from the major European languages, which a goodly number of English people had been swallowing wholesale in his time. The swallowing metaphor anticipates the translator George Pettie (1548–99), who, in his Preface to *The Ciuile*

Conuersation of M. Steeuen Guazzo (1581), uses a rather more vivid expression to express his distaste of those who penalize him for choosing to write in English:

> There are some others yet who wyll set lyght by my labours, because I write in Englysh: and those are some nice Trauaylours, who returne home with such quæsie stomackes, that nothyng wyll downe with them but Frenche, Italian, or Spanishe.

French, it seems – and Latin even more – was still associated with high style, scholarship, and rhetorical excellence. English was not.

The solution to the problem seemed straightforward. If languages like French and Latin were superior to English, then English would automatically improve its quality by adopting their properties, such as their vocabulary, balanced sentence construction, and features of rhetoric. Several writers expressed their need. The poet John Skelton made the point vividly and succinctly in *The Boke of Phyllyp Sparowe* (1545, l. 777):

> Our Language is so rustye,
> So cankered and so ful
> Of frowardes [ugly things] and so dul
> That if I wold apply
> To write ornatly
> I wot [know] not where to finde
> Termes to serve my minde

And as early as 1531 we find the writer and diplomat Sir Thomas Elyot (in *The Boke named the Governour*) commending 'the necessary augmentation of our language', pointing out that once people started using 'strange and darke' words they would soon become 'facile [easy] to vnderstande'.

Latin was the chief source where people looked for words to 'serve their minds'. There had been a steady trickle of Latin borrowings into English throughout the Middle English period, but during the fifteenth century their number greatly increased, and in the sixteenth century they became so numerous, along with words from Greek, that the character of the English lexicon was permanently altered. The linguistic development reflected a cultural and cognitive shift. The period from the time of Caxton until around 1650 was later to be called the 'Renaissance'. It included not only a 'rebirth of learning', in the sense of a renewal of connection with Classical languages, literatures, and the arts, but also a rethinking of religious and scientific values, as seen in the Reformation and the discoveries of Copernicus, as well as an expansion of global horizons through the European explorations of Africa, the Americas, and the Far East. There were few words in English to talk precisely about the new perspectives, concepts, techniques, and products which were being seen in Europe or further afield; but the Classical languages, increasingly encountered through translations, presented a solution, offering hundreds of Latin and Greek words which could be readily adapted. Writers such as Elyot went out of their way to 'enrich' the language with classically derived words, to enable the new learning to become accessible to the English public.

The serving of minds also related to the new varieties of discourse which were developing in the language as English took over the range of functions previously performed by French and Latin (Chapter 8). Legal, scientific, religious, educational, medical, and other 'institutions' were developing their distinctive modalities of expression. The 'language of law' is one domain which had begun to develop its own stylistic norms during Middle English (p. 152), and parallel developments were taking place elsewhere. From anatomy, biology, and medicine, for example, we find *larynx*, *pancreas*, *pneumonia*, *skeleton*, *tibia*, *ulna*, and *virus*. The glossaries compiled by translators show the range of specialist usage which was emerging, in such fields as alchemy, architecture, fencing, grammar, heraldry, hunting, navigation, and military science (see panel 12.1). Borrowings greatly facilitate stylistic differentiation because they provide synonyms with different sense associations and tonal resonances. Although *hearing* (from the early twelfth century) and *audition* (first recorded use, 1599) basically mean the same thing, the later word came to be used in more intellectual and scientific settings, and developed a greater formality of tone and eventually a distinctive range of meanings. The same distinction applies to *praising* (which goes back to Wycliffe, 1382) and *laudatory* (1555), *loving* (from Old English) and *amatory* (1599), and many more. There was a real concern for definition as the period progressed, as Cawdrey's first efforts show (p. 283).

It is difficult to be definite about the rate at which the neologisms came into Early Modern English. Traditional linguistic indices, such as the *Oxford English Dictionary*, have weaknesses because, although there are many more texts available to study, some periods have been covered more thoroughly than others, and the literary biases of the work privilege the later part of the period, when authors such as Spenser, Shakespeare, and Jonson had begun to write. There is no doubt, however, that this was an age of particularly rapid vocabulary growth, and that Latin was the dominant source: about two thirds of all borrowing at the time was from that language – a momentum which continued until late in the seventeenth century, when still a third of all borrowing was from Latin.[3] Latin was also the means of entry for many words which ultimately came from Greek. A huge number of words from these two languages entered the general vocabulary, as this short selection illustrates:

12.1 The emerging linguistic lexicon

A number of Classical borrowings between 1500 and 1700 helped to form the technical lexicon for describing the properties and uses of spoken and written language. At the same time, several neologisms were helping to form the related lexicons of literary language (e.g., *elegy, eclogue, irony*) and publishing (e.g., *quarto, folio*), as well as providing everyday expressions for talking about language (e.g., *innuendo, dictum, diatribe, topic, amanuensis, literati, lingo*).

The following selection illustrates the range of items involved, though not the senses and derived forms of each word. *Alphabet* (1580), for example, gave rise to the following forms at the time: *alphabetarian* (1614), *alphabetary* (1569), *alphabetic* (1642), *alphabetical* (1567), and *alphabetically* (1567). And *linguist* developed its familiar ambiguity during the period: in the sense of 'skilled in the use of languages', the *Oxford English Dictionary* records its first use by Shakespeare (in *The Two Gentlemen of Verona*, IV.i.57); in the sense of 'student of language', it is first recorded in 1642 in Bishop John Wilkins' *Mercury*. A third sense – someone with the 'gift of the gab', a chatterer – is recorded from 1588, but apparently not used after the end of the seventeenth century. From *linguist* was derived *linguacity, linguacious,* and *linguister* ('interpreter'). Regrettably, none of these last three survived either.

alphabet	dissonance	parenthesis	semi-vowel
acrostic	elision	philological	strophe
adjective	hyphen	phrase	substantive
alphabet	inflection	polysyllable	syllabary
caesura	lexicon	pronoun	syntax
colon	lingua franca	rhetoricize	trochee
comma	linguist	rhythm	trope
consonance	monosyllable	semi-colon	

absurdity, adapt, anonymous, appropriate, benefit, chaos, climax, commemorate, crisis, critic, disability, emancipate, encyclopedia, enthusiasm, exaggerate, exist, expensive, explain, fact, frequency, habitual, immaturity, immediate, impersonal, inveterate, invitation, malignant, offensive, official, relaxation, relevant, skeleton, species, susceptible, temperature, thermometer, vacuum

The presence of suffixes should be noted – and of some suffixes in particular. For example, two thirds of all verbs which came into the language at the time ended in *-ate*, as did many adjectives. This was part of a more general trend, which will be discussed below (p. 303).

Elyot had described the Classical words as 'strange and darke', and it was precisely those properties which made them appeal to many writers and speakers. Then as now, some people had a penchant for arcane neologism – they liked to use hard words – and a moderate use of learnèd vocabulary is probably found in everyone who has achieved an advanced level of education. Most people of the time would have agreed wholeheartedly with Ben Jonson's aphorism (in *Timber: or, Discoveries made upon Men and Matter*, published posthumously in 1640), 'Words borrow'd of Antiquity, doe lend a kind of Majesty to style'. The problem came when people overdid it, using too many elaborate coinages, thereby attracting the criticism of such scholars as Thomas Wilson in *The Arte of Rhetorique* (1553):

> Among all other lessons this should first be learned, that wee never affect any straunge ynkehorne termes, but to speak as is commonly received ... Some seeke so far for outlandish English, that they forget altogether their mothers language. And I dare sweare this, if some of their mothers were aliue, thei were not able to tell what they say; and yet these fine English clerkes will say, they speake in their mother tongue, if a man should charge them for counterfeiting the Kings English.

And Robert Cawdrey (p. 280) copies the Wilson passage almost word for word (without acknowledgement) in his address to the reader in *A Table Alphabeticall*. Cawdrey was a pragmatist. If there were hard words out there, the public needed dictionaries to help them out. And his little *Table* did indeed sell very well.

The maternal theme was one which appealed to several writers. Thomas Nashe alludes to it in his Preface to Greene's *Menaphon* (1589):

> how eloquent our gowned age is growen of late, so that euerie mœchanicall mate abhorres the english he was borne too, and plucks with a solemn-periphrasis his *vt vales* [how are you?] from the inkhorne.

But all kinds of dismissive metaphors were used. The Preface to Edmund Spenser's *The Shepheardes Calender* (1579), written by a friend of the poet, uses some specially vivid terms. After talking about the way some writers have found English prose and poetry to be 'bare and barren', he launches into an extended image in which the language is likened to a piece of cloth:

> they patched vp the holes with peces and rags of other languages, borrowing here of the french, there of the Italian, euery where of the Latine, not weighing how il, those tongues accorde with themselues, but much worse with ours: So now they haue made our English tongue, a gallimaufray or hodgepodge of al other speeches.

Gallimaufry: a term from cooking, referring to a dish made up of all kinds of odds and ends of food.

As most of these quotations show, the term which captured the character of the argument was *ink-horn* (= 'inkpot'), a word first known to have been used two centuries earlier, in Wycliffe's translation of the Bible (p. 239): 'The man that hadde an enk-horn in his rigge [belt]' (Ezekiel 9.11). In the fifteenth century, other words had been used to describe Classical borrowings, such as 'ornate' and 'aureate' (p. 157), but the phrase 'ink-horn terms' seemed to appeal more to the imagination, in its scornful suggestion that the words were lengthy and therefore used up more ink. The writer George Gascoigne, in *Certayne notes of Instruction concerning the making of verse or ryme in English* (1575), explicitly makes the connection:

> The most auncient English wordes are of one sillable, so that the more monosyllables that you use the truer Englishman you shall seeme, and the less you shall smell of the Inkehorne.

The word was invariably found in a disparaging context – 'smelling of the ink-horn' was a common way of talking about a pedant. And Shakespeare picks up the connotation when he has one of the duke of Gloucester's men describe the bishop of Winchester as an 'inkhorn mate' (*Henry VI Part 1*, III.i.99).

As with all controversies, both sides had a point. Some writers had certainly been overdoing it, if this extract from the beginning of a letter cited by Thomas Wilson is anything to go by. It is supposed to be from a Lincolnshire gentleman asking for help in obtaining a vacant benefice, though it may well be a parody composed by Wilson himself. Even if it is an invention, it well captures the character of the kind of ornately obscure language which was attracting the ire of the ink-horn critics at the time:

> Ponderyng expendyng ['weighing'], and reuolutyng ['revolving'] with my self your ingent ['enormous'] affabilitee, and ingenious capacitee, for mundane affaires: I cannot but celebrate and extolle your magnificall dexteritee, aboue all other.

Faced with examples like this, it is not difficult to see why some people went to the opposite extreme, condemning all borrowings, or demanding their removal. Sir John Cheke, for example, writes in a letter to Thomas Hoby (1557):

> I am of the opinion that our tung shold be written cleane and pure, vnmixt and vnmangeled with borowing of other tunges.

Loanword antipathy, as we have seen (p. 186), is a long-standing complaint; and, as in previous centuries, Cheke would have been unable to achieve the desired purity even in his own writing. In this sentence alone Cheke used four words of Latin or French origin: *opinion, mix, mangle,* and *pure*.

Even though purity is a myth, it plays an important part in forming social attitudes, and in the sixteenth century the feeling was widely held that borrowing had gone too far, and that the Germanic word stock was at risk. Some, indeed, tried to restore an Anglo-Saxon character. Edmund Spenser revived obsolete

Anglo-Saxon words – what were sometimes called 'Chaucerisms' – and made use of little-known words from English dialects: a small selection is *algate* 'always', *eld* 'old age', *hent* 'seize', *sicker* 'certainly', *yblent* 'confused', and *yode* 'went'. The Preface to *The Shepheardes Calender* praises the role of 'auncient solemne wordes' in poetry, as long as they are 'good and naturall English words, as haue ben long time out of vse'. John Cheke replaced Classical terms whenever he could: he preferred *crossed* to *crucified* and *gainrising* for *resurrection*. Ralph Lever in his *Arte of Reason* (1573), a study of logic, subtitles his work: *rightly termed Witcraft*. He replaces Latin logical terms by Anglo-Saxon ones, such as *conclusio* by *endsay* and *negatio* by *naysay*. But his neologisms had no greater success than those of William Barnes, who tried to do the same thing in the nineteenth century.[4] Evidently the Classical importations, notwithstanding their overuse by fashionable wits and ink-horn scholars, met a real need.

A little-understood system of checks and balances operates in language, as the centrifugal forces which introduce variation and change compete with the centripetal forces which keep people communicating with each other. It is a theme which will arise again in the twentieth century, in relation to World English (Chapter 20), but we can see it operating in Early Modern English in the way that a natural selection of Latinate vocabulary seemed to take place. According to one survey, over a third of all neologisms which entered the language at that time are not recorded after 1700. Some of the items which didn't survive are:

> accersite 'summon', adnichilate 'destitute', cohibit 'restrain', concernancy, deruncinate 'weed', disaccustom, dominicall 'lordly', eximious 'excellent', omittance, suppeditate 'supply'

Some further examples are given on p. 326. It remains a lexicological puzzle why some words were accepted and some rejected. We do not know how to account for the linguistic 'survival of the fittest'. Both *impede* and *expede* were introduced during the period, as well as *disabuse* and *disadorn*, but in each of these pairs the first item stayed in the language and the second did not. In some instances, the prior existence of another word may have motivated the rejection – the presence of *visible*, for example, would have made it more difficult to promote *aspectable* – but we know from earlier periods of English that this is not an obligatory state of affairs, for many doublets arrived in English during the Middle Ages and both survived, developing different senses or nuances (p. 151). Some neologisms doubtless became popular because of their use in an influential text or word list. Some (such as those associated with a particular religious view, p. 240) might have conveyed connotations which prevented their being widely taken up. In literary contexts, a coinage might have been made solely to meet the needs of the metre, as in the Shakespearean use of *cursorary* ('cursory', p. 364). In many cases, the adaptation of a previously existing word (i.e., giving it a new sense) would have seemed a more natural solution. There are several other possible explanations. An important step will be the construction of a historical and stylistically aware thesaurus to give us a first sense of the 'competition' which exists between words during a time of rapid lexical growth in a language; and such projects are still in their early stages.[5] The understanding of communal lexical decision-making has hardly begun.

As the century progressed, more balanced views began to appear, along with defences of the increasingly mixed character of the language. The matter was put into its historical perspective by William Harrison, whose *Description of Britaine* (1587) was printed as prefatory material in the second edition of Holinshed's *Chronicles*, and thus achieved a wide readership (including Shakespeare). In Chapter 6, 'Of the languages spoken in this Iland', he sums up the contemporary situation. He first draws attention to how English had grown in estimation since the days when the 'French rascall' had failed in his effort to get English exiled:

> for in the time of king Edward the first, to wit, toward the latter end of his reigne, the French it selfe ceased to be spoken generallie, but most of all and by law in the midst of Edward the third, and then began the English to recouer and to grow in more estimation than before; notwithstanding that mong our artificers, the most part of their implements, tooles and words of art reteine still their French denominations euen to these our daies, as the language it selfe is vsed likewise in sundrie courts, bookes of record, and matters of law; whereof here is no place to make any particular rehearsall.

(Nor here, for these matters were discussed in Chapter 6 above.) He then compliments some writers, such as Chaucer, for their skill in improving the language, but finds others wanting:

> not a few other doo greatlie seeke to staine the same, by fond affectation of forren and strange words, presuming that to be the best English, which is most corrupted with externall termes of eloquence, and sound of manie syllables.

And eventually he arrives at a balanced conclusion:

> ours is a meane ['in-between'] language, and neither too rough nor too smooth in vtterance . . .

Richard Carew goes further, in *The Excellencie of the English Tongue* (1614). For him, the lexicon was in a state of perfect balance:

> the longe wordes that wee borrowe, being intermingled with the shorte of our owne store, make vp a perfitt harmonye.

Carew at one point refers to 'the miracle of our age Sir Philip Sidney', whose early death at thirty-one, as a result of a gunshot wound gained when fighting the Spanish, caused national mourning for the loss of someone seen as the ideal of a courtier. Sidney, too, was in no doubt about the way English was developing. In his *Defence of Poesie* (1595), he says:

> our language giueth us great occasion, being indeed capable of any excellent exercising of it. I knowe some will say it is a mingled language: And why not, so much the better, taking the best of both the other? Another will say, it wanteth Grammer. Nay truly it hath that praise that it wants not Grammar; for Grammer it might haue, but it needs it not, being so easie in it selfe, and so voyd of those combersome differences of Cases, Genders, Moods, & Tenses, which I thinke was a peece of the Tower of Babilons curse, that a man should be put to schoole to learn his mother tongue. But for the uttering sweetly and properly the conceit of the minde, which is the end of speech, that hath it equally with any other tongue in the world.

And in his *Remaines Concerning Britain* (1605), William Camden – a friend of Sidney and the tutor of Ben Jonson – draws attention to the linguistic point that English is now no different from any other language:

> Whereas our tongue is mixed, it is no disgrace, whenas all the tongues of *Europe* doe participate interchangeably the one of the other, and in the learnèd tongues, there hath been like borrowing one from another.

Chief among the defenders of English was the teacher Richard Mulcaster (p. 268), who adopts a firmly sociolinguistic perspective (*Elementarie*, p. 80):

> For the account of our tung, both in pen and speche, no man will dout thereof, who is able to iudge what those thinges be, which make anie tung to be of account, which things I take to be thré, the autoritie of the peple which speak it, the matter & argument, wherein the speche dealeth, the manifold vse, for which the speche serueth. For all which thré, our tung nedeth not to giue place, to anie of her peres.

The passage deserves to be quoted at length, for its prescience (see panel 12.2). A few years later Camden reaches the same conclusion. Reflecting on the way that 'learning after long banishment was recalled in the time of King *Henry* the eight', he reflects on the benefits for the language:

> it hath beene beautified and enriched out of other good tongues, partly by enfranchising and endenizing [making a citizen of] strange words, partly by refining and mollifying olde words, partly by implanting new wordes with artificiall composition . . .

12.2 Mulcaster's defence

Mulcaster clearly saw the association between language and (especially economic) power, and pointed out the way English (as always, a metonym for the speakers of English) readily accepts words from other languages. This next paragraph (here presented in modern spelling) could have been written as a gloss on the twentieth-century global expansion of English vocabulary:

> Will all kinds of trade, and all sorts of traffic, make a tongue of account? If the spreading sea, and the spacious land could use any speech, they would both show you, where, and in how many strange places, they have seen our people, and also give you to wit, that they deal in as much, and as great variety of matters, as any other people do, whether at home or abroad. Which is the reason why our tongue doth serve so many uses, because it is conversant with so many people, and so well acquainted with so many matters, in so sundry kinds of dealing. Now all this variety of matter, and diversity of trade, make both matter for our speech, and mean to enlarge it. For he that is so practised, will utter that, which he practiseth in his natural tongue, and if the strangeness of the matter do so require, he that is to utter, rather than he will stick in his utterance, will use the foreign term, by way of premunition, that the country people do call it so, and by that mean make a foreign word, an English denizen (p. 81).

He sees no problems in the small size of English (at the time numbering some 4 millions) or the fact that it had not travelled overseas.

> But it may be replied again, that our English tongue doth need no such pruning, it is of small reach, it stretcheth no further than this Island of ours, nay not there over all. What though? (p. 256)

'So what?', as we would say. (By 'not there over all' he was thinking of Wales, Scotland, and Cornwall, where Celtic languages were still used.)

> Yet it reigneth there, and it serves us there, and it would be clean brushed for the wearing there. Though it go not beyond sea, it will serve on this side. And be not our English folks finish, as well as the foreign I pray you? And why not our tongue for speaking, and our pen for writing, as well as our bodies for apparel, or our tastes for diet? But our state is no Empire to hope to enlarge it by commanding over countries. What though? though it be neither large in possession, nor in present hope of great increase, yet where it rules, it can make good laws, and as fit for our state, as the biggest can for theirs, and oft times better too, because of confusion in greatest governments, as most unwieldiness in grossest bodies (p. 256).

He knows his argument is likely to be interpreted as an attack on the value of other languages, especially the role of Latin as a scholarly lingua franca, so he adds a paragraph on the point:

But will ye thus break of the common conference with the learnèd foreign, by banishing the Latin, and setting over her learning to your own tongue. The conference will not cease, while the people have cause to interchange dealings, and without the Latin, it may well be continued: as in some countries the learneder sort, and some near cousins to the Latin itself do already wean their pens and tongues from the use of Latin, both in written discourse, and spoken disputation, into their own natural, and yet no dry nurse, being so well appointed by the milch nurse's help. The question is not to disgrace the Latin, but to grace our own (p. 257).

'Our state is no Empire to hope to enlarge it by commanding over countries.' Here Mulcaster's prescience deserted him, for two years later Walter Ralegh's first expedition landed at Roanoke Island, Virginia (p. 300).

As a result, he concludes:

> our tong is (and I doubt not but hath beene) as copious, pithie, and significative, as any other tongue in *Europe* . . .

He allows that it cannot do everything:

> our *English* tongue is (I will not say as sacred as the *Hebrew*, or as learnèd as the *Greeke*,) but as fluent as the *Latine*, as courteous as the *Spanish*, as courtlike as the *French*, and as amorous as the *Italian* . . .

None the less the comment is noteworthy. To call English 'as courtlike as the French' – a Middle English aristocrat would have recoiled in horror at the thought – was still a remarkable claim.

By the end of the century, it was widely held that the language had succeeded in making good its deficiencies. Handbooks of rhetoric, modelled on Latin, had shown how English could be made more ornate, and a literature of impressive poetry and drama was accumulating (Chapter 13). A principle of decorum was widely advocated, characterized by such properties as proportion, harmony, brevity, order, naturalness, and vitality. As a result, a sharper sense of stylistic differentiation emerged. Robert Cawdrey drew attention in his Preface to the distinction between 'learnèd' and 'rude' English – he also called it 'Court talke' and 'Country-speech'. In George Puttenham's view (p. 263), there were actually three English styles, *high*, *mean*, and *low*, associated with courtiers, citizens, and country folk, respectively. These distinctions were based on literary content more than language (the 'low' style included poetic pastorals and eclogues, for example), but they none the less fostered a fresh prejudice against provincial speech. The prestige of the south-east of England was now undisputed. As William Harrison, put it:

> this excellencie of the English toong is found in one, and the south part of this Iland . . .

And regional variation was evaluated accordingly:

> The Scottish english hath beene much broader and lesse pleasant in vtterance than ours, because that nation hath not till of late indeuored [endeavoured] to bring the same to any perfect order . . .

A clear sense of a Southern standard now existed in people's minds. And during the sixteenth century the use of regional dialect for the literary expression of serious subject-matter went into a long period of hibernation.

The most dramatic effect was in Scotland. From the early literary growth of a Scottish variety of English in the Middle Ages, and its use in local administration (p. 202), we might have expected an independent standard form of the language to have continued developing there, with Scottish words, grammatical constructions, and spellings. This did not happen: we have to wait until the eighteenth century before we see the emergence of a regional variety in Scotland with significant literary and social backing to enable it to function as a recognized standard (p. 488). There were several reasons. At the end of the Middle English period, the leading Scottish creative writers were very much influenced by the literary models of their southern counterparts, so much so that literary critics later referred to them as the 'Scottish Chaucerians' (p. 206). The Protestant Reformation, strong in Scotland, looked towards Europe, and the Wycliffe translation of the Bible (p. 239) found a welcome there. Later, the Geneva Bible and the King James Bible would be authorized for use in Scotland. Southern words and spellings became increasingly evident in Scottish writing, first in religious texts and then in official correspondence and other genres.[6] Writers, anxious to reach a wide and influential readership, opted to use the variety which they sensed would be more accessible. Printers began to Anglicize material presented to them in Scots; after around 1600, reprints of texts originally written in Middle Scots would be published in a Southern English spelling (see panel 12.3). Another factor is that the Scottish forms were never taught in the school system – always an important means of consolidating a standard. But the underlying reason was the changing power relationships between Scotland and England. The loss of Scottish autonomy after the Battle of Flodden (1513) was followed ninety years later by the union of the two crowns under James VI of Scotland and I of England, and the move to London of the Scottish court. No local variety could retain its identity as a formal medium of discourse after such a serious loss of regional prestige. And for some 200 years Scots was reduced to the level of any other local British dialect, 'lewed' and not 'lered' (p. 151).

12.3 Quhat a question

In about 1617, the Scottish spelling reformer Alexander Hume wrote a treatise intended for use in Scottish schools, *Of the Orthographie and Congruitie of the Britan Tongue*. A staunch defender of a regional spelling for Scotland, he tells the story of how he had an argument during a meal with some Englishmen over the best way of spelling such words as *who* and *what*, which in Scottish would have begun with *qu* – *quho, quhat* (p. 205). He has a hard time from his dinner companions, who evidently found a lot to laugh at, much to Hume's disgust:

> I wil tel quhat befel myself quhen I was in the south with a special gud frende of myne. Ther rease [rose], upon sum accident, quither [whether] quho, quhen, quhat, etc., sould be symbolized with q or w, a hoat [hot] disputation betuene him and me. After manie conflictes (for we oft encountered), we met by chance, in the citie of baeth [Bath], with a doctour of divinitie of both our acquentance. He invited us to denner. At table my antagonist, to bring the question on foot amangs his awn condisciples [fellow-scholars], began that I was becum an heretik, and the doctour spering [asking] how, answered that I denyed quho to be spelled with a w, but with qu. Be quhat reason? quod the Doctour. Here, I beginning to lay my grundes of labial, dental, and guttural soundes and symboles, he snapped [interrupted] me on this hand and he on that, that the doctour had mikle a doe [ado] to win me room for a syllogisme [good argument]. Then (Said I) a labial letter can not symboliz a guttural syllab [syllable]. But w is a labial latter, quho a guttural sound. And therfoer w can not symboliz quho, nor noe syllab of that nature. Here the doctour staying them again (for al barked at ones), the proposition, said he, I understand; the assumption is Scottish, and the conclusion false. Quherat al laughed, as if I had bene dryven from al replye, and I fretted to see a frivolouse jest goe for a solid answer.

The story tells us a lot about Early Modern English dialect attitudes. But it also tells us something about the way Scottish spelling was being pulled in the direction of the English standard. Hume knows what is going on: the *wh-* forms, he says, are 'an errour bred in the south, and now usurped by our ignorant printeres'.

Hume is making a point about *qu-*, so this spelling stays in the passage; and there are a few other Scottish spellings, such as *sould* (for *should*), *amangs* (for *amongst*), and *denner* (for *dinner*). But the text shows many Southernisms: in an earlier Scottish version (p. 204), we would have found *ane* instead of *an*; the *-ed* ending on a verb would have been *-it*; and there would have been *-ch-* forms where now we find *-gh-*, such as *laucht* for *laughed*. It would take only a few decades more (by about 1660) to see all signs of a distinctive Scottish spelling disappear from texts printed north of the border.

Widening horizons

Latin and Greek were not the only sources of loanwords in the sixteenth century. The Renaissance brought a widening of horizons – indeed, English horizons had never reached so far or in so many directions. Words were introduced from all the major European languages. French continued to be a source of supply, either directly or as a 'relay' language, channelling words from further afield. They include:

> anatomy, battery, bayonet, bizarre, cabaret, chocolate, colonel, comrade, detail, duel, entrance, equip, explore, grotesque, invite, moustache, muscle, naive, passport, probability, progress, repartee, shock, soup, ticket, tomato, vogue, volunteer

Here are some which came in from or via Italian:

> argosy, balcony, ballot, cameo, carnival, concerto, cupola, design, giraffe, grotto, lottery, macaroni, opera, piazza, portico, rocket, solo, sonata, sonnet, soprano, stanza, stucco, violin, volcano

And here are some from or via Spanish and Portuguese:

> alligator, apricot, armada, banana, barricade, bravado, cannibal, canoe, cocoa, corral, creole, desperado, embargo, guitar, hammock, hurricane, maize, mosquito, mulatto, negro, potato, sherry, sombrero, tank, tobacco, yam

In this last list, many of the words ultimately come from South or Central American Indian languages: *canoe* and *potato*, for example, are from Haitian via Spanish. The first Amerindian word in English is very early, in 1533: it is in Paynell's English translation of Ulrich von Hutten's treatise *De Guiaci Medicina et Morbo Gallico*, on the medical properties of guaiac wood, thought to be a cure for syphilis. There we find *guaiacum*, a Latin form of Spanish *guayaco*, from Haitian.

In these last examples, the atmosphere of global exploration is unmistakable. By 1600 there had been plenty of time for words to arrive via Spanish or Portuguese: the first voyages of Columbus and Cabot had been a century before, in 1492 and 1497. Direct loans into English, however, had to wait for the first English settlement. The first expedition from Britain to Virginia was not until 1587, and it took another twenty years before there was a permanent English presence. Even so, that initial contact introduced a few words from North American Indian (Algonquian) languages; the first records of *skunk, cashaw* (a squash), and *manitou* (a deity) are 1588. After 1607 we find a number of other Algonquian words, such as *totem, moose, opossum, tomahawk, caribou,* and *moccasin.* The new vocabulary can be seen even in the first written accounts which reached Britain, demonstrating the speed with which languages adapt to new circumstances (see panel 12.4).[7]

The explorations on the other side of the world likewise brought in new vocabulary from several languages, in some cases expanding the presence of a language source known from earlier times. Quite a few Arabic words, for example, had come into Middle English, especially reflecting scientific notions (p. 161), but in the sixteenth century there is a significant expansion, reflecting the contacts with North Africa and the Middle East. In many cases, the Arabic words enter English through another language: *assassin*, for example, is ultimately from Arabic *hashshashin* 'hashish-eaters', but came to English via Italian *assassino*. The new words generally reflect an encounter with the various aspects of culture and religion, as in these examples:

12.4 An early Amerindian loanword

In 1608 a London printer published a recently written account by Captain John Smith (*c.* 1580–1631) of the early exploration of Virginia:

> A True Relation of Such Occurrences and Accidents of Note as Hath Hapned in Virginia Since the First Planting of that Colony, which is now resident in the South part thereof, till the last returne from thence.
>
> Written by Captaine Smith one of the said Collony, to a worshipfull friend of his in England

Smith, who had been a soldier in European campaigns, had joined the expedition to Virginia, where he became a member of the first Council and later (1608–9) governor. He then returned to England, where he became known for his writings about the colony.

His story contains many Amerindian place-names, and at one point – during a visit to the Powhatan Indians – a new noun:

> Arriving at Weramocomoco, their Emperour proudly lying uppon a Bedstead a foote high, upon tenne or twelves Mattes, richly hung with Manie Chaynes of great Pearles about his necke, and covered with a great Covering of Rahaughcums.

Rahaughcums? The first spelling of *racoons* in English. And in Smith's later writings we find such words as *persimmon, moccasin, terrapin, moose, pow-wow,* and *wigwam*.

Not surprisingly, there is an apology in the Preface from the printer:

> the Author being absent from the presse, it cannot be doubted but that some faults have escaped in the printing, especially in the names of Countries, Townes, and People, which are somewhat strange unto us

> alcove, civet, emir, fakir, harem, hashish, hegira, jar, magazine, mameluke, muezzin, sheikh, sherbet, sofa, tariff

Other countries of the region also became a lexical source, sometimes directly, sometimes via another European language or Latin:

> cabbala, caftan, coffee, horde, janissary, kiosk, koumiss, vizier, yoghurt (Turkish)
> hallelujah, midrash, mishna, Sanhedrin, shekel, shibboleth, torah (Hebrew)
> bazaar, caravan, cummerbund, dervish, divan, lascar, shah, turban (Persian)

The *Edward Bonaventure*, the first English ship to reach the East Indies by way of the Cape, left Plymouth in 1591, on the way visiting such places as Zanzibar (1592). The British East India Company was established in India in 1600, and travel to the region greatly increased. From the north of the Indian subcontinent, where Indo-European languages are spoken (e.g., Hindi), we accordingly find such seventeenth-century words as the following:

> bungalow, chintz, cot, dhoti, dungaree, guru, juggernaut, mahout, nabob, punch (the drink), pundit, rupee, sahib

And from the south, where Dravidian languages are spoken (e.g., Tamil), we find words such as these:

> atoll, calico, catamaran, cheroot, copra, curry, mango, pariah, teak

In the Far East, Tibetan, Malay, Chinese, Japanese, and other languages all began to supply new items:

> bamboo, cockatoo, gingham, ginseng, junk (a ship), ketchup, kimono, lama, litchi, sago, shogun

The African connection, via the Portuguese or French, was less productive. It did bring a few English loans by the end of the sixteenth century, such as *yam* and *banana*, and during the following century we find a few more, such as *drill* (a baboon), *harmattan*, and *zebra*. But significant borrowing from African languages does not take place until the 'scramble for Africa' in the nineteenth century.

Other perspectives

It is not surprising that sixteenth-century writers focused on the way English vocabulary was developing through the use of loanwords. These are usually very recognizable items, often highly distinctive, using unfamiliar combinations of sounds, and thereby motivating unfamiliar spellings. We can see this in the words used by the Dutch explorers, such as *cruise*, *keelhaul*, *knapsack*, and *yacht*. This was a time when the already stretched orthography gained a great deal of its irregular appearance, as words like *yacht*, *sheikh*, and *yogurt* illustrate. For example, when *yogurt* arrived in 1625, it was first spelled *yoghurd*, and later citations record *yogourt*, *yahourt*, *yaghourt*, *yogurd*, *yoghourt*, *yooghort*, *yughard*, *yohourth*, *yoghurt*, and *yogurt*. Indeed, the uncertainty still exists: looking in three modern dictionaries, we find:

> in the *Longman Dictionary of Contemporary English* (2003) *yoghurt* is the headword, with one variant, *yogurt*;
> in the *Encarta Dictionary* (1999) *yoghurt* is the headword, with two variants, *yogurt* and *yoghourt*;
> in the *New Penguin Dictionary* (2000) *yogurt* is the headword, with two variants, *yoghurt* and *yoghourt*.

There is still quite a bit of variation in so-called 'Standard' English (see further, p. 476).

More surprising, however, is that nobody paid any attention to other processes of word creation which were also very common at the time – the formation of new words through the addition of prefixes and suffixes, and through compounding and conversion:

> adding a prefix: *mount* > *dismount* (1533)
> adding a suffix: *drink* > *drinkable* (1611)
> making a compound word: *green* + *house* > *greenhouse* (1664)
> converting a word class: *nose* (noun) > *nose* (verb = 'perceive a smell') (1577)

These were the common types of word formation. There were also some minor word-creating processes in operation. For example, we find reduplicated words being coined throughout the period, such as *helter-skelter* (1593) and *shilly-shally* (1700). And new words are formed through abbreviation, as in the case of *miss* from *mistress*, known from 1645 and possibly earlier (for the word was often abbreviated in writing before it was spoken). It seems that abbreviation became something of a fashion in England during the later part of the Early Modern English period, judging by the way Joseph Addison, for example, complains in 1711 about the way words are being 'miserably curtailed' – 'as in *Mob. rep. pos. incog.* and the like'.[8] But earlier on, it was sporadic.

Although processes of word formation had been much used in previous stages of the language (p. 150), they were particularly active between 1500 and 1700, accounting for almost a half of all new words.[9] Suffixation was the primary means employed, chiefly in the formation of new nouns and adjectives (e.g., *-ness, -er, -tion, -ment, -ship*), but also helping to form verbs (notably with *-ize*) and adverbs (with *-ly*). The suffixes were added to words of all three main historical origins: Latin, French, and Anglo-Saxon. The *-ness* and *-er* endings (the latter in various senses) were especially popular, appearing in about half of all the new nouns (e.g., *delightfulness, bawdiness, kind-heartedness, togetherness; caterer, villager, seafarer, disclaimer*). The literary authors of the period massively exploited the expressive potential of affixation and compounding (see panel 12.5). Moreover, affixes were used to coin words even if a perfectly satisfactory word for the same concept already existed, as in the case of *immenseness* (1610) alongside *immensity* (1450), *frequentness* (1664) alongside *frequency* (1553), and *delicateness* (1530) alongside *delicacy* (1374). Usually, in such competitions, the earlier form won; but the naturalness of the *-ness* ending still surfaces today: in casual speech, we occasionally hear nonstandard forms such as *immediateness* and *immenseness*.

12.5 *Un-* verbs

The story of any affix can take us in some unexpected directions. Here is the Shakespearean chapter in the story of *un-*, which was one of the most productive prefixes of the Early Modern English period.

Holofernes, complaining about Dull's misunderstanding of Latin (in *Love's Labour's Lost*, IV.ii.16), describes his manner as an 'undressed, unpolished, uneducated, unpruned, untrained, or, rather, unlettered, or, ratherest, unconfirmed fashion'. Shakespeare seems to have had a penchant for using *un-* in interesting ways. There are 314 instances in the *Oxford English Dictionary* where he is the first citation for an *un-* usage. Most of them are adjectives (e.g., *uncomfortable, uncompassionate, unearthly, uneducated*), and there are a few adverbs (e.g., *unaware, unheedfully*) and nouns (e.g., *an undeserver*), but there are as many as sixty-two instances where the prefix has been added to an already existing verb, such as *unshout, unspeak, uncurse, unswear,* and *undeaf*:

> *Coriolanus* (V.v.4: First Senator to all) Unshout the noise that banished
>   Martius
> *Macbeth* (IV.iii.123: Malcolm to Macduff) I . . . Unspeak mine own detraction
> *Richard II* (III.ii.137: Scroop to Richard) Again uncurse their souls

King John (III.i.245: Philip to Pandulph) Unswear faith sworn . . . ?
Richard II (II.i.16: John of Gaunt to York) My death's sad tale may yet undeaf his ear.

The verbs well illustrate Shakespeare's remarkable lexical inventiveness. But what is also interesting, from the point of view of stylistic variation, is that eighteen of the *un-* verbs (about 30 per cent) appear in just four plays – *Richard II*, *Macbeth*, *Troilus*, and *Hamlet*. Some of the novel uses, of course, apply only to just one sense of a verb. For example, *unbend* in other meanings ('release, relax') is known from well before Shakespeare; but his is the first recorded use of its sense of 'weaken', when Lady Macbeth says to her husband, 'You do unbend your noble strength' (II.ii.45). The eighteen verbs are as follows:

> *Richard II*: uncurse, undeaf, undeck, unhappy
> *Hamlet*: uncharge, unhand, unmask, unpeg
> *Troilus*: unlock, untent, untie, unveil
> *Macbeth*: unbend, unfix, unmake, unprovoke, unspeak, unsex

The last three of these plays are all 1600 or later, that year felt to be so significant for the development of Shakespeare's language by the critic Frank Kermode.[10] Is there any difference in Shakespeare's usage, pre- and post-1600? There seems to be. Using the *OED*'s dates, there are twenty-four instances in the twenty plays pre-1600, with seven plays not containing any instance at all. Post-1600 there are thirty-eight instances in eighteen plays, with just four not having any examples (*Henry VIII*, *Two Noble Kinsmen*, *Antony and Cleopatra*, and *All's Well*). Half the lexical creativity with this form, in fact, appears between 1600 and 1607.

The odd one out, in this scenario, is *Richard II*. But what does Kermode say? Commenting on the famous 'I have been studying . . .' speech (V.v), he observes: 'one might foretell, from this point of vantage, a hugely different style'. And Stanley Wells, in his Penguin edition, describes the language of *Richard II* as both 'immensely complex and unusually self-conscious'. *Un-*, in its tiny way – not even 'one little word', a prefix only – has a part to play in fuelling these grander linguistic intuitions.

The Early Modern English period is still at an early stage of survey investigation, compared with Middle English, but a number of studies[11] suggest that it was a period of particular significance, especially in the creation of English vocabulary. The indications are that about four times as many words were introduced between 1500 and 1700 as between 1200 and 1500. The increase is partly a function of the greater number and survivability of texts, as a result of printing: nearly 160,000 early printed titles are listed in the standard catalogues of the period.[12] But it is also a matter of authorial inventiveness, for the late sixteenth and early seventeenth centuries contain some of the most lexically creative authors in English literature. After their attentions, the language emerges with a new and confident character. And several basic linguistic notions – such as dialect, variety, and style – would come to be viewed in a fresh light at the end of the literary 'golden age'.

Interlude 12
Choosing *thou* or *you*

In the beginning, in Old English, the rules controlling the use of the second-person pronouns were straightforward:

> *thou* and its variant forms (*thee*, *thy*, *thine*) were used in talking to one person (*singular*);
>
> *you* and its variant forms (*ye*, *your*, *yours*) were used in talking to more than one (*plural*).

And within sentences:

> *thou* and *ye* were used as the *subject* of a clause: *thou/ye saw me*;
>
> *thee* and *you* were used as the *object* of a clause: *I saw thee/you*.

But things began to change during Middle English.

The first change was the emergence of *you* as a singular, noticeably during the second half of the thirteenth century. The same kind of development had already taken place in French, where *vous* had come to be used as a polite form of the singular, as an alternative to *tu*; and it seems likely that the usage began in English because the French nobility began to think of the English pronouns in the same way.

The second change took place some time later: during the sixteenth century the difference between the subject and the object forms gradually disappeared, and *you* became the norm in both situations. *Ye* was still in use at the end of the century, but only in contexts which were somewhat literary, religious, or archaic.

So, for anyone talking to one person, there was a choice in Early Modern English: *thou* or *you*. And quite quickly the language evolved a set of social norms, based on the distinction. We can see them already present in *Le Morte Darthur*, written between 1461 and 1470.[13] In Book VII, we read of Gareth arriving at Arthur's court. The king asks Gareth what he wants, addressing him with *ye*, which would be the expected polite form to an apparently upper-class visitor:

> Now ask, said Arthur, and ye shall have your asking.

Gareth then demands food and drink, as if he were a beggar, and this makes the king immediately change his tone, shown by a switch to *thou/thee*:

> Now, sir, this is my petition for this feast, that ye will give me meat and drink sufficiently for this twelvemonth, and at that day I will ask mine other two gifts.
>
> My fair son, said Arthur, ask better, I counsel thee, for this is but a simple asking; for my heart giveth me to thee greatly, that thou art come of men of worship, and greatly my conceit faileth me but thou shalt prove a man of right great worship.

Gareth's robust reply temporarily restores the king's confidence – but not for long:

> Sir, he said, thereof be as it be may, I have asked that I will ask.
>
> Well, said the king, ye shall have meat and drink enough; I never defended [denied] that none, neither my friend nor my foe. But what is thy name I would wit?
>
> I cannot tell you, said he.
>
> That is marvel, said the king, that thou knowest not thy name, and thou art the goodliest young man that ever I saw.

Only when Gareth later reveals himself to be the king's nephew, does *ye* return as Arthur's normal mode of address.

The social basis of the *thou/you* distinction was established by the sixteenth century. The *you* forms would normally be used:

- by people of lower social status to those above them (e.g., ordinary people to nobles, children to parents, servants to masters);
- by the upper classes when talking to each other, even if they were closely related;
- as a sign of a change (contrasting with *thou*) in the emotional temperature of an interaction.

The *thou* forms would normally be used:

- by people of higher social status to those below them (e.g., nobles to ordinary people, parents to children, masters to servants);
- by the lower classes when talking to each other;
- in addressing God;
- in talking to ghosts, witches, and other supernatural beings;
- in an imaginary address to someone who was absent;
- as a sign of a change (contrasting with *you*) in the emotional temperature of an interaction.

The old singular/plural distinction could still be expressed, of course. For example, in the Book of Common Prayer (p. 278), the *thou* forms tend to be used (there is some variability) when the minister is addressing an individual member of the congregation, whereas the *you* forms tend to be used when the minister is talking to the congregation as a whole. Thus we find the individual communicant addressed with *thee*: 'The Body of our Lord Jesus Christ which was given for thee'; by contrast, *you* is used in the general absolution: 'pardon and deliver you from all your sins'.

In the theatrical setting, the interest focuses on what is meant by a 'change in the emotional temperature', which applies to both forms. It is often the case that a switch from *you* to *thou* signals special intimacy or affection between two characters, whereas the reverse switch would signal extra respect or distance. But it all depends on context. Often, a switch to *thou* expresses social condescension or contempt. The use of *thou* to a person of equal rank would usually be an insult, in fact, as Sir Toby Belch is well aware when he advises Sir Andrew Aguecheek on how to write a challenge to an enemy: 'if thou thou'st him some thrice, it shall not be amiss' (*Twelfth Night*, III.ii.42), ironically using a disparaging *thou* to Sir Andrew in the process.

The crucial role of the context is clear in the opening scene of *King Lear*, when Lear is giving away his kingdom to his three daughters. He addresses his first two daughters, Gonerill and Regan, using *thou*: this would be the normal pronoun of parent to child. 'Of all these bounds . . . / We make thee lady', he says to Gonerill (I.i.76); and 'To thee and thine hereditary ever / Remain this ample third of our fair kingdom', he says to Regan (I.i.80). But when he turns to his favourite daughter, Cordelia, he switches to *you*: 'what can you say to draw / A third more opulent than your sisters?' (I.i.85). Here, *you* is being used as a sign of special intimacy. But when Cordelia does not behave as he wishes, he is taken aback. He cannot quite believe it, persisting with *you*:

Mend your speech a little / Lest you may mar your fortunes.

When Cordelia continues in her attitude, he hardens his tone, and the *thou* forms show it:

LEAR But goes thy heart with this?
CORDELIA   Ay, my good lord.

And he eventually explodes in anger:

LEAR So young, and so untender?
CORDELIA So young, my lord, and true.
LEAR Let it be so! Thy truth then be thy dower!

From affection to anger: within just a few lines, we can see *thou* being used in totally contrasting ways.

The *thou/you* distinction was quite well preserved until about 1590, when Shakespeare was beginning to write. It seems to have earlier been disappearing in everyday prose, for the Pastons (p. 178) make very little use of it, even in their more intimate exchanges. We might expect to find it in the more heightened emotional atmosphere of a play; but even there, at the turn of the century, it was by no means universal. Shakespeare makes great dramatic use of the distinction,[14] but Jonson, for example, uses it much less. Perhaps it was more a part of Shakespeare's linguistic intuition, having been brought up in Warwickshire, where *thou* forms were a feature of regional speech.

Thou disappeared from Standard English completely during the first half of the seventeenth century. It remained widespread in regional dialect (and would continue so into Modern English), and continued to be used in plays as an archaism. The distinction was sufficiently alive in the popular mind for it to become an issue mid century, when the Society of Friends movement began. Quakers disapproved of the way in which singular *you* had become part of an etiquette of social distance, and used *thou* forms to everyone, believing that this better reflected the spirit of the exchanges Christ would have had with his disciples. One of the first Quakers, Richard Farnsworth, in *The Pure Language of the Spirit of Truth* (1655), considers that anyone who 'cannot bear thee and thou to a single person, what sort soever, is exalted proud fresh, and is accursed'. He also had a grammatical reason: *thou* was a more exact usage, being a 'particular, single, pure proper unto one'.

Because *thou* forms were now rural and nonstandard, the Quaker usage offended many. The authorities, and people with high social positions or pretensions, considered it an insult to be addressed using these forms. George Fox, in his *Journal*, reports that he and his followers were

> in danger many times of our lives, and often beaten, for using those words to some proud men, who would say, 'Thou'st "thou" me, thou ill-bred clown', as though their breeding lay in saying 'you' to a singular

No other organization copied the practice.

The second-person pronoun system may have simplified in Standard English; but throughout the English-speaking world variant forms continued to be used. Some of these are described in Interlude 17 (p. 449).

Chapter 13 Linguistic daring

Whatever the feelings writers expressed about the inferiority of English compared to other languages, at the beginning of the sixteenth century, these had
largely disappeared by the end. As we have seen in the two previous chapters,
English experienced a huge lexical growth. The Classical origins of much of
this vocabulary sharpened writers' sense of style, widening the range of choices
which were available to characterize 'high' and 'low' levels of discourse, and
offering the option of intermediate levels. Professional domains, such as science,
law, and medicine, developed their expressive capabilities, becoming increasingly standardized. And standardization within the language as a whole made
significant progress. All this was reinforced by an increased awareness of the
nature of language and of linguistic performance, as seen in such treatises as
Thomas Wilson's *Arte of Rhetorique* and Philip Sidney's *Defence of Poesie*
(p. 295). The language was undoubtedly richer, in quantitative terms, than it
had ever been. In 1600, a John Skelton could not have complained about a lack
of words to 'serve his mind' (p. 288).

It is only to be expected that an age when linguistic resources are increasing
so much in richness would be immensely stimulating to creative writers.
Authors, we may suppose, have a particular ability to observe and assimilate
into their work details of the contemporary scene, and the period was one which
provided unprecedented opportunities for linguistic exploitation. Because
lawyers, for example, had developed a standard style of discourse, this could
be imitated, exaggerated, and parodied, and its vocabulary used in a range of
appropriate and inappropriate contexts restricted only by the limitations of
authorial imagination.[1] A good example occurs in the middle of Shakespeare's
Merry Wives of Windsor (IV.ii.192). A disguised Falstaff has just been beaten
out of the house by Frank Ford, who thinks he is having an affair with his wife.
Falstaff has indeed been making advances to both Mistress Ford and Mistress
Page, much to their disgust, and at this point in the play they have already
found two successful ways to humiliate him. Mistress Ford then wonders
whether they have done enough:

> What think you – may we, with the warrant of womanhood and the witness of a
> good conscience, pursue him with any further revenge?

And Mistress Page replies using a legal figure of speech.

> The spirit of wantonness is sure scared out of him. If the devil have him not in
> fee-simple, with fine and recovery, he will never, I think, in the way of waste
> attempt us again.

There are three legal expressions exploited here, in fact, and we need to disentangle their senses in order to work out what the sentence means. *Waste* meant
'damage to property by a tenant'. Mistress Page is basically saying that, if she
and Mistress Ford are thought of as pieces of property, then Falstaff will never
try to harm them again. But this will happen only, *if the devil have him not in
fee-simple*. *Fee-simple* meant a private estate belonging to an owner and his heirs
for ever; so, *in fee-simple* meant 'in permanent leasing' or 'in full possession'. She
is saying: 'We're safe as long as the devil doesn't have a permanent hold on
Falstaff'. But there is more. What sort of hold might the devil have? *With fine
and recovery* – two terms to do with transferring property. *Fine* refers to an
agreement to transfer land possession; *recovery*, a procedure for transferring
property into full ownership. Put the two terms together, and the meaning is
essentially 'with everything transferred to him'. In modern idiom, Mistress Page
is saying that if the devil doesn't own Falstaff lock, stock and barrel, so that he
can never stop being wicked, they are safe enough.

The greatest creativity in an author's exploitation of a linguistic variety
comes in such contexts – not when its language is being used in its normal
setting, but when it is used in unexpected situations. If a lawyer appears
professionally on stage, we expect legal language to be part of the characterization, as in the courtroom climax of *The Merchant of Venice*. But we do not
expect legal language to be used by a Windsor housewife, so that when we
encounter it there the ingenuity and subtlety of the allusions can add an
intellectual layer of enjoyment to our general appreciation of the humour. In
the Mistress Page example, that extra layer depends on our ability to understand
as well as to recognize the specific legalisms. But in the gravedigger scene in
Hamlet (V.i.98), we need only recognize the general presence of legal terminology in order to appreciate its effect. Hamlet has observed the gravedigger's
unceremonious treatment of a skull in the grave he is digging, and observes:

> Why does he suffer this rude knave now to knock him about the sconce with a
> dirty shovel, and will not tell him of his action of battery? H'm! This fellow
> might be in's time a great buyer of land, with his statutes, his recognizances, his
> fines, his double vouchers, his recoveries. Is this the fine of his fines and the

recovery of his recoveries, to have his pate full of fine dirt? Will his vouchers vouch him no more of his purchases, and double ones too, than the length and breadth of a pair of indentures? The very conveyances of his lands will hardly lie in this box; and must th'inheritor himself have no more, ha?

HORATIO: Not a jot more, my lord.

Horatio, perhaps, is somewhat bemused by all this legalinguistic dexterity, and so probably were the groundlings at the Globe. But they would have recognized the legal language for what it was, as do we; and that is the important point, when thinking about the significance of growing stylistic awareness in the sixteenth century. Here we have an instance of legal language out of context. None of it is strictly necessary, at this point in the play. It did not have to be a lawyer's skull that Hamlet speculated about in the scene; it might have been a doctor's or a soldier's or a clergyman's. But the 'action of battery' pun seems to have caused the association, and, having chosen the law, we then get a ludic celebration of legal language, with pun piling on top of pun. And even though the individual terms may mean little to us today, our general awareness of the nature of legal language allows us to recognize the accumulation of effects, and appreciate its dramatic impact.

Manipulating the styles used by a community is one way an author can exploit the resources of a language. In such cases, the creativity lies in the writer's ability to adapt already existing vocabulary to a fresh character or setting. It is another example of the 'bending and breaking of rules' (p. 182): until legal language has achieved a certain level of community recognition, authors cannot use it to make special effects. By the end of the sixteenth century, several such varieties were available for use in this way. The arcane language of the ink-horn pedant is parodied in the speech of the schoolteacher Holofernes in *Love's Labour's Lost* (V.i), as is the overfastidious language of the courtier, Don Armado:

ARMADO Sir, it is the King's most sweet pleasure and affection to congratulate the Princess at her pavilion in the posteriors of this day, which the rude multitude call the afternoon.

HOLOFERNES The posterior of the day, most generous sir, is liable, congruent, and measurable for the afternoon. The word is well culled, choice, sweet, and apt, I do assure you, sir, I do assure.

Later in the scene, following an erudite conversation with Armado and Nathaniel, Holofernes turns to constable Anthony Dull:

HOLOFERNES Thou hast spoken no word all this while.

DULL Nor understood none neither, sir.

It is a highly comic moment, based on the conflict of comprehension which arises when speakers of 'high' and 'low' varieties meet each other.

A rather different kind of creativity takes place when a writer does not just adapt but actually adds to the resources of the language, by devising new styles of expression (such as fresh literary forms), inventing new words, or using old words in new senses. All the leading authors of the period played a part in the lexical expansion taking place in English, adapting the vocabulary to their own ends, often with strikingly evocative results, as we have already seen in the creative use of the *un-* prefix (p. 304; see also panel 13.1). But before illustrating the point, several words of caution are needed. In particular, we should note that it is not usually possible to be definite about a writer's personal role in the introduction or creation of a new word. A common procedure – used repeatedly in earlier pages of this book – is to look at the citations of earliest recorded uses in the leading historical record, the *Oxford English Dictionary*. But it is not a straightforward exercise, as can be illustrated from Shakespeare, acknowledged to be the leading creative lexical mind of this age.

13.1 A lexical thought experiment

Imagine being an Elizabethan author wanting to create an adjective from the noun *discord*, so that you can say 'characterized by discord', and thus write such phrases as (what in modern English would be) *discordant times* or *discordant multitude*. There is no way you can check to see if the word already exists, because there are no large-scale dictionaries in which to look it up. You might be familiar with its use from an earlier author, but, even if you are, the usage might not capture the nuance that you have in mind. Either way, you find yourself disposed to coin your own word.

You have two options. One is to make an adjective by simply changing the part of speech: *the discord times*. The other is to add a suffix. Here you have a dozen or so alternatives to choose from, but only two or three of these really capture the sense 'full of discord'. In alphabetical order, these are:

> discordable, discordal, discordant, discordful, discordic, discording, discordish, discordive, discordly, discordous, discordsome, discordy

There is nothing to stop you using any of these, other than your sense of what the suffix means. There are no sanctions. Everyone is coining. And there are no dictionaries to say that one usage is right and another wrong. Which would you choose?

Now imagine a dozen authors all faced with the same task. Given that there are so few real alternatives, it would not be surprising to see more than one author going for the same word.

The *Oxford English Dictionary* records show Bishop Joseph Hall opting for *discordous* in his *Satires* (1597–8), Father James Dalrymple using *discordeng* (i.e., *discording*) in his Scots translation of John Leslie's Latin history of Scotland (1596), Shakespeare going for *discordant* in the Induction to *Henry IV Part 2*, and Spenser trying out *discordfull* in *The Faerie Queene* (1596). No one seems to have gone for the other suffixes. There are two recorded cases of *discord* as an adjective, a century apart (1509, 1606).

Discordful seems to be the obvious choice – 'full of discord' – but today we say *discordant*. This turns out to have been the oldest usage, known from the thirteenth century, and the commonest, found in Chaucer (just once, in Book II of *Troilus and Criseyde*) and other late Middle English writers. We know this, because we have the *OED* at our disposal. It is a moot point how far Elizabethan authors were familiar with the earlier usages, though *Troilus* was by then a classic. There are two other sixteenth-century citations, apart from Shakespeare, in the *OED*, which suggests a certain community of use. However, if the word *was* well known, it is difficult to see why writers would coin other forms using the same root, producing alternatives which are all equally 'high style'. As ever, the factors which make a word most fit to survive remain obscure (p. 293).

Quantifying innovation

The problem with Shakespeare is that his literary greatness has led enthusiastic linguistic amateurs to talk absolute rubbish about his role in the development of the English language. For example, in contributions to a television programme on the bard in early 2000, such comments were made as 'Shakespeare invented a quarter of our language' and 'Shakespeare *is* our language'.[2] At another point, Shakespeare was said to have four times as many words as the average undergraduate, who – the 'expert' opined – has a vocabulary of 5,000 words. In another television programme at the end of 2002, adult average vocabulary was said to be 10,000 words.[3] And here is a published statement:

> Shakespeare had one of the largest vocabularies of any English writer, some 30,000 words. (Estimates of an educated person's vocabulary today vary, but it is probably half this, 15,000.)[4]

In a different connection, I have lost count of the number of times I have heard people say that the *Sun*, one of Britain's tabloid daily newspapers, uses a vocabulary of only 500 words – presumably to avoid straining the supposed limited comprehension ability of its readers. All of this goes to show that people have very poor intuitions about vocabulary size, though no inhibitions about expressing them. They are all miles away from the truth. What is the reality?

First, a point of terminology. When we estimate vocabulary size, what we count is the number of 'different words' being used – what in semantics are technically called *lexemes*. For example, the different forms of the lexeme GO are *go*, *goes*, *going*, *gone*, and *went* – and, in Elizabethan English, it would include such forms as *goest* and *go'st* as well. The different forms of the lexeme BOY are *boy*, *boys*, *boy's*, and *boys'*. Dictionaries list lexemes, and lexemes are what we look up. We do not search for *taking*; we search for *take*, and expect to find *taking* mentioned within the entry. The distinction is crucial: if we counted all the variant forms of Shakespeare's words, we would reach 29,066 (that is where the rounded-up 30,000 figure quoted above comes from); but if we count lexemes, the figure is less than 20,000.[5] It is the lexemes which are the important thing. In the First Folio we find the following forms:

> take, takes, taketh, taking, tak'n, taken, tak'st, tak't, took, took'st, tooke, tookst

It would be absurd to think of these 'twelve words' as showing us twelve aspects of Shakespeare's lexical creativity. They are simply twelve forms of the *same* word, varying for grammatical, metrical, and orthographic reasons.

Bearing this in mind, what are the true lexeme counts for the various contexts referred to above? Let us take the newspaper first. A count of the lexemes used in 100 articles spread across just one issue of Britain's tabloid daily, the *Sun*, produced a total of 5,190. The first twenty items from the list were:

> abandon, abdicate, abdominal, ability, ablaze, able, abnormal, aboard, about, above, abroad, absence, absinthe, absolutely, absorb, abstain, abuse (as a verb), academic, academy, accent

Life is too short to count the whole paper: my impression is that there would be at least 6,000 lexemes in any complete issue of the *Sun*. Certainly, an estimate of 500 is nowhere near the truth. It is disturbing that pundits are so ready to write off the linguistic competence of the general public in this way. Doubtless it is partly because they have noted that a great deal of the vocabulary in the *Sun* is not Standard English. My lexeme count brought to light such nonstandard word forms as the following (see further, p. 481):

> bruv 'brother', dammit, dunno, fecking, fella, footie 'football', gotta, missus, nah 'no', nosh, pressie 'present', puddin', sarnies, skint, tater 'potato', wanna, yep 'yes', yer 'your'

Such words are often given positional prominence as headlines, and sometimes appear in huge type on the front page. A culture which underprivileges non-standard varieties would inevitably interpret the use of such forms as a measure of expressive inadequacy. Ours is, unfortunately, such a culture.

Determining the size of an adult's vocabulary has to be approached in a different way. In one study, adults were asked to take a 1 per cent selection of pages throughout a college-size English dictionary (i.e., about 100,000 entries) and identify the words they actively used, as well as the ones they knew but did not use.[6] Extrapolating from their results, estimates of active vocabulary for an office secretary, a businesswoman, and a university lecturer were 31,500, 63,000, and 56,250 – the large second total probably because the person was, by her own account, a voracious reader. The average is 50,000. Estimates of passive vocabulary were roughly 25 per cent larger. This is an exercise anyone can do, and it demonstrates immediately that modern vocabularies are much larger than is generally thought.

Another interesting estimate is the size of the English lexicon as a whole. This, too, is much larger than most people think. If we combine all the lexemes found in the largest British dictionary (over half a million in the *OED*), the largest US dictionary (just under half a million in *Webster's Third New International Dictionary*), and add a selection of specialized dictionaries (such as botany and chemistry), even allowing for overlap we easily reach a million.[7] Not all the lexemes are in current use, of course: the *OED* in particular is a historical dictionary, with *c.* 100,000 of its senses marked as obsolescent or obsolete. But let us assume that the remaining 400,000 lexemes in the *OED* accurately represent Modern English vocabulary. This allows us to reach an interesting statistic, relating it to the 50,000 figure from the previous paragraph: a reasonably well-educated person actively uses about 12 per cent of the word stock of the language. The figures are inevitably very approximate, but they will not be wildly out.

All of this sets the scene for a re-valuation of the Shakespearean contribution. The English lexicon grew, during the Early Modern English period, from 100,000 to 200,000 lexemes (p. 162). (It would double again, as a result of the Industrial Revolution and twentieth-century global expansion.) As already noted, the size of Shakespeare's vocabulary is somewhere between 17,000 and 20,000 lexemes. This means that – as someone living midway through the period, when we might imagine the vocabulary to have grown to around 150,000 items – he was using something over 13 per cent of the total word stock. This was probably much higher than his contemporaries (I do not know of any counts). It is certainly well ahead of the other major work of the period, the linguistically conservative King James Bible (p. 276), which has around 8,000 lexemes.

In passing, we should note that it will never be possible to reach a definitive figure for Shakespeare's – or anyone's – vocabulary, for several reasons. In particular, there are many differences of opinion over what counts as a lexeme. How many are there in 'three suited, hundred pound, filthy worsted stocking knave' (*King Lear*, II.iii.14, with hyphens removed)? Editors have to decide just how many compound words there are, in such cases. They cannot rely on the hyphenation introduced by the Elizabethan compositors, which was decidedly erratic. A second point is that there are many different editorial views as to what lexemes are actually being represented by some of the textual forms printed in the Quartos and Folios: what exactly is being 'sledded' in *Hamlet*, I.i.63 – *poleaxe*? *Polacks*? The emendations proposed by successive generations of editors steadily increase the theoretical size of Shakespeare's lexicon. Also, a number of decisions about method have to be taken, when counting lexemes. It is usual to exclude proper names from a lexeme count, for example, unless they have a more general significance (such as *Ethiop*). A decision has to be made over whether to count foreign words (from Latin, French, etc.), and if so, does this also exclude the franglais used in *Henry V*? Should onomatopoeic sounds be excluded (e.g., *sa*, *sese*). And what about humorous forms, such as malapropisms: should they be counted separately or as variants of their supposed targets (e.g., *allicholly* as a variant of *melancholy*)? In each case there is room for debate about what items should be included and what excluded.

But despite the difficulties, it is still possible to hazard an estimate of the amount of personal lexical innovation in Shakespeare's work. Let us begin with the traditional procedure, looking in the *OED* for lexemes where Shakespeare is the first recorded user. Excluding 54 cases of humorous malapropisms and nonsense words, such as *gratility* and *impeticos*, we find a total of 2,035 instances.[8] (The total is broken down in panel 13.2[a] into yearly subtotals, between 1588 and 1613, using the play and poem dates assigned by the *OED*.) A figure of around 2,000 may not seem very large, but as a personal total it is really very impressive, being much greater than the totals assigned to any of his contemporaries: a similar search for Spenser produces *c*. 500, Sidney *c*. 400, Marston *c*. 200, and the King James Bible *c*. 50 (see further below). The 2,035 total is also some 10 per cent of the 20,000 lexemes in his total output. I have not found another English author coming anywhere near such a percentage for first recorded uses of individual lexemes. In this respect, at least, Shakespeare stands supreme.

Noting the appearance of a lexeme is one aspect of potential lexical creativity. Noting the appearance of different *senses* of a lexeme is another. The figure of 2,035 refers to lexemes being used for the first time, regardless of the sense they have – *rascally*, *rat-catcher*, *rated*, *ratifier*, *ravelled*, *raw-boned*, and so on. It does not include cases where an earlier writer is known to have introduced a lexeme in one sense, but Shakespeare uses it in a new sense. For example, if we look up the adjective *confident* in the *OED* we find that it is recorded in the meaning of 'self-reliant' from 1576, well before (one imagines) Shakespeare started to write. Since then it has developed a number of other

13.2 Shakespearean statistics

Panel 13.2(a) shows a new count of the total number of earliest recorded uses of a lexeme assigned to Shakespeare (according to the *OED*). The *OED* editors used the traditional canon of thirty-seven plays (excluding *The Two Noble Kinsmen* and *King Edward III*) and poems, and extracted items from Quarto texts as well as from the First Folio. (That is the chief reason why some texts turn up in more than one year; there are also a few dating inconsistencies.)

Year	Total	Plays and poems
1588	140	*Love's Labour's Lost, Titus*
1589	0	
1590	82	*Comedy of Errors, Midsummer Night's Dream*
1591	73	*Henry VI(1), Two Gentlemen*
1592	99	*Henry VI(2), Romeo, Venus*
1593	137	*Henry VI(2), Henry VI (3)*, 'Lover's Complaint', *Lucrece, Richard II, Venus*
1594	38	*Richard III*
1595	46	*King John*
1596	162	*Henry IV(1), Merchant, Taming*
1597	94	*Henry IV(2)*, 'Lover's Complaint', 'Passionate Pilgrim', *Romeo*
1598	69	*Henry IV(1), Merry Wives, Romeo, Richard III, Two Gentlemen*
1599	91	*Henry V, Much Ado*, 'Passionate Pilgrim'
1600	87	*As You Like It, Henry V*, 'Lover's Complaint', Sonnets, *Titus*
1601	122	*All's Well, Julius Caesar, Pericles*, 'Phoenix', *Twelfth Night*
1602	99	*Hamlet*
1603	60	*Measure, Hamlet*
1604	78	*Othello, Hamlet*
1605	164	*Lear, Macbeth, Hamlet*
1606	158	*Antony, Troilus*
1607	104	*Coriolanus, Timon*
1608	23	*Lear, Pericles*
1609	1	*Troilus*
1610	51	*Cymbeline, Tempest*
1611	86	*Cymbeline, Winter's Tale*
1612	0	
1613	15	*Henry VIII*
Grand total	2,079	[2,035, excluding malapropisms, etc.]

Panel 13.2(b) shows the number of earliest recorded usages assigned to Shakespeare by the *OED*, grouped into five categories.

Category	Number of instances
A No usage of the word recorded by anyone other than Shakespeare	309
B1 Usage of same word in same sense recorded after a gap of at least a generation (twenty-five years)	1,035
B2 Usage of same word in different sense recorded after a gap of at least a generation	48
C Usage of same word in same sense recorded within a generation	464
D Usage of same word in different sense recorded within a generation	179
Total	2,035
E Excluded words (malapropisms, etc)	44 [2,079]

Panel 13.2(c) shows the time it takes for a lexeme to appear in another writer's usage, within a generation (twenty-five years) following its first recorded use by Shakespeare (a breakdown of categories C and D above).

The year in which a word is used after its first recorded usage in Shakespeare	Number of words
Same year	36
1 year later	30
2 years later	36
3 years later	27
4 years later	32
5 years later	33
6 years later	36
7 years later	29
8 years later	31
9 years later	36
10 years later	29
11 years later	33
12 years later	20
13 years later	20
14 years later	27
15 years later	18

The year in which a word is used after its first recorded usage in Shakespeare	Number of words
16 years later	13
17 years later	21
18 years later	18
19 years later	29
20 years later	17
21 years later	18
22 years later	20
23 years later	16
24 years later	18
Total	643

Panel 13.2(d) shows the time it takes for a lexeme to appear in another author's usage, following its first recorded use by Shakespeare.

Period after Shakespeare	Number of words	Average per year	Cumulative total
1588–99	167	13.8	167
1600s	222	22.2	389
1610s	197	19.7	586
1620s	114	11.4	700
1630s	130	13.0	830
1640s	95	9.5	925
1650s	88	8.8	1,013
1660s	75	7.5	1,088
1670s	46	4.6	1,134
1680s	39	3.9	1,173
1690s	34	3.4	1,207
1700s	207	2.1	1,414
1800s	285	2.8	1,699
1900s	17	0.17	1,716
Total	1,716		

senses – eight in all – and Shakespeare seems to have been responsible for three of them: 'trustful' and 'impudent' (both of which have now died out), and 'sure'. I have not found an easy way of extracting a complete list of these sense innovations from the OED database, so cannot give a figure for the number of sense developments in which Shakespeare was involved. There is no doubt that, when this task is carried out, the extent of his contribution to the character of English vocabulary will turn out to be very much greater than my 2,035 figure suggests. However, this kind of semantic investigation remains to be done – for any author.

It is universally believed that Shakespeare is pre-eminent in the history of English lexical creativity, but this is for a whole host of semantic and stylistic reasons (discussed below), and not just because of his lexical coinage. In fact, when that figure of 2,035 is put under the sociolinguistic microscope it turns out to be less significant than it seems. To begin with, a 'first recorded usage', for any author, actually tells us very little about whether that author coined the word. Shakespeare may have been the first person recorded as using the oaths *'sblood* ('God's blood') and *'slid* ('God's eyelid') but he certainly did not invent such everyday expressions. Nor did he invent the word *Newgate*, even though it is first used as an adjective in his work (referring to people walking *Newgate fashion* in *Henry IV Part 1*), for the prison had been around at least since the time of King John. Nor is he likely to have invented *clack-dish* (a wooden dish with a lid that beggars 'clacked' as they invited contributions). On the other hand, the coinages *anthropophaginian* and *exsufflicate* are so unusual that they do suggest a personal touch. And when we see a particular pattern of interesting word formation recur, we do begin to develop a sense of personal creative energy: *out-Herod, outfrown, outpray, outswear, outvillain* . . . The problem for the lexicologist is plain: how to decide which of the various 'first recorded usages' are like *'sblood* and *clack-dish* and which are like *anthropophaginian* and *outswear*?

One approach is to look for other instances of supposed new lexemes in the writings of other authors of the period. If a lexeme really was in common use when Shakespeare was writing, we would expect to find it being used at around the same time by the other authors sampled in the OED. At the opposite extreme, we might find instances which were so unusual or imaginative that nobody ever used them again, other than by way of quotation. We would be on dangerous ground asserting that the items in the former category were all Shakespearean innovations; we would be on much safer ground in thinking of the latter group in this way. Panel 13.2(b) gives the relevant statistics, beginning with the unique cases. In Category A we find 309 lexemes where Shakespeare is the only user (as far as we know from the texts sampled by the OED). They vary from vivid and imaginative coinages (such as *out-craft* and *unshout*) to 'workhorse' items needed to express an everyday meaning (such as *well-saying* and *unimproved*). Here is a selection from the first half of the alphabet for this category:

> acture, anthropophaginian, attemptable, bepray, besort, bitter-sweeting, candle-holder, chirurgeonly, conceptious, correctioner, demi-puppet, directitude, dis-property, enschedule, felicitate, fustilarian, incardinate, insultment, irregulous

We might say with a fair degree of confidence that Shakespeare coined these lexemes. Plainly they were not in everyday usage.

And we might feel equally confident that Shakespeare was the originator of lexemes which were not used again until centuries later. A number of items have no further recorded uses until 'rediscovered' by nineteenth-century romantic writers, such as Scott, Byron, and Elizabeth Barrett Browning, who gave them a new lease of life: examples include *antre, cerements, overteem, rubious, silverly, unchary,* and *water-drop.* The influence continued into the twentieth century, and still exists today: a writer in the 1905 *Athenæum* talks rather self-consciously about readers 'ready to expend their testril on such an attractive booklet', taking up a usage of Sir Andrew Aguecheek in *Twelfth Night* (II.iii.32). The number of lexemes that were not used again until the 1800s or later (see the last two lines of panel 13.2[d]) is 302. We could add these to our list of 'Shakespearean definites' with reasonable confidence.

Now let us turn to the other end of the time continuum when Shakespeare was writing. Here we find several cases where other writers are recorded as using a 'new' lexeme in the same year as Shakespeare, or soon after. For example, both Shakespeare and Jonson used *tightly* in 1598; both Shakespeare and Marston used *condolement* in 1602; *bandit* is used by Shakespeare in 1593 and by Nashe in 1594; Shakespeare's use of *ruttish* in 1601 is followed by a Middleton usage in 1602; his use of *charmingly* in 1610 is followed by a Cotgrave usage in 1611.[9] In such cases, we must surely conclude that the lexeme was in general use – part of the linguistic consciousness of the time. This is not to deny the possibility that two writers might coin a new word independently and simultaneously. Indeed, given the creative lexical tendencies of the later Elizabethan age, and the collaborative world to which writers belonged, it probably happened fairly often. The pros and cons of competing linguistic fashions must constantly have been debated in the playwright corners of taverns, and it is easy to conceive how something which came up in an evening's conversation might influence two authors to coin the same lexeme the next day. However, when two authors do use the same lexeme at about the same time it is rather more likely that they are reflecting a wider community usage. Indeed, the point can sometimes be demonstrated: the study of texts which did not form part of the OED database often brings to light an earlier usage (*lonely,* for example, has been found fifteen years earlier). But we do not yet have a concordance of all the texts from this period, and only when we do will we know just how original to an author the earliest recorded usages are.

In the absence of this information, all we can do is make some educated guesses about what might have been the linguistic consciousness of the time. If we allow that most of the lexemes used by other writers in the same year as Shakespeare is known to have used them were in common usage, as were those recorded in the following year, what about the year after that? And the year after that? And what about a lexeme next recorded five years later, or ten years later? At what point might we say that the linguistic climate in which Shakespeare lived, and from which he learned his basic lexicon as a child, would have changed so much that it would have to be considered a different climate, in which people spoke noticeably differently, and had different intuitions about what counted as modern or old-fashioned usage? The common assumption in sociolinguistics is that such linguistic intuitions last for a generation before they evolve into something distinctively different.[10] That seems reasonable: people born or working in London within the same generation as Shakespeare – writers such as Jonson and Middleton – would have been exposed to the same linguistic climate, and have acquired similar linguistic intuitions. Although Shakespeare would have brought to London a certain Warwickshire background, he would soon have accommodated (p. 83) to London norms. There is in fact hardly any sign in his general writing of his regional background, other than what we can infer from the occasional dialect items put into the mouths of his rural or regional characters (p. 361).

A 'generation' in Elizabethan England was about twenty-five years, much as it is now; the average age of marriage for women was twenty-four and for men was twenty-seven (Juliet at fourteen was quite the exception).[11] Moreover, it was a relatively young population, compared with today: life expectancy varied greatly at the time, averaging around thirty-eight years for the country as a whole, with London much lower (around thirty-five years) because of the spread of disease caused by crowding and poor sanitation.[12] We might thus expect new lexemes to diffuse through the community (at least in London) more rapidly than they would today, helped along by a youthful society sensitive to the latest linguistic fashions, the 'new tuners of accent' (as Mercutio describes Tybalt, in *Romeo and Juliet*, II.iv.29). A Jacobethan 'linguistic generation' might therefore have been much shorter – perhaps twenty or even fifteen years – but I shall stay with the more conventional time-frame of twenty-five years for the present exercise.

We can assume that writers born in the same decade as Shakespeare would have begun to take up their pen during the 1580s, at the earliest, and that their output during the next twenty-five years (i.e., until the 1610s) would very much reflect the language of their youth. Apparently innovative usages in their writing during that period could just as easily have been a reflection of what they heard around them as anything personally creative, so this is a period when we may rightly be suspicious about lexemes being claimed to be Shakespearean in origin. How many of his first recorded usages would be affected? Categories C and D in panel 13.2 (b) show that there were 643 lexemes which were used by other writers within twenty-five years of the usage first appearing in Shakespeare. A breakdown is shown in panel 13.2(c). We see in its first line that thirty-six lexemes used by Shakespeare in a given year were also used by another author in the same year (as in the *tightly* and *condolement* examples noted above); thirty were used one year later (as in the *bandit* and *charmingly* examples); and so on, up to twenty-five years. There is a noticeable evenness of diffusion over the first eleven years, with an average of thirty-two words each year; there is then a drop to an average of twenty per year over the remaining part of the period.

If we now extend this perspective into the seventeenth century as a whole, we can link up with the conclusion already reached above for later centuries. The figures are laid out in panel 13.2(d), which shows the gap which occurs between a first recorded use of a lexeme (in any of its senses) in Shakespeare and the next recorded use of that lexeme (in any of its senses) by some other author. We have already noted that lexemes not recorded again until the 1800s could hardly have been in common usage. But the same conclusion would also apply to lexemes not again recorded until the 1700s, and likewise for much of the 1600s. The interesting period is the beginning of the seventeenth century, as we come closer to Shakespeare's generation. The cumulative totals show that 586 of 'his' lexemes were in circulation by 1620, and the total of 643 mentioned above is reached by 1628. How many of these would have been in common use?

To deny Shakespeare a formative role in all of these lexemes would be going too far, because they are actually a mix of the mundane and the creative, as this selection from the two ends of the alphabet shows:

> abode (as a verb), abstemious, adulterate, affecting (as an adjective), after-time, a-height, a-high-lone, ajax 'jakes', ambassy, ambuscado, anchovy, apoplex (as a verb), arch-villain, assailing (as an adjective), atomy, attorneyship . . . weather-bitten, well-beseeming, well-conceited, well-foughten, well-ordered, well-read, well-refined, widen, wind-shaked, winnowed, wittolly 'cuckoldy', worm-hole, zany

Sometimes there are clues, such as when we find two structurally related innovations attributed to the same author. A person who coins *crimeful* is likely to coin *crimeless*; and we find this pairing in the list of Shakespeare attributions, as well as *useful/useless*, *upstairs/downstairs*, *skyey/skyish*, and *unshunned/unshunnable*. Using a lexeme in two grammatical functions is another clue: *besort* as a noun and a verb; *impress* as a noun and a verb; *grumbling* as an adjective and a noun. But for the most part, there are no clues; and it would be a foolish person indeed who would try to impose a criterion of imaginative creativity on such a list, and decide which usages were Shakespeare reporting everyday usage and which were his personal coinages. On the other hand, it would be naive to think of them all as everyday, or all as personal. The answer will lie somewhere in between.

This lengthy excursus can now be summarized. If we accept all recorded first usages as being individual Shakespearean innovations, we have a total of 2,035. If we deny him all 643 lexemes which had a presence within twenty-five years of his first using the lexeme, we have a total of 1,392. How to interpret 'somewhere in between'? If we arbitrarily halve the difference, we end up with 1,712. It is a figure which corresponds to impressionistic estimates which have often been made,[13] so we might accept ±1,700 as a reasonable middle-of-the-road figure. It would be incautious to be any more precise; nor, from the point of view of the history of English, is it necessary. The important point to appreciate is that lexeme-coining was normal practice in Jacobethan England. The creative writers played their part, probably more than most, but we must not discount the role of the translators, historians, scientists, and others who made up the linguistic character of the age.

A final observation, before ending this excursus. A complete assessment of the significance of an author's lexical coining ability for the history of a language has to take into account its long-term impact. From this point of view, the 309 cases where Shakespeare is the only user of a lexeme are only of stylistic interest – telling us something about him as a creative language-using individual, but making no further contribution to the language (apart from the occasional instance where they might form part of a well-known quotation). But far more than these unique uses are involved. When we examine all 2,035 of Shakespeare's first recorded usages, we find that over 900 of them sooner or later fall out of use: *adoptious, agued, aidance, allayment, annexment,* and so on. Only about 1,100 still have any use today, and to reach that figure we have to include such words as *buskined, dog-weary, tetter,* and *well-flowered,* as well as word-class changes such as the verb uses of *belly* and *bower,* whose present-day status as living items might well be queried (none has any twentieth-century OED citations). Some 300 lexemes fall into this uncertain category.

That leaves about 800 clear-cut cases – such as *abhorred, abstemious, accessible, accommodation, acutely,* and *assassination* – and even some of these might be excluded, on the grounds that there has been a major change of meaning between Shakespeare's time and now. *Mountaineer* in *Cymbeline* and *The Tempest* meant 'mountain-dweller', not 'mountain-climber'. His adjectival use of *counterfeiting* meant 'pretending' or 'role-playing' (the *counterfeiting actors* of *Henry VI Part 3*), not 'forging'. Most lexemes display later semantic development of this kind. Lexical history is a multifaceted thing, involving much more than a single line of descent from an older form: the modern senses of a lexeme contain all kinds of semantic elements and nuances which have interacted throughout its history, resulting from the accumulated creativity of an unknown number of users. Etymology is a collective responsibility. It is very rare indeed to find a single person responsible for a modern lexeme in all its current senses. (US humorist Gelett Burgess' *blurb* is one of them.) And few Shakespearean coinages have remained uninfluenced by later usage.

Even though we may chip away like this at Shakespeare's supposed linguistic significance, a monument of respectable size none the less remains. Whether we assess his lexical contribution as 800 or 1,700, it is still hugely impressive, compared with the contribution of other writers. Most modern authors I imagine would be delighted if they contributed even one lexeme to the future of the language. And certainly, if we compare Shakespeare with his contemporaries, we can immediately see the contrast:

- The playwright John Marston has over 200 *OED* attributions, including *actorship, discursive, disunion, downcast, extracture, fashion-monger, flop* (as a verb), *gloating, musicry, pathetic, petulant, rivalry, strenuous, stutterer,* and *yawn*. He evidently achieved something of a reputation among his contemporaries for his coining – a reputation which seems justified if we reflect upon *gargalize* 'gargle' and *propensitude*, as well as this fine nonsensical creation from *The Dutch Courtesan* (II.i.): 'my catastrophonicall fine boy'. However, about a third of his lexemes failed to become a permanent part of the language.

- Sir Philip Sidney is represented by about 400 lexemes, including *amorousness, appassionate, artist, beautified, bookishness, counterbalance, harmfulness, hazardous, outflow, praiseworthiness,* and *refreshing*. Among the coinages which did not catch on are *disinvite, endamask, hangworthy, rageful,* and *triflingness*. He seemed to have a particular liking for compounds beginning with *well*, such as *well-choosing, well-created, well-defended, well-followed, well-framed, well-inclined, well-liked, well-met, well-succeeding,* and *well-trusted*.

- Edmund Spenser has over 500 attributions. Among those which entered the language are *amenable, baneful, blandishment, cheerless, chirruping, dismay, heart-piercing, heedless, indignant, jovial, lambkin, lawlessness, life-blood, suffused, tambourine, thrilling,* and *violin*. Among those which did not are *avengeress, disadventurous, jolliment, schoolery,* and *weetless* 'meaningless'. He had a great liking for new adjectives in *-ful*, adding it to verbs as well as the more usual nouns, but hardly any survived:

  adviceful, avengeful, baneful, chanceful, choiceful, corruptful, deviceful, discordful, dislikeful, dueful, dureful, entreatful, gazeful, grudgeful, groanful, listful, mazeful, rewardful, sdeignful, senseful, spoilful, toilful, tradeful, tuneful, vauntful, wreckful

Spenser is a good example of how an individual author's stylistic preferences do not always have a permanent effect on a language. There can be a big gap between what an author wants to say and what the community thinks is routinely worth saying.

- Quantitatively, the playwright and satirist Thomas Nashe comes closest to Shakespeare, with nearly 800 attributions, but the majority of his creations were, like Marston's, too ink-horn in character to have had a general appeal, for they quickly fell out of use. Typical of his style are:

adequation, apophthegmatical, baggagery, clientry, collachrymate ('accompany with weeping'), confectionate, discernance, intermedium, oblivionize

I personally regret the passing of some Nashisms: there ought to be a place in Modern English for *bodgery* 'botched work', *tongueman* 'good speaker', and *chatmate* ('person to gossip with' – a word ripe for Internet rediscovery), and there have been times when I could have used *sparrow-blasting* ('being blighted with a mysterious power of whose existence one is sceptical'). Among the lexemes which did succeed are:

Chaucerism, conundrum, grandiloquent, harlequin, impecunious, Latinize, Mediterranean, memorize, multifarious, plausibility, seminary, silver-tongued, terminate, transitoriness

They include some of the more frequently used words of educated discussion. But some everyday and down-to-earth items are also attributed to him, such as *balderdash*, *earthling* (for which science-fiction writers should ever give thanks), *helter-skelter*, *motherhood*, *cum-twang* (a term of contempt), *ninny-hammer* ('simpleton'), *temptress*, and *windfucker* (a name for the kestrel, though soon after used as a generalized insult). Only Shakespeare exceeds Nashe in the quantity and range of his lexical innovation.

- Finally, by way of comparison, here are all the items which have a first recorded usage in the King James Bible of 1611, including the marginal notes and the translators' Preface. Two of them (marked with *) also appear in the translations to entries in Randall Cotgrave's 1611 *Dictionarie of the French and English tongues*:

abased (as an adjective), accurately, afflicting (as a noun), almug 'algum tree', anywhither, armour-bearer, backsliding (as an adjective), battering-ram, Benjamite, catholicon, confessing (as a noun), crowning (as an adjective), dissolver, dogmatize, epitomist, escaper, espoused (as an adjective), euroclydon (type of wind), exactress, expansion, free-woman, Galilean (as a noun), gopher, Gothic (as an adjective), granddaughter, Hamathite, infallibility,* Laodicean (as noun), lapful, light-minded, maneh (Hebrew unit of account), moistening (as a noun), narrowing (as a noun), night-hawk, nose-jewel, oil-tree, omer (unit of capacity), onewhere, oppressing (as an adjective), palmchrist, panary 'pantry', pannag (type of confection), phrasing (as a noun), pruning-hook, putrefying (as an adjective), respecter, retractate 'retract', ring-straked 'colour-banded', rosebud, rose of Sharon, Sauromatian, shittah (type of tree), skewed, taloned* (as an adjective), way-mark 'traveller guide'

The total is small (fifty-five) because of the conservative bias of the translators, and because many of the distinctive lexemes had already been introduced by previous translators, notably Wycliffe and Tyndale (p. 273).

The story continues

It is time to leave lexeme counting behind – and indeed to return the *lexeme* to its linguistic cage, as for most purposes the everyday term *word* is unambiguous. Word counts, despite the fascination they seem to exercise on the popular imagination, are not as illuminating as people think. They are extremely crude ways of characterizing an author's linguistic creativity, are usually serious over- or under-estimates, and have a limited impact on the language as a whole. Admittedly, when a well-known author uses a word in a work which ends up being read by many people, it may influence its frequency of use, or even give it a presence which it would not otherwise have received (as seen in the Romantic revival of Shakespearisms, p. 323). But for the most part an author's words join others in the melting-pot of an age's linguistic consciousness, and emerge in a later age having been shaped by countless other intuitions.

Word counts also distract attention from other aspects of an author's language and style which are much more important for an understanding of creative identity. What counts is not what you use, but the way that you use it. Linguistic originality is much less a matter of creating new words and much more a matter of taking familiar words and doing fresh things with them. This book is about the development of the language as a whole, and is not an account of the linguistic creativity of individual authors, but the principle is the same. If we look at the Shakespearean expressions which have achieved an idiomatic or quasi-proverbial status in the language (see panel 13.3), we find hardly any employing the neologisms discussed in the previous section (the exceptions are *bated, be-all, dickens, end-all, foregone,* and *green-eyed*). And when we look for striking uses of language, there is far less to be said about Shakespeare's use of *appertainment* and *assassination* than there is about his *grace me no grace, and uncle me no uncle* (*Richard II*, II.iii.86).

13.3 Influencing idioms

The longer the utterance, the easier it is to show the influence of an individual writer on the language. This list shows many of Shakespeare's phrases and sentences which – often after some modification – have become part of general English idiomatic expression. Some of the expressions must have been in prior proverbial use, as we know from the Nurse's comment in *Romeo and Juliet*: 'if ye should lead her in a fool's paradise, as they say . . .'; but their use in Shakespeare certainly gave them an unprecedented public hearing.

your lord and master (*All's Well that Ends Well*, II.iii.185)
my salad days (*Antony and Cleopatra*, I.v.73)
it beggared all description (*Antony and Cleopatra*, II.ii.203)
she . . . hath at fast and loose beguiled me (*Antony and Cleopatra*, IV.xii.28)
we have seen better days (*As You Like It*, II.vii.121)
neither rhyme nor reason (*As You Like It*, III.ii.381)
can one desire too much of a good thing (*As You Like It*, IV.i.112)
the game is up (*Cymbeline*, III.iii.107)
I have not slept one wink (*Cymbeline*, III.iv.102)
in my mind's eye (*Hamlet*, I.ii.185)
more in sorrow than in anger (*Hamlet*, I.ii.232)
I doubt some foul play (*Hamlet*, I.ii.256)
I am . . . to the manner born (*Hamlet*, I.iv.15)
brevity is the soul of wit (*Hamlet*, II.ii.90)
'twas caviare to the general (*Hamlet*, II.ii.435)
hold . . . the mirror up to nature (*Hamlet*, III.ii.22)
I must be cruel only to be kind (*Hamlet*, III.iv.179)
to have the engineer hoist with his own petard (*Hamlet*, III.iv.208)
I'll send him packing (*Henry IV Part 1*, II.iv.290)
tell truth and shame the devil (*Henry IV Part 1*, III.i.55)
set my teeth . . . on edge (*Henry IV Part 1*, III.i.127)
thy wish was father . . . to that thought (*Henry IV Part 2*, IV.v.93)
give the devil his due (*Henry V*, III.vii.113)
knit his brows (*Henry VI Part 2*, I.ii.3)
dead as a door-nail (*Henry VI Part 2*, IV.x.38)
be it as it may (*Henry VI Part 3*, I.i.194)
it was Greek to me (*Julius Caesar*, I.ii.281)
I never stood on ceremonies (*Julius Caesar*, II.ii.13)
play fast and loose (*King John*, III.i.242)
I beg cold comfort (*King John*, V.vii.42)
more sinned against than sinning (*King Lear*, III.ii.60)
the be-all and the end-all (*Macbeth* I.vii.5)
stretch out to the crack of doom (*Macbeth*, IV.i.116)
at one fell swoop (*Macbeth*, IV.iii.218)

all our yesterdays (*Macbeth*, V.v.22)
with bated breath (*The Merchant of Venice*, I.iii.121)
in the end, truth will out (*The Merchant of Venice*, II.ii.74)
mine own flesh and blood (*The Merchant of Venice*, II.ii.85)
love is blind (*The Merchant of Venice*, II.vi.36)
a blinking idiot (*The Merchant of Venice*, II.ix.54)
green-eyed jealousy (*The Merchant of Venice*, III.ii.110)
let us not be laughing-stocks (*The Merry Wives of Windsor*, III.i.77)
what the dickens (*The Merry Wives of Windsor*, III.ii.17)
as good luck would have it (*The Merry Wives of Windsor*, III.v.76)
pomp and circumstance (*Othello*, III.iii.351)
a foregone conclusion (*Othello*, III.iii.425)
make a short shrift (*Richard III*, III.iv.95)
I dance attendance here (*Richard III*, III.vii.56)
a tower of strength (*Richard III*, V.iii.12)
if ye should lead her in a fool's paradise (*Romeo and Juliet*, II.iii.155)
I'll not budge an inch (*The Taming of the Shrew*, Induction I.12)
the more fool you (*The Taming of the Shrew*, V.ii.128)
keep a good tongue in your head (*The Tempest*, III.ii.34)
melted . . . into thin air (*The Tempest*, IV.i.150)
I have been in such a pickle (*The Tempest*, V.i.282)
the incarnate devil (*Titus Andronicus*, V.i.40)
a good riddance (*Troilus and Cressida*, II.i.119)
'tis but early days (*Troilus and Cressida*, IV.v.12)
'tis fair play (e.g., *Troilus and Cressida*, V.iii.43)
you will laugh yourselves into stitches (*Twelfth Night*, III.ii.64)
make a virtue of necessity (*The Two Gentlemen of Verona*, IV.i.62)
with bag and baggage (*The Winter's Tale*, I.ii.206)

This last example illustrates again (p. 303) the important process of word creation through changing a word from one word class (part of speech) into another – what is often called *conversion* or *functional shift*. It is something which many Jacobethan authors experiment with, and some constructions – such as the one used by the duke of York in *Richard II* – are repeatedly encountered:

Thank me no thankings, nor proud me no prouds (*Romeo and Juliet*, III.v.152)

Philip Massinger uses it several times in *A New Way to Pay Old Debts* (published in 1633)

Cause me no causes (I.iii)
Virgin me no virgins (III.ii)
End me no ends (V.i)

It turns up regularly in the work of other dramatists:

> O me no O's (Ben Jonson, *The Case is Altered*, V.i)
> Pancridge me no Pancridge (Ben Jonson, *A Tale of a Tub*, II.i)
> Sir me no sirs (Lewis Machin, *The Dumb Knight*, III.i)
> Vow me no vows (Beaumont and Fletcher, *Wit without Money*, IV.iv)

It threads its way through later English literature:

> Petition me no petitions (Henry Fielding, *Tom Thumb*, 1730, I.ii)
> Map me no maps (Henry Fielding, *Rape upon Rape*, 1730, I.v)
> Play me no plays (Samuel Foote, *The Knights*, 1749, II)
> Diamond me no diamonds . . . prize me no prizes (Tennyson, *Launcelot and Elaine*, 1859, ll. 502–4)

And it continues to be used today. *Poem Me No Poems* is the title of a Web site collection of poetry. *But Me No Buts* is the name of a 2001 punk rock group. This group's self-exposé contains the comment: 'Our name comes from a line that i read in a book i have long since forgotten (possibly by Clive Barker).' This may be so, but the ancestry of the construction long predates that fantasy author.

Functional shift is one of the features which makes the English language distinctive. Virtually any word class can be shifted to any other, but most writers content themselves to a noun > verb conversion, as in all the above examples except one – Old Capulet's use of the adjective *proud* as a verb. In Shakespeare we see a much wider range of shift opportunities being exploited, as this further selection illustrates:

> adverb > noun: Thou losest *here*, a better *where* to find (*King Lear*, I.i.261)
> adverb > verb: they . . . from their own misdeeds *askance* their eyes (*Lucrece*, l. 637)
> numeral > verb: what man / *Thirds* his own worth (*The Two Noble Kinsmen*, I.ii.96)
> verb > adjective: he . . . / Nor dignifies an *impair* thought with breath (*Troilus and Cressida*, IV.v.103)
> verb > noun: Achievement is command; ungained, *beseech* (*Troilus and Cressida*, I.ii.293)[14]

And even in the common category, of noun > verb conversions, we see a much more daring use of the option, involving a remarkable range of semantic types of noun – proper names, categories of people, animals, body-parts, behavioural descriptions, locations, and abstract nouns:

> Petruchio is *Kated* (*The Taming of the Shrew*, III.ii.244)
> She *Phebes* me (*As You Like It*, IV.iii.40)

he *childed* as I *fathered* (*King Lear*, III.vi.108)
The hearts / That *spanieled* me at heels (*Antony and Cleopatra*, IV.xii.21)
a hand that kings have *lipped* (*Antony and Cleopatra*, II.v.30)
Dost *dialogue* with thy shadow? (*Timon of Athens*, II.ii.55)
his discernings are *lethargied* (*King Lear*, I.iv.225)
give us the bones . . . that we may *chapel* them (*The Two Noble Kinsmen*, I.i.50)
whilst you do *climate* here (*The Winter's Tale*, V.i.169)
if her fortunes ever stood *necessitied* to help (*All's Well that Ends Well*, V.iii.85)

Vividly expressive literary conversions, such as those used by Shakespeare, tend not to become standard usage: we do not usually *jaw* or *ear* people. The common conversions in use today (such as *to father* or *to arm*) have a history that long predates Shakespeare. What these usages illustrate is an imaginative extension of a general process rooted deep within the language. They show people being linguistically daring. And Shakespeare, above all, shows us how to dare with language. It is our main linguistic legacy from the Jacobethan age.

Interlude 13
Avoiding transcriptional anaemia

Language histories spend much of their space illustrating their points from writing of literary merit. The emphasis is understandable. Anyone interested in language is bound to respond to the magnetic pull of imaginative writing, which explores a wider range of linguistic expressiveness than any other genre, and offers an unparelleled diversity of analytical challenges. It is a delight to explore the development of a usage in, say, a Shakespeare play, because even though attention is focused on the linguistic dimension, there is always another level of consciousness which appreciates the text as a work of art, and greedily assimilates the pinpricks of illumination that the linguistic perspective can provide.

At the same time, it is important to step back, every now and again, and recognize that literature is but the icing on a huge linguistic cake. It is impossible to put a figure on what counts as 'literature' in a culture, but even if we give it its broadest definition – going beyond the imaginative to include intellectual essays, memoirs, biographies, speeches, sermons, and other genres – we have to recognize that it comprises only a very small amount compared to a language's total tally of daily spoken communication. And even if we restrict ourselves to the written medium, the combined output of all 'authors' writing in a language in a given year is only going to be a fraction of the year's total output from all written genres, most of which is ephemeral in character.

Ephemeral writing is the oil which keeps a society's daily encounter with literacy running smoothly. It includes most of the letters and emails we send and receive, postcards, Christmas and birthday cards, newsletters, note-taking, and a great deal of self-information and personal organizational texts, such as shopping lists, diary notes, filofaxes, and computer notebooks. At a business level, it includes more letters and emails, faxes, memos, minutes, agendas, stock lists, planners, order forms, notices, flyers, advertisements, reports, proposals, presentations, and a huge range of informational texts. At a social institutional level, it includes all items from organizations of government (national and local), law, religion, the forces, charities, leisure bodies, and societies. At an educational level, it includes essays, prospectuses, timetables, course information, lecture notes, exam papers and answers, notices, and museum leaflets. Transactionally, it includes transport tickets, parking tickets, theatre programmes, membership cards, and all kinds of permits. It includes daily newspapers and weekly magazines, most chat-room interaction, and the bulk of the World Wide Web.

Very little of this has ever been studied, in the history of a language. Most of it, by its nature, has been lost. Certain types of records (political and legal proceedings, in particular) might be carefully collected for potential future reference, but are usually stored away. A practical reason for choosing literary texts for study is that they are simply much more readily available. And in the early period of English, it is virtually all we have to go on. Only a scattering of wills, charters, and other ephemera have survived from Old English.

However, from the early Middle Ages, the amount of routine documentation significantly increases, beginning with Domesday Book (p. 121). National and local records begin to be kept, and more material survives involving a wider range of people. Defendants, witnesses, constables, judges, and others are reported in court proceedings. Several members of a family interact in letter sequences (p. 178) – displaying what have sometimes been called 'familects'. Organizations of all kinds keep regular accounts (p. 140). Facets of domestic life – such as health remedies and recipes (p. 153) – come to be written down. There are more minutes, more wills, more memoirs. An increasing amount is becoming accessible via the Web and the occasional anthology. The deficiency is no longer in the data but in the scholars available to analyse it.

And, it has to be said, in the states of mind willing to analyse it. For there is still a curious reluctance to take seriously genres of language written in anything other than the more formal varieties or sanctioned by a criterion of literary excellence. If a court record, for example, uses colloquial, dialectal or informal English, or if it contains inconsistencies and errors (as shown by manuscript crossings-out), for some people this is enough to make it an unworthy object of linguistic study. Or, if the text is to be used, it is silently emended so that inconsistencies are eradicated, changes of mind eliminated, abbreviations expanded, informal contractions filled out, dialectisms replaced, and spelling, punctuation, grammar, and vocabulary generally brought into line with the editor's conception of what counts as 'correct' English. In such ways is the linguistic life-blood of an original manuscript sucked out, and its real character hidden from public view.

It is understandable that people interested only in the core content of what a text says – such as historians, or professionals interested in the history of ideas of their subject[15] – should wish to remove from it anything which would act as a barrier to comprehension. But for anyone interested in the history of their language, such sanitization is unacceptable. And even historians in general take a great risk, for so much information is lost when manuscripts are presented in an anaemic transcription.

The extract in panel 13.4 is taken from Bridget Cusack's invaluable anthology of 'everyday' Early Modern English, and illustrates the dynamic character both of the transcription and of the people it reports.[16] It is a courtroom clerk's record (in 1615) of a witness's account of an alleged defamation of character between a William Delve and a Hugh Mill and his wife Elinor. The language is a fascinating mix of legal and colloquial styles, at one extreme using such formal and formulaic locutions as *the said* and *deponent* (i.e., the person making the deposition) and at the other reporting everyday vocabulary (*to doe with*, *whore*) and syntax (*hast minde, wentes to leache, thancke mee for it*). The two styles meld in such phrases as *as farre as this deponent ever hearde*, which presumably is a transcription of 'as far as I ever heard'.

13.4 A courtroom record

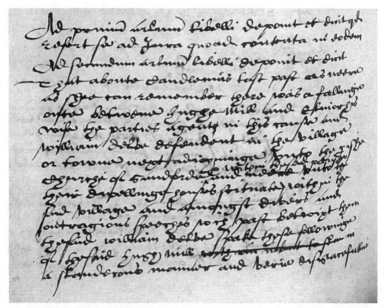

Transcription conventions
{ } indicates words written above the line as an afterthought
italics (as in agent*es*) show the expansion of a word which is abbreviated in the manuscript
strikethroughs (as in ~~do~~) show forms which the clerk crossed out in the manuscript
[ ] enclose glosses of unfamiliar words

The first few lines of the translation can be seen in the photograph, commencing at line 4.

. . . aboute Candlemas last past as neere as shee can remember there was a fallinge oute betwene Hughe Mill and Elinor his wife the parties agent*es* in this cause [the people bringing the suit in this case] and William delve defendent in t̶h̶ their village or towne next adioyninge vnto the p*a*rishe Churche of Sundforde {& within the said paryshe} and neere vnto the dwellinge houses situate within the said village and amongst divers and outragious speches wch past betwixt them thesaid william delve spake these followinge of thesaid Hugh mill w̶i̶t̶h̶ ̶a̶n̶ ̶i̶n̶t̶e̶n̶t̶ ̶t̶o̶ ̶s̶l̶a̶ in a slanderous manner and verie disgracefullie v*i*d*elicet* [that is to say] Thou arte no Cuckolde holdinge oute two of his fingers to thesaide Mill in the manner of hornes, Then thesaid Hughe Mill demanded of thesaide delue what hee meante therby and why hee did so, and delve scoffinglie replied againe thou arte no cuckolde poyntinge at the said Hughe Mill, sayenge that hee did give fortie suche armes [gestures] in a yeare as thesaid hornes were wch hee made and shewed to thesaid Mill with his fingers, and this deponente verilie belieueth that the saide delve meante by poyntinge vnto thesaid Mill in suche sorte with his two fingers as before shee d̶o̶ hath deposed that Hugh mill was a Cuckolde and his Wife an vnhonest [immoral] woman and she saith that it is so generallie vnderstoode of all as farre as this deponent ever hearde v̶p̶ ̶t̶h̶a̶t̶ ̶a̶n̶y̶o̶n̶e̶ when one man poynt*es* to another in suche sorte with his fingers that is a married man ffurther Hughe mill saide vnto thesaid delve I thinke I have an honest woman to my wife, vnto wch d̶l̶e̶ delve replied thou mayst thancke mee for it for I might have had to doe with her if I wolde, for shee vntrussed my poynt*es* [unfastened my hose-laces] and then hee spake vnto A̶g̶n̶ Elinor Mill Hughe Mills wife hast minde [do you recall] when thou vntrust my poynt*es* and thou quothe the said delve speakinge still vnto thesaid Elinnor wentes to leache [doctor] for thyne vncomlie [indecent] part*es* and neither [nether] part*es* meaninge therby a̶s̶ ̶t̶h̶i̶s̶ that shee was a whore and that shee had bin cured of some filthie disease . . .

Even a minimal amount of standardization (such as the omission of alterations, and the use of punctuation and capital letters) can significantly alter the style of a passage. Here is an edited version of the last few sentences:

> Ffurther, Hughe Mill said vnto the said Delve, 'I thinke I have an honest woman to my wife,' vnto which Delve replied, 'Thou mayst thancke mee for it, for I might have had to doe with her if I wolde, for shee vntrussed my poyntes.' And then hee spake vnto Elinor Mill, Hughe Mill's wife: 'Hast minde when thou vntrust my poyntes, and thou' – quothe the said Delve speakinge still vnto the said Elinor – 'wentes to leache for thyne vncomlie partes and neither partes?', meaninge therby that shee was a whore and that shee had bin cured of some filthie disease . . .

If, in addition, the spelling were modernized, and the grammar regularized (e.g., *hast a mind*, *went to a leech*), as often happens in quoting from historical documents, the effect would be to distance us from the original even more. The differences will not always be very significant, of course; but often they can seriously influence the way we interpret a text, affecting the way we judge a speaker's status or credibility, and perhaps even altering our sense of its authorship or authenticity.

Chapter 14 Dialect fallout

The linguistic climate of a community changes as a standard language grows. Before a standard arrives, and is recognized as such, there is actually no justification at all for talking about usage as being 'nonstandard'. Dialect forms, colloquialisms, class-restricted slang, divergent spellings, and alternative conventions of capitalization and punctuation, even if they provoke attitudes, are no more than variations reflecting the society's diverse structure and differing practices. Only when one dialect achieves a special social position, associated with power and prestige, and begins to be described using such terms as 'correct', 'proper', and 'educated', can we really justify referring to other varieties as *nonstandard*. Even then, this is an academic attempt to use an unemotional designator. The opposite of 'standard' for most people is not 'nonstandard': it is 'substandard'. The nonstandard varieties – the regional varieties, in particular – become ridiculed and condemned.

There was no necessary inferiority complex attached to dialect variation in Shakespeare's time. Indeed, there are some famous cases of people achieving the highest positions in society while retaining their regional speech. A contemporary of Walter Ralegh, the judge Sir Thomas Malet, observed:

> that notwithstanding his so great mastership in style, and his conversation with the learnedest and politest persons, yet he spoke broad Devonshire to his dyeing day.[1]

And when James I of England (and VI of Scotland) and his entourage arrived in London, they brought their Scottish way of talking with them. Francis Bacon describes James' speech as 'swift and cursory, and in the full dialect of his country', and Sir John Oglander describes the reaction of the crowds flocking to see the king: 'Then he would cry out in Scottish, "God's wounds! I will pull down my breeches and they shall also see my arse." '[2] Although there was considerable anti-Scottish sentiment at the time, we can imagine it would not have been wise to pass remarks about the king's accent – at least, not within his hearing.

Although negative attitudes were growing (p. 343), there was no universal assumption that regional accents and dialects portrayed people who were uneducated or naively provincial or both. The speech forms were just distinctive, reflecting a particular part of the country. If a comedy rustic was portrayed on stage with a rustic accent, people might laugh at his rural ways, attitudes, and behaviour, but not at his speech as such. They would expect a rustic to speak in a rustic way. It would be the character – and especially the pretentious character who tries to speak 'above himself' – which would provoke the laughter. Indeed, although someone like Constable Dogberry, in *Much Ado About Nothing*, is usually portrayed in a rural accent, there would be nothing to stop an actor presenting him in some other way. The humour would be the same. Here is Dogberry, responding with malaproprietorial pomposity to Conrade's calling him an ass:

> Dost thou not suspect my place? Dost thou not suspect my years? O that he [the Sexton] were here to write me down an ass! But masters, remember that I am an ass; though it be not written down, yet forget not that I am an ass. No, thou villain, thou art full of piety, as shall be proved upon thee by good witness. I am a wise fellow, and, which is more, an officer; and, which is more, a householder; and, which is more, as pretty a piece of flesh as any is in Messina; and one that knows the law, go to; and a rich fellow enough, go to; and a fellow that hath had losses; and one that hath two gowns and everything handsome about him. Bring him away. O that I had been writ down an ass!

There is in fact nothing regional about this speech. Today, we read in extra values, depending on whether the character is acted as rural or urban, northern or southern, English or Celtic. These were not the values in Shakespeare's time. Richard Carew, in *The Excellencie of the English Tongue* (printed in 1614), sums up the variety and the attitude in one sentence:

> the Copiousnes of our Languadge appeareth in the diuersitye of our dialectes, for wee haue court, and wee haue countrye Englishe, wee haue Northern and Southerne, grosse and ordinary, which differ ech from other, not only in the terminacions, but alsoe in many wordes, termes, and phrases, and expresse the same thinges in diuers sortes, yeat all right Englishe alike.

Yet all are right English alike.

We have to disregard the widespread modern way of thinking, which rejects that last sentence out of hand, if we are to evaluate correctly Shakespeare's dialect speakers. There are not many of these, but they are by no means uneducated yokels. We have already seen how the Northern dialect in *The Reeve's Tale* is given to college students (p. 163). The people in Shakespeare's most famous dialect scene are educated, too – in *Henry V* (III.ii), where we find a dialogue between Welsh, Irish, and Scots captains.[3] Fluellen, Macmorris, and

Jamy are labelled respectively, in the First Folio, simply as *Welch*, *Irish*, and *Scot*, and they are represented as speaking to some extent in a regional way. (The English captain, Gower, is simply called *Gower*, and his speeches display no features that might be considered as nonstandard.) But while their regional origins are the source of the humorous dimension of the scene, they are also portrayed as well educated – intellectual, even, in the case of Fluellen:

> Captain Macmorris, I beseech you now, will you vouchsafe me, look you, a few disputations with you, as partly touching or concerning the disciplines of the war, the Roman wars, in the way of argument, look you, and friendly communication? Partly to satisfy my opinion and partly for the satisfaction, look you, of my mind.

This would not have been unusual for Elizabethan captains. The rank was prestigious. Senior company commanders, knights, and nobles (Talbot, Falstaff, Alençon) could be 'captains', and the notion of leadership involved could even allow the term to be applied to royalty (as when the Chorus describes Henry V himself as a 'royal captain').

It is difficult to read or hear this scene today without inserting modern values, and seeing the regional characters as comic simply because of the way they speak. But there is no difference between Gower and the others in that respect. The captains are equal in status and dramatic role; their regional diversity is generally taken to symbolize the way King Henry was uniting a kingdom in a glorious cause. If we are meant to laugh at Fluellen, it is primarily because of his explosive temperament and his obsession with military history. His Welshisms reflect the honest enthusiasm of a non-native speaker, and if they make us laugh (as doubtless they did at the time), it is a sympathetic, not malevolent, laughter. Shakespeare did not poke fun at a person's natural language of expression, at a native accent and dialect. He chose as his main target people who put on linguistic airs and graces, who tried to be what they were not, and who used language as part of the affectation. It is the pretentiousness of the speech which makes him satirize the courtier Osric (in *Hamlet*) or the pedant Holofernes and the braggart Don Armado (in *Love's Labour's Lost*). People who try to use big words and get them wrong are a target, too – as in the case of Mistress Quickly, Dogberry, Bottom, and Launcelot Gobbo. And foreigners from outside Britain attempting to speak English, as we shall see, were felt to be fair game. But regional speech as such was not. I would not expect it to be otherwise, in a writer of real insight.

However, not everyone maintained the linguistic egalitarianism of Carew and Shakespeare. Indeed, from the early 1500s we can see a growing association between the use of regional dialect and several demeaning social values. There had been little sign of this earlier: medieval comments about regional speech had focused on its unpleasantness to the ear or its relative unintelligibility (p. 168), but in the sixteenth century we find a different set of connotations emerging. For example, following Caxton's translation of *Æsop's Fables* in 1484, a new genre of story-books evolved, many of them translations from European languages, but also including home-grown collections such as *A Hundred Mery Talys* (1526). They have come to be called *jest-books* – a term which had a much broader meaning in Early Modern English than it has today (p. 136), including short tales which were entertaining rather than simply humorous. They often involved characters from outside London, as can be seen from some of the titles: 'Of the Welshman that confessed him he had slain a friar', 'Of the northern man that was all heart'. The stories introduce the reader to the behaviour of a range of provincial characters, many of whom are portrayed as naive, simple-minded, ignorant, or untrustworthy, and thus inculcate a set of negative attitudes about rural folk which would in due course come to be associated with the way they spoke. Dialect speech is introduced only sporadically, such as when a Welshman is presented as cursing with *Cot's bloot* instead of *God's blood*, or a rustic is made to say *chadde* or *ich hadde* for *I hadde*. But even a sprinkling of dialect forms, in such a widely read context, is enough to help form a climate of opinion (see further, panel 14.1).

14.1 Accent and dialect

The growing awareness and use of regional variation in the sixteenth century eventually manifested itself in terminology, notably in the arrival in English of the words *dialect* and *accent*. *Accent* came first, from Latin via French, recorded in 1538 in a very general sense of 'tone of voice' or 'pronunciation': call with a 'timorous accent', Iago tells Roderigo, in the opening scene of *Othello* (I.i.75). And from the 1580s we find writers such as Sidney and Spenser using it with reference to the accentual beat of poetry and to the diacritical marks used to represent it.

Shakespeare, typically (p. 321), takes the word in different directions. He uses the plural form in *Julius Caesar* to mean a spoken language as a whole, when Cassius ruminates about the way Caesar's assassination will one day be represented (III.i.112):

How many ages hence
Shall this our lofty scene be acted over,
In states unborn and accents yet unknown!

And in the singular Shakespeare is the first recorded user in the general sense of this book – a manner of pronunciation typical of a person or social group. The locus is *As You Like It* (III.ii.328), when Orlando meets the disguised Rosalind in the Forest of Arden, and finds her speech unexpectedly non-rustic:

ORLANDO Are you native of this place?

ROSALIND As the coney [rabbit] that you see dwell where she is kindled.

ORLANDO Your accent is something finer than you could purchase in so removed a dwelling.

ROSALIND I have been told so of many; but indeed an old religious uncle of mine taught me to speak, who was in his youth an inland man.

Her explanation gets her out of trouble, and incidentally provides historical socio-linguists with an indication of the way town and country accents were coming to be polarized.

Dialect, referring to the whole manner of speaking typical of a person or group – including grammar and vocabulary as well as pronunciation – is also a borrowing from Latin via French, first recorded in the dedication to Spenser's *Shepheardes Calender* (1579). The notion of a dialect as a variety of a language – with a first hint of a subordinate status – is also present from the 1570s, when a writer talks of 'Hebrew dialects'. And there is a third usage, in which the term was used for *dialectic* – a confusion which may still be heard today, when people talk of *dialectical* (instead of *dialectal*) variation.

By the early 1600s, the term must have become so familiar that it was possible to begin playing with it, as Shakespeare does in *Measure for Measure*, when Claudio hopes that his sister Isabella will intercede for him with deputy-duke Angelo (I.ii.170):

> for in her youth
> There is a prone and speechless dialect
> Such as move men.

And in *King Lear*, we even find it becoming part of the discussion almost as a standard technical term. The disguised Duke of Kent, now in Lear's service, has given Regan's steward Oswald a beating. When asked why, he says bluntly, 'His countenance likes me not' (II.ii.87), and when Cornwall remonstrates with him, he adds ''tis my occupation to be plain'. Cornwall is having none of this, and condemns Kent's bluntness as the speech of a crafty and corrupt knave. This provokes Kent into a 'high style' response which so takes Cornwall aback that he interrupts:

> KENT
> Sir, in good faith, in sincere verity,
> Under th'allowance of your great aspect
> Whose influence like the wreath of radiant fire
> On flickering Phoebus' front –
> CORNWALL
> What mean'st by this?

Kent then switches into prose, to say that there is more to him than his plain speech shows. The implication is that anyone who can switch between high and low styles cannot be a knave.

> KENT To go out of my dialect which you discommend so much. I know, sir, I am no flatterer. He that beguiled you in a plain accent was a plain knave; which, for my part, I will not be, though I should win your displeasure to entreat me to't.
>
> This is *accent* and *dialect* both being used metalinguistically, it seems for the first time, in English literature.

In any case, the jest-books were not alone. Between Chaucer and Shakespeare, an increasing amount of dialect representation appeared in English literature. This was a perfectly natural development. We do not have to wait for the arrival of a standard before we can start representing regional speech. There was no Standard English in Chaucer's day, yet the dialect features are there in *The Reeve's Tale* clearly enough. And during the fifteenth and sixteenth centuries we see a slow, sporadic, but increasing utilization of dialect features in prose, poetry, and plays, as authors became more aware of the possibilities and a broader coverage of subject-matter offered fresh opportunities to exploit them. Several of these works experimented with dialect forms. For example, as early as 1505–6 we find the Suffolk poet Stephen Hawes writing a long poem of nearly 6,000 lines called *The Passetyme of Pleasure*, which was printed by Wynkyn de Worde. The narrator-hero, Graund Amour, having met Lady Fame, falls in love with La Bel Pucelle, and travels to the tower of Doctrine, where he receives instruction from – appropriately enough – Lady Grammar. The language displays no regional features until Graund Amour meets a foolish dwarf, a despiser of women, Godfrey Gobylyve, who lives in Kent and who introduces himself in a local dialect:

> 'Sotheych,' quod he, 'whan I cham in Kent
> At home I cham though I be hyther sent.
> I cham a gentylman of moche noble kynne
> Though Iche be cladde in a knaues skynne.'

The crucial point, for the present book, is that by his own admission he has a knave's skin. He also comes from Kent, which in those days was a part of the country known for its low life, roughness, and rebelliousness (the Peasants' Revolt had begun there in 1381, and Jack Cade had styled himself 'Captain of Kent' in 1450). The implication is obvious. Dialect speech = trouble-maker.

Forms such as *I cham* and *sotheych* ('soothly') identify the speech as regional – though they are not used very consistently, even in this short extract, and they are not specifically restricted to Kent. The *ch* forms were in fact more associated with the south-west of England, but by the middle of the sixteenth century they had become a stereotyped marker of dialect speech from any locality – much as today *ain't* is a nonstandard feature which could originate in any part of the English-speaking world. In Thomas Deloney's novel *Jack of Newbury* (1597), the hero's parents-in-law are from Buckinghamshire, but they say such things as *chill giue you twenty Nobles*. And the elderly nurse Madge Mumblecrust slips into this 'stage dialect' briefly in Nicholas Udall's *Ralph Roister Doister* (*c.* 1550), when she excitedly takes up Ralph's offer of a kiss.

> ROISTER DOISTER ... mistress nurse, I will kiss you for acquaintance.
> MUMBLECRUST I come anon, sir.
> TALKAPACE Faith, I would our dame Custance saw this gear! [business]
> MUMBLECRUST I must first wipe all clean, yea, I must.
> TALKAPACE I'll 'chieve it, doting fool, but it must be cust! [kissed]
> MUMBLECRUST
>> God 'ield you, sir! Chad [I had] not so much i-chotte [I know] not whan [when], Ne'er since chwas [I was] born, chwine [I believe], of such a gay gentleman!

Madge's surname suggests someone with a speaking problem – it hints at a lack of teeth – but she lacks the malapropisms of her later alter-ego, the Nurse in *Romeo and Juliet*, and there is no other sign of an impediment. As she normally speaks in a non-regional way, the switch to a dialect is perhaps due to her forgetting herself, in the heat of the kissing moment, and betraying her origins. It wouldn't be the first or last time for an accent to go out of control. Duke Theseus reports that his arrival could put clerks into such a state of confusion that they 'Throttle their practised accent in their fears' (*A Midsummer Night's Dream*, V.i.97). Here, dialect speech = artlessness.

Early representations of literary dialect tend to be isolated moments in an otherwise non-regional text. Even in plays where the use of local accents must have been routine, such as for rustic and wicked characters in the cycles of mystery plays, there is little sign of anything regional in the writing. Just occasionally, we see some dialect features, and in one case they are actually commented upon (p. 247). But during the sixteenth century, the presence of dialect becomes more noticeable. The morality plays and interludes offered greater scope for a contrast between non-regional and regional speech, as they generally presented a confrontation between good and evil through the allegorical personification of abstract qualities such as Vice, Mercy, Knowledge, and Good Deeds. And whenever these characters were portrayed as dialect speakers, the distinctive features appear more consistently in what they say.

A good example of dialect presence can be seen in the character of People in a political morality play generally ascribed to Nicholas Udall, *Respublica*, which was performed by a troupe of boys in 1553 to celebrate Queen Mary's accession. People speaks in a stylized stage dialect throughout – and is also clownish and ignorant in behaviour. He calls the lady Respublica 'Rice puddingcake' as soon as he arrives on stage (III.iii), and when Adulacion claims not to know such a person, People replies (punctuation and capitalization have been modernized):

> PEOPLE Masse, youe liest valeslye in your harte. She is this waie. Che wart [warrant] a false harlot youe arte.
>
> ADULACION I knowe Respublica.
>
> PEOPLE Yea, marie, whare is shee?
>
> ADULACION She is buisie nowe.
>
> PEOPLE Masse, ere iche goe chill hir zee [before I go I'll see her], for this waie she came.

The *ch* forms are apparent again, as is the voicing of initial consonants typical of the West Country (p. 129) – *falsely* becoming *valeslye*, *see* becoming *zee*. It is not entirely consistent (e.g., *for* remains *for*, not *vor*), but it is enough to contrast the two kinds of speech, and it characterizes everything People says.

A similar stylization is found in the character of Ignorance in John Redford's *Wit and Science* (*c*. 1550). Idleness calls him in, and asks him to spell his name.

> IDLENESS Go to, than; spell me thilt same. Wher was thou borne?
>
> IGNORANCE 'Chwas ibore [born] in Ingland, Mother sed.
>
> IDLENESS In Ingland?
>
> IGNORANCE Yea.

There is then a long dialogue in which Idleness tries to teach Ignorance the word *England* using his fingers and thumbs, and then his name. When he finally does it,

> IDLENESS How'ayst now, foole? Is not there thy name?
>
> IGNORANCE Yea.
>
> IDLENESS Well than, con [repeat] me that same. What hast thow lern'd?
>
> IGNORANCE Ich cannot tell.
>
> IDLENESS Ich cannot tell! Thow sayst evyn very well; For if thow cowldst tell, then had not I well towght the [thee] thy lesson, which must be tawghte: To tell all, when thow canst tell righte noght.
>
> IGNORANCE Ich can [know] my lesson.
>
> IDLENESS Ye, and therfore shalt have a new cote, by God I swore.

The speech shows the *ch* form again, as well as the use of the prefix *i-* to form the past participle form *ibore*, but *sed* does not have a *z*. The new coat is significant, for when Ignorance comes in he is wearing a fool's coat, ass's ears, and a coxcomb. The implication is plain. Here, dialect speech = ignoramus.

The rather thin use of dialect features in these works is understandable, if we consider that the writers had a broad audience or readership in mind. It was enough for a dialect to be recognizable as such, not that it should be reproduced accurately. A thorough representation would in fact have made a text un-interpretable, given the considerable differences between dialects at the time. Sixteenth-century travellers routinely reported the difficulties they had in under-standing local speakers, and linguistic observers reflected upon it. 'The commen maner of spekynge in Englysshe of some contrc [region] can skante [scarcely] be vnderstondid in some other contre of the same londe,' remarked one commen-tator in 1530.[4] The spelling reformer John Hart observed in 1551 that local people would be scornful about the way their neighbours talked even if they were from the next town or just one or two days' journey away.[5] And the antiquarian and publisher Richard Verstegan commented in 1605 that when a group of Englishmen from different parts of the country were talking together, 'others being present and of our own nation, and that naturally speak the English toung, [they] are not able to vnderstand what the others say, notwith-standing they call it English that they speak'.[6] In such circumstances, any author wanting his work to be widely understood would need to keep dialect features to the bare minimum – enough to make the character recognizable, but no more.

To make this happen – at any period of history – one or two of the most noticeable features of a dialect are chosen to represent the dialect as a whole, and these gradually come to be seen as its characteristic features, even though other features might actually be just as salient or more frequent. The over-simplification then substitutes for the reality, as far as the public at large are concerned, and we end up with the artificial mental conception of a person or group which we refer to as a *stereotype*. We then expect people from that group to conform to that stereotype – whether in real life or on stage or in a novel – and are surprised, and may even be critical, when they do not. In the case of speech, a single feature may be enough to identify a whole group – such as the *l/r* confusion which supposedly identifies Japanese speakers of English, or the 'ooh-aar, Jim laad' which is the expected vocalization of all pirates since Robert Newton.[7] In the case of dialects, however, the stereotyping extends well beyond the noting of particular sounds, words, and grammatical constructions to include the set of attitudes which people associate with them. And when the associations are those of naivety, clownishness, ignorance, and wickedness, the social danger is evident.

In modern times, accent and dialect stereotyping has grown to be a major social disease, in which different groups are nationally perceived to be, for example, of lower intelligence or higher criminality purely on the basis of how they sound (the issue is addressed in the final chapter). The operative word is 'nationally'. At a personal level, people have always liked or disliked the accents and dialects they hear around them, and held opinions about individual speakers. That is human nature. The problem arises when these attitudes become generalized, and lose touch with social reality. Polarized thinking especially fosters stereotyping, and by the sixteenth century there were plenty of dichotomies reflecting the 'lered' vs 'lewed' mentality which had been around since medieval times (p. 174), such as Carew's 'court' vs 'country', 'northern' vs 'southern'. To these, the morality confrontations added the contrast between 'good' and 'evil'. The problem becomes particularly acute when the attitudes are institutionalized in literary form. Literature has a special responsibility, in this connection. As Disraeli would later say: 'Fiction, in the temper of the times, stands the best chance of influencing opinion.'[8] And it was during the sixteenth century that the literary foundations of modern dialect stereotyping were laid down.

Not that the features associated with dialect speakers were actually all regional in character. What is usually represented is a generalized colloquial speech containing a scattering of genuine regional features. Indeed, because our knowledge of the language of the time is inevitably partial, it is sometimes impossible to be sure whether a distinctive feature is dialect in origin or not (see panel 14.2). But the informal character of the language is clear enough, shown by such conventions as the use of apostrophes or respellings to mark omitted sounds (*'chieve* for *achieve*, *'a* for *he*, *fippence* for *fivepence*), contracted forms (*ile* 'I'll'), and simplified spellings (*sed* for *said*, *cum* for *come*). Also typical of the informality is the use of short and elliptical sentences, as seen in the extracts above, and of blunt and down-to-earth expressions – such as this exchange in *Everyman* between the hero and his kinsman:

EVERYMAN My Cosyn, wyll you not with me go?

COSYN No, by our Lady! I haue the crampe in my to.

The dialogues uninhibitedly portray everyday conversation among ordinary folk, with all its exclamations, vulgarisms, oaths, coarse wordplay, malapropisms, and insults. In *Wit and Science*, Idleness gives Ignorance's excuses short shrift in a suitably direct language:

IGNORANCE Um, Mother will not let me cum.

IDLENESS I woold thy mother had kis't thy bum!

and when he doesn't make any progress, threatens him with 'Shal I bete thy narse now?'

The emergence of dialect features in literature is strong evidence of the growing awareness of a standard variety of the language (Chapter 10). After all, the whole point of using nonstandard forms in a play, poem, or story is for them to be recognized as such, and this cannot happen until a language has achieved a reasonably standardized state. With spelling being so inconsistent in

14.2 Dialect words?

The Oxford poet laureate John Skelton (*c.* 1460–1529), in his search for 'terms to serve his mind' (p. 288), looked in both directions – high and low. In some of his writing we find a down-to-earth, colloquial style, in which he seems to have taken words from lower-class speech and regional dialect, or simply made them up himself. Words like *blinkard blowboll* 'blinking drunkard', *gup* (an expression of angry chiding to a horse), and *trym-tram* 'pretty trifle' are plainly colloquial. Coinages such as *Let us syppe and soppy / And not spyll a droppy* (i.e., of ale) are plainly playful. The alliteration conveys an informal tone, too. But informal or ludic usage does not necessarily mean that a word is dialectal in origin, and it is often difficult to be sure.

What are we to make of some of the words in, for example, 'Womanhod, wanton, ye want', a poem in a collection of *Dyuers Balletys and Dyties Solacyous* (*Various Ballads and Solace-giving Ditties*), dedicated:

> To mastres Anne, that farly swete,
> That wonnes [dwells] at the Key in Temmys strete.

The third verse runs:

> Though angelyk be youre smylyng,
> Yet is youre tong an adders tayle,
> Full lyke a scorpyon styngyng
> All those by whom ye haue auayle:
> Good mastres Anne, there ye do shayle:
> What prate [say] ye, praty [pretty] pyggysny?
> I truste to quyte [quit, 'repay'] you or [before] I dy.

Was *shail* in this sense a low-class word, or a dialect word? It meant 'blunder, go wrong', a figurative extension of an earlier use of the word meaning 'stumble', known from *c.* 1400. Skelton is the only recorded user, in this sense, and he employs it several times. And what about *pyggysny* – or *pigsney*, as it was often later spelled? It is etymologically 'pig's eye', perhaps in origin a children's nursery word, and used at the time as a term of endearment for a woman, 'darling, pet'. An earlier user had been Chaucer, in *The Miller's Tale*, where it helped to describe the carpenter's wife, and perhaps Skelton borrowed it from there. It certainly became dialectal later, but whether it had dialect resonance in the early sixteenth century is a matter of speculation.

late Middle English and at the beginning of Early Modern English, there was little hope of portraying regional identities consistently – which is why Chaucer's experiment is so unexpected and striking (p. 163). Only during the sixteenth century do we see spelling settling sufficiently to enable a consensus to emerge among authors about how nonstandard usage should be written down. And, as we would expect, it is the literary authors who lead the way, for theirs is the world where nonstandard-speaking characters live. There are few other occasions when we find nonstandard forms in writing – an example being trial records, where there is pressure to write down exactly what a speaker says (p. 336). But there is a big difference between nonstandard features which happen to turn up in a trial record and those which appear in imaginative literature: in the former case, the features are entirely incidental to the proceedings,[9] whereas in the latter case they are in special focus, part of the literary effect.

For an author, accordingly, it is crucial that nonstandard features of language are readily identifiable, if their effect is to be appreciated by the general public. Nonstandard language has a variety of functions: it can mark a type of character; it can identify a regional setting; it can add extra colour to an otherwise standard-language text (as when fictional characters are introduced into an educational dialogue);[10] and it can display an element of directness, humour, or irony in an otherwise standard-language setting (a modern example is the famous *Sun* newspaper headline, *Gotcha*).[11] In all such functions, the effect depends on our ability to recognize that the writer is deviating from the rules of the standard language, and to interpret the social direction of the deviation – such as towards lower-class city speakers, country dwellers, foreigners, vagrants, or members of the underworld. As already mentioned, recognition does not depend on accuracy or consistency, at any linguistic level. The stereotype is enough. Usually, writers opt for distinctive vocabulary, a few variations in spelling, and the occasional nonstandard grammatical inflection (such as *I were, they goes*). As nineteenth-century dialect writers demonstrate (Chapter 19), a great deal can be done with even a limited range.

We can see this in the way foreigner-talk was represented. This is in fact the most noticeable use of nonstandard English in the Jacobethan period. For example, in Thomas Dekker's *The Shoemaker's Holiday* (1599) we see a foreign language which is spoken both by a genuine foreigner (a Dutch sea-captain) and a disguised one (the Englishman, Richard Lacy). Asked if he can mend shoes, Lacy's Dutchlish receives an acerbic comment from Firk, a journeyman (II.iii.31):

> LACY   *Yaw, yaw, yaw; ick can dat wel doen.* [Yes, yes, yes; I can do that well.]
>
> FIRK   *Yaw, yaw!* He speaks yawing like a jackdaw that gapes to be fed with cheese-curds.

On the other hand, when later (III.i.), known as Hans, Lacy meets a real Dutch skipper, we find very little linguistic difference between the two:

HANS *Godden day, mester. Dis be de skipper dat heb de skip van marchandice; de commodity ben good; nempt it, master, nempt it.* [Good day, master. This is the skipper that has the ship of merchandise; the commodity is good; take it, master, take it.]

EYRE Godamercy, Hans; welcome, skipper. Where lies this ship of merchandise?

SKIPPER *De skip ben in revere; dor be van Sugar, cyvet, almonds, cambrick, and a towsand, towsand tings, gotz sacrament; nempt it, mester: ye sal heb good copen.* [The ship lies in the river; there are sugar, civet, almonds, cambric, and a thousand thousand things. By God's sacrament; take it, master; you shall have a good bargain.]

FIRK To him, master! O sweet master! O sweet wares! Prunes, almonds, sugar-candy, carrot-roots, turnips, O brave fatting meat! Let not a man buy a nutmeg but yourself.

Shakespeare too has his foreigner-talk, but only in relation to French, and not very often. Most foreigners speak a high English style with no nonstandard features, showing their foreignness only by the occasional French expression – as in the case of the French lords in *Henry V*. But when a nonstandard ('broken') English is used, it is made to perform a range of functions. With Princess Katherine in *Henry V* it is a sweetly sympathetic style, part innocence, part coquetry. With Alice, the princess's lady-in-waiting, who is supposed to be the English teacher, the language is fractured to the point of comedy:

ALICE I cannot tell wat is baiser en Anglish.

KING HENRY To kiss.

ALICE Your majestee entendre bettre que moi.

Her franglais is in some ways worse than Katherine's. She gets in a muddle over English auxiliary verbs, whereas Katherine has apparently mastered the modals (V.ii):

ALICE De tongues of de mans is be full of deceits . . .

KATHERINE Is it possible dat I sould love de ennemi of France?

And with the pompous physician, Dr Caius, the broken English forms part of a satirical portrait of a Frenchman which at times descends to low comedy. Accepting Page's invitation to accompany him on a birding expedition, both Evans and Caius remark (*The Merry Wives of Windsor*, III.iii.221):

EVANS If there is one, I shall make two in the company.

CAIUS If there be one or two, I small make-a the turd.

In all these cases, there is no especial consistency. At the beginning of the sentence, Caius can apparently pronounce the English *th* sound, but not at the end, where the joke depends upon it. Here as elsewhere, transcriptional consistency is necessarily subordinate to dramatic effect, and the selection of linguistic features which go to make up the character is entirely within the hands of the author.

The authors have the power. Until the arrival of the grammarians and lexicographers, who would usurp this power (Chapter 15), it is they who decide which linguistic features shall identify a nonstandard way of speaking, and they who choose the manner of its representation. Although the divide between standard and nonstandard originates in social realities, it is ultimately arbitrary and conventional. Any linguistic feature – any vowel or consonant, any word or phrase, any aspect of grammatical expression – can become nonstandard by being routinely put into 'low' mouths or regularly associated with 'low' subject-matter; and vice versa. Even such 'neutral' features as alliteration and rhyme can go one way or the other, over the course of time, depending on how authors treat them. In Old and early Middle English, as we saw in earlier chapters, highly alliterative verse was associated with the highest possible styles of expression, but by the time of Skelton it was frequently used as a sign of 'low' subject-matter (p. 348). And it characterizes some of the most abusive slanging matches in English literary history, such as William Dunbar's *Flyting of Dunbar and Kennedie* (1508).

It is also the authors who decide which personalities, groups, or domains of society, whether originating within or outside the country, shall be given a nonstandard literary representation. In principle any setting or subject-matter could receive a nonstandard treatment; in practice, only certain ones do. It is the author's choice of context which counts. And in the sixteenth century, nonstandard usage was increasingly contextualized in comedic, uneducated, or morally suspect subject-matter. A serious topic would be expressed in the standard language, even if the characters were lower class. The rustic people in this love scene speak formally and non-regionally to each other:

> Sweet Phebe, do not scorn me, do not, Phebe.
> Say that you love me not, but say not so
> In bitterness. The common executioner,
> Whose heart th'accustomed sight of death makes hard,
> Falls not the axe upon the humbled neck
> But first begs pardon: will you sterner be
> Than he that dies and lives by bloody drops?

It could be any Shakespearean lover talking – a Romeo or an Orlando. It is in fact a shepherd, Silvius, addressing his love, who replies in a comparably 'high' style (*As You Like It*, III.v.1). And when, at the end of the play (V.i.78), all the lovers are brought together, from high and low social ranks, there is no distinguishing them from a linguistic point of view:

PHEBE
Good shepherd, tell this youth what 'tis to love.
SILVIUS
It is to be all made of sighs and tears,
And so am I for Phebe.
PHEBE
And I for Ganymede.
ORLANDO
And I for Rosalind.
ROSALIND
And I for no woman.

It would have been possible to write the rustic parts in a nonstandard style, but that was not the way of love scenes. And death scenes – or reports of death – likewise demanded a high level of speech. Just occasionally an author dares to break the conventions – such as when the Hostess reports the passing of Falstaff in colloquial and prosaic tones (*Henry V*, II.iii.12):

'a parted e'en just between twelve and one, e'en at the turning o'th'tide; for after I saw him fumble with the sheets, and play with flowers, and smile upon his fingers' ends, I knew there was but one way; for his nose was as sharp as a pen, and 'a babbled of green fields.

That is perhaps why it is so moving. It takes a highly skilled dramatist to get away with it.

These examples illustrate how, by the early seventeenth century, we find a much sharper division in English being drawn between the standard and nonstandard language. The process of standardization in spelling and grammar had made great progress, resulting in a much increased consistency of representation, and the amount of regionalism in the public record had dramatically diminished. The only place where regional speech could now be publicly acknowledged was in works of literature, and even there its presence was muted, its varied character distorted by the use of stereotyped features, and its positive functionality lost to view under the weight of a century of negative associations. But it is impossible to keep dialects down, and even as regional dialect was disappearing from public view, the seeds of its rebirth were being sown.

Some consequences

A standard language is, by definition, supra-regional. When you see it written, or hear it spoken, you cannot tell which part of the country it comes from. But this situation itself allows certain trends to operate in the reverse direction. In particular, the emergence of a standard puts the nonstandard language into sharper relief, so that authors begin to see its properties more clearly. Because words are now being written in a consistent – or, at least, reasonably consistent – way, it becomes much more straightforward to devise alternative spellings which represent nonstandard speech. If *would* is always spelled *would* in the standard variety, then any alternative spelling (*wou'd*, *wood*, *wud*, etc.) will be an immediate sign of nonstandardness, even if no change in pronunciation is involved.

Several of the spelling conventions showing nonstandard speech are purely visual in character, as they continue to be today. In Received Pronunciation (p. 468), *sez* is pronounced the same as *says*, *sed* as *said*, *cum* as *come*, *enuf* as *enough*, and *wot* as *what*; but the former in each case would immediately suggest a nonstandard speaker. Leaving out a letter is interpreted as nonstandard, even if in standard speech that letter would never normally be pronounced – as in *show'd* for *showed* or *fish 'n' chips*. If someone says *I asked her to go*, at a normal conversational speed, the *h* of *her* is never pronounced, no matter how well educated the person is; and if someone were to write that sentence down in a play script in that way, it would be considered a normal Standard English utterance. But if it were written down as *I asked 'er to go*, the implication would immediately be that this was a nonstandard speaker – even though the pronunciation would be exactly the same. Once spelling conventions become standardized, any departure from them is considered nonstandard, whether they reflect pronunciation differences or not. Distinctions of this kind begin to be a regular feature of literary writing in the sixteenth century, and become routinely exploited in later dialect literature (Chapter 19).

But in sixteenth-century England we see a second consequence of the emergence of a standard language. As dialects began to disappear from the public record, they became objects of curiosity, and prompted an antiquarian interest which extended well beyond the domain of literature. Professional people – historians, physicians, lawyers, politicians, scholars – who travelled about the British Isles began making lists of dialect words and collected dialect poems and aphorisms. In the seventeenth century, John Aubrey – one of the most assiduous collectors of regional miscellanea – would reflect on 'How these curiosities would be quite forgott, did not such idle fellowes as I am putt them down'.[12] Doubtless William Lambarde, Richard Stanihurst, Andrew Boorde,

Richard Carew, and Sir Thomas Browne were the sort of idle fellow he was thinking of. At the same time, interest grew in word etymologies, archaic usage, professional jargons, the argots of subcultures (such as vagrants and criminals), and the older periods of the English language – a somewhat surprising development in an age when Latin was still the dominant language of education and scholarship (see panel 14.3).

14.3 Archaisms

Archaisms are usages from an earlier stage of a language which have been given a further lease of life. They may be words, idioms, pronunciations, grammatical constructions, or patterns of discourse. Such medieval words as *eyne* 'eyes', *iwis* 'indeed', *hight* and *yclept* 'called', *wight* 'person', *shoon* 'shoes', *sain* 'said', *forthy* 'therefore', and *eke* 'also' are used upon occasion by several Shakespearean characters, such as Gower, Ophelia, Pistol, Holofernes, Bottom, and Armado.

However, although an interest in archaisms grew during the sixteenth and seventeenth centuries, as part of the general antiquarian spirit of the times, their use in literature was not always well received. Philip Sidney was one who criticized Edmund Spenser for their copious use in *The Shepheardes Calender* (p. 293). A typical illustration is the dialogue between two shepherds in the opening verse of April:

> Tell me good Hobbinoll, what garres thee greete?
> What? hath some Wolfe thy tender Lambes ytorne?
> Or is thy Bagpype broke, that soundes so sweete?
> Or art thou of thy loved lasse forlorne?

What garres thee greete – 'What causes thee to lament' – is Northern dialect. *Forlorne* ('abandoned') and *ytorne* (the old past participle form of the verb *tear*, p. 166) look back to early Middle English. The distinction between dialectism and archaism is not always clear.

Spenser himself probably anticipated the reaction, if we can judge from the apologia appended to the work written by the person known only as E. K.

> And firste of the wordes to speake, I graunt they be something hard, and of most men vnused, yet both English, and also vsed of most Authors and most famous Poetes.

He thinks that 'those auncient solemne wordes are a great ornament', adding great grace and authority to the poetry:

> But whether he Vseth them by such casualtye and custome, or of set purpose and choyse, as thinking them fittest for such rusticall rudenesse of shepheards, eyther for that theyr rough sounde would make his rymes more ragged and rusticall, or els because such olde and obsolete wordes are most vsed of country folke, sure I think,

and think I think not amisse, that they bring great grace and, as one would say, auctoritie to the verse.

The introduction of archaisms is also a service to the language as a whole:

> For in my opinion it is one special prayse, of many which are dew to this Poete, that he hath laboured to restore, as to theyr rightfull heritage such good and naturall English words, as have ben long time out of vse and almost cleane disinherited.

On the other hand, E. K. appreciates the problem: if readers do not understand the words, the work will fail. He therefore takes it upon himself to add a glossary – apparently with direct access to Spenser's intuition:

> Hereunto haue I added a certain Glosse or scholion [explanatory note] for thexposition of old wordes & harder phrases . . . I thought good to take the paines vpon me, the rather for that by meanes of some familiar acquaintaunce I was made privy to his counsell and secret meaning in them, as also in sundry other works of his.

Today, the use of archaic words and phrases on the whole has a 'good press', though their use in religious and legal settings regularly prompts a debate about the relative merits of tradition vs intelligibility. They are also quite frequent in general usage,[13] being found in many kinds of professional and intellectual subject-matter: *What Doth It Profit a Bank Manager?* is a representative headline from the economics pages of a daily paper (see further, p. 515).

Because archaisms were generally part of an earlier 'high' or standard variety of the language, and tend to be used today in formal written contexts, they would usually be included within the notion of Standard English (though marked as *archaic* in dictionaries). On the other hand, if *archaism* is interpreted synchronically, the fact that they are no longer part of the contemporary language would suggest they are, by definition, nonstandard. Archaisms occupy a somewhat uneasy position within the standard–nonstandard continuum.

Old English was an early focus of attention. Robert Talbot (*c.* 1505–68), a prebendary of Norwich Cathedral with wide antiquarian interests, was the first to compile a mini-dictionary – a short list of thirty-two Anglo-Saxon words with Latin equivalents. In the 1560s, we find the first real dictionary of Anglo-Saxon, *Vocabularium Saxonicum*, compiled by Laurence Nowell, dean of Lichfield and the earliest known owner of the *Beowulf* manuscript. Another dictionary was later compiled by John Joscelyn (1529–1603), Archbishop Parker's secretary. And in 1605 we find a general work, *A Restitution of Decayed Intelligence in Antiquities*, published in Antwerp by the exiled Catholic publisher and antiquarian Richard Verstegan (*c.* 1548–1636) – the first real attempt to bring Anglo-Saxon customs, laws, and language into the public domain. Its wide-ranging content includes the earliest account in English of the

Pied Piper legend, the history of the white horse of Kent, and several other topics of English heritage. He gives dialect examples, too. 'Lo heer three different pronountiations in our own country in one thing,' he remarks at one point, illustrating from three dialect areas (punctuation modernized):

> For pronouncing according as one would say at London, 'I would eat more cheese yf I had it,' the northern man saith, 'Ay sud eat mare cheese gin ay hadet,' and the western man saith, 'Chud eat more cheese an chad it.'

In all, some thirty scholars are known for their interest in Anglo-Saxon manuscripts and language during the sixteenth century.

The investigation of regional dialects fell naturally into place alongside this antiquarian interest. However, dialects were not usually viewed as a living medium of expression, offering a window into cultural diversity; rather, they were thought of as relics of past times, quaint curiosities to be cherished and preserved. The spirit was very much that of the butterfly hunter, with enthusiasts keeping their ears open for interesting specimens, and writing them down. The transcriptions were invariably stylized and stereotyped (though as the seventeenth century progressed, some more detailed versions appeared). A typical example comes from a Devonshire gentleman, William Stoude, who transcribed a bouncing poetic dialogue – the final -*a* in the opening lines is a rhyming tag – between two rustics, Tom and Tan:

> Ruddle, ruddle, nebour Tan
> Whare ich a late a benn [been] a
> Why ich a benn to Plymouth man,
> The lik wah neuer zeene [seen] a.
> Zutch streates, zutch men, zutch hugeous zeas,
> Zutch gunns wth things ther tumblinge.
> Thy zul [soul] wth me woudst blest to zee,
> Zutch bomination rumblinge.[14]

By 1674 enough was known for the first dialect dictionary to be published, by the Essex botanist John Ray: *A Collection of English Words, Not Generally Used, with Their Signification and Original*, who used informants from various parts of the country. An expanded edition appeared in 1691. There was then a century-long lull – dialects did not exercise the same fascination on refined eighteenth-century sensibilities – before the revitalization of dialect study in a philological age (p. 484) and a flowering of English dialect literature.

Other dimensions of language variation attracted interest, too. People began to collect the specialized vocabularies of farmers, shepherds, farriers, fishermen, miners, seafarers, lawyers, physicians, and from many other kinds of occupational activity, and began to circulate them both privately and through publication.[15] Seafaring, for example, was of special significance in the seventeenth century, which saw the three Anglo-Dutch Wars and several other naval conflicts. In 1626, Captain John Smith produced the first of several explanatory books:

> An Accidence, or The path-way to experience. Necessary for all young sea-men, or those that are desirous to goe to sea, briefly shewing the phrases, offices, and words of command, belonging to the building, ridging, and sayling, a man of warre; and how to manage a fight at Sea. Together with the charge and duty of every officer, and their shares: also the names, weight, charge, shot, and powder, of all sorts of great ordnance. With the vse of the petty tally [record of ship's provisions].

The book was popular, going into five editions by the end of the century, and followed up with a *Sea Grammar* (1627) as well as a combined grammar and dictionary (1641). At around the same time, Sir Henry Manwayring, captain of the *Unicorn* in the Ship Money fleet of 1636, compiled a seafaring dictionary (see panel 14.4). Although not published until 1644, it must have been written earlier, for George Villiers – the lord high admiral of the dedication – was murdered in 1628:

> The Sea-mans Dictionary: Or, An Exposition and Demonstration of all the Parts and Things belonging to a Shippe: Together with an Explanation of all the Termes and Phrases used in the Practique of Navigation. Composed by that able and experienced Sea-man S[r] Henry Manwayring, Knight: And by him presented to the late Duke of Buckingham, the then Lord High Admirall of England.

This, too, was reprinted several times.

Another example, interesting from a linguistic point of view, comes from the pen of Edward Manlove, a mid seventeenth-century magistrate from Ashbourne, Derbyshire, who was steward of the local lead-mining court, the Great Barmote Court. The jurisdiction of this court dated from 1288, when Edward I called an inquisition for the King's Field of the High Peak at Ashbourne, setting up a grand jury of twenty-four true men to establish the laws of lead mining, and this court operated separately from the rest of the British legal system. In 1653, Manlove compiled 'the liberties and customs of the lead mines within the Wapentake of Wirksworth' (a town that had become the centre of jurisdiction for the area's lead industry), but he decided to write them out in rhyme, to help illiterate miners to remember them. The laws governed such matters as where lead could not be mined (in churchyards, highways, orchards, gardens), the payments that had to be made for mining rights, and the punishments which would be meted out if laws were broken. Manlove's 'Rhymed Chronicle' made things perfectly clear (the text is modernized):

14.4 Careening along

The flavour of early seventeenth-century compilations of specialist nomenclature can be judged from the entries on *careening* in the books by Smith and Manwayring (p. 357). Smith's entry is short and to the point.

> careen; which is to make her so light, as you may bring her to lie on the one side so much as may be, in the calmest water you can, but take heed you overset her not. And this is the best way to bream [clean] ships of great burthen, or those [that] have but four sharp floors, for fear of bruising or oversetting.

Manwayring provides a much more extensive essay:

> Careening is the best way of trimming a ship under water, both for that the carpenters may stand upon the scaffolds, most commodiously to caulk the seams, or do any other thing that shall be requisite; also for the saving of the ground timbers, which, especially in ships of great burthen and weight, must needs be much wrung, though they be laid never so strong; besides, it is a most necessary trimming for great ships, which are either old or weak-built, and also for any ships that have but small float, and are built so sharp under water, that they will be in danger of overthrowing when they shall be brought aground. This careening is to be done in harbour, where the slower the tide runs the better. And it is most commonly used in such places, where there are no docks to trim a ship in, nor no good places to grave [clean the bottom of] a ship on, or else that it does not ebb so much that a ship may shew dry.

There is then a 240-word encyclopedic excursus on careening procedures, in relation to different types of ship, before he returns to some strictly lexicographical points, including two examples of usage:

> Any kind of bringing the ship over to lie on one side (she being afloat) is called careening, though it be but a few strakes [plank-breadths]; as we say, she was careened three, four or five strakes. If a ship lie down much with a sail, they will say, she sails on the careen.

The verb had an interesting later history. In the early twentieth century, chiefly in the USA, it became associated with *career*, and developed a usage of 'hurtle unsteadily' or 'rush along while swaying from side to side'. People, cars, dogs, logs, and teardrops are some of the entities that have since careened, as well as ships.

For stealing ore twice from the minery
The thief that's taken fined twice shall be,
But the third time that he commits such theft,
Shall have a knife stuck through his hand to th'haft,
Into the stow, and there till death shall stand.
Or loose himself by cutting loose his hand,

And shall forswear the franchise of the mine,
And always lose his freedom from that time.

Lead-mining jargon comes to the fore in a section which ingeniously weaves together over eighty technical terms – shown here in original spelling, with several words presumably reflecting local dialect use:

Bunnings, polings, stemples, forks, and slyder,
Stoprice, yokings, soletrees, roach, and ryder,
Water holes, wind holes, veyns, coe-shafts, and woughs,
Main rakes, cross rakes, brown-henns, budles, and soughs,
Break-offs and buckers, randam of the rake,
Freeing, and chasing of the stole to th'stake,
Starting of oar [ore], smilting, and driving drifts,
Primgaps, roof works, flat-works, pipe-works, shifts,
Cauke, sparr, lid-stones, twitches, daulings, and pees,
Fell, bous, and knock-barke, forstid-oar, and tees,
Bing-place, barmoot court, barghmaster, and stowes,
Crosses, holes, hange-benches, turntree, and coes,
Founder-meers, taker-meers, lot, cope, and sumps,
Stickings, and stringes of oar, wash-oar, and pumps,
Corfes, clivies, deads, meers, groves, rake-soil, the gange,
Binge oar, a spindle, a lamptum, a fange,
Fleaks, knockings, coestid, trunks, and sparks of oar,
Sole of the rake, smytham, and many more.

By the end of the Early Modern English period, we see the standard variety of the language taking on a very definite shape. At the same time, the maintained interest in regional dialect, along with the proliferation of publications of a specialized kind, led to an enormous increase in the public sense of linguistic variety. Terminology evolved to talk about it: the words *accent* and *dialect* arrived towards the end of the sixteenth century (p. 341), and *creole* (from the West Indies) is recorded in 1604. The term *variety* was itself developing its range of applications, being used from around the 1590s with reference to qualitative variation in the arts, music, and literature. 'The more varietie you shew the better shal you please,' observed the composer Thomas Morley in *A Plaine and Easie Introduction to Practicall Musick* (1597). In the middle decades of the seventeenth century we find the first usages of *vernacular*, in the sense of a local variety, and of *jargon* and *nomenclature*, both in the sense of terminology used in a restricted domain. Also during this period, terms appear with contemptuous overtones: *lingo*, *patois*, and *cant* (a musical term applied to the whining speech of beggars) are also all mid seventeenth century. And by the end of the century we see the first use of a word which would dominate linguistic thinking for the next 300 years. Gilbert Burnet comments in the Preface to his 1684 translation of Sir Thomas More's *Utopia* about 'the fidelity of the Translation, and the correctness of the English'.

The correctness of the English. The speed with which this notion of 'correct English' was taken up, promulgated, and institutionalized during the eighteenth century is one of the most remarkable developments in the history of the language. Evidently the notion was too important to continue being left to the uncontrolled intuitions of literary authors and enthusiastic amateurs. Important as these may have been in the compilation of early manuals and in the formation of attitudes towards the distinction between standard and nonstandard, it seems that people now felt the need for more authoritative custodians, if the language were to progress. Accordingly, as we leave the Early Modern English period, we enter the age of the grammarians.

Interlude 14
A beggarly portrayal

Rural dialect speech is conspicuous by its absence in Shakespeare. His country people are honest, well-meaning, dignified folk – the shepherds in *As You Like It*, the play-troupe in *A Midsummer Night's Dream*, the villagers in *The Winter's Tale* – and to portray them through a demeaning rustic speech style, we might imagine, would not have been appropriate. There is just one occasion when Shakespeare uses a 'stage dialect', and this is in *King Lear*, when Edgar, in the guise of a mad country beggar, defends his blinded father against the approach of Gonerill's steward Oswald. Normally, the disguised Edgar speaks in a non-regional way, though in an accent that prevents his father recognizing him. But when he confronts Oswald, he switches into a regional persona.

Here are the relevant passages, taken from the Oxford edition of the First Folio text prepared by Stanley Wells and Gary Taylor (IV.vi.230):

OSWALD
Wherefore, bold peasant,
Durst thou support a published traitor? Hence,
Lest that th'infection of his fortune take
Like hold on thee. Let go his arm.

EDGAR
'Chill [I'll] not let go, sir, without vurther 'cagion [occasion].

OSWALD
Let go, sir, or thou diest.

EDGAR
Good gentleman, go your gate, and let poor volk pass. An 'chud ha' been swaggered [should have been bullied] out of my life, 'twould not ha' been so long as 'tis by a vortnight. Nay, come not near th'old man. Keep out, 'che vor' ye [warrant/warn you], or I's' try whether your costard [head] or my baton be the harder; I'll be plain with you.

OSWALD
Out, dunghill!

EDGAR
'Chill pick your teeth, sir. Come, no matter vor your foins [sword-thrusts].

The speeches amount to a mere seventy-five words, but they raise a number of interesting questions about how regional and colloquial forms were being represented at the time.[16]

There are two main texts: a Quarto printed in 1608, thought to be Shakespeare's original version, and a heavily revised Folio. The distinctive words which appear in the two versions are compared in panel 14.5, alongside the decisions made by Wells and Taylor. There is evidently a mixture of colloquial and regional forms.

The most noticeable feature is the stage use of regional *ch-* in *chill*, *che*, and *chud*, along with the voicing of initial *f* seen in both versions of 'folk' (*voke/volke*) and of *vortnight*. But the Folio compilers seem to have been dialect-aware

---

14.5 Dialect variants in Edgar's speech

Quarto	First Folio	Wells and Taylor
Chill	Chill	'Chill
sir	Zir	sir
	vurther	vurther
cagion	'casion	'cagion
gate	gate	gate
voke	volke	volk
chud	'chud	'chud
haue	ha'	ha'
beene	bin	been
swaggar'd	zwaggerd	swaggered
it would	'twould	'twould
haue	ha'	ha'
beene	bin	been
so	zo	so
	'tis	'tis
vortnight	vortnight	vortnight
the old	th'old	th'old
cheuore ye	che vor'ye	'che vor' ye
ile	ice	I's'
whether	whither	whether
bat	Ballow	baton
ile	chill	I'll
Chill	Chill	'Chill
sir	Zir	sir
for	vor	vor

(as some of Chaucer's scribes were, p. 167): they extended this practice to include *vor*, and applied it to all the words beginning with *s* – *zir*, *zo*, and *zwaggerd*. What is odd, given this awareness, is that they printed *foynes*, not *voynes*. The word (shown as *foins* in the above extract) was not new: it had been in English since the fifteenth century. Perhaps it was felt to be too specialized or too 'high' a level for dialect treatment. But there is another possible explanation (see below).

The colloquial features of the speech, though less immediately noticeable, are actually more frequent. They are shown by abbreviations and contractions, as in *'casion* and *ile*, much as they would be today, with letter omissions normally indicated by an apostrophe. (*Bin* for *been* might also be viewed as a colloquial spelling-pronunciation, but it is used elsewhere in the Folio text in formal contexts.) The apostrophe is not the normal practice in the Quarto version, but it is widely introduced in the Folio: *haue* > *ha'*, *the old* > *th'old*, *chud* > *'chud*, *cagion* > *'casion*, *cheuore ye* > *che vor'ye*, *it would* > *'twould*. The extra Folio *'tis* has an apostrophe, too. However, the practice is not consistent. The Folio does not add an apostrophe in other places where letters have been left out – the omitted *I* before *che* and the two instances of *chill*, and it omits the apostrophe in the case of *zwaggerd*, where the Quarto version includes one. This last instance is an especially surprising omission, as the contracted *-ed* ending is commonly marked in this way; indeed, the apostrophe turns up in the Folio text in just such a context only half a dozen lines previously (*a publish'd traitor*).

Probably here we have a case of a dialect stereotype (p. 346) influencing publishing practice. The editors would certainly have noticed the unusual use of language, and tried to work out how best to print it. Realizing that the author was representing a rural manner of speech, they might easily have concluded that it was unnecessary to use more than one distinguishing feature in the same word – hence *zwaggerd* rather than *zwagger'd*. The same thinking might have been behind the decision to print Quarto *voke* as *volke*. The spelling with *l* had long been normal practice, so that the Quarto version actually contains two dialect markers, an instance of *f* > *v* and an omitted *l*. The Folio version reduces them to one.

A few features introduced often: that is how a stereotype works. But something else may have been going on, for there is evidence that Edgar was not accommodating to his new accent very well. (As a nobleman, he would hardly have had much opportunity to practise.) If we assume the text to reflect authorial intention, his failure to say *foins* as *voins* is suggestive of someone who is unsure what to do. He shows a similar uncertainty over the use of 'I'll', which turns up as *chill* and *ile* in the Quarto. In earlier speeches in the play, Edgar only uses *Ile*, so he is definitely trying to be different when talking to

Oswald. The Folio version takes this intent a step further, regionalizing the *ile* forms as *chill* and (an unexpected but none the less possible dialect form) *ice*. Given the determined way in which Edgar approaches the dialect, we might expect him – as a non-native dialect speaker – to overuse one regionalism rather than to opt for several (this is what tends to happen in the phenomenon of hypercorrection). The fact that he does not do so suggests that he may not be as good at dialects as he thinks he is.

A more prosaic explanation is of course possible: *ice* may be a compositor error, a misreading of *l* for the elongated *s* graph which was normal at the time, followed by a sound association which caused the substitution of a *c*. Such two-stage errors, though somewhat unusual, do happen in typesetting. But there is one piece of textual evidence which supports the hypothesis that Edgar could have done with some dialect coaching. When he is accompanying Gloucester to a Dover cliff-top, he evidently loses his accent altogether (IV.vi.7):

GLOUCESTER
    Methinks thy voice is altered, and thou speak'st
    In better phrase and matter than thou didst.

EDGAR
    Y'are much deceived. In nothing am I changed
    But in my garments.

GLOUCESTER
    Methinks y'are better spoken.

Edgar then changes the subject.

The Edgar passages are neither a consistent nor a complete representation of regional speech. A Jacobethan dialectologist on the case would have pointed to other words which would have been pronounced distinctively in Edgar's adopted dialect, such as *life*, *try*, and *night*. What we have here is a piece of colloquial speech with some stereotypical dialect features added. In fact it is the colloquial element which more clearly contrasts the passages with Edgar's usage elsewhere in the play, where he hardly uses contracted forms at all. As himself, there are just a few isolated instances, mostly in poetic passages, where they are needed by the metre; and as Poor Tom we see only the occasional item, such as *is't* and *'tis*. Although Tom speaks madness, it is not colloquial madness: 'Wine loved I deeply, dice dearly, and in woman out-paramoured the Turk – false of heart, light of ear, bloody of hand . . .' (III.iv.87). This is high speech, for a mad beggar. Only in the Oswald interaction do we find a concentration of colloquialisms.

The Edgar speeches are probably the most famous example we have of a literary rural stereotype in Jacobethan drama. Despite their brevity, they are full of sociolinguistic interest and intrigue.

Chapter 15 Stabilizing disorder

'The maker of a sentence launches out into the infinite and builds a road into Chaos and old Night, and is followed by those who hear him with something of wild creative delight.' Thus Ralph Waldo Emerson, in his *Journal* for 1834. By the end of the Early Modern English period there were many who felt that there had been just a little too much 'wild creative delight' in the English language, and that a road had been built which indeed was pointing firmly in the direction of chaos.

Who said there was chaos? Virtually everyone, judging by the statements of the literary elite which have come down to us. By the mid eighteenth century, people were in no doubt. The statesman Philip Stanhope, earl of Chesterfield, for example, wrote in 1754: 'It must be owned that our language is at present in a state of anarchy.'[1] And Samuel Johnson, in the Preface to his *Dictionary* (1755), concurred:

> When I took the first survey of my undertaking, I found our speech copious without order, and energetick without rules: wherever I turned my view, there was perplexity to be disentangled, and confusion to be regulated; choice was to be made out of boundless variety, without any established principle of selection.

Earlier in the century, Jonathan Swift had been so unimpressed by the state of the language, as he perceived it, that he formulated 'A proposal for correcting, improving and ascertaining the English tongue' (1712), sending it to the leader of the government, Robert Harley, earl of Oxford. A complaint could hardly have been phrased more formally or more powerfully:

> My LORD; I do here, in the Name of all the Learnèd and Polite Persons of the Nation, complain to your LORDSHIP, as *First Minister*, that our Language is extremely imperfect; that its daily Improvements are by no means in proportion to its daily Corruptions; that the Pretenders to polish and refine it, have chiefly multiplied Abuses and Absurdities; and, that in many Instances, it offends against every Part of Grammar.

Swift's solution was an Academy (which I discuss below), and he hoped Lord

Oxford would deign to be a founder member. Unfortunately, the Tory ministry fell in 1714, Harley was dismissed, and after the Hanoverian succession spent two years in prison. In Lord Chesterfield's view, this had actually been a blessing in disguise. Whoever might be the members of an Academy, he opined, it ought not to be politicians – 'precision and perspicuity not being in general the favourite objects of ministers, and perhaps still less of that minister than of any other'.

Words like 'anarchy' and 'chaos' were not being used lightly, and were by no means restricted to the language issue. They reflected a period of unprecedented social and political upheaval. The 150 years before Swift had seen the impact of the Reformation on English religious practice, the dissolution of the monasteries (1536–9), the Gunpowder Plot (1605), two civil wars (1642–6, 1648–51), the execution of a king (1649), Irish and Scottish rebellions (1649–50), three Dutch wars (between 1652 and 1674), the Restoration (1660), the Great Plague and Fire (1665–6), and the 'glorious' revolution (1688). The word *anarchy* is first recorded in English in 1539. The Stuart era has been called the 'century of revolution'. A summarizing statement from a historian is perhaps in order:

> Although there is much that is controversial and uncertain about social change between 1450 and 1625, there is one feature on which most historians would agree: that over that time-span a period of relative stability was replaced by one of obvious instability ... people at the end of the period saw themselves in a society beset with uncertainties and continuous flux, and they spent a good deal of time proclaiming the virtues of 'order' and 'degree' against dangers which seemed to lurk all around.

And the next section in the historical encyclopedia in which this article appears, relating to the period 1625 to 1783, is headed: 'Disorder to Stability'.[2]

The fear of disorder had been a common theme in the plays of the Jacobethan period. *Chaos*, in its political sense of civil breakdown, is first found in Shakespeare: Ulysses complains to Agamemnon of the 'chaos' which has arisen in Troy, as a result of failing to maintain proper degrees within society (*Troilus and Cressida*, I.iii.125). Indeed, in his view the whole universe is founded on degree:

> The heavens themselves, the planets, and this centre [the earth]
> Observe degree, priority, and place,
> Insisture [constancy], course, proportion, season, form,
> Office, and custom, in all line of order.

And 'when degree is shaked', he goes on, 'the enterprise is sick'.

Take but degree away, untune that string,
And hark what discord follows!

Everything – the organization of schools and cities, the practice of commerce, the structure of the family and precedence within society – is affected. This is what has happened to Troy. And when Agamemnon asks what is the remedy, Ulysses gives an answer entirely focused on the bad behaviour of Achilles, who 'in his tent / Lies mocking our designs'. His friend Patroclus lies on a lazy bed and 'breaks scurril [coarse] jests' and 'pageants' (impersonates) his seniors. Ulysses calls him a 'slanderer', and compares him to a strutting actor producing 'wooden dialogue and sound'. When he speaks,

'Tis like a chime a-mending, with terms unsquared [unbecoming]
Which, from the tongue of roaring Typhon dropped,
Would seem hyperboles.

What is interesting, from the point of view of this book, is that the thrust of Ulysses' attack is entirely couched in linguistic terms. Achilles and Patroclus are men behaving badly, and showing this through their unconstrained language. It is this link between unsociable behaviour, the breakdown of society, and language which so disturbed men like Chesterfield and Swift (and some modern politicians, too, as we shall see, p. 526).

Any breakdown of society involves far more than specifically political issues. Economic issues are critical, and here also we see an increasingly chaotic situation, with a huge price inflation in food and land rents throughout the period. The cost of living rose fivefold between 1510 and 1625. Demographic issues become critical, for the size of a population has obvious economic and social implications, and at the end of the Early Modern English period there was a remarkable doubling of the population of England. From about 2.5 million in 1550, we see a rise to some 5 million by 1650, and a further significant increase to about 6 million by 1700. Immigration to London continued (p. 244), so that by 1650 the number of people living in the capital had reached 400,000, and 575,000 by 1700, making it the largest city in Western Europe. But more dramatic than this was the rise in urban growth which was beginning to take place outside London. It is in the Hanoverian era (after 1714) that we encounter the rise of cities in Central Scotland and South Wales, the ports of Liverpool, Bristol, and Glasgow, the manufacturing centres of Birmingham, Leeds, and Manchester, and the leisure resorts of Bath, Scarborough, and Brighton. Nor should we forget Ireland, part of Britain at the time: in the seventeenth century, Dublin was the second-largest city in the British Isles.

Population growth has obvious implications for language, too. As social groups grow within a township, sub-groups proliferate, based on geography, social structure, and social networks. Notions such as 'East End', 'south of the river', and 'well-to-do area' become current. *Ghetto* is first recorded in 1611, with reference to the Jewish quarter of a city; *well-to-pass* (i.e., 'well-to-do') in 1610; *suburban* in 1625. Differences between townships become more marked, and more noticeable, as people move more widely about the country and encounter how 'other people' live. In the 1700s we see improved roads and methods of transportation significantly reducing travel times and increasing the number of journeys. Over a thousand Turnpike Acts (permitting road-tolls to be levied on travellers) were introduced in the eighteenth century, enabling roads to be better maintained. Although stage-coaches had been introduced into England in 1640, their impact was limited by the poor roads during the subsequent century, but the improvements, when they came, had an immediate effect. In 1740, the London–Birmingham road saw just one coach a day; by the 1760s there were thirty.

Accents and dialects exist to give a vocal identity to regional and social communities. It is a particularly powerful method, because the voice – unlike, say, distinctive clothing, facial features, or ornaments – is perceptible around corners and in the dark. We can speculate that a distinctive accent would have been of especial evolutionary value to early hominids, as they heard voices outside their cave, and needed to establish whether the owners were friendly or not. Things were not so different in eighteenth-century caves, where voices continued to identify members of the same and alien tribes. Nor is there any essential difference today. Accents and dialects continue to have their two functions: they are inward-looking, fostering group solidarity, and they are outward-looking, fostering group distance. 'We are like us, and we are not like them.' The more speakers there are, of course, and the more they encounter each other, the more the distinctive features of an accent or dialect become noticed, imitated, exaggerated, and satirized. Stereotypes (p. 346) become more frequent and more widely recognized. Swift seems to have been an early-day Professor Higgins, in this respect:

> Not only the several Towns and Countries of *England*, have a different way of Pronouncing, but even here in *London*, they clip their Words after one Manner about the Court, another in the City, and a third in the Suburbs.

Britain had never seen such an increase in the numbers of regional speakers as took place in the seventeenth and eighteenth centuries. We might interpret this as a sign of linguistic vitality. But what one person sees as an enriching diversity another person sees as a divisive fragmentation. To the observers of the time, such as Swift and Chesterfield, this was further evidence that the language was headed for disaster.

It was not just the increase in numbers which was significant; it was the increase in the social character of those numbers. These were not all rustics. They were businessmen, merchants, and industrialists, an increasingly powerful sector of society, whose numbers would be further swelled as the Industrial Revolution progressed. They were an increasingly literate section of society: by 1700 nearly half of the male population and a quarter of the female population of England were able to read and write.[3] And they were an increasingly genteel section of society. The growth of the gentry, a class below the peerage, had been one of the most important developments of the late Middle Ages, and it became a major feature of life in the seventeenth and eighteenth centuries. It was a very broad and disparate group, chiefly including anyone who had an income derived from land that was physically worked by others. Such people usually had local government responsibilities, for example acting as magistrates. They and their sons would probably have spent time at a university or one of the Inns of Court. Their gentility could be registered in the College of Arms: 4,000 such grants of arms were made between 1560 and 1640. The social elite was further broadened when James I introduced in 1611 the category of baronet – 'a new Dignitie between Barons and Knights' – with the aim of making money for the Crown. Although the numbers were at first limited and expensive, by 1640 you could purchase a baronetcy for as little as £400.

And how were you to behave, if you had become a member of this new class of gentry? Books of etiquette, conduct guides, and courtesy manuals came to be written, defining gentility. Some adopted a Puritan vision of a godly household; others introduced French notions of politeness. The Anglican divine Richard Allestree (1619–81) illustrates the spiritual and moral approach: *The Gentleman's Calling* (1660) went through eighteen editions by 1700; the sequel, *The Ladies' Calling* (1673), went through eight; both were popular in England and America. Another influential author was George Savile, Lord Halifax, who wrote *Lady's New Year's Gift; or, Advice to a Daughter* (1688). All aspects of behaviour had to be dealt with – how to bow, shake hands, wear a hat, hold gloves, eat with a fork, use a napkin, blow one's nose in public, pour tea (see panel 15.1). Also, what not to do: no spitting, chewing with the mouth open, eating with one's hands. It is in one of Lord Chesterfield's *Letters to His Son* (19 March 1750) that we first encounter the word *etiquette* in English, and he does not beat about the bush. In that same letter we read:

> For instance: do you use yourself to carve, eat, and drink genteelly, and with ease? Do you take care to walk, sit, stand, and present yourself gracefully? Are you sufficiently upon your guard against awkward attitudes, and illiberal, ill-bred, and disgusting habits; such as scratching yourself, putting your fingers in your mouth, nose, and ears? Tricks always acquired at schools, often too much neglected afterwards; but, however, extremely ill-bred and nauseous.

15.1 *Tea* time

On 25 September 1660, Samuel Pepys' *Diary* records: 'I did send for a cup of tee (a China drink) of which I never had drunk before.' Nothing better represents the linguistic consequences of politeness than the proliferation of tea terminology which began to enter English during the later decades of the seventeenth century. The first recorded reference to the word is 1655. In 1661, tea-taking was introduced into the Restoration Court by Queen Catherine, the Portuguese wife of Charles II, and it immediately became the fashion. At high social levels, it became a formal ritual accompanied by an elegant apparatus of silver spoons, pots, stands, tongs, and caddies, and an occasion for polite conversation. But the innovation was taken up by other levels of society, too. As its price fell, everyone adopted the habit, upstairs and downstairs alike, taking tea usually twice a day. House inventories in the eighteenth century show twice as many items relating to tea than to coffee or chocolate (previously the favourite drinks). The following selection of compound words shows its progress both at home and in the fashionable streets.

Item	First recorded usage	Item	First recorded usage
tea-pot	1662	tea-time	1741
tea-spoon	1666	tea-shop	1745
tea-table	1688	tea-things	1747
tea-house	1689	tea-treats	1748
tea-water	1693	tea-box	1758
tea-stand	1697	tea-saucer	1761
tea-cup	1700	tea-visit	1765
tea-room	1702	teaware	1766
tea-equipage	1702	tea-cloth	1770
tea-dish	1711	tea-tray	1773
tea-canister	1726	tea-set	1786
tea-tongs	1738	tea-urn	1786

It did not take long for the first conduct guides to become thoroughly assimilated into society. By the end of the seventeenth century, several such books had become standard texts in schools. And their established status was tacitly confirmed when authors began to satirize them. The novelist Jane Collier (?1709–54) wrote one such text: *An Essay on the Art of Ingeniously Tormenting, with Proper Rules for the Exercise of that Pleasant Art ... with Some General Instructions for Plaguing All Your Acquaintance* (1753). Its subversion of the Golden Rule is especially memorable: 'Remember always to do unto everyone, what you would least wish to have done unto yourself.'

In an era where there is so much emphasis on social hierarchy as part of a stable state, degrees in society become especially important. And social ranks need to be recognized, otherwise they cease to have any value. Far more is involved than being able to demonstrate status through possessions – housing, gardens, furnishing. In the seventeenth century, we find special attention being paid to codes of appearance, notably in dress, hair-style, and body decoration, and in all aspects of behaviour, especially language. There are several words which capture the spirit of the age – 'polish', 'refinement', 'propriety', and 'manners'; but the most important watchword for behaviour was 'politeness', recorded in this sense in 1702 (though the adjective, *polite*, was several decades earlier). A social historian, Amanda Vickery, sums up its significance:

> Politeness in the eighteenth century meant much more than mere etiquette, and minding your ps and qs. It was an all-embracing philosophy of life, and a model for a harmonious society. It promoted openness and accessibility in social behaviour, but at the same time set strict standards of decorum for merchants and manufacturers to live up to. Politeness demanded that people should make themselves agreeable to others, to give pleasure as well as take it. Indeed the social lubrication which politeness offered was one of its great attractions, because it offered a way for very different sorts of people to get along without violence, and helped heal the wounds of civil war. Politeness was an intellectual response to the uncompromising religious fanaticism of the civil war years, and the political hatreds which lingered afterwards.[4]

Dr Johnson's definition of politeness was 'elegance of manners; gentility; good breeding' adding an illustrative quotation from Swift about 'politeness in manners and discourse'. And Swift would know, having carried out a pioneering study in conversational pragmatics (see panel 15.2).

The term permeated society. Swift had described his century as 'this Age of Learning and Politeness'. Literature, science, education, the arts, entertainment could all be described as 'polite'. So could scholars and wits, nations and languages. In each case, the implication is that the behaviour is part of a broad network of cultivated and refined social interaction. A 'polite poem' would be one which could be understood and enjoyed by anyone with a cultured background. A 'polite lecture' would be one which avoided specialized or arcane learning. And 'polite language' would be a use of English which was widely intelligible and acceptable – polished, elegant, correct. It was the correctness which was the ultimate guarantor of its politeness. 'Every polite tongue [language] has its own rules,' affirmed the grammarian Lindley Murray (p. 396).[5] And it was the job of the grammarians, lexicographers, pronunciation analysts, and usage stylists to make sure that these rules were known, appreciated, and followed. The polite people themselves could not help; for, it

15.2 Having a polite conversation

Simon Wagstaff – or Jonathan Swift, as he is better known – published his satirical *Polite Conversation*, as it is usually called, in 1738. Its full title is more impressive: *A Complete Collection of Genteel and Ingenious Conversation, According to the Most Polite Mode and Method Now Used at Court, and in the Best Companies of England*. It consists of three dialogues – at breakfast, dinner, and tea – between 'the Polite persons, of both Sexes', five men and three women, at Lord Smart's house in St James' Park.

According to his Introduction, Swift did what any present-day linguist does: compile a corpus. He would visit 'the most polite Families':

> I always kept a large Table-Book in my Pocket; and as soon as I left the Company, I immediately entred the choicest Expressions that passed during the Visit; which, returning home, I transcribed in a fair Hand, but somewhat enlarged.

This he did for twelve years, but delayed publication until he could 'present a compleat System to the World'. In fact, by the time the book appeared, he had been observing for thirty-six years, so that his claim – 'the whole Genius, Humour, Politeness, and Eloquence of *England*, are summed up in it' – may not be so far from the truth.

The openings of the morning and afternoon conversations illustrate the style and content:

COLONEL Well met, my Lord.

LORD SPARKISH Thank ye, Colonel; a Parson would have said, I hope we shall meet in Heaven. When did you see *Tom. Neverout*?

COLONEL He's just coming towards us. Talk of the Devil. –

[*Neverout comes up*]

COLONEL How do you do *Tom*?

NEVEROUT Never the better for you. [No better for your asking]

COLONEL I hope you're never the worse. But where's your Manners? Don't you see my Lord *Sparkish*?

NEVEROUT My Lord, I beg your Lordship's Pardon.

LORD SPARKISH *Tom*, How is it? what, you can't see the Wood for Trees? What Wind blew you hither?

NEVEROUT Why, my Lord, it is an ill Wind that blows no Body Good; for it gives me the Honour of seeing your Lordship.

* * *

LADY SMART Well, Ladies, now let us have a Cup of Discourse to our selves. [cup of tea and talk]

LADY ANSWERALL What do you think of your Friend, Sir John *Spendall*?

LADY SMART Why, Madam, 'tis happy for him that his Father was born before him. [i.e., he is not thrifty]

MISS NOTABLE They say, he makes a very ill Husband to my Lady.

LADY ANSWERALL Well, but he must be allowed to be the fondest Father in the World.

LADY SMART Ay, Madam, that's true; for they say, the Devil is kind to his own.

MISS NOTABLE I am told, my Lady manages him to Admiration.

LADY SMART That I believe, for she's as cunning as a dead Pig; but not half so honest.

LADY ANSWERALL They say, she's quite a Stranger to all his Gallantries.

LADY SMART Not at all; but you know, there's none so blind, as they that won't see.

MISS NOTABLE Oh, Madam, I am told, she watches him as a Cat would watch a Mouse.

The text is crammed full of contemporary catch-phrases, colloquialisms, pieces of slang, oaths, exclamations, greetings, farewells, and all kinds of banality. Swift points out that the reader will find them extremely helpful, for the expressions can be used over and over on all occasions. They 'will easily incorporate with all Subjects of genteel and fashionable Life. Those which are proper for Morning Tea, will be equally useful at the same Entertainment in the Afternoon', and 'will indifferently serve for Dinners, or Suppers'.

A reading of Swift's *Polite Conversation* is the quickest and most enjoyable way to obtain an insight into the linguistics of eighteenth-century polite society.[6] Eric Partridge thought that the work 'forms by far the best single record of polite English spoken at any given period, not merely up to and including that of Swift himself, but also, indeed, after him'. He is probably right.

transpired, it was precisely that section of society which was perpetually getting them wrong.

Understanding the mindset

In tracing the history of English during the eighteenth century, there is nothing more important than to understand the mindset of the language professionals, for this would colour our entire way of thinking for the next 300 years. Indeed, it was only in the latter part of the twentieth century that we began to free ourselves from it, and started to give language realities the sort of recognition which was routine in earlier ages (Chapter 20). And because the mindset is grounded in the social climate of the period, it has been necessary to begin this chapter with an excursus into social history. But we must turn now to examine how this climate totally conditioned the way in which the language professionals approached their subject. The argument can be summarized in four steps:

- Left to themselves, polite people do not speak or write correctly.
- Grammars, dictionaries, and other manuals are therefore needed in order to instruct polite society in the correct ways of speaking and writing.
- No-one is exempt. Even the best authors, such as Shakespeare, break the rules from time to time.
- And if even Shakespeare breaks the rules, this proves the need for guidance, because lesser mortals are even more likely to fall into the same trap.

Exactly the same argument continues to be used today, except that for 'polite' read 'educated'.[7]

How was it that polite people had got themselves into such a mess? Where had the chaos come from? The literary pundits were in no doubt. It was because the language had been left to take care of itself. Individuals of all kinds and abilities had been allowed to use it in any way they wanted. As a result it had changed in countless unpredictable ways. There was uncontrolled variation everywhere, in writing as well as in speech. Vocabulary, as always (p. 170), was the primary focus of attention, with pronunciation a close second. New words were coming into the language from all kinds of sources. People – not least, famous authors – had been coining words as never before, and idiosyncrasy seemed to rule. Situations like the case of *discordant* (p. 314), where there were half a dozen different coinages competing for the adjective form of *discord*, filled people with horror. Above all, there was the danger of words entering the language from 'below' – cant words, which Swift called 'the most ruinous Corruption in any Language'.

Who was to blame? Virtually everyone, according to Swift. The recent playwrights, to begin with, who had been badly influenced by the 'licentiousness' of the Restoration court:

> the Plays, and other Compositions, written for Entertainment within Fifty years past; filled with a Succession of affected Phrases, and new, conceited Words.

The poets were just as bad in their lack of responsibility, abbreviating words to fit the metre of their verse (*drudg'd, rebuk't*) in a manner which Swift found especially irritating:

> There is another Sett of Men who have contributed very much to the spoiling of the *English* Tongue; I mean the Poets, from the Time of the Restoration.

Then there were the spelling reformers:

> a foolish Opinion, advanced of late Years, that we ought to spell exactly as we speak; which beside the obvious Inconvenience of utterly destroying our Etymology, would be a thing we should never see an End of.

His reasoning here was that there was so much variation and change in speech that any attempt to reflect this in spelling 'would entirely confound Orthography':

> the Words are so curtailed, and varied from their original Spelling, that whoever hath been used to plain *English*, will hardly know them by sight.

And the university people must take their share of the blame:

> Several young Men at the Universities, terribly possessed with the fear of Pedantry, run into a worse Extream, and think all Politeness to consist in reading the daily Trash sent down to them from hence: This they call *knowing the World*, and *reading Men and Manners*. Thus furnished they come up to Town, reckon all their Errors for Accomplishments, borrow the newest Sett of Phrases, and if they take Pen into their Hands, all the odd words they have picked up in a Coffee-House, or a Gaming Ordinary [gambling-house], are produced as Flowers of Style.

It is difficult to see how any writers could have escaped Swift's wide-ranging censure.

Swift was not the first to place the blame for linguistic deterioration firmly on the shoulders of the literary writers. Ironically, the same sentiments had been expressed, a generation before, by the poet laureate John Dryden. The irony lies in the fact that Dryden would have been one of those whom Swift had in mind when he castigated the poets' 'barbarous Custom of abbreviating Words, to fit them to the Measure of their Verses', perhaps thinking of lines like these:

> the Day approach'd when Fortune shou'd decide
> Th' important Enterprize, and give the Bride.[8]

Swift's scorn would have included Dryden; Dryden's scorn, as we shall see, included his predecessors; and the grammarian Robert Lowth would later be scornful of Swift's 'carelessness' (p. 397). This has always been the way, with those who set themselves up as authorities prescribing correct usage. One generation's linguistic pedant is the next generation's critical butt. Indeed, it need not take a generation. In modern times, it is commonplace to see a newspaper complainant condemning one linguistic sin, only to be condemned in turn for committing another. What puzzles me is why people fail to make the appropriate deduction from this behaviour, and see the pointlessness and counter-productiveness of being prescriptive about language.

But this is to anticipate Chapter 20. At the end of the seventeenth century, a prescriptive approach was perceived to be the only remedy for the disease which had infected the language. No writers had proved to be immune, no matter how great. Dryden illustrates the point at length in an essay he wrote in

1672, 'Defence of the Epilogue' – the reference is to a verse Epilogue he had written for *The Conquest of Granada* (the essay was included in the play's first edition). Referring to the way Shakespeare and other Jacobethan writers expressed themselves in 'sense and language', he comments: 'I dare almost challenge any man to show me a page together, which is correct in both.' He gives a number of examples of 'errors' in Ben Jonson, such as the use of the double comparative (*Contain your Spirit in more stricter bounds*), which he calls 'gross'. (It was a perfectly normal construction in Jonson's day, but by Dryden's it was falling out of standard use, and would eventually become nonstandard.) One of Dryden's syntactic condemnations would later become famous:

> *The Waves, and Dens of beasts cou'd not receive*
> *The bodies that those Souls were frighted from.*
>
> The Preposition in the end of the sentence; a common fault with him, and which I have but lately observ'd in my own writings.

And indeed, Dryden took pains to eradicate it from his style. But at least Jonson was learnèd, and someone Dryden venerated. As for people with less learning, what hope for them?

> And what correctness after this, can be expected from *Shakespear* or from *Fletcher*, who wanted that Learning and Care which Johnson had? I will therefore spare my own trouble of inquiring into their faults: who had they liv'd now, had doubtless written more correctly.

Doubtless, if Shakespeare had lived later, he would have written more correctly. This sums up the literary mindset at the turn of the century. It would be adopted in due course by the influential grammarians Robert Lowth and Lindley Murray (Chapter 16).

What was Dryden's solution? He had been a member of the Royal Society's 'committee for improving the English language', set up in December 1664 – a group which also included the poet Edmund Waller and the polymath John Evelyn (see Interlude 15). At a series of meetings in Gray's Inn, they explored the idea of founding an institution to look after the language. This was not the first time such a proposal had been made, but the French Academy, founded in 1634, had provided a model. A letter from Evelyn survives in which he enthusiastically proposes some of the enterprises which an English Academy might undertake, such as a grammar, a dictionary, spelling reform, collections of dialect words, and translations to act as models of elegance. Nothing happened. The meetings petered out in early 1665, perhaps because of indifference from other members of the Society, perhaps because of a dawning sense that the scale of the enterprise was beyond them. The arrival of bubonic plague in the spring of 1665 would certainly have curtailed debate, for in subsequent months everyone who could left London for the country. Survival was more important than syntax.

But the idea of an Academy did not go away. Wentworth Dillon, the earl of Roscommon, is said to have resuscitated the enterprise in about 1783 – at least, according to Samuel Johnson, who in the Preface to Roscommon's works, says this:

> He now busied his mind with literary projects, and formed the plan of a society for refining our language, and fixing its standard; 'in imitation,' says Fenton, 'of those learnèd and polite societies with which he had been acquainted abroad.' In this design his friend Dryden is said to have assisted him.

What if anything his friend did, we do not know; but the turbulent and short reign of James II was no time for a monarch to be reflecting on linguistic matters, and we hear nothing more of it. Daniel Defoe, however, certainly ran with the idea, for he develops it at some length in an article 'Of Academies' included in *An Essay upon Projects*, written in 1697. Here we have a specific proposal that the king should establish a society for the purpose:

> The Work of this Society shou'd be to encourage Polite Learning, to polish and refine the *English* Tongue, and advance the so much neglected Faculty of Correct Language, to establish Purity and Propriety of Stile, and to purge it from all the Irregular Additions that Ignorance and Affectation have introduc'd; and all those Innovations in Speech, if I may call them such, which some Dogmatic Writers have the Confidence to foster upon their Native Language, as if their Authority were sufficient to make their own Fancy legitimate.

Who should rule, in this society? Not the scholars, first of all:

> Into this Society should be admitted none but Persons Eminent for Learning, and yet none, or but very few, whose Business or Trade was Learning: For I may be allow'd, I suppose, to say, We have seen many great Scholars, meer Learnèd Men, and Graduates in the last Degree of Study, whose *English* has been far from Polite, full of Stiffness and Affectation, hard Words, and long unusual Coupling of *Syllables* and Sentences, which sound harsh and untuneable to the Ear, and shock the Reader both in Expression and Understanding.
>
> In short, There should be room in this Society for neither *Clergyman*, *Physician*, or *Lawyer* . . .

So who is left?

> I wou'd therefoe have this Society wholly compos'd of Gentlemen; whereof Twelve

> to be of the Nobility, if possible, and Twelve Private Gentlemen, and a Class of
> Twelve to be left open for meer merit.

And women?

> though I would by no means give Ladies the Trouble of advising us in the
> Reformation of our Language; yet I cannot help thinking, that since they have
> been left out of all Meetings, except Parties at Play, or where worse Designs are
> carried on, our Conversation hath very much degenerated.

And how would they proceed?

> The Reputation of this Society wou'd be enough to make them the allow'd Judges
> of Stile and Language; and no Author woul'd have the Impudence to Coin without
> their Authority . . . There shou'd be no more occasion to search for Derivations
> and Constructions, and 'twou'd be as Criminal then to *Coin Words*, as *Money*.

Thus the ideal. But the king's attention was elsewhere, what with European
wars, Whig vs Tory conflicts, and assassination plots. English language proposals were the least of a Dutch Stuart king's worries.

And so we reach Jonathan Swift, and his 1712 proposal, which, as we
have already seen, fared no better in its timing than its predecessors. Nobody
took up the idea in any serious way thereafter. Johnson, in his Preface to
Roscommon's works, sums up the reasons why Swift's idea never caught on:

> it has never since been publickly mentioned, though at that time great expectations
> were formed, by some, of its establishment and its effects. Such a society might
> perhaps without much difficulty be collected; but that it would produce what is
> expected from it may be doubted.

Citing the French model is all very well, but Swift's idea – that an Academy
would 'fix language for ever' – evidently had not worked in that country:

> The French academy thought that they refined their language, and doubtless
> thought rightly: but the event has not shewn that they fixed it; for the French of
> the present time is very different from that of the last century.

And Johnson is well aware of the British temperament:

> In this country an academy could be expected to do but little. If an academician's
> place were profitable it would be given by interest; if attendance were gratuitous
> it would be rarely paid, and no man would endure the least disgust. Unanimity is
> impossible, and debate would separate the assembly.
>
> But suppose the philological decree made and promulgated, what would be its
> authority? In absolute governments there is sometimes a general reverence paid to
> all that has the sanction of power and the countenance of greatness. How little

this is the state of our country needs not to be told. We live in an age in which it is a kind of publick sport to refuse all respect that cannot be enforced. The edicts of an English academy would probably be read by many, only that they might be sure to disobey them.

That our language is in perpetual danger of corruption cannot be denied; but what prevention can be found? The present manners of the nation would deride authority, and therefore nothing is left but that every writer should criticise himself.[9]

But of course, by the time Johnson had written this Preface, in 1779, he had already done more than most to provide an alternative, for his *Dictionary* was by then in its fourth edition.

The suggestion that 'every writer should criticise himself' was really not an option: that way could only lead to anarchy. Swift has serious doubts about leaving ordinary people to do the decent thing. Left to themselves, they will descend into barbarism. 'I am afraid', he says at one point in his proposal, 'we are naturally not very Polite.' Such features as abbreviating words 'is nothing else but a tendency to lapse into the Barbarity of those *Northern* Nations from whom we are descended, and whose Languages labour all under the same Defect'. And so, with all proposals for an Academy having come to nothing, and with the motivation and judgement of individuals suspect, it was going to be up to the professionals to do something.

The enthroning of Standard English

Enthrone, according to the *Oxford English Dictionary*, is 'to set on a throne as a formal induction to office', and there is no better way of characterizing what happened to the language in the middle decades of the eighteenth century. The age, as we have seen, was one which readily affirmed the existence of linguistic standards, but opinions varied as to what the best models were. The speech of the court continued to be seen as pre-eminent. The notion of the 'King's English' was widespread. This term had come to the fore some 200 years earlier, being first recorded in Thomas Wilson's *Arte of Rhetorique* in 1553, where he talks of 'counterfeiting the king's English' (p. 291). It had become the Queen's English in Thomas Nashe's satirical pamphlet *Strange Newes* (1592). And responsibility varied between king and queen thereafter, along with their court, which, according to Swift, was 'the Standard of Propriety and Correctness of Speech'. Or rather, it should have been, for Swift felt it left a great deal to be desired in its actual linguistic practices.

An alternative was the Bible. Swift again: 'For those Books being perpetually read in Churches, have proved a kind of Standard for Language, especially to the common People.' And the grammarians Lowth and Murray (p. 396) agreed: 'The present translation of the Bible is the best standard of the English language.'[10] On the other hand, Puritanism and the other religious movements of the age had made that notion uncertain, too, for there were now many competing translations and different interpretations of theological terms. A third alternative was the dictionary, a genre which had grown substantially since Cawdrey's first effort (p. 280): John Kersey's *New English Dictionary* (1702), for example, had contained 28,000 words; Nathaniel Bailey's *Universal Etymological English Dictionary* (1721) had contained 60,000 by its 1736 edition. But these, in Lord Chesterfield's opinion, were of little help either. He dismisses them, in his letter of support for Johnson's project (see below), as mere 'word-books' in which 'all words, good and bad, are there jumbled indiscriminately together'. He concludes:

> I cannot help thinking it a sort of disgrace to our nation, that hitherto we have had no such standard of our language . . . The time for discrimination seems to be now come. Toleration, adoption and naturalization have run their lengths. Good order and authority are now necessary.

Despite the genius of English authors being recognized abroad, he adds, 'a grammar, a dictionary, and a history of our language through it's several stages were still wanting at home, and importunately called for from abroad' – the latter point relating to the increasing demand for English teaching materials in Europe at this time.[11]

What Chesterfield was driving at was the lack of authority in these earlier publications. Bailey's entries were certainly much fuller, compared with those in the 'hard-word' books, but his definitions lacked illustrative support from prestigious authors, and he gave little guidance about usage. And there had been so many rows between early lexicographers. For example, in 1656, the lawyer Thomas Blount had produced his own dictionary of hard words, *Glossographia*; its 11,000 entries made it the largest dictionary to date, and its innovations included the routine use of etymologies (Cawdrey had included only the occasional hint) and the first dictionary illustrations. Two years later, Edward Phillips – John Milton's nephew – produced *The New World of Words*, a bigger book than Blount's (20,000 words) but containing a great deal of Blount's material. The extent of the borrowing, in Blount's view, far exceeded the levels of acceptable pirating which had been traditional in dictionary-writing (p. 284), and the greater sensitivities of the age – the word *plagiarism* is recorded in English from 1621 – led to an early dictionary war.[12] In 1673 Blount published a furious condemnation of Phillips: *A World of Errors Discovered in the New World of Words*, pointing out what he considered to be its many lexical blunders. Phillips replied in like terms. When even the lexicographers are accusing one another of including 'barbarous and illegally compounded words', it is hardly surprising that observers such as Chesterfield should feel confused.

The demand for a standard involved all aspects of language structure, in both writing and speech – spelling, pronunciation, grammar, and vocabulary. Everything needed to be 'fixed' – a term which meant both 'specify, determine' and 'give stability to, secure against change'. Johnson, at the outset, had both meanings in mind, when he sent his Plan for his *Dictionary of the English Language* to Lord Chesterfield (published in 1747):

> This, my Lord, is my idea of an English dictionary, a dictionary by which the pronunciation of our language may be fixed, and its attainment facilitated; by which its purity may be preserved, its use ascertained, and its duration lengthened.

The Plan explored each of the areas which the *Dictionary* would address. It would begin with spelling:

> When all the words are selected and arranged, the first part of the work to be considered is the ORTHOGRAPHY . . . [in which] there is still great uncertainty among the best critics.

Johnson was right. There was still a lot of variation. But given the amount of orthographic standardization which had taken place over the previous 300 years, this was the least of his worries. A bigger problem was pronunciation:

> Closely connected with orthography is PRONUNCIATION, the stability of which is of great importance to the duration of a language . . . [therefore] care will be taken to determine the accentuation of all polysyllables by proper authorities . . . [and] to fix the pronunciation of monosyllables.

The history of the word would come next:

> When the orthography and pronunciation are adjusted, the ETYMOLOGY or DERIVATION is next to be considered.

And then the way words vary in their grammatical form – what grammarians had for some time been referring to as *accidence* (i.e., the 'accidents' affecting their grammatical shape), and what in the nineteenth century would come to be called *morphology* (p. 43):

> When the etymology is thus adjusted, the ANALOGY of our language is next to be considered . . . by what rules [words] are governed, and how they are inflected through their various terminations.

Another area would provide information about the correct way words intercon-
nect, such as by using prepositions (*die of wounds* not *die with wounds*). This
Johnson felt to be a particular innovation:

> Words having been hitherto considered as separate and unconnected, are now to
> be likewise examined as they are arranged in their various relations to others by
> the rules of SYNTAX or construction, to which I do not know that any regard
> has been yet shewn in English dictionaries, and in which the grammarians can give
> little assistance.

A further dimension would handle what later linguists would call *collocation* –
make love, make a bed, make merry, make good, and so on:

> When the construction of a word is explained, it is necessary to pursue it through
> its train of PHRASEOLOGY, through those forms where it is used in a manner
> peculiar to our language, or in senses not to be comprised in the general expla-
> nations.

Then, and only then will it be possible to get to the meat of the work, the
definitions. One can almost sense Johnson taking a deep breath:

> The great labour is yet to come, the labour of interpreting these words and phrases
> with brevity, fulness and perspicuity; a task of which the extent and intricacy is
> sufficiently shewn by the miscarriage of those who have generally attempted it.

And even then, it is not all over:

> There remains yet to be considered the DISTRIBUTION of words into their
> proper classes . . . words of general use; words employed chiefly in poetry; words
> obsolete; words which are admitted only by particular virtues, yet not in them-
> selves improper; words used only in burlesque writing; and words impure and
> barbarous.

The first of Johnson's amanuenses began work on Midsummer Day, 1746. It
took Johnson three years to read his source works and mark the citations to be
used. These were copied onto slips of paper and filed alphabetically. He then
began to draft definitions. The first sheets were printed in 1750, beginning at
letter A. It was complete by 1754, and an edition of 2,000 copies appeared in
1755, price £4.10s. Johnson himself was responsible for seeing four editions
through the press, the last in 1773.

The *Dictionary* was the first attempt at a truly principled lexicography. It
portrayed the complexity of the English lexicon more fully than ever before:
42,773 entries in the first edition, with 140,871 definitions and 222,114
quotations. The quotations initiated a practice of citation which has informed
high-quality English dictionaries ever since. The definitions for the most part

are admirably succinct; this was an area where Johnson had a real talent. And his ability to discriminate senses was exemplary, as in his sixty-six definitions of *take*, supplemented by some fifty further senses of its phrasal verbs and idioms (*take away, take care*, etc.) – though he ruefully reflects at the end of the fourth-edition entry, 'that is hardest to explain which least wants explication. I have expanded this word to a wide diffusion, which, I think, is all that could be done.' Some of his entries display an attractive frankness: of *stammel*, for example, he says 'Of this word I know not the meaning' (though he had worked it out by the fourth edition, where it is glossed as 'a species of red colour').

The *Dictionary* would receive its share of criticism in due course. There is a certain unevenness of treatment, because words at the beginning of the alphabet were more generously handled than those at the end. The quotations were chosen more for their literary or moral value than for their linguistic clarity: half of them come from just seven sources – Shakespeare, Dryden, Milton, Addison, Bacon, Pope, and the Bible. As he says in his Preface:

> I have studiously endeavoured to collect examples and authorities from the writers before the restoration, whose works I regard as *the wells of English undefiled*, as the pure sources of genuine diction.

None the less, some of the words selected for inclusion had doubtful status in English – cumbersome Latinate forms such as *cubiculary* and *incompossibility*, for example. Also, some of his definitions became famous for their impenetrability, such as *cough* 'A convulsion of the lungs, vellicated by some sharp serosity' – though he then adds, as if by way of apology, 'It is pronounced *coff*.' But none of these difficulties stopped the *Dictionary* achieving the authoritative status which Chesterfield, at the outset, acknowledged it to have.

Johnson's focus on the need to institutionalize the lexicon of the standard language was unwavering. 'I have laboured', he says in the *Rambler*, 'to refine our language to grammatical purity, and to clear it from colloquial barbarisms, licentious idioms, and irregular combinations.'[13] But as the task progressed, he became a realist. His Preface contains a famous statement of retraction:

> When we see men grow old and die at a certain time one after another, from century to century, we laugh at the elixir that promises to prolong life to a thousand years; and with equal justice may the lexicographer be derided, who being able to produce no example of a nation that has preserved their words and phrases from mutability, shall imagine that his dictionary can embalm his language, and secure it from corruption and decay, that it is in his power to change sublunary nature, and clear the world at once from folly, vanity, and affectation.

'Fixing' is out. This is one of the lessons which etymology quickly teaches you – and Johnson's etymologies were scrupulous and detailed: you cannot stop language change. Nor, if you are taking your job as a lexicographer seriously, can you turn away from language variation. It is in fact possible to sense the dynamic of the English language from the way Johnson writes his entries, frequently reflecting on the nature of change, including notes on the vagaries of English usage, and taking account of regional forms more often than his contemporaries might have expected (see panel 15.3). But it could hardly have been otherwise. Johnson was linguistically omnivorous, interested in all varieties of language and indeed in all languages. His respect for other languages is often acknowledged:

> There is no tracing the connection of ancient nations, but by language; and therefore I am always sorry when any language is lost, because languages are the pedigree of nations.[14]

15.3 Dialects in Johnson

DIALE'CT. *n. f.* [διάλεκτ⊙.]
1. The fubdivifion of a language; as the Attic, Doric, Ionic, Æolic dialects.
2. Stile; manner of expreffion.
      When themfelves do practife that whereof they write, they change their *dialect*; and thofe words they fhun, as if there were in them fome fecret fting.   *Hooker, b.* v. *f.* 22.
3. Language; fpeech.
                    In her youth
      There is a prone and fpeechlefs *dialect*,
      Such as moves men.   *Shakefp. Meafure for Meafure.*
      If the conferring of a kindnefs did not bind the perfon, upon whom it was conferred, to the returns of gratitude, why, in the univerfal *dialect* of the world, are kindneffes ftill called obligations?   *South's Sermons.*

Although some of Johnson's definitions are famous for their personal prejudices – as in his *excise* entry: 'A hateful tax levied upon commodities . . .' – he was singularly objective when it came to the treatment of linguistic notions. Notwithstanding his concern to promote a standard language, variation is simply recognized as a fact of life, and there is no hint of dialect disapproval. The definition of *idiom* reads, equably, 'A mode of speaking peculiar to a language or dialect.' And the entry on *dialect* itself is just as neutral.

His focus on a standard gave him little motivation or scope for including regional words. This was not to be a dialect dictionary. But he none the less included a number of items, mostly from Scotland (doubtless because several of his amanuenses were Scottish). They include:

> algates, anent, auld, bonny, by-gone, by-past, cibol, drotchel, feague, freak, gawntree, halsening, laird, loch, marrow, scambler, scelerat, stuckle, succumb, syb, thrapple, tyke

and specific senses of *affront*, *bourn*, *duck*, *ever*, *harry*, *having*, and *lift*. Irish words include:

> booly, brehon, carrows, coigne, coshering, creaght, glyn, kern, sept, shamrock, stocah, tanist

And there are a few joint assignations, such as *sorn* (Irish and Scottish), and *scraw*, *skean*, and *usquebaugh* 'whiskey' (Irish and Erse). Reference is also occasionally made to terms restricted to occupational varieties, again chiefly Scottish. We find the Scottish academic term *laureation*, and legal words such as *holograph*, *intromission*, *minute*, and *fabricate*:

> FABRICATE 2. To forge; to devise falsely. This sense is retained among the Scottish lawyers; for when they suspect a paper to be forged, they say it is a *fabricate*.

And just occasionally, a non-Scottish occupational term finds its way in:

> HANDSEL. The first act of using any thing; the first act of sale. It is now not used, except in the dialect of trade.

Although relatively few in number, the dialect references do add a distinctive dimension to the character of the *Dictionary*. That they are there at all should not surprise us, given Johnson's broad linguistic interests (p. 386). A quotation from Boswell's *Life of Samuel Johnson* (Chapter 20) seems apposite. On Thursday, 19 October 1769,

> I passed an evening with him at his house. He advised me to complete a Dictionary of words peculiar to Scotland, of which I showed him a specimen. 'Sir,' said he, 'Ray has made a collection of north country words. By collecting those of your country, you will do a useful thing towards the history of the language.' He bade me also go on with collections which I was making upon the antiquities of Scotland. 'Make a large book – a folio.' BOSWELL: 'But of what use will it be, sir?' JOHNSON: 'Never mind the use; do it.'

If only all dictionaries treated nonstandard words with the same respect.

There is a nice anecdote in Boswell's *Life* which shows Johnson's linguistic temperament well:

> Somebody found fault with writing verses in a dead language, maintaining that they were merely arrangements of so many words, and laughed at the Universities

of Oxford and Cambridge for sending forth collections of them not only in Greek and Latin, but even in Syriac, Arabic, and other more unknown tongues. JOHNSON: 'I would have as many of these as possible; I would have verses in every language that there are the means of acquiring.'[15]

And just in case anyone might still miss the point, there is an explicit statement in an earlier letter:

> My zeal for languages may seem, perhaps, rather overheated, even to those by whom I desire to be well esteemed. To those who have nothing in their thoughts but trade or policy, present power or present money, I should not think it necessary to defend my opinions; but with men of letters I would not unwillingly compound, by wishing the continuance of every language, however narrow in its extent, or however incommodious for common purposes, till it is reposited in some version of a known book, that it may be always hereafter examined and compared with other languages, and then permitting its disuse.[16]

Can one ever be overheated with a zeal for languages? I think not.

Johnson is the first to take on board the dual perspective which is essential for an integrated and sociolinguistically aware account of language variation. On the one hand, we have to recognize that all varieties of language have their value as a reflection of a segment of society, and are alike fascinating as objects of study. On the other hand, we have to recognize that some varieties of language – and one in particular, Standard English – have acquired special roles which give them privileged status in the eyes of society. That is just as much a fascinating linguistic fact. Johnson respected all varieties, while seeing the need for a standard:

> In literate nations, though the pronunciation, and sometimes the words of common speech may differ, as now in England, compared with the south of Scotland, yet there is a written diction, which pervades all dialects, and is understood in every province. But where the whole language is colloquial, he that has only one part, never gets the rest, as he cannot get it but by change of residence.[17]

He was able to maintain a balance. Where things go wrong is when that balance is lost, and an exclusive focus on the latter dimension is accompanied by a denigration of the former. This is the real harm that the prescriptivism of the mid eighteenth century did to English. It prevented the next ten generations from appreciating the richness of their language's expressive capabilities, and inculcated an inferiority complex about everyday usage which crushed the linguistic confidence of millions. We have begun to emerge, at the beginning of the twenty-first century, from this linguistic black hole, notwithstanding the purist temperaments which continually try to suck us back into it. The dual perspective is in sight again.

But in the eighteenth century Johnson was virtually alone in seeing it. And the authors who carried most sway, in promoting an exclusive concentration on Standard English, certainly did not. These were the grammarians.

Interlude 15
Delusions of simplicity

The Royal Society was established in 1660, and received its charter in 1662, calling itself 'The Royal Society of London for Improving Natural Knowledge'. The word 'natural' was chosen to contrast with the 'supernatural' concerns of scholarship in the days before Francis Bacon (1561–1626), whose vision of science and learning was the Society's inspiration. In 1667, Bishop Thomas Sprat wrote a *History of the Royal-Society of London*, in which, after censuring the 'schole-men's' philosophy and content, he turns his attention to 'the Barbarousness of their style' and 'want of good Language'. In Section 20, 'Their manner of Discourse', he condemns what he sees as their chief defects – ornateness and eloquence:

> there is one thing more, about which the *Society* has been most sollicitous; and that is, the manner of their *Discourse*: which, unless they had been very watchful to keep in due temper, the whole spirit and vigour of their *Design*, had been soon eaten out, by the luxury and redundance of *speech*. The ill effects of this superfluity of talking, have already overwhelm'd most other *Arts* and *Professions*; insomuch, that when I consider the means of *happy living*, and the causes of their corruption, I can hardly forbear recanting what I said before; and concluding, that *eloquence* ought to be banish'd out of all *civil Societies*, as a thing fatal to Peace and good Manners.

A proper scientific approach, he argues, needs to avoid rhetoric, metaphors, and Classical vocabulary, which get in the way of clear thinking:

> Who can behold, without indignation, how many mists and uncertainties, these specious *Tropes* and *Figures* have brought on our Knowledg? How many rewards, which are due to more profitable, and difficult *Arts*, have been still snatch'd away by the easie vanity of *fine speaking*? For now I am warm'd with this just Anger, I cannot with-hold my self, from betraying the shallowness of all these seeming Mysteries; upon which, *we Writers*, and *Speakers*, look so bigg. And, in few words, I dare say; that of all the Studies of men, nothing may be sooner obtain'd, than this vicious abundance of *Phrase*, this trick of *Metaphors*, this volubility of *Tongue*, which makes so great a noise in the World.

Sprat is in despair at the way the English language has deteriorated and continues to deteriorate. He sees the decay in language skills as part of the other evils of the time, such as wars and the decline of religious practice (a not unfamiliar contention today: p. 525):

> But I spend words in vain; for the evil is now so inveterate, that it is hard to know whom to *blame*, or where to begin to *reform*. We all value one another so much, upon this beautiful deceipt; and labour so long after it, in the years of our education: that we cannot but ever after think kinder of it, than it deserves. And indeed, in most other parts of Learning, I look on it to be a thing almost utterly desperate in its cure: and I think, it may be plac'd amongst those *general mischiefs*; such, as the *dissention* of Christian Princes, the *want of practice* in Religion, and the like; which have been so long spoken against, that men are become insensible about them; every one shifting off the fault from himself to others; and so they are only made bare common places of complaint.

The Royal Society, he says, is the most professed enemy of these excesses. And they have a solution:

> They have therefore been most rigorous in putting in execution, the only Remedy, that can be found for this *extravagance*: and that has been, a constant Resolution, to reject all the amplifications, digressions, and swellings of style: to return back to the primitive purity, and shortness, when men deliver'd so many *things*, almost in an equal number of *words*. They have exacted from all their members, a close, naked, natural way of speaking; positive expressions; clear senses; a native easiness: bringing all things as near the Mathematical plainness, as they can: and preferring the language of Artizans, Countrymen, and Merchants, before that, of Wits, or Scholars.

Brave words. A fine ideal. But it was all a delusion. Sprat's own discourse was full of the very language he was complaining about. Under no stretch of the imagination could it be described as 'the language of artisans, countrymen, and merchants'. We do not know whether the members of the Society in their everyday discourse achieved a use of language which might plausibly be described as 'a close, natural, naked way of speaking'; but there is no sign of it in their writing, which, though often admirable in its clarity, is heavily dependent on Classical vocabulary and metaphor, containing sentences of great elegance but of structural complexity.

The point can be illustrated from the very first book published by the Society, in 1664. This was a 'green' treatise on timber preservation: John Evelyn's *Sylva; or, a Discourse of Forest-Trees, and the Propagation of Timber in His Majesties Dominions, &c.* His argument is forceful and persuasive, but it is couched in language which is full of the 'amplifications and swellings of style' which the Society was condemning. There is hardly a paragraph which does not have its allusion to Latin or Greek authors, or make references to Classical mythology. It is a literary tour de force. But no one could possibly say that it presented a 'native easiness' of style.

15.4 From Evelyn's *Sylva*

But to turn this just indignation into Prayers, and address my self to our better-natur'd Country-men: May such Woods as do yet remain intire be carefully Preserv'd, and such as are destroy'd, sedulously Repair'd. It is what every Person who is Owner of Land may contribute to, and with infinite delight, who are touch'd with that laudable Ambition of imitating their most illustrious Ancestors, whose Names we find mingl'd amongst Kings and Philosophers, Patriots and good Common-wealths-Men: For such were of old Solomon, Cyrus, and Numa; Licinius sir-named Stolo, Cato, and Cincinnatus; the Pisoes, Fabii, Cicero, Plinies, and a thousand more whom I could ennumerate, that disdain'd not to exercise themselves in these Rusticities, as esteeming it the greatest accession of Honour to dignifie their lasting Names with such Rural marks as have consecrated their Memories, and transmitted them to us through so many Ages and Vicissitudes of the World.

Let none therefore repute this Industry beneath him, or as the least indignity to the rest of his Qualities, which so great Persons have honour'd and cultivated with that affection and ingenuity.

The famous Answer which Cyrus gave to Lysander will sufficiently justifie that which I have said, and what I farther recommend to such Gentlemen as resolve to be Planters, *viz.* That they do not easily commit themselves to the sole Distastes of their ignorant Hinds and Servants, who are (generally speaking) more fit to Learn then to Instruct. *Male agitur cum Domine quem Villicus docet*, was an Observation of old Cato's; and 'twas Ischomachus who told Socrates (discoursing one day upon a like subject): That it was far easier to Make than to Find a good Husband-man: I have often prov'd it so in Gard'ners; and I believe it will hold in most of our Country Employments: We are to exact Labour, not Conduct and Reason, from the greatest part of them; and the business of Planting is an Art or Science (for so Varro has solemnly defin'd it) and That exceedingly wide of Truth, which (it seems) many in his time accounted of it; *facillimam esse, nec ullius acuminis Rusticationem*, an easie and insipid Study.

There is no simple relationship between clarity and language. Apart from well-known political exceptions, everyone wants to be clear and admires clarity of expression in others. But clarity cannot be achieved by forbidding the use of whole areas of language, such as figures of speech or Classical vocabulary, for it may well be precisely those areas which best express a thought. Notions such as 'plain speech' and 'simple style' are notoriously deceptive, especially when it comes to explaining complex thinking. Where would a modern popular scientist, such as Richard Dawkins, be without his reliance on metaphors of blind watchmakers and digital rivers flowing out of Eden?

Clarity depends on our making judicious use of all of a language's resources, and the blanket condemnation of any of these resources is as undesirable as it is unwise. For, when we find such stylistic condemnation itself using the very style which it is condemning, there is no other word for it but linguistic hypocrisy. It is not the first time we have encountered linguistic self-delusion in this book (pp. 57, 292), and unfortunately it will not be the last.

Chapter 16 Standard rules

When it comes to creating a standard language, three groups of people come into the limelight: the orthographers, the orthoepists, and the grammarians. *Orthography* was known from the late Middle Ages, a branch of language study which dealt with the writing system, and especially the way in which words were spelled. Bishop Wilkins is recorded in 1668 using the corresponding notion of *orthoepy*, which dealt with the pronunciation system (what would later be called *phonology*), and especially with how sounds and spellings were interrelated. Both domains would have a place within a *grammar* of English, though the bulk of any grammatical study would be taken up with other matters – with the structure of words, especially their inflectional variation (handled under such headings as *etymology* or *accidence*, p. 381), and the arrangement of words in sentences (handled under *syntax*).

It is these three domains which are central to the definition of a standard language, because, as distinct from vocabulary, they are finite and highly rule-governed. There are only so many sounds and letters, and the ways in which they combine to produce syllables and words, although intricate, are limited. Likewise, there are only so many ways in which words vary their grammatical shape, and only so many ways in which they are arranged into sentences. As has often been said, language makes infinite use of finite means. Apart from stylistic felicities, children normally complete the learning of their phonology and grammar by the time they reach puberty. But in vocabulary, we are dealing with a dimension which is beyond complete learning, potentially infinite in scope (at least a million words in English, p. 455), with new items added to the lexicon every day. Vocabulary is also unpredictable in its presence, as we have seen (p. 44). If we take a book at random, and try to predict which sounds, spellings, grammatical patterns, and words a page contains, we will make good progress under the first three headings, but quickly find failure under the fourth. Apart from a few very common words, the choice of vocabulary is too much bound up with subject-matter and style for us ever to be confident that a particular word is going to appear.

These factors strongly influence the way a standard language is created.

A focus on vocabulary is of limited use when it comes to getting a message about the desirability of standardization across to a general public. Despite all the care and attention Samuel Johnson devoted to 'fixing' the meaning of contentious English words (p. 381), most of those words would only occasionally have been encountered in daily linguistic interaction. An analogy from modern usage is the dispute over the use of *uninterested* as opposed to *disinterested*. Whatever view we take about the matter, the fact remains that it is not a problem we are likely to encounter very often. Hitherto, in this book, I have used *uninterested* just once, and *disinterested* not at all. Whatever energy I might have devoted to getting this distinction fixed in my mind, it benefits me not a bit when it comes to dealing with the rest of the language. Other lexical problems – the distinction between, say, *refute* and *deny* or between *biannual* and *biennial* – raise fresh issues. If people are to be persuaded about the value of a standard variety of English, little progress will be made by concentrating on individual words which, by their nature, are only occasionally encountered. It is much better to draw attention to problems which turn up on every page and in every conversation. If Standard English is to be a badge of politeness (p. 374) or education, then people need to be able to show it continually in their writing and speech. And that means showing it in spelling, in pronunciation, and especially in grammar.

Of the three, in the eighteenth century, it was grammar that was considered to be the most powerful means of drawing attention to the importance of linguistic standards. Grammar transcends the divide between speech and writing: both rely equally on the processes of grammatical construction. And it was grammar which had received the least treatment – a point affirmed by Johnson when he made his acerbic remark about grammarians' negligence of syntax (p. 382). By contrast, orthography *had* received a great deal of attention. Indeed, despite Johnson's belief that there was still 'uncertainty' in this domain, the fact of the matter was that 300 years of steady standardization in spelling had resulted in enormous consensus, and little further need for change. Put any eighteenth-century text through a modern spellchecker, and relatively little will be highlighted (see panel 16.1). Standard English already existed, very largely, as far as spelling was concerned. And people were now very ready to talk about 'bad spelling', as illustrated by Lord Chesterfield, in one of his letters to his son (19 November 1750):

> I come now to another part of your letter, which is the orthography, if I may call bad spelling *orthography*. You spell induce, *enduce*; and grandeur, you spell grand*ure*; two faults, of which few of my house-maids would have been guilty. I must tell you, that orthography, in the true sense of the word, is so absolutely necessary for a man of letters, or a gentleman, that one false spelling may fix a

ridicule upon him for the rest of his life; and I know a man of quality, who never recovered the ridicule of having spelled *wholesome* without the *w*.

There was still some sorting out to be done in relation to punctuation, especially regarding the apostrophe, and there was still some uncertainty over whether compound words should be written solid (*flowerpot*), hyphenated (*flower-pot*), or spaced (*flower pot*) – Swift's *now a-days* illustrates the point – but a great deal of that variation remains today, either in the form of regional differences (e.g., British *humour* vs American *humor*) or alternatives in house style (e.g., *judgment* vs *judgement*). In the eighteenth century, the orthography was almost as standard as it would ever be. And relatively few writers seemed to be especially worried about it. It was a very different situation with grammar, in the 1760s.

16.1 Spelling checking

How far had the eighteenth century to go before its spelling system was equivalent to that found in Modern English? From three texts, written at roughly thirty-year intervals, I have extracted all the spellings that are different from those found in British English today, and list them below. From 1 variant spelling per 50 words in 1672, we find 1 per 150 in 1712, and 1 per 400 in 1747. Older spellings steadily decrease as we approach modern times. By the mid eighteenth century there is very little distance still to travel.

By Johnson's time there is no real evidence of serious 'uncertainty' in orthography. Nor is there much variation within an individual author: there are just six instances in the earlier samples where two spellings of a word appear in the same text. Punctuation is the main feature which is still variable, notably in relation to the apostrophe, which is sometimes present and sometimes not (*Jonson's* and *Jonsons* both used by Dryden) and used in places where it would not occur today (e.g. *embrio's* for *embryos*, *it's* for *its*, p. 380). The seventeenth-century fashion for capitalizing nouns had gone by the time of Johnson.

If we were to classify the variant forms into types, the impression of nonstandard usage would be even less: over half the items in Dryden's list are due to his abbreviating tendency in verbs – *'d* for *-ed* (p. 375). And many of the others are due to a small number of repeated patterns, such as *-our* where we now have *-or*, *-ick* for *-ic*, consonant doubling, an additional *-e*, and changes in the spacing and hyphenation of compound words. Most of present-day orthography was fixed long before Johnson.

1672: Dryden's 'Defence of the Epilogue', c. 5,000 words

acknowledg'd, admir'd, aim'd, allow'd, arriv'd, Black-Friars, blam'd, Bug-bear, call'd, caus'd, censur'd, confest 'confessed', confineing, constrain'd, constru'd, custome, daies 'days', defin'd, deny'd, doe 'do', drest, dy'd 'died', equallity, e're, errours, every where, excell, excell'd, extreamly, farr, fix'd, follow'd, Fopps, forc'd, fore mention'd, form'd, gayety, groveling, height'ning, Heroe, horrour, improv'd, inferr, ingag'd, Inscrib'd, intitled, introduc'd, it self [*also* itself], Judgment [*also* Judgement], justifie, kill'd, labor, Latine, laught 'laughed', liv'd, loosen'd, maintain'd, Master-piece, meaness [*also* meanness], mention'd, misfortunes, Mistriss, mortifi'd, my self, oblig'd, observ'd, onely, our selves, perplex'd, plac'd, Playes [*also* Plays], pleas'd, plyant, polish'd, practic'd, preheminence, propos'd, prov'd, Raggs, receiv'd, refin'd, reform'd, requir'd, reserv'dness, retrench'd, reverenc'd, satisfy'd, sayes, scatter'd, seldome, Sence, Shakespear, shew, show'd, somuch, Tallent, tax'd, tir'd, Unaffraid, unpolish'd, us'd, vigor, waken'd, wonder'd

1712: Swift's 'Proposal', *c.* 5,000 words

alledging, allow'd, Antients [*also* Ancients], any Thing, attone, Candor, Chearfulness, Domestick, dropt, encountring, encreasing, Enthuiastick, Expence, Extream, Fanatick, favorite, forein [*also* Foreign], Honor, Humor, intrinsick, joyned, mouldring, now a-days, our selves, Panegyrick, Publick, refus'd, rendring, Sett, shew, Suedes, tho', Topick, wondred, Your Self

1747: Johnson's 'Plan of a Dictionary', *c.* 8,000 words

antient, bewildred, camæleon, croud, design'd, encrease, enter'd, fix'd, hyæna, Italick, oftner, perswade, phænomena, physick, publickly, registred, shew, suffer'd, synonimous, tho'

Grammars in English and on English were by no means new in the eighteenth century. Such books had been around since William Bullokar's *Pamphlet for Grammar* in 1586 (p. 265), and nearly thirty such books had been published in the following 150 years. Ben Jonson, for example, wrote *An English Grammar . . . for the Benefit of all Strangers, out of his Observations of the English Language now Spoken and in Use* (published in 1640, after his death). The 'strangers' were the foreign learners, becoming increasingly interested in English because 'they want to be able to understand the various important works which are written in our tongue' (a translation from *Grammatica Linguae Anglicanae* [*Grammar of the English Language*], published by the mathematician John Wallis in 1653). And partly because of the interest coming primarily from abroad, there was a focus on the way the language was actually used by educated people. Jonson, recalling Classical models, cites the general usage of the learnèd: '*Custome*, is the most certaine Mistresse of Language, as the publicke stampe makes the current money.'[1]

The change in the grammatical climate, when it came, was really quite sudden and dramatic. The two decades between 1750 and 1770 proved to be the turning-point. The half-century between 1750 and 1800 saw more English grammars published than in the whole of the previous two centuries, with a number going into several editions. All played their part in fostering a new attitude towards grammar, which in the twentieth century would come to be called the *prescriptive* or *normative* approach, because of the way it formulated rules defining what was to count as correct and incorrect usage.[2] Two of these grammars had particular influence. The most important of the early prescriptivists was the clergyman Robert Lowth (1710–87), professor of poetry at Oxford and bishop of London at the height of his career, whose anonymously published *Short Introduction to English Grammar* appeared in 1762. This was the inspiration behind an even more widely used book, Lindley Murray's *English Grammar* of 1795. Murray (1745–1826) was a New York lawyer and businessman who in *c.* 1784 retired to Holgate, near York, England, because of ill-health. There, as a result of a request to provide material for use at a local girls' school, he wrote his *English Grammar, adapted to the different classes of learners; With an Appendix, containing Rules and Observations for Promoting Perspicuity in Speaking and Writing.* Both works went into many editions. Lowth had forty-five by 1800. But it was Murray's *Grammar* which had the greater influence.[3] It became the second bestselling work (after Noah Webster's spelling-book, p. 420) in the English-speaking world, with 200 editions by 1850, selling over 20 million copies, even more popular in the United States than in Britain, and translated into many languages. Twentieth-century school grammars – at least, until the 1960s (p. 523) – would all trace their ancestry back to Murray.

The writer Thomas De Quincey was one who grudgingly acknowledged Murray's supremacy. After listing a series of grammars from Ben Jonson's to Noah Webster's, including Lowth's, he concludes:

> We have also, and we mention it on account of its great but most unmerited popularity, the grammar of Lindley Murray ... This book, full of atrocious blunders (some of which, but with little systematic learning, were exposed in a work of the late Mr Hazlitt's), reigns despotically through the young ladies' schools, from the Orkneys to the Cornish Scillys.[4]

Indeed it did. Murray and English Grammar became synonymous in the early nineteenth century, and – the fate of all institutions – his name eventually began to appear in satirical magazines (such as *Punch*) and in novels. Here is Charles Dickens in *The Old Curiosity Shop* (1840–41), describing Mrs Jarley's efforts to attract a new class of audience to her waxworks (Chapter 29):

> And these audiences were of a very superior description, including a great many young ladies' boarding-schools, whose favour Mrs Jarley had been at great pains

to conciliate, by altering the face and costume of Mr Grimaldi as clown to represent Mr Lindley Murray as he appeared when engaged in the composition of his English Grammar, and turning a murderess of great renown into Mrs Hannah More – both of which likenesses were admitted by Miss Monflathers, who was at the head of the head Boarding and Day Establishment in the town, and who condescended to take a Private View with eight chosen young ladies, to be quite startling from their extreme correctness.

Articles on grammar would routinely give Murray pre-eminence, whether supporting his approach or condemning it. As late as 1869, we find in an issue of *Athenæum* an article headed 'The Bad English of Lindley Murray and other Writers on the English Language'.[5]

The prescriptive grammars perfectly illustrated the eighteenth-century mindset summarized on p. 374. Here is Lowth, taking up the theme of politeness and condemning the whole of English major literary output hitherto:

> The English language as it is spoken by the politest part of the nation, and as it stands in the writings of our most approved authors, oftentimes offends against every part of grammar.

No one was exempt, including all who had in previous generations themselves been critical of contemporary usage and put themselves forward as models of excellence. Lowth's book was indeed a 'short introduction' – fewer than 200 pages – but it managed to pack into its scope criticisms of the language of Shakespeare, Milton, Dryden, Pope, Addison, Swift, and others, all of whom, in his opinion, had offended. It was not that there was any inherent defect in the English language, in his view; these were simply people failing in their efforts to speak or write properly. Murray, who takes much of his material from Lowth, held the same view. The very first sentence of his book reads: 'English Grammar is the art of speaking and writing the English language with propriety.' And the three chapters forming the first part of his Appendix are headed: 'Of purity', 'Of propriety', and 'Of precision'.

Reading through these early grammars, we cannot but be impressed by the detailed grammatical knowledge they display. A great deal of the analysis is accurate and perceptive, and might appear – with minor terminological adjustments – in any modern descriptive grammar. For example, Murray recognizes only two noun cases, nominative and possessive (*a mother / a mother's; mothers / mothers'*), and rejects those grammars which insisted on applying all the Latin terms to the description of English nouns (vocative *O mothers*, ablative *By mothers*, etc.). He writes:

> If these relations were to be so distinguished, the English language would have a much greater number of cases than the Greek and Latin tongue: for, as every

preposition has its distinct meaning and effect, every combination of a preposition and article with the noun, would form a different relation, and would constitute a distinct case. This would encumber our language with many new terms, and a heavy and useless load of distinctions.

None of this would be out of place in a modern introduction to linguistics. And the same point applies to most of the analytical statements, printed in large type, which open each chapter or section. There is only the occasional sign of prescriptivism here. The problems which provoked De Quincey, the *Athenæum* writer referred to above, and many other later language commentators lie in the commentaries, printed in a smaller type, which follow each of these introductory statements. It is the imbalance between descriptive analytic statement and prescriptive interpretive commentary which is so striking.

For example, Rule 5 in Murray's chapter on syntax begins innocuously enough, with a ten-line section on pronoun agreement:

> Pronouns must always agree with their antecedents, and the nouns for which they stand, in gender and number; as 'This is the friend whom I love;' 'That is the voice which I hate' . . .

But this is then followed by a 160-line section of commentary which begins:

> Of this rule there are many violations to be met with; a few of which may be sufficient to put the learner on his guard.

And he then works his way through the various problems of usage, dealing with such issues as the choice between *Give me them books* (wrong) vs *Give me those books* (right), or the use of *who* vs *which* vs *that*. Reasons are not usually given for the choice, other than a personal impression that one construction is 'harsh', 'improper', or 'preferable' compared to another. When reasons are given, they are often (to modern readers) bizarre. Violation 7 of Rule 5, for example, begins:

> We hardly consider little children as persons, because that term gives us the idea of reason and reflection: and therefore the application of the personal relative *who*, in this case, seems to be harsh: 'A child *who*'.

In this case, the rule was eventually ignored, though doubtless several generations of schoolchildren were penalized for getting it wrong.

Many of the famous shibboleths of grammatical usage which continued to be taught in schools throughout the twentieth century derive from Murray's *Grammar*. An example is his Rule 16:

> Two negatives, in English, destroy one another, or are equivalent to an affirmative: as, 'Nor did they not perceive him;' that is, 'they did perceive him'.

His commentary concludes that such cases as 'Nor let no comforter approach me' are improper; they should be rewritten as 'Nor let any comforter approach me'. The reasoning is of course based on the combining value of negative expressions in mathematics and logic – a value which is indeed sometimes implemented in English. When someone says *My childhood was not unhappy*, the meaning is close to *My childhood was happy*, though the negative phrasing suggests some degree of qualification – 'It was not perfectly happy'. But the usual way in which the language as a whole (and many other languages) uses multiple negatives is based on a different principle – one of accumulating emphasis. The more negatives in a sentence, the more emphatically negative the meaning is. This is a usage which can be traced back to Old English, and is strongly present in earlier writers. There are two in Hamlet's advice to the players:

> *Nor* do *not* saw the air too much with your hand . . .

and four in this description of Chaucer's knight:

> He *nevere* yet *no* vileynye [villainy] *ne* sayde
> In al his lyf unto *no* maner wight [person]

This is very close to such examples as *He never said nothing to nobody* in modern nonstandard English, which by Murray's rule are excluded. It was, of course, his exclusion that institutionalized them as nonstandard in the first place.

Another example of a twentieth-century shibboleth occurs in his Section 7 on auxiliary verbs. He picks up on a usage which had bothered grammarians at least since John Wallis (p. 395):

> *Will*, in the first person singular and plural, intimates resolution and promising: in the second and third person, only foretells. . . . *Shall*, on the contrary, in the first person, simply foretells; in the second and third persons, promises, commands, or threatens.

On the basis of this, we find among the illustrations:

> The following passage is not translated according to the distinct and proper meanings of the words *shall* and *will*: 'Surely goodness and mercy shall follow me all the days of my life; and I will dwell in the house of the Lord for ever;' it ought to be, '*Will* follow me;' and 'I *shall* dwell.'

And thus Psalm 23 from the King James Bible is condemned, alongside most contemporary practice in the use of *shall* and *will*, then and now. (A third shibboleth is discussed in panel 16.2.)

It is important to appreciate why such statements are prescriptive, and why prescriptivists have had such a bad press. It is because they select, from the range of expressive opportunities found in the language, one of the options to the exclusion of the others, on the basis of reasoning which, upon investigation, turns out to be spurious. The chosen option is *prescribed* as the 'correct' usage, and the excluded options *proscribed* as 'incorrect', and all the sanctions of educational practice are brought to bear on instilling a proper sense of the former in child intuitions, as well as an antipathy towards the latter – and, of course, a correspondingly critical attitude towards those people (the less well-educated majority) who continue to use them. It hardly needs to be pointed out that all the 'incorrect' options are used within the English-speaking community; indeed, the rejected options may actually be far more commonly used than the favoured one. But in an age where the aim is to support class distinction by linguistic criteria, considerations of frequency are of no relevance. Nor, in an age of authority, is any other reasoning needed, other than by fiat. If the grammarian says that X is correct and Y is incorrect, then it must be so.

16.2 Up with which we will not put

Lowth amplified Dryden's anxiety over placing a preposition at the end of a sentence (p. 376):

> The preposition is often separated from the relative which it governs, and joined to the Verb at the end of the Sentence, or of some member of it: as, 'Horace is an author, whom I am much delighted *with*'.

He is well aware that this is a normal English-speaking practice in informal usage.

> This is an idiom, which our language is strongly inclined to: it prevails in common conversation, and suits very well the familiar style in writing:

The 'strong inclination' can in fact be traced back to early Middle English. But doubtless the etymology of the word weighed heavily with him: if it is a *pre*position, it must go before, not after; and he concludes:

> but the placing of the preposition before the Relative is more graceful, as well as more perspicuous; and agrees much better with the solemn and elevated style.

The last part of this sentence is accurate enough: it is indeed the case that the difference between the two constructions is one of formality. *That's the bus I was travelling in* is much more informal than *That is the bus in which I was travelling*. And if Lowth had gone on to recommend that both be used in their appropriate circumstances, informal and formal, there would be no quarrel today.

But that is not what prescriptive grammarians are for. Their role is not to recognize and applaud variety, but to condemn and eliminate it. Lowth, as Murray after him, wants only the formal alternative to be used. The argument about perspicuity is totally beside the point: it is not the case that one version is any more or less clear than the other. The two sentences are synonymous. And the argument from gracefulness is irredeemably subjective: what Lowth might consider graceful another writer might consider graceless.

Nor are prescriptive grammarians very good at avoiding the practices that they are in the process of condemning. In the above prescription, Lowth actually ends one of his sentences with a preposition: . . . *which our language is strongly inclined to.* Murray, taking over the point wholesale, must have noticed, for in his *Grammar* he corrects it: *This is an idiom to which our language is strongly inclined.* But even Murray lets his guard down from time to time: on p. 40 of his book we read *so convenient is it to have one acknowledged standard to recur to.*

Lowth then lists a number of bad examples, which ought to be avoided in an age of politeness. They include two Shakespearean instances: *Who servest thou under?* from *Henry V*, and *Who do you speak to?* from *As You Like It.* The implication is plain: if even Shakespeare can get it wrong, what chance do ordinary people have? But there is a solution: face can be saved by following the practices recommended by the grammarian.

And good practice could be achieved only by practice. Here are two of the test sentences relating to end-placed prepositions in Lindley Murray's follow-up book: *English Exercises, Adapted to the Grammar Lately Published,* which appeared in 1797. Section 5 (p. 174) adumbrated: 'A fifth rule for the strength of sentences, is, to avoid concluding them with an adverb, a preposition, or an inconsiderable word.'

> By what I have already expressed, the reader will perceive the business which I am to proceed upon.
> Generosity is a showy virtue, which many persons are very fond of.

The Key at the back of the book tells us that the correct versions are *upon which I am to proceed* and *of which many persons are very fond.* The examples are plainly formal in character, and if we sense a stylistic inelegance, especially in the first sentence, it is due to the inconsistency of using both preposed and postposed prepositions in the same construction (*by what . . . proceed upon*). The utterance is plainly part of a discourse of some intellectual content, requiring carefully articulated expression, and it is disturbing to see it change stylistic level halfway through. Such observations could form part of an instructive lesson on English style, in which the stylistic force of the alternative constructions would be compared and contrasted.

But that is not how things went. Schoolchildren learned a black-and-white rule: one should *never* end a sentence with a preposition. As Winston Churchill was later to remark: that kind of English was something up with which he would not put.

In actual fact Murray and the other grammarians did sometimes give reasons for choosing X rather than Y. The choice was usually based on a notion of aesthetics (one construction being more elegant or harmonious than another), or on clarity (one construction being clearer or more precise than another), or on some undefined conception of the character of the English language (one construction being more natural than another). All of these have an initial plausibility, but upon examination they evaporate into subjective impressionism. Nobody would ever deny that it is important for speakers to be clear and precise; and some of Murray's examples do draw attention to genuine dangers of ambiguity which would apply to any writer, regardless of regional background. What is fallacious about the prescriptive approach is its attempt to restrict notions such as clarity and precision to the choice of one alternative when choosing between other alternatives which would convey the same idea just as well.

The last sentence of that paragraph provides an illustration: 'choosing between other alternatives', it said. If you were brought up in the prescriptive tradition, you would have balked at my use of the word *alternative* to refer to more than two options, and of *between* (rather than *among*) as the appropriate preposition. Prescriptive grammar insisted on the prepositional distinction: we choose *between* two options and *among* three or more options. The reasoning is etymological: *between* derives from a word in which the meaning of 'two' is primary (as does *alternative*). But this is spurious reasoning, for etymology can never be a guide to contemporary usage; most of the words in the language have changed their meaning over the past thousand years, their original meanings long forgotten. *Between* has been used with reference to more than two entities at least from early Middle English. Nor is there any lack of clarity in saying *I have to choose between three courses of action*, or (as Gladstone did in one of his essays) *My decided preference is for the fourth and last of these alternatives*. If you do not like these usages, the only reason is that, once upon a time, a grammarian told you otherwise, and may even have beaten the distinction into you. As one correspondent to a BBC radio programme put it:

> The reason why the older generation feel so strongly about English grammar is that we were severely punished if we didn't obey the rules![6]

This says a great deal about English society and educational practice but nothing at all about the real nature of English grammar.

It took time to build up the accumulation of rules which defined 'correct' grammatical usage. Some of these rules predate Murray – such as Dryden's concern about end-placed prepositions (p. 400). Some of the rules most widely debated today postdate Murray, such as the one which says it is wrong to split an infinitive by inserting an adverb between the *to* and the verb – to say *I want to really understand what they are saying* rather than *I want really to understand what they are saying* or *I want* **to understand** *really what they are saying.* But if we count them all up, they do not amount to very many – a few dozen points only, which form a very small part of the grammar of English.[7] Yet, despite their paucity, the set of rules which comprised the prescriptive element in English grammar proved to be immensely powerful as class discriminators, and by the early nineteenth century they were unquestioned as indicators – along with the rules of the spelling system – of a standard variety of the language. From then on, to speak or write Standard English meant primarily to spell it according to the norms, and to construct sentences according to the norms.

The question of pronunciation

And to speak it according to the norms? This was going to be more difficult. Johnson had been particularly worried about pronunciation. Realizing that English had a 'double pronunciation; one, cursory and colloquial; the other, regular and solemn', he despaired of ever being able to handle the former, because of the way it was 'made different, in different mouths, by negligence, unskilfulness, or affectation'. In his Preface he described the task as trying 'to enchain syllables, and to lash the wind'. As a lexicographer, however, he had to make a decision, so he opted for a representation of the solemn variety, taking the written language as a guide:

> For pronunciation the best general rule is, to consider those as the most elegant speakers who deviate least from the written words.

Lindley Murray made the same point, when recommending the pronunciation of verb forms ending with -*ing*:

> it is a good rule, with respect to pronunciation, to adhere to the written words, unless custom has clearly decided otherwise.[8]

On this basis, someone who pronounced the *t* in *often* would be preferred to someone who did not, as would someone who pronounced *singing* instead of *singin'*.

But this was not good enough for his contemporary John Walker (1732–1807), who felt that, somehow, *all* aspects of pronunciation had to be brought within the fold:

> if a solemn and familiar pronunciation really exists in our language, is it not the business of a grammarian to mark both?

Walker acknowledges the difficulty of the task:

> to all works of this kind there lies a formidable objection; which is, that the pronunciation of a Language is necessarily indefinite and fugitive, and that all endeavours to delineate or settle it are in vain

Still, it had to be attempted. Pronunciation was perceived to be a critical faculty, when it came to the presentation of self within society. Lord Chesterfield advised his son to aim for 'an agreeable and distinct elocution; without which nobody will hear you with patience; this everybody may acquire, who is not born with some imperfection in the organs of speech'.[9] And everybody talked about it and worried about it, as James Boswell records (see panel 16.3).

16.3 Provincial disadvantages

On Saturday, 27 March 1772, James Boswell introduced Samuel Johnson to the Scottish gentleman Sir Alexander Macdonald. Part of their conversation provides a fascinating insight into contemporary attitudes about eighteenth-century pronunciation. (The text is from Chapter 24 of Boswell's *Life of Samuel Johnson*. I have added some paragraph divisions.)

> SIR A.: I have been correcting several Scotch accents in my friend Boswell. I doubt, sir, if any Scotchman ever attains to a perfect English pronunciation.
>
> JOHNSON: Why, sir, few of them do, because they do not persevere after acquiring a certain degree of it. But, sir, there can be no doubt that they may attain to a perfect English pronunciation, if they will. We find how near they come to it; and certainly a man who conquers nineteen parts of the Scottish accent, may conquer the twentieth.
>
> But, sir, when a man has got the better of nine-tenths he grows weary, he relaxes his diligence, he finds he has corrected his accent so far as not to be disagreeable, and he no longer desires his friends to tell him when he is wrong; nor does he choose to be told. Sir, when people watch me narrowly, and I do not watch myself, they will find me out to be of a particular county. In the same manner, Dunning [Lord Ashburton] may be found out to be a Devonshire man. So most Scotchmen may be found out. But, sir, little aberrations are of no disadvantage. I never catched Mallet in a Scotch accent; and yet Mallet, I suppose, was past five-and-twenty before he came to London.
>
> Upon another occasion I talked to him on this subject, having myself taken some pains to improve my pronunciation, by the aid of the late Mr. Love, of Drury Lane Theatre, when he was a player at Edinburgh, and also of old Mr. Sheridan. Johnson said to me, 'Sir, your pronunciation is not offensive.' With this concession I was pretty well satisfied; and let me give my countrymen of North Britain an advice not

to aim at absolute perfection in this respect; not to speak *High English*, as we are apt to call what is far removed from the *Scotch*, but which is by no means *good English*, and makes 'the fools who use it' truly ridiculous. Good English is plain, easy, and smooth in the mouth of an unaffected English gentleman. A studied and facetious pronunciation, which requires perpetual attention, and imposes perpetual constraint, is exceedingly disgusting. A small intermixture of provincial peculiarities may perhaps have an agreeable effect, as the notes of different birds concur in the harmony of the grove, and please more than if they were all exactly alike.

I could name some gentlemen of Ireland to whom a slight proportion of the accent and recitative of that country is an advantage. The same observation will apply to the gentlemen of Scotland. I do not mean that we should speak as broad as a certain prosperous member of Parliament from that country [the Lord Advocate, Mr Dundas]; though it has been well observed that it has been of no small use to him, as it rouses the attention of the House by its uncommonness, and is equal to tropes and figures in a good English speaker. I would give as an instance of what I mean to recommend to my countrymen, the pronunciation of the late Sir Gilbert Elliot; and may I presume to add that of the present Earl of Marchmont, who told me, with great good humour, that the master of a shop in London, where he was not known, said to him, 'I suppose, sir, you are an American!' 'Why so, sir?' said his lordship. 'Because, sir,' replied the shopkeeper, 'you speak neither English nor Scotch, but something different from both, which I conclude is the language of America.'

BOSWELL: It may be of use, sir, to have a Dictionary to ascertain pronunciation.

JOHNSON: Why, sir, my Dictionary shows you the accent of words, if you can but remember them.

BOSWELL: But, sir, we want marks to ascertain the pronunciation of the vowels. Sheridan, I believe, has finished such a work.

JOHNSON: Why, sir, consider how much easier it is to learn a language by the ear than by any marks. Sheridan's Dictionary may do very well, but you cannot always carry it about with you; and when you want the word, you have not the Dictionary. It is like a man who has a sword that will not draw. It is an admirable sword, to be sure; but while your enemy is cutting your throat, you are unable to use it.

Besides, sir, what entitles Sheridan to fix the pronunciation of English? He has, in the first place, the disadvantage of being an Irishman; and if he says he will fix it after the example of the best company, why, they differ among themselves. I remember an instance: when I published the plan for my Dictionary, Lord Chesterfield told me that the word *great* should be pronounced so as to rhyme with *state*; and Sir William Yonge sent me word that it should be pronounced so as to rhyme with *seat*, and that none but an Irishman would pronounce it *grait*. Now here were two men of the highest rank, the one the best speaker in the House of Lords, the other the best speaker in the House of Commons, differing entirely.

Elocution was the watchword. The 'Old Sheridan' referred to by Boswell was Thomas Sheridan (1719–88), the father of the playwright, who was famous for his countrywide lectures on elocution, speaking to packed halls. John Watkins, the editor of Richard Brinsley Sheridan's memoirs, reflects on the 'incredible' success of his courses – 'upwards of sixteen hundred subscribers, at a guinea each, besides occasional visitors',[10] in addition to hardback copies selling at half-a-guinea a time (*A Course of Lectures on Elocution,* 1763). Translated into modern values, that is equivalent to a course fee per person of about £75. One of Sheridan's courses must have brought him in (in today's money) well over £150,000. Elocution was big business, and people were prepared to pay for it: it would have cost an up-and-coming clerk a quarter of his weekly salary to attend one of Sheridan's courses. The book sold well in the United States, too, where anxiety over correct speech was just as marked.

Sheridan went on to compile a *General Dictionary of the English Language* (1780), which, with its systematic respelling of words, was a great influence on John Walker, who in due course would hugely exceed him in influence – just as, in the same decade, Murray would exceed Lowth in the field of grammar. Walker eventually earned his own sobriquet – 'Elocution Walker', following a tradition begun by Johnson, who by the 1760s had already acquired the nickname 'Dictionary Johnson'.[11] The book which earned Walker this accolade had been planned as early as 1774, when he published an idea for an English pronouncing dictionary, with the aim of doing for pronunciation what Johnson had done for vocabulary and Lowth for grammar. It finally appeared, in 1791, under the title:

> A Critical Pronouncing Dictionary and Expositor of the English Language: to which are prefixed, Principles of English Pronunciation: Rules to be Observed by the Natives of Scotland, Ireland, and London, for Avoiding their Respective Peculiarities; and Directions to Foreigners for Acquiring a Knowledge of the Use of this Dictionary. The Whole Interspersed with Observations Etymological, Critical, and Grammatical.

'Walker' became a household word, both in Britain and the USA, where in the mid nineteenth century it influenced another bestselling textbook, by Lyman Cobb. Dickens, never one to miss a fashionable trick, picks it up. In Chapter 14 of *Dombey and Son,* Miss Blimber begins her 'analysis of the character of P. Dombey'.

> 'If my recollection serves me,' said Miss Blimber breaking off, 'the word analysis as opposed to synthesis, is thus defined by Walker. "The resolution of an object, whether of the senses or of the intellect, into its first elements."'

Miss Blimber, we have earlier learned (Chapter 11), was 'dry and sandy with working in the graves of deceased languages. None of your living languages for Miss Blimber. They must be dead – stone dead – and then Miss Blimber dug them up like a Ghoul.' Another Dickensian dig at the prescriptive tradition, perhaps.

Dombey appeared in 1848. Walker would have been delighted to know his book had lasted so long, as he had been somewhat taken aback by the unexpected success of the early editions. He complains in the Advertisement to the fourth edition how the rapid sale of the third had made him take up his pen again 'at a time of life, and in a state of health, little compatible with the drudgery and attention necessary for the execution of it'. Dictionary-writing as harmful drudgery, indeed. But he did it, and the book would see over a hundred subsequent editions, and do for pronunciation what Murray and Johnson had done for grammar and the lexicon: provide a polite public, hungry for prescriptions to guarantee the social safety of all aspects of their language, with a recognized authority.

Walker's prescriptive temperament plainly reflects the mindset which we have seen to be a defining feature of the eighteenth century (p. 374). In the final analysis, his belief can be characterized quite simply: he did not believe in the relevance or desirability of linguistic change and variation. He cites two objections to attempting to write a pronouncing dictionary: pronunciation changes too rapidly for a dictionary to remain relevant for long, and there is too much variation among speakers to enable entries to remain under control. Both he dismisses. To the first point he answers:

> the fluctuation of our Language, with respect to its pronunciation, seems to have been greatly exaggerated

he lists a few exceptions, such as the way people now pronounce the word *merchant* differently, but then adds:

> the pronunciation of the Language is probably in the same state in which it was a century ago; and had the same attention been then paid to it as now, it is not likely that even that change would have happened.

This is the 'fixing' motif again (p. 381): a pronouncing dictionary would have stopped change in its tracks. And he displays the same attitude in relation to the second point. The availability of a controlling influence would also have reduced the amount of synchronic variation:

> The same may be observed of those words which are differently pronounced by different speakers: if the analogies of the Language had been better understood, it

is scarcely conceivable that so many words in polite usage would have a diversity of pronunciation, which is at once so ridiculous and so embarrassing.

Ridiculous and embarrassing. The words might have been Johnson's or Boswell's (p. 404). And Sheridan took the same line, in *A Dissertation on the Causes of Difficulties, Which Occur, in Learning the English Tongue*:

> The consequence of teaching children by one method, and one uniform system of rules, would be an uniformity of pronunciation in all so instructed. Thus might the rising generation, born and bred in different Countries and Counties, no longer have a variety of dialects, but as subjects of one King, have one common tongue.[12]

Anything further away from the mindset of the present book, which gives admiring recognition to the centrality of language variation and change in human affairs, can hardly be imagined.

All prescriptivists have to highlight a model to act as an authority, and Walker is in no doubt where that model lies for pronunciation. It is the same as the one intimated by George Puttenham and others 200 years before: London. He says in his various Prefaces:

> Accent and Quantity, the great efficients of pronunciation, are seldom mistaken by people of education in the Capital.

and he introduces an important word into the discussion:

> though the pronunciation of London is certainly erroneous in many words, yet, upon being compared with that of any other place, it is undoubtedly the best; that is, not only the best by courtesy, and because it happens to be the pronunciation of the capital, but the best by a better title – that of being more generally received.

'Received' – an early use of a term which would become a dominant feature of later pronunciation studies (p. 468). He means 'received among the learnèd and polite' – the cultured society which made up the universities, the court, and their associated social structure.

Then we encounter the other side of the coin. What about everyone else? Walker sees them as inhabiting a phonological wilderness.

> the great bulk of the nation, and those who form the most important part in it, are without these advantages, and therefore want such a guide to direct them as is here offered.

The further away they live, the worse their situation:

> harsh as the sentence may seem, those at a considerable distance from the capital,

do not only mispronounce many words taken separately, but they scarcely pronounce, with purity, a single word, syllable, or letter.

And that means the Scots and the Irish are in the worst danger of all, which is why they receive special mention in the subtitle to his book. He relies on Dublin-born Sheridan for his section on the quality of Irish pronunciation – something which, by all accounts (p. 405), would not have received the approval of Dr Johnson.

When Walker gets down to phonetic detail, his approach is unequivocally patronizing and stigmatizing. He begins his section on Ireland in an uncompromising tone:

> The chief mistakes made by the Irish in pronouncing English, lie . . . for the most part in the sounds of the two first vowels, *a* and *e* . . .

and he works his way through a long list of faults. He then deals with Scotland in the same way. After noting that the Scots lengthen their accented vowels, he gives advice on 'the best way . . . to correct this', and then illustrates a series of 'errors' in vowel quality. With both the Scots and the Irish, he notices a distinct tone of voice:

> an asperity in the Irish dialect, and a drawl in the Scotch, independent of the slides or inflections [intonation patterns] they make use of.

The Irish accent 'abounds' with a falling inflection, he says, and the Scottish accent with a rising. So how should a teacher 'remedy the imperfection'? By getting people to practise talking using a tone which is the complete opposite of their natural manner of speech:

> I would advise a native of Ireland, who has much of the accent, to pronounce almost all his words, and end all his sentences with the rising slide; and a Scotchman, in the same manner, to use the falling inflection: this will, in some measure, counteract the natural propensity, and bids fairer for bringing the pupil to that nearly equal mixture of both slides which distinguishes the English speaker, than endeavouring at first to catch the agreeable variety.

Although any of the regional dialects might be discussed in the same way, in the final part of his Preface Walker focuses on Cockney speakers in London. He gives a particular reason for this: Cockney is in an especially bad position, as it is so close to the court and the City. Because 'people of education in London are generally free from the vices of the vulgar', they notice Cockney more. It may have fewer faults than are found in provincial dialects, he says, but it is always to be heard, thrusting itself harshly into the ears of the polite. As a consequence:

> the vulgar pronunciation of London, though not half so erroneous as that of Scotland, Ireland, or any of the provinces, is, to a person of correct taste, a thousand times more offensive and disgusting

In fact he identifies only four 'faults':

- pronouncing *s* indistinctly after *st* (as in *posts*)
- pronouncing *w* for *v* and vice versa (as in *winegar*, a feature of Dickens' Sam Weller some years later)[13]
- not sounding *h* after *w*, so that the distinction between *while* and *wile* is lost
- not sounding *h* where it ought to be and vice versa

Looking back at this list from the standpoint of modern Received Pronunciation (p. 468), it is a curious mixture. The omission of a *t* in the consonant sequence *sts* is common in educated colloquial speech now, in such words as *cyclists*. And the loss of the *wh* vs *w* distinction eventually became part of the standard accent; RP speakers do not distinguish between *Wales* and *whales*. The *v/w* substitutions were already on their way out, in Walker's time; by Dickens, they were no more than a literary stereotype; and they are no longer a Cockney feature.[14] The only long-standing feature of London speech is the issue of *h*, so it is not surprising to see this cited as a special 'vice' (see panel 16.4). Curiously, no mention at all is made of the glottal stop (see further, Interlude 16).

It is all a matter of mindset once again. Walker is well aware of the variable nature of language: 'a degree of versatility seems involved in the very nature of language', he says, and he knows there is such a thing as 'vernacular instinct'. He has a good ear, as shown by his detailed illustration of the way vowel quality changes between stressed and unstressed syllables – 'the *o* in *obedience* shortened and obscured, as if written *uh-be-di-ence*'. Yet the climate of the age will not let him accept the normality, let alone the value, of variation. A few years earlier, Johnson had been much more tolerant. He was a Staffordshire man, with a recognizable accent: 'Johnson himself never got entirely free of those provincial accents,' says Boswell of Johnson in his sixties.[15] As someone who believed that the inhabitants of his birthplace Lichfield 'spoke the purest English', we might expect Johnson to show some signs of accent appreciation – notwithstanding his castigation of Sheridan and others – and so he does (p. 405). But there is no hint of this in Walker.

16.4 *h*-sinking and -sounding

John Walker, after identifying three 'bad habits' of London speech, leaves the worst fault till last:

> A still worse habit than the last prevails, chiefly among the people of London, that of sinking the h at the beginning of words where it ought to be sounded, and of sounding it, either where it is not seen, or where it ought to be sunk.

This 'vice', he adds, is commonly heard among children, who pronounce *heart* as *art* and *arm* as *harm*. It is a feature which, along with the use of the glottal stop, continues to identify Cockney speech today.

Although *h* variation starts getting a bad press in London in the eighteenth century, there is evidence that it is a much older and more widespread process. The anonymous writer of an early fifteenth-century concordance (p. 227) happens to mention one of his problems in passing: *Sum man writeþ sum word wiþ an h, which saame word anoþir man writiþ wiþouten an h.*

> A certain man writes a certain word with an *h*, which same word another man writes without an *h*. [and he continues] Thus it is with the English word which the Latin word *heres* signifies: some write that word with *h* thus, *here*, and some thus, *eir*, without *h*.

And throughout the Middle English period, from the early thirteenth century, we find texts from various parts of the country showing variation in the presence or absence of an initial *h*. Examples of an omitted *h* are *aue* 'have', *ate* 'hate', *elles* 'hell', and *ail* 'hail'. Examples of an inserted *h* are *hic* 'I', *ham* 'am', *herðe* 'earth', and *hunkinde* 'unkind'.[16] There are many more.

The conclusion is plain: *h*- variation is not specifically a London feature. Most people in England and Wales drop their *h*'s some of the time (p. 353) – an observation which supports the notion that the process has been around a long time. It did not start in the eighteenth century. It simply became noticed then, and labelled a vulgarism. It was Cockney's bad luck to be in the firing line, when the polite revolution came.

But once a pronunciation feature is chosen as a class marker, its history becomes irrelevant. Within a few decades of Walker's judgement, societies were being formed for the protection of the letter *H*, and people were paying their sixpences in droves to learn from such booklets as *Poor Letter H, Its Use and Abuse. Addressed to its little vowels a, e, y, o, u, and the millions who use them. Poor Letter H* appeared in 1854, and had sold 30,000 by the following year. Evidently, to drop an *h* was now a social disaster.

Punch writers and cartoonists had a field-day. Virtually all the jokes at the expense of 'Arry and 'is friends in the turn-of-the-century collection, *Mr Punch's Cockney Humour*, involve the *h*. Says a doctor: 'I can tell what you're suffering from, my good fellow! You're suffering from acne!' 'Ackney?' replies the patient. 'I only wish I'd never been near the place!'[17]

But even the *Punch* writers were aware that things weren't so simple. At the very end of the collection we read:

COCKNEY HOBSERVATION. – Cockneys are not the only people who drop or exasperate the 'h's.' It is done by common people in the provinces, and you may laugh at them for it. The deduction therefore is, that a peasant, with an 'h', is fair game.

POOR LETTER 'H'
'Have you got any *whole* strawberry jam?'
'No, miss. All ours is quite new!'

A century of contradictions

It may seem remarkable, today, that writers, scholars, and senior figures in the British establishment of the 1760s should have been prepared to follow the dictates of a very small number of self-appointed language pundits, such as Johnson, Lowth, and Sheridan. The sentiments of Lord Chesterfield, in his 1754 letter to the *World* (p. 365), now seem absurd in the extremity of their subservience. We must choose a 'dictator' to sort out the language, he says:

> I give my vote for Mr Johnson to fill that great and arduous post. And I hereby declare that I make a total surrender of all my rights and privileges in the English language, as a freeborn British subject, to the said Mr Johnson, during the term of his dictatorship. Nay more; I will not only obey him, like an old Roman, as my dictator, but, like a modern Roman, I will implicitly believe in him as my pope, and hold him to be infallible while in the chair; but no longer.

This attitude was by no means unusual. And on the other side of the Atlantic, Noah Webster looked at Britain in disbelief. In his *Dissertations on the English Language* (1789) he writes:

> strange as it may seem, even well-bred people and scholars, often surrender their right of private judgement to these literary governors. The *ipse dixit*[18] of a Johnson, a Garrick, or a Sheridan, has the force of law, and to contradict it is rebellion.

Webster hadn't seen anything yet. He would have to add Walker and Murray to his canon in the next decade.

It was a curious century of contradictions. Pundits saw nothing wrong with pontificating themselves while castigating the efforts of others. 'What entitles Sheridan to fix the pronunciation of English?' Dr Johnson had asked, while trying to do the same sort of thing himself. Society had ignored proposals for an authoritative Academy, several times, yet was evidently ready to accept an unofficial 'academy' of language writers. There were perceptive critics from the outset. Joseph Priestley, for example, saw through the prescriptive mindset straight away. In *The Rudiments of English Grammar* (1761) we read: 'Our grammarians appear to me to have acted precipitately . . . It must be allowed, that the custom of speaking is the original and only just standard of any language.' But his objections, and those of later writers such as De Quincey and Hazlitt (p. 396), hardly caused a ripple in the groundswell of prescriptive opinion which characterized the study and teaching of the English language during the nineteenth century and the first half of the twentieth. And even though times have changed in modern educational practice (Chapter 20), the embedding of prescriptive rules within the intuitions of older people (and thus, the more senior people within society) gives them a continuing influence.

Looking back, we might interpret the precipitance of the grammarians as a response to an issue of much deeper concern. Several of the language writers saw their subject as forming part of a vision of an ordered and unified society which must have seemed unarguably desirable, following the rebellions of 1715 and 1745, the growing uncertainties in British–American relations from the 1760s, and the 1789 French Revolution. Sheridan in particular saw the need for an identifying unity. In 1756 he published *British Education* – the very title is significant (he did not call it *English Education*) – in which he argued that the 'Immorality, Ignorance and false Taste' of contemporary Britain were the result of poor education. He believed that only a 'Revival of the Art of Speaking and the Study of our Language' would solve the problem. The study of elocution, oratory, and rhetoric, in his view, was central to the successful functioning of law, religion, politics, and the whole cultural basis of civilized society. Language norms would guarantee social normality and the avoidance of civil discord. And improved elementary education – with its grammars, dictionaries, and elocution manuals – was the means through which all this would be achieved.

In the eighteenth century, the logic was persuasive, and rarely denied. Its influence remained supreme throughout the nineteenth century, as the British Empire grew, and into the first part of the twentieth. In 1872, William White, talking about the many languages of India, comments:

> As we link Calcutta with Bombay, and Bombay with Madras, and by roads, railways, and telegraphs interlace province with province, we may in process of time fuse India into unity, and the use and prevalence of our language may be the register of the progress of that unity.[19]

English, as the register of unity. This meant Standard English, of course, as the expression of an internationally expanding polite British presence. The colonial mentality through which Walker saw the outlying areas of the British Isles now had world horizons. Standard English was about to go global.

Interlude 16
Glottal stops

The glottal stop is one of the most widely recognized features of a regional accent – not just in England, but in many parts of the English-speaking world. The reason is probably that it is so acoustically obvious. If a consonant is articulated as a glottal stop, it is perceived to have been 'left out', and is widely interpreted as a sign of 'lazy' or 'slovenly' speech. In fact, of course, it is not lazy at all: the amount of energy it takes to produce a glottal stop is considerable – as reflected in the way singers and elocutionists talk about it using the phrase 'hard attack'. But that is neither here nor there, when it comes to the sound's social status. Few other sounds have attracted quite so much vilification in recent years.

Although the sound may be familiar, its name may not be. The term *glottal stop* describes both the location of the sound in the vocal tract and the type of sound it is. The *glottis* is the space between the vocal cords, which are located behind the Adam's apple in the throat. A *stop* is the kind of sound which is made when two vocal organs come tightly together (the sound is 'stopped'); air pressure builds up behind the closure, and when this is released the sound pops out in a mini-explosion – hence *plosive*, an alternative name for stop. The consonants [p] and [b], for example, are stops, with the closure made by the two lips.

In a glottal stop, the closure is made at the glottis: the two sides of the vocal cords come together, holding in the air from the lungs; and you hear a glottal stop when they are suddenly separated. In a cough, for example, the very first thing you hear is a noisy glottal stop. In speech the sound is much quieter. Between vowel-like sounds, it comes out so quickly that you hardly hear the 'catch' in the voice, and the effect is one of a short sharp silence – as in the way London Cockneys say the /t/ sound in *bottle* or in such phrases as *not much* or *get a cab*. The effect is difficult to write in ordinary spelling. It has no letter of the alphabet. Phoneticians show it with a special symbol: [ʔ]. In a phonetic transcription, *bottle* would be written [bɒʔl]. This makes it clear that the word has four distinct sounds in it. Nothing is actually being 'left out' at all: one sound, [t] has simply been replaced by another, [ʔ].

This is the most noticeable type of glottal effect. A more subtle type occurs when a consonant is not *replaced* by a glottal stop but *reinforced* by it. You can hear this kind of articulation when people pronounce a word like *Gatwick* with a glottal stop after the /a/ but with a /t/ articulation immediately following it *as well* – so that it comes out as [gaʔ-twik]. Words ending in a /t/, /k/, /p/, or /tʃ/ (as in *watch*) will often be heard with a glottal reinforcement of the final consonant: *hot*, for example, comes out as [hɒʔt]. This kind of reinforcement is a very noticeable feature of some accents, such as Newcastle (Geordie) English.

You will hear glottal replacement and reinforcement in many British regional accents, especially urban ones. The effects have been around for a long time, though scholars have only begun to talk about them in the last hundred years or so. Nineteenth-century phoneticians, such as Henry Sweet, commented on their existence in some Scottish accents, and by the beginning of the twentieth century their presence in the speech of Londoners was being routinely noted. In addition to London and Newcastle, the glottal stop is common in Edinburgh, Glasgow, Cardiff, Belfast, Bristol, Birmingham and the Midlands, and East Anglia. Outside the British Isles it has been noted in several places such as New York, parts of southern USA, Hawaii, Newfoundland, and Barbados. On the other hand, it is not heard much in most northern English accents, southern Ireland, most of the USA, Australia, New Zealand, and South Africa, though it seems to be coming into the speech of younger people in such cities as Liverpool, Manchester, and Dublin.

Because of its associations with regional and working-class urban speech, glottal stops would be avoided in the prestige accent, Received Pronunciation (RP, p. 468) – and their apparent increase in RP in recent years, along with other changes in pronunciation, has accordingly attracted a great deal of comment. If the glottal stop is entering RP, there could be only two explanations: either it is being less used in these non-prestige accents (thus 'freeing it up' for use in RP) or the RP accent is itself changing, and moving 'downmarket'. There is no evidence for the first explanation: the glottal stop is still frequent everywhere. It is the second explanation which seems to be the case.

However, this change in RP is not as recent as many people think. It is a popular impression that the change is happening now, but as early as 1921 the British phonetician Daniel Jones was remarking on the use of the glottal stop as a noticeably spreading fashion among educated speakers all over the country. He actually predicted that in a hundred years' time everybody would be pronouncing *mutton* as [mʌʔn]. And phoneticians in the middle decades of the century often remarked on the trend.

Is there any direct evidence of the use of the glottal stop in the early years of the twentieth century? Cylinder recordings of voices can be found from the

1890s; there are recordings in the London Science Museum which let us hear what Florence Nightingale and others sounded like. These are too poor in quality for us to hear if any glottal stops are present; but by the 1910s, recording quality had improved greatly. A 1996 study looked for glottal stops in early recordings of a number of people, such as actress Ellen Terry (born in 1848), Daniel Jones (born in 1881), and Bertrand Russell (born in 1870).[20] They were found to be widespread, with some speakers using glottal stops in nearly 80 per cent of all the locations where such an effect would be possible. Daniel Jones, for example, is heard to say *le?me see* and *you ge?some idea*. Ellen Terry even begins the famous speech from *The Merchant of Venice* by saying *The quality of mercy is no?strained*. There is a great deal of variation among the speakers, but they all use it. And the important point to note is that they are all upper-class speakers, speaking in formal contexts, and using an accent which these days many people would describe as 'refined'.

We know that accents are established early on in life. Most people have their accent fixed by their teens, and in the days when geographical mobility was limited, this accent would probably stay throughout their lives. So, if Ellen Terry was using glottal stops in the 1910s she was almost certainly using them in the 1860s. Moreover, although these sounds are not especially common in her dramatic renderings, the fact that they are there at all suggests that they would be even more common in her everyday speech. And the fact that upper-class and well-educated speakers used glottal stops suggests that they must have been even more widespread in the speech of other classes, too.

So the view that the arrival of the glottal stop in Received Pronunciation is something recent is not correct. Certainly, there has been an increase in the spread of the feature since the middle decades of the twentieth century. It is one of the features of so-called Estuary English (p. 472), which people have been talking about since the early 1990s. But this aspect of Estuary (as so many other aspects) is nothing new. It has been around for at least a century. And in places where it is really well known, such as Tyneside, it has probably been part of the pronunciation for much longer. A feature of pronunciation takes time to be established, and the glottal stop is so prevalent in the UK that it must have been in the language for a long time.

Just how long is difficult to say. It is hard to find evidence for older use. Because it has no letter of the alphabet, its presence in speech would not be routinely recorded. And it is difficult to represent in a literary style using the usual way of showing an omitted letter, the apostrophe: *bu'on*, for example, is not a very clear rendition of *button*, so novelists tend to avoid it. There are intriguing hints. We find Abraham Tucker mentioning in his book *Vocal Sounds* (1773, published under the name of Edward Search) the way 'stop' sounds often disappear at the end of a sentence, being replaced by 'a very faint blowing which might be called the ghost of an "h"'. He may well have been talking about glottal stops. On the other hand, John Walker, in his *Critical Pronouncing Dictionary*, published in 1791, lists the four main 'faults' of Cockney speech (p. 410), but these do not include *t* being dropped. If *he* didn't notice it, maybe it wasn't there to be noticed.

The glottal stop isn't a notable feature of the English accents of Australia and New Zealand. And as those accents were formed by emigrants from Britain at the end of the eighteenth century, it suggests that glottal stops were not a feature of their accents. On that basis, the glottal stop would be a nineteenth-century development in England. But where would it have come from? It is heard in Ulster Scots, which suggests that it could have travelled over with the Scots to the Ulster Plantations in the early seventeenth century, and that would make it a sixteenth-century Scottish feature. Maybe it began a slow journey into England after the uniting of the Scots and English crowns. Interesting thought – but pure speculation.

By contrast, some interesting facts have emerged from the scientific study of glottal stops as carried out by sociolinguists in recent years. They have discovered that there is a great deal of variation between the different accents that use them. The stops can appear before /l/ (as in *bottle*), before /n/ (as in *button*), before a vowel (as in *got it*), and so on, but not all accents use them in all of these contexts. Some use them throughout the whole of the pronunciation system; others use them in a very restricted way. Also, men and women use glottal stops differently.

Another discovery is that the two types of glottal effect – replacement and reinforcement – are not used in exactly the same way. Some accents replace and reinforce; some reinforce only. Indeed, people who reinforce only may actually dislike the sound of a full glottal replacement, and avoid it. This difference in social evaluation indicates that the two effects are not just variations in degree – weak and strong glottal versions of the same thing. They are different in kind.

An interesting conclusion follows. If glottal stops are a sign of nonstandard speech, then some accents are more nonstandard than others, in this respect. As we shall see again (p. 531), the terms standard and nonstandard turn out not to be in stark contrast to each other, but to be two points on a continuum of (non)standardness. Moreover, some types of people seem more ready to use the effect than others. If glottal stops are increasing in an accent, there is growing evidence that the change is being led by young middle-class women, who seem more ready to use the most noticeable type – glottal replacement between vowels. This in turn leads to the intriguing conclusion drawn by some sociolinguists: it is the pronunciations which women use that become the prestige forms in a language. Men may be the dominant voice in society, but their accent has been given a female sanction.

Chapter 17 New horizons

The rise of the standard language out of the dialectal diversity of Middle English forms the heart of the traditional 'story' of English. Its starting-point, as we have seen in Chapter 10, lies in a complex network of interrelated factors, which recent studies have done a great deal to disentangle. Its development, also as we have seen, is a steady process of decreasing regionalism and increasing uniformity in the use of spelling and grammar, and to a lesser extent in vocabulary and pronunciation among an elite – 'polite', 'educated' – class of the population (Chapter 15). But what of its maturity? When might we say with confidence that a standard variety of English arrived? The end of the eighteenth century is usually cited, when influential dictionaries, grammars, and pronunciation manuals had 'institutionalized' the variety (Chapter 16), and it had begun to be taught routinely in schools. A recent book title reads: *The Development of Standard English 1300–1800*.[1] And certainly, by this time the process of standardization had resulted in a variety whose character was genuinely supraregional within Britain. The books and teaching were initially influential in America, too. For just a few brief decades, the English-speaking world – from about 1760 to 1800 – was more unified in the way it was taught spelling, grammar, and vocabulary than it had ever been before.

Or would ever be again. Standard English, conceived as a uniform mode of linguistic behaviour uniting English speakers everywhere, began to fragment almost as soon as it had appeared. While Johnson, Lowth, Walker, Sheridan, and the other prescriptivists were busy inserting the remaining bars into a cage which they thought would keep English under proper control in Britain, on the other side of the Atlantic the cage-door was about to be opened by Noah Webster, who was proposing a different set of linguistic norms for American English (see panel 17.1). Webster saw the arrival of American independence in 1776 as an opportunity to get rid of the linguistic influence of Britain. The new nation needed new language – rationalized and refined as British English had been, but with a fresh identity. In his *Dissertations on the English Language* (1789) he therefore proposed the institution of an 'American standard'. It was hardly possible, he reasoned, for British English to continue to be the model for

17.1 Noah Webster (1758–1843)

Webster was born in West Hartford, Connecticut, served briefly in the US War of Independence, and graduated from Yale in 1778. He worked as a teacher, clerk, and lawyer, becoming dissatisfied with the lack of an American perspective in the texts he had to use. His general attitude can be found in an essay he wrote in 1785, included in a pamphlet called *Sketches of American Policy*. In his 'Plan of policy for improving the advantages and perpetuating the Union of the American States' he complains: 'Nothing can be more ridiculous than a servile imitation of the manners, the language, and the vices of foreigners.'

Webster published a spelling guide (which became a bestseller in its own right), a grammar, and a reader as part of *A Grammatical Institute of the English Language* (1783–5), and in 1800 began work on his first dictionary. *A Compendious Dictionary of the English Language* appeared in 1806, containing *c.* 28,000 words. Then, in 1828, appeared *An American Dictionary of the English Language*, in two volumes, with *c.* 70,000 words.

The 'American' in the title does not refer to a distinctive American lexicon, for very few words in the dictionary were not available in both the United States and Britain; it is more a reflection of the American authors used as sources for the vocabulary. None the less, the book did contain words to do with US culture and institutions, such as *congress, caucus, statehouse,* and *plantation*, and it contained a great deal of encyclopedic information, such as names of towns and data on population – an emphasis which distinguishes American and British lexicography to this day. Nearly half the words which are included (especially in science and technology) were not to be found in Johnson's *Dictionary* (p. 382).

The *American Dictionary* made Webster a household name in the USA, and it rapidly became the authority in matters of spelling, pronunciation, meaning, and usage. It was fiercely attacked in Britain for its Americanism, but it gave US English an identity and status comparable to that given to the British English lexicon by Dr Johnson.

the American people. England was too far away. British English was too corrupt and in a state of decline. But above all, it was a matter of honour 'as an independent nation ... to have a system of our own, in language as well as government'.

The English language bird was not freed by the American manoeuvre. Rather, it hopped out of one cage into another. The new nation was just as prescriptively minded as the old one. The idea had already been raised for the formation of an Academy to safeguard the (American) language. America, as Britain, had let the language develop 'by itself' (p. 374). Since 1600, a large number of new words had entered American English, and variant pronunciations, spellings, and usage had developed as naturally as in Britain. This was far too haphazard for many people. America thought it could succeed where Britain had failed. A proposal for an 'American Society of Language' was made to the *Royal American Magazine* as early as 1774, but nothing happened. In 1780, John Adams (US president 1797–1801) wrote to Congress hoping that it would form 'the first public institution for refining, correcting, and ascertaining the English language'. The letter might have come from the pen of Swift (p. 365). Nothing happened. A Philological Society was founded in New York in March 1788, with Webster a leading light, with the aim of 'ascertaining and improving the American tongue'; but it lasted less than a year. And then, temporary success, in 1820, when an American Academy of Language and Belles Lettres was launched in New York, with John Quincy Adams (John Adams' son) as president. Its aim was 'to promote the purity and uniformity of the English language', and it had plans for a dictionary – though of a rather different kind from Webster's, as its members strongly disapproved of American neologisms. Its committee on Americanisms was told:

> collect throughout the United States a list of words and phrases, whether acknowledged corruptions or words of doubtful authority, which are charged upon us as bad English, with a view to take the best practical course for promoting the purity and uniformity of our language.

But disagreements grew. After only two years, having received little support from government or public, the group broke up. Thomas Jefferson, who had refused the offer of the honorary presidency of the Academy, was one who was not surprised:

> Judicious neology can alone give strength and copiousness to language, and enable it to be the vehicle of new ideas.[2]

A refreshingly modern view.

All this seems to have taken the British by surprise. There had been a largely unspoken assumption that the linguistic identity emerging among the elite class in England would naturally transfer to the rest of the English-speaking world, as the British Empire grew, and that it would take more than the occasional independence movement to stop it. But as English began its journey around the globe, the same pressures of identity which had promoted a standard variety in England began to operate again, except now they operated in different directions. Initially, views were mixed. Some of the first settlers in America were quite happy to retain their historical and linguistic links with Britain; the colonists in Virginia wanted to continue their lives as English people, and they maintained ways of life and family connections in Britain for several generations. On the other hand, the colonists in Massachusetts were driven by a sense of new destiny, and evolved a cultural milieu which would later be called the 'New England Way'. It was this spirit of independence and fresh purpose which had become the dominant ethos by the time Webster and his contemporaries began to intervene.

The British reacted with consternation. The *Monthly Review*, in March 1808, condemned 'the corruptions and barbarities which are hourly obtaining in the speech of our transatlantic colonies' – though 'colonies' was by then a somewhat nostalgic term. And the next month, the *British Critic* concurred: 'the common speech of the United States has departed considerably from the standard adopted in England'. This was mild language compared with some critics, who railed against the 'spurious dialect' which was emerging, condemning everything as linguistic 'perversions'.[3] Although some earlier travellers had been impressed by what they heard, the remarks of the Scottish visitor, Thomas Hamilton, were more typical:

> The amount of bad grammar in circulation is very great; that of barbarisms enormous . . . The privilege of barbarizing the King's English is assumed by all ranks and conditions of men.[4]

And he was one of the first to make the prediction which would be made at regular intervals over the next century:

> Unless the present progress of change be arrested by an increase of taste and judgment in the more educated classes, there can be no doubt that, in another century, the dialect of the Americans will become utterly unintelligible to an Englishman.

Two hundred years on, this prediction continues to be made.

Webster approached his self-appointed task by focusing on spelling, which he felt to be the heart of the matter. In his *Dissertations* he observed:

> a difference between the English orthography and the American . . . is an object of vast political consequence.

After reviewing the disastrous way in which spelling had been left to look after itself in Britain, resulting in a highly irregular system and 'an orthography very ill suited to exhibit the true pronunciation', he asks:

> The question now occurs; ought the Americans to retain these faults which produce innumerable inconveniencies in the acquisition and use of the language, or ought they at once to reform these abuses, and introduce order and regularity into the orthography of the AMERICAN TONGUE?

Such a small change would have major consequences. Uniformity would foster unity.

The alteration, however small, would encourage the publication of books in our own country. It would render it, in some measure, necessary that all books should be printed in America . . . The inhabitants of the present generation would read the English impressions; but posterity, being taught a different spelling, would prefer the American orthography.

Besides this, a national language is a band of national union. Every engine should be employed to render the people of this country national; to call their attachments home to their own country; and to inspire them with the pride of national character.

And, as a member of the first generation of a newly independent country, Webster is in no doubt:

> *Now* is the time, and *this* the country, in which we may expect success, in attempting changes favorable to language, science and government . . . Let us then seize the present moment, and establish a *national language*, as well as a national government.[5]

In the event, the new spelling system was not as radical a departure from the old one as he had initially envisaged. Although at first in favour of radical reform, his original proposals received little support, and he eventually opted for a more moderate solution, avoiding the introduction of new letters and diacritics. Indeed, in his later work he became less concerned about the British/American divide, and spoke out in favour of an international language.

His full range of proposals was published in the 1806 *Compendious Dictionary*. The approach employed two main principles: 'the omission of all superfluous and silent letters'; and the 'substitution of a character that has a certain definite sound, for one that is more vague and indeterminate'. By no means all of his suggestions caught on. Many final -*e*'s (as in *definite*) and 'silent' vowels (as in *feather*) stayed. On the other hand, he was successful in changing -*re* words to -*er* (*center*) and omitting *u* from words ending in -*our* (*color*). Today, most of the differences between American and British spelling are due to the American words having fewer letters – in two thirds of cases, one vowel instead of two (*anemic* for *anaemic*, *armor* for *armour*, *caldron* for *cauldron*, *diarrhea* for *diarrhoea*, *smolder* for *smoulder*) or dropping a vowel (*ax* for *axe*, *catalog* for *catalogue*, *largess* for *largesse*, *story* [of a building] for *storey*). Consonant changes included the use of *z* for *s* in verb endings (*advertize*, *analyze*), replacing -*ce* by -*se* (*defense, offense*), the dropping of a final -*k* from words ending in -*ick* (*musick, physick* – something that had already begun to happen in Britain), and simplifying the double consonant before a suffix (*traveling, appareled*). A number of other changes can be seen in this further selection of graphological differences (the British form is in parentheses):

424 THE STORIES OF ENGLISH

check (cheque), donut (doughnut), draftsman (draughtsman), [roadside] curb (kerb), jail (gaol), program (programme), maneuver (manoeuvre), mollusk (mollusc), mustache (moustache), plow (plough), pajamas (pyjamas), sulfur (sulphur), thruway (throughway), tire (tyre)

Most of the changes were rejected out of hand in Britain as being 'American' and condemned with considerable emotion. As a result, they stayed firmly on the US side of the Atlantic – at least, until a twentieth-century wave of borrowing changed the situation (p. 477).

It might be thought odd that a few orthographic differences would cause such controversy and bitterness; but that is the way, with spelling, as Lord Chesterfield among many others had remarked the century before (p. 393). Good spelling is a badge of identity – originally a symbol of polite breeding and education, now a badge of being American as well. Webster in fact was only doing what Johnson and the others had done before him: he was turning the language he spoke and wrote into an institution. He actually called one of his books *A Grammatical Institute of the English Language* – the word meant no more than 'digest of principles', but it had the overtones of earlier meanings of 'established law' and 'institution'. However, Webster had a fresh constituency in mind. He used the same reasoning that had been used by the British and other Europeans the century before – a standard language is needed to symbolize status, stability, and political unity (p. 366) – but it was a new nation that now needed the symbol.

Webster provided the published institutions that allowed this nation to develop a sense of linguistic identity – a spelling-book, a dictionary, and a grammar. It seems remarkable today that one man might wield such extensive and long-lasting linguistic influence, but, as we have seen in relation to Britain (p. 412), the climate of the age was ready for authoritative statement, even if coming from a self-appointed few. America, blinking in the light of freshly achieved independence (1776), was looking for linguistic direction even more than Britain had been. And a distinctive written American English provided an important and far-reaching part of the solution. Terminology soon emerged to capture the fresh direction. The term *Americanism* was first used by Scottish clergyman James Witherspoon in 1781, an analogy with the word *Scotticism*. Robert Ross published an *American Grammar* in 1782. Congress used the phrase *American language* in 1802.

Yet despite the new mood, there was also a great deal of cultural and linguistic continuity. The US schools in the early nineteenth century were much influenced by their British forebears, and in their linguistic practices continued to teach using the leading British textbooks in rhetoric (composition) and grammar, such as those of Lowth and Murray (p. 396). They also promoted the study of English literature, using the same range of recognized authors as would have been taught in Britain. American literature was in any case a much later development, with such authors as Washington Irving and James Fenimore Cooper not publishing until the mid nineteenth century. Most well-known American authors, such as Longfellow, Hawthorne, Poe, Melville, Whitman, and Twain, were not even born by 1800. And American literature, when it eventually emerged, did not begin to be studied in US schools until the twentieth century.

Some commentators rather overstated the continuities. They drew attention to such usages as *gotten*, *I guess* 'suppose', *flapjack*, *beef* (for the animal), *loan* 'lend', *mad* 'angry', *homely* 'plain-featured', *fall* 'autumn', and the use of an *a-* prefix (as in *a-running*) in order to suggest a closeness to the language of Shakespeare, Chaucer, and their contemporaries which they claimed British English had lost (for such usages were either provincial or obsolete in Britain). This led to a hugely popular myth that some isolated American rural dialects, especially in Appalachian 'hillbilly' territory, had actually managed to preserve Elizabethan English. In fact, there were relatively few such usages. Although some dialects had changed less rapidly than others, all had changed significantly over the two centuries of settlement – as is only to be expected. The view that a colony is somehow inherently more conservative in its linguistic usage than its mother country (sometimes referred to as *colonial lag*)[6] is a considerable oversimplification.

It is important to be aware of this mixture of reactions and continuities when taking a view about the nature of language change, and of attitudes to the language, in the early decades of the new nation. On the one hand, there was indeed a huge amount of continuity. The common core of the language was still there. There are no obvious Americanisms in the Declaration of Independence, and they are hard to find even in such mid nineteenth-century authors as Emerson and Longfellow. On the other hand, there was a huge amount of difference. At a very early stage, people were focusing on the contrasts and predicting the emergence of a new standard. In a 1781 article, James Witherspoon predicted that the Americans would 'find some center or standard of their own', and he began to make a collection of Americanisms from all social classes and educational backgrounds. He was an accurate prophet. The distinction between Old World and New World would in due course have its linguistic dimension, and a dual standard would emerge.

The relationship between sameness and difference is at the heart of historical linguistics. There is always convergence and there is always divergence, operating simultaneously. Both processes are subject to many influences – too many, indeed, for them to be capable of control by any one person or by an Academy. Even Webster, one of the most ardent enthusiasts for change, eventually recognized that there needed to be a balance. In the introduction to his 1828 *Dictionary* he wrote: 'although the body of the language is the same as in England, and it is desirable to perpetuate that sameness, yet some difference must exist'. Although there was a conscious effort on Webster's part to foster change, change would have happened anyway. American and British had been diverging from the moment the first English-speaking settlers arrived in North America, and his orthographic innovations simply added a fresh dimension to the process, albeit a highly visible one.

It is important to recognize that there are always two sides to divergence. It is misleading to think of all the movement as being on the American part. When English arrived in America, it continued to evolve on *both* sides of the Atlantic but in different directions, as the second diagram in panel 17.2 illustrates. There were variations in American English which were unknown in Britain, and variations in British English which were unknown in America. This is hardly surprising. Transportation between Britain and America was very slow and expensive, and the opportunities for ongoing linguistic influence were extremely limited. When they did arise, there was no symmetry. Thanks to the cultural continuities with Britain, and that country's economic pre-eminence (in the eighteenth century), linguistic changes in Britain were more likely to be picked up in America than the other way round. Influential British publications, such as the grammars and dictionaries, achieved considerable sales in America, as we have seen (p. 396). Only in the twentieth century do we see the process in reverse, and the former empire striking back.

17.2 Two views of American and British English

The late eighteenth-century view, held on both sides of the Atlantic, was that American English was diverging from the standard language found in contemporary Britain.

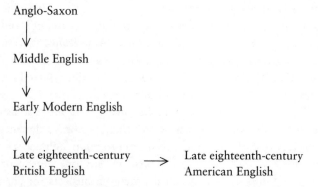

Anglo-Saxon

↓

Middle English

↓

Early Modern English

↓

Late eighteenth-century   →   Late eighteenth-century
British English   American English

A more accurate view emphasizes the common continuity between these two varieties and older states of the language. From this standpoint, it is not strictly proper to talk about 'British English' until the seventeenth century, because only then is there something to contrast it with. There was no 'American English' previously. Before 1607 there was only 'English' – in its various varieties within the British Isles.

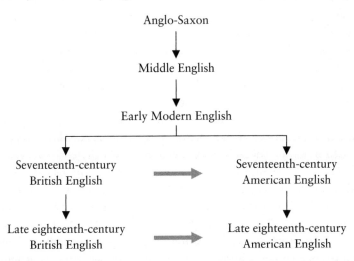

The block arrows indicate the ongoing influence of Britain upon America throughout the period. In the twentieth century, of course, the direction of these arrows reversed.

Growing diversity

From the second half of the eighteenth century, in the United States as in Britain, the prescriptive temperament ruled. Writers believed in the value of a uniform variety of English to be taught in school and to be used in writing and speech by people throughout the country as a sign of their educated upbringing. At the same time, the spread of English throughout North America had led to an unprecedented linguistic diversity. The linguistic contrast between an educated and an uneducated class was therefore very much in evidence. But the contrast was much more marked in America than it was in Britain, because significantly greater areas and more types of speaker were involved.

Everything was on a larger scale. We are, after all, talking about a country some thirty times the size of the British Isles, and a population whose growth would soon vastly exceed that of Britain. By 1700, the colonial American population numbered around 220,000. At the time of the first census, in 1790, there was a total population of 3.9 million (in sixteen states) – more or less the size that England's had been in 1600. This total would rise to over 5 million in 1800, and double again by 1820 (in twenty-four states). By 1860, the American population of 31 million (in thirty-six states) had passed that of Britain's 30 million, and fifty years later, with 91 million (in forty-eight states), it was twice the British total. With such numbers, distributed over such a huge area, the scene was set for an unprecedented amount of language variation.

A number of factors shaped the growing diversity, each of which had immediate linguistic consequences. There was great popular mobility, as the search for land moved westwards, with families and communities splitting and combining in multifarious ways. The political structure of the United States evolved into a loosely decentralized federation, which fostered notions of regional identity. Communication routes did not all lead to a single centre, as they had in England, where London had acted as a cultural, political, and economic magnet. The immigrants entered a world where there was no inherited social structure; they had to devise their own, using class criteria other than those of inherited privilege. New pressures were placed upon English, as settlers adapted it to cope with an unprecedented range of physical and environmental conditions – deserts, deltas, forests, prairies, high mountains – as well as new fauna and flora, patterns of indigenous behaviour, and the customs of settlers from different cultural backgrounds. Here is a small selection from the vocabulary which appeared:

> backwoodsman, bayou (French), bury the hatchet, cache (French), canoe, coleslaw (Dutch), corn 'maize', eggplant, groundhog, hominy, log cabin, moccasin, moose, noodle (German), peace pipe, pecan, pretzel (German), raccoon (p. 301), scalp, skunk, squatter, stoop (Dutch), tapioca, toboggan

Above all, the settlers represented in their origins a far wider set of language and dialect backgrounds than had ever before been made to cohabit within the short time-frame of a century.

There were, to begin with, dialect differences originating in the various parts of Britain from which the original settlers came (see panel 17.3). By the time of the first census, in 1790, just over 2 million were recorded as having come from England or Wales. The eighteenth century had additionally seen a marked increase in the number of immigrants from other parts of the British Isles, notably the Irish and Scots-Irish (from northern Ireland). The Irish had been migrating to America from around 1600, but the main movement began during the 1720s. By 1776, it is thought that one in seven of the colonial population was Celtic in origin. Many stayed along the coast, especially in the Philadelphia area, but most moved inland through the mountains to find land. They were seen as frontier people, with an accent which at the time was described as 'broad'. The opening up of the south and west was largely due to the pioneering spirit of this group of settlers, and their numbers rapidly grew. Over 37,000 Irish are recorded in the 1790 census, and over 162,000 Scottish (nearly a third of them living in Pennsylvania).

17.3 Early accent origins

The first permanent English settlement in North America dates from 1607, when an expedition arrived in Chesapeake Bay. The hundred or so colonists called their settlement Jamestown (after James I) and the area Virginia (after Elizabeth, the 'Virgin Queen'). Further settlements followed along the coast, and also on nearby islands, such as Bermuda. Then, in November 1620, the first group of Puritans, thirty-five members of the English Separatist Church, arrived on the *Mayflower* in the company of sixty-seven other settlers. Prevented by storms from reaching Virginia, they landed at Cape Cod Bay, and established a settlement at Plimoth (now Plymouth, Massachusetts). By 1640, about 25,000 immigrants had come to the Massachusetts area.

The southern and northern settlements had different linguistic consequences. The southern colonists came mainly from England's 'West Country' – such counties as Somerset and Gloucestershire – and brought with them its characteristic accent, a chief feature being the *r* pronounced after vowels. Most of the northern colonists came from counties in the east of England, such as Norfolk, Suffolk, Essex, and London, with some from further afield. These eastern accents tended not to sound an *r* after vowels, and this proved to be the dominant influence in the area. *Harvard*, for example, would be pronounced 'Haava'd'. Although a few settlers came from the south-west – such as Alice Bradford, the wife of the first governor of the colony, who hailed from Somerset – their accent did not prevail.

During the seventeenth century, new groups of immigrants brought an increasing variety of British linguistic backgrounds. From the 1640s, colonists to Virginia included some 40,000 cavaliers and their servants, escaping the anti-royalist sentiments of the English Civil War; two thirds of these settlers came from the English south and west. And after the Restoration, some 23,000 Quakers arrived, chiefly settling in Pennsylvania; their origins were mostly from the North Midlands, Lancashire, and Yorkshire, though they also included some Welsh and Scots-Irish (p. 438).

Resonances of these early distinctions can still be heard today, but mainly along the eastern seaboard of the United States. In 1973, in a joint broadcast for the BBC and Voice of America, Princeton professor Albert H. Marckwardt summed it up like this:

> As one moves west, particularly beyond the Appalachian Mountains, the more obvious distinctions tend to level out, and the language is much more uniform.[7]

The popular notion of a 'General American' accent comes from this impression of uniformity.

However, the British and Irish immigrants were not the only influences on the character of American accents and dialects. A very significant amount of regional distinctiveness arose from within the country itself – from mutual influences between varieties, interaction between English and other languages, and spontaneous processes of change affecting the pronunciation of individual sounds, words, and grammatical constructions. As one scholar has put it:

> no variety of British or Irish English found itself replicated in North America, and no American dialect, however conservative, derives largely from the British Isles. In all types of American English the indigenous character is dominant.[8]

The dialect mix becomes more complex when we add the speech of settlers from non-English backgrounds. During the seventeenth and eighteenth centuries, immigrants arrived from all parts of Europe, started to learn English, and evolved distinctive 'Dutch English', 'German English', 'French English', and other speech varieties. The chief nationalities of non-English-speaking origin in 1790 were the Dutch (c. 56,000, 90 per cent of them living in the New York area) and the Germans (c. 139,000, about 80 per cent of them living in the Pennsylvania area). There were also some 11,000 people of French background. Nor must we forget the English spoken by an increasingly bilingual indigenous Indian population – reduced to a small but resilient number by conflict with the incomers and European-introduced diseases.[9]

Finally there was the English spoken by the growing black population, well on its way to evolving as a distinctive creole variety. By 1800 there were over 750,000 people of African-American origin, chiefly in the southern part of the country, where they far outnumbered the southern whites. The vast majority were slaves, but a small and steadily growing proportion (about 14 per cent in 1800 – some 108,000) were free. A consequence was the emergence of a wide range of accents and dialects, collectively usually called 'Southern', affecting both black and white populations (see Interlude 17). And within this, a black vernacular was evolving which would later come to be called African-American Vernacular English, and whose distinctive grammatical properties – such as the omission of forms of the verb *be* (*she going, he ready*) – have now received a great deal of study.[10] However, the early history of this variety is complex, controversial, and only partially understood. Records of speech forms are sparse, so that it is unclear, for example, exactly how much influence black speech had on the pronunciation of southern whites, and vice versa. Information is fuller from the mid nineteenth century, when the abolitionist movement focused national attention on black civil rights, and sympathetic representations of black English began to appear in literary works, such as those by Harriet Beecher Stowe and Mark Twain (p. 500).

Linguistic variation lay at the heart of the new nation, though the extent of the regional diversity became evident only during twentieth-century dialect studies. As in Britain, the true extent of spoken variety was obscured by a focus on the written standard, and by a natural process of cultural accommodation, as people hammered out a new way of life. The drive for nationhood readily fostered a corresponding linguistic accommodation (p. 83). As people speaking very different kinds of English found themselves living alongside each other, sharing common aspirations, a great deal of accent and dialect levelling took place. The concept of the 'melting pot' must have applied very early on to immigrant speech. One result was the foundation of the accent which came to be heard across the country throughout the northern and central regions – sometimes loosely referred to as 'General American' (though its generality is not as widespread as is often assumed). It was this accent which came to be represented in the dictionaries and pronunciation manuals, and which is most commonly used as a convenient standard of reference for the study of American speech. A standard of reference is all it is. There has never been a standard accent in the United States corresponding to the supra-regional educated accent (Received Pronunciation) which came to the fore in Britain during the nineteenth century (p. 468).

Although certain parts of the United States display considerable admixture, and despite the fact that in some areas very little descriptive work has been done, there is clear support for three, and probably four, major dialect divisions, each containing several subdivisions (see panel 17.4).[11] *Northern* is found in the north and north-east, historically focusing on New England and New York City, but extending west to include the upper regions of Pennsylvania and of the Midwestern states (Ohio, Indiana, Illinois), and north-west into the Dakotas, with significant influence in the northern Pacific states, where it mixes with Western. *Southern* is found from Virginia along the Atlantic coast and then along the Gulf coast states, as well as some way inland into Texas, Oklahoma, and Arkansas, where it mixes with Midland. A *Midland* area – the rest of the country – is now often divided into two, with a *Western* region identified to include most of the Pacific coast, the Rockies, the Great Plains, and the western Mississippi Valley. A narrower notion of *Midland* then occupies the eastern central area, from Pennsylvania to the eastern Mississippi region. Several subdivisions within these areas have also been proposed. However, cutting across the geographical classification are the three primary social dialects of American English: *Anglo* (of European ancestry), *African-American* (of African ancestry), and *Hispanic* (of Central American ancestry). The Northern region is predominantly Anglo in character. The Southern region is very mixed, but is distinctive for its African-American presence. Hispanic presence is chiefly notable throughout the south-west, from southern California through Arizona,

17.4 Some US regional dialect items

Northern

angleworm 'earthworm', *brook* 'stream', *comforter* 'quilt', *darning needle* 'dragon-fly', *johnnycake* 'corn bread'; *wun't* 'wasn't', *dove* 'dived', *hadn't ought* 'shouldn't'

Midland

blinds 'roller shades', *coal oil* 'kerosene', *green beans* 'string beans', *skillet* 'frying pan', *spouting* 'drainpipes'; *clum* 'climbed', *all the further* 'as far as'

Southern

chifforobe 'wardrobe', *clabber* 'curdled milk', *goobers* 'peanuts', *polecat* 'skunk', *tote* 'carry', *varmint* 'small predator'

Creole forms
they gone, we ready, might could, I done gone, right fine – and see also: *y'all* (p. 449), *gumbo* (p. 531)

Western

Mississippi Valley
boulevard 'grass strip at roadside', *spider* 'frying pan', *Dutch cheese* 'cottage cheese'

South-West
calaboose 'jail', *arroyo* 'dry creek', *trap* 'enclosure for livestock', *hackamore* 'rope halter'

New Mexico, to southern Texas, and also in southern Florida. Falling outside of this classification are the geographically separate Alaska and Hawaii, with their distinctive indigenous populations.

Such levels of linguistic diversity could never have been anticipated. In the Elizabethan period, a development of this magnitude was unimaginable. Even Richard Mulcaster, one of the strongest proponents of the role of English as a valid language of the intellect (p. 296), was reluctant to grant it any international potential at the time:

> our English tongue . . . is of small reach, it stretcheth no further than this Island of ours, nay not there over all[12]

He was right, for the Celtic languages were still strongly present in the sixteenth century, and relatively few people engaged in foreign travel. When they did go abroad, they found other languages more useful. Some time later, in the 1650s, the Irish priest, poet, and traveller Richard Flecknoe reported on his ten-year journey through Europe, Asia, Africa, and America. He found that the really useful languages to know were Spanish and Dutch, with English being only occasionally helpful – as he put it, 'to stop holes with'.[13]

Mulcaster made his comments in 1582 – not really the year to be asserting that English 'stretcheth no further than this island of ours', given that two years later Walter Ralegh would send the first of his expeditions to America, and within a generation a permanent settlement would be established in Virginia. Mulcaster had gone on to say, 'our state is no Empire to hope to enlarge it by commanding over countries'. Events soon proved him wrong. Indeed, because of the developments in America, by the middle of the eighteenth century the position of English as an international language had already changed perceptions about its future. In 1767 the philosopher David Hume – writing at a time when French was indisputably the first language of international diplomacy – felt able to say:

> Let the French, therefore, triumph in the present diffusion of their tongue. Our solid and increasing establishments in America . . . promise a superior stability and duration to the English language.[14]

This was a view, of course, which Americans in the 1760s would have found most congenial. And after 1776 they did not hesitate to assert that the future of the language lay very much in their hands. In 1780, as part of his address to Congress for an Academy, John Adams said:

> English is destined to be in the next and succeeding centuries more generally the language of the world than Latin was in the last or French is in the present age. The reason of this is obvious, because the increasing population in America, and

their universal connection and correspondence with all nations will, aided by the influence of England in the world, whether great or small, force their language into general use, in spite of all the obstacles that may be thrown in their way, if any such there should be.

As we have seen, the Academy proposal failed; but he was right about the rest.

Further horizons

During the late eighteenth and early nineteenth centuries, the geographical horizons of the language steadily expanded as the British Empire grew. To the dialect situation within the British Isles and the United States was now added the foundation of new varieties, as English began to be adapted to meet the communicative demands of new locations. Nothing happened overnight. The power-wielders who took the language around the world – the governors, officers, diplomats, senior civil servants, schoolteachers, missionaries, and their entourages – initially worked through the medium of Standard British English, and in many parts of the English-speaking world, 200 years on, still do. But within fifty years of Johnson's *Dictionary*, it was possible to see the language adapting in several different directions at once as it came to be taken up by people in the new imperial dominions. The process of expansion would continue throughout the nineteenth century and beyond, and would in due course add further complications to the notion of Standard English (p. 522).

It does not take long for a language to show the effect of being in a new location, when we are dealing with such dramatically different parts of the world as India, West Africa, and Australia. A country's biogeographical uniqueness will generate potentially large numbers of new words for animals, fish, birds, insects, plants, trees, rocks, rivers, and so on – as we have already seen in relation to North America – as well as for all the issues to do with land management and interpretation, which is an especially important feature of the lifestyle of many indigenous peoples. There will be words for foodstuffs, drinks, medicines, drugs, and the practices associated with eating, health-care, disease, and death. The country's mythology and religion, and practices in astronomy and astrology, will bring forth new names for personalities, beliefs, and rituals. The country's oral and perhaps also written literature will give rise to distinctive names in sagas, poems, oratory, and folk-tales. There will be a body of local laws and customs, with their own terminology. The culture will have its own technology with its own technical terms – such as for vehicles, house-building, weapons, clothing, ornaments, and musical instruments. The whole world of leisure and the arts will have a linguistic dimension – names of dances, musical styles, games, sports – as will distinctiveness in body appearance (such as hair-styles, tattoos, decoration). Virtually any aspect of social structure can generate complex naming systems – local government, family relationships, clubs and societies. A regionally distinctive English vocabulary involving thousands of items can emerge within just a few years (see panel 17.5).[15]

As the eighteenth century reached its close, English had either been established, or was about to be established, in as many as seven regions outside the British Isles and the United States. In each case, a distinctive variety (more accurately, group of varieties) would emerge in due course, chiefly through pronunciation and vocabulary, and some areas would develop norms of educated usage which would eventually attract the designation of 'regional standard' (p. 506). In the earliest literature of these regions, sparse though it often is, we can see both a backwards-looking and a forwards-looking identity. People who have arrived in a new territory remember their roots, and often incorporate a dialectal dimension into what they write. At the same time, they are looking towards a new future for themselves, and their language begins to be shaped by fresh forces.

17.5 How long does it take?

How long does it take for a new variety of English to grow? Not long, especially if it exists in relative isolation. A good example is Pitcairnese, spoken on Pitcairn Island in the South Pacific, where the nine *Bounty* mutineers landed in 1790. Its population today is around fifty. In such a situation, even individual speakers can have an influence on the way a variety develops.

There was dialect variation from the beginning, and it was a remarkable mix. The leader, Fletcher Christian, was from Cumbria; midshipman Edward Young was from St Kitts, West Indies; William Brown, the botanist's assistant, was from Leicester; Isaac Martin was from Philadelphia, USA; two of the others were from Scotland, two were from London, and one was from Cornwall. Few of the men had received much education.

Within thirty years of the mutineers' arrival, visitors to the island were noting that the English had changed. As time went by, the islanders' English was pulled strongly in an American direction, following regular visits by US whalers and in 1890 conversion to Seventh Day Adventism. The missionaries may also have encouraged the use of biblical language; one visitor commented in 1916 on hearing 'the pure Elizabethan English of the Bible and Prayer Book'. Certainly, within a century, there were problems of mutual intelligibility between islanders and visitors.

Today, a wide range of influences can be heard in pronunciation, grammar, and vocabulary. Grammatical conversions include *to crazy* and *to hypocrite*. The vocabulary displays archaisms (*musket* 'fire-arm', *pin* 'clothes-peg'), mariners' expressions (*heave* 'throw', *all-hands* 'everybody'), and missionary expressions (*sabbath* 'Saturday'), as well as words from American (*candy* 'sweets', *corn* 'maize'), Australian (*billy* 'cooking-pot'), and British dialectal English (*iwi* 'small' – cf. Scottish *wee*). Polynesian loanwords are used for some local fauna and flora, especially fish. A particularly interesting feature is the way the names of historical individuals live on in the general lexicon: *Dicky* is used for haemorrhoids, apparently after a Dick Fairclough who lived there in the 1920s; *Fredfeet* is used for very big feet, it seems after one Fred Christian.

Studies of the island in the late twentieth century show that the younger members are now much more aware of standard varieties of English, and are beginning to be influenced by them.[16] But even in older people, there is now an admixture of standard and local forms, as can be seen in this extract from a woman in her fifties explaining how to make Pitcairn's national dish, pilai. Examples include 'because' expressed as Pitcairnese *said* and colloquial standard *'cause*. Some verb forms are quite full, whereas others are reduced; and concord varies greatly.

Dumain [it doesn't matter] what kind of pilai you want . . . You want we learn you watawe [teach you how] we make? Well, fer making a tete [sweet potato] pilai and a plun [banana] pilai . . . es the . . . most kind people will . . . will like it, will like them the best 'cause . . . fer making a tete pilai the first thing we gwen [going to] do we take one taal'e [basket] we go up there in our ground [plantation] and we dig our tete, then we come down, we peel it, then we jolo [grate] it and then we want some leaf [leaves] fer wrap it up, fer wehe [wrap] it so . . . if . . . fer wrap it up we go over there in our valley cut some leaf, then we come home we pehe [scrape] it, then take em jolo [grated] tete, mix it up, put it in and then we wehe [wrap] it, then we put ha oven on, ala burn [or bake] it in em big-oven [the old-fashioned stone oven], and then we put it in till se cook [it is baked] and take it out you can eat it. Daa's you's tete'an. [That's your sweet potato pilai.] But if you want some plun'an [banana pilai], we go peel 'em plun and then we udi [rinse] it up and then . . . said [because] if you not udi it good not gwen jolo good [won't be easy to grate], gwen . . . gwen not mix up, so you have to make sure that you udi it good and then we take it, jolo it, then mix it up in ha water fer quite thin [until it is quite watery], and you take you's leaf, you meme [soften in the sun] it first, said ell put it down [so that they can be put down] in a tin, and then you spill [pour] you's plun down in 'em tin . . .

The Caribbean

During the early years of American settlement, a highly distinctive kind of speech was emerging in the islands of the West Indies and the southern part of the mainland, spoken by the incoming black population. This was a consequence of the importation of African slaves to work on the sugar plantations, a practice started by the Spanish as early as 1517. The policy of the slave-traders was to bring people of different language backgrounds together in the ships, to make it difficult for groups to plot rebellion. The result was the growth of several *pidgin* forms of communication, and in particular a pidgin between the slaves and the English-speaking sailors. Once arrived in the Caribbean, this pidgin English continued to act as a means of communication between the black population and the new landowners, and among the blacks themselves. Then, when their children were born, the pidgin gradually began to be used as a mother tongue, producing the first black *creole* speech in the region.

It is this creole English which rapidly came to be used in the southern plantations of the American mainland, in many of the coastal towns and islands, and throughout the whole of the West Indies. Each territory evolved a creole with local variations, reflecting the different traditions and social mix to be found in such areas as Jamaica, Grenada, Trinidad and Tobago, the Virgin Islands, Dominica, and Antigua. English-based creoles also spread onto parts of the mainland of Central and South America, especially in Belize. At the same time, the standard variety of British English was becoming a prestige variety throughout the area, because of the growing political influence of Britain. A continuum of varieties soon emerged: at one extreme there was the voice of political power, speaking and writing in Standard English; at the other extreme, there were the street varieties of creole, only spoken; and in between, various mixtures of standard and local dialect, depending on a person's social level, occupation, and amount of education.

Most of the historical records from the area are in Standard British English, but it is possible to obtain a glimpse of early linguistic diversity from the occasional piece of creative literature. An example is E. L. Joseph's *Warner Arundell: The Adventures of a Creole*, a novel of some 200,000 words published in London in 1838. The hero is a white creole of British descent, born in Grenada and brought up in Antigua and Trinidad, who travels to various West Indian settings as he seeks his fortune. Most of the book is written in the standard variety, in various styles, but several of the characters use other varieties. One black character, Quashy, uses Grenadian English Creole mixed with some French Creole. It is a variety readily understood by the local white and mulatto characters. At one point, he tells Monsieur Louis how Monsieur Victor had made him volunteer for the army:

> *Ma foi* [my honour], Monsieur Louis, he take me from massa [master's] plantation, and tell me to fight for liberty and 'quality. Me been a tell him me no good for soldier, 'cause me so lame dat me no sabby [cannot] run away. When he heare me say dis, he call out, 'Ah! bah!' like one man-sheep dat choke wid him fat; 'ha! bah! citoyen!' [citizen] he say, ' 'spose you no sabby run away, you go make the most

best soldier in a world. Me want soldier for fight, no for run away; so me no take you *lame* excuse'. So him send me to Monsieur Fedon, who make me brave man, 'cause he go shoot me if me coward.[17]

Canada

The first English-language contact with Canada was as early as 1497, when John Cabot is thought to have reached Newfoundland; but English migration along the Atlantic coast did not develop until a century later, when the farming, fishing, and fur-trading industries attracted English-speaking settlers. During the eighteenth century, French claims in the area were gradually surrendered, and during the 1750s thousands of French settlers were deported from Acadia (modern Nova Scotia) and replaced by settlers from New England. The numbers were then further increased by many coming directly from England, Ireland, and Scotland (whose earlier interest in the country is reflected in the name *Nova Scotia* – 'New Scotland'). Following the US Declaration of Independence in 1776, loyalist supporters of Britain (the 'United Empire Loyalists') emigrated from the new United States in large numbers, settling first in what is now Nova Scotia, then moving to New Brunswick and further inland. They were soon followed by many thousands (the 'late Loyalists') who were attracted by the cheapness of land, especially in the area known as Upper Canada (above Montreal and north of the Great Lakes). Within fifty years, the English-speaking population of Canada had reached 100,000.

Although the *Halifax Gazette* had been in existence since 1752, the Tory refugees introduced a fresh literary dimension to late eighteenth-century Canada. However, the early literature of pre-confederation Canada (1867) has received little study from a linguistic point of view. *Roughing it in the Bush* (1852), by Susanna Moodie (1803–85), is one of the best-known books from that period. She and her sister, Catharine Parr Traill, emigrated with their husbands from Scotland in 1832, settling in the backwoods of Ontario, near modern Lakefield. Her book records their pioneering experiences. It is written in Standard British English, with occasional Americanisms (*fall crop of wheat*, *steam-boat stock*), but the dialogue of her Scottish servant Jenny is written in a country-of-origin dialect that is as plausible as that found in any British nineteenth-century novel (p. 488). At this point in the story, John Moodie has decided to leave his farm and join the militia in the 1837 rebellion.

> Before the cold, snowy morning broke, we were all stirring. The children, who had learned that their father was preparing to leave them, were crying and clinging round his knees. His heart was too deeply affected to eat; the meal passed over in silence, and he rose to go. I put on my hat and shawl to accompany him through

the wood as far as my sister Mrs. T—'s. The day was like our destiny, cold, dark, and lowering. I gave the dear invalid his crutches, and we commenced our sorrowful walk. Then old Jenny's lamentations burst forth, as, flinging her arms round my husband's neck, she kissed and blessed him after the fashion of her country.

'Och hone! och hone!' she cried, wringing her hands, 'Masther dear, why will you lave the wife and the childher? The poor crathur is breakin' her heart intirely at partin' wid you. Shure an' the war is nothin' to you, that you must be goin' into danger; an' you wid a broken leg. Och hone! och hone! come back to your home – you will be kilt, and thin what will become of the wife and the wee bairns?'[18]

Australia

Expansion of English into the southern hemisphere also began at the end of the eighteenth century. Australia was visited by James Cook in 1770, and within twenty years a penal colony had been established at Sydney, thus relieving the pressure on the overcrowded prisons in England. About 130,000 prisoners were transported during the fifty years after the arrival of the 'first fleet' in 1788. Many of the convicts came from London and Ireland, especially following the 1798 Irish rebellion. 'Free' settlers, as they were called, also began to enter the country from the beginning, but they did not achieve substantial numbers until the mid nineteenth century. By 1850 the population had reached 400,000.

Captain Cook had also charted the New Zealand islands on his 1770 expedition, and European whalers and traders began to settle there in the 1790s, expanding the developments already taking place in Australia. Christian missionary work began among the Maori from about 1814. However, the official colony was not established until 1840, and the main increase in European immigration is after that date: about 2,000 in 1840 had become 25,000 by 1850.

Several early nineteenth-century works give accounts of colonial life, both historical and fictitious. Like her Canadian contemporary, Caroline Louisa Atkinson (1834–72) shows the dialect mix which was part of early colonial settlement. In *Gertrude the Emigrant: A Tale of Colonial Life* (1857), Gertrude has just arrived from England and is on her way to the farmstead where she is to be employed as a housekeeper. She soon encounters an early Australianism. She is telling her new mistress about the way her father had received an injury before he died:

'. . . he was so changed – so – so' – she paused.

'He was cracked,' suggested the listener.

Gertrude gathered the meaning of the colonialism from the look, and nodded.

Then she meets an Irish fellow-domestic, Mary:

> It was Saturday afternoon. Gertrude was busy making apple tarts for the coming Sabbath's dinner, and musing, not unpleasantly on the active life she had led since the Monday evening previous.
>
> 'Be them for to-morrow?' inquired Mary O'Shannassy leaving a pot she was scouring, and coming up to the table.
>
> 'Yes. What a beautiful oven we have,' and she glanced at the glowing coals and bricks.
>
> 'Them pies 'ill be could to-morrow.'
>
> 'Certainly, why not?'
>
> 'I never seed a could dinner in this house on a Sunday, that's all I know, but ye'll do as ye like sure,' and she bounced back to the pot.
>
> Gertrude stood uncertain. The larder could already boast of one of those huge joints of salt meat which appeared three times a day upon the table, and a good piece of cold bacon purely white and red, and veined like choice marble.
>
> 'We will boil some potatoes Mary, and we have had cold meat before.'
>
> 'I mind that: but on Sunday Missus looks for a better dinner than common. Thim taters are getting low in the bin, and ye must tell the "super" to send up another bag.'[19]

Irish, English, and Australian together. A *super* was a station superintendent. The inverted commas suggest its newness; Wilkes' *Dictionary of Australian Colloquialisms*[20] has its first recorded usage in 1857, the same year Atkinson published her book.

South Africa

Although Dutch colonists arrived in the Cape as early as 1652, British involvement in the region dates only from 1795, during the Napoleonic Wars, when an expeditionary force invaded. British control was established in 1806, and a policy of settlement began in earnest in 1820, when some 5,000 British were given land in the eastern Cape. English was made the official language of the region in 1822, and there was an attempt to Anglicize the large Afrikaans-speaking population. English became the language of law, education, and most other aspects of public life. Further British settlements followed in the 1840s and 1850s, especially in Natal, and there was a massive influx of Europeans following the development of the gold and diamond areas in the Witwatersrand in the 1870s.

The English language history of the region thus has many strands. There was initially a certain amount of regional dialect variation among the different groups of British settlers, with the speech of the London area prominent in the Cape, and Midlands and northern British speech strongly represented in Natal; but in due course a more homogeneous variety emerged. At the same time, English was being used as a second language by the Afrikaans speakers, and many of the Dutch colonists took this variety with them on the Great Trek of 1836, as they moved north to escape British rule. An African variety of English also developed, spoken by the black population, who had learned the language mainly in mission schools, and which was influenced in different ways by the various language backgrounds of the speakers. In addition, English came to be used, along with Afrikaans and often other languages, by those with an ethnically mixed background ('coloureds'); and it was also adopted by the many immigrants from India, who arrived in the country from around 1860. South Africa thus quickly became one of the most diverse English-speaking areas outside of Britain. Much of the vernacular literature which survives from the early nineteenth century was published by Lovedale Press, established in 1823 primarily as a missionary and educational press. Printing equipment was brought to South Africa from Britain by a Scottish missionary, and transported to a mission station at Lovedale. Though twice destroyed in wartime, it was rebuilt, and published the work of most early African writers.

The distinctive South African landscape and cultural mix is well illustrated in *Story of an African Farm* (1883), by Olive Schreiner (1855–1920). Born in South Africa, she began her novel while working as a teacher in Kimberley, but published it after later moving to England. Her portrait of a strong, independent-minded female protagonist, Lyndell, working on an isolated ostrich-farm, greatly impressed the early women's movement, and she became part of the social activism of the time. The book is preceded by a Glossary (see panel 17.6), though not all the local vocabulary is included within it. Here are its atmospheric opening paragraphs.

The full African moon poured down its light from the blue sky into the wide, lonely plain. The dry, sandy earth, with its coating of stunted karoo bushes a few inches high, the low hills that skirted the plain, the milk-bushes with their long finger-like leaves, all were touched by a weird and an almost oppressive beauty as they lay in the white light.

In one spot only was the solemn monotony of the plain broken. Near the centre a small solitary kopje rose. Alone it lay there, a heap of round ironstones piled one upon another, as over some giant's grave. Here and there a few tufts of grass or small succulent plants had sprung up among its stones, and on the very summit a clump of prickly-pears lifted their thorny arms, and reflected, as from

17.6 Schreiner's glossary

'Several Dutch and Colonial words occurring in this work, the subjoined Glossary is given, explaining the principal,' says Olive Schreiner before the opening chapter of her novel, aware of the linguistic limitations of her English readers. The items she selected, with her definitions, are listed below.

Alle wereld! – Gosh!
Aasvogels – Vultures.
Benauwdheid – Indigestion.
Brakje – A little cur of low degree.
Bultong – Dried meat.
Coop – Hide and Seek.
Inspan – To harness.
Kapje – A sun-bonnet.
Karoo – The wide sandy plains in some parts of South Africa.
Karoo-bushes – The bushes that take the place of grass on these plains.
Kartel – The wooden-bed fastened in an ox-wagon.
Kloof – A ravine.
Kopje – A small hillock, or 'little head'.
Kraal – The space surrounded by a stone wall or hedged with thorn branches, into which sheep or cattle are driven at night.
Mealies – Indian corn.
Meerkat – A small weazel-like animal.
Meiboss – Preserved and dried apricots.
Nachtmaal – The Lord's Supper.
Oom – Uncle.
Outspan – To unharness, or a place in the field where one unharnesses.
Pap – Porridge.
Predikant – Parson.
Riem – Leather rope.
Sarsarties – Food.
Sleg – Bad.
Sloot – A dry watercourse.
Spook – To haunt, a ghost.
Stamp-block – A wooden block, hollowed out, in which mealies are placed to be pounded before being cooked.
Stoep – Porch.
Tant or Tante – Aunt.
Upsitting – In Boer courtship the man and girl are supposed to sit up together the whole night.
Veld – Open country.
Velschoen – Shoes of undressed leather.
Vrijer – Available man.

mirrors, the moonlight on their broad fleshy leaves. At the foot of the kopje lay the homestead. First, the stone-walled sheep kraals and Kaffer huts; beyond them the dwelling-house – a square, red-brick building with thatched roof. Even on its bare red walls, and the wooden ladder that led up to the loft, the moonlight cast a kind of dreamy beauty, and quite etherealized the low brick wall that ran before the house, and which inclosed a bare patch of sand and two straggling sunflowers. On the zinc roof of the great open wagon-house, on the roofs of the outbuildings that jutted from its side, the moonlight glinted with a quite peculiar brightness, till it seemed that every rib in the metal was of burnished silver.[21]

South Asia

The first regular contact with the subcontinent of India came in 1600, with the formation of the British East India Company – a group of London merchants who were granted a trading monopoly in the area by Queen Elizabeth I. The Company established its first trading station at Surat in 1612, and by the end of the century others were in existence at Madras (Chennai), Bombay (Mumbai), and Calcutta (Kolkata). During the eighteenth century, it overcame competition from other European nations, especially France. As the power of the Mughal emperors declined, the Company's influence grew, and in 1765 it took over the revenue management of Bengal. Following a period of financial indiscipline among Company servants, the 1784 India Act established a Board of Control responsible to the British Parliament, and in 1858, after the Indian Mutiny, the Company was abolished and its powers handed over to the Crown.

During the period of British sovereignty (the *Raj*), from 1765 until independence in 1947, English gradually became the medium of administration and education throughout the subcontinent. The language question attracted special attention during the early nineteenth century, when colonial administration debated the kind of educational policy which should be introduced. A recognized turning-point was Lord William Bentinck's acceptance of a Minute written by Thomas Macaulay in 1835, which proposed the introduction of an English educational system in India. When the universities of Bombay, Calcutta, and Madras were established in 1857, English became the primary medium of instruction, thereby guaranteeing its status and steady growth during the next century.

Anglo-Indian literature in English can be traced back to the end of the sixteenth century, consisting of letters from missionaries and accounts of travels in the subcontinent. The first English newspaper, *Hicky's Bengal Gazette* (named after its founder, James Augustus Hicky), began in 1780. Poetry and fiction written in English began to appear from the 1830s, much influenced by British models, but from the outset distinguished by a strong colouring of local vocabulary and idiom. Although the following sonnet, 'Baugmaree', is Classical in its form and sentiment, its diction relies on the evolving regional lexicon of India. Toru Dutt (1856–77) has been called the Keats of Anglo-Indian literature, due to her early death from consumption. Born in Bengal, she was educated in England and France, made a number of translations, and published a single volume of poetry in 1876. Baugmaree (modern Bagmari) is a district in northern Calcutta where her family had a country house.

> A sea of foliage girds our garden round,
> But not a sea of dull unvaried green,
> Sharp contrasts of all colours here are seen;
> The light-green graceful tamarinds abound
> Amid the mango clumps of green profound,
> And palms arise, like pillars gray, between;
> And o'er the quiet pools the seemuls lean,
> Red – red, and startling like a trumpet's sound.
> But nothing can be lovelier than the ranges
> Of bamboos to the eastward, when the moon
> Looks through their gaps, and the white lotus changes
> Into a cup of silver. One might swoon
> Drunken with beauty then, or gaze and gaze
> On a primeval Eden, in amaze.

Several local flora are mentioned, of which the *seemul*, from the Hindi name for the silk-cotton tree, is the most distinctive – a word still not recorded in the *Oxford English Dictionary*, though known in India from *c.* 1807.[22]

West Africa

The English began to visit West Africa from the end of the fifteenth century, and soon after we find sporadic references to the use of the language as a lingua franca in some coastal settlements. By the beginning of the nineteenth century, the increase in commerce and anti-slave-trade activities had brought English to the whole West African coast. With hundreds of local languages to contend with, a particular feature of the region was the rise of several English-based pidgins and creoles, used alongside the standard varieties spoken and written by colonial officials, missionaries, soldiers, and traders. Each country in the region developed its own linguistic character as a consequence, and for Sierra Leone, Gambia, and Liberia this happened relatively early on. It was not until the second half of the nineteenth century that English made significant inroads into Nigeria and Ghana (formerly Gold Coast), following their establishment as colonies in 1861 and 1874 respectively, though documents such as the one illustrated below show that pidgin-like varieties were in place much earlier.

The thread which unites Sierra Leone, Gambia, and Liberia was the rise of the anti-slavery movement. The situation in Sierra Leone developed as early as the 1780s, when philanthropists in Britain bought land to establish a settlement for freed slaves, the first groups arriving from England, Nova Scotia, and Jamaica. The settlement became a Crown Colony in 1808, and was then used as a base for anti-slave-trading squadrons, whose operations eventually brought some 60,000 'recaptives' to the country. The chief form of communication was an English-based creole, Krio, and this rapidly spread along the West African coast. In Gambia, English trading began along the Gambia River during the early seventeenth century. A period of conflict with France was followed in 1816 by the establishment of Bathurst (modern Banjul) as a British base for anti-slaver activities, and the area became a Crown Colony in 1843. Liberia, Africa's oldest republic, was founded in 1822 through the activities of the American Colonization Society, which wished to establish a homeland for former slaves. Within fifty years it received some 13,000 black Americans, as well as some 6,000 slaves recaptured at sea. The settlement became a republic in 1847, and adopted a constitution based on that of the USA, managing to retain its independence despite pressure from European countries during the nineteenth-century 'scramble for Africa'.

This letter from a West African king to a British naval commander was written on 4 December 1842 from Old Calabar, an area of south-eastern Nigeria settled by the Efik people, and is interesting for the way it demonstrates the way literate forms of nonstandard English were already in routine use.

> To Commander Raymond.
>
> Now we settle treaty for not sell slaves, I must tell you something, I want your queen to do for we. Now we can't sell slaves again, we must have too much man for country, and want something for make work and trade, and if we could get seed for cotton and coffee we could make trade. Plenty sugar cane live here, and if some man come teach we way for do it we get plenty sugar too, and then some man must come for teach book proper, and make all men saby God like white man, and then we go on for same fashion. We thank you too much for what thing you come do for keep thing right. Long time we no look Man-of-war as Blount promise, and one Frenchman come make plenty palaver for slave when he can't get them. You been do very proper for we, and now we want to keep proper mouth. I hope some Man-of-war come some time with proper captain all same you to look out and help we keep word when French man-of-war come. What I want for dollar side is fine coat and sword all same I tell you and the rest

in copper rods. I hope Queen Victoria and young prince will live long time, and
we get good friend. Also I want bomb and shell.

I am, your best friend,

King Eyamba V, 'King of all Black Man'.[23]

The letter displays a number of distinctive grammatical abbreviations and
substitutions as well as some lexical features (*saby* 'savvy', *palaver* 'talk') typical
of an emerging pidgin, though it is unclear just how far texts of this kind, which
are extremely variable in their language, can be said to be the precursors of
modern pidgins.

South-East Asia and the South Pacific

British influence began through the voyages of English sailors towards the end
of the eighteenth century, notably the journeys of Captain Cook in the 1770s.
The London Missionary Society sent its workers to the islands of the South
Pacific some fifty years later. In South-East Asia, the development of a British
colonial empire grew from the work of Stamford Raffles, an administrator in
the British East India Company. Centres were established in several locations,
notably Penang (1786), Singapore (1819), and Malacca (1824). Hong Kong
island was ceded to Britain in 1842. Within a few months, the population of
Singapore had grown to over 5,000, and by the time the Federated Malay States
were brought together as a Crown Colony (in 1867) English had come to be
established throughout the region as the medium of law and administration,
and was being increasingly used in other contexts. An English-language newspaper, the *Straits Times*, began publication in 1845. The introduction of a
British educational system exposed learners to the standard variety of British
English very early on, and this dominated literary expression during the century.
English-medium schools began in Penang (now Malaysia's leading port) in
1816, with senior teaching staff routinely brought in from Britain – carrying
their Murray, Walker, and Johnson with them (Chapter 16). Although at the
outset these schools were attended by only a tiny percentage of the population,
numbers increased during the nineteenth century as waves of Chinese and
Indian immigrants entered the area. English rapidly became the language of
professional advancement and the chief literary language. Only in the mid
twentieth century do we find the development of varieties of English which
begin to express the local spoken language of the region (p. 502).

During the later part of the nineteenth century, further expansion took
place as British and American colonial interests grew, notably in East Africa
and the Pacific. Under the former heading, we find the presence of British
English in Kenya, Tanzania (formerly Tanganyika and Zanzibar), Uganda,

Malawi (formerly Nyasaland), Zambia (formerly Northern Rhodesia) and Zimbabwe (formerly Southern Rhodesia). Under the latter heading, we find American English introduced (after the Spanish-American War of 1898) into the Philippines, Guam, and Hawaii, as well as into Puerto Rico in the Caribbean. By the end of the nineteenth century, nearly a quarter of the earth's land mass was part of the British Empire, containing a population of over 400 million. In 1829, the Scottish essayist John Wilson, writing under his pseudonym of Christopher North, referred to 'Her Majesty's dominions, on which the sun never sets'.[24] The locution could just as well have referred to the English language, and indeed we do find some writers later giving it a linguistic adaptation: 'the language on which the sun never sets'.[25] When we look at a map of the world which shows the territories where the language developed a significant presence (see panel 17.7), we can understand why.

17.7 World English

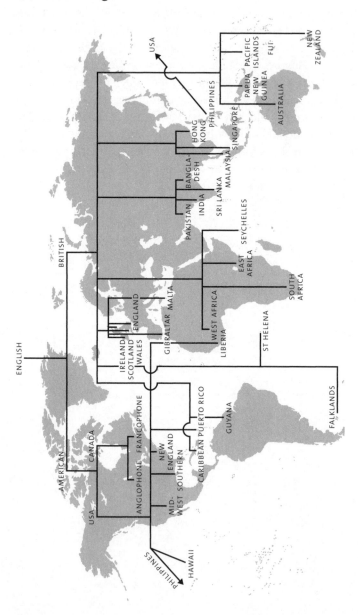

A family-tree representation (after Peter Strevens) of the way English has spread around the world. It shows the influence of the two main branches of British and American English.

Interlude 17
Tracking a change: the case of *y'all*

It was in 1969, during my first visit to the United States, that I had my earliest face-to-face encounter with *y'all*. I was in Fort Worth, Texas, and went into a store to buy a Stetson hat for my son. The assistant greeted me with a *Howdy y'all* and a *What can I do for y'all*, and it was so unexpected that I actually looked round to see who else he was referring to, thinking that someone must have come into the store behind me. But I was the only one there. As I left, he said, *Y'all take care now*.

Outside I began listening seriously to the use of *y'all*. On the whole it did seem to be used when addressing more than one person, though sometimes the people were being viewed as a single body. And all kinds of people used it. A professor at the university used it when addressing her class of students, *I hope y'all managed to read my paper*. A cab driver addressed two of us in the back with a general *Where y'all going?* Most of the users were African-American; but many were white.

The use of a nonstandard second-person pronoun, as such, was not a new experience for me. I had spent my teenage years in Liverpool, where *youse* was a perfectly normal form. *Youse* also could be used for either singular or plural: *Can I give youse a lift?* might be said by a lorry-driver to either a group of hitch-hikers or a single hitch-hiker. And such forms were common in Ireland and Scotland, too, where both *youse* and *y'all* can be heard alongside *ye*, *yiz*, and others. *Youse* travelled to America that way, probably via Liverpool, and one strand in the history of *y'all* probably has an Irish origin.

Y'all first comes to notice in the southern states of the USA, chiefly among African-Americans around the turn of the nineteenth century, and rapidly established its presence among southern whites of all social classes (some of whom would also have been familiar – through immigration – with the analogous Irish usage). From there it became more widely encountered in American English, especially as black people moved into northern states after the Civil War, and its active use spread. Eventually it found its way, via novels and stories written in Southern dialect, and later through movies and television serials reflecting life in the US south, all over the world. I have heard *y'all* used in the UK by a number of people, of various ages and ethnic backgrounds.

It is worth noting that dialects which make use of words like *y'all* and *youse* are in fact richer, in their possibilities of expression, than Standard English. This can come as a shock to those who cannot see beyond the stand-ard variety: to realize that regional dialects often allow options that the standard never had or has lost. Early Modern English, of course, did have a more expressive second-person pronoun system (p. 307), using *thou* (for singular) and *ye* (for plural).

There are still fascinating puzzles surrounding American *y'all*. Did it originate exclusively among the southern black population, as many have suggested, or did it have earlier antecedents? Some have looked for its origins in local creoles, especially Gullah. Some think that its origins lie within early Scots or Irish usage in the USA – and indeed, it is interesting to note that those parts of the country where we find the widest range of *y'all* usages do seem to be where black and Celtic immigrant populations have long coexisted.

Doing research into *y'all* is not easy, because the written records cannot always be trusted. As it is a feature of colloquial English, it often would not have been written down: there would have been a tendency to write 'correctly', and substitute *you*. When it *was* written down, it might not have been written accurately – there would have been a tendency to write *you all*, or to omit the (often difficult to hear) final *'s* in *y'all's*. And we cannot even trust the feature when it *was* written down correctly: many writers saw *y'all* as a feature stereo-typing black speech, and made their characters use it more than would happen in real life. We always have to be sensitive to the presence of parody and exaggeration in early writing – as we do today.

Y'all seems very straightforward, but there are in fact some quite complex linguistic factors governing its use, and only some of them are well understood. In pronunciation it is a monosyllabic variant of *you all*, rhyming with words like *call*; but in spelling it is quite variable. A 1993 study found it turning up in several spellings over the past 200 years, such as *you all*, *you-all*, *ya'll*, *yawl*, and *yo-all*.[26] And there are some subtle differences in usage. It tends to occur more often with certain verbs – *hope*, *think*, and *want* are notable. It can be used in most parts of the sentence where *you* and *your* can go, but there are some exceptions. Here are some examples taken from a corpus, with the grammatical function noted:

> What kind o' hair yawl want? [subject]
> Ah mean to carry y'all to Palatka. [object]
> How many of y'all wanna live to an old age? [after a preposition]

I feel pretty good, y'all. [vocative]
I passed y'all's house. [possessive]

In each of these cases, we could substitute the word *you* or *your*. But the parallel is not complete: *y'all's selves*, the equivalent to *yourselves*, is hardly ever heard.

There are also constraints, not fully understood, governing the way in which multiple instances of *y'all* turn up in a discourse. In Standard English it is perfectly possible to use *you-* forms several times in the same sentence:

You will need your coat if you are going out.

But 'translating' this into *y'all* forms is not straightforward, as these examples show:

Y'all are moving y'all's legs too much. [said by a swimming teacher]
Y'all left your lights on.

Why did the first speaker use *y'all's* and the second use *your*?

One factor must be that *y'all* is much stronger in stress than *you*: it has a greater impact in a sentence. *You* is a word which can be reduced to just the consonant, as when people say *y'know*. We can't make this kind of reduction with *y'all*. For the same sort of reason, *y'all* is generally not heard at the very end of a sentence, as a tag question. We can often hear:

Y'all come back now, won't you?

but only very rarely

Y'all come back now, won't y'all?

So maybe the swimming teacher repeats *y'all* because he is wanting his listeners to pay serious attention to using their legs, and (unconsciously, of course) uses the stronger form to make his point. And maybe in the second instance, the speaker is making more of a routine observation. Or maybe it is that 'legs' have a closer notion of possession to a person than 'lights' (which strictly belong to cars) and therefore prompt the stronger form. These are the kind of hypotheses that linguists love to investigate.

There are other factors – pragmatic ones (p. 524). If *you* vs *y'all* doesn't convey a contrast of number (singular vs plural), then what does it convey? Speakers plainly have the choice of both in a sentence: *What can I do for y'all?* or *What can I do for you?* Why use the one and not the other? A plausible suggestion is that *y'all* is 'warmer', a sign of familiarity, friendliness, informality, and rapport, at least among young people. A 1970s study found it being commonly used by younger Virginians to convey this kind of warmth.[27]

However, many older people are still somewhat suspicious of it, and do not use it, perhaps associating it with past ethnic tensions, or finding it patronizing. As for my store assistant, I certainly felt that he was being 'customer-friendly'. I bought the Stetson. I wonder whether his farewell would have been *You take care now*, if I hadn't?

Chapter 18 Linguistic life goes on

Meanwhile, back at the (British) ranch . . . the rest of the language was continuing its development as if nothing had happened. During the nineteenth century, processes of linguistic change continued to operate, in pronunciation, grammar, and vocabulary, and imperceptibly Early Modern English became Modern English. The variation which prescriptive scholars had attempted to eliminate at the end of the eighteenth century continued to manifest itself, and would eventually be reinforced as the new alternatives introduced into American English began to spread beyond the United States. And, as we shall see in the next chapter, regional and social variation continued to poke its head above the literary parapet in the form of an increasingly realistic dialect portrayal of contemporary life, most noticeably at first in the plays of Sheridan and his contemporaries and later in the nineteenth-century novel. The appearance of nonstandard English continued to receive a critical reaction from the Standard English pundits, but it was carrying on regardless. Or rather, people were carrying it on. And by the end of the nineteenth century it had received a fresh lease of life from novelists, Romantic poets, playwrights, Anglo-Saxon enthusiasts, dialectologists, and philologists.

Ongoing change

The ongoing processes of change affected all aspects of English structure. As always (p. 170), the most noticeable sign of change is in vocabulary, which in this period reflected the multiple social, scientific, technological, and economic developments that cumulatively comprised the Industrial Revolution. By 1800, Britain had become the world's leading industrial and trading nation. Its population of 5 million in 1700 had increased to over 9 million (in England and Wales) by the time of the first census in 1801. London was approaching its first million – 948,000 people – and other cities were rapidly expanding. Dublin, for example, had reached nearly 200,000 in 1801. During that century, no country could equal Britain's economic growth, with a gross national product rising, on average, at 2 per cent a year. Exports and imports doubled between 1700 and 1770. The merchant marine increased by a factor of three during the same period – over 3,000 ships in 1700, over 9,000 in 1770.

Most of the innovations of the Industrial Revolution were of British origin: the harnessing of coal, water, and steam to drive heavy machinery; the development of new materials, techniques, and equipment in a wide range of manufacturing industries; and the emergence of new means of transportation. We find coke smelting in 1709, steam engines in 1712, the spinning jenny in 1768. By 1800, the chief growth areas, in textiles and mining, were producing a variety of manufactured goods for export which led to Britain being called the 'workshop of the world'. The inventions of people such as Thomas Newcomen, James Watt, Matthew Boulton, Richard Trevithick, George Stephenson, Charles Wheatstone, Michael Faraday, Humphry Davy, Thomas Telford, and Henry Bessemer demonstrate the British achievement of that time. Similar developments then took place in America, which, by the end of the nineteenth century, had overtaken Britain as the world's fastest-growing economy. There is a corresponding litany of US inventors who maintained the momentum of the European Industrial Revolution, such as George Westinghouse, Benjamin Franklin, Thomas Edison, Samuel Morse, and Alexander Graham Bell. Gradually, the United States acted as a magnet for European scholars, attracting in an early 'brain drain' such researchers as the glaciologist Jean-Louis Agassiz (in 1844) and the electrical engineer Nikola Tesla (in 1884).

Vocabulary

The linguistic consequences of this achievement were far-reaching. The new terminology of technological and scientific advance had an immediate impact on the language, adding tens of thousands of words to the English lexicon. Indeed, 'hundreds of thousands' is a better way of expressing this approximation. The bulk of Modern English vocabulary lies in its scientific and technological nomenclature, and most of this arrived during and after the Industrial Revolution. More precise estimates of the size and rate of the lexical growth are hindered by the sampling selectivity of historical lexicographers, who have tended to look at literary rather than scientific sources (p. 289). But it is obvious, from an examination of any modern professional scientific work in, say, botany, medicine, or chemistry, that we are dealing with an unprecedented increase in the size of the English lexicon, which continued into the twentieth century as specialized domains (such as interactive television or New Age medicine) proliferated. There are nearly half a million compounds identified in the Chapman and Hall/CRC *Combined Chemical Dictionary*, for example.[1]

It is impossible to know just how much specialized vocabulary there is in Modern English. The dictionaries capture only a small part of it. I looked in the *Oxford English Dictionary* for the presence of terms describing just one tiny domain from within the subject I know best, linguistics – terms to do with the description of tone of voice. In one technical treatment of this subject, which was sufficiently influential for some of its terminology to be referenced in standard introductions to phonetics a generation later, there were seventy-four terms or new uses of terms.[2] However, only four of these were included in the *OED* – and none at all in *Webster's Third New International*. Admittedly, linguistics is a more neologistic subject than many others, its practitioners (perhaps by their nature) being a terminologically inventive crowd; but emergent academic vocabulary is routinely neglected in all subjects. The implication is plain. If this proportion of exclusion is typical of all domains of science and technology, the size of the English lexicon will multiply several times. A total of a million will then seem rather small. However, figures of this kind do not really mean very much, for lexicons by their nature are intrinsically indeterminate in size, with new words arriving and old words dying out on a daily basis. More important is to look at the linguistic means through which the remarkable increase in specialist terminology took – and continues to take – place. The same word-formation processes which we have seen operating in earlier chapters appear again: borrowing, affixation, compounding, and abbreviation.

Borrowings from Greek and Latin continued to perform the role they had been assigned in Renaissance English (Chapter 12), introducing a large number of forms to science and scholarship. Any subject would provide hundreds of examples; panel 18.1 contains a small sample taken from a few sciences. More important than borrowing, however, was compounding. Most of the terminological 'monsters' of modern science arise from the stringing together of separate roots – in chemistry or medicine, for example:

chlorofluorocarbon (chloro+fluoro+carbon)
benzoylnitroacetanilide (benzoyl+nitro+acet+anilide)
systemic lupus erythematosus

The words that tend to get into the record-books are usually from chemistry: the full name for *deoxyribonucleic acid (DNA)*, cited as the longest scientific name by the *Guinness Book of Records*, contains 16,569 elements. Rather more usual are compounds of just two or three elements, sometimes printed solid or hyphenated:

agoraphobia, crankshaft, daisy-wheel, kleptomania, radioisotope, steady-state, turboprop, wavelength

18.1 Scientific nomenclature

Term	Source	Subject	First recorded usage
bacillus	Latin	biology	1883
caffeine	French	chemistry	1830
calcaneum	Latin	anatomy	1751
calcar	Latin	botany	1832
cloaca	Latin	physiology	1834
corolla	Latin	botany	1753
femur	Latin	anatomy	1799
fibula	Latin	anatomy	1746
flagellum	Latin	zoology	1852
hibiscus	Greek	botany	1706
hydra	Latin	zoology	1798
influenza	Italian	medicine	1743
lamina	Latin	geology	1794
latex	Latin	botany	1835
loess	German	geology	1833
moraine	French	geology	1789
nickel	German	mineralogy	1755
ovum	Latin	zoology	1706
pipette	French	chemistry	1839
quartz	German	mineralogy	1756
radula	Latin	zoology	1877
rhizome	Greek	botany	1845
thallus	Greek	botany	1829
tibia	Latin	anatomy	1726

and sometimes spaced:

> ammonium chloride, atomic mass unit, bar code, central nervous system, Parkinson's disease, shock absorber

Affixation was also important, using both prefixes and suffixes. Scientific and technical vocabulary of course continued to use everyday prefixes, such as *pre-*, *dis-*, *un-*, and *co-*, and suffixes such as *-al*, *-ful*, *-ous*, and *-less*, but several prefixes were of special scientific relevance:

- numerical prefixes, such as *bi-*, *di-*, *mono-*, *multi-*, *poly-*, *semi-*, *tri-*, *uni-*
- metrical prefixes: *micro-*, *nano-*, *pico-*, *femto-*, *atto-*, *mega-*, *giga-*, *tera-*
- orientation prefixes, such as *anti-*, *auto-*, *contra-*, *counter-*, *pro-*

Different domains had their 'favourite' suffixes, as can be seen from the following selections of terms:

geology: Pliocene, Miocene; Jurassic, Triassic; Silurian, Cambrian; Cretaceous, Carboniferous
botany: mesocarp, pericarp; fusiform, napiform; antherozoid, spermatozoid; bacterium, sporangium
chemistry: acetylene, benzene; oxalic, acetic; methane, alkane; ethanol, alcohol; chromium, sodium; chlorine, fluorine; nitrate, sulphate

The domain names themselves, of course, were distinctive, the majority using *-ology*, but not forgetting *-ography*, *-metry*, *-onomy*, and *-ics*:

entomology, petrology; photography, crystallography; telemetry, audiometry; taxonomy, astronomy; mechanics, genetics

Ology, as a noun for a science, is first recorded in 1811. By Dickens' time, it was in routine use. Mrs Gradgrind, on her death-bed, reflects to her daughter about her husband, 'a man of facts and calculations':

You learnt a great deal, Louisa, and so did your brother. Ologies of all kinds from morning to night. If there is any Ology left, of any description, that has not been worn to rags in this house, all I can say is, I hope I shall never hear its name.[3]

Abbreviation has grown in importance, in the age of modern science. It is sometimes said that we live in an age of abbreviations; and certainly, when we look at a volume such as Gale's *Acronyms, Initialisms and Abbreviations Dictionary*, with 586,000 entries in its 2001 edition, it is hard to disagree.[4] Abbreviated forms are now so many and varied that their study has evolved its own nomenclature:

- *initialisms* or *alphabetisms* (spoken as individual letters): *BBC, DJ, GM, EU, USA*
- *acronyms* (initialisms pronounced as single words): *NATO, UNESCO, laser, radar*
- *clippings* (part of a word serves as the whole): *ad, demo, flu, fridge, max, phone, pub*
- *blends* (a word made from two shortened forms): *brunch, heliport, infotainment, motel, Muppet* (marionette + puppet), *Oxbridge, numeracy, smog*

In 1711 the essayist Joseph Addison gloomily reflected on the linguistic temper of his time:

It is perhaps this Humour of speaking no more than we needs must, which has so miserably curtailed some of our Words, that in familiar Writings and Conversations they sometimes lose all but their first Syllables, as in *Mob. rep. pos. incog.* and the like.[5]

What he would have made of *URLs* and *FAQs* on the Internet, or *imnsho* and *cul8r* in the language of present-day texting,[6] I dare not imagine. There seems to be no lessening of the motivation to abbreviate in present-day society, thanks to the double function of abbreviation as an energy-saver and rapport-builder. Abbreviations most obviously save the expending of unnecessary articulatory or graphic energy; but more subtly they identify networks of social relationships, for insiders and outsiders differ in their awareness and use of abbreviated forms. Only people who need to refer frequently to urinary tract infections actually refer to them as *UTIs*, and to do so automatically signals that you belong to a particular background. If you say *UTI* you are more likely to be treating it than suffering from it.

Everyday usage has employed all these processes, of course, and extended them in various ways. Borrowing has continued from an increasingly diverse range of languages, following the spread of English around the world. Over 350 languages are identified as sources for the present-day lexicon in the *OED*, and the arrival of English in a country where there are many contact languages (over 400 in Nigeria; ten other official languages in South Africa) immediately increases the rate of lexical borrowing in those countries (p. 502). Only a small proportion of these words actually end up in Standard English, in its British or American incarnations, but they are none the less a significant element in the lexical mix. For example, the following words appear towards the beginning of the alphabet in one dictionary of South African English; just two are known in British or American English:

> aardvark (Afrikaans), abafazi (Nguni 'women'), afdak (Afrikaans, 'shed'), agter-skot (Afrikaans, 'final payment'), amabutho (Zulu, 'fighter for a cause'), amadhlozi (Xhosa, 'ancestral spirit'), apartheid (Afrikaans), askoek (Afrikaans, 'dough cake')[7]

The amount of borrowing is always influenced by the number of cultures which coexist, and the status which their languages have achieved. In a highly multilingual country, such as South Africa, Malaysia, or Nigeria, where issues of identity are critical, we might expect a much greater use of loanwords. There is already evidence of this in the range of words collected by lexicographers. In the South African dictionary, depending on the initial letter-preferences of the contributing languages, there are long sequences of loanwords: *aandag, aandblom, aap, aar, aardpyp, aardvark, aardwolf, aas,* and *aasvoël* (all from Afrikaans) are immediately followed by *abadala, abafazi, abakhaya, abakwetha, abantu, abaphansi, abathagathi,* and *abelungu* (all from Nguni languages). Only on the next page of the dictionary do we encounter items from British English with local senses, such as *administrator* and *advocate*. The influence of local languages is also apparent in hybrid forms, where a foreign root is given an English affix (as in *Afrikanerdom* and *Afrikanerism*), or where two languages are involved in a blend (as in *Anglikaans*).

There was a salient loanword presence in South African English even before the 1994 constitution recognized eleven languages as official. We might therefore expect the status of these languages to be reflected in due course by a further significant growth in the number of loanwords into this variety; but the linguistic outcome will depend on such factors as the extent to which the newfound official status of these languages is supported by economic and political realities, and the extent to which their lexical character itself changes as a result of Anglicization. Some cultural domains are likely to manifest this growth sooner than others. Restaurant menus, for example, are always a good source of lexical nourishment. In an English menu at a restaurant in Nigeria one researcher – doubtless using his time well while waiting for the arrival of his meal – noted *agidi, gari, eba, iyan, edikagong, suya, dodo, foofoo, moin-moin,* and *efo elegusi.*[8] On the *English* menu.

Although the amount of borrowing into the two standard varieties was less in the nineteenth and twentieth centuries than it had been in earlier periods, it remained an important feature of lexical growth in English. We find French continuing to exercise its traditional influence, especially on British English (see panel 18.2). But words continued to arrive from all parts of the world. Of particular note are words from the East, relating to Chinese philosophy and alternative medicine (such as *an mo, feng shui, qi*), Indian philosophy and religion (such as *chakra, karma, mantra, mandala*), and Japanese business, culture, technology, and sport:

> aikido, aiki-jutsu (type of martial art), basho (in sumo wrestling), futon, honcho, kaizen 'work philosophy', kanban, karaoke, karate, karoshi 'death by job-related exhaustion', sushi, zaitech 'financial engineering'

A sense of other regional contributions can be obtained from this mixed-bag of last-century examples:

> autobahn (German), balti (Urdu), bhangra (Punjabi), blitz (German), bolshy (Russian), cappuccino (Italian), ciabatta (Italian), conga (Spanish), dunk (German), espresso (Italian), fatwa (Arabic), flak (German), glasnost (Russian), intifada (Arabic), juggernaut (Hindi), kalashnikov (Russian), kung-fu (Chinese), lambada (Portuguese), latte (Italian), Lebensraum (German), macho (Spanish), mah-jong (Chinese), moussaka (Turkish), paparazzo (Italian), paso doble (Spanish),

18.2 French loans

Eighteenth century

Notable for its loans in the domains of social institutions and behaviour.

> bouquet, canteen, clique, connoisseur, coterie, cuisine, debut, espionage, etiquette, glacier, liqueur, migraine, nuance, protégé, roulette, salon, silhouette, souvenir, toupee, vignette

Nineteenth century

More French loans arrived in this century than at any time since Middle English, especially in relation to the arts, food, and dress.

> acrobat, baroque, beige, blouse, bonhomie, café, camaraderie, can-can, chauffeur, chef, chic, cinematography, cliché, communism, croquet, debutant, dossier, en masse, flair, foyer, genre, gourmet, impasse, lingerie, matinée, menu, morgue, mousse, nocturne, parquet, physique, pince-nez, première, raison d'être, renaissance, repertoire, restaurant, risqué, sorbet, soufflé, surveillance, vol-au-vent, volte-face

Twentieth century

New art forms and technology supplement traditional trends.

> art deco, art nouveau, au pair, auteur, blasé, brassiere, chassis, cinéma-vérité, cinematic, coulis, courgette, crime passionnel, détente, disco, fromage frais, fuselage, garage, hangar, limousine, microfiche, montage, nouvelle cuisine, nouvelle vague, questionnaire, tranche, visagiste, voyeurism

> perestroika (Russian), putsch (German), robot (Czech), rumba (Spanish), safari (Swahili), schlep, schlock, schmaltz (Yiddish), slalom (Norwegian), taramasalata (Greek), wok (Chinese)

A particular feature of the modern period is the way extensive 'families' of compound words have grown up, as a particular cultural or technological notion developed or became fashionable. Here is a selection related to the arrival of aeroplane technology:

> air ambulance, airbus, air cavalry, air force, air hostess, air-lift, airmail, air miles, airport, air-raid, airspace, air support, air supremacy, air terminal, airworthy

And a tiny selection from the hundreds of compound terms beginning with *sex*:

> sex aid / awareness / clinic / discrimination / distinction / drive / education / fiend /

instruction / life / machine / mad / magazine / maniac / manual / object / problem / show / starvation / symbol

In the same way, certain forms developed a fashionable period of use, as is evident from the way *mega-*, *tele-*, *-gate*, *-aholic*, and *-friendly* came to be used in the twentieth century. *Mega-*, for example, became popular during the 1980s (*megastore, megabrand, megabucks, megamerger* . . .) and soon developed an independent existence as an adjective (*That band is mega in Europe!*).

Word-class conversion is a long-standing means of making new words in English (p. 303), and it continued to be an important process in the nineteenth and twentieth centuries. Present-day examples include *spend* as a noun, or *handbag, text, out, spam,* and *surf* as verbs. The process began to incorporate trade names, which developed generic meanings, such as *Hoover* (in the UK), *filofax, Band-Aid, Zimmer, Levis, perspex,* and *Xerox*. And there were many instances of personal or place-names developing uses as common nouns – *ampere, biro, joule, mae west, ohm, quisling, watt* – or being used as the root for a general concept: *Blairite, Californium, Chaplinesque, Clintonite, Darwinism, Dianamania, Einsteinium, Kremlinology, Leninist, Pinteresque, Reaganomics, Thatcherism.*

The modern period is also notable for the way certain types of word formation, sporadic in earlier periods, became widespread. An example is the proliferation of nouns composed of a combination of verb and particle: *knock-out* and *stand-by* are examples from the eighteenth century, *stick-up* and *take-off* from the nineteenth, *check-up* and *fly-past* from the twentieth. The type of word formation known as a *back-formation* also seems to have increased in popularity during the past century. Back-formations occur when a shorter word is made by removing the affix from a longer word. Illustrating from agentive nouns, we find *edit* formed from *editor* in the eighteenth century, and *swindle* from *swindler*. Later examples are *shoplift, housekeep,* and *sculpt* in the nineteenth century, and *sleepwalk, name-drop,* and *therap* in the twentieth. Several types of back-formation exist, with hundreds of examples within each category. The adjectival endings *-pathic* or *-pathological*, for example, have generated a large number of nouns – *homoeopath, telepath, osteopath, psychopath* . . .

Grammar

During the Modern English period, the grammar of Standard English continued to change, but at a very much slower rate than in previous centuries. Indeed, a comparison of an early nineteenth-century text with one from the present-day seems to show very little difference, from a grammatical point of view. When we read a Jane Austen letter or a Charles Dickens novel we do not feel the need to make regular allowances for points of grammar, such as we do when reading Chaucer or Shakespeare (see panel 18.3). But some allowances do have to be made, for the grammar is not exactly the same. Whenever we sense that the phrasing of a passage is somewhat 'awkward' or 'old-fashioned', or a conversation is in some way 'stilted' or 'unidiomatic', we are probably noting a difference in grammatical norms between the beginning of the Modern English period and today. Usually, a sense of difference can be explained as a matter of frequency – a rare usage becoming common, or vice versa. It is also often a matter of stylistic change – a usage becoming more formal or polite, or vice versa, or altering its status with respect to a particular stylistic domain.

18.3 Yʳˢ affec:ˡʸ J. A.

This opening page of a letter from Jane Austen to Cassandra Austen (17 October 1815) requires no grammatical glossing, but at the same time there are points (underlined) where the grammar is subtly different from present-day usage. Spelling and punctuation are as in the original.[9]

> Thank you for your two Letters. I am very glad the new Cook begins so well. Good apple pies are a considerable part of our domestic happiness.—Mʳ Murray's Letter is come; he is a Rogue of course, but a civil one. He offers £450— but wants to have the Copyright of MP. & S&S included. It will end in my publishing for myself I dare say.—He sends more praise however than I expected. It is an amusing Letter. You shall see it.— Henry came home on Sunday & we dined the same day with the Herrieses—a large family party—clever & accomplished.—I had a pleasant visit the day before. Mʳ Jackson is fond of eating & does not much like Mʳ or Miss P.—What weather we have!—What shall we do about it?—The 17ᵗʰ of Octʳ & summer still! Henry is not quite well—a bilious attack with fever—he came back early from H.Sᵗ yesterday & went to bed—the comical consequence of which was that Mʳ Seymour and I dined together tète a tète.—He is calomeling* & therefore in a way to be better & I hope may be well tomorrow. The Creeds of Hendon dine here today, which is rather unlucky—for he will hardly be able to shew himself—& they are all Strangers to me. He has asked Mʳ Tilson to come & Take his place. I doubt our being a very agreable pair.—We are engaged tomorrow to Cleveland Row.

> *The use of *calomel* as a verb is not recorded in the *OED*.

Sometimes the difference is easy to see, because the actual structure of a word or sentence varies noticeably.[10] In the verb phrase, there are several differences in the way people expressed negation in the late eighteenth and early nineteenth centuries:

- in *The School for Scandal* (1777), Sheridan has one of his characters say: *an't I rather too smartly dress'd*; today we would say: *aren't I* or *am I not*;
- in one of his letters (1819), Keats writes: *I look not forward with any pleasure to what is call'd being settled*; today: *I don't look forward*;
- in another letter (1819), Keats writes: *I wonder your Brother don't put a monthly bulleteen in the Philadelphia Papers*; today: *doesn't*.

Some of these usages continued throughout the century:

- in *Mary Barton* (1848), Mrs Gaskell writes: *I have it not by me*; today: *I don't have it by me* or *I haven't got it by me*;
- in *The Eldest Son* (1912), John Galsworthy writes: *Caste don't matter*; today: *doesn't*;
- in *Cranford* (1851–3), Mrs Gaskell writes: *I had better ring the bell, my dear, had not I?*; today: *hadn't I*.

Some of the other auxiliary verbs were also used differently, especially *shall*:

- in *Middlemarch* (1871–2), George Eliot writes: *shall you let him go to Italy?*; today: *will*;
- in a letter (1813), Jane Austen writes: *Shall not you put them into our own room?*; today: *won't*.

After negative adverbials in Modern English, we find inversion of the subject and verb (*Never did I see . . .*), but here we find it after other kinds of adverbial:

- in *The Critic* (1779), Sheridan writes: *Now will he go and vent his philosophy*; today: *Now he will go*;

Some 'double' usages involving the verb *to be* were quite normal:

- in *Mansfield Park* (1816), Jane Austen writes: *You will **be to visit** me in prison*;
- in a letter (1818), Keats writes: *No snuff **being to be** had in the village*;
- in a letter (1807), Jane Austen writes: *we have scarcely a doubt of her **being** actually **staying** with the only Family in the place whom we cannot visit*.

And this piece of dialogue, from Austen's *Northanger Abbey* (1818), shows an ellipsis of the verb *to be*:

'He is very handsome indeed.'
'Handsome! – Yes, I suppose he may.'

Today, we would have to say, 'I suppose he may be.'

The way in which verb phrases express their tenses and aspects has also subtly changed:

- in a letter (1804), Jane Austen writes: *Jenny & James are walked to Charmouth this afternoon*; today: *walked/have walked*;
- in a letter (1861), John Richard Green writes: *I was glad to find Mrs Ward returned*; today: *has/had returned*;
- in a letter (1818), Keats writes: *Now I will return to Fanny – it rains*; today: *it is raining*;
- in *Mary Barton* (1848), Mrs Gaskell writes: *What do they say?*; today: *What are they saying?*

And some nonstandard usages which are believed to be of twentieth-century origin in fact appear much earlier, and from literary pens. For example:

- in a letter (1819), Keats writes: *I should not of written*.

In the noun phrase, there are several indications of change. Johnson uses *informations* as a plural in his *Dictionary* Plan. Walter Scott talks about *accommodations*. Jane Austen suffered from *the headach*. Also:

- in a letter (1819), Keats writes: *when none such troubles oppress me*; today we would say: *no such troubles*;
- in a letter (1830), the lawyer Joseph Jekyll writes: *the new police has defeated the canaille* [rabble]; today: *have defeated*;
- in *Essays of Elia* (1823), Charles Lamb writes: *any the most intricate accounts*; today: *any of the most*.

Adverbs, too, have changed, as illustrated by such former constructions as *a monstrous fine young man* (1840) and *she is absolutely fatter* (1836). Combinations of adverbs appear which would not be used today, other than in a pastiche of an earlier speech style, such as *quite too adorable* (1890) and *dreadfully too early* (1838). And comparison of adjectives, distinctively different in Early Modern English (p. 376), continues to display a contrast with modern usage, as with *properer* and *scornfullest*.

Less noticeable are cases where there is a difference in the frequency of usage between then and now. Instances of increased frequency are not too difficult to spot. *Mayn't*, for example, is rare today, but it was a normal polite usage in the nineteenth and early twentieth centuries: *please, mayn't we have another?* is an example from 1902. We would also be likely to notice the much greater use of the subjunctive construction:

- in *Money* (1840), Bulwer-Lytton writes: *It were madness*; today: *It would be madness*;

- in *Waverley* (1814), Scott writes: *how different had been my present situation!*; today: *would have been.*

On the other hand, it is extremely difficult to spot the opposite trend: usages which have developed *since* the earlier period, and therefore do not occur in early nineteenth-century texts. It is always difficult to notice something that *isn't* there, or which is used with much less frequency. The progressive passive, as in *John is being promoted*, is an example. We would never notice that Jane Austen does not use it. It was a new usage in the nineteenth century, and when it did begin to appear it attracted considerable criticism, with pundits widely condemning the construction as a 'monstrous absurdity'. Cardinal John Henry Newman wrote in a letter (*c.* 1871) 'I have an undying, never-dying hatred to *is being.*' Today, it attracts not the slightest notice.

Some of the new grammatical usages of the time were so violently attacked that, even nearly 200 years on, they remain contentious. The use of *get* and *got* increased, probably because of American influence, and generations of schoolchildren were – and still are – taught that these are 'ugly' words. An early example is Sheridan's *These Londoners have got a gibberage* [gibberish] *with 'em* (in *Scarborough*, 1777). The use of *get* in the passive construction was particularly criticized, despite receiving considerable literary use:

- in a letter (1819), Keats writes: *he gets beaten;*
- in *The Moonstone* (1871), Wilkie Collins writes: *after they had got released from prison;*
- in the continuation of the letter quoted on p. 462, Jane Austen uses *get* twice: *I want to get rid of some of my things . . . I want to get to Keppel Street again.*

And the split infinitive 'arrived', in the sense that this usage – illustrated by *to boldly go* or *to really try* (p. 402) – though common in English since the Middle Ages, attracted the attention of prescriptive grammarians, and quickly became one of the leading usage shibboleths of the century. A famous example of the extraordinary sensitivity surrounding this construction is reported in Andrew Lang's *Sir Stafford Northcote: Life, Letters and Diaries* (1890), the biography of the British statesman who was much involved in foreign affairs in the 1860s. Lang describes how the British government was prepared to make several concessions in negotiating a treaty with the United States, but 'telegraphed that in the wording of the treaty it would under no circumstances endure the insertion of an adverb between the preposition *to* . . . and the verb'. In the 2000s, the contentiousness surrounding this construction is thankfully diminishing, for it was never sanctioned by the leading usage pundits.[11] George Bernard Shaw called it 'fatuous'. Henry Fowler referred scathingly to the 'non-split diehard' –

'bogey-haunted creatures'. And Ernest Gowers said simply: 'It is a bad rule.' But it is still one of the most commonly cited prescriptive rules. Purists have surprisingly long memories sometimes.

Pronunciation

Pronunciation still had some way to go to reach its present-day position. We know this because more information is available about the way words were pronounced during the nineteenth century, compared with previous periods. Writers were much fuller in their descriptions, and in the last few decades of the century the first cylinder recordings of speech came to be made. The subjects of phonetics and philology (p. 53) introduced a level of expertise that had previously been missing, and there were more informal reports, as people wrote about the speech patterns they recalled from an earlier generation. Thus we find observers talking about the pronunciation of *oblige* as *obleege*, *daughters* as *darters*, *gold* as *goold*, *seven* as *sivin*, and *china* as *chayney*, as well as many words where the stress pattern was different from what it is today, as in *balcony, compensate*, and *Trafalgar*. We can even date the change, in such cases as *balcony*: dictionaries before 1800 show the older stress pattern only, there is then some mixed reporting, and those after the 1850s show the new pattern only.[12] Additional evidence comes from the complaints. In *Recollections of the Table-talk of Samuel Rogers*, published just after his death in 1855, we read:

> The now fashionable pronunciation of several words is to me at least very offensive: *cóntemplate* – is bad enough; but *bálcony* makes me sick.

It is also possible to identify trends affecting individual segments. One example is the distinction between a voiced and a voiceless *w* – as in *Wales* vs *whales* – which was maintained in educated speech until the second half of the nineteenth century. That the change was taking place during that period is evident from the way people began to notice it and condemn it. For example, Cardinal Newman's younger brother, Francis, writing in his seventies in 1878, comments: 'W for Hw is an especial disgrace of Southern England.'[13] Today, it is not a feature of Received Pronunciation (see below), though it is kept in several regional accents (including my own). Another example is the pronunciation of final *-ng* in words like *singing*. In 1791, John Walker affirmed that the 'best speakers' pronounced such words as *singin'*, and echoes of this accent could be heard in upper-class speech in the early decades of the twentieth century. However, there was always a lot of variation. Received Pronunciation today requires the sounding of the *-ng*, and 'dropping the *g*' is usually condemned as a nonstandard feature. But it will quite often be heard in informal educated speech, and it still carries some resonance of its former status, especially in stereotyped contexts such as *huntin', shootin', and fishin'*.

Probably the most important change during this period affected the pronunciation of *r* after a vowel.[14] Present in English since Anglo-Saxon times, John Walker had already noted that it was weakening, referring to it as a 'soft' sound in words like *farm*, though he none the less continued to mark it as present in all his entries. There was a great deal of inconsistency throughout the nineteenth century, with many people replacing the *r* with a vowel glide (i.e., turning the main vowel of the word into a diphthong – *calm* as 'kah-um'). But in the early part of the century, we find rhymes and respellings suggesting that *-r* had actually disappeared: *harm* is said to rhyme with *calm*, and *alms* with *arms*. Also, when people wrote *calm* in a mock-phonetic way they sometimes spelled it *karm*, which they would never have done if the *r* had continued to be sounded. The perception that the language was 'losing a letter' was a cause of profound upset to some writers, who bitterly condemned poets who made use of such 'Cockney rhymes' (as they were called). Keats was one who placed aural considerations above visual, producing such rhymes as *thoughts / sorts, thorns / fawns*, and *higher / Thalia* – but he was heavily censured throughout the nineteenth century for his pains. Today, the controversy is in the other direction: the omission of a 'postvocalic *r*', as it is technically called, is accepted as a standard feature of Received Pronunciation – indeed, it is one of its most distinctive characteristics.

The 'other direction' refers to the rise of the so-called 'intrusive *r*' – the insertion of an *r* consonant into the pronunciation to ease the transition between adjacent vowels. Examples include *Africa[r] and Asia, the idea[r] of it*, and *draw[r]ing*. The crucial point is that there is no letter *r* in the spelling. The usage seems to have emerged in the late eighteenth century, and quickly attracted condemnation, given the prevailing view that it was important to make pronunciation as much as possible a reflection of writing (p. 403). Educated speakers were recommended to avoid it; doubtless it carried some echoes of the Cockney pronunciation of such words as *window*, which would often be written as *winder*. In fact intrusive *r* had never been restricted to lower-class usage. The late nineteenth-century phonetician Henry Sweet made a point of listening out for it, and he heard it everywhere, in educated and non-educated usage alike. In an 1889 letter, he says:

> I have made special observations on this point, & I am now certain that the insertion of the r . . . is absolutely universal in educated southern English speech & has been for the last 50 years. I hear it from old as well as young . . . Yet they all deny it.[15]

He later clarified his view, suggesting that the effect was frequent only in rapid colloquial speech; and all phoneticians since have concurred that it is especially common in this style, even in Received Pronunciation. However, phonetic realities never persuade those who believe in the power of a shibboleth. Today, the use of an intrusive *r* – especially in a noticeable context, such as after a long open vowel (as in *drawing*) – continues to attract strong criticism, and leads some radio broadcasters, anxious to avoid irate letters from listeners, to mark up their scripts in advance to identify any problem cases.

Received Pronunciation has now been mentioned several times – the non-regional educated British accent of the twentieth century, variously labelled 'RP', an 'Oxford accent', a 'BBC accent', the 'King's/Queen's accent', and a 'public-school accent'. This did not exist at the end of the eighteenth century. On the contrary, features of regional pronunciation were a normal characteristic of educated speech, and attracted no comment. John Walker acknowledged the point in his 1791 Preface (p. 408):

> The best educated people in the provinces, if constantly resident there, are sure to be strongly tinctured with the dialect of the country in which they live.

But the tone of his Preface suggests that he was sensing its emergence, and the reference to 'the provinces' leaves little doubt as to where this new accent was to be found. Several language writers of the time had already begun to acknowledge that the norms of acceptable pronunciation had moved from the court to polite London society. One 1784 work, by William Kenrick, makes it plain:

> By being properly pronounced, I would be always understood to mean, pronounced agreeable to the general practice of men of letters and polite speakers in the Metropolis.[16]

By the 1830s, writers were advising provincials to speak like Londoners.

In due course phoneticians began to make descriptions of this desirable London speech. Although Walker had already used the term 'received' (p. 408) it was the pioneering phonetician Alexander Ellis who first introduced it as a technical term, as part of a classification of types of pronunciation. He distinguished six kinds: Received, Correct, Natural (Untamed), Peasant, Vulgar (Illiterate), and Dialect. This is how he characterized the 'Received' type, which he abbreviated as *r.p.* (the capitalized abbreviation came later):

> In the present day we may . . . recognise a received pronunciation all over the country . . . It may be especially considered as the educated pronunciation of the metropolis, of the court, the pulpit and the bar . . .[17]

and he later added other categories, such as the universities and the stage. 'Received' for Ellis was not a completely homogeneous notion. In the omitted section of the above quotation he had said that it exists 'all over the country not widely differing in any particular locality, and admitting a certain degree of variety'. He demonstrated the variety by carrying out a detailed analysis of several individual accents, showing how, for example, people from the same background might say *across* or *acrorss*, *Bath* or *Bahth*, *God* or *Gawd*, *gal* or *girl*, *dooty* or *duty*, *umbrella* or *umberella*, and so on. He especially pointed out the contrast between formal and informal speech styles, and also recognized the presence of a 'thread' of regional colouring in many people's speech. The novelists and social commentators of the period picked up the point repeatedly, recognizing the variation in their portrayal or condemnation of it. Dickens captures three such features in his account of Mr Sparkler, who would remark 'of every successive young lady to whom he tendered a matrimonial proposal that she was "a doosed fine gal – well educated too – with no biggodd nonsense about her" '.[18] And Lady Agnes Grove writes in her etiquette guide: 'Nothing . . . is more irritating than the sedulous pronunciation of mid-verbal "h's" [in words like *adhere*] or the sounding of the "t" in often.'[19]

There was never total uniformity, therefore, but this new accent was certainly one which was much more supra-regional than any previous English accent had ever been. The regional neutrality, Ellis believed, had come from a natural process of levelling (p. 246), with educated people from different regional backgrounds increasingly coming into contact and accommodating to each other's speech. Greater social mobility had brought urban and rural dwellers together more than before. University education had brought people from many different regional backgrounds together. Schoolteachers were exercising an increased influence on their charges, and a momentum was building up within the schools themselves, especially in the private system. The new accent eventually did come to be associated with a 'public-school education' – at such schools as Eton, Harrow, Winchester, and Westminster – followed by higher education at Oxford or Cambridge. And the accent then rapidly spread through the career structure which such an education opened up – in the civil and diplomatic service (especially abroad, as the Empire expanded) and the Anglican Church. The immense pressure from the public-school system was probably the chief reason why the regional colouring which Ellis had noted in educated speech largely died out between 1860 and 1890, so much so that by 1894 Richard Lloyd was able to talk about 'perfect' English being that which gives 'the least possible indication of local origin'.[20] It was because there was such a link with the public schools that when the phonetician Daniel Jones carried out his first description of r.p. he called it *Public School Pronunciation* (PSP): 'that most usually heard in everyday speech in the families of Southern English persons whose menfolk have been educated at the great public boarding schools'.[21] He went for *RP* in 1926.

By then, of course, it had been further institutionalized by being adopted by the BBC. Lord Reith, the founder of the BBC, expressed his policy in this way:

> Since the earliest days of broadcasting the B.B.C. has recognised a great responsibility towards the problems of spoken English. These are vexed but intriguing. They might have been evaded, leaving both general principles and particular words to chance. Tendencies might have been observed and either reinforced or resisted. As the broadcaster is influential, so also is he open to criticism from every quarter in that he addresses listeners of every degree of education, many of whom are influenced by local vernacular and tradition. There has been no attempt to establish a uniform spoken language, but it seemed desirable to adopt uniformity of principle and uniformity of pronunciation to be observed by Announcers with respect to doubtful words. The policy might be described as that of seeking a common denominator of educated speech.[22]

The 'common denominator' was of course RP. And to help put this policy into practice, in 1926 the BBC appointed an Advisory Committee on Spoken English, chaired by the poet laureate Robert Bridges, and including George Bernard Shaw, Daniel Jones, and A. Lloyd James, who made a set of recommendations about variant forms (see panel 18.4).

18.4 Announcing pronouncing

A list of recommended pronunciations for BBC announcers appeared in the second edition of *Broadcast English* (1931). The first edition, published in 1928, had contained 332 words; the second, 503. Even in that short period, though, the editors found it necessary to make changes in their recommendations, such as in *fragile, iodine, decadence*, and *garage*. For example, in relation to the last of these, they say:

> *Garage* has been granted unconditional British nationality, and may now be rhymed with *marriage* and *carriage*.

The perpetually changing stress pattern in English words (p. 466) will be noted in the list below, where *acumen, allies, anchovy, antiquary, artisan,* and *aspirant* are among those which have been affected since the 1920s. The Committee also backed the wrong horse for British use in *airplane*.

accessory	stress on 2nd syllable
accomplish	accómplish, not -cúm-
acetic	aséetic
acoustic	acóostic
acumen	akéwmen

adherent	adhéerent
adieu	adéw
adults	áddults
aerated	áy-erayted
aerial	(a) noun – 1st syllable to be pronounced áir; (b) adjective – ay-éerial
aeroplane	áiroplayn; but the Committee advises the use of *airplane*
alabaster	stress on 1st syllable
allied	allíed, but *állied forces*
allies	allíes
altercate	aẃltercayt
amateur	ámaterr; final syllable rhymes with *fur*
amenable	améenable
amenities	améenities
anchovy	an-chŏvy
anglice	ánglissy
antiquary	stress on 1st syllable
apothegm, apophthegm	áppothem ('th' as in *thin*)
apparatus	apparáytus
apparent	appárrent
applicable	stress on 1st syllable
appreciation	appreeshiáyshon
aquatic	akwátic; 2nd syllable rhymes with *hat*
arbitrary	árbitrăry
arid	árrid
armistice	stress on 1st syllable
artisan	principal stress on last syllable
aspirant	stress on 2nd syllable, which is pronounced as *spire*
ass	*a* as in *hat*
associate	assŏshiayt
ate	rhymes with *bet*, not with *bait*
athwart	athwárt; last syllable as in *wart*
auld lang syne	*Syne* is to be pronounced like *sign*: the *s* must not be pronounced *z*
autogyro	awtojýro
automobile	áwtomobeel
azure	ázhure; *a* as in *hat*

But almost as soon as RP arrived, it began to fragment. It already contained a great deal of personal variation, and it was subject to change, as any other accent. By the beginning of the twentieth century it was displaying a range of chiefly age-related differences which the phonetician A. C. Gimson would describe in the 1960s as 'conservative' (used by the older generation), 'general' (or 'mainstream'), and 'advanced' (used by young upper-class and professional people), the last often being judged as 'affected' by other RP speakers.[23] It retained its upper and upper-middle social-class connotation, as a supra-regional standard, but from the 1960s it slowly came to be affected by the growth of regional identities, resulting in the re-emergence of regional colouring – a phenomenon now described as 'modified RP'. There was also a reduction in the extent of the country which recognized the accent as a desirable standard. From a characterization in terms of 'Britain' it came to be restricted to 'England'. The British phonetician John Wells described it in 1982 as 'a standard through-out southern Britain (i.e., in England and perhaps Wales, but not in Scotland)'.[24] These days, following devolution, we would have to exclude Wales as well as Northern Ireland. In these constituencies, RP survives in most educated voices only with a considerable regional modification.

Even in England, the character of the accent as spoken by the educated class has dramatically altered, incorporating a number of features previously associated with local London speech to produce the accent that the media have happily designated 'Estuary English'.[25] Although first noticed in the 1980s with reference to the accent emerging around the River Thames estuary, it soon became apparent that this name would not do as a means of characterizing an accent several of whose features were spreading around the country, as far north as Yorkshire and as far west as Dorset. Moreover, the trend had been around for quite a while. As early as 1949, in one of his BBC talks, Daniel Jones had commented that 'it seems quite likely that in the future our present English will develop in the direction of Cockney unless special influences come in to counteract this tendency'.[26] No such influences arrived. By the 1970s, accents showing a mixture of RP and Cockney were becoming noticeable, motivated by an upmarket movement of originally Cockney speakers and a downmarket trend towards 'ordinary' (as opposed to 'posh') speech by the middle class. By the 1990s, attitudes had begun to change, with conservative RP attracting negative attitudes, such as 'posh' and 'distant', and modi-fied varieties (such as Estuary) eliciting such positive evaluations as 'warm', 'customer-friendly', and 'down to earth'. For many people, no further evidence of the rehabilitation of regional accents is required than the voices heard at the ends of phones in call-centres throughout the UK, where varieties of Edinburgh Scots, Yorkshire, and other regional forms are routinely encountered, but traditional RP hardly ever. The number of people using a non-regionally tinged RP accent has fallen greatly, as a consequence. Estimates of usage in the 1980s were that between 3 and 5 per cent of the British population still used it – around 2 million. This must be now less than 2 per cent and falling.

Although the BBC held out until the 1970s against the use of regional colouring in the accents of its announcers, the eventual demise of the RP monopoly had been anticipated from the beginning. In 1926, the *Daily Chronicle* expressed its anxieties:

> Is there not some danger that the uniform system of training in pronunciation as well as voice production, which the B.B.C. is planning, may lead to a tiresome and possibly infectious monotony of utterance? We see no reason why the B.B.C. should not rather cultivate a variety of accent, intonation and blend of sound, so long as each variety is good of its kind.[27]

Some twenty years later, broadcaster Wilfred Pickles made the same point in an eloquent defence of regional dialect:

> While I have the greatest respect for the many achievements of the B.B.C., I believe they are guilty of the offence of trying to teach Great Britain to talk standard English. How terrible it is to think that we may some day lose that lovely soft Devonshire accent or the bluff and very wonderful Scots brogue or the amusing flatness and forthrightness of the North-countryman's speech, or the music of the Welsh voice. May it be forbidden that we should ever speak like B.B.C. announcers, for our rich contrast of voices is a vocal tapestry of great beauty and incalculable value, handed down to us by our forefathers.[28]

And he hit out at stereotypes:

> The view that if a man speaks in a North-country accent he must necessarily wear a cloth cap and keep a whippet under the table should be quashed; we must see to it that we don't speak in one language.

Pickles rather overestimated the potential power of radio to change community accents, but he certainly knew what happened when a regional voice disturbed the RP hegemony, because he had taken part in an experiment in the early part of the Second World War, when he had been asked to read the national news. According to the BBC announcer John Snagge, the minister of Information had felt that Pickles' Northern accent could be a useful security measure, because it 'might not be so easily copied by the Germans'. The decision caused headline news in the national press, with Pickles' 'short *a*' repeatedly picked upon: *Lahst a Thing of the Pahst* said one. Although the BBC's Listener Research Department found his reading to be surprisingly popular, a torrent of abuse came through the post. People complained that they were unable to believe the news read in such an accent. Although Pickles claimed he enjoyed the fuss, he eventually decided to give it up, preferring to carry on with other broadcasting work 'up north' in Manchester.

There were other famous cases of accent rejection. In 1937 Charles Chilton began to present a programme of popular music, but his 'Cockney voice' led to his being taken off the air. Even in 1980, listeners to Radio 4 were expressing concern over the Scottish accent of the presenter Susan Rae. But by then, the RP monopoly had already been placed in its coffin. In 1977 the Annan Report on the future of broadcasting commented 'We welcome regional accents.'[29]

Ongoing variation

The eighteenth-century prescriptivists (p. 396) had two impossible aims: they wanted to stop the language changing, and they wanted to eliminate usage variation. In neither case were they successful. They could not have been, for it is in the nature of language to change and to vary. And the evidence of their failure – as Johnson himself had sagaciously noted, expressing his distaste of Academies (p. 378) – is all around us today. We have already identified several of the changes which have taken place in the vocabulary, grammar, and (for Britain) pronunciation of English. In each case, however, we are talking about trends, never uniformity. Linguistic change does not take place all at once: it gradually diffuses – both geographically, throughout a region, and socially, throughout the various classes out of which the society is comprised, with the rate at which the change is taken up very much affected by the gender and age of the speakers. As a result, at any one point in time, there is inevitably a great deal of variation, as old forms compete with new. Not only is there variation among speakers, there is variation within individuals, with people taking time to get used to new forms. Random variation exists, with language users pulled in different directions at once. I am a case in point: I currently pronounce the word *schedule* both with and without a [k] consonant. I am traditionally a 'shedule' user, but quite often say 'skedule', influenced partly by the content of what I am saying (American subject-matter might trigger it), by the need to accommodate to the accent of my interlocutor (my children are all [k] users), and, often, for no apparent reason other than the whim of the moment. The same variability, as we shall see, also applies to spelling. And I am not alone. Everyone is pulled in multiple directions when it comes to language, because we interact within a multifaceted society.

The chief evidence of the prescriptivist failure to control variation lies in the hundreds of manuals giving guidance on usage, style, and linguistic etiquette, which became increasingly common in the nineteenth century and which are still regularly published. These manuals would never have had a reason to be compiled at all if variation had been successfully eliminated. Especially influential works from the last 150 years include *The Queen's English* (1860) by Henry Alford, dean of Canterbury, followed a few decades later by Henry and Francis

Fowler's *The King's English* (1906). A generation on and we have Henry Fowler's *Dictionary of Modern English Usage* (1926). Another generation on and we find Eric Partridge's *Usage and Abusage* (1942) and Ernest Gowers' *Plain Words* (1948). A proliferation of titles appear over the next few decades, such as the Washington Square Press *Handbook of Good English* (1982), the Reader's Digest manual, *The Right Word at the Right Time* (1985), and the Longman *Guide to English Usage* (1988). Few of these books are less than 400 pages. Fowler's *Dictionary* is over 700. And as the international use of English grows (Chapter 19), the usage books get bigger. Pam Peters' *Australian Style Guide*, adding an antipodean perspective to the already considerable vacillation over formal and informal British and American usage, is 850 pages, and an even larger work is in progress.[30] Even if we were to leave all international variation out of account, a usage manual would still need to be several hundred pages long if it was (were?) to contain every single feature of pronunciation, orthography, grammar, vocabulary, and discourse which (that?) have been sources (has been a source?) of dispute (dis*pute*? *dis*pute?) upon occasion. For a supposedly standard language, this is an awful lot of variation.

Why are there so many usage guides? It is not as if the issues change very much, from one generation to the next. Most of the contentious points which Dean Alford addressed are the same as those which face usage pundits today. He, the Fowlers, and the rest all worry about ending sentences with prepositions, how to avoid splitting infinitives, whether to say *will* or *shall*, and what to do about all the other grammatical prescriptions dating back to Lowth and Murray. Contemporary changes in pronunciation attract the same kind of dissatisfaction and abuse, from one generation to the next. The specific examples may change, but the usage issue does not. For example, a change in the stress pattern of a word is guaranteed to cause disquiet, and this lasts a few decades before it dies away. In the first half of the nineteenth century, as we saw above, there was a dispute over the new pronunciation of such words as *balcony* and *contemplate*. This is a long-since-forgotten controversy: *balcony* and *contemplate* are uncontroversial now. But each generation has its new examples of stress-shift to complain about. Old *illustrate* competed with new *illustrate* in the early decades of the twentieth century. That is over now. Old *promulgate* competed with new *promulgate* in the 1940s, as did old *controversy* with new *controversy*. The former is over; the latter rumbles on. A dispute between old *research* (as a noun) and new *research* began in the 1980s. That still causes letters to the press.

Plainly, lexical stress-shifting is a regular feature of the English language. Indeed, we can trace variations in word stress back to beyond Shakespeare and Chaucer. But people do not seem able to accept them as a normal feature of the language – as a natural variation in linguistic fashion. The irony is that each generation tends to look back at earlier generations (especially the one two generations earlier) as if they were some kind of golden linguistic age. 'Things were not so bad when I was a child' is the common grandparental refrain. But of course, they were. The Bullock Report of 1975, investigating the use of English in British schools, began by quoting some comments from employers about poor standards, such as: 'it is a great surprise and disappointment to us to find that our young employees are so hopelessly deficient in their command of English'.[31] However, this is a quotation from an employer in 1921, not the 1970s. No doubt people in the 1920s in their turn looked back nostalgically at the 1860s. But Henry Alford was in gloom even then:

> Look, to take one familiar example, at the process of deterioration which our Queen's English has undergone at the hands of the Americans.[32]

And if he was thinking of sixty years earlier as a golden age, at a time before the Americans had begun to carve out their own linguistic road, he would have found Lindley Murray and the other early prescriptivists very ready to disagree with him (p. 397).

Even in orthography, the area that is often said to have become completely standardized by 1800, we find a remarkable amount of variation, as Sidney Greenbaum established in 1986.[33] He carried out a survey to estimate how much spelling variation there was in Modern English. He took a medium-sized (1,690-page) desk dictionary, and identified all the words spelled in more than one way under letter A. He found an average of three variant forms per page – 296 entries. Extrapolating from this to the dictionary as a whole, he estimated there would be nearly 5,000 variants altogether. As a percentage of all the entries in the dictionary, this was a remarkable 5.6 per cent (see panel 18.5). What is especially interesting is to note the way the variation appears in all stylistic levels. We might expect a certain amount of variation at the most informal levels of the language (*auntie* vs *aunty*) or in general everyday use (*aging* vs *ageing*). Nor might we be too surprised to find spelling variation in poetry, such as *aery* and *airy*. But it is somewhat unexpected to see the most scholarly, scientific, and technical texts varying so much. This is a formal level of language, where we would expect prescriptive pressure to be operating most strongly.

Greenbaum's study opens up a can of words. The amount of spelling variation in scientific and technical words in the language as a whole is bound to be much greater than can be found in the pages of a general-purpose desk dictionary. For instance, in one of the dictionaries Greenbaum consulted, there are eleven words beginning with *paed-* or *paedo-*; but if we go to a scientific dictionary, or an unabridged dictionary, we find many more. There are twenty-seven such entries in the unabridged *OED*, for example – an increase of 150 per cent. About a third of the words in Greenbaum's sample were technical

18.5 Spelling variation

The following selection of doublets from Greenbaum's spelling survey illustrates the type of variation which exists in Standard English orthography.

abetter	abettor	aegis	egis
abridgable	abridgeable	aerogram	aerogramme
absinthe	absinth	aesthesia	esthesia
abulia	aboulia	aga	agha
accessory	accessary	ageing	aging
acclimatize	acclimatise	aide-de-campe	aid-de-camp
acouchi	acouchy	albumin	albumen
adieus	adieux	all right	alright
adrenalin	adrenaline	amok	amuck

Most variants operate in pairs, but triplets can also be found:

acronychal, acronycal, acronical

aerie, aery, eyrie

Even, at times quadruplets:

anaesthetize, anaesthetise, anesthetize, anesthetise

And if we add to Greenbaum's list proper names transliterated from a foreign language (p. 478), the variants can become extensive:

Tschaikovsky, Tchaikovsky, Tschaikofsky, Tchaikofsky, Tshaikovski, Chaikofski...

terms. If this increase is typical of the language as a whole, we might expect our 5.6 per cent figure to rise to around 14 per cent. Although some of these variants were originally due to the differences between American English and British English, the situation is no longer so simple. The influence of American textbooks in Britain has caused US spellings to become common in the UK – such as the often encountered -z- for -s- in such words as *atomize, atomizer, atomizable, atomization*. The -ae- and -oe- spellings have been widely replaced by -e- spellings in scientific texts, such as (in medicine) *etiology* for *aetiology*, *pediatrician* for *paediatrician*, and *fetus* for *foetus*. The impression of frequency is much increased when there is a widely used prefix, such as *ped-* for *paed-* and *arche-* for *archae-*. But even if we exclude all the variations due to American influence, this only eliminates just under a quarter of them: 231 entries in Greenbaum's sample (78 per cent) were variations within British English alone.

Nor does our account stop here, because Greenbaum did not deal with variations in capitalization (*Bible* vs *bible*, *Moon* vs *moon*, etc.) or in the spacing and hyphenation of compound words (*dark room* vs *dark-room* vs *darkroom*). In dictionaries, we regularly see the heading 'often capitalized' or 'sometimes hyphenated'. No one (No-one?) has ever worked out just how many capitalization or hyphenation variants there are – one reason being that the usage situation is so fluid. Increased familiarity with a compound form increases the likelihood that users will move from a spaced version (*dark room*) to a hyphenated one (*dark-room*) to a solid one (*darkroom*). In the 1990s it was usually *e-mail*; in the 2000s it is increasingly *email*. None the less, the total amount of variation under these headings must be quite high. In this illustration – part of the entry on Tony Blair from the *New Penguin Encyclopedia* (2002) – the words are underlined which could vary in their capitalization:

> Educated in Edinburgh, he studied law at Oxford, and was called to the bar in 1976. He was elected Labour MP for Sedgefield in 1983, becoming his party's spokesperson on Treasury affairs (1985–7) and trade and industry (1987–8). He joined the shadow cabinet in 1988, becoming responsible for energy (1988), employment (1989), and home affairs (1992). He was elected leader of the Labour Party in 1994 and led it to power in a landslide victory in 1997 and 2001, the first Labour prime minister to win a second full term.

Ignoring numerical dates, there are seventy-nine words in this passage, and eighteen of them might be capitalized or not, depending on the house style of a publisher and other factors – nearly 23 per cent.[34]

And there is still one further strand to this story of orthographic variation in Standard English. If we extend the inquiry to include encyclopedic knowledge – allowing in people, animals, vehicles, geographical locations, historical events, special days, and other such 'proper names' – our estimate must increase yet again. There is considerable variation here, too, especially when we are dealing with transliteration from a foreign alphabet. Is it *Aqaba* or *Akaba*? Is it *Tutankhamen, Tutankhamun, Tut'ankhamun*, or a hyphenated version reflecting the structure of the original language, such as *Tut-ankh-amun*? Shall we spell the fourteenth-century Arabic poet and biographer *Ibn al-Khatib* in that way, or as one of the many other variant forms of his name, such as *ibn al-Khatib, Ibn Al-Khatib, Abenaljatib*, and *Ben al-Hatib*? Most people would not think twice about the matter (the people who do notice the lack of this kind of standardization are the publishing professionals – the copy-editors, proof-readers, and book indexers). Most people would not even notice that there was an issue here, that systems of transliteration exist, or that a choice had been made. Very few readers would be able to say, at this point, which of the following forms has been chosen as standard for the present book: *judgment* or *judgement*? *authorise* or *authorize*? *medieval* or *mediaeval*?[35] All of which makes the point that we are quite used to variation; we live with it and accept it. Unfortunately, every now and then, someone gets upset about it, and assigns it responsibilities which it cannot bear (see Chapter 20).

It is ironic that the turn of the nineteenth century saw the beginning, as well as the beginning of the end, of the idea of a single monolithic variety of English used throughout the educated English-using world. In the eighteenth century, for just a few decades, a genuinely universal Standard English did exist, assiduously constructed by a team of linguistic master-builders. However, as we saw in Chapter 17, it was soon split into two wings by the emergence of American English, and further extensions began to appear with the growth of other global variations in educated usage. Nor was the building as permanent or stable as might have appeared. The present chapter demonstrates that there is a perpetual instability within the notion of a standard. The conception of an ever-lasting uniform Standard English is a myth. Within the emerging regional norms the language has continued to change and to display considerable variation.

However, none of this is sufficient to cause the building to collapse: the demand for a standardized variety of English to promote intranational and international intelligibility is urgent, and the forces which publish and teach through the medium of English are sufficiently strong to guarantee its core stability for the foreseeable future. If English is to remain a world language, then it needs a variety as a reference standard. But, as a result of the processes which have taken place – and which are an inevitable consequence of the nature of language – the character of the building has changed. Whereas Standard English was once viewed as a cathedral or monument, now it has to be seen more as a skyscraper, with a specific function of facilitating intelligibility, coexisting in a city of other tall buildings which perform other functions, such as the facilitation of local identity. It is no longer the only building in the city, and certainly no longer the only building thought to be worth a visit.

The new millennium has brought new ways of regarding the many buildings in the linguistic city we call English. And for this fresh vision we have to thank two remaining nineteenth- and twentieth-century developments – one national, the other global.

The grammatical heart of nonstandard English

Grammatical variation is at the heart of the distinction between standard and nonstandard English because it cuts across the divide between speech and writing. Although a standard orthography is a critical feature of the written language, this obviously does not apply to speech (except insofar as it leads people to pronounce words in a particular way, p. 467), and there is nothing in pronunciation quite like the standardization we see in orthography (p. 393). Nor is vocabulary of any relevance to the distinction: although there are many words which distinguish formal and informal varieties of speech and writing, there are none which might be unequivocally called standard – that is, *never* used by people who in other respects are nonstandard English users – or universally nonstandard (see panel 18.6). Only grammar has the capacity to operate with equivalent diagnostic power in both spoken and written language.

There are just a few dozen grammatical features commonly identified as nonstandard English. Not all of them appear in all regional dialects.

In the noun phrase

- *them* is used as a determiner instead of *those*, as in *them mice*[36]
- there is an additional demonstrative form: *yon*, in addition to *this/these* and *that/those*
- some comparative and superlative forms are different, as in *worser, more bigger, bestest*
- singular forms are used for plurals in numerical expressions, as in *twenty year, three pound*
- there is a second-person distinction between *thou* and *you*
- *you* is replaced by alternative personal forms, such as *yiz* and *youse* (p. 449)
- possessive forms are used in the third-person reflexive pronouns, as in *hisself* and *theirselves* (Standard English uses the objective form in this person – *himself, themselves*)

18.6 Nonstandard spelling

The following words in nonstandard spelling were noted in one issue of the *Sun* newspaper. If we imagine them spoken, rather than written, there are none which would be unavailable to a speaker of Standard English who wanted to be maximally informal or jocular.

Nonstandard spelling	Standard spelling
bruv	brother
dammit	damn it
dunno	don't know
fella	fellow
gotta	got to
Missus	Mrs
nah	no
puddin	pudding
wanna	want to
yep	yes
yer	your

In addition, there were several colloquialisms which added to the paper's informal tone, but any of them might be heard – depending on personality and taste – in colloquial Standard English: *fecking* (euphemistic intensifier for *fucking*, popularized by the television series *Father Ted*), *f'ing* (euphemisic intensifier for *fucking*), *footie* 'football', *hols* 'holidays', *info* 'information', *nosh* 'meal', *oomph* 'energy', *pal* 'friend', *phew* (interjection expressing admiration or exhaustion), *pic* 'picture', *pressies* 'presents', *no probs* 'no problems', *puke* 'vomit', *quickie* 'rapid sexual encounter', *skint* 'lacking money', *snazzy* 'flashily beautiful', *splat* (noise of something wet hitting a surface), *swig* 'drink', *tater* 'potato', *tummy* 'stomach', *undies* 'underwear'.

In the verb phrase

- a singular form of *be* is used with a plural subject after 'existential' *there*, as in *there's lots, there was lots*
- *of* is used for auxiliary have, as in *should of* (p. 464)
- *ain't* and *in't* replace *am not, are not*, and *is not*[37]
- the same form is found throughout the present tense: *I likes, you likes*, etc., *I be, you be*, etc.

- the same form is found throughout the past tense: *I was, we was*, etc.; *I were, we were*, etc.
- several irregular verbs display alternative past tense and past participle forms, as in *I done it, I seen it* (see panel 18.7)
- certain verbs use a past-tense form for the present participle, as in *she was sat there, I was stood there.*
- *never* is used as a past-tense negative, as in *I never did it*

18.7 Dialect tenses

The kinds of difference which distinguish dialect past forms of verbs from Standard English can be seen in this selection of items from north-east England (Tyneside).[38] It is noteworthy that in some cases the paradigm is simplified (*give . . . give . . . give*), compared with Standard English, whereas in others it is more complex (*get . . . got . . . getten*).

Standard English			Tyneside English		
I speak	I spoke	I've spoken	I speak	I spoke	I spoke
I take	I took	I've taken	I take	I took	I've took
I see	I saw	I've seen	I see	I seen	I've saw
I spin	I span	I've spun	I spin	I spun	I spun
I go	I went	I've gone	I go	I went	I've went
I get	I got	I've got	I get	I got	I've getten
I treat	I treated	I've treated	I treat	I tret	I tret
I say	I said	I've said	I say	I sayed	I've sayed
I give	I gave	I've given	I give	I give	I've give
I do	I did	I've done	I do	I done	I've done

In a clause

- there can be multiple negation, as in *I didn't want no trouble* (p. 398)
- some relative pronouns vary, as in *the play what he wrote*
- *-ly* adverbs appear without the ending, as in *the time went really quick*
- some complex prepositions vary, as in *going up my mate's house* ('up to'), *got off of the bus* ('off')

A few of these features are now so widely encountered in informal educated usage that they could probably be seen as part of colloquial Standard English, avoided only by people who are particularly sensitive about maintaining a school-taught rule. Within this category would fall the usages illustrated by *there's lots of apples in the box, I never saw him last week, three pound of potatoes,* and *the time went really quick.* The list could also be extended somewhat by incorporating those usages condemned by prescriptive grammarians even though they have long had a presence in educated English, such as the use of *and* at the beginning of a sentence, split infinitives, and end-placed prepositions (p. 400). But they are still only a tiny number compared with the 3,500 or so features described in major reference grammars (p. 403).

Chapter 19 And dialect life goes on

When Johnson died in 1784, Wordsworth was fourteen, Coleridge was twelve, Jane Austen was nine, and Charles Dickens had not yet been born. These names herald the impending arrival of a new literary age, in which authors recognized and exploited a much fuller range of English varieties and modes of expression than had been the case in the preceding century, and brought to maturity an alternative set of linguistic attitudes to those which had characterized the Johnsonian era. The new writing would prove to be a turning-point. Regional dialects, and positive attitudes towards these dialects, would once again be placed before the reading public, and there would be a growing criticism of the straitjacket within which prescriptively minded writers had attempted to enclose the language. Gradually, as a result of the status and respectability conferred by creative literature, nonstandard English would begin to reassert itself as a viable and expressive medium of communication, its position further supported by studies and statements from new breeds of dialectologists, philologists, and Anglo-Saxon enthusiasts. Although the prescriptive tradition would continue to be the dominant voice in the nineteenth century, maintaining an artificial account of Standard English which was widely taught and practised, its days were numbered. When Becky Sharp, on leaving school, throws out of her coach-window her presentation copy of Johnson's *Dictionary*, she unwittingly reflects the spirit of a new age.[1]

It was an age which received its first characterization from the Romantic poets, Wordsworth and Coleridge, whose *Lyrical Ballads* were published in 1798. The prefatory statement, published in the 1800 edition, was unequivocal.

> The principal object, then, proposed in these Poems, was to choose incidents and situations from common life, and to relate or describe them, throughout, as far as was possible, in a selection of language really used by men, and, at the same time, to throw over them a certain colouring of imagination, whereby ordinary things should be presented to the mind in an unusual aspect.

A selection of language really used by men? The notion is enticing, though the reality, as encountered in the poems themselves, is rather different. The

Romantics never actually got their syllables dirty; there is no sign of the earthy colloquialism of Chaucer's Host or the regional directness of a Fluellen or a disguised Edgar (p. 361). In fact, there is no local dialect at all. When we hear a character such as the shepherd Michael talking, we are actually presented with someone who is speaking in Standard English, with an elegant command of sentence structure and quite a large vocabulary. This is the opening of Michael's farewell words to his son Luke (in 'Michael: A Pastoral Poem', l. 331):

> Tomorrow thou wilt leave me: with full heart
> I look upon thee, for thou art the same
> That wert a promise to me ere thy birth,
> And all thy life hast been my daily joy.
> I will relate to thee some little part
> Of our two histories . . .'

No shepherd ever spoke like that. The language certainly conveys an impression of artless simplicity, but this is the result of Wordsworth's artistry, not his character's naturalness. As he says in another part of the Preface:

> There will also be found in these volumes little of what is usually called poetic diction; as much pains has been taken to avoid it as is ordinarily taken to produce it; this has been done for the reason already alleged, to bring my language near to the language of men.

The quotation makes it perfectly clear that the new 'Romantic' mood was a reaction against the perceived artificiality of the preceding poetic age. By 'real language' Wordsworth had in mind a kind of writing which would avoid the elaborate syntax and elegant diction employed by the 'Augustan' poets, such as Pope and Dryden, and capture the direct simplicity of expression he saw in Chaucer. His achievement is outstanding; but the result was still some considerable distance away from the realities of early nineteenth-century every-day speech. The stylistic innovation of the Romantic poets was to create the *illusion* that writing was a reflection of speech – a linguistic impressionism whose influence was profound.

The Romantic reaction did not result – could never have resulted – in a return to the linguistic norms of the English Middle Ages, when authors could write in whatever dialect they wanted, introducing spelling conventions which reflected the sounds of their accent. The arrival of the standard language had changed everything. Because Standard English was now a pervasive presence, it dictated the terms of literary encounter. All accents had to be 'heard' through the prism of the standard orthography, which reflected a sound system that, by the nineteenth century, was moving steadily in the direction of Received Pronunciation (p. 468). The best an author could do was to make an accent 'look' regional, by deviating from the standard norms in conventional ways, chiefly by respelling words or adding and omitting letters. In some cases the deviant form might capture a feature of regional pronunciation, as when *might* is represented as *micht* in Scots (p. 489), because in such cases there is a happy coincidence between the sound we associate with *ch* and the sound which actually occurs in the accent. On the other hand, to capture the sound which occurs in Scots *either*, there is no obvious representation, and several alternatives are found in local writing from Scotland, such as *ayther, aither, ather, ayther, ether, eather, eyther, adir*, and *edder*. None of these reflects the sound with any phonetic accuracy; rather, they reflect a *belief* about the sound. In many dialect representations, indeed, there is no pronunciation difference involved at all, but the nonstandard spelling conveys a regional resonance none the less. These are examples of the *Wot 'e wuz giv'n* type (p. 353). This sentence is actually an accurate representation of the utterance *What he was given* as it would be pronounced by a speaker of Received Pronunciation, but that is not how anyone would interpret it. The deviant spelling conveys a nonstandard accent – albeit one of no specific character. We are not talking about real accents or dialects, in such cases. They are dialects for the eye rather than the ear – and the technical term for them is in fact *eye-dialects*.

We have to bear in mind the inherent artificiality – though artistry would be a better word – in all the dialect representations which enter English literature after the emergence and international recognition of British and American Standard English. Authors have to resort to subterfuge to get their characterizations across. Sometimes they do no more than hint at a speaker's dialect background by choosing one or two features and letting these carry the weight of the whole – what we earlier (p. 346) referred to as stereotyping. Simply by increasing or decreasing the frequency with which a dialect feature is used in a character's speech can convey a message about the person's regional identity, level of education, or degree of solidarity with a local community. An upper-class rural speaker, such as a squire or parson, might have only one or two nonstandard spellings, just to 'remind' the reader, as it were, of the person's origins; a local rustic would have many. But even the rustic would be some distance away from real speech. According to Thomas Hardy, this was not only unavoidable, it was positively desirable:

> In the printing of standard speech hardly any phonetic principle at all is observed; and if a writer attempts to exhibit on paper the precise accents of a rustic speaker he disturbs the proper balance of a true representation by unduly insisting upon the grotesque element.[2]

Hardy was himself a master of dialect manipulation in the service of art. Despite attempts to localize the dialect of his rustic speakers, his Wessex was a fictitious area, much larger than the Dorset with which it is sometimes identified; more-over – despite its Anglo-Saxon name – it was not coincident with the area covered by historical Wessex (p. 24). He sensed, as did most other nineteenth-century novelists, that dialect realism in a literary work is part of the fiction. The dialect must seem credible, and the conventions must relate to the perceptions and expectations of the reader, but that is all.

Once such conventions become recognized, the opportunity is then avail-able for the writer to explore a world of dialect relativity, in which a change between standard and nonstandard, or between one set of nonstandard forms and another, represents much more than just a switch in regional identity. It can reflect a change in narrative perspective – the author, for example, adding a background comment in a dialect that is different from that of the characters. It can reflect a change in a character's attitude, point of view, or state of mind. It can reflect a change in a character's consciousness – a contrast between outer and inner voices, for example, or from present opinion to past reminiscence. It can reflect a change in the dynamic of character relationships, as people accommodate to each other (p. 83), signalling a shift in their intimacy or hinting at a new tone or atmosphere in an encounter. We have already seen this happening through a device as simple as switching between the pronouns *thou* and *you* (p. 307), and nineteenth-century novelists greatly exploited the expressive potential of this kind of code-switching. A modernist metaphor refers to the many 'voices' that comprise a literary work, emanating from the author as well as from the author's characters; and this polyvocalism is much facilitated by the availability of nonstandard forms.

During the nineteenth century, nonstandard English significantly increased its presence in national literature, moving from simple attempts at regional representation to subtle manipulations of dialect forms for literary effect. In the twentieth century, international developments in the use of English as a global language reinforced these trends, resulting in a blossoming of literary regional representations so multifarious and far-reaching in character that it would be no exaggeration to say we are entering a golden age of literary dialectology. The emphasis on literature is deliberate. The story of this remark-able turnaround in the fortunes of nonstandard English is chiefly a literary story – though not exclusively. Literature can give a dialect a public presence and confer prestige on it, as we have seen in the history of Standard English itself (Chapter 11); but if there is no 'live' dialect behind the literature, which readers can recognize and relate to, the exercise becomes surreal and can appear contrived (as in the 'droog' speech – Nadsat – of the characters in Anthony Burgess' *A Clockwork Orange*, 1962). What authors actually do is discover – and dis-cover – dialects. The sociolinguistic importance of Wordsworth and Coleridge is that they drew the attention of the literary world in England to the existence of living dialects – even though they did not try to portray them accurately themselves – and laid the foundations of the intellectual and emotional climate in which a more realistic dialect representation could flourish.

Literary dialects and dialect literature

The English Romantics were behind the times in one respect: literary dialect was already alive and well north of the border. In Scotland, the eighteenth century had already seen a resurgence of regional literature that had conferred a fresh level of national prestige upon the Scottish variety of nonstandard English. Three centuries before, Scottish English had achieved literary distinction, and had it not been for adverse political circumstances it might have evolved as a regional standard (p. 298). But even though the centre of linguistic gravity remained in the south, regional dialects in Scotland continued to flourish and change. The vernacular revival, associated primarily with the poetry of Robert Burns (1759–96), could not otherwise have taken place. 'The twa dogs (Cæsar and Luath)' provides an illustration of the kind of language Burns employed. The poem opens with a philosophical comment from one of the house-dogs:

> 'I've notic'd, on our Laird's [Lord's] court-day,
> An' mony a time my heart's been wae [sorrowful],
> Poor tenant bodies, scant [short] o' cash,
> How they maun thole a factor's snash: [must endure an agent's abuse]
> He'll stamp an' threaten, curse an' swear,
> He'll apprehend them, poind their gear; [seize their property]
> While they maun stan', wi' aspect humble,
> An' hear it a', an' fear and tremble!
> I see how folk live that hae [have] riches;
> But surely poor folk maun be wretches.'

And at the end of the poem, the animals conclude they would rather be dogs than men.

People responded to Burns' writing because they were able to recognize it and identify with it, and could appreciate its potential power as a way of legitimizing a variety which for so long had been obscured by southern literary dominance. For Scottish English, Burns opened the floodgates. Two centuries later, and some of the most powerful and successful writing in nonstandard English would be emanating from north of the border (see panel 19.1). But we are not talking about regional standards, with these examples. There is no uniformity. The authors are creating their own individual linguistic identities, wholly dependent on the use of nonstandard forms, but choosing different modes of representation and allowing (consciously or unconsciously) varying amounts of influence from Standard English. Words appear in a range of spellings: what we see in the panel as *weill* might in other writers appear as *well, wel,* or *weel; juist* might appear as *just, jist,* or *duist.* And there is variation, too, in the choice of lexicon and grammatical construction. Indeed, when William Laughton Lorimer was translating the Bible, he deliberately avoided a uniform representation, choosing several varieties of Scots to reflect the fact that the original text came from different writers using different styles.

19.1 The resurgence of Scots

The brilliance of Scotland's older poetry has rather diverted attention from the steadily increasing functionality of present-day Scottish English, which can now be read in several varieties of prose, both fiction and non-fiction.[3] The extracts below illustrate the range of the medium, which in the twentieth century, under the designation of *Scots*, began to attract claims that it was less a dialect of English and more an independent language.

The New Testament (1983)

The opening of the St John Gospel, in William Laughton Lorimer's translation (1983), as revised by his son, Robin Lorimer:

> In the beginnin o aa things the Wurd wis there ense, an the Wurd bade wi God, an the Wurd wis God. He wis wi God i the beginnin, an aa things cam tae be throu him, an wiout him no ae thing cam tae be. Aathing at hes come tae be, he wis the life in it, an that life wis the licht o man; an ey the licht shines i the mirk, an the mirk downa slocken it nane. There kythed a man sent frae God, at his name wis John. He cam for a witness, tae beir witness tae the licht, at aa men micht win tae faith throu him. He wisna the licht himsel; he cam tae beir witness tae the licht. The true licht, at enlichtens ilka man, wis een than comin intil the warld. He wis in the warld, an the warld hed come tae be throu him, but the warld miskent him. He cam tae the place at belanged him, an them at belanged him walcomed-him-na. But til aa sic as walcomed him he gae the pouer tae become childer o God; een tae them at pits faith in his name, an wis born, no o bluid or carnal desire o the will o man, but o God. Sae the Wurd becam flesh an made his wonnin amang us, an we saw his glorie, sic glorie as belangs the ae an ane Son o the Faither, fu o grace an trowth.

Academic discussion

John Thomas Low, 'Is Scots English?', is one of a series of contributions by Scottish academics experimenting with nonstandard prose:

'Is Scotch no juist [just] orra [shabby] English?' That's whit [what] a dominie [schoolmaster] in Scotland micht [might] still say, the kind o dominie that is sae [so] taen [taken] up wi [with] the 'richt' [right] educational policy o the high heid yins [head ones] in the gouvernment. Ye maun ken [must know] that dominies and schule-teachers in Scotland are no telt verra muckle [told very much] – if onything ava [at all] – aboot the auld leids [old languages] o their ain kintra [own country]. It's pairt o [part of] their trainin juist to haud [hold] on to Standard English and stop the bairns frae yasan [children from using] eyther Scotch in the Lallans [Lowlands] or Gaelic in the Heilans [Highlands]. I ken fu weill [full well] we maun aa [all] lairn English – a warld [world] leid wi a weill-gethert [well-gathered] and bien [rich] literatur; but we shairly sudna [surely should not] look doon [down] on oor ain [our own] auld leids.[4]

The novel

The mainstream Edinburgh-based dialect has now been supplemented by writing from other areas, especially Glasgow, as seen in the earthy realism of modern Scots novels. Here are the opening lines of two of them:

Irvine Welsh, *Trainspotting* (1993)

The sweat wis [was] lashing oafay [off of] Sick Boy; he wis trembling. Ah wis jist sitting thair [their], focusing oan [on] the telly, tryin no tae [not to] notice the cunt. He wis bringing me doon [down]. Ah tried tae keep ma [my] attention oan the Jean-Claude Van Damme video.

James Kelman, *How late it was, how late* (1994)

Ye wake in a corner and stay there hoping yer [your] body will disappear, the thoughts smothering ye; these thoughts; but ye want to remember and face up to things, just something keeps ye from doing it, why can ye no do it; the words filling yer head: then the other words; there's something wrong; there's something far far wrong; ye're no [not] a good man, ye're just no a good man.

This last book was the 1994 winner of the Booker Prize – an indication of the progress nonstandard English has made in being accepted by the literary establishment.

It is plain, from the way regional speech came to public attention in the nineteenth century, that dialects had not been overwhelmed by the bad press they had received since the Middle Ages, nor had they lost any of their vitality from their mistreatment by prescriptive writers. They had, as it were, simply been lying low, biding the time when attitudes would change, and they would no longer be viewed solely from an upper-class point of view as corrupt versions of the standard language, used only by people of poor upbringing, lowly status, or malevolent character. The moment had been a long time coming. For 200 years the standard language had been monopolizing prestige, internationally as well as nationally, in speech as well as in writing. By 1800, with the prescriptive foundation of Standard English universally acknowledged and respected, the position of nonstandard variation could hardly have been lower and its future less assured. But that is not how things turned out. Just when you think it has disappeared, linguistic variation has a habit of reasserting itself.

The positive reaction given to the portrayal of nonstandard speech in literature is perhaps not so surprising when we realize that dialects had their strong defenders as well as their critics, on both sides of the Atlantic. At the same time as Wordsworth and Coleridge were making the case for the rehabilitation of rural language, Thomas Jefferson was flying the American dialect flag – and remembering Britain as he did so. Jefferson was one who had no truck with the newfound prescriptivism. In a letter to John Waldo (16 August 1813) he affirms the priority of usage:

> I have been pleased to see that in all cases you appeal to usage, as the arbiter of language; and justly consider that as giving law to grammar, and not grammar to usage. I concur entirely with you in opposition to Purists, who would destroy all strength and beauty of style, by subjecting it to a rigorous compliance with their rules.

He then affirms the importance of language change:

> I have been not a little disappointed, and made suspicious of my own judgment, on seeing the Edinburgh Reviewers, the ablest critics of the age, set their faces against the introduction of new words into the English language; they are particularly apprehensive that the writers of the United States will adulterate it. Certainly so great growing a population, spread over such an extent of country, with such a variety of climates, of productions, of arts, must enlarge their language, to make it answer its purpose of expressing all ideas, the new as well as the old. The new circumstances under which we are placed, call for new words, new phrases, and for the transfer of old words to new objects.

And he concludes with a pro-dialect rhetorical outburst, citing precedent after precedent:

> An American dialect will therefore be formed; so will a West-Indian and Asiatic as a Scotch and an Irish are already formed. But whether will these adulterate, or enrich the English language? Has the beautiful poetry of Burns, or his Scottish dialect, disfigured it? Did the Athenians consider the Doric, the Ionian, the Aeolic, and other dialects, as dis-figuring or as beautifying their language? Did they fastidiously disavow Herodotus, Pindar, Theocritus, Sappho, Alcaeus, or Grecian

writers? On the contrary, they were sensible that the variety of dialects, still infinitely varied by poetical license, constituted the riches of their language, and made the Grecian Homer the first of poets.

Jefferson's views about usage had parallel expression in Britain, too, in the opinions of William Hazlitt, Thomas De Quincey, and others (p. 396).

As the nineteenth century progressed, language pundits added their voices to those of their literary counterparts in defence of the realities of everyday speech. The concept of a 'language pundit' was itself rather novel, emerging out of the subject of comparative philology which had come into being at the end of the eighteenth century. In 1785 Sir William Jones had proposed the common origin of Sanskrit, Latin, and Greek as part of an Indo-European family of languages. Scholars, especially in Germany, then investigated the detail of how the European linguistic situation had evolved, looking closely at the way sounds changed as languages moved through time and space. The result was a renewed interest in speech, and in the changes it displayed – not only between countries, but within a country, from one place to another. From the middle of the century, linguistic atlases began to be compiled to record regional differences, and a whole new domain of academic study, *dialectology*, evolved. Alexander Ellis was one of the pioneers, looking especially at pronunciation (p. 468). Another was the philologist Walter William Skeat, who became professor of Anglo-Saxon at Cambridge (1878). He had founded the English Dialect Society in 1873, with the aim of producing a dialect dictionary. Joseph Wright, later professor of comparative philology at Oxford (1901), took this task on, eventually completing the multi-volume *English Dialect Dictionary* (1898–1905). Wright also founded the Yorkshire Dialect Society in 1897, and several other dialect societies followed. By the middle of the twentieth century, when Harold Orton and Eugene Dieth began their major Survey of English Dialects (1948–61), rural varieties had attracted a huge amount of publication and developed an honourable tradition of study and debate.

The focus was definitely rural: the concern was to get country dialects recorded before they disappeared. Urban dialects received little attention. Apart from anything else, these did not fit into the nostalgic frame of reference which the Romantic idyll had fostered. A great deal of the *dialect literature* of the period (that is, literature wholly written *in dialect*) testifies to this nostalgia. In 1854, Samuel Bamford presented an edition of Tim Bobbin's 'Tummus and Meary' in a book called *The Dialect of South Lancashire*. (Tim Bobbin was the pseudonym of an eighteenth-century schoolteacher, John Collier.) In his Introduction, Bamford talks about 'a pleasure in the contemplation, the remembrance, as it were, through history, of old people who have left the place we live in'. He regrets their absence, and accordingly values a book in which 'we find, not only the portraiture of those we have been regretting, but their old stories, their uncouth words, and almost the tones of their voice are therein preserved for us'.[5] Many such works appeared in the second half of the nineteenth century; indeed, hardly any part of England failed to have its 'local dialect book'. Here are two brief extracts, to characterize the genre. The first is from Cheshire – 'Betty Bresskittle's Pattens, or Sanshum Fair' (a fair held at Altrincham on St James' Day):

> Jud [George] sprung upo' th' stage leet [light] as a buck an' bowd [bold] as a dandy-cock [Bantam cock], an' th' mon [man] what were playingk th' drum (only it wer'nt a gradely [proper] drum) gen [gave] him a pair o' gloves. Jud began a-sparringk, an' th' foaks shaouted, 'Hooray! Go it, owd [old] Jud! Tha'rt a gradely Cheshire mon!'[6]

The second is from Wiltshire – 'Extracts from the Genuine Remains of William Little' – a story turning upon the way the town of Cirencester is pronounced.

> 'How far d'e cal't to Zirencester [Cirencester], my friend?' zays a Cockney genelman one day to owld Pople, as a wor [were] breakin stwones on th' road. 'Dwont kneow zich a place [place],' zays he, scrattin's yeard [head], 'never yead [heard] on't avore [before]!' – 'What!' zays the genelman, 'never heard o' Zirencester?' – 'Noa', zays he, 'I aint.' – 'Why, it's the next town.' 'Haw! haw!' zays Pople; 'you means Ziszeter; why didn't e zay so? it's about vower mile off.'[7]

It is difficult to know just how genuine this kind of literature is. Most of it is recorded by well-meaning well-educated people – such as local clergymen or schoolteachers – who, in the absence of any phonetic or linguistic training, tend to spot only the most noticeable features and to over-represent them. There is certainly a marked contrast between these pieces and the basic level of functional literacy glimpsed when working-class people put pen to paper. A case in point is William Borrow, who kept a daybook in the mill where he worked, at Knaresborough, Yorkshire, in the 1790s. His sentences – examples are *their Childer hath done their work as Usial today* and *I is very ill set with them* – display erratic capitalization, little punctuation, local dialect forms (*bide* 'need', *miln* 'mill'), and a mixture of standard and nonstandard spelling. The use of *hath* in the first sentence is notable: it could be a local regionalism; but it could also be a borrowing from the King James Bible. There is a naivety and inconsistency about his writing which is very different from the language found in pieces designed for publication, where writers are 'showing off' their local dialects.[8]

That professional authors took their dialect responsibilities seriously can be seen in Tennyson, who wrote seven poems in Lincolnshire dialect. He was especially concerned about their phonetic accuracy, devising a special transcription in which diacritics changed the sounds of several letters, as seen in the opening lines of 'Northern Farmer, Old Style', a dramatic monologue from a dying farmer:

> Wheer 'asta beän saw long and meä liggin' 'ere aloän?
> Noorse? thoort nowt o' a noorse: whoy, Doctor 's abeän an' agoän:
> Says that I moänt 'a naw moor aäle: but I beänt a fool:
> Git ma my aäle, fur I beänt a-gawin' to breäk my rule.[9]

> Where hast thou been so long and me lying here alone? Nurse? Thou art nothing of a nurse: why, Doctor's a-been and a-gone: Says that I mustn't have no more ale: but I'm not a fool: Get me my ale, for I'm not a-going to break my rule.

He puzzled over the best way of representing the accent, making several changes at the proof stage of publication. At one point (in 1881) he even arranged to read the poems to Alexander Ellis, who made various suggestions which Tennyson later incorporated (e.g., *yeäd* becoming *eäd* 'head'). He perhaps need not have worried so much. Joseph Wright was sufficiently impressed to include five of the poems in his Lincolnshire source material. On the other hand, because Tennyson gave no guidance about the values of his diacritics, it is difficult today to know exactly how to read them.[10]

Most of the growing representation of English dialects appears not in poetry, or even in drama, but in the novel; and when it arrives, it carries with it a fresh set of attitudes. This can be seen in the first regional novel in English, Maria Edgeworth's *Castle Rackrent: An Hibernian Tale taken from the Facts and from the Manners of the Irish Squires Before the Year 1782* (1800). Not only does the author effectively capture the idiom of Irish speech, she uses the variety for a serious purpose – a satire directed at Anglo-Irish landlords, in an era long before the Reform Act of 1832. Irish English was no longer just a comic dialect (see further, panel 19.2).

> Sir Patrick died that night – just as the company rose to drink his health with three cheers, he fell down in a sort of a fit, and was carried off – they sat it out, and were surprised, on enquiry, in the morning, to find it was all over with poor Sir Patrick – Never did any gentleman live and die more beloved in the country by rich and poor – his funeral was such a one as was never known before nor since in the county! – All the gentlemen in the three counties were at it – far and near, how they flocked! – my great grandfather said, that to see all the women even in their red cloaks, you would have taken them for the army drawn out. – Then such a fine whillaluh! [lamentation over the dead] you might have heard it to the farthest end of the county, and happy the man who could get but a sight of the hearse! – But who'd have thought it? Just as all was going on right, through his own town they were passing, when the body was seized for debt – a rescue was apprehended

from the mob – but the heir who attended the funeral was against that, for fear of consequences, seeing that those villains acted under the disguise of the law – So, to be sure, the law must take its course – and little gain had the creditors for their pains.

The author is aware of a possible dialect problem, and draws the attention of the non-Irish reader to it in a Preface. The fault – she asserts – lies with the narrator, Thady Quirk, 'an illiterate old steward' who 'tells the history of the Rackrent family in his vernacular idiom'. So she adds a Glossary, in which such terms as *whillaluh* are explained:

> For the information of the ignorant English reader a few notes have been subjoined by the editor, and he had it once in contemplation to translate the language of Thady into plain English; but Thady's idiom is incapable of translation, and besides, the authenticity of his story would have been more exposed to doubt if it were not told in his own characteristic manner.

In fact there is very little that would be unintelligible to the English reader; but the explanation was evidently needed in an age when a prescriptive notion of Standard English ruled.

19.2 Less obvious dialect grammar

The rhythmical lilt of Irish English (Hiberno-English) is evident in *Castle Rackrent*, even though there are few apparent signs of nonstandard English grammar. This is because some of the most important grammatical features of regional dialects are extremely subtle. An example is the way Gaelic influences the word order of modern Hiberno-English so that different words receive a degree of emphasis that would be unlikely to be heard in Standard British English.

> It's meself was there first.
> Is it off to work you are?
> Would it be a drink you're wanting?
> All over the place they're going.

There are several such variations in emphasis in the literary extract on pp. 494–5:

> never did any gentleman live and die more beloved
> far and near, how they flocked
> happy the man who could get but a sight of the hearse
> through his own town they were passing
> little gain had the creditors for their pains

Sometimes it is easy to see the equivalent word order in the standard language – such as *they were passing through his own town*. But it is actually quite difficult to provide a straightforward equivalent for some sentences. To capture the exact sense of this next one in Standard English would require a great deal of restructuring:

> to see all the women even in their red cloaks, you would have taken them for the army drawn out

Examples of this kind indicate that the grammatical basis of a regional dialect lies in much more than the immediately noticeable nonstandard features, such as (in Irish) the distinctive forms *yiz, youz, them'ns*, and *amn't*, or the alternative forms of the preposition *to*:

> a quarter till three
> you'll have till wait
> I went for ti get some bread.

These are easy to spot. Far more difficult is to note any differences in the meaning of a regionally distinctive form.[11] For example, the use of *after* in modern Hiberno-English expresses such notions as a recent action or the recent completion of an action:

> I was after asking he could I have a loan of it.
> We're after bein livin there for the past twenty-one years.
> There's a dog after flying up the road.

And the use of *do be* expresses a habitual activity:

> I do be half asleep in the morning.
> It does be colder at nights.
> There does be nobody there.

As a result, there is a contrast in meaning between the following three sentences:

> *She's playing* means 'She's playing now.'
> *She be's playing* means 'She plays regularly.'
> *She does be playing* means 'She plays regularly and continuously.'

However, the study of the semantics of regional varieties remains one of the neglected areas in present-day dialectology.

Whereas in earlier periods we have to hunt to find good examples of nonstandard English in literature, in the nineteenth century there is an embarrassment of riches. Walter Scott developed archaic and regional varieties in no fewer than three directions, to reflect contemporary Scotland (as in *Guy Mannering*, 1815), medieval Scotland (as in *The Monastery*, 1820), and medieval England (as in *Ivanhoe*, 1819).[12] Emily Brontë provided a noticeable increase in dialect presence in *Wuthering Heights* (1847), where it is used by the old servant Joseph, young Hareton, and people from the nearby village.

Mrs Gaskell used dialect speech as an expression of working-class solidarity in such novels as *North and South* (1855). George Eliot – another writer with an interest in philology – took pains to follow North Midlands speech in *Adam Bede* (1859). Charles Dickens portrayed a wide range of dialects in his novels – even varieties of American English in his *American Notes* – and was the chief mover in the rehabilitation of Cockney, long viewed as the arch-enemy of good usage (p. 409). Sam Weller, in *The Pickwick Papers* (1836), uses several of the classic features of Cockney English, such as the omission of *g* and *h*, and the substitution of *w* for *v*, but he is presented sympathetically, as witty and brave, and he and his family are by no means caricatures. Here he has just read aloud his valentine to Mary:[13]

> ' "Except of me Mary my dear as your walentine and think over what I've said.
> – My dear Mary I will now conclude." That's all,' said Sam.
> 'That's rather a sudden pull up, ain't it, Sammy?' inquired Mr Weller.
> 'Not a bit on it,' said Sam; 'she'll vish there wos more, and that's the great art o' letter writin'.'
> 'Well,' said Mr Weller, 'there's somethin' in that; and I wish your mother-in-law 'ud only conduct her conwersation on the same gen-teel principle.'

Dickens' Cockney characters represent a cross-section of human life, from the most wicked to the most high-minded; they display comedy and pathos, and evoke a full range of emotions, from delight to disgust. Nor are they always minor characters. In *Hard Times* (1854), Stephen and Rachael are the Lancashire-speaking heroes of the book. Here is their conversation when we first meet them, set out below as a dialogue:

> Ah, lad! 'Tis thou? . . .
> I thought thou wast ahind me, Rachael?
> No.
> Early t'night, lass?
> 'Times I'm a little early, Stephen! 'times a little late. I'm never to be counted on, going home.
> Nor going t'other way, neither, 't seems to me, Rachael?
> No, Stephen . . .
> We are such true friends, lad, and such old friends, and getting to be such old folk, now.
> No, Rachael, thou'rt as young as ever thou wast.
> One of us would be puzzled how to get old, Stephen, without t'other getting so too, both being alive . . . but, anyways, we're such old friends, that t'hide a word of honest truth fro' one another would be a sin and a pity.[14]

If there is a bias in Dickens' portrayals, it is that dialect is more often put into the mouths of characters who are honest, genuine, sincere, and down-to-earth – characters like Rachael and Stephen, or Joe Gargery in *Great Expectations*, or Mrs Gamp in *Martin Chuzzlewit* – but the bad guys use dialect, too. And that is what any variety of English should do, of course, whether standard or nonstandard. Varieties are spoken by communities which contain all types of people, and they should be available to express the thoughts of any of them. It is the character stereotype which has to be avoided. And Dickens – with his shorthand-reporter's ear and his childhood experience of different social classes – did more than any other nineteenth-century novelist to break down those stereotypes.

It was not always easy, getting dialect representation into print, and in several cases we cannot be sure that the version as we have it is what the author originally intended. There were many printing errors and inconsistencies in the first edition of *Wuthering Heights*, for example, and the situation was made more complicated when Charlotte prepared a second edition after Emily's death (1848). Further variants were introduced, and in some cases local forms were replaced by standard forms. But these problems do not negate the overall effect, as can be seen in this early encounter between Joseph and the narrator:

> 'Whet are ye for?' he shouted. 'T' maister's dahn i' t' fowld. Goa rahned by th' end ut' laith, if yah went tuh spake tull him.'
>
> 'Is there nobody inside to open the door?' I hallooed, responsively.
>
> 'They's nobbut t' missis; and shoo'll nut oppen 't and ye mak yer flaysome dins till neeght.'[15]

> What are you for? . . . The master's down in the fold. Go round by the end of the laith [barn], if you want to speak to him . . . There's no one but the Mrs; and she'll not open it and [even if] you make your flaysome [frightening] din until night.

The frequent use of such forms as *ye*, *shoo* 'she', and *t'* 'the' capture well the general character of Yorkshire regional speech, notwithstanding the various inconsistencies (such as *ye* vs *yah*, *tull* vs *till*). In any case, as we have seen, a totally consistent dialect representation is a chimera.

The notion of 'dialect presence' in a novel refers to more than the nonstandard representation of what the characters say; it also refers to any comments that the author makes about the kind of language being used. By the end of the nineteenth century, we regularly encounter narrator observations such as this one:

> Mrs Durbeyfield habitually spoke the dialect; her daughter, who had passed the Sixth Standard in the National School under a London-trained mistress, spoke two languages; the dialect at home, more or less; ordinary English abroad and to persons of quality.[16]

Even the characters enter into metadiscussion at times. Margaret Hale has the following exchange with her mother, in *North and South* (1854):

> 'But Margaret, don't get to use those horrid Milton words. "Slack of work"; it is a provincialism. What will your Aunt Shaw say if she hears you use it on her return?'
>
> 'Oh, mamma! don't try and make a bugbear of Aunt Shaw,' said Margaret, laughing. 'Edith picked up all sorts of military slang from Captain Lennox, and Aunt Shaw never took any notice of it.'
>
> 'But yours is factory slang.'
>
> 'And if I live in a factory town, I must speak factory language when I want it.'[17]

And a point of usage is foregrounded in this dialogue initiated by the newly genteel Pip, who visits his old home and criticizes Biddy for calling him 'Mr Pip':

> 'Biddy,' said I, in a virtuously self-asserting manner, 'I must request to know what you mean by this?'
>
> 'By this?' said Biddy.
>
> 'No, don't echo,' I retarded. 'You *used not* to echo, Biddy.'
>
> '*Used not!*' said Biddy. 'O Mr Pip! *Used!*'[18]

Biddy is evidently shocked to hear such a refined usage coming out of the mouth of someone who, once upon a time, would have said *You did not use to echo*.

Such comments, whether made by authors or their characters, are a sign of increasing confidence in using the medium. By the mid twentieth century, they have become routine, even bridging the gap between upper and lower class, as in the post-coital dialect dialogue of Lady Chatterley and her gamekeeper lover:

> 'Tha mun come one naight ter th'cottage, afore tha goes; sholl ter?' . . .
>
> 'Sholl ter?' she echoed, teasing.
>
> He smiled.
>
> 'Ay, sholl ter?' he repeated.
>
> 'Ay!' she said, imitating the dialect sound.
>
> 'Yi!' he said.
>
> 'Yi!' she repeated.
>
> 'An slaip wi' me,' he said. 'It needs that. When sholt come?'
>
> 'When sholl I?' she said.
>
> 'Nay,' he said, 'tha canna do't. When sholt come then?'
>
> ''Appen Sunday,' she said.
>
> ''Appen a' Sunday, Ay!'

> He laughed at her quickly.
> 'Nay, tha canna,' he protested.
> 'Why canna I?' she said.
> He laughed. Her attempts at the dialect were so ludicrous, somehow.
> 'Coom then tha mun go!' he said.
> 'Mun I,' she said.
> 'Maun Ah!' he corrected.
> 'Why should I say *maun* when you said *mun*,' she protested. 'You're not playing fair.'[19]

> Thou must come one night to the cottage, before thou goes, shalt thee? . . . Thou cannot do it . . . Perhaps Sunday . . . Come, then, thou must go.

Dialect is no longer simply part of the characterization, in such cases; it is part of the subject-matter.

Although literary developments were later in the United States (p. 425), when they arrived they followed a similar path with respect to the way they portrayed nonstandard speech. Joel Chandler Harris represented black speech in his Uncle Remus tales (from 1879), and southern white as well as black speech is found in much of Mark Twain's writing. The nonstandard colouring of the opening lines of *Huckleberry Finn* (1884) attunes the reader to what is to come:

> You don't know about me, without you have read a book by the name of *The Adventures of Tom Sawyer*, but that ain't no matter. That book was made by Mr Mark Twain, and he told the truth, mainly. There was things which he stretched, but mainly he told the truth . . .

The first piece of black speech, from the slave Jim, occurs soon after:

> 'Say – who is you: Whar is you? Dog my cats ef I didn' hear sumf'n. Well, I knows what I's gwyne to do. I's gwyne to set down here and listen tell I hears it agin.'

And when the white boys start talking to each other, we find utterances like this:

> 'Here's Huck Finn, he hain't got no family – what you going to do 'bout him?'[20]

The nonstandard grammatical features are very similar to those already noted for British speech (p. 481). We find the use of such verb forms as *ain't, hain't, warn't,* and *dasn't,* omission of the auxiliary verb (as in *what you going to do*), multiple negation (as in *ain't got no*), an extended use of an -*s* ending (*upwards, northards, whiles, on accounts of*), and nonstandard tenses (*seed, drownded, a-saying*) and forms of comparison (*faithfuller, powerfullest*). Pronunciations are also similarly distinctive. There is *d* for *th* in such words as *de, dem,* and *wid*; initial unstressed syllables are dropped or clipped (*'bout* 'about', *'deed* 'indeed', *b'long*) as are medial syllables (*considable, diffunt*); and consonants are omitted medially (*on'y, chillen, consekence*) and finally (*fren', bes', yo'*). Local pronunciations are seen in several words, such as *sholy* 'surely', *shet* 'shut', *nussery* 'nursery', *sich* 'such', and *agin* 'again'. There is also a great deal of eye-dialect, as in *reck'n* and *wuz* 'was'. Several of these nonstandard forms are shared by the characters, regardless of their colour. It is chiefly the density of forms in Jim's speech which marks him out as a black speaker.[21]

As the twentieth century progresses, we find a steady growth in the use of nonstandard English in literary work – in the number of authors wanting to use it, the range of dialects represented, and the extent to which dialect speech is actually used. Among the leading authors who devote significant space to regional speech are Rudyard Kipling, George Bernard Shaw, D. H. Lawrence, Arnold Bennett, John Galsworthy, Joseph Conrad, Arnold Wesker, and Edward Bond. A genre of ludic nonstandard usage also emerges. Its origins can be traced back to Mistress Quickly, Dogberry, and Mrs Malaprop (p. 318), but it flowers in the comic writing of Josh Billings (Henry Wheeler Shaw) and Artemus Ward (Charles Farrar Browne) in the nineteenth century and in the writing of James Joyce in the twentieth. Billings and Ward were the leading proponents of a comic-spelling genre which was extremely popular in the later nineteenth century in the USA, in which homespun wit and down-to-earth sentiments were expressed in a style which seemed to reflect the sounds and rhythms of local speech. The operative word is 'seemed'; as with Wordsworth, we are in a world of ingeniously contrived illusion. This is part of a letter from Artemus Ward to Mr Punch, during his visit to London.

> You didn't get a instructiv article from my pen last week on account of my nervus sistim havin underwent a dreffle shock. I got caught in a brief shine of sun, and it utterly upsot me. I was walkin in Regent Street one day last week, enjoyin your rich black fog and bracing rains, when all at once the Sun bust out and actooally shone for nearly half an hour steady. I acted promptly. I called a cab and told the driver to run his hoss at a friteful rate of speed to my lodgins, but it wasn't of no avale. I had orful cramps, my appytite left me, and my pults went down to 10 degrees below zero. But by careful nussin I shall no doubt recover speedy, if the present sparklin and exileratin weather continners.[22]

There is no real accent or dialect behind these misspellings, but the humour succeeds none the less.

A global presence

The most notable development in the twentieth-century use of nonstandard English was the extension and flowering of the global literature whose origins were illustrated in Chapter 17, chiefly in those regions which became part of the British Commonwealth. It was a remarkably rapid process, in many cases emerging only since the 1940s, prompted by a need to develop an indigenous literature following the arrival of political independence. The recognition of English as an official language or lingua franca in several territories introduced a creative tension among local writers. The choice was stark: on the one hand, there was Standard British English, unpalatable as the language of the former colonial masters, but guaranteeing an international readership; and there was the indigenous language or languages of the community, appropriately national in spirit, but providing a public voice of limited reach. Authors initially went in both directions: some chose Standard English; some chose to write in their mother tongue. But it was not long before a possible solution to the dilemma came into view. West African writer Chinua Achebe is one who expresses it:

> I feel that the English language will be able to carry the weight of my African experience. But it will have to be a new English, still in full communion with its ancestral home but altered to suit its new African surroundings.[23]

And 'New Englishes' became the dominant development in the second half of the twentieth century.[24]

Singapore is a case in point, displaying a literature which began by using only Standard English, then slowly becoming more confident, introducing features of English dialect use from there or Malaysia. An illustration is Catherine Lim's short story 'The Taximan's Story' (1978), in which the driver talks colloquially to a lady passenger, at one point describing the behaviour of some schoolgirls:

> They tell their Mum got school meeting, got sports and games, this, that, but they really come out and play the fool. Ah, madam, I see you surprise, but I know, I know all their tricks. I take them about in my taxi. They usual is wait in bowling alley or coffee house or hotel, and they walk up, and friend, friend, the European and American tourists, and this is how they make fun and also extra money. Madam, you believe or not when I tell you how much money they got?[25]

Another example is Chinua Achebe's own short story 'Uncle Ben's Choice' (1973), written in an emergent Nigerian English:

I was playing this record and standing at the window with my chewing stick. People were passing in their fine-fine dresses to one church near my house. This Margaret was going with them when she saw me. As luck would have it I did not see her in time to hide. So that very day – she did not wait till tomorrow or next-tomorrow – but as soon as church closed she returned back.

Outsiders find it difficult to know, in such cases, whether the style is a representation of a genuine local dialect or whether it is an authorial stylistic manipulation to achieve a particular effect. It may approximate to real life, or it may not. There is a great deal of literary experimentation about, as can be seen in the style developed by Nigerian writer Gabriel Okara in his novel *The Voice* (1964) – a deliberate attempt to create a style following the syntax of his native language, Ijaw:

> I have killed many moons, many years in that hut thinking of the happening things in this town. My feet know not the door of a school but Woyengi who all things created gave each of us human beings an inside and a head to think. So the many years I have killed in the hut have put many thoughts into my inside which have made me see differently. To speak the straight thing, I was beginning to see things as if through a harmattan fog when they called me a witch and I was put out of the way by the Elders like a tree that has fallen across a path.

In the final analysis, the need for accuracy is no greater here than it was in the literary portrayals from Britain and America during the nineteenth century; but because issues of national and ethnic identity are involved, questions of representation have been hotly debated.

There has been an enormous maturing of literary expression in Commonwealth literature during the past fifty years. Often, in early writing, there was a certain mechanical manner of exposition. Authors would take pains to let their readers know what language or dialect their characters were using, or they would feel it necessary to gloss an expression in Standard English. Texts contained such phrases as 'she replied in pidgin English' or 'he said, switching into the local patois'. This is much less usual today. Authors confidently let the local language speak for itself, and manipulate voices and effects within it as required by the story. With careful writing, even the problems of intelligibility caused by using local dialect words can be avoided, as in this example from *Ice-Candy Man* (1988) by the Pakistani writer Bapsi Sidhwa:

> A tonga waits in the porch. Hollow-eyed and dazed with the heat we pile perspiring into the tonga. Mother and Ayah in back and Adi and I up front with the tongaman. We sit back to back on a bench divided by a quilted backrest. A flimsy canvas canopy shelters us from the sun. The tonga is held together by two enormous wooden wheels on either side of the shaft and is balanced by the harnessed horse.

In a discussion of this passage, Sidhwa comments: 'I do not like to describe a *tonga* as a carriage. It robs it of its jaunty, two-wheeled, one-horse character.' Nor does she need to – the context explains it perfectly.[26]

Examples such as the following illustrate the way in which a writer can manipulate different voices without making any explicit comment about the kind of dialect being used. Darrell Lum's play *Oranges are Lucky* (1983) is set in Hawaii. At one point we hear an old Chinese woman, Ah Po, hoping her grandsons Ah Jiu and Ah Gnip will marry. She speaks in Hawaiian Pidgin English; but when she recalls her own marriage long before, she switches into Standard English – representing her thoughts in Chinese.

> Aie, I no bring coconut candy fo Ah Jiu. Maybe next time he tell me he get married. You tell him no need be Chinese girl. Now modern days, okay marry Japanese, maybe haole [foreigner], anykine girl okay. Ah Jiu get married be happy, den Ah Gnip get married. I go temple and pray for Ah Jiu. Maybe da Buddha help me find one nice girl fo Ah Jiu. Bumbye [later on] no marry, no have children fo da family name . . . (*lights dim*). Mama, who is that man who came to talk to Daddy? Am I to marry him, he is old! That is Chew Mung's father? Am I to marry Chew Mung?[27]

This is an example of code-switching between contemporary dialects. The switch can be backwards in time, too, as in the opening lines from 'Spring Cleaning' (1992), by Jamaican-born poet Jean 'Binta' Breeze:

> de Lord is my shepherd
> I shall not want
>
> an she scraping
> de las crumbs
> aff de plate
> knowing ants will feed
>
> maketh me to lie down
> in green pastures
> leadeth me beside de still
> waters
>
> an she han washing clothes
> spotless
> lifting dem outa de water
> drying she han careful slow
> pon she apron[28]

And in this next example, we have a switch between cultures, with the local dialect being made to carry the weight of traditional British literary allusion along with an almost Joycean linguistic playfulness. Author Karen King-Aribisala was born in Guyana and moved to Nigeria. One section of her novel *Kicking Tongues* is headed 'The Tale of the Palm-wine Tapster: in search of the fine tree gentlewoman'. It begins using an unsophisticated local variety:

> That day when my Palm-wine Tree Wife did die was the baddest most worstest day of my life. Her tree-trunk body did fall for ground making sound like atomic nuclear explosion . . .

But when she describes the meeting with a new lady, Mademoiselle Willow, a whole new variety opens up, mixing regional and standard sources:

> I did follow follow this fine complete tree gentlewoman with Great Expectations and she have no branch bone of Pride or Prejudice in she tree body. She all the time turning Nigerian environment into Mansfield Park with too too much gentility. And when she Shake she Speare-hand branch at me and she begin for to talk, it be like menthol peppermint did come out like it did Chaucering me to stand still and to listen to what she did say and she be too too clean like Milton solution and fresh is fresh for to fresh I am feeling.[29]

As a final example, in 'Sonny's Lettah', by Linton Kwesi Johnson, we have a verse letter which mixes standard and nonstandard graphology. It is described as an 'Anti-Sus Poem' – *sus* 'suspicion' referring to British legislation which led to a disproportionate number of black youths being arrested. The address and salutation mimic the conventions of Standard English letter-writing, but these are subverted by the nonstandard spelling, adding a satirical dimension to the treatment of its underlying theme.

> Brixtan Prison
> Jebb Avenue
> Landan south-west two
> Inglan

> Dear Mama,
> Good Day.
> I hope dat wen
> deze few lines reach yu,
> they may find yu in di bes of helt.

> Mama,
> I really dont know how fi tell yu dis,
> cause I did mek a salim pramis
> fi tek care a likkle Jim
> an try mi bes fi look out fi him.

Mama,
I really did try mi bes,
but nondiles
mi sarry fi tell yu seh
poor likkle Jim get arres.[30]

I hope that when these few lines reach you, they may find you in the best of health
. . . I really don't know how to tell you this, because I did make a solemn promise
to take care of little Jim, and try my best to look out for him . . . I really did try
my best, but none the less, I'm sorry to tell you poor little Jim got arrested.

Towards a brave new world

This chapter has been unable to do more than hint at the way varieties of
nonstandard English are used in modern English literature. Thousands of such
texts have now been published. They illustrate the way people all over the
English-speaking world have adapted the language to express new identities
and attitudes. Regional dialects have fought back against the hegemony of, first,
a single standard language, and then a dual standard, British and American. In
most places, they exist in a range of nonstandard varieties. In some countries,
though, there are already clear signs of further 'regional standards' emerging,
such as Australian English and Indian English. This is not surprising. There is
no reason why the same processes which governed the consolidation of a
standard variety within Britain and America should not manifest themselves in
Australia, India, South Africa, or wherever a country is sufficiently concerned
about its linguistic identity to institutionalize its usage in the form of regional
dictionaries, grammars, pronunciation guides, and style manuals. Ironically,
prescriptive attitudes once again arise, in these circumstances. The debates
surrounding a question of what is the 'correct' form of Australian or Indian
English can be just as heated as anything seen in eighteenth-century Britain. But
there is a difference. In a pluricentric world, there is no longer a notion of
general ownership.

Linguistic pluricentrism reflects the fact that, in the twenty-first century,
nobody can be said to 'own' English any more. Or rather, everyone who has
opted to use it has come to have a part-ownership in it. That is what happens
to a language when it achieves an international or global presence. It belongs
to all who use it. And when people adopt a language they immediately adapt
it, to make it suit their needs. Chinua Achebe saw this: 'The price a world
language must be prepared to pay is submission to many different kinds of

use.'[31] English has now become a pluricentric language – one whose norms and functions vary globally and develop independently according to sets of forces that no longer reflect the influence of a single (British or American) point of origin. Even a native-speaking point of origin is becoming less relevant as time goes by. The centre of gravity of the English language is steadily shifting from the native speaker to the non-native speaker. People who use English as a second or foreign language are now very much in the majority, with three non-native speakers in the world for every one native-speaker.[32]

The literary implications are profound. Most English literature hitherto has come from people who speak English as a first or second language – that is, they learned their English in a country where the language had some kind of special status arising out of its colonial history. Commonwealth literature was one of the consequences of this situation. It remains to be seen what contribution will one day be made by those who have learned English as a foreign language – that is, from countries where English has had no colonial history but where fluent levels of competence are increasingly routine, such as Sweden, the Netherlands, and Denmark. Writing in English from such countries is currently always in Standard (British or American) English, but it will not always be that way. One day we will surely be reading Swedish English novels – that is, novels written by people who have Swedish as a mother tongue but who choose to write in a Swedish-coloured variety of English, analogous to the Commonwealth examples shown above. There could be poetry in Japanese English or Russian English. Perhaps an Egyptian English short story will one day be called 'Welcome in Egypt'.[33]

The concept of English as a pluricentric language has worried some people. It scared some of the British when the centre of linguistic gravity seemed to move to the United States. They listened to the words of the American writer Brander Matthews in 1900 with considerable trepidation:

> What will happen to the English language in England when England awakes to the fact that the centre of the English-speaking race is no longer within the borders of that little island? . . . Will the British frankly accept the inevitable . . . Will they follow the lead of the Americans when we shall have the leadership of the language, as the Americans followed their lead when they had it?[34]

There was a flurry of British reaction. The Society for Pure English was founded by poet laureate Robert Bridges in 1913. Pamphlets were produced. The BBC stressed the importance of British English (p. 470). Letters to the press proliferated. One to the *New Statesman* (25 June 1927) began:

> The English language proper belongs to the people who dwell south of Hadrian's Wall, east of the Welsh hills and north of the English channel.

As for everyone else:

> Their choice is to accept our authority or else make their own language.

The irony, of course, is that this was exactly what everyone around the world was already doing. And the double irony is that this process proved eventually to be bigger than any nation, even the United States. American English would in due course be put in its place just as much as the Americans thought British English had been. For even the United States – with some 230 million English speakers in the year 2000 – must now be seen as using a minority dialect of World English, with its total of over 1,500 million speakers of English as a first, second, or foreign language. Or rather, we see a set of minority dialects, for as the ethnic mix within the United States has grown, so has the range of regional and ethnic varieties of American English (p. 431), and these are steadily broadening their presence in creative and functional domains such as the press, advertising, and broadcasting. And although the influence of American English on other countries remains far greater worldwide than that of any other kind of English, it has not prevented the progress or fresh emergence of local varieties. The numbers are sometimes extremely significant: there are probably more English speakers in India today than in the whole of America and Britain combined. But even in places where the numbers are small, such as Singapore, the literary output displays an impressive vitality.

It is important to emphasize that Standard English, as manifested in its two main varieties, is not threatened by all these regional developments. That could hardly be, given that the vast majority of the world's printed English output is in either the British or American standard, or in a standard heavily influenced by one or the other (as in the case of Australia and Canada). Nor should we underestimate the common core of linguistic identity which unites them. Every few decades someone predicts that British and American English are one day going to become mutually unintelligible, but there is very little sign of this happening as far as the written language is concerned. When we add up all the differences between these two varieties – all the points of contrast in spelling, grammar, and vocabulary – we are talking about a very small part of the language as a whole. That, of course, is why we usually find the term 'Standard English' used without any regional qualification. We sense the common core.[35]

But there is a second reason why the burgeoning of nonstandard varieties is no threat to the standard. Their function is different. Nonstandard varieties exist in order to express local identities, at a regional level. A standard variety exists to foster intelligibility, at a supra-regional level. In a world where there is an increasing need for international communication the role of a Standard English, whether in its British or American incarnation, remains secure. We need both kinds of variety, nonstandard and standard, if we are to participate fully in a local as well as an international world. And that is why, in the final chapter of this book, we can achieve a rapprochement between the apparently conflicting domains of the nonstandard and standard stories of English.

Interlude 19
Dialect in Middle Earth

English dialect representations are now found in every domain of English fiction – even including the fantasy worlds, where traditionally it was conspicuous by its absence. In many science fiction works, for example, we would get the impression that time, linguistically, stands still. A spaceship leaves earth for some distant star, and the author takes pains to deal with the problems of life maintenance and transmission as time passes between the generations; yet the language of the emigrants somehow remains exactly the same when they reach the star as when they left Earth. There has been no linguistic change – an impossible state of affairs. Fantasy stories take similar liberties with language variation. Groups of giants, elves, fairies, and earthlings are typically all portrayed as speaking the same English dialect, even though they presumably live in totally different societies.

Dramatic licence, of course. And everyone – linguists included – is happy to make allowances, in the interests of enjoying a good story. But from time to time we find authors taking the trouble to do something a little more difficult, introducing language variation and change to suit the circumstances of the plot, and this can add a greater dramatic realism and a deeper level of characterization. Some add a colouring of archaic language as the story moves back in time (as with the novels of Walter Scott); some introduce novel constructions and vocabulary as time moves forward (as in George Orwell's *1984*); and some incorporate dialect variation when presenting a cross-section of a fictitious society (as in Emily Brontë, p. 496). We might expect authors who are philologists to be especially sensitive to such matters, and in the case of J. R. R. Tolkien, professor of Anglo-Saxon at Oxford, so it proves to be.

The hobbit domain created by Tolkien (in *The Hobbit* and *The Lord of the Rings*), the Shire, was quite extensive. He describes it as being some forty leagues in one direction and fifty leagues in another (120 × 150 miles) – an area equivalent to the whole of England north of Birmingham. It contains several regional divisions – four 'farthings', each of which contains several 'folklands'. The hobbit inhabitants are of all ages and occupations, of different social classes, and of both sexes, and they interact with a wide range of racially different groups, such as orcs, goblins, and elves. In such circumstances, dialect distinctions ought to abound.

In fact, there is not as much as we might have expected. Most of the characters speak Standard English (in a variety of accents, in the 2001–3 filmed version), regardless of race. However, Tolkien is quite scrupulous in distinguishing characters of a higher and lower class among the hobbits. Standard English is used by the hobbit heroes (Bilbo and Frodo Baggins, Pippin, and Merry), as well as by the wizard Gandalf and the noble supporters whom the hobbits meet on their journey. A nonstandard English is used by Frodo's man Sam Gamgee, the Gaffer (Sam's father), Tom Bombadil, and other rustic characters. The only other nonstandard-speaking character in the novel is Gollum, who has an accent and dialect all of his own, a curious mixture containing some regional dialect constructions, the occasional sigmatism (*yess*), and the kind of deviant usage associated with the four-year-old stage of child language acquisition:

> They won't hurt us will they, nice little hobbitses? We didn't mean no harm, but they jumps on us like cats on poor mices, they did, precious . . .

The English used by the hobbits would with few exceptions not be out of place in the part of the country where Tolkien himself lived and worked (Oxfordshire and Warwickshire), but several of its features are found widely in English rural dialects.[36] There is no attempt at a systematic or totally consistent representation. In some cases, Tolkien seems to have aimed for no more than a dialect colouring. For example, at the beginning of *The Lord of the Rings* (Book I, Chapter 1), the Gaffer is discussing the Baggins family with his friends. It is entirely in a colloquial variety hardly distinguishable from the standard language until the very last word:

> Mr. Frodo is as nice a young hobbit as you could wish to meet. Very much like Mr. Bilbo, and in more than looks. After all his father was a Baggins. A decent respectable hobbit was Mr. Drogo Baggins; there was never much to tell of him, till he was drownded.

By contrast, some other characters get a fuller representation. Mr Butterbur, the landlord of the Prancing Pony, uses a wide range of dialect forms. Here he is apologizing for not sending on a letter from Gandalf to Frodo (Book I, Chapter 10):

> and I'm mortal afraid of what Gandalf will say, if harm comes of it. But I didn't keep it back a-purpose. I put it by safe. Then I couldn't find nobody willing to go to the Shire next day . . .

And Sam Gamgee uses a similarly wide range of nonstandardisms, as when he talks to his horse (Book II, Chapter 3):

> Bill, my lad . . . you oughtn't to have took up with us. You could have stayed here and et the best hay till the new grass comes.

or when he tells himself off in delight at having forgotten he was carrying some rope (Book IV, Chapter 1):

> Well, if I don't deserve to be hung at the end of one as a warning to numbskulls! You're nowt but a ninnyhammer, Sam Gamgee.

or when he talks to Frodo about the time of day and their breakfast (Book IV, Chapter 4):

> About a couple of hours after daybreak . . . and nigh on half past eight by Shire clocks, maybe. But nothing's wrong. Though it ain't quite what I'd call right: no stock, no onions, no taters. I've got a bit of a stew for you, and some broth, Mr. Frodo. Do you good. You'll have to sup it in your mug; or straight from the pan, when it's cooled a bit. I haven't brought no bowls, nor nothing proper.

For a literary dialect representation, quite a large number of different forms are used (compare the listing in Interlude 18, p. 481) – certainly more than enough to represent a social contrast between Frodo and Sam. They include nonstandard verb agreement (*they has, they goes, he don't*), auxiliary verbs (*ain't, durstn't*), past tenses (*etten, took* 'taken'), pronouns (*hisself, ee* 'you' as in *thank 'ee*), prepositions (*nigh on, agin* 'near', *a* 'on', as in *a-purpose*), adverbs (*leastways, yonder*), and multiple negatives. There are also some well-known nonstandard lexical uses, such as *lay* ('lie') and *learn* ('teach'), dropped consonants (*Lor bless you, o'* 'of'), and eye-dialect words (*dunno, et* 'ate', *jools* 'jewels').

The portrayal is not entirely consistent. For example, Sam sometimes uses *ain't* and sometimes *'s not*, and he uses *nowt* in one of the examples above (which is a little surprising, given that this is chiefly a word from the North and North-east Midlands) but *nought* in other places. He also seems to be bidialectal. He is capable of speaking a (slightly archaic) Standard English when occasion demands it, as in this example (Book IV, Chapter 10):

> Good bye, master my dear . . . Forgive your Sam. He'll come back to this spot when the job's done – if he manages it. And then he'll not leave you again. Rest you quiet till I come; and may no foul creature come anigh you! And if the Lady could hear me, and give me one wish, I would wish to come back and find you again.

Treebeard, the Ent, is also sufficiently bidialectal to be able to make a slightly apologetic dialect joke about the name of his race (Book III, Chapter 4):

there are Ents and things and things that look like Ents but ain't, as you might say.

However, issues of consistency and realism are beside the point. We are not dealing with a true regional dialect here. We are dealing with hobbits, and we do not expect hobbits to speak a consistent dialect of British English. I suspect we would be mildly disappointed if they did come out with a realistic Cockney or Geordie or Scouse. Middle Earth is not of our world, and its dialect representations should also be a step removed from human experience. Perhaps this is why Tolkien gives us an insight into their different way of thinking at the very beginning of the book. Bilbo Baggins is using the hobbit counting-system above 100 when he declares, in the opening chapter: *I am eleventy-one today.* English speakers from upper-earth, unless they are Tolkien fans, don't usually calculate like that.

Chapter 20 Times a-changin'

Nonstandard English in a chapter heading? Such a thing would never have been seen in a serious book a century ago; but it is not unusual today. Indeed, nonstandard language is often found even in book titles. A brief search of Web booksellers brought to light hundreds of examples. Here are a few recent titles using *ain't* or double negatives or both:

> *Ain't No Makin' It: Aspirations and Attainment in a Low-Income Neighborhood* (1995)
>
> *Ain't Nobody's Business If You Do: The Absurdity of Consensual Crimes in Our Free Society* (1996)
>
> *Ain't Misbehavin': A Good Behaviour Guide for Family Dogs* (1997)
>
> *You Ain't Seen Nothing Yet: the Future of Media and the Global Expert System* (2002)
>
> *It Ain't No Sin . . . Springsteen* (2001)
>
> *It Ain't Necessarily So: Investigating the Truth of the Biblical Past* (2002)

It is plain from the quotative element in these titles that an element of acceptable nonstandard English is part of our everyday consciousness. We have stored away in our memory such phrases as *ain't misbehavin'*, and can bring them out as required, confident that other people will recognize the allusions. It is a common practice on the part of title creators, who are always on the lookout for the attention-grabbing phrase, and it is by no means restricted to the book trade. Popular songs and record albums do the same thing – as is evident from 'Ain't Misbehavin'', the name of a Louis Armstrong hit from the 1929 musical comedy *Hot Chocolates*. More recent musical examples include 'Age Ain't Nothing But a Number' (1994), 'Ain't Life Grand' (2000), 'Ain't No Sunshine' (2001), and 'It Ain't Safe No More' (2002).

People do not fuss about this sort of thing: they accept the nonstandard usage for what it is – a special effect, embedded within a Standard English frame of reference. And it is this same notion of a shared, community memory for language which allows newspaper subeditors to write such lines as:

There's silver in them there hills

introducing a travel piece about visiting a ghost town in Australia's Blue Mountains where there is an old silver mine.[1] Very few people will have heard anyone actually say *them there hills* (or *tham thar hills*) in real life, and certainly not in Australia, but they are aware of its cinematic history, spoken by prospectors in films about the days of the American gold-rush. It makes a good headline. Similarly, community memory holds a large store of archaic forms (all of which have to be considered nonstandard in present-day English) upon which headline writers and journalists frequently rely, usually to produce a catchy headline or to add an element of humour or parody to an article. These next examples were collected in a study of newspaper language in the mid 1990s:

> What doth it profit a man to gain the Dow Jones Industrial Average and lose his own soul?
>
> Hark, all ye with thy ears thus tilted.
>
> Taxman cometh, but can't getteth
>
> For yea verily, I say unto thee, just as Elton John's career is dead . . .[2]

The Bible and Shakespeare are primary sources, but often no specific text is implied: usages commonly rely only on a general sense of older speech patterns, such as the use of *thou* or an *-eth* ending. Often the usage is wrong. No Early Modern English author could ever have said 'all ye with thy ears'. But accuracy, as we have repeatedly seen (Chapter 19), is beside the point, when it comes to literary effect.

What is important about these examples is that they provide evidence of a growing presence of nonstandard English outside the domain of creative literature (Chapter 19). We might expect to find nonstandard usage in literary genres, where so much of the purpose is to reflect identities and relationships. For example, it is unusual, but not out of place, to find a poet using nonstandard language for the title of a collection, as did Linton Kwesi Johnson in *Mi Revalueshanary Fren* (p. 505). And we might expect to find nonstandard usage in the titles of humorous books, especially those which focus on parodies of regional dialect, such as *Let Stalk Strine* or *Yacky Dar, Moy Bewty!*.[3] What is much less expected is to find it in the titles of serious books on sociology or technology, or in newspaper articles from the 'quality' press. None the less, it is a noticeable feature of recent years to see nonstandard usages acting as a subtle counterpoint to the predominantly standard language. Often, blink and you'd miss it – as in this single-word example from a theatre review which mentions a character, the goddess Isis, 'who lives on the seashore, in disguise, selling – geddit? – ices'.[4] But just as often you can't avoid it, for it is in large type. An item in the travel section of one newspaper is headed *Finns ain't what they used to be* – a report on a new architectural style in Finland – and in the same edition we find a review of the film *Ali G Indahouse*, whose headline capitalizes on the nonstandardisms associated with its leading character:

> Respect to da right honourable gangsta. But Ali G, why is you sold out so soon?[5]

These examples suggest that the rehabilitation of nonstandard English has made considerable progress. However, its public presence is still quite limited. The history of association of nonstandard English with informal, jocular, and intimate settings currently restricts it to certain kinds of subject-matter where these resonances do not clash. In newspapers, nonstandard English grammar and orthography are generally found only in the creative and leisure pages, such as the review section, the sports section, or sections providing comment, letters, and other personal reactions to events. They hardly ever appear in news articles; and we can feel uneasy when we see them used there. It was a daring moment indeed when the *Sun* used *Gotcha* ('Got you') to refer to the sinking of the *General Belgrano* in the Argentinian conflict, with the loss of many lives.[6] For many people, this was taking nonstandard usage too far, for the playful connotations of *Gotcha* – said, for example, when we have caught someone out in an argument, or discovered someone in a game of hide-and-seek – resonated uncomfortably in a story dealing with matters of life and death (see further, panel 20.1).

20.1 Bible stories

Uncertainty over the role of nonstandard English can also be seen when it is used in domains from which it has traditionally been excluded. Retellings of the Bible are an example (see also p. 489). In *God is For Real, Man* (1967), by New York prison chaplain Carl Burke, we find Bible stories 'translated' into the language of the city streets. Here are the first three of the Ten Commandments:

> 1. *You shall have no other gods before me* . . . Means God's the leader – nobody, but nobody, man, gets in the way. This is the top. He is Mr. Big, real big.
> 2. *You shall not make for yourself a graven image* . . . This means no making things that look like God in the craftshop at the settlement house. No worship things like rabbits' foots and lucky dice and, damn it, dolls.
> 3. *You shall not take the name of the Lord your God in vain* . . . It means knock off the swearing, or you better watch out.[7]

In Arnold Kellett's *Ee By Gum, Lord*, we find the New Testament turned into broad Yorkshire. Here is the announcement of the birth of Jesus from Saint Luke's Gospel:

Nah ther' wor a two-a-thri shepherds 'oo t' same neet 'appened ter bi aht i' t' fields near Bethle'em, sitting rahnd the'r campfire, keepin' watch ovver the'r sheep. All of a sudden, says Sent Lewk, these 'ere shepherds see t' sky breeten up wi' a gloorious blaze o' leet 'at shines all rahnd 'em. Well, the'r flaid ter deeath! An' while the're cahrin' theeare on t' grahnd, as weak as watter, an' all of a dither, t' Angil o' t' Lord says tul 'em: 'Nay, there's nowt ter bi affeared on! Ah've come ter bring thi some reight cheerful neews . . .'.

Now there were a two or three shepherds who the same night happened to be out in the fields near Bethlehem, sitting round their campfire, keeping watch over their sheep. All of a sudden, says Saint Luke, these here shepherds see the sky brighten up with a glorious blaze of light that shines all round them. Well, they're frightened to death! And while they're cowering on the ground, as weak as water, and all of a dither [tremble], the Angel of the Lord says to them: No, there's nothing to be frightened about. I've come to bring thee some right cheerful news . . .

Criticism of such experiments is diminishing, with the rise of global English, and the production of biblical texts in international varieties of nonstandard English, such as the various pidgins and creoles of the English-speaking world. Some translations are in fact quite old. Here is a version of the Ten Commandments in Queensland Kanaka Pidgin dating from 1871.

1. Man take one fellow God; no more.
2. Man like him God first time, everything else behind.
3. Man no swear.
4. Man keep Sunday good fellow day belong big fellow master.
5. Man be good fellow longa father mother belonga him.
6. Man no kill.
7. Man no take him Mary belong another fellow man.
8. Man no steal.
9. Man no tell lie bout another fellow man.
10. Spose man see good fellow something belong another fellow man, he no want him all the time.

We ain't seen nothin' yet

The book title cited above referred to the future of broadband technology. Its theme was that, however impressed we are at the way Internet technology, in particular, has progressed during the past few years, this is nothing compared with the advances which have still to take place. It is the same with language. However impressed we are at the evolution of regional standards and the re-emergence of nonstandard English over the past century or so, this is nothing compared with the linguistic developments which are about to take place as a result of the new technology. In a way, this should not surprise us. Technological progress affecting the media has always had a significant impact on language variety and language change. But there is something about the Internet which takes us into a new era.

The impact of technology on variety has been evident at every stage in English linguistic history. Printing added a whole new dimension to written language, as is evident from a moment's reflection on the range of variation in style, graphic design, and typography encountered in books, magazines, newspapers, advertisements, and all kinds of printed ephemera (p. 334). The telephone introduced new techniques of spoken communication, and the telegraph added a distinctive written style (the words *telegrammic* and *telegrammatic* entered the language in the 1860s). Radio broadcasting did for the spoken language what print had done for the written, adding a new dimension in the form of talks, announcements, sports commentaries, news broadcasts, weather forecasts, and all the genres which can be found in the pages of any channel guide. The advent of television added yet another dimension: televisual speech varieties are not the same as radio ones, nor is the written language of television (as found, for example, in commercials) the same as that found elsewhere. Most recently, the advent of the mobile phone (or cellphone), with its space-restricted screen, has motivated the development of a further variety based on linguistic abbreviation, in the form of text-messaging.

Media technology inevitably generates linguistic variety. But it also speeds up the process of language change – in three ways. Most obviously, each innovation introduces a new terminological domain into the language: the technical terms of printing and broadcasting, for example, are very numerous. Less obviously, several of these terms come to be used outside of the technical domain, developing figurative or popular senses, and becoming available for allusive use in satirical, comedic, and other dramatic contexts. *You're broadcasting to the whole restaurant,* one person might say to another, who has been making a point rather too loudly. And several comedy sketches rely on an awareness of broadcasting varieties for their effect, as in this opening to a Monty Python sketch:

> Good evening. Here is the news for parrots: No parrots were involved in an accident on the M1 today when a lorry carrying high-octane fuel was in collision with a bollard. That's a bollard and *not* a parrot. A spokesman for parrots said he was glad no parrots were involved . . .[8]

Least obviously, the technology introduces novel linguistic forms to public attention more rapidly and universally than the traditional method – word of mouth. On 4 October 1957, the first sputnik was launched; on 5 October 1957, the word *sputnik* was known everywhere, thanks to broadcasting and the press. A twentieth-century phenomenon is the proliferation of catch-phrases, from – to take just the cinematic genre – *What's up, doc?* to *May the Force be with you!* With the simultaneous (or near-simultaneous) production of films, television programmes, radio broadcasts, and newspapers all over the world, we can now see language change operating 'top down' at a global level. The Internet, of course, offers an unprecedented potential for speed of transmission of language change. A new usage can be on millions of screens within seconds.

Although the Internet is still in its early stages (the World Wide Web began to function only in 1991, and most people who now use email did not begin to do so until the mid 1990s), we can already see the emergence of a new range of language varieties. Emails, synchronous (real-time) chat-rooms, asynchronous discussion groups, and the many types of Web-based text show English moving in new stylistic directions, partly in response to the personalities and group dynamics of the participants, and partly because of the constraints introduced by the screen size and the controlling software (as in the asterisked sentence in this extract from a chat-room interaction):

Orc: i thought it was his best gig yet
Mikie: anyway i wouldnt want to see it again
M3: i think he was better when he played in Glasgow
Dop: i gotta go
see ya
***DOP has left Channel 33
Orc: i never went to Glasgow
i saw him in Manchester tho
Orc: and in Birmingham
M3: how you get around so much?

There are plainly considerable differences between the kind of language used on the Internet – *Netspeak*, as I have elsewhere called it[9] – and those used in other forms of speech and writing. Indeed, the extent of the difference is so great that it amounts to the arrival of a new medium – often called *computer-mediated communication* – which blends properties of traditional spoken and written language. Netspeak is, firstly, not like traditional speech. It lacks the simultaneous feedback which is an essential part of face-to-face conversation. It permits the carrying on of several conversations simultaneously in chat-rooms, where it is possible to attend to many interlocutors at once, and to respond to as many as taste and typing speed permit. And it is unable to communicate the dynamic aspects of speech, such as intonation and tone of voice – notwithstanding the primitive attempts to do so, in the form of emoticons, or 'smileys', such as :-) and :-(. Nor is Netspeak like traditional writing. It permits people to do things routinely to the written language which were not possible before, such as to interpolate responses into a message (as in emails) or to cut and paste from one document to another without the results clashing graphically. And it offers new dimensions of contrast which were not previously available, notably in animated graphic presentation.

In addition to its roles in fostering variety and facilitating change, the Internet is performing a third function, and it is in this respect that its impact on the future of the English language is likely to be most dramatic. It offers an unprecedented degree of written public presence to individuals and small-scale community groups, and thus a vast potential for representing personal and local identities. Minority languages have already benefited. Although an exclusively English-language medium at the outset, because of its origins in the USA, the Internet has steadily developed a multilingual identity, so much so that in 2003 estimates suggest that less than 50 per cent of cyberspace was occupied by English. At least a quarter of the world's languages have an Internet presence now,[10] and many of these are minority and endangered languages. For a small speech community, the Internet therefore offers a linguistic lifeline, enabling its scattered members to keep in touch with each other through emails and chat-rooms, and through Web sites giving their language a world presence which it would have been impossible to achieve using traditional media, such as broadcasting or the press. And the Internet privileges individuals, too, allowing anyone with access to the medium to present a personal diary-type statement to the world, in the form of a *blog*, or 'Web log' – one of the most proliferating functions of the Web in the early 2000s.

But the emergent multilingual character of the Internet must not blind us to the impact that the medium is also having on English. The majority of Web pages in English are in British or American Standard English, as we would expect, given that the Web holds a mirror up to the linguistic proportions found in the 'real' world; however, other varieties are growing. Any intranational regional dialect which has a history of enthusiastic support will have its Web pages now. A search for sources on Newcastle English ('Geordie'), for example, produced over a hundred sites, including several which offered transcriptions of dialect usage and sound-recordings in support. And at an international level, the 'New Englishes' in the world (p. 502) now have available a written electronic identity which previously it was possible to achieve only through conventional creative literature (Chapter 19). I do not know of any studies of the way the processes of accommodation (p. 83) operate on the Internet; but it seems likely that, with a much greater frequency of informal written interaction taking place than at any previous stage in the history of the language, we will see the rapid emergence and consolidation of local group norms of usage – several of which will privilege nonstandard forms (see panel 20.2). These new varieties are bound to achieve a more developed written representation than would ever have been possible before, and through the global reach of the Internet they may well extend their influence beyond their country of origin.

20.2 New online Englishes

It does not take long for nonstandard expressions to achieve a normative status in a chat-room interaction. Each group has a collective memory of usage arising out of repeated online contacts, and new members of the group are expected to conform. Some of the conventional nonstandardisms in a chat-room include:

- unusual symbol combinations, as in personal nicknames which use upper- and lower-case letters unpredictably: *daViD, aLoHA*
- omission of capitalization within sentences, even including *i* for *I*
- omission of internal sentence punctuation and full stops (though question marks and exclamation marks are usually kept)
- abbreviations, often involving rebuses (as in text-messaging), such as *sat* for *Saturday*, *C U* 'see you', *l8* 'late'
- emotive punctuation sequences, such as *yes!!!!!!!!, Jim??!!??*
- spellings, such as *outta* 'out of', *wanna* 'want to', *cee ya* 'see you', *seemz* 'seems'
- grammatical constructions, such as omitting a verb (*he lovely*), or breaking a concord rule (*me am feeling better*)
- eye-dialect forms (p. 486), such as *it wuz lotsa lafs, i got enuf*
- nonce formations, such as running words together (*igottanewcar*) or abnormal hyphenation (*what-a-helluva-mess*)
- misspellings or lexical substitutions which achieve a fashionable privileged status in a particular group, such as the deliberate spelling of *computer* as *comptuer* (originating in an individual error which caught the group's fancy)

As New Englishes come increasingly online, regional nonstandard variations are bound to proliferate. An example of this already happening is from Hong Kong, where a sample of internet chat (via ICQ, 'I Seek You') between two university students produced the following exchange:

> Philip: will u go to library on fri?
> Gary: i'm not sure. haven't decided yet but probably coz i have bought the text book of econ112. i need to borrow the 2-hr reserve as a reference.
> Philip: see u on lib on fri ar? ok? as my friend will not stay ma . . . find sb to study la . . . to push me up ar.
> Gary: so do i.[11]

The exchange contains several international nonstandardisms and abbreviations:

> *u* 'you', *fri* 'Friday', *i'm*, *coz* 'because', *i*, *hr* 'hour'

and some abbreviations evidently in regular use among these students:

lib 'library', *sb* 'someone'

But it is also characterized by the use of three Cantonese particles: *ar* has an assertive force ('then', 'in short'); *ma* has an explanatory nuance ('as you know'); and *la* has an affirmative force ('so you see'). Other dialogues can contain even more code-mixing, so that it is difficult at times to know whether the language is English or Chinese. In such cases, of course, we may be seeing the birth of a new language, as yet without a name.

The newest New Englishes – as opposed to the older new Englishes, such as Indian English or South African English (Chapter 17) – are often identified by blend names, reflecting their mixed-language character, as with *Singlish* ('Singaporean English' – chiefly a mix of English and Chinese), *Tex-Mex* (English and Mexican Spanish in the south-western USA), and *Taglish* (in the Philippines, a mix of English and Tagalog).[12] Introducing words and phrases into one language from another is a perfectly normal feature of linguistic history, as we have often seen in this book; and switching between two (or more) languages is no less normal when people from different linguistic backgrounds come into regular contact with each other. These 'hybrid languages' seem to be on the increase, as English extends its global presence, and they will undoubtedly become more noticeable on the Internet as their speakers develop greater confidence in manipulating the new medium to express themselves. A whole new range of Internet-mediated regional written standards is the likely outcome. And as the amount of written language on the Internet will eventually far exceed that available in traditional print form, a new type of relationship between nonstandard varieties and Standard English will one day emerge.

Or perhaps I should call it a new manifestation of an old relationship. Once upon a time, England was a triglossic and then a diglossic nation (Chapter 6), and the consequences of that continued in the distinction between 'high' and 'low' varieties of English throughout Middle English, and still reverberate in the contrast between standard and nonstandard today. In such parts of the world as Singapore, where we find Standard English now coexisting with a local variety (Singlish), new forms of diglossia seem to be appearing, and functioning along with other languages to express complex sets of multi-ethnic cultural relationships. The way the Internet will help to shape these emergent diglossias is as yet unclear, but it is bound to play a dominant role. Several Internet varieties are inherently informal in character, and the more these are given written expression, the more the medium heightens the contrast with Standard English, which as we have seen (p. 224) is essentially a manifestation of language in its written form. It is a volatile, unprecedented, unpredictable, and altogether fascinating linguistic situation.

A period of transition

At the beginning of the twenty-first century, the relationship between standard and nonstandard language is, evidently, still an uncertain one. We are at a transitional point between two eras. We seem to be leaving an era when the rules of Standard English, as selected and defined by prescriptive grammarians, totally conditioned our sense of acceptable usage, so that all other usages and varieties were considered to be inferior or corrupt, and excluded from serious consideration. And we seem to be approaching an era when nonstandard usages and varieties, previously denigrated or ignored, are achieving a new presence and respectability within society, reminiscent of that found in Middle English, when dialect variation in literature was widespread and uncontentious (Chapter 9). But we are not there yet. The rise of Standard English has resulted in a confrontation between the standard and nonstandard dimensions of the language which has lasted for over 200 years, and this has had traumatic consequences which will take some years to eliminate. Once people have been given an inferiority complex about the way they speak or write, they find it difficult to shake off.

However, it is only a matter of time. Institutionalized prescriptivism began to come to an end in the later decades of the twentieth century. Primarily, this meant a change in educational practice, for it was only through the school system that prescriptivism had been able to propagate itself (p. 396). In the UK, from the 1970s, changes in school syllabuses and examination systems heralded a new dispensation, with an unthinking adherence to mechanical sentence analysis and old-style canons of correctness gradually being replaced by a broad-based investigation of the forms and functions of language in all their social manifestations. By the 1990s, in the new National Curriculum, as well as in the syllabuses which were being devised for higher examinations, there was a complete change in emphasis. Similar educational changes took place, also, in other parts of the English-speaking world, with Australia and Canada early innovators.

In this new dispensation, exam papers no longer asked students to parse sentences or to make decisions about correctness in relation to such issues as end-placed prepositions and split infinitives. Instead, the questions began to make students *explain* what happens when language is used – to go beyond the mere identifying of a linguistic feature (an infinitive, a metaphor, a piece of alliteration) to a mode of inquiry in which they explored the reasons lying behind the choices of words in such contexts as a scientific report, a news broadcast, or an advertising slogan. It was no longer enough to say, 'I see a passive verb in that science report.' The interesting question – and the one which gained the marks in an exam – was to be able to say why it was there. Only in that way, it was reasoned, would students be able to develop a sense of the consequences of choosing one kind of language rather than another (such as formal vs informal), when it came to using language themselves or evaluating the effect of a language choice upon other people. The aim, in short, was to promote a more responsive and responsible approach to language, in which students would come to understand why people use language in the way they do, and would put this knowledge to active use to become more able to control language for themselves.

There is no agreed term to summarize this change in emphasis. It is not a matter of a 'prescriptive' approach being replaced by a 'descriptive' one, as has sometimes been suggested, for this pedagogy goes well beyond description into a world of explanation and evaluation. A better term would be 'pragmatic' (as opposed to 'dogmatic'), with all that this implies – an ability to adapt knowledge to meet the needs of differing circumstances and a readiness to judge cases on their merits. From the viewpoint of the present book, the pragmatic approach instils an awareness that variation and change are normal features of linguistic life, demanding recognition and respect. And it carries with it the corollary that those who make use of this variation must themselves be recognized and respected. In its strongest and most positive manifestation, the pragmatic approach replaces the concept of 'eternal vigilance' (beloved of prescriptivists and purists) by one of 'eternal tolerance'.

Although the educational perspective is crucial, in moving away from an institutionalized prescriptivism towards a more egalitarian linguistic era, it cannot operate alone. Other social institutions need to be involved. Indeed, without a sense of linguistic disquiet within society as a whole, it is unlikely that any change in educational practice would have taken place at all. What is interesting about the later decades of the twentieth century is the way that different social trends began to reinforce pragmatic educational linguistic thinking. To take just a few examples from the UK. Leading media organizations such as the BBC opened their doors to regional speech, partly as a result of the emergence of local radio and television stations (p. 474). Business management recognized the importance of speech variation in interacting with clients: the accents of a new linguistic order may be heard now at the end of a telephone in many a call-centre (p. 472). Organizations such as the Plain English Campaign began to demand a rethink in the way governmental, legal, and medical institutions operated linguistically. Political correctness, in the best sense, fostered notions of gender and racial equality. And there was a fresh awareness of the nature of regional and ethnic identity, which led to a greater valuing of linguistic diversity. These trends had their parallels in other English-speaking countries.

But changes in linguistic attitudes and practices do not come to be accepted overnight, or even overdecade. The cumulative effects of ten generations of prescriptive teaching are still around us. Organizations which were set up to 'safeguard' the English language, founded in the prescriptive era, continue to exist and to attract members. Usage manuals presenting a vision of Standard English as a uniform, unchanging, and universal norm of correctness continue to be published. And senior managers today, whether in government, law, medicine, business, education, or the media, cannot rid themselves entirely of prescriptive thinking, because they are the last generation to have experienced this approach in their schooling. Their influence is considerable, because they unconsciously pass on their linguistic anxieties and precoccupations, often half remembered and poorly understood, to subordinates who, in the absence of linguistic knowledge of their own, accept their opinions as dictates. In a few years' time, the new generation of schoolchildren, well grounded in pragmatic principles, will be out there in society, able to counter unthinking prescriptive attitudes; and once they are in senior positions, the confrontation will be over. Criticism of split infinitives will be gone for ever. But in the meantime, innumerable schoolchildren and adults have developed feelings of inadequacy and inferiority about their natural way of speaking, or about certain features of their writing, being led to believe that their practice is in some way 'ugly' or 'incorrect'. We are coming towards the close of a linguistically intolerant era, but – as happens in last-ditch situations – conservative reaction can be especially strong.

One reason for the strength of feeling is that there is still a widespread belief that the closest of connections exists between linguistics and morality. This belief came to the fore in the nineteenth century. The Anglican theologian and archbishop, Richard Chenevix Trench, was one of the most outspoken about the matter:

> How deep an insight into the failings of the human heart lies at the root of many words; and if only we would attend to them, what valuable warnings many contain against subtle temptations and sins![13]

Trench was making his point with reference to the meaning of words; but the age saw the whole of language as a mirror of community standards, ethics, and behaviour. In particular, grammar (which is at the heart of Standard English, p. 393) came to be seen as the mouthpiece of propriety and was linked to right living. It therefore followed that a failure to enforce grammatical rules would lead to a breakdown of the social order. The sentiment was reiterated throughout the nineteenth century and continued to be affirmed in the twentieth. In recent times, we find it expressed by a headteacher in a 1982 newspaper article, regretting the demise of old-style grammatical analysis in schools:

> As nice points of grammar were mockingly dismissed as pedantic and irrelevant, so was punctiliousness in such matters as honesty, responsibility, property, gratitude, apology and so on.[14]

The suggestion here is that the relationship is one of cause and effect. And his point was echoed by the politician Norman Tebbit in a 1985 broadcast on BBC Radio 4. To lose standards in English, he argued, 'cause[s] people to have no standards at all, and once you lose standards then there's no imperative to stay out of crime' (see further, panel 20.3).

It is indeed a long jump from not splitting infinitives to not splitting skulls; but, as we have seen before (p. 371), people do attribute huge amounts of significance to points of grammatical usage. It therefore has to be firmly stated: there is no simple or direct relationship between grammar and behaviour. Some of the most respectable people I know speak nonstandard grammar; and conversely, there are several villains around whose standard grammar is impeccable. Vocabulary is a different matter. There *is* a relationship between language and behaviour in the use of vocabulary – the use of insulting words (such as racist names), gender-biased terms, antagonistic obscenities, and other such denigrating lexical choices is clearly related to a person's temperament and belief. But even here, there is no simple link between linguistic cause and social effect. Racist words do not cause racist beliefs. It is the other way round. And in any case, as we have seen (p. 480), lexical choice is not a matter of Standard English.

Of course, it also has to be firmly stated that certain standards do need to be maintained in linguistic schooling. It is important for students to be able to write and speak clearly, to avoid ambiguity, to be precise, to develop a consistent style, to spell properly, to suit their language to the needs of the situation, and to bear in mind the needs of their listeners and readers. Everyone needs help to shape their own personal style and to develop their ability to appreciate style in others, and the role of teachers and of good linguistic models (the 'best authors') is crucial. The more people read widely, acquire some analytical terminology, adopt a critical perspective, and try their hands (and mouths) at different genres, the more they will end up as linguistically well-rounded individuals. But none of this has anything to do with the perceptions that were inculcated by the prescriptivist account of Standard English. There is no problem of intelligibility if I say *to boldly go* instead of *to go boldly,* or *between you and me* instead of *between you and I.* Nor is there a difference in clarity between *The time went really quickly* and *The time went really quick.* Nor is there any

20.3 The latest thing in crime

The contributors to the satirical magazine *Punch* were among the first to draw attention to the absurdity of suggesting that there is an inevitable link between bad grammar and bad behaviour. This dialogue is taken from an anthology, *Mr Punch in Society*, from *c.* 1870.

THE LATEST THING IN CRIME
(A Dialogue of the Present Day.)

SCENE – *Mrs Featherston's Drawing-room.*
Mrs Thistledown discovered calling.

MRS THISTLEDOWN [*taking up a novel on a side-table*] 'The Romance of a Plumber,' by Paul Poshley. My dear Flossie, you don't mean to tell me you read *that* man?
MRS FEATHERSTON I haven't had time to do more than dip into it as yet. But why, Ida? *Oughtn't* I to read him?
IDA Well, from something Mr. Pinceney told me the other day – but really it's too bad to repeat such things. One never knows, there *may* be nothing in it.
FLOSSIE Still, you might just as well *tell* me, Ida! Of course I should never dream –
IDA After all, I don't suppose there's any secret about it. It seems, from what Mr. Pinceney says, that this Mr. Poshley – you must *promise* not to say I told you –
FLOSSIE Of course – of course. But do go on, Ida. what *does* Mr. Poshley do?
IDA Well, it appears he *splits his infinitives.*
FLOSSIE [*horrified*] Oh, not *really*? But how *cruel* of him! Why, I met him at the Dragnet's only last week, and he didn't look at *all* that kind of person!
IDA I'm afraid there's no doubt about it. It's perfectly notorious. And of course any one who once takes to *that* –
FLOSSIE Yes, indeed. *Quite* hopeless. At least, I *suppose* so. Isn't it?
IDA Mr. Pinceney seemed to think so.
FLOSSIE How sad! But can't anything be *done*, Ida? Isn't there any law to punish him? By the bye, how do you split – what is it? – infinitudes?
IDA My dear, I thought you knew. I really didn't like to ask any questions.
FLOSSIE Well, whatever it is, I shall tell Mudies not to send me anything more of his. I *don't* think one ought to encourage such persons.

ambiguity between *There's lots of apples in the box* and *There are lots of apples in the box*. Training someone to avoid split infinitives is not going to improve a child's communicative abilities one jot. There are better ways of using the time in a classroom than worrying about how to maintain a 200-year-old conception of grammatical correctness, condemning nonstandard English, and complaining about linguistic variation and change.

The 'complaint tradition', in particular, is something we need to consign to history. It is something which seems to have grown up with the standard language (see Interlude 10), and especially in relation to the prescriptive approach, manifesting itself in each generation since the eighteenth century, and focusing on the same points of grammar, lexicon, orthography, and pronunciation.[15] The complaints are made to the press, to the BBC, or to anyone who the complainant thinks is likely to listen. Some issues attract more complaints than others because by their nature they occur more often in the language. The varying stress pattern in polysyllabic words is a case in point. Because stress see-saws backwards and forwards over time within many words in English – such as *dispute* vs *dispute, controversy* vs *controversy* (p. 466) – it is often noticed, and people who do not like this change therefore find themselves with many opportunities to complain about it. But even infrequent points of usage can attract a great deal of emotion – as is typically the case with grammatical issues. None of the 'top ten' grammatical complaints to the BBC in the 1980s – citing such constructions as *to boldly go* and *between you and me* – in fact turn up very often, in speech or writing; but they evoked great strength of feeling none the less.[16] The complaints are generally made with a single-mindedness of purpose and passionate concern that forces admiration: one complainant to my Radio 4 series *English Now* in the 1980s tabulated all split infinitives heard on that channel for a week, and, judging by the dozen or so pages of neat handwriting he submitted, he had spotted most of them. Regrettably, such enthusiasm is generally accompanied by a harmful narrowness of vision. In its worst excesses, when it focuses on the usage of particular minority groups, it amounts to ethnolinguistic cleansing. It is intolerance masquerading as vigilance.

The complainants are the legatees of the eighteenth-century prescriptivists, sometimes writing in anger, but more often in anxiety – concerned and confused about what they perceive to be their own linguistic inadequacies. The intellectual achievement of the prescriptive writers of the eighteenth century was to give definition to the future character of the standard (Chapter 15); but their emotional legacy was to instil in everyone a great deal of guilt about everyday usage, and a fear of 'breaking the rules' which can reach paranoid proportions. It was they, and they alone, who chose which features of grammar were to be the sign of an educated writer, and their prescriptions were sufficiently powerful to persuade generations of writers how to behave, right up to the present. Their success – if that is what it can be called – is evident on every page of this book. The third sentence of this paragraph might just as clearly have begun: 'It was them, and them alone, that chose . . .'. There is no difference in clarity of expression, but a world of difference in grammatical acceptability in the eyes of society, and those whose role it is to monitor prevailing standards on behalf of society, such as teachers and copy-editors, would not tolerate it. Only in certain kinds of fiction (Chapter 19) might it be allowed to stand. In these respects, we would have to acknowledge that the prescriptive aim was successful, and recognize that we have all been turned into linguistic automata (*OED* definition 5: 'a human being acting mechanically or without active intelligence in a monotonous routine'). Nor are we alone. The same prescriptive climate affected language writers in all the leading countries in eighteenth-century Western Europe. Nations voluntarily placed themselves into a linguistic prison-house from which, in the English-speaking world, we are just beginning to escape.

There is actually only one escape-route: we have to maintain the literary momentum of the nineteenth and twentieth centuries, and develop a more accepting frame of reference for handling nonstandard English. And this means that at the same time we have to develop a fresh conception of Standard English – one which gets away from its prescriptive preoccupations, occupying as they do only a tiny proportion of grammatical 'space', and allows us to concentrate on the core areas of grammatical structure that actually govern the way we express and respond to meaning and style. In a typical reference grammar of 1,500 pages, only a dozen or so will be taken up with the issues that so worried the prescriptive grammarians. It is time to focus on the topics covered by the remaining pages – topics which turn out to be much more closely bound up with questions of intelligibility, clarity, precision, and elegance of expression than could ever be found in the pages of a prescriptive grammar.

The way forward

A transition between linguistic eras is not a comfortable stage. It takes time to get away from the complaint tradition. It takes time before people adjust their mindsets to assimilate new ways of thinking. It takes time for teachers to be prepared to cope with this thinking.[17] It took half a century for the prescriptive era to become firmly established, and I expect it will take a similar period to be fully weaned away from it. In 2004 we are perhaps halfway through this period. A new social climate has emerged, and a new intellectual sociolinguistic climate is beginning to be formed, to which the present book hopes to make a contribution.[18] This climate is based on a rationalization in which certain principles are central, and it will perhaps be helpful, at this point in the book, to summarize what they are.

1. Language change is normal and unstoppable, reflecting the normal and unstoppable processes of social change.
2. Language variation is normal and universal, reflecting the normal and universal diversity of cultural and social groups.

3. A highly diversified society needs a standard variety ('the standard language') to facilitate intelligible supra-regional communication, nationally and internationally. This variety needs to be respected and studied, and the points of contrast with nonstandard varieties appreciated.

4. A highly diversified society needs nonstandard varieties ('nonstandard language') to enable groups of people to express their regional or cultural identity, nationally and internationally. These varieties need to be respected and studied, and the points of contrast with the standard language appreciated.

5. Neither standard nor nonstandard language is homogeneous. Both are continually subject to the processes of language change, and they display variation arising from the different mediums they exploit (speech, writing, electronic), the different ranges of formality they employ (informal to formal), and the different occupational domains in which they are used (law, technology, religion, literature, etc.).

6. There is an intimate relationship between standard and nonstandard language. Standard language users can make use of nonstandard forms, as occasion requires, and nonstandard language users can be influenced by the standard in varying degrees. Over time, nonstandard forms frequently influence the way the standard language develops.

7. Standard and nonstandard language are primarily differentiated by choices in grammar. In its written manifestation, the standard language (Standard English)[19] is additionally characterized by choices in orthography. In its spoken manifestation, there is no additional feature: Standard English is not characterized by choices in pronunciation; it has no associated accent, either nationally (though RP came close at one time in the UK) or internationally.

8. Everyone who receives a school education needs to learn to read and write Standard English, and to understand its spoken use, because this is the variety which carries most prestige in English-speaking national and international society and which gives greatest access to high-status positions at these levels. Some children also learn to use the associated grammar as a spoken dialect in addition to their mother dialect; and a small minority, from higher-class backgrounds, use it as a mother dialect at home.[20] A spoken form of Standard English is the traditional expectation of use in certain careers, such as the civil service, teaching, and national broadcasting.

9. Everyone who receives a school education needs to learn about varieties of nonstandard English, because these are the varieties which express a person's identity as part of a national or international community and which give greatest insight into community values and attitudes. The

first dialect learned by most English-speaking children is a nonstandard variety, and the importance of this should be recognized when the children arrive in school, respect for it being reinforced through opportunities to use their variety in writing as well as in speech.

10. As English becomes an increasingly global language, we need to re-appraise the concept of a single Standard English, giving due recognition to the emergence of 'regional standards'. British and American English – the first to emerge at an international level and the source of all other global English varieties – are already well established; and others will follow as the 'New Englishes' of the world acquire local prestige.

The chief message to be extracted from these ten sociolinguistic principles is the intimate and complex relationship which exists between standard and nonstandard varieties. The two notions define each other, not just in a simple terminological manner, but in the way that each takes its distinctive character-istics from a common 'pool' of linguistic features that make up the language as a whole. Any of the features which identify a regional accent or dialect – distinctive sounds, words, or grammatical features – can 'cross the divide' and lose their regional status, becoming incorporated into the speech of people who would consider themselves to be users of Standard English. And the same thing can happen in the other direction – a feature of Standard English can be picked up by nonstandard speakers. In fact, 'can' is the wrong verb: exchanges in both directions are so commonplace that they have to be considered the norm (see panel 20.4).

20.4 What we learn from gumbo

Vocabulary is the most obvious bridge between standard and nonstandard varieties, but it is not a symmetrical relationship. Regional vocabulary plainly exists – words which are used only in a particular regional dialect – as has often been illustrated in this book. But there is no such thing as a 'standard vocabulary', in the sense that there are words used by a speaker of Standard English which would *never* be used by speakers of a nonstandard variety. It is a commonplace to hear people using a broad local dialect to discuss matters to do with politics, religion, technology and using the relevant vocabulary in the process. Some typical examples:

There's too many administrators, if you ask me, and none of 'em know nowt about t' new health service reform proposals.

The gas ain't got to go far – just through them needle valves into the manifold, what links up with your laser.

Just because nonstandard speech contains regional dialect words and slang does not mean that local people with the appropriate interests and knowledge cannot be technical when they need to be. If they lack the background, of course, then they will not use the words – but that is a matter of education or personal taste, not linguistics.

The intimate relationship also works in the other direction. Regional vocabulary is often assimilated into the standard language. *Gumbo* is a case in point. Originally a Bantu word, from Angola, it identified okra, a type of tropical annual plant with fleshy green seed-pods. It is recorded in the USA from the early nineteenth century as the name of a thick spicy soup prepared in New Orleans – 'made of every eatable substance', according to a writer in *American Pioneer* (1805).

The *Dictionary of American Regional English* lists it as a regional form from the Gulf States and Louisiana, though recognizing that it has become much more widely known, spreading outward from its original home.[21] The *Dictionary of Americanisms on Historical Principles* shows that during the nineteenth century it extended its meaning, being applied to several dishes involving a mixture of ingredients, and then going beyond food, referring at various times to people of mixed blood and to mixed forms of speech. Along the Mississippi Valley and into the Great Plains it also came to refer to a type of soil, named for an apparent similarity to the texture of the soup. And several combining forms emerged, such as *gumbo town* (a contemptuous name for a small town) and *gumbo ball* (a type of social gathering).

It is just one of the local details which makes Tom Stoppard's account of an American rail journey so vivid (in *New-Found-Land*). Here is the train approaching New Orleans.

> The train slows, crawling through the French quarter of the City on the Delta. The sun hangs like a copper pan over boarding houses with elaborately scrolled gingerbread eaves. In the red-lit shadow of wrought-iron balconies octaroon Loreleis sing their siren songs to shore-leave sailors, and sharp-suited pimps push open saloon doors, spilling light and ragtime to underscore the street cries of old men selling shrimp gumbo down on the levee . . .

There are no inverted commas, no special explanations, no apologies for using a humble dialect word. The word has silently become part of the Standard English of the play.

Examples like these show that there is no sharp dividing line between nonstandard and standard. Indeed, Standard English obtains much of its vitality by sucking linguistic energy from local dialects. And in the present instance, the nutritional metaphor has a second application, for when users of Standard English go out to eat, gumbo may well be on the menu, gracing the pages of many a high-class recipe book.

The Interlude on the glottal stop (p. 415) illustrated this process in action, with reference to accents. The glottal stop is inside us all, part of our phonetic ability as human beings, waiting to be put to use. We use one every time we cough. At a certain point in the history of English it began to replace or reinforce consonants by speakers of various regional backgrounds. When Received Pronunciation emerged as a prestige accent, its speakers 'chose' not to use the glottal stop in this way, because this was one of the means whereby they could distance themselves from regional speakers. As it turned out, they were not successful. Very early on, glottal stops of various kinds began to be heard in RP, and have steadily increased in frequency in recent years, the incidence depending on such factors as the age, sex, and social background of the speaker. The outcome is that we can obtain a sample of speech from a speaker and find within it no glottal stopping, or a little, or a lot. Or we find glottal stops used in certain words or contexts (e.g., between vowels) and not in others. It is a multidimensional process, with the effects appearing at different rates in different parts of the language. Dialectologists who have studied these processes at work encounter an extremely messy picture. It is not enough to say that there is a continuum in the use of such features as the glottal stop. There are several continua, operating simultaneously, relating to different uses of the sound – and, similarly, dozens more continua relating to other sounds, words, and grammatical constructions.

As social interaction increases, nationally and internationally, it becomes increasingly difficult to maintain a clear distinction between 'standard' and 'nonstandard', at least in speech. Most people seem to use an amalgam of the two, especially when they speak informally. The distinction may even be unclear in writing, if we recollect the mixed varieties which can now be found throughout Commonwealth literature (Chapter 19). Accordingly, a better model of the relationship is to replace the opposition 'standard–nonstandard' by a scale of standardness or nonstandardness. At one end of the scale we have the 'most standardized' variety, which we call Standard English; at other points along the scale we have the various regional and ethnic varieties, some of which display more standardness than others. Scales of this kind have long been recognized in creole-speaking communities, where we find some varieties very close to Standard English and others very distant from it.[22] It is time to recognize that such scales exist everywhere.

A halfway house

All that has happened in the past century makes me believe that we are travelling along a road which leads to a brave new linguistic world. We have seen the emergence of new literary discourses, on a global scale, characterized by a fresh regional linguistic diversity. Many authors now routinely use standard alongside nonstandard language as part of their work. We have seen fresh social recognition and respect being given to linguistic identities within communities that are becoming increasingly multicultural. Many people now realize that labels such as 'substandard' and 'broken English' are just as insulting and out of order as any set of racist or sexist names. We have seen a move away from the linguistic subjugation of the prescriptive era, with people asserting their right to be in control of their language rather than to have it be in control of them. For many, prescriptivism has come to be seen as a bad dream from which we are only now beginning to awake. The operative word, in all these sentences, is 'many'. We are only halfway along the road, and not everyone is yet persuaded that it is a road they ought to take. But, as I have argued above, it is only a matter of time. A major step has been taken in schools, where the renaissance in linguistic study has already begun to produce generations of schoolchildren who are aware of the importance and relevance of Standard English without seeing any need to dismiss or condemn nonstandard English.

These children, I hope, will grow up in a world which is intelligent, responsible, and mature, in its linguistic beliefs and attitudes – a world in which people are given reasons for the way things are, in language, and are not expected to follow self-appointed authority blindly. It will be a world which will recognize a federation of standard and nonstandard varieties, performing different life functions. And it will be a world which will affirm the central role that regional dialects have played – and continue to play – in linguistic history. It has not been my world, or even my children's world; but it is certainly my grandchildren's world. And it is a world which needs its history written.

The Stories of English is a first attempt to write that history, from within this new perspective. I have tried to draw attention to the inherent vitality of the English language as manifested in its variety, which was there from the outset with the arrival of the Anglo-Saxons, and which was recognized and exploited by such authors as Chaucer, Shakespeare, and Dickens. I have tried to demonstrate how it has been impossible to keep the nonstandard language down, despite many efforts to do so. There is an energy in the language – in any language – which derives from its diversity, and this is something which needs to be recognized and celebrated. Ideally, the subject deserves large-scale treatment in encyclopedias, sound archives, and text galleries, allowing the unique attractiveness of each linguistic variety to be admired – just as we can enjoy the varieties on show in botanical gardens. One day, perhaps. In the meantime, I have brought together some of the best displays I know for *The Stories of English*.

Appendix

Locations in the British Isles referred to in this book (several county boundaries reflect the situation before local government changes in 1972)

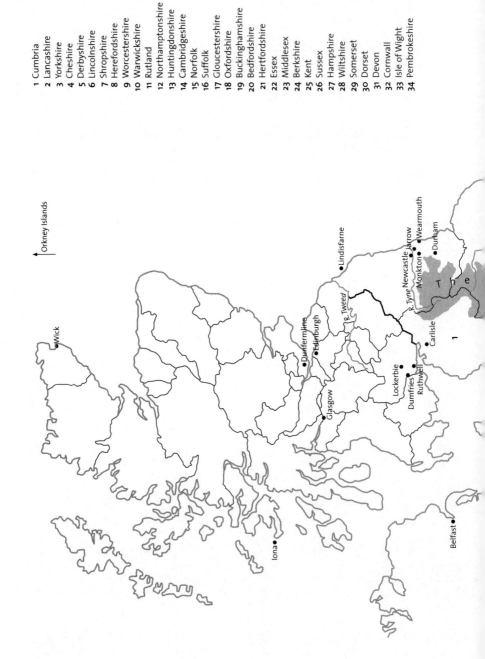

1 Cumbria
2 Lancashire
3 Yorkshire
4 Cheshire
5 Derbyshire
6 Lincolnshire
7 Shropshire
8 Herefordshire
9 Worcestershire
10 Warwickshire
11 Rutland
12 Northamptonshire
13 Huntingdonshire
14 Cambridgeshire
15 Norfolk
16 Suffolk
17 Gloucestershire
18 Oxfordshire
19 Buckinghamshire
20 Bedfordshire
21 Hertfordshire
22 Essex
23 Middlesex
24 Berkshire
25 Kent
26 Sussex
27 Hampshire
28 Wiltshire
29 Somerset
30 Dorset
31 Devon
32 Cornwall
33 Isle of Wight
34 Pembrokeshire

Orkney Islands

Wick

Iona

Belfast

Glasgow

Dunfermline
Edinburgh

R. Tweed

Lindisfarne

Lockerbie
Dumfries
Ruthwell

Carlisle

R. Tyne Newcastle
Jarrow
Monkton Wearmouth
Durham

The

Notes

Introduction

1. The quotes about dialects come from the third edition of Wyld (1927), §§ 209, 211. For a more detailed analysis of the tradition, see Milroy (1999, 2002).
2. Classical accounts of English linguistic history include Jespersen (1905), Brook (1958), and Baugh (1935). I include myself, in earlier incarnations, within this tradition: Crystal (1988: see 2002a; 1995: see 2003: Part 1). There have been occasional efforts to break away from the usual approach, such as Strang (1970), who told the story backwards, beginning with 'changes in living memory', then proceeding in 200-year retrograde steps until, in her final chapter, she reached the origins of Old English; but her focus was still on the standard language.
3. Wyld (1927), §§ 5, 6, 7. This book displays all the biases we might expect from someone writing in a society ruled by class distinction, and there is a persistent theme of denigration of anything nonstandard. Even in the case of 'sophisticated villagers', he avers in §211, we are a long way from the English heard 'in an Oxford Common Room, or in an Officers' Mess'; and even in the cases of those 'town vulgarians [who] speak a form of the standard language', this is 'far removed from the most refined and most graceful type'.
4. Other sociolinguistically informed accounts of the history of English include Smith (1996), Fennell (2001), Watts and Trudgill (2002), Mugglestone (forthcoming), and many of the chapters in the *Cambridge History of the English Language*, edited by Richard Hogg in six volumes (1992–2001). For an example of the new climate emphasizing variation on a global scale, see McArthur (1998). For nonstandard language in English literature, see Blake (1981). For a general discussion on issues surrounding the notion of 'standard', see Bex and Watts (1999). Collections of articles include Bolton (1966) and Lass (1969). Useful collections of data sources are Burnley (2000), Cusack (1998), Diamond (1970), Dickins and Wilson (1951), Mitchell (1995), Rigg (1968), Sisam (1959).

Chapter 1 and Interlude

1. The translation is from the Everyman Library edition (Bede, 1910), originally an eighteenth-century translation by J. Stevens, later revised.
2. Blair (1977: 10–11).
3. The genetic study is reported in Weale, Weiss, Jager, Bradman, and Thomas (2002).
4. Page (1987: 32).
5. For further reading on Anglo-Saxon England and its prehistory, see Blair (1977) and Partridge (1982). The history and archaeology are copiously illustrated by texts and translations in Mitchell (1995). Dialect origins are debated in DeCamp (1958) and Toon (1992).
6. For South African English, see Branford and Branford (1991).
7. Weale, et al. (2002).

Chapter 2 and Interlude

1. Dictionary of Old English Project, Centre for Medieval Studies, University of Toronto.
2. The panel is based on Toon (1992: 427).
3. The text of the *Parker Chronicle* used for this chapter is Smith (1951).
4. The text and lineation follow Dickins and Ross (1954).
5. The Abba will is Cotton Aug.ii.64, reprinted in Sweet (1885: 447–9).
6. Toon (1992: 432–3).
7. Schabram (1965).
8. The text of Ælfric's *Colloquy* is that of Garmondsway (1947).
9. The full text of the Cædmon event, and the hymn he composed, is given in Crystal (2003: 20, 29).
10. The Klaeber comment is on p. lxxxviii of his edition (Klaeber, 1922).
11. See further Kastovsky (1992: 346ff.).

Chapter 3 and Interlude

1. Serjeantson (1935: Appendix A).
2. The Latin words are: *belt, bin, cook, cup, pan, pit, post, pot, sack, sock, stop, wall.*
3. This translation is from Garmondsway (1953: 54).
4. Partridge (1984: 792).
5. Lindkvist (1978).
6. On the importance of wool in Anglo-Saxon times, see Biddle (1985: 80).
7. For the influence of the Vikings on English, see Geipel (1971). On foreign loans in Old English, see Serjeantson (1935), Kastovsky (1992).

Chapter 4 and Interlude

1. Exeter Dean and Chapter MS 3501, f. 76v.
2. For mnemonic techniques, see Smith (1983: Chapter 6).
3. For the importance of rhyme and alliteration in children's learning of a language, and in relation to reading, see Crystal (1998: Chapters 5–6).
4. In order: rake, key, bookworm.
5. Corpus Christi College, Cambridge, 201.
6. Bodleian, Ashmole 328, 94.
7. On Old English literature in general, see Godden and Lapidge (1991), especially Chapters 2–4. On Old English grammar, see Quirk and Wrenn (1955) and Kispert (1971). For a general exposition, including textual illustrations and translations, see Diamond (1970), Rigg (1968), and the early items in Farnham (1969) and Finnie (1972). Essays on all aspects of the language are found in Hogg (1992).
8. The statistical data are selected from Shores (1971: 220).
9. For a discussion of the variables involved, see Fischer (1992: 370–83).

Chapter 5 and Interlude

1. 'Sumer is icumen in' is in the British Library, MS Harley 978, f. 11b. 'Thirty dayes' is MS Harley 2341. A comprehensive collection of Middle English lyrics is found in Luria and Hoffman (1974).
2. The *Kentish Homilies* are in the British Library, London: MS Cotton Vespasian D.xiv. The

Lambeth Homilies are at Lambeth Palace, London: MS Lambeth 487. The *Trinity Homilies* are at Trinity College, Cambridge: MS 335 B.14.52.

3. The use of the male pronoun deserves a comment. The vast majority of the scribes would have been monks, but increasingly in the Middle Ages nuns would have been employed in the copying task. Occasionally we find a fragment of evidence to show that a text was being used by a woman. An annotation to a late twelfth-century Latin prayer to the Virgin Mary reads *ego ancilla tua* ('I your servant'), the significance lying in the fact that the inflectional ending of the last two Latin words is feminine, not masculine. The same point applies to a copy of the Salisbury Psalter, where in one of the prayers someone has changed the masculine form *famulum tuum* ('your family') to the feminine *famulam tuam*. See Irvine (2000: 53).

4. See Swan (2000).

5. Lambeth 487 and Royal 7 c.xii, respectively. The examples are taken from Swan (2000: 72–5).

6. The copy is in Lambeth 487. The examples are from Wilcox (2000: 90, 94).

7. Irvine (2000: 52).

8. Liuzza (2000).

9. The examples are from Teresi (2000).

10. Proud (2000: 120).

11. The observation is made by Ker (1957: xlix) referring to Cambridge University Library Ii.1.33.

12. The *Peterborough Chronicle* is in the Bodleian Library, Oxford: MS Laud Misc. 636.

13. A longer extract from the year 1137 is given in Crystal (2002a: 185–6; 2003: 33); the text of the whole year is reproduced in Dickins and Wilson (1951: 4–6).

Chapter 6 and Interlude

1. The writ of William I is preserved in the Corporation of London Records Office. See Bates (1998).

2. See the discussion in Berndt (1965).

3. The translation (with some punctuation changes) is that of Henderson (1910).

4. The extract is taken from the translation by Forester (1854).

5. The translation is from Attwater (1957).

6. See Burton (1994).

7. See Gillingham (1991: 109–11).

8. See Clanchy (1993).

9. See Rothwell (2001).

10. Reported in Jenkyns (1833: 109).

11. There are several trilingual manuscripts, e.g., British Library Egerton 613, from *c.* 1300. See further, Turville-Petre (1996: Chapter 6).

12. The Lay Subsidy Rolls are located in class E179 at the Public Record Office. See Jurkowski, Smith, and Crook (1998). The Lincolnshire data is taken from E179/133.

13. Kristensson (1995: Map 15), with statistics added from the data provided on pp. 143–6.

14. The Worcestershire data is from Amphlett (1900).

Chapter 7 and Interlude

1. The earlier, *c.* 1200–25, is Cotton Caligula A.ix; the latter, *c.* 1250, is Cotton Otho C.xiii, both in the British Library.

2. The *Gawain* text is MS Nero A.x in the British Library.

3. The extract is from f. 105r of Corpus Christi College, Cambridge, MS 402.

4. There are fifty-six prefixes and fifty suffixes (ignoring variant forms) listed in the Appendix on word formation in Quirk, Greenbaum, Leech, and Svartvik (1985). 'Everyday' is intended to exclude specialized affixes, such as those in chemistry. The percentage of use in word types is based on a series of samples taken from the headword lists in the *OED*. The percentage varies greatly depending on the letter of the alphabet being examined: there are over 10,000 words beginning with *un-* or *under-* alone, whereas only a handful of scientific prefixes begin with *z-* (e.g., *zoo-, zinco-, zirco-*).

5. Sources are: *The Merchant's Tale*, l. 1,908; *The Man of Law's Tale*, l. 163; *The Wife of Bath's Tale*, l. 1,256; *General Prologue*, l. 471.

6. Mellinkoff (1963: Preface). See also his account of the Middle English period in Chapters 8 and 9, especially §71.

7. Both recipes are from Harleian MS 4016; see Austin (1888).

8. Estimates in textbooks vary greatly, because of differences in the methodology of counting: see the comparison of estimates in Coleman (1995). Coleman's own approach finds a peak of French influence in the late thirteenth century.

9. See Crystal (2003: Chapter 19).

10. Kučera and Francis (1967: 5).

11. Scribal practice in this *Tale* is considered in Horobin (2001).

Chapter 8 and Interlude

1. [I] *rekke nat a bene*, as the Host would say: Prologue of *The Nun's Priest's Tale*, l. 2,814.

2. For discussion of the lered / lewed distinction in terms of social roles (chiefly, the Latin-using cleric vs the non-Latin-using layman), see Turville-Petre (1996: Chapter 2).

3. Prologue of *The Nun's Priest's Tale*, l. 2,808.

4. In *The Miller's Tale*, l. 3,740. Chaucer's 'dirty words' are discussed by Eliason (1972: 107ff.).

5. There is a selection of royal and aristocratic letters in Fisher, Richardson, and Fisher (1984). Most of the Paston letters are in the British Library, Add. MS 27,466. For an analysis of address formulae in letters of the period, see Nevalainen and Raumolin-Brunberg (1995).

6. The translation is from Attwater (1957). Earl Randolph was one of those who fought against King Stephen in 1140, according to the *Peterborough Chronicle*.

7. Ware (1909: 171/1).

8. Blake (1992: 517).

9. In a letter to *The Times*, 1961.

10. British Library Royal 13.E.ix, f. 287a. The letter is included in the collection of fourteenth-century texts by Sisam (1959: 160–61).

11. *De Officio Pastorali*, Chapter 15. MS Ashburnham 27.

12. For the growth of literacy, see Cressey (1980), Thompson (1939/63), Gellrich (1985). The figures are from Cressey.

13. Steiner (1967).

14. For examples of early dictionaries, see Collison (1982: 48).

15. Orwell (1946).

16. 'The English Language', *Blackwood's Magazine*, April.

17. For a further discussion of *well* in conversation, see Svartvik (1980); for a historical perspective, Jucker (1997).

Chapter 9 and Interlude

1. MS Bodley 34, one of three extant manuscripts containing texts of this group. The group is named after Katherine because her life is the only one to appear in all three. For a discussion of the factors involved, see Logan (1973: Chapters 1–2).

2. The single surviving manuscript is Bodleian MS Junius I.5113. The reference to 'full' lines contrasts with line counts which represent the text in terms of half-lines.

3. The texts referred to are all in Dickins and Wilson (1951).

4. For the early history of English in Ireland, see Kallen (1994: 150–51); in Wales, Thomas (1994); and in Scotland, McClure (1994).

5. St John's College, Cambridge, MS G 23, 1487.

6. The only manuscript is Bodleian MS Arch. Selden. B.24, late fifteenth century. The prefatory sentence is on f. 191. For a selection of other Scottish 'ballattis of luve', see MacQueen (1970).

7. The charter lists names are from Sweet (1885: 439); the *Liber Vitae* from Sweet (1885: 156–7).

8. Scribe A of MS Cambridge University Library Gg.4.27. The matter is discussed in Burnley (1989: 26–7).

9. The procedure outlined here lies behind the four-volume *Linguistic Atlas of Late Medieval English*, and a wide range of associated papers (McIntosh, Samuels, Benskin, et al., 1986). For the reproduction of a map showing all the variant forms of *church*, see Crystal (2003: 51). See also Kristensson (1997).

10. The Parson gives the Host a telling off for his bad language in the Epilogue of *The Man of Law's Tale*, l. 1,171: 'What eyleth the man, so synfully to swere?'

11. In the Prologue to Book III of *Gesta Pontificum Anglorum* (*Deeds of the English Bishops*); see Hamilton (1870: 209).

12. This story of early code-mixing or -switching (it is unclear which) is told in Clark (1981). The actual words are: *mutuavit modum loquendi fingendo se aliquendo Anglicum Australem, aliquando Borialem mere, et aliquando Scoticum per modum Scotorum sonando ydioma Anglicanum, et ideo videtur examinatoru quod minor fides est sibi adhibenda.* '. . . changed his way of speaking, forming it sometimes in Southern English, sometimes entirely Northern, and sometimes Scottish by speaking the English tongue in the manner of the Scots, and therefore the magistrates consider that less trust be placed in it.' A more malicious translation would appear if *fingendo* were translated as 'feigning'.

Chapter 10 and Interlude

1. Its role in relation to the medium of electronic communication, which has properties that are neither exclusively spoken nor written, has yet to emerge: see Crystal (2001).

2. There can be hints of it in the writing system of a community exposed to two different spelling systems, such as in Canada. See the pictorial examples in Crystal (2003: 284–5).

3. See the account in Kuhn (1968) of British Library MS Royal 17.B, an East Midlands text dated *c.* 1425; the extracts are from ff. 5a,b, with abbreviations expanded.

4. Robbins (1970); see also Jones (2001).

5. For further examples of the contemporary social scene, see Christianson (1989), from which several of the following examples are taken.

6. This and several other examples are discussed in Richards (1989: 10–12).

7. See Christianson (1989).

8. See Taavitsainen (2000).

9. For this exercise, I used the electronic version of the 241 texts in the Chancery anthology

collected by Fisher, Richardson, and Fisher (1984), ranging from 1384 to 1462, made available through the Middle English Collection at the Electronic Text Center, University of Virginia.
10. By Samuels, in an influential paper (1963).
11. Samuels (1963) cites manuscript examples from Dorset and Somerset.
12. National Library of Scotland, Advocates' MS 19.2.1. For information about a new transcription and digitized version of the manuscript, see www.shef.ac.uk/auchinleck/auchleck.htm
13. For the historical background, see Bolton (1985). For a demographic account, see Keene (2000).
14. Populations were never very great during the fourteenth century: in 1300 few towns were larger than two or three thousand, and almost all of these would have been in the south-east. London was the only centre of any real size, with a population in 1300 of 30–40,000; York, some way behind, might have had 10,000.
15. See Wright (2001).
16. For example, Labov (1966), Trudgill (1974), and the sociolinguistic perspective presented in Milroy and Milroy (1991).
17. See the analysis in Moerenhout and van der Wurff (2000).
18. A two-stage analysis is presented by Johnston (1992). The dialectal perspective is further emphasized by, for example, Chevillet (1997).

Chapter 11 and Interlude

1. The allusion is to the last line of Dylan Thomas' radio story 'Reminiscences of Childhood'.
2. Trudgill (1999: 124); see further, p. 530.
3. Blake (1969: Chapter 9); the quotation is from p. 176. See also the word listings in the introduction to Blake (1973).
4. See the survey in Parkes (1992: Chapter 6).
5. There is a comparative study of several editions of *Reynard* in Blake (1965).
6. For examples of fashion change in language, see Crystal (2003: 392).
7. Facsimiles of the two surviving copies, Bodleian MS Tanner 67 and the MS at Christ Church College, Oxford, are reproduced in Turner (1980). The illustration on p. 267 is page 1 of the Christ Church text.
8. These quotations are taken from the edition of Hart's works by Danielsson (1955), pp. 121–2.
9. See Brooke (1965: 97). For biblical translation generally at this time, see Partridge (1973).
10. Furnivall and Cowper (1871: 89). For further context, see Brooke (1965).
11. 'A Description of England', in Pine (1947: 35).

Chapter 12 and Interlude

1. 'The Confutacion of Tyndale's aunswere, made Anno 1532', in Skeat (1886: 192).
2. Quoted in Pollard (1911: 94).
3. See Coleman (1995: 115), Nevailainen (1999: 336ff.).
4. See examples in Crystal (2003: 125).
5. Current projects include the Early Modern English Dictionary Database at the University of Toronto. See also Schäfer (1989).
6. Devitt (1989).
7. See Mencken (1963: Chapter 3).
8. In the *Spectator*, 135, 4 August 1711: *mob* (from *mobile vulgus*), *rep* (from *reputation*),

pos (from *positive*), *incog* (from *incognito*); see further, p. 457. Nor did Jonathan Swift like the 'barbarous Custom of abbreviating Words' (in his 1712 *Proposal*): see p. 378.

9. See Nevalainen (1999: 350).

10. Kermode (2000). The quotation is on pp. 45–6.

11. Barber (1976: Chapter 4); Nevalainen (1999).

12. Over 37,000 in the revised and enlarged Pollard and Redgrave (1976–91), and over 120,000 in the revised and enlarged Wing (1972–88).

13. See Field (1971). The passage is in Book VII, Chapter 1.

14. For further illustration of the *thou/you* contrast, see Crystal and Crystal (2001: 450–51), Ronberg (1992: 75–88).

Chapter 13 and Interlude

1. For a further discussion of legal language in Shakespeare, see Crystal (2002b), Sokol and Sokol (2000).

2. *The South Bank Show*, ITV London, January 2000.

3. *The Adventure of English*, programme 1, ITV London, 1 December 2002.

4. McCrum, Cran, and MacNeil (1986: 102).

5. The word-form count is from Spevack's concordance research (see 1973), which identifies 884,647 words in the traditional Shakespeare canon. If *Two Noble Kinsmen* and *King Edward III* are included, that total would rise to *c*. 930,000. By way of comparison, Hart (1943) lists 17,677 different words.

6. The procedure is explained in detail in Crystal (2002a: 46–9); see also Crystal (2003: 123), from which these figures are taken.

7. See Crystal (2002a: 119).

8. The vocabulary counts for this section were carried out using the CD-ROM version of the second edition of the *OED*. The full lists of lexemes underlying the various counts are being made available at www.shakespeareswords.com, along with the criteria for identifying lexemes.

9. The dates of course are suspect: *condolement* occurs in *Hamlet*, which some editors think was written as early as 1600. But the general point stands, regardless of a date being a year or so out, one way or another.

10. The notion is widely assumed but has received very little discussion. Distinctions such as 'old age' vs 'middle age' are normal, and generally assume a generational difference of around 25 years. Among the few references to the notion of 'generation' is Eckert (1997: 188).

11. See Coward (1997: 23).

12. See Wrigley and Schofield (1981: 234), Finlay (1981: 108).

13. For example, by Shipley (1977: 28), Lederer (1991), and on many Shakespeare Web sites. See also Schäfer (1973: Appendix 3).

14. For a fuller listing, see Crystal and Crystal (2002a: 191–3).

15. Moore (1999: 358) makes the point with reference to what she calls the 'airbrushing' practices of oral historians in removing informants' hesitations and other discourse features: 'oral historians may theoretically wish to bring forth the voices of the unheard, the impoverished, but we are silencing and further suppressing the speech of these same speakers by wiping out the cues to their emotions, feelings and social relationships'.

16. Cusack (1998: 24). Devon Record Office MS Chanter 867.

Chapter 14 and Interlude

1. Reported in Wyld (1936: 109).
2. The first quotation is from Spedding (1870: 77), the second from Bamford (1936: 197). I am indebted to Jenny Wormald for these references.
3. At least, in the First Folio; Jamy and Macmorris do not appear in the 1600 Quarto text, now generally regarded as an actor's reconstruction from memory.
4. Several such remarks are reported in Fox (2000).
5. In *The Opening of the Unreasonable Writing of our Inglish Toung*; see p. 266.
6. In *A Restitution of Decayed Intelligence in Antiquities*.
7. The point is developed humorously by Miles Kington in 'It's the way you say it', *Independent Review*, 12 February 2003, p. 3.
8. Preface to *Coningsby* (1844).
9. Nonstandard features can, however, become centre-stage in a forensic linguistic era: see Crystal (1997: 69).
10. An example is in medicine: 'A Dialogue against the Feuer Pestilence' (1584), discussed in Taavitsainen and Nevalainen (1999).
11. On the occasion of the sinking of the *General Belgrano* in 1982: see Essery (1993), and below, p. 481.
12. In 'Venetia Digby', *Brief Lives* (published in 1813).
13. Minugh (1999) found over 3,000 instances in a small newspaper corpus from the mid nineties.
14. This example is from Fox (2000).
15. For an analysis of the medical vocabulary of the time, see McConchie (1997).
16. There is a detailed discussion of these issues in Blake (1989).

Chapter 15 and Interlude

1. Letter to the *World*, 28 November 1754. The letter is reprinted in Bolton (1966), as are the pieces by Defoe, Swift, and Johnson referred to below.
2. Slack (1985: 181). For general background to the period covered by this chapter, see Brewer (1997), and the relevant section in Haigh (1985).
3. Slack (1985: 187).
4. Vickery (2001). See also Langford (1989), Arditi (1998).
5. 5th edition, I.174.
6. The most useful edition is the one with Eric Partridge's annotations: Partridge (1963).
7. See Watts (2002) for the development of this relationship.
8. Opening lines of Book III, 'Palamon and Arcite', in *Fables Ancient and Modern* (1700).
9. Preface to Roscommon is in *Prefaces, Biographical and Critical to the Works of the English Poets*, Vol. 6, 1779.
10. Murray, quoting Lowth approvingly in his *English Grammar*, p. 161.
11. It is likely that readers will suppose there to be an error in *it's*, so it is perhaps worth a note to explain that the use of the apostrophe was still fluid at this time. Because it was developing its use as a marker of possession (the genitive case, as in *the dog's bone*), it was felt perfectly logical to extend the usage to the pronoun (*it's bone*). An attempt at standardization did not take place until the following century, when this particular point was lost sight of by the pundits – with the result that *its* and *hers* now stand out as exceptions to the possessive rule – to the infinite puzzlement of children who thought they had worked the rule out. Nor has the

standardization process been particularly successful, judging by the amount of variation which is still encountered today (*St Paul's* vs *St Pauls*, *1940's* vs *1940s*, etc.).

12. For the later 'dictionary war' between Noah Webster and Joseph Worcester, see Crystal (2003: 82).

13. 14 March 1752, p. 208.

14. 18 September 1773, in James Boswell, *The Journal of a Tour to the Hebrides.*

15. 1775, in James Boswell, *The Life of Samuel Johnson* (1791), Chapter 32.

16. 13 August 1766, letter to William Drummond, in James Boswell, *The Life of Samuel Johnson* (1791), Chapter 18.

17. 1773, 'Ostig in Sky', in *A Journey to the Western Islands of Scotland.*

Chapter 16 and Interlude

1. In his essay 'Timber: or, Discoveries' (1640).

2. These two decades are highlit in a study of English reference grammars written between 1577 and 1898: the Ottawa Grammar Resource on Early Variability in English (OGREVE): Poplack, Van Herk and Harvie (2002). Taking a number of variable past-tense forms (e.g., *I saw* vs *I seen/seed*, *I did* vs *I done*), they show that before this turning-point the variability is attested but not condemned, whereas after it the vast majority of the grammars stigmatize the nonstandard usages as vulgar or provincial.

3. For a discussion of Murray's life and work, see Tieken-Boon van Ostade (1996).

4. In *Blackwood's Magazine*, April 1839. The reference to Hazlitt is to an essay in the *Atlas*, 'English Grammar', 15 March 1829. Both pieces are reprinted in Bolton (1966).

5. G. W. Moon, 23 January 1869, p. 128.

6. See Crystal (2000a: 27).

7. The Index to *The Comprehensive Grammar of the English Language* (Quirk, Greenbaum, Leech, and Svartvik, 1985) contains some 3,500 entries dealing with general (as opposed to lexical) points of English morphology and syntax.

8. *English Grammar*, Part 1, Chapter 1, Section 2, under *N.*

9. *Letters of Lord Chesterfield to His Son*, 18 January 1750.

10. In *Memoirs of R. B. Sheridan* (1817), p. 79; cited in Mugglestone (2003: 37).

11. Boswell's *Life of Johnson*, Chapter 14, in relation to 1763.

12. Published in 1761, p. 36.

13. In *The Pickwick Papers*. Mr Weller Senior illustrates *v*-substitution (Chapter 27): 'Wen you're a married man, Samivel, you'll understand a good many things as you don't understand now; but vether it's worth while goin' through so much, to learn so little, as the charity-boy said ven he got to the end of the alphabet, is a matter o' taste.' Another illustration is on p. 497.

14. See Wells (1982: 332–3).

15. Boswell's *Life of Johnson*, Chapter 35, in relation to 1775.

16. The examples are from Milroy (1992: 197–201).

17. One of the volumes in the *Punch Library of Humour*, p. 137. For the non-British: *Hackney* is a suburb of London's East End. The cartoon below is on p. 168 of the same volume.

18. A Latin translation of the Greek phrase used by the Pythagorean philosophers: he – that is, the Master – said it.

19. In an article for the *Schoolmaster*, 28 December: 'Reasons for a Phonetic Representation of the English Language'.

20. Collins and Mees (1996). See also Milroy, Milroy, and Hartley (1994).

Chapter 17 and Interlude

1. Wright (2000) – a book whose orientation influenced my Chapter 10 above.
2. Letter of 21 January 1821; see also the quotation on p. 491. Further details of the Academy proposals of the period can be found in Mencken (1963: 11–13).
3. See the extracts reported in Mencken (1963: 18–20).
4. In *Men and Manners in America* (1833), pp. 127–9.
5. In an essay on spelling reform appended to *Dissertations on the English Language* (1789).
6. On the myth of colonial lag, see Görlach (1987).
7. Marckwardt and Quirk (1963: 64).
8. Montgomery (2001: 151).
9. See Crystal (2000b: 72).
10. For the history of African-American Vernacular English, see Harrison and Trabasso (1976).
11. For details, see Pederson (2001), especially for the distinction between Western and Midland.
12. In the Peroration to the *First Part of the Elementarie* (1582).
13. In *A Relation of Ten Years Travells in Europe, Asia, Affrique, and America* (1656).
14. Letter to Edward Gibbon, 24 October 1767.
15. See Crystal (forthcoming) for relevant statistics. There are, for example, 20,000 items in the *Dictionary of Caribbean English Usage* (Allsopp, 1996). A study of Trinidad and Tobago alone produced some 8,000 (Winer, 1989).
16. See Källgård (1993), which contains several transcribed texts.
17. The varieties of English found in this and three other novels is discussed in Winer and Rimmer (1994), from which the quotation is taken (p. 30 of the novel).
18. Chapter 10, 'The Outbreak' (1852), p. 189.
19. Chapter 2 (1857), p. 18.
20. Wilkes (1985).
21. Published under the name of Ralph Iron. The extract is from Chapter 1, 'Shadows from Child-life'.
22. According to *Hobson-Jobson*, the first major glossary of Anglo-Indian words (Yule and Burnell, 1886).
23. Reprinted in Görlach (1994: 250).
24. In 'Noctes Ambrosianae', *Blackwood's Magazine*, no. 42 (April).
25. For example, Quirk (1985: 1).
26. Lipski (1993).
27. Spencer (1975).

Chapter 18 and Interlude

1. Chapman and Hall's *Dictionary of Analytical Reagents, Dictionary of Carbohydrates, Dictionary of Inorganic and Organometallic Compounds, Dictionary of Natural Products, Dictionary of Organic Compounds*, and *Dictionary of Pharmacological Agents*.
2. See Crystal (2000c). The book in question, *Systems of Prosodic and Paralinguistic Features in English*, by myself and Randolph Quirk, was actually used as a source text by the OED editors, who extracted twenty citations from it; but these citations were for other words than those which had been given a new usage by this monograph.
3. *Hard Times* (1854), Book II, Chapter 9. The noun use of *ism* is much earlier, from 1680.
4. Gale Research Company (Michigan: Farmington Hills), 29th edn, 2001.

5. In an essay in the *Spectator* 135, 4 August 1711; reprinted in Bolton (1966). He was echoed by Swift the following year (p. 368).

6. 'in my not so humble opinion'; 'see you later'.

7. Branford and Branford (1991).

8. Awonusi (1990).

9. Reprinted in Le Faye (1995: 291).

10. Examples in this section are adapted from the illustrations in the extensive survey in Denison (2001).

11. See the selection of comments in Crystal (2003: 195).

12. A large number of words have their changing stress pattern described in this way in MacMahon (1998: 493ff.).

13. Newman (1878).

14. See the discussion in Mugglestone (2003: 86ff.).

15. 7 April, quoted by MacMahon (1998: 476).

16. *A Rhetorical Grammar of the English Language*, p. 56.

17. Ellis (1869–89: 23). The distinction between *Received* and *Correct* was based on regional distribution: *Received* was supra-regional, whereas *Correct* referred to the speech of a well-educated group in a particular part of the country. Educated Scots, for example, spoke correctly, on this criterion, but did not use r.p. Ellis thought r.p. was a somewhat artificial accent, which is why he contrasted it with 'natural' pronunciation, where people spoke without being influenced by dictionaries, authors, style manuals, and the like.

18. *Little Dorrit* (1855–6), Book I, Chapter 21.

19. In *The Social Fetich* (1907), p. 9. For other examples, see Phillipps (1984: Chapter 3).

20. Lloyd (1894: 52).

21. Jones (1917: Preface).

22. Foreword to Lloyd James (1928).

23. Gimson (2001: 88).

24. Wells (1982: 117).

25. Following its baptism with this name by Rosewarne (1984).

26. See Juul and Nielsen (1985).

27. Issue of 24 July 1926.

28. Pickles (1949: 146–7). The quotation below is from p. 133.

29. *Future of Broadcasting* (London: HMSO, 1977), p. 259.

30. Peters (1995). A series of usage questionnaires, called Langscape, was published in the journal *English Today* in the late 1990s.

31. Department of Education and Science (1975: 3).

32. Alford (1860: 6).

33. Greenbaum (1986).

34. For another example, see Crystal (2003: 122).

35. I use *judgement, authorize,* and *medieval.* (But *judgment* for a legal decision.)

36. This was the most widespread feature across Britain in a 1989 survey: see Cheshire, Edwards, and Whittle (1989).

37. These forms were found to be functionally distinguished in one study (Cheshire, 1982): *in't* was preferred in tag questions, especially when the speaker was expressing hostility (*You're a hard nut, in't you!*); *ain't* was preferred in declarative sentences (*I ain't going*).

38. Data from Beal (no date [mid 1980s]: 5).

Chapter 19 and Interlude

1. William Thackeray, *Vanity Fair* (1848), Chapter 1.

2. In Orel (1967: 91).

3. See the discussion in McClure (1993).

4. Taken from McClure, Low, Annand, Mackie, and Graham (1981).

5. *The Dialect of South Lancashire* (1854), pp. xi–xii.

6. *Cheshire Glossary* (English Dialect Society, 1886), p. 466.

7. In J. Y. Akerman, *Wiltshire Tales* (1853). This item is reprinted along with other examples in Jones and Dillon (1987: 168).

8. See further, García-Bermejo Giner and Montgomery (2001).

9. Written in 1861, published in 1864. There is a corresponding poem called 'Northern Farmer: New Style', which he began in 1861 and published in 1869.

10. See the discussion in Tilling (1972).

11. For further examples, see Kallen (1989).

12. See Tulloch (1980).

13. *The Pickwick Papers* (1836–7), Chapter 33. See also p. 410.

14. *Hard Times* (1854), Book I, Chapter 10.

15. *Wuthering Heights* (1847, edition by David Daiches, Penguin 1965), Chapter 2.

16. Thomas Hardy, *Tess of the D'Urbervilles* (1891), Chapter 3.

17. Mrs Gaskell, *North and South* (1854), Chapter 29.

18. Charles Dickens, *Great Expectations* (1860–61), Chapter 35.

19. D. H. Lawrence, *Lady Chatterley's Lover* (1928), Chapter 12.

20. Mark Twain, *Huckleberry Finn* (1884), quotations from Chapters 1 and 2.

21. See further, Ives (1955), and other papers in Williamson and Burke (1971: Part 3).

22. 'A visit to the British Museum', *Artemus Ward in London* (1866), Chapter 8. For further examples, see Crystal (2003: 84–5).

23. In Achebe (1965: 29–30).

24. See McArthur (1998, 2002).

25. For other examples, see Platt (1980).

26. Sidhwa (1993: 216).

27. Example from Romaine (1994: 538).

28. In *Spring Cleaning*, p. 12.

29. *Kicking Tongues* (London: Heinemann, 1998), p. 53.

30. *Mi Revalueshanary Fren* (London: Penguin, 2002), p. 27.

31. Achebe (1965: 29).

32. See Crystal (2003), Graddol (1999).

33. The point being that this locution (as distinct from 'Welcome to Egypt') is so widespread in that country that it has developed the status of a regional standardism, used by educated and uneducated alike, and recognized in at least one English grammar published there. As a distinctive use of a preposition, it is no more unusual than, for example, the difference between British *quarter to four* and American *quarter of four*.

34. Matthews (1900).

35. Adamson (1998: 608) argues for a 'vision of Standard English as the lowest common denominator rather than the highest common factor'.

36. For a further perspective on Tolkien's dialect world, see Johannesson (1994).

Chapter 20

1. In the *Independent*, 1 March 2003.

2. Minugh (1999).

3. Lauder (1965); Llewellyn (1985). For a further selection, see Crystal (2003: 410).

4. In the *Independent*, 21 August 2002.

5. Both examples from the *Independent*, 21 March 2002.

6. The *Sun*, 4 May 1982.

7. The first two extracts in this panel are from Burke (1967: 20) and Kellett (1996: 3). The Kanaka example is reported in Dutton and Mühlhäusler (1984).

8. 'News for Parrots', *Monty Python's Flying Circus* (BBC), Series 2, Episode 20.

9. Crystal (2001).

10. Crystal (2001: Chapter 7).

11. For more of this conversation, see James (2001).

12. The range is explored in McArthur (1998, 2002).

13. In Lecture 3 of Trench (1851), 'On the Morality in Words', p. 89.

14. John Rae, the *Observer*, 7 February 1982, 'The Decline and Fall of English Grammar'.

15. For an analysis of the complaint tradition, see Milroy and Milroy (1991).

16. The poll is reported in 'How dare you talk to me like that', the *Listener*, 2,719, 9 July 1981, pp. 37–9. See also Crystal (2000a).

17. The National Curriculum in English was in many ways a breakthrough in educational linguistic thinking, but its successful implementation was seriously hindered by insufficient provision being made to train teachers in the new way of looking at language. Even ten years on, considerable confusion remains.

18. A great deal of work in twentieth-century sociolinguistics laid the foundations of this climate, but it is only recently that there has been a specific focus on reinterpreting the relationship between standard and nonstandard in the history of English: see Watts and Trudgill (2002).

19. The name of the standard variety is capitalized as Standard English, as is normal practice with other named varieties (Cockney English, American English, etc.). As 'nonstandard' refers to an unspecified number of varieties, it is not capitalized.

20. The number of adult speakers of Standard English in the UK is thought to be between 12 and 15 per cent of the population (p. 254).

21. For gumbo, see Kretzschmar (1996: 197–8). The dictionaries are Cassidy and Hall (1985) and Mathews (1951). The Stoppard extract is from *New-Found-Land*. In Stoppard (1996: 127).

22. See the various papers in Hymes (1971).

References

Achebe, Chinua. 1965. English and the African Writer. *Transition* 4, 27–30

Adamson, Sylvia. 1998. Literary Language. In Romaine (1998), 589–692

Alford, Henry. 1860. *A Plea for the Queen's English: Stray Notes on Speaking and Spelling.* London: Strahan

Algeo, John. (ed.) 2001. *The Cambridge History of the English Language*, Vol. 6. Cambridge: Cambridge University Press

Allsopp, Richard. 1996. *Dictionary of Caribbean English Usage.* Oxford: Oxford University Press

Amphlett, John. (ed.) 1900. *Lay Subsidy Rolls, AD 1346, and AD 1358 for the County of Worcester.* Oxford: Parker

Arditi, Jorge. 1998. *A Genealogy of Manners: Transformations of Social Relations in France and England from the Fourteenth to the Eighteenth Century.* Chicago: University of Chicago Press

Attwater, Rachel. (ed.) 1957. *The Book Concerning Piers the Plowman*, trans. Donald and Rachel Attwater. London: Dent

Austin, Thomas. 1888. *Two Fifteenth-century Cookery-Books.* London: Early English Text Society

Awonusi, Victor O. 1990. Coming of Age: English in Nigeria. *English Today* 22, 31–5

Bamford, Francis. 1936. *A Royalist's Notebook: The Commonplace Book of Sir John Oglander.* London: Constable

Barber, Charles. 1976. *Early Modern English.* London: Deutsch

Bates, David. (ed.) 1998. *Regesta Regum Anglo-Normannorum: The Acta of William I 1066–1087.* Oxford: Clarendon Press

Baugh, Albert C. 1935. *A History of the English Language*, 4th edn 1993 with Thomas Cable. New York: Appleton-Century-Crofts

Beal, Joan. [no date]. The Grammar of Tyneside and Northumbrian English. In James Milroy and Lesley Milroy, *Regional Variation in British English Syntax.* Economic and Social Research Council, UK

Bede. 1910. *The Ecclesiastical History of the English Nation.* London: Dent (Everyman's Library 479)

Berndt, Rolf. 1965. The Linguistic Situation in England from the Norman Conquest to the Loss of Normandy 1066–1204. *Philologica Pragensia* 8, 145–63; reprinted in Lass (1969), 369–91

Bex, Tony and Richard J. Watts. (eds.) 1999. *Standard English: The Widening Debate.* London: Routledge

Biddle, Martin. 1985. Economy: Farming, Trade, and Manufacture. In Haigh (1985), 78–80

Blair, Peter Hunter. 1977. *An Introduction to Anglo-Saxon England*, 2nd edn. Cambridge: Cambridge University Press

Blake, Norman F. 1965. English Versions of 'Reynard the Fox' in the Fifteenth and Sixteenth Centuries. *Studies in Philology* 62, 63–77

Blake, Norman F. 1969. *Caxton and His World*. London: Deutsch

Blake, Norman F. 1973. *Caxton's Own Prose*. London: Deutsch

Blake, Norman F. 1981. *Non-standard Language in English Literature*. London: Deutsch

Blake, Norman F. 1989. Standardizing Shakespeare's Non-Standard Language. In Trahern (1989), 57–81

Blake, Norman F. (ed.) 1992a. *The Cambridge History of the English Language*, Vol. 2. Cambridge: Cambridge University Press

Blake, Norman F. 1992b. The Literary Language. In Blake (1992a), 500–541

Bolton, J. L. 1985. The economy of Britain: An Age of Crisis? In Haigh (1985), 124–30

Bolton, W. F. (ed.) 1966. *The English Language: Essays by English and American Men of Letters, 1490–1839*. Cambridge: Cambridge University Press

Bolton, W. F. and D. Crystal. (eds.) *The English Language. Vol. 2: Essays by Linguists and Men of Letters 1858–1964*. Cambridge: Cambridge University Press

Branford, Jean and William Branford. 1991. *A Dictionary of South African English*, 4th edn. Oxford: Oxford University Press

Brewer, John. 1997. *The Pleasures of the Imagination: English Culture in the Eighteenth Century*. New York: HarperCollins

Brook, G. L. 1958. *A History of the English Language*. London: Deutsch

Brooke, Stella. 1965. *The Language of the Book of Common Prayer*. London: Deutsch

Burchfield, Robert. (ed.) 1994. *The Cambridge History of the English Language*, Vol. 5. Cambridge: Cambridge University Press

Burke, Carl. 1967. *God is For Real, Man*. London: Fontana

Burnley, J. D. 1989. Sources of Standardization in Later Middle English. In Trahern (1989), 23–41

Burnley, J. D. 2000. *The History of the English Language: A Source Book*, 2nd edn. London: Longman

Burton, Jane. 1994. *Monastic and Religious Orders in Britain 1000–1300*. Cambridge: Cambridge University Press

Cassidy, Frederic and Joan Hall. 1985 (and ongoing). *Dictionary of American Regional English*. Cambridge, MA: Belknap/Harvard University Press

Cheshire, Jenny. 1982. *Variation in an English Dialect: A Sociolinguistic Study*. Cambridge: Cambridge University Press

Cheshire, Jenny, Viv Edwards and Pamela Whittle. 1989. Urban British Dialect Grammar: The Question of Dialect Levelling. *English World-Wide* 10, 185–225

Chevillet, François. 1997. The Great Vowel Shift: Theories and Problems. *Dialectologica and Geolinguistica* 5, 49–63

Christianson, C. Paul. 1989. Chancery Standard and the Records of Old London Bridge. In Trahern (1989), 82–112

Clanchy, M. T. 1993. *From Memory to Written Record: England 1066–1307*, 2nd edn. Oxford: Blackwell

Clark, Cecily. 1981. Another Late-Fourteenth-Century Case of Dialect-Awareness. *English Studies* 62, 504–5

Coleman, Julie. 1995. The Chronology of French and Latin Loan Words in English. *Transactions of the Philological Society* 93, 95–124

Collins, Beverley and Inger M. Mees. 1996. Spreading Everywhere? How Recent a Phenomenon is Glottalisation in Received Pronunciation? *English World-Wide* 17, 175–87

Collison, Robert L. 1982. *A History of Foreign-Language Dictionaries.* London: Deutsch

Coward, Barry. 1997. *Social Change and Continuity: England 1550–1750,* 2nd edn. London: Longman

Cressey, David. 1980. *Literacy and Social Order: Reading and Writing in Tudor and Stuart England.* Cambridge: Cambridge University Press

Crystal, David. 1997. *The Cambridge Encyclopedia of Language,* 2nd edn. Cambridge: Cambridge University Press

Crystal, David. 1998. *Language Play.* London: Penguin

Crystal, David. 2000a. *Who Cares About English Usage?* 2nd edn. London: Penguin

Crystal, David. 2000b. *Language Death.* Cambridge: Cambridge University Press

Crystal, David. 2000c. Investigating Nonceness: Lexical Innovation and Lexicographic Coverage. In Robert Boenig and Kathleen Davis. (eds.) *Manuscript, Narrative and Lexicon: Essays on Literary and Cultural Transmission in Honor of Whitney F. Bolton.* Lewisburg: Bucknell University Press; London: Associated University Presses, 218–31

Crystal, David. 2001. *Language and the Internet.* Cambridge: Cambridge University Press

Crystal, David. 2002a. *The English Language,* 2nd edn. London: Penguin

Crystal, David. 2002b. Speak, in the Name of the Law. *Entertainment Law* 1, 103–16

Crystal, David. 2003. *The Cambridge Encyclopedia of the English Language,* 2nd edn. Cambridge: Cambridge University Press

Crystal, David. forthcoming. English World-wide. In Richard Hogg and David Denison. (eds.) *The Cambridge Shorter History of the English Language.* Cambridge: Cambridge University Press

Crystal, David and Ben Crystal. 2002. *Shakespeare's Words: A Glossary and Language Companion.* London: Penguin

Cusack, Bridget. 1998. *Everyday English 1500–1700: A Reader.* Edinburgh: Edinburgh University Press

Danielsson, B. 1955. *John Hart's Works on English Orthography and Pronunciation.* Stockholm: Almqvist and Wiksell

DeCamp, David. 1958. The Genesis of the Old English Dialects: A New Hypothesis. *Language* 34, 232–44

Denison, David. 1998. Syntax. In Romaine (1998), 92–329

Department of Education and Science. 1975. *A Language for Life.* London: Her Majesty's Stationery Office

Devitt, Amy J. 1989. *Standardizing Written English: Diffusion in the Age of Scotland 1520–1659.* Cambridge: Cambridge University Press

Diamond, Robert E. 1970. *Old English: Grammar and Reader.* Detroit: Wayne State University Press

Dickins, Bruce and Alan S. C. Ross. (eds.) 1954. *The Dream of the Rood,* 4th edn. London: Methuen

Dickins, Bruce and R. M. Wilson. (eds.) 1951. *Early Middle English Texts.* London: Bowes and Bowes

Dutton, Tom and Peter Mühlhäusler. 1984. Queensland Kanaka English. *English World-Wide* 4, 231–63

Eckert, Penelope. 1997. Age as a Sociolinguistic Variable. In Florian Coulmas. (ed.) *The Handbook of Sociolinguistics.* Oxford: Blackwell, 151–67

Eliason, Norman E. 1972. *The Language of Chaucer's Poetry.* Copenhagen: Rosenkilde and Bagger

Ellis, Alexander J. 1869–89. *On Early English Pronunciation*, 5 vols. London: Asher

Essery, John. 1993. *Classic Headlines from* The Sun. Harmondsworth: Penguin

Farnham, Anthony E. (ed.) 1969. *A Sourcebook in the History of English*. New York: Holt, Rinehart and Winston

Fennell, Barbara. 2001. *A History of English: A Sociolinguistic Approach*. Oxford: Blackwell

Field, P. J. C. 1971. *Romance and Chronicle: A Study of Malory's Prose Style*. London: Barrie and Jenkins

Finlay, Roger. 1981. *Population and Metropolis: The Demography of London 1580–1650*. Cambridge: Cambridge University Press

Finnie, W. Bruce. 1972. *The Stages of English: Texts, Transcriptions, Exercises*. Boston: Houghton Mifflin

Fischer, Olga. 1992. Syntax. In Blake (1992a), 207–408

Fisher, John H., Malcolm Richardson, and Jane L. Fisher. 1984. *An Anthology of Chancery English*. Knoxville: University of Tennessee Press

Forester, Thomas. 1854. *The Ecclesiastical History of Ordericus Vitalis*. London: George Bell

Fox, Adam. 2000. *Oral and Literate Culture in England 1500–1700*. Oxford: Oxford University Press

Furnivall, F. J. and J. Meadows Cowper. (eds.) 1871. *Four Supplications 1529–53 AD*. London: Early English Text Society

García-Bermejo Giner, María F. and Michael Montgomery. 2001. Yorkshire English Two Hundred Years Ago. *Journal of English Linguistics* 29, 346–62

Garmondsway, G. N. (ed.) 1947. *Ælfric's Colloquy*, 2nd edn. London: Methuen

Garmondsway, G. N. (ed.) 1953. *The Anglo-Saxon Chronicle*. London: Dent (Everyman's Library 624)

Geipel, John. 1971. *The Viking Legacy*. Newton Abbot: David and Charles

Gellrich, Jesse. 1985. *The Idea of the Book in the Middle Ages: Language Theory, Mythology, and Fiction*. Ithaca: Cornell University Press

Gillingham, John. 1991. *The Oxford Illustrated History of England*. Oxford: Oxford University Press

Gimson, A. C. 2001. *An Introduction to the Pronunciation of English*, 6th edn. London: Arnold

Godden, Malcolm and Michael Lapidge. (eds.) 1991. *The Cambridge Companion to Old English Literature*. Cambridge: Cambridge University Press

Görlach, Manfred. 1987. Colonial Lag? The Alleged Conservative Character of American English and Other 'Colonial' Varieties. *English World-Wide* 8, 41–60

Görlach, Manfred. 1994. Broken English from Old Calabar. *English World-Wide* 15, 249–52

Graddol, David. 1999. The Decline of the Native Speaker. In David Graddol and Ulrike H. Meinhof. (eds.) *English in a Changing World*. AILA Review 13: International Association of Applied Linguistics, 57–68

Greenbaum, Sidney. 1986. Spelling Variants in British English. *Journal of English Linguistics* 19, 258–68

Haigh, Christopher. (ed.) 1985. *The Cambridge Historical Encyclopedia of Great Britain and Ireland*. Cambridge: Cambridge University Press

Hamilton, N. (ed.) 1870. *Willelmi Malmesbiriensis Monachi de Gestis Pontificium Anglorum, Libri Quinque*. London: Rolls Series

Harrison, Deborah Sears and Tom Trabasso. 1976. *Black English: A Seminar*. Hillsdale: Erlbaum

Hart, Alfred C. 1943. The Growth of Shakespeare's Vocabulary. *Review of English Studies* 19, 128–40, 242–54

Henderson, Ernest F. 1910. *Select Historical Documents of the Middle Ages*. London: George Bell

Hogg, Richard M. (ed.) 1992. *The Cambridge History of the English Language*, Vol. 1. Cambridge: Cambridge University Press

Horobin, S. C. P. 2001. J. R. R. Tolkien as a Philologist: A Reconsideration of the Northernisms in Chaucer's *Reeve's Tale*. *English Studies* 82, 97–105

Hymes, Dell. (ed.) 1971. *Pidginization and Creolization of Languages*. Cambridge: Cambridge University Press

Irvine, Susan. 2000. The Compilation and Use of Manuscripts Containing Old English in the Twelfth Century. In Swan and Treharne (2000), 41–61

Ives, Sumner. 1955. Dialect Differentiation in the Stories of Joel Chandler Harris. *American Literature* 17, 88–96

James, Gregory. 2001. Cantonese Particles in Hong Kong Students' English E-mails. *English Today* 17, 9–16

Jenkyns, H. (ed.) 1833. *The Remains of Thomas Cranmer*, 4 vols. Oxford: Oxford University Press

Jespersen, Otto. 1905. *Growth and Structure of the English Language*, 9th edn 1962. Oxford: Blackwell

Johannesson, Nils-Lennart. 1994. Subcreating a Stratified Community. On J. R. R. Tolkien's Use of Non-standard forms in *The Lord of the Rings*. In Gunnel Melchers and Nils-Lennart Johannesson. (eds.) *Nonstandard Varieties of Language*, Stockholm: Almqvist and Wiksell, 53–63

Johnston, Paul. 1992. English Vowel Shifting: One Great Vowel Shift or Two Small Vowel Shifts. *Diachronica* 9, 189–226

Jones, Claire. 2001. Elaboration in Practice: The Use of English in Medieval East Anglian Medicine. In Jacek Fisiak and Peter Trudgill. (eds.) *East Anglian English*. Cambridge: Brewer, 163–77

Jones, Daniel. 1917. *English Pronouncing Dictionary*. London: Dent

Jones, Malcolm and Patrick Dillon. 1987. *Dialect in Wiltshire*. Trowbridge: Wiltshire County Council

Jucker, Andreas H. 1997. The Discourse Marker *well* in the History of English. *English Language and Linguistics* 1, 111–33

Jurkowski, M., C. Smith, and D. Crook. 1998. *Lay Taxes in England and Wales 1188–1688*. London: Public Record Office

Juul, A. and H. F. Nielsen. (eds.) 1985. *Our Changing Speech. Two BBC Talks by Daniel Jones*. Copenhagen: Landscentralen for Undervisningsmidler

Kallen, Jeffrey L. 1989. Tense and Aspect Categories in Irish English. *English World-Wide* 10, 1–39

Kallen, Jeffrey L. 1994. English in Ireland. In Burchfield (1994), 148–96

Källgård, Anders. 1993. Present-day Pitcairnese. *English World-Wide* 14, 71–114

Kastovsky, Dieter. 1992. Semantics and Vocabulary. In Hogg (1992), 290–408

Keene, Derek. 2000. Metropolitan Values: Migration, Mobility and Cultural Norms, London 1100–1700. In Wright (2000), 93–114

Kellett, Arnold. 1996. *Ee By Gum, Lord* (with tape). Otley: Smith Settle

Ker, N. R. 1957. *Catalogue of Manuscripts Containing Anglo-Saxon*. Oxford: Clarendon Press

Kermode, Frank. 2000. *Shakespeare's Language*. London: Penguin

Kispert, Robert J. 1971. *Old English: An Introduction*. New York: Holt, Rinehart and Winston

Klaeber, F. (ed.) 1922. *Beowulf*. London and Boston: Heath

Kretzschmar, William A. 1996. Dimensions of Variation in American English Vocabulary. *English World-Wide* 17, 189–211

Kristensson, Gillis. 1995. *A Survey of Middle English Dialects 1290–1350: The East Midland Counties*. Lund: Lund University Press

Kristensson, Gillis. 1997. Middle English Dialects. In Raymond Hickey and Stanislaw Puppel. (eds.) *Language History and Language Modelling*. Berlin: de Gruyter, 655–64

Kučera, Henry and W. Nelson Francis. 1967. *Computational Analysis of Present-day American English*. Providence: Brown University Press

Kuhn, Sherman M. 1968. The Preface to a Fifteenth-century Concordance. *Speculum* 43, 258–73

Labov, William. 1966. *The Social Stratification of English in New York City*. Washington: Center for Applied Linguistics

Langford, Paul. 1989. *A Polite and Commercial People: England 1727–1783*. Oxford: Oxford University Press

Lass, Roger. (ed.) 1969. *Approaches to English Historical Linguistics*. New York: Holt, Rinehart and Winston

Lass, Roger. (ed.) 1999. *The Cambridge History of the English Language*, Vol. 3. Cambridge: Cambridge University Press

Lauder, Afferbeck. 1965. *Let Stalk Strine*. Sydney: Ure Smith

Lederer, Richard. 1991. *The Miracle of Language*. New York: Simon and Schuster

Le Faye, Deirdre. (ed.) 1995. *Jane Austen's Letters*, 3rd edn. Oxford: Oxford University Press

Lindkvist, Karl-Gunnar. 1978. *At versus On, In, By: On the Early History of Spatial At*. Stockholm: Almqvist and Wiksell

Lipski, John M. 1993. Y'all in American English: From Black to White, from Phrase to Pronoun. *English World-Wide* 14, 23–56

Liuzza, Roy Michael. 2000. Scribal Habit: The Evidence of the Old English Gospels. In Swan and Treharne (2000), 143–165

Llewellyn, Sam. 1985. *Yacky Dar, Moy Bewty!* London: Elm Tree Books

Lloyd, R. J. 1894. Standard English. *Die Neueren Sprachen* 2, 52–3

Lloyd James, A. 1928. *Broadcast English*. London: British Broadcasting Corporation

Logan, H. M. 1973. *The Dialect of the Life of Saint Katherine*. The Hague: Mouton

Luria, Maxwell S. and Richard L. Hoffman. 1974. *Middle English Lyrics*. New York: Norton

McArthur, Tom. 1998. *The English Languages*. Cambridge: Cambridge University Press

McArthur, Tom. 2002. *Oxford Guide to World English*. Oxford: Oxford University Press

McClure, J. Derrick. 1993. Varieties of Scots in Recent and Contemporary Narrative Prose. *English World-Wide* 14, 1–22

McClure, J. Derrick. 1994. English in Scotland. In Burchfield (1994), 23–93

McClure, J. Derrick, John Thomas Low, J. K. Annand, A. D. Mackie, and John J. Graham. 1981. Our ain leid? The Predicament of a Scots Writer. *English World-Wide* 2, 3–28

McConchie, R. W. 1997. *Lexicography and Physicke: The Record of Sixteenth-century English Medical Terminology*. Oxford: Clarendon Press

McCrum, Robert, William Cran, and Robert MacNeil. 1986. *The Story of English*. London: Faber and Faber/BBC Publications

McIntosh, Angus, M. L. Samuels, and M. Benskin, with M. Laing and K. Williamson. 1986. *A Linguistic Atlas of Late Mediaeval English*. Aberdeen: Aberdeen University Press

MacMahon, Michael K. C. 1998. Phonology. In Romaine (1998), 373–535

MacQueen, John. (ed.) 1970. *Ballattis of Luve: The Scottish Courtly Love Lyric 1400–1570*. Edinburgh: Edinburgh University Press

Marckwardt, Albert H. and Randolph Quirk. 1963. *A Common Language: British and American English*. London: British Broadcasting Corporation

Mathews, Mitford M. 1951. *A Dictionary of Americanisms on Historical Principles*. Chicago: University of Chicago Press

Matthews, Brander. 1900. The Future Literary Centre of the English Language. *Bookman* 12, 238–42

Mellinkoff, David. 1963. *The Language of the Law*. Boston: Little, Brown

Mencken, H. L. 1963. *The American Language*. New York: Knopf; London: Routledge and Kegan Paul

Milroy, James. 1992. Middle English Dialectology. In Blake (1992), 156–206

Milroy, James. 1999. The Consequences of Standardisation in Descriptive Linguistics. In Bex and Watts (1999), 16–39

Milroy, James. 2002. The Legitimate Language: Giving a History to English. In Watts and Trudgill (2002), 7–25

Milroy, James and Lesley Milroy. 1991. *Authority in Language*, 2nd edn. London: Routledge

Milroy, James, Lesley Milroy, and Sue Hartley. 1994. Local and Supra-local Change in British English: The Case of Glottalisation. *English World-Wide* 15, 1–33

Minugh, David C. 1999. *What Aileth Thee, to Print So Curiously?* Archaic Forms and Contemporary Newspaper Language. In Taavitsainen, Melchers, and Pahta (1999), 285–304

Mitchell, Bruce. 1995. *An Invitation to Old English and Anglo-Saxon England*. Oxford: Blackwell

Moerenhout, Mike and Wim van der Wurff. 2000. Remnants of the Old Order: OV in the Paston Letters. *English Studies* 81, 513–30

Montgomery, Michael. 2001. British and Irish Antecedents. In Algeo (2001), 86–153

Moore, Kate. 1999. Linguistic Airbrushing in Oral History. In Taavitsainen, Melchers, and Pahta (1999), 347–60

Mugglestone, Lynda. 2003. *Talking Proper: The Rise of Accent as Social Symbol*, 2nd edn. Oxford: Oxford University Press

Mugglestone, Lynda. forthcoming. *The Oxford History of the English Language*. Oxford: Oxford University Press

Nevalainen, Terttu. 1999. Early Modern English Lexis and Semantics. In Lass (1999), 332–458

Nevalainen, Terttu and Helena Raumolin-Brunberg. 1995. Constraints on Politeness: The Pragmatics of Address Formulae in Early English Correspondence. In Andreas H. Jucker. (ed.) *Historical Pragmatics: Pragmatic Developments in the History of English*. Amsterdam: Benjamins, 541–601

Newman, Francis William. 1878. The English Language as Spoken and Written. *Contemporary Review* 31, 689–706

Orel, H. 1967. *Thomas Hardy's Personal Writings*. London: Macmillan

Orwell, George. 1946. Politics and the English Language. *Horizon* 13; reprinted in Bolton and Crystal (1969), 217–28

Page, R. I. 1987. *Runes*. London: British Museum

Parkes, M. B. 1992. *Pause and Effect: An Introduction to the History of Punctuation in the West*. Aldershot: Scolar Press

Partridge, A. C. 1973. *English Biblical Translation*. London: Deutsch

Partridge, A. C. 1982. *A Companion to Old and Middle English Studies*. London: Deutsch

Partridge, Eric. 1961. *Adventuring Among Words*. London: Deutsch

Partridge, Eric. (ed.) 1963. *Swift's Polite Conversation*. London: Deutsch

Partridge, Eric. 1984. *A Dictionary of Slang and Unconventional English*, 8th edn (ed. Paul Beale). London: Routledge

Pederson, Lee. 2001. Dialects. In Algeo (2001), 253–90

Peters, Pam. 1995. *The Cambridge Australian English Style Guide*. Cambridge: Cambridge University Press

Phillipps, K. C. 1984. *Language and Class in Victorian England*. Oxford: Blackwell

Pickles, Wilfred. 1949. *Between You and Me*. London: Werner Laurie

Pine, Edward. (ed.) 1947. *The Pauline Muses*. London: Gollancz

Platt, John T. 1980. Varieties and functions of English in Singapore and Malaysia. *English World-Wide* 1, 97–121

Pollard, A. W. 1911. *Records of the English Bible*. Oxford: Oxford University Press

Pollard, A. W. and G. R. Redgrave. 1976–91. *A Short-title Catalogue of Books Printed in England, Scotland, and Ireland and of English Books Printed Abroad 1475–1640*, 2nd edn (eds. W. A. Jackson, F. S. Ferguson, and Katharine F. Pantzer). London: Bibliographical Society

Poplack, Shana, Gerard Van Herk, and Dawn Harvie. 2002. 'Deformed in the Dialects': An Alternative History of Non-standard English. In Watts and Trudgill (2002), 87–110

Proud, Joana. 2000. Old English Prose Saints' Lives in the Twelfth Century: The Evidence of the Extant Manuscripts. In Swan and Treharne (2000), 117–31

Quirk, Randolph. 1985. The English Language in a Global Context. In Randolph Quirk and H. G. Widdowson. (eds.) *English in the World*. Cambridge: Cambridge University Press, 1–6

Quirk, Randolph, Sidney Greenbaum, Geoffrey Leech, and Jan Svartvik. 1985. *A Comprehensive Grammar of the English Language*. London: Longman

Quirk, Randolph and C. L. Wrenn. 1955. *An Old English Grammar*. London: Methuen

Richards, Mary P. 1989. Elements of a Written Standard in the Old English Laws. In Trahern (1989), 1–22

Rigg, A. G. (ed.) 1968. *The English Language: A Historical Reader*. New York: Appleton-Century-Crofts

Robbins, Rossell Hope. 1970. Medical Manuscripts in Middle English. *Speculum* 45, 393–415

Romaine, Suzanne. 1994. Hawai'i Creole English as a Literary Language. *Language in Society* 23, 527–54

Romaine, Suzanne. (ed.) 1998. *The Cambridge History of the English Language*, Vol. 4. Cambridge: Cambridge University Press

Ronberg, Gert. 1992. *A Way with Words: The Language of English Renaissance Literature*. London: Arnold

Rosewarne, David. 1984. Estuary English. *The Times Educational Supplement*, 19 October, 29

Rothwell, W. 2001. English and French in England after 1362. *English Studies* 82, 539–59

Samuels, M. L. 1963. Some Applications of a Middle English Dialectology. *English Studies* 44, 81–94; reprinted in Lass (1969)

Schabram, H. 1965. *Superbia*. Munich: Fink

Schäfer, Jürgen. 1973. *Shakespeares Stil: Germanisches und romanisches Vocabular*. Frankfurt: Athenäum

Schäfer, Jürgen. 1989. *Early Modern English Lexicography*. Oxford: Clarendon Press

Scieszka, Jon. 1989. *The True Story of the Three Little Pigs*. London: Viking Kestrel

Serjeantson, Mary S. 1935. *A History of Foreign Words in English*. London: Routledge and Kegan Paul

Shipley, Joseph T. 1977. *In Praise of English: The Growth and Use of Language*. New York: Times Books

Shores, David. 1971. *A Descriptive Syntax of the Peterborough Chronicle from 1122 to 1154*. The Hague: Mouton

Sidhwa, Bapsi. 1993. New English Creative Writing: A Pakistani Writer's Perspective. In Robert J. Baumgardner. (ed.) *The English Language in Pakistan*. Oxford: Oxford University Press, 212–20

Sisam, Kenneth. 1959. *Fourteenth-century Verse and Prose*. Oxford: Clarendon Press

Skeat, W. W. 1886. *Specimens of English Literature*, Vol. 3. Oxford: Oxford University Press

Slack, Paul. 1985. A Divided Society. In Haigh (1985), 181–7

Smith, A. H. 1951. *The Parker Chronicle (832–900)*, 3rd edn. London: Methuen

Smith, Jeremy. 1996. *An Historical Study of English*. London: Routledge

Smith, Steven B. 1983. *The Great Mental Calculators*. New York: Columbia University Press

Sokol, B. J. and Mary Sokol. 2000. *Shakespeare's Legal Language: A Dictionary*. London: Athlone

Spedding, James. 1870. *The Letters and the Life of Francis Bacon*, Vol. 3. London: Longman

Spencer, Nancy. 1975. Singular *y'all*. *American Speech* 50, 315–17

Spevack, Marvin. 1973. *The Harvard Concordance to Shakespeare*. Cambridge, MA: Harvard University Press

Steiner, George. 1967. F. R. Leavis. In George Steiner, *Language and Silence*. London: Faber and Faber, 249–66

Stoppard, Tom. 1996. *Plays*, Vol. 1. London: Faber and Faber

Strang, Barbara M. H. 1970. *A History of English*. London: Methuen

Svartvik, Jan. 1980. *Well* in Conversation. In S. Greenbaum, G. Leech, and J. Svartvik (eds.) *Studies in English Linguistics*. London: Longman, 167–77

Swan, Mary. 2000. Ælfric's *Catholic Homilies* in the Twelfth Century. In Swan and Treharne (2000), 62–83

Swan, Mary and Elaine M. Treharne. (eds.) 2000. *Rewriting Old English in the Twelfth Century*. Cambridge: Cambridge University Press

Sweet, Henry. (ed.) 1885. *The Oldest English Texts*. London: Oxford University Press, for the Early English Text Society

Taavitsainen, Irma. 2000. Scientific Language and Spelling Standardization 1375–1550. In Wright (2000), 131–54

Taavitsainen, Irma, Gunnel Melchers, and Päivi Pahta. (eds.) 1999. *Writing in Nonstandard English*. Amsterdam: Benjamins

Taavitsainen, Irma and Saara Nevanlinna. 1999. 'Pills to Purge Melancholy' – Nonstandard Elements in *A Dialogue Against the Feuer Pestilence*. In Taavitsainen, Melchers, and Pahta (1999), 151–70

Teresi, Loredana. 2000. Mnemonic Transmission of Old English Texts in the Post-Conquest Period. In Swan and Treharne (2000), 98–116

Thomas, Alan R. 1994. English in Wales. In Burchfield (1994), 94–147

Thompson, James Westfall. 1939/63. *The Literacy of the Laity in the Middle Ages*. Berkeley: University of California Press, 1939; New York: Franklin, 1963

Tieken-Boon van Ostade, Ingrid. (ed.) 1996. *Two Hundred Years of Lindley Murray*. Münster: Nodus

Tilling, Philip M. 1972. Local Dialect and the Poet: A Comparison of the Findings in the Survey of English Dialects with Dialect in Tennyson's Lincolnshire Poems. In Martyn F. Wakelin. (ed.) *Patterns in the Folk Speech of the British Isles*. London: Athlone, 88–108

Toon, Thomas E. 1992. Old English Dialects. In Hogg (1992), 409–51

Trahern, Joseph B. (ed.) 1989. *Standardizing English*. Knoxville: University of Tennessee Press

Trench, Richard Chenevix. 1851. *The Study of Words*. London: Kegan Paul, Trench, Trubner

Trudgill, Peter. 1974. *The Social Differentiation of English in Norwich*. Cambridge: Cambridge University Press

Trudgill, Peter. 1999. Standard English: What It Isn't. In Bex and Watts (1999), 117–28

Tulloch, Graham. 1980. *The Language of Walter Scott: A Study of His Scottish and Period Language*. London: Deutsch

Turner, J. R. 1980. *The Works of William Bullokar*, Vol. 2. Leeds: University of Leeds School of English

Turville-Petre, Thurlac. 1996. *England the Nation: Language, Literature, and National Identity 1290–1340*. Oxford: Clarendon Press

Vickery, Amanda. 2001. *In Pursuit of Pleasure*. Milton Keynes: Open University Press

Ware, J. Redding. 1909. *Passing English of the Victorian Era: A Dictionary of Heterodox English, Slang, and Phrase*. New York: Dutton

Watts, Richard. 2002. From Polite Language to Educated Language: The Re-emergence of an Ideology. In Watts and Trudgill (2002), 155–72

Watts, Richard and Peter Trudgill. (eds) 2002. *Alternative Histories of English*. London: Routledge

Weale, Michael E., Deborah A. Weiss, Rolf F. Jager, Neil Bradman, and Mark G. Thomas. 2002. Y Chromosome Evidence for Anglo-Saxon Mass Migration. *Molecular Biology and Evolution* 19, 1,008–21

Wells, John. 1982. *Accents of English, Vol. 1: An Introduction. Vol. 2: The British Isles*. Cambridge: Cambridge University Press

Wilcox, Jonathan. 2000. Wulfstan and the Twelfth Century. In Swan and Treharne (2000), 83–97

Wilkes, G. A. 1985. *A Dictionary of Australian Colloquialisms*, 2nd edn. Sydney: Sydney University Press

Williamson, Craig. 1977. *The Old English Riddles of the Exeter Book*. Chapel Hill: University of North Carolina Press

Williamson, Juanita V. and Virginia M. Burke. (eds.) 1971. *A Various Language: Perspectives on American Dialects*. New York: Holt, Rinehart and Winston

Winer, Lise. 1989. Trinbagonian. *English Today* 18, 17–22

Winer, Lise and Mary Rimmer. 1994. Language Varieties in Early Trinidadian Novels 1838–1907. *English World-Wide* 15, 225–48

Wing, Donald. 1972–1988. *Short-title Catalogue of Books Printed in England, Scotland, Ireland, Wales, and British America, and of English Books Printed in Other Countries 1641–1700*, 2nd edn (eds. John J. Morrison, et al.). New York: Modern Language Association of America

Wright, Laura. (ed.) 2000. *The Development of Standard English 1300–1800*. Cambridge: Cambridge University Press

Wright, Laura. 2001. Some Morphological Features of the Norfolk Guild Certificates of 1388/9. In Fisiak and Trudgill (2001), 79–162

Wrigley, E. A. and R. S. Schofield. 1981. *The Population History of England 1541–1871: A Reconstruction*. Cambridge, MA: Harvard University Press

Wyld, H. C. 1927. *A Short History of English*, 1st edn 1914. London: Murray

Wyld, H. C. 1936. *A History of Modern Colloquial English*. Oxford: Blackwell

Yule, Henry and A. C. Burnell. 1886. *Hobson-Jobson: A Glossary of Anglo-Indian Colloquial Words and Phrases*. London: Routledge and Kegan Paul

Acknowledgements

p. 39 Archivio e Biblioteca Capitolare, Vercelli.

p. 91 Reproduced by kind permission of the Dean and Chapter of Exeter Cathedral.

p. 109 British Library.

p. 122 Corporation of London Records Office.

p. 267 The Governing Body of Christ Church, Oxford.

p. 282 Bodleian Library, University of Oxford, Arch. A. f. 141 (2).

p. 336 Reproduced by kind permission of the Diocese of Exeter, Chanter 867.

p. 505 Quotation from 'Sonny's Lettah', copyright © Linton Kwesi Johnson, reproduced by kind permission of LMJ Music Publishers Ltd.

Person Index

Subject Index